Worlds of Work: Peasants and Artisans, Engineers and Theorists

Library of Economic History

VOLUME 19

The titles published in this series are listed at *brill.com/lehi*

Worlds of Work: Peasants and Artisans, Engineers and Theorists

By

Carlo Poni

Edited by

Vivian R. Gruder, Patrick Leech and Roberto Scazzieri

With translations by

Gabriella Gruder-Poni and Carolyn Kadas

BRILL

LEIDEN | BOSTON

SEPS
SEGRETARIATO EUROPEO PER LE PUBBLICAZIONI SCIENTIFICHE

The translation of this book has been funded by SEPS—Segretariato Europeo per le Pubblicazioni Scientifiche, Via Val d'Aposa 7,40123 Bologna (Italy), seps@seps.it, www.seps.it.

This book has been funded by the Dipartimento di Scienze Economiche, and the Dipartimento di Interpretazione e Traduzione, Alma Mater Studiorum, Università di Bologna.

Cover illustration: *Model of the silk mill machine "alla bolognese"* (*mulino da seta*). The *mulino da seta* twists the threads. Source: Archivio Fotografico, Museo del Patrimonio Industriale di Bologna; originally published in the periodical of the Museum, *"ScuolaOfficina"*, nos. 4-5-6, July-December 1985. The mill "alla bolognese" was constructed under the direction of Carlo Poni and Roberto Curti with the assistance of students of the Aldini Valeriani School.

The Library of Congress Cataloging-in-Publication Data is available online at https://catalog.loc.gov
LC record available at https://lccn.loc.gov/

Typeface for the Latin, Greek, and Cyrillic scripts: "Brill". See and download: brill.com/brill-typeface.

ISSN 1877-3206
ISBN 978-90-04-29434-9 (hardback)
ISBN 978-90-04-71327-7 (e-book)
DOI 10.1163/9789004713277

This book is printed on acid-free paper and produced in a sustainable manner.

Contents

Acknowledgments IX
List of Illustrations XI
Notes on the Chapters XIII

Introduction: In Homage to Carlo Poni 1
Steven L. Kaplan

PART 1
Peasants, Landonwners, Agronomists

1 Peasant Tricks and Landlord Strategies in the Bolognese Countryside 11
Carlo Poni

2 Between Agriculture and the Manor: Structure, Strategy and Ambiguity in Agostino Gallo's *Dialogues* 26
Carlo Poni

3 Environmental Crisis and the Shifting Practice of Property Rights: The Bolognese Marshlands, 17th to 19th Centuries 55
Carlo Poni and Roberto Scazzieri

4 Family and *Podere* in Emilia-Romagna: Peasant Sharecroppers 71
Carlo Poni

PART 2
Artisans, Workers, Merchants

SECTION 1
Crafting Shoes

5 Norms and Disputes: The Shoemakers' Guild in Eighteenth-Century Bologna 113
Carlo Poni

6 Local Market Rules and Practices: Three Guilds in the Same Line of Production in Early Modern Bologna 143
Carlo Poni

SECTION 2
Manufacturing Silk

7 'Measure for Measure': From Fine Thread to Rigid Labor Control. Changing Conditions of Work in Silk Factories 179
Carlo Poni

8 Technology, Organization of Production, and the Gender Division of Labor 214
Carlo Poni

9 Fashion as Flexible Production: Strategies of the Lyon Silk Merchants in the Eighteenth Century 238
Carlo Poni

PART 3
Engineers and Theorists

10 The Synergy between Two Innovations: Canals and Silk Mills in Bologna 289
Alberto Guenzi and Carlo Poni

11 Behind the Scenes: The Staging of a Theater of Machines 304
Carlo Poni

12 The Craftsman and the Good Engineer: Technical Practice and Theoretical Mechanics in J.T. Desaguliers 351
Carlo Poni

13 The Worlds of Work: Formal Knowledge and Practical Abilities in Diderot's *Encyclopédie* 375
Carlo Poni

PART 4
Methods

14 The Name and the Game: Unequal Exchange and the Historiographic Marketplace 399
Carlo Ginzburg and Carlo Poni

15 The Silk Mill: A Path of Research 408
Carlo Poni

Postscripts

16 Remembering Carlo Poni 417
Carlo Ginzburg

17 In Praise of Carlo Poni 422
Edmund Leites

18 Between Practice and Theory: An Appraisal 426
Roberto Scazzieri

Index, *Worlds of Work* 441
Index, *Postscripts* 450

Acknowledgments

The project to publish a selection of articles by the late Carlo Poni, Emeritus Professor of the University of Bologna, relating to the various forms and experiences of the world of work, was first proposed by Roberto Scazzieri. The editorial work was subsequently carried out by the three editors: Roberto Scazzieri, Vivian Gruder and Patrick Leech. One of the first to be informed was Maxine Berg, Professor of History of the University of Warwick. She recommended contacting Giorgio Riello, also Professor of History at the University of Warwick; he in turn recommended that we contact Brill Publishers. And so this book project came to be a book publication under the auspices of Brill.

Deepest gratitude goes to former students of Carlo Poni: Fabio Giusberti, Professor at the University of Bologna, and Alberto Guenzi, Professor at the University of Parma, for their help in explaining multiple technical aspects of silk-making—the principal parts of machines and their operations—and the changes silk making introduced to the infrastructure of Bologna. Silvio Fronzoni, sadly no longer with us, also a former student and former Director of the Museo della Civiltà Contadina in San Marino di Bentivoglio, Bologna, was an inestimable guide in explaining the multiple facets of sharecropping life; his kindness and generosity in responding to question after question will not be forgotten. Antonio Campigotto and Gian Michele Alessio Zoeddu of the Museo del Patrimonio Industriale of Bologna offered their generous help in explaining the meaning of technical terms in silk manufacturing. Davide Beccia and Francesca Rina Gabbrielli, while students at the Department of Economics of the University of Bologna, were unfailing in helping to carry out multiple translating and editing tasks.

Roberto Scazzieri would like to thank those closely involved in intellectual exchanges with him and with Carlo Poni around the themes of this book, and primarily Patrizio Bianchi, Craig Muldrew, and Frank Perlin. He is also grateful to Cambridge University Library and to the Library of the Whipple Museum of the History of Science in Cambridge for providing resources essential to the editing of this volume.

Andrea Cristiani provided much help on the article on Agostino Gallo's *Dialogues* and the article on peasant sharecroppers. Massimo Fornasari gave valuable help on questions of terminology relating to silk.

Carolyn Kadas had the heavy responsibility of translating five chapters, which she did with great skill, especially in translating into English the many technical terms in Italian. Thanks as well to Gabriella Gruder-Poni for the translation into English of the "Postscriptum" in Chapter 14, and for the translations of the many Latin quotations in several chapters, as well as other editorial suggestions and aid in obtaining several of the illustrations included in this volume.

Danio Maldussi helped to clarify translations from Diderot. Nelia Dias helped in understanding an allusive statement by Diderot. And Myriam Maayan "decoded" a French allusion about a silk merchant.

We thank Ugo Berti, former editor of Il Mulino Publishers of Bologna, who graciously gave permission to our requests to reprint a number of articles and chapters in books that Prof. Poni wrote.

Grateful thanks to Paul Friedman, Research Librarian at the New York Public Library who, during the years of Covid isolation, sent digital copies of whatever was requested—documents, books, pages from books—which advanced the tasks of editing this book.

We wish to express our gratitude to those who have given their support for the publication of the volume: SEPS (Segretariato per le Pubblicazioni Scientifiche) and its Chairman, Fabio Alberto Roversi Monaco; the Department of Economics of the University of Bologna and its former Director, Giorgio Bellettini; and the Department of Interpreting and Translation and its former director, Silvia Bernardini. The editors would also like to give heartfelt thanks to all those at Brill who have worked on the publication of this volume, in particular Melissa Allieri and Fem Eggers.

Illustrations

Figures

4.1 Model sharecropping farm divided into four sections 75
7.1 Silk imported and exported from the city of Bologna 185
10.1 Hydraulic macrosystem of Bologna (16th–19th centuries) 291
10.2 Typology of underground conduits supplied by the Reno canal in the city (Bologna, 17th– 18th centuries) 294
10.3 Silk mill "alla bolognese" (external) 301
10.4 Pedini silk mill (internal) 302
11.1 The scale in a sketch 308
11.2 "Mill moved by animal power" 309
11.3 "Mill moved by animal power" 310
11.4 Water-powered silk mill I 335
11.5 Water-powered silk mill II 336
12.1 Postures of the body I 373
12.2 Postures of the body II 374
13.1 Clockmaking, the gearwheel and teeth of a tower bell 391
13.2 Silkmaking, geometrical image of the silk mill of Piedmont producing organzine 395

Centre Fold Figures

Sharecroppers' house 211
Ploughing a field with oxen 211
Threshing wheat and machine baling of straw 212
Model of the silk mill machine "alla bolognese" (mulino da seta) 212
Silk factories, Bologna 213
Silk mill, Bergamo 213

Maps

4.1 Distribution of sharecropping farms in Emilia Romagna, 1961 107
4.2 Distribution of sharecropping farms in Emilia Romagna, 1970 107

Graphs

4.1 Daily work hours: temporary workers and sharecroppers, hemp farm A 87
4.2 Daily work hours: temporary workers and sharecroppers, hemp farm B 87
4.3 Daily work hours: women, boys, adult males, hemp farm A 88
4.4 Daily work hours: women, boys, adult males, hemp farm B 88
4.5 The distribution of female household labor between farmwork and housework, (farm A) 90
4.6 The distribution of female household labor between farmwork and housework, (farm B) 90
4.7 Daily work hours, farm C for one hectare 91
7.1 Cocoons brought into Bologna, 1568–1840 188

Tables

2.1 *Crop Rotation in Gallo, GIORNATE* 40
4.1 Household members in agricultural work, communes of the Bolognese plain, 1847 78
4.2 Size of *poderi* and members per household in six districts of the province of Bologna, mid-19th century 80
4.3 Size of labor force and size of *podere* in six districts of the province of Bologna, mid-19th century 81
4.4 Reduction of male and female working hours to a common unit 85
5.1 Licences granted to the rural shoemakers, 1747–1796 123
5.2 Urban shoemakers' shops and journeymen employed, 1697 132
5.3 Urban shoemakers' shops and number of calfskins worked, 1745 133
6.1 Weight and price variations of fresh and dry hides 161
6.2 Distribution of hides among three classes of tanners 169
6.3 Purchases of hides among three classes of tanners, 1577–1604 170
6.4 Skin quotas (*comparti*) and (attributed) incomes within the hierarchy of the tanners guild 175
9.1 Organization of the *Communauté des Marchands* and the *Maîtres Ouvriers* (1732) 252
10.1 Hydraulic plants in Bologna (1393–1797/98) 298
10.2 Water wheels in the hydraulic plants in Bologna (1393–1797/98) 298
10.3 Licenses for water to power silk mills in Bologna (1491–1620) 299
10.4 Groups who made their living from the silk industry in Bologna (1591) 299
11.1 'Force' or 'Form' of mills (grain mills) 323
11.2 Operation of machines 324

Notes on the Chapters

Chapters 4, 5, 6, 9, 12, 13 and 14 in this volume have already appeared in different publications in English. The editors of the present volume have avoided, as far as possible, modifying these essays in any substantial manner. They have limited their interventions to correcting typographical errors or minor errors of fact, ensuring a homogeneous format congruent with the other essays in the volume and, on a few occasions, making minor stylistic adjustments.

Part 1: Peasants, Landowners, Agronomists

Chapter 1. "Peasant Tricks and Landlord Strategies in the Bolognese Countryside, 17th to 19th Centuries."

Paper presented at the Institute of Advanced Study, Princeton, New Jersey, 1980. Translated by Vivian R. Gruder.

Chapter 2. "Between Agriculture and the Manor: Structure, Strategy and Ambiguity in Agostino Gallo's *Dialogues.*"

Originally published as "Struttura, strategie e ambiguità delle 'Giornate': Agostino Gallo fra l'agricoltura e la villa," in *Agostino Gallo nella Cultura del Cinquecento*, M. Pegrari, ed. (Brescia, 1999), pp. 73–108; also in *Intersezioni*, 2 (1989). Translated by Carolyn Kadas.

Chapter 3. Carlo Poni and Roberto Scazzieri, "Environmental Crisis and the Shifting Practice of Property Rights: the Bolognese Marshlands, 17th to 19th Centuries."

Originally published in *The Rules of the Game: Institutions, Law and Economics*, Aloys Prinz, Albert E. Steenge, Jörg Schmidt, eds. (Berlin, LIT, 2007), pp. 81–101; initially presented at the Seminar in Economics, Wettringen-Rothenberge, December 7–8, 2006.

Chapter 4. "Family and *Podere* in Emilia-Romagna: Peasant Sharecroppers."

The period covered is mainly the nineteenth century.

Written at the suggestion of the *Fondazione delle Casse di Risparmio dell'Emilia Romagna* and originally published in Italian in *Cultura popolare nell'Emilia-Romagna. Struttura rurale e vita contadina* (Milan, 1977). An English version, "Family and 'Podere' in Emilia Romagna," appeared in *The Journal of Italian History*, 1 (2, Autumn, 1978), 201–34. A third publication, "La famiglia contadina e il podere in Emilia Romagna", *Fossi e cavedagne benedicon le campagne* (Bologna, 1982) provides a more extensive analysis and bibliographical information. This chapter is an edited and revised version of the previous publications.

Part 2: Artisans, Workers, Merchants

Chapter 5. "Norms and Disputes: The Shoemakers' Guild in Eighteenth-Century Bologna."

First presented at a workshop on "Work and Family in Pre-Industrial Europe" at the European University Institute of Florence and at a seminar at the Arbeitsbericht Wirtschafts-und Sozialgeschichte at the Free University of Berlin. It then was published in *Past and Present*, no. 123 (May, 1989), 80–108. The author benefited from the comments of Wolfram Fischer, Alberto Guenzi, Hartmut Kaelble, Reinhold Reith, Annamarie Kleinert, Gunther Teubner, Stuart Woolf and Chris Woodall. The author thanked Vivian Gruder who provided useful comments on the earliest draft, and to Philippe C. Schmitter for his acute suggestions and criticisms. Translated by Patrick Leech.

Chapter 6. "Local Market Rules and Practices: Three Guilds in the Same Line of Production in Early Modern Bologna."

Originally published in *Domestic Strategies: Work and Family in France and Italy 1600–1800*, Stuart Woolf, ed. (Cambridge and Paris, 1991). © Maison des Sciences de l'Homme and Cambridge University Press 1991, reproduced with permission. It was first presented and discussed at the workshop on "Work and Family in Pre-industrial Europe" at the European University Institute of Florence (1984), and later during a seminar at the University of Pisa (1985), at the Wissenschaftkolleg zu Berlin (1986), and at the Department of Economics of the University of Bologna (1988). The author benefited from the stimulating comments and suggestions of Wolfram Fischer, Vivian Gruder, Abdellah Hammoudi, Christopher H. Johnson, Patrick Leech, Mario Mirri, Massimo Riccottilli, Michael Sonenscher, Heinrich A. Winkler, Stefano Zamagni. The author thanked Gunther Teubner, Philippe C. Schmitter and Terence Daintith who first introduced him to the idea of long-term contracts and negotiations; Wolf Lepenies for making difficult but fruitful criticisms; Patrizio Bianchi for suggesting useful tools of economic analysis; and Stuart Woolf who read carefully and provided many improvements to the text. Translated by Patrick Leech.

Chapter 7. "'Measure for Measure': From Fine Thread to Rigid Labor Control. Changing Conditions of Work in Silk Factories."

Originally published in *Quaderni storici*, vol. 16, no. 47 (1981), 385–422; it was republished and translated from "Misura contro misura: come il filo di seta divenne sottile e rotondo," in *La seta in Italia. Una grande industria prima della rivoluzione industriale* (Bologna, 2009), pp. 405–441. Translated by Carolyn Kadas.

Chapter 8. "Technology, Organization of Production and the Gender Division of Labor."

Originally published as "Tecnologie, organizzazione produttiva e divisione sessuale del lavoro," in *Il lavoro delle donne*, ed. Angela Groppi (Roma-Bari, 1996), pp. 269–296; it was republished in *La seta in Italia. Una grande industria prima della rivoluzione industriale* (Bologna, 2009), pp. 443–471. Translated by Carolyn Kadas.

Chapter 9. "Fashion and Innovation: Strategies of Lyon Silk Merchants in the Eighteenth Century."

Originally published in French in *Revue d'histoire moderne et contemporaine*, XLV, no. 3 (1998), 589–625; then published in English in *World of possibilities: flexibility and mass production in western industrialization*," eds. C.F. Sabel and J. Zeitlin (Cambridge, 1997, reproduced with permission), pp. 37–44; and published in Italian in *La seta in Italia. Una grande industria prima della rivoluzione industriale* (Bologna, 2009), pp. 497–542. Translated by Patrick Leech. This essay benefited from the criticisms and suggestions of many of the author's colleagues and friends, and in particular Fernand Braudel, Immanuel Wallerstein, Mario Mirri, Vivian Gruder, Peter Laslett, and Emma Rothschild. In the final phase, the author discussed the text both with Jonathan Zeitlin and colleagues in the Department of Economics of the University of Bologna. The author thanked in particular Roberto Scazzieri, Patrizio Bianchi and Gianpaolo Rossini for their stimulating suggestions and criticisms. The author benefitted from the help of Leonard Wetzler, who permitted a comparison of the notes and photocopies he had made in the Archives Nationales de Paris with the author's own notes.

Part 3: Engineers and Theorists

Chapter 10. Alberto Guenzi and Carlo Poni, "The Synergy between Two Innovations: Canals and Silk Mills in Bologna."

Originally published as "Sinergia di due innovazioni. Claviche e Mulini da Seta a Bologna," in *Quaderni storici*, vol. 22, no. 64 (1987), 111–127. Translated by Carolyn Kadas.

Chapter 11. "Behind the Scenes: The Staging of a Theater of Machines."

Originally published as "Scenari e fuori scena di un teatro di macchine," introduction to the first modern edition of Vittorio Zonca, *Novo teatro di machine et edificii, 1607*, Carlo Poni, ed. (Milan, 1985), pp. IX–LIII. Translated by Carolyn Kadas.

Chapter 12. "The Craftsman and the Good Engineer: Technical Practice and Theoretical Mechanics in J.T. Desaguliers."

Originally published in *History and Technology*, vol. 10, no. 4 (1993), 215–232 (www.tandfonline.com). The author expressed his gratitude to the following friends and colleagues for their advice and comments: Patrick Chorley, Roberto Curti, Patrick Leech and Paolo Galluzzi. Translated by Patrick Leech.

Chapter 13. "The Worlds of Work: Formal Knowledge and Practical Abilities in Diderot's *Encyclopédie*."

Originally published in *Jahrbuch für Wirtschaftsgeschichte, Economic History Yearbook* (Munich, De Gruyter, 2009/1), 135–149 (http://www.degruyter.com).

Part 4: Methods

Chapter 14. Carlo Ginzburg and Carlo Poni, "The Name and the Game: Unequal Exchange and the Historiographic Marketplace."

Originally published in *Microhistory and the Lost Peoples of Europe: Selections from Quaderni Storici*, eds. Edward Muir and Guido Ruggiero (Baltimore, 1991), pp. 1–10. Reprinted with permission of Johns Hopkins University Press; in Italian, published as "Il nome e il come: scambio ineguale e mercato storiografico," *Quaderni storici*, vol. 14, no. 40 (1979), 181–190; and originally presented as a paper at the conference on "The *Annales* and Italian Historiography," Rome, January 1979.

Chapter 15. "The Silk Mill: A Path of Research."

Originally published as "Il mulino da seta: percorso di una ricerca," in *ScuolaOfficina*, Museo de Patrimonio Industriale di Bologna, June–December 1985 and republished in *La seta in Italia. Una grande industria prima della rivoluzione industriale* (Bologna, 2009), pp. XV–XXII. Translated by Vivian Gruder.

Postscripts

Chapter 16, "Remembering Carlo Poni" by Carlo Ginzburg, was originally published in Italian with the title "Ricordando Carlo Poni: Una rilettura de 'Il nome e il come," *Quaderni storici*, vol. 54 (2019), 552-556. Translated by Gabriella Gruder-Poni.

Introduction: In Homage to Carlo Poni

Steven L. Kaplan

Employing a binary cadence, I would say that Carlo Poni often seemed "double": simultaneously elegant and disheveled, intensively focused and heuristically dispersed, patient and restless, disinterested and engaged, eager and discreet, tolerant and exigent, supple and tenacious, forthright and wry, pluralistic on many issues, yet intransigent on some. Who else could make of silk thread an object of mechanical precision and of unbounded sensuality, of fashion a vain caprice and a vector of rational action, of disputes a privileged avenue of reconciliation, of subaltern irony a mode of vengeful seduction, of guilds both stifling monopolies and startup incubators, of norms both internalized standards and performative exceptions, of property rights both forms of tyranny and redistribution, of innovation both creativity and occlusion? Where an inimical critic might denounce otiose paradox, I see neither languorous evasiveness nor idle playfulness, but method, an agile expression of the epistemological reflexivity that marks all of Carlo's work. He was not an historiographical quietist; I see him rather as infused with the spirit of the implacable *enquêteur* that Diderot imputed to Galiani.

Conventionally speaking, Carlo's investigations fall under the somewhat multivocal—it would have been curmudgeonly to say muddy—rubric of the "economic historian." This "field" denotes and connotes different things in different moment and places. In its most professionally instrumentalized, combative and exclusivist embodiment, economic history involves scholars trained first in economics, deploying theory called economic, and applying it to historical questions in which they are also versed. Cliometrics is the maximalist expression. This approach interested Carlo, who was endlessly inquisitive, but it was not the history he practiced. He criticized rather sharply, with others, an earlier and far more rudimentary form of quantitative research, the "Galilean" temptation in scholarship associated with the *Annales* school, whose long-run compilation of moving averages and other central measures of tendency risked obfuscating certain of the fleshy human elements, that convulsed with urgent appetite Marc Bloch's celebrated ogre, certain kinds of social practice and social relations that, beyond their intrinsic interest, helped to shape structures and inflect conjunctures. Carlo was never an historiographical luddite; without ever embracing a positivist posture, he worried about the administration of proof, the question of causality, the demonstration of claims. Traces and indices galvanized him and fascinated him, but I don't think they ever satisfied

 | DOI:10.1163/9789004713277_002

him. His rendezvous with Marxism perhaps predisposed him to look sympathetically at its laicized structural riff incarnated by the *Economies. Sociétés. Civilisations.* that for so long accompanied the title *Annales* and announced its colors. I think, however, that the "three-levels" mustered his enthusiasm more elliptically than the less procrustean approach of *histoire-problème*, a way of thinking about and problematizing notions, relations, institutions, behaviors, etc., and I believe that he evinced sympathy for the "critical turn" that the next generation of *Annalistes* engineered, in part in reaction to Italian influence to which Poni contributed.

The methodological agenda changed significantly, and not merely in scale and angle of approach or as a function of the emancipation—it was more like a deliverance—of the cultural, the famous level three in *E.S.C.* Heralding the end of the long hegemony of social history, stilted by its overweening triumphalism, this transformation also dislodged the economic, putative *primum mobile*, on which the social heedlessly surfed. I do not think that Carlo ever took an oath, in Richard Cobb's cruel sense, as a *frère-ès-conjoncture*, nor chanted *mea culpa* for his robust investment in what was (and still is) commonly called social history. Certainly Poni never abandoned the economic. It is tempting to say he relativized it, but in some ways, I esteem that it is more fruitful to suggest that, increasingly, he coded the economic as being simultaneously material and cultural (or symbolic). This conceptualization made it more difficult to isolate or stigmatize or—worse—flee from the economic; and it made it more difficult for culturalists, thereafter riding their tsunami of domination, to ignore or scorn or—worse—farm out the economic to highly-skilled journeymen enrolled as a specialized chapel.

Whether Carlo dealt with technology or with fashion or with markets, he was preoccupied with representations: with the assumptions of the diverse actors, with their fears, their aspirations, their capacity to apprehend and comprehend. Attitudes were not the biproducts of underlying, in some way ontologically prior economic or technological factors; they were independent as well as dependent variables, depending on the situation. Even as he refused to worship at the market-as-altar, he regarded the graven images with which that altar was adorned as at least as significant as the power the market was supposed to wield. The market did not enjoy a sanctuarized status, a transcendental, ahistorical standing, its self-referential "meta-ness" conveyed by the portentous definite article, the very "the" rendering actors more or less helpless to resist its "forces" or its "laws." It seems to me that Carlo's market was plural or multiple and variable, that it was, at least for centuries, at least through the early modern period, a socially embedded institution, that it was deeply shaped by cultural and political representations that chastened its imperious teleological claims. Market "forces" or "laws" needed to be contextualized, situated, interrogated, deconstructed, defined, mapped, measured, constantly evaluated and then reassessed. They did not stand outside of history or upstream of society. Efficiency and equilibria are metrics, or instruments or even objectives rather than predicates or self-evident, self-actuating Truths. Sometimes markets were specific constellations of relations; sometimes they bespoke material constraints imposed upon culture, and sometimes they were cultural constraints that shaped economic factors. Markets were at once about imagining, implementing and undermining regulations. In any event, they were not conceivable outside the realms of rules, norms, collective memory, and a repertory of tricks as well as canonical collective action. Supply and demand were about discourse as well as practice, about mechanisms (if not systems) of thinking as well as producing, distributing and consuming. In this manner, market coordination was about maximizing security as much as about maximizing profit. In terms as much Weberian as Polanyian, Poni's markets make society and his society makes markets.

Many theoretical currents enrich and inflect Carlo's thinking across the years. If I had to characterize them crudely, I would say that they were a blend (nevertheless) distinguished less by *cépage* than by *terroir*, and that the terroir was more often anthropological than not, but diversely anthropological, from Mary Douglas to Clifford Geertz, from Victor Turner to Terry Turner, from Levi-Strauss's structuralism to Philippe Descola's taxonomical implosion and ontological multiplicity. Much of this reflection acquired a specifically Italian flavor, extending from Emilia-Romagna to Liguria and beyond.

The range of Carlo Poni's interests is staggering; here I will confine myself to a few examples from historiography, only one of myriad sectors that mobilized his passion. Cloths and clothes fascinated him because they were at the core of the economic in the double sense that I just adumbrated: the material and the cultural or symbolic. The dominant expression of the industrial economy, spilling over from agriculture, textiles weighed massively in religious, social and civic life: draping churches and representing the Christian mystery in the Italian pictorial tradition, fabricating and broadcasting social status, demarcating political claims, etc. Carlo looked fruitfully at many dimensions of this sway of textiles. He deployed it to explore technology in its relations to ways of living as well as ways of doing, to issues of gender as well as of technique, to the mill as an embodiment of community as well as of capitalism. He showed us how cloth mediated relations between rival powers on the international stage and between city and countryside in the Bologna region (not merely an affair of unilateral urban colonialism). He demonstrated how proto-industrialization empowered and trammeled rural communities, how cloth-making reinforced certain barriers while displacing others, how cloth-making structured social relations of production in fresh and unlikely ways and altered the ways in which input and output markets operated. Even as he restituted a granular texture to the lives of proto-industrial actors, through his manner of thick description, he contested the idea that they lived in a rigid heteronomy that utterly deprived them of voice. With other scholars, he made of "proto" a phenomenon not reducible to technology or demography, nor susceptible to an imaginative economistic treatment turning, say, on something resembling principal-agents issues or moral hazard. Navigating these sites and spaces induced him to forge several telling ways of practicing *microstoria*, which I am inclined to view, to the chagrin of many revisionist colleagues, as an expression of a certain *histoire totale* on a human scale. Moving between town and country, between production and consumption, attuned him quite precociously to ecological questions. Nor did Carlo ever confine environmental questions to the residual rubric of externalities. They constituted the vital center of a new *problématique* that he left for others to elaborate.

Finally, textiles opened a further vista, testing and deepening his taste for transnational comparison (not only with France, but with England and Germany) and for a Bolognese sport called semiotics. From machines and mills, from silkworms and threads, from the sexual division of labor to the sexualization of cloth, Carlo inexorably found himself grappling with the notion and the modalities of fashion, a system of signs as well as a complex protocol of production based upon a play of forward and backward linkages. Carlo brilliantly scrutinized the stages, tensions and aporias in the fashion-making process, at once a commercial and cultural story, a collusion and/or collision between psychology and technology. He looked closely at the formation and transmission of information, of its multiple idioms, and of its perfidious asymmetries. Then he unpacked the connections between fashion and types of innovation in manufacture that had a variable influence on esthetic and moral representations.

Though his research defies pigeon-holing because his purview was unbounded, it does not seem to me unjust to cast Carlo, in one of his sundry guises, as an historian of work. Of work in the countryside and in the city, in the tensions and negotiations between them that structured and tested their relations; of work in the interstices, in the spaces not covered or discovered by guilds, in the streets, the attics, the backrooms, the so-called privileged places; of work as productive enterprise and the congealing of valuable capital; of work as suffering, subordination and/or social control; of work as creation and blossoming; of work as *tekhnikos*, in which craft and art compete to capture the notion of skill. In the world of work, his interest in technology intersected with his social concerns. It mattered to him immensely upon what workers worked: the grand oppositional solidarities or the (later) extreme divisions of labor did not dispense the historian from gauging the specific activities on the floor (or the table) of a workshop. It made a difference to sensibility, attitude and engagement whether a worker dealt with leather or gold or flour or wood or metal or silk or cotton or wool or hemp or wheat or beef or pork. There is an argument today that skills were often common to many professions, that professions overlapped, that transmission was less crucial than often imagined. Without overlooking these intersections, I think that Carlo was more struck by differences than similarities in the theory and the practice of most crafts (though he was more sanguine than I about the positive connections between formal knowledge and craft practice and manifestly less inclined than I to see in many parts of the Encyclopedist project a form of proto-Taylorism that denied durable value to the trade "secrets" that constituted much of work culture).

In any event, he took the trouble, whether in silk or leather or elsewhere to learn precisely how workers made things, how they constructed themselves even as they fabricated goods, how they refined their identities over time, and how these identities played out in the various arenas of daily life. For reasons that I believe were at once historical/historiographical and political. Carlo was deeply interested in the social relations of production, whether they took the form of the classic urban corporate trinity (master-journeyman-apprentice), or less formally institutionalized arrangements (entrepreneur-worker, journeyman-journeyman, owner-laborer, etc.) or more frankly capitalist configurations, for example, in one of many possible putting-out templates. He was struck both by the leverage and the limits of guilds, by their ambitions and their frustrations, by their mobilizing fictions (unity, harmony, monopoly) and their murkier realities. In the recent controversies, I reckon that he would have been closer in method and mood to the late Larry Epstein than to Sheilagh Ogilvie. If there was abundant work life outside the guilds, Carlo did not view those institutions as universally crabbed, cankered, clannish, cohesive, conservative, or as structurally inimical to innovation and inhospitable to economic growth. He argued that guilds did not characteristically or inexorably do what they said (thus the impossibility of extrapolating comportment from statutes, lived experience from prescriptive guidelines), that guilds often had a quite heterogeneous membership, that the artisans who acceded to mastership did not all march to the same drumbeat, and that they often competed, sometimes aggressively, in raw materials markets and labor markets as well as in the markets for finished goods.

That said, masters defended privileges and entitlements, though not all in the same way or with the same resources; and they benefitted from advantages that were not narrowly commercial or financial. Engaged in trades, often in complex ways and with astute strategies, these corporations were also quintessentially socio-cultural institutions (producers and products of social capital, more in the sense of Pierre Bourdieu than of Robert Putnam). Not coterminous with the world of work—far from it—yet influential in sketching out the premises of most regulatory paradigms, the guilds exercised considerable influence on the unincorporated players, and not just by oppressing/repressing them. Neither *Ganz Haus* patriarcho-paternalism nor top-down moral economy, the guilds often remained remarkably attractive for reasons that Carlo attentively noted, not only to its current membership, but to many journeymen and apprentices. Thus, the guild was invested in reproduction as well as production, replete with the contradictions that marked each stream.

The guilds that Carlo examined closely enjoyed both a coherence and a certain suppleness. They were capable of abject forms of arrogance, but also of a genuine capacity and will for negotiation. Masters manifested ambivalence towards rules and norms: they could not do without them, inside their own shops, inside their corporation, and in the various markets in which they were involved. Yet they frequently sought to evade, undermine or modify them when their interests shifted or the opportunity costs for compliance seemed exorbitant. The guilds contrived to settle disputes on the basis of regnant norms and institutional apparatuses. But they generated alternate mechanisms to resolve discord, compromises based on accommodating exegeses of recognized norms or contrived to offer compensations of various sorts (material, moral, judicial). Given his remarkable knowledge of supply channels, quality control, evolving divisions of labor, sub-contracting systems, and political connections between various corporations—notably in the same line of production—and monitoring authorities, particularly at the municipal level, Carlo has given us vivid portraits and probing studies of entire processes, running from upstream heights to diverse downstream applications.

With which side did Carlo feel a stronger affinity, intellectual and/or emotional? Urbane and sophisticated, logically he would identify with the city. Yet much of his finest research dealt with peasants, directly or obliquely. He was no physiocrat, but agriculture had allure for him because it framed so large a part of daily life everywhere. His study of household structure and sharecropping is an excellent example of a sympathetic and rigorous examination of how work forms and deforms rural life. My favorite "rural" Poni is "Peasant Tricks," a remarkable long-run gaze at social relations of production between rural workers and landlords (he insisted tirelessly on the great heterogeneity of the peasantry, on a complicated taxonomy, sticky but not entirely immutable). The tricks of the Bolognese region are, after a fashion, Carlo's Balinese cockfight: a deep plunge into the intersecting webs of sociocultural assumptions and relations. There is a dense semiology here that needs to be decoded, a repertory of actors, individual and collective, that both structures and subverts relations with authority. The tenacity of the peasants in their refusal to submit passively is redolent of certain of James Scott's resilient and rebellious Southeast Asian peasants. Poni's peasants need subsistence and dignity, not necessarily always in that order, and are tenacious in their refusal to submit passively. Their tricks are inventive, yet—to be durably efficacious—they are also reasonably transparent, or at least not opaque. Through their tricks, Carlo shows how the peasants recover agency, a tangled expression of volition, force and wagering. The tricks are meant more as leverage than vengeance. They are supposed to build the grounds for some sort of entente that is both face-saving and useful (or advantageous). The Bolognese cockfight, as it were, reveals the resourcefulness of the peasants, their capacity to identify and articulate their interests, and their determination *not* to humiliate their adversary (or rather antagonist), but merely to bring him to reason. A *tour de force*, for the peasants and their historian-anthropologist.

Eminently important as a major force in historiography, Carlo Poni was also a breaker and a broker: a *breaker* of stereotypes, clichés, bromides, received ideas, simplistic formulae, occluded interpretation, insularity and sectarianism; a *broker* of provocative ideas, of risk-taking, of relations among people unknown to each other, of fresh and nimble ways of thinking and doing. Voraciously curious, he was not just an accomplished scholar; he was a broad-ranging intellectual as well. Everything interested him (he was born enemy of the cult of the expert), and he believed that citizens generally should be interested in everything in their eco-system, writ large. He was a deeply humane person, warm, welcoming, excessively generous. Over so many years, I benefitted from the movements of his head and his heart. For having frequented Carlo Poni, I became a little better. In the parlance of my hometown, for me he was above all a *mensch*.

PART 1

Peasants, Landonwners, Agronomists

CHAPTER 1

Peasant Tricks and Landlord Strategies in the Bolognese Countryside

Carlo Poni

My aim is to analyse the link between the deceits of peasants (that is, petty crimes of the peasantry) and the development of productive techniques, the nature of social relations and the form of the rural landscape. A work of unification which proceeds in a dual path between the moral and the deviant, the visible and the invisible, and which not only uncovers the contradictions in the relations of production between landowners and peasants, but also analyzes the contradictions within the very system of productive forces expressed in the daily practice of work and of the control of workers.

From the end of the sixteenth century to the first half of the seventeenth century, the agronomists of northern Italy – in the Po Valley – drew a sharp distinction between the agronomy of the landed proprietor and the agricultural practices of the peasants.

Certainly learned agronomy maintained its traditional character, descriptive and didactic. It continued to describe agricultural practices according to the models of the Latin writers (Varro, Cato, Columella). It still taught agricultural "know-how": what must be done to cultivate wheat, beans and vines; but also new plants such as corn and mulberry trees. While retaining such traditional features, at the same time it was tending to become and in an increasingly explicit manner, the agronomy of control over the peasants, a body of ideological knowledge of inquiry into and denunciation of peasant cunning – of their tricks and deception.

The key figure in promoting this transformation in the sharecropping area of the Po Valley (basically the southern plain of the Po Valley) was the Bolognese agronomist, Vincenzo Tanara, author of *L'economia del cittadino in villa* (*The Economy of the City-Dweller in the Countryside*) published in 1644. The title of this book already reveals the author's intention, which was not to write a simple treatise on agriculture but to instruct the landed proprietors, who lived in the cities and towns, to take care of their interests on their land. Tanara developed this theme quite consistently, especially in chapter VI, where he wrote on the cultivation of land and the cunning of peasants in performing their labor. *L'economia del cittadino in villa* had an extraordinary success. Between the

 | DOI:10.1163/9789004713277_003

seventeenth and eighteenth centuries it was reprinted at least seven times (no less than four times in Venice, then the center of printing in Italy and a major publishing city of Europe). It inspired or influenced almost all the succeeding literature on agronomy for over a century. Among the followers of Tanara or those close to his view in the southern Po Valley (present day Emilia-Romagna) we may include the Bolognese Antonio Bianchi and the anonymous author of *Il Cavalier de passeggia la campana col suo fattore*; Codevilla of Reggio Emilia; two Modenese, Righi and Domenico Aimi; Battarra of Romagna; and two agronomists from Ferrara, Chendi and Farina. In the following analysis I shall refer especially to Tanara who offers the most insights about the deceptive practices of the peasants.

The break in the agronomist tradition which these authors carried out was to transform into conscious knowledge pieces of information already available in the oral tradition but previously neglected in written works, thereby giving life to a new paradigm which would have considerable influence at least until the second half of the eighteenth century.

This "new" paradigm could be represented, in the first instance, as a system of binary oppositions of either/or situations in which each alternative was the extreme of the other. On the one hand, there is the agriculture of the city dweller (*il cittadino* – landowner), presented as the "true" agriculture, as hard-working agriculture, the noble agriculture of the ancient Romans. On the other hand, there is the agriculture of the peasant, described as the agriculture of cunning, of laziness, an agriculture fallen from its ancient excellence, and sometimes characterized as new or modern. To understand the reason for this break, which also expresses and deforms an opposition that has deep roots, it is necessary to analyze the material and subject of this agronomy: the agriculture of sharecropping.

Here I limit myself to analyzing the fundamental character of sharecropping in the Bolognese plain. We may consider that all types of sharecropping resemble each other. For example, sharecropping supposes the existence of landless peasants, the land belonging to proprietors living in the city (nobles, urban bourgeois, the church). In the Bolognese region the landowners provided the land, the small house, the stable – which constituted the *podere* (farm), the unit of agricultural production – and half of the seed; they also chose the crops to be grown and the fields for their cultivation. The peasants provided all the labor – their personal labor, that of their families, and when needed live-in farmhands and hired day-workers especially for the summer harvesting and ditch-digging; all the instruments – the plough, the wagon, the wheelbarrow, the spades, the hoes, the flails; all the oxen and cows for tilling the land; and half of the seed.

In return for their contribution to production, the landowners claimed for themselves half of the annual gross production, while the sharecroppers retained the other half. The landowners' share often included an important part of the produce necessary for the peasants' subsistence. The peasants therefore were forced to borrow grain, beans or corn to eat or for sowing, and thus also became the debtors of the landowners. In this situation the sharecropping contract was altered. At the end of the annual cycle of production, in October, when the produce was to be divided, the peasants had to pay their debts in kind. The result was that the proportion the sharecroppers paid was increased and their own share diminished, a practice that perpetuated their debts. Often in an unequal exchange, peasants paid in wheat and received loans in inferior cereals (barley and millet) and beans.

By custom, the sharecropping contract was annual and was renewed tacitly every year. But sharecroppers burdened with debts and unable to produce a quantity of crops equal to the average rent were often threatened with termination of the lease and eviction. According to the municipal statutes, the eviction notice had to be sent by May for the following November, but it became a common practice (though its origins are unknown) to serve notice of eviction five months earlier, before the preceding Christmas, leaving a period of almost one year for the family to find another farm. The peasants won a small advantage that the landowners sought, with little success, to eliminate.

Apart from the half the peasants had to provide to the town-dwelling landowners, they also had to make additional contributions called *patti* (compacts):

1. Free services, such as the transportation of the owner's share of the harvest to the warehouse in the city.
2. Payments in kind as specified by the municipal statutes: a pair of capons or hens for Christmas; 100 eggs for Easter; chickens during the feast of Ascension in August; and a duck for All Saints Day. In addition, half of any pigs raised beyond the legal limit, which was set at one pig for each two hectares of cultivated land with a maximum of four pigs.

These contributions were probably of limited economic importance. But they tended to increase between the seventeenth and nineteenth centuries. In the first half of the nineteenth century a Bolognese agronomist calculated that these payments increased the share of the landowners by an average of seven percent, even reaching a maximum of twenty-five percent according to certain writers favorable to the peasants. If this were true, then the landowner's share might be not one-half but two-thirds of gross production. This increase resulted not only from raising traditional contributions (demanding, for example, more fowls, more pigs), but also from introducing new compacts, such as a money rent for the house or a fee for the use of pasturage.

The economic weight and significance of the compacts can be linked to the patterns of labor productivity over long periods. The work incorporated permanently in the land improved its productivity, and created the conditions for increasing the contributions, as did the landowner's investments in fixed capital (in the house, stables, new plantings of trees and vines, improvements in the drainage, etc.). One may say that these compacts were an instrument tending to hinder the accumulation of surpluses by the peasants and to keep their remuneration (save for a small minority) at the level of subsistence.

Within this economic structure profound contradictions were at work. On the one hand, the landowners – who avoided all the short-term investments in the means of production whose total profit would not be returned to him – sought to compel the peasants to supply, without limit, the means of production, including their labor-power. In other words, the landowners sought to increase gross production at the expense of the peasants, in order to obtain the agreed half, or additional production, even if this surplus of production was obtained through a reduction in the productivity of labor to minimal levels of remuneration.

On the other hand, the peasants were forced to resist this pressure of the landowners. They willingly did the necessary work for the cultivation of cereals and vegetables in order to satisfy the food needs of their families. But they defended the productivity of their work and their contribution to the means of production (such as the livestock) on the basis of an instinctive comparison between the marginal cost of work and the marginal productivity. In any event, they interrupted their labor every time that effort was incorporated in a permanent way in the land and thus increased its productivity (one should recall that the sharecropping contract was annual). In particular the Bolognese peasants sought to terminate their productive efforts in the cultivation of hemp, a commercial and industrial crop cultivated over large expanses of fertile land in rotation with wheat, and requiring great physical effort. This plant was favored by the landowners because through its sale it brought in an income for a given amount of land that was higher than for wheat. In extending the cultivation of hemp from the nineteenth century onward over large areas previously limited to small plots, landowners asserted their right to select the plants to be grown and so to introduce a major innovation.

In contrast, the Bolognese peasants hated the cultivation of hemp and for good reason. First, the entire production of hemp, including the peasants' portion, was seized by the landowners and its value was deducted from the sharecroppers' debt. Secondly, this plant demanded a productive effort – in work and in the means of production – five times greater than that of wheat. And third, the amount of labor required a large number of salaried workers whom the peasants traditionally had to pay.

The chronic insufficiency in diet also pushed peasants to avoid the heaviest work and according to Poggi, a nineteenth-century agronomist, to resort to thievery, an almost "inseparable companion of sharecropping," a sort of "hidden compensation" against the vexations of the landowners.

In light of this brief sketch of the economic structure that operated as a code for the organization of work, there is no difficulty in understanding why the Bolognese peasants, like the other sharecropping peasants in Emilia Romagna, sought to replace the heaviest work with less demanding productive techniques. But the ruse of less work had to satisfy other particular and very essential demands. The peasants could not openly refuse to obey the landowners' orders for fear of expulsion or of a fine which had been carefully inserted into the statutes of the city. They could only respond with cunning, deceit and fraud. The lightest and easiest work had to imitate the heaviest work and leave a similar impression on the surface of the field. The peasants' aim was to make the landowners and their stewards believe that they had worked according to the stipulated rules and as a good and honest worker (*bonus vir*). Thus they sought to replace digging with the spade in the fields where hemp was cultivated, a real "yoke" for the peasants according to the agronomist Zucchi, with ploughing interspersed with spade-work at every third or fourth furrow, so that the field looked as if it had been completely dug.[1] Again in order to spare their physical labor, the peasants tended to replace the toilsome ploughing of furrows that were close and deep with less toilsome ploughing of furrows that were wider apart and superficial. In the latter case between every two furrows the peasants left a strip of land unploughed which they covered over with the earth from the ploughed furrow. The result was that the entire field had the appearance of being completely ploughed.

Tanara insisted that the landowners compel their peasants to plough the fields three times in three different months prior to the sowing of winter cereals, as stipulated in the statutes of the city and in the sharecropping contracts. The peasants, on their part, tried to reduce ploughing to a minimum. Both Tanara and the author of *Il Cavalier* condemned those peasants who sowed on unploughed land.

The peasantry's cunning use of agricultural techniques did have its limits. Their ingenuity never extended beyond the intelligent use of traditional instruments. If the ways of using these instruments became more varied, those

1 C. Zucchi, *Il duce agrario* (Bologna, 1848), pp. 20–21.

same tools, so far as we know, remained basically unchanged at least until the end of the eighteenth century.

In sum, the sharecroppers consciously used productive techniques as a means of producing on the land the effects of simulation – and dissimulation – with the aim of escaping the control (a control dangerous for them) of the landowners. Furthermore, the secret technical "tricks" of the peasants were not limited to ploughing. They included also a range of practices that tended to parallel the entire work process. According to a description in the writings of several agronomists, the sharecroppers dug the ditches – important for draining the fields of excess water – only as far as the landowners' eye could see. Tanara stated that the peasants dug only those ditches close to the path (the headland) where the landowners walked, with the intention of making them believe that the rest of the ditches were also dug in the same way.

The use of these productive techniques embodies the peasant's perception of the landowner's eye, his range of vision. These techniques were employed as a system of signs that produce metonymies (paradigmatic relations, according to the definition of Hjelmslev, or associative relations according to Saussure).[2] The peasant knew (in his own language) that the support of metonymy was nothing but an error of perception. His strategy of simulation was based on "error," what Charles Bally called "sluggishness of thought."[3] To understand the nature and style of these metonymies is fundamental for understanding the peasant's universe of images, for understanding the particular skill with which the peasant constructs his theatrical inventions. One can define these metonymies as opaque, because they hide the real meaning and as transparent because they transmit the imaginary meanings. The agricultural landscape appears as an immense scenography in "trompe-l'oeil," a masked space; a point of equilibrium between the visible and the invisible, the latter hidden behind a thin strip of soil or beyond the horizon of the landowner's eye. The peasant possesses the interpretive keys of his language. He understands it because he made it, because it is the result of his own work.

But the eye, the gaze of the landowner, is not a disinterested and inattentive eye. It is a suspicious eye that does not trust appearances but is vigilant as it watches over the process of work. "The eye of the landowner fattens the horse," says an old proverb. According to Tanara, the landlord should not remain at home but should circle the fields "in order to draw the greatest profit. If he

2 Louis Hjelmslev, *Prolegomena to a Theory of Language*. trans. Francis J. Whitfield (Madison, 1963), and Ferdinand de Saussure, *Course in General Linguistics*, introd. Jonathan Culler, eds. Charles Bally and Albert Sechehaye, trans. Wade Baskin (London, 1974), pp. 122–139.

3 Charles Bally, *Traité de stylistique française*, 2nd edition (Heidelberg, 1921), pp. 188–189.

approaches the strip where the peasant is ploughing, he will see the peasant stop the plough and maneuver it in such a way as to make a deeper and straighter furrow." In short, the landowner's eye becomes skilled. It changes and develops through the information it receives, and the control and analysis it carries out. It enters into the invisible space, uncovers it and makes it visible. But to attain this result it must decode the peasant's cryptography, uncover the indicators, conceive of new instruments of control, or use traditional agricultural tools in a different manner. According to Tanara, it was sufficient to open the center of the strip with the hoe to discover the "hidden tricks."

Agronomy was thus losing the didactic innocence of classical "georgic" agronomy. It was becoming the agronomy of denunciation, of inquisition, of control that seeks out the invisible behind the effects on the surface. In the work of Tanara, in particular, the relation between visible and invisible is, from the conceptual point of view, at the heart of the discourse. Under his penetrating gaze emerges what for a long period of time had remained behind or outside the bounds of knowledge. A new relationship is established between words and their objects. Old instruments like the hoe, traditionally used to cultivate the land, are employed in order to discover under the surface of the field the secret plot, the proof of the tricks and deceptions.

The landowner and his steward – the latter of peasant origin who played a complicated role as intermediary but also as a spy between the proprietor and the sharecropper – did not limit themselves to suppressing the peasant's tricks with fines and evictions (in the most serious cases) or to condemning the "modern" practices of the peasant and exalting the "good" agriculture of the ancients. Towards the second half of the eighteenth century, in some cases, the landowner improved upon the cunning innovations that the peasants had adopted to reduce their physical effort and incorporated these improvements into the productive process. One example is the *ravagliatura*, a new form of ploughing based upon the combined use of the plough and the spade. This technique was a clear modification and improvement of the technique invented by the peasant to replace digging with the spade. In the course of the nineteenth century digging with the spade was officially abandoned, especially on the large farms, and replaced by this new technique. This change, and the introduction of a mechanical device for crushing the hemp broke the bottleneck that had prevented the extension of hemp cultivation. Within eighty years the cultivation of hemp increasingly occupied larger land areas. From an average of 8 to 10 million *libbre* at the end of the eighteenth century the volume of hemp rose to 30 million *libbre* by 1870. This was a resounding defeat for the peasants.

The peasant's response to the landowner's challenge audaciously shifted to a terrain more susceptible to conflict. He learned to leave "an empty space in the center of the hemp-field for cultivating onions and other edible plants, and the hemp, grown tall [almost 5 yards] covered the secret."[4] The peasant's ruse, probably with limited success, modified the choice the landowner made for agricultural production. The space for the vegetable garden was enlarged, but "deceptively" hidden amid the hemp. Onions, squash and tomatoes ripened behind the dense vegetation of the hemp.

This conflict over agricultural cultivation and crop rotation ran deeply through the entire history of agriculture in the Bolognese area. Thus, according to Tanara, the peasants tended to fertilize their gardens with the manure that was supposed to be used on the *podere* and to substitute millet for hemp "if the landlord was not careful." Together with the author of the *Cavalier*, Tanara in particular denounced the peasants' practice of reducing arable land in favor of grazing land. For the peasants who owned livestock, the meadows were entirely within their portion of the sharecropping contract, the fodder being consumed on the farm to feed their cattle. But if the peasants tended to enlarge the grazing areas, on the other hand the landowners tended to oppose these practices. Not by chance the statutes of the city of Bologna stipulated that the peasants had to pay to the landowner 20 *soldi* and two *corbe* (equal to one quintal and a half) of wheat for every fifth of a hectare not ploughed and sown, or not sown within the required time. As early as 1454, and for the similar purpose of limiting the land set aside for grazing, the law set a maximum on the quantity of cattle, equal to one pair of oxen and one cow for an area up to two hectares; for every additional two hectares it was permitted to have one oxen or cow, one goat and one pig up to a limit of four goats and four pigs. In essence the landowner employed political authority to impose legal limits on the development of productive forces in one of the key sectors of the agrarian economy, cattle-breeding, because that development did not immediately result in an increase in the landowner's income but rather in its fall.

The Bolognese peasants not only sought to escape from the heaviest labor and to make the system of crop rotation less contrary to their interests. They also tried to take a proportion of the crops that was greater than prescribed in their contracts, in order to meet the subsistence needs of their families and to offset the weight of indebtedness.

4 [This chapter is based on an oral communication delivered by the author, and the source for this quotation is not cited. - Eds.]

Before delivering the landowner's portion the peasants took from the undivided stock – hemp, wheat, wood, grape must and beans. The stolen hemp they used to pay part of the salaries of the day-laborers and to barter with itinerant peddlers. The wheat which they hid under piles of logs and branches in the stable was their reserve, especially in times of scarcity. The wood they sold in the local market. And the grapes they ate in abundance and gave away generously, in accordance with an old tradition originating in the Bible (Deuteronomy), which the Catholic Church openly recognized and approved. These "deductions" from the landowners' part, generally small in amount, were done in secret. The peasants who were discovered stealing faced the risk of fines and expulsion.

But the weapon of eviction was double-edged. From the moment notice was given to the date of expulsion almost one year passed, during which time the peasants could ravage the land. They could cut up trees, vines and hedges to supply themselves with firewood, carry off manure and hay for their new farms, refuse to dig ditches, change the course of rotation, damage the house in an act of desperation or vengeance. As did the peasant Barba-Plin, a character in a play of the early seventeenth century who hoped that, after his departure, the house, stable and oven would collapse and fire destroy the piles of straw and hay. A new peasant might also be worse than the one evicted. The landowner had to consider this possibility and cautiously weigh his alternatives before deciding on eviction. Even he faced limits on his action. Tanara knew this well. After having revealed and condemned the peasants' deceits and thefts, the author of *L'economia del cittadino in villa* wrote in the concluding chapter of his work that it is "better to solicit, correct, and make the peasant work with loving words than ill-treat him with insults and humiliations, because they ... always find a way to cheat you without your being aware." He exhorted the landowner to have compassion for the peasants in their misery, to tolerate or ignore what they did or failed to do, to spur them out of their laziness, to help them overcome their baseness and master their ignorance, to defend them in time of need, to be their "godfathers and protectors." A paternalistic discourse on the one hand attributed negative traits to peasants – misery, failures, laziness, baseness, ignorance – and on the other hand, positive ones to landlords – compassion, tolerance, charity and protection. Yet Tanara was sincere in his views, being aware that social control cannot be purely repressive, and even sought to justify, in a limited way, the peasants' transgressions. It was natural for them to avoid fatigue, while the landowners lived in leisure; theft, if moderate, was their form of appropriating goods to meet the needs of their families, "to live, dress and provide for subsistence ... with the income from the farm they worked." These arguments contained hints of peasants' laments and offered concessions to certain norms of peasant culture, which may be called, adopting E.P. Thompson's term, "the moral economy of labor": a set of customs fluctuating over time but having deep roots in the cultural tradition especially represented by the Catholic Church.[5]

What did the Catholic church teach, in particular the church in Bologna, in books promoted by one of the most important ecclesiastical authorities, Cardinal Prospero Lambertini, himself a member of the Bolognese nobility and later to become Pope Benedict XIV? It taught, through numerous examples designed for confessors and according to the doctrine of Thomas Aquinas, that in time of extreme necessity all goods are common, as in the state of nature. This being the case, a "very poor" peasant, "abandoned by all," had the moral right "in time of dearth" to take flour stealthily, provided the amount did not exceed the extreme needs of his family. This portion did not have to be restored even if in subsequent years abundant harvests yielded sufficient supplies of food to enable the peasant to return what he had taken and still have enough for his family's subsistence. In normal years, those not considered years of extreme necessity, the servants – here assimilated to the peasants – who received "a less than just compensation" could resort to the practice of "occult compensation," stealing secretly from their employers' goods to a value equaling "a just salary." In short the Catholic Church devised a theological stratagem to rescue from the flames of hell those peasants who stole, but stole moderately and according to precepts of justice, in times of extreme misery.

The argument most sympathetic to the peasants is found in a work entitled *Dialogo sopra le mancanze de' padroni, e contadini* printed in 1785 and addressing conditions in the Bolognese countryside.[6] The anonymous author was unquestionably a cleric with a deep knowledge of works on agronomy and of the reality of rural life. He sharply attacked "unjust landowners, who searched for ways to cheat and overburden the poor peasants." In particular the author condemned the "compacts" when they were too heavy: excessive payments of fowls and pigs, excessive demands for free labor service, excessive rent for the house. The peasants, he argued, were constrained to make the payments prescribed in the compacts "in the manner of someone assaulted on the street and robbed of his money." It was not a surprise that they (the peasants) paid by robbing from the crops before their division, applying their rules – a *massima regolatrice* (a general guideline) – whereby they had the right to obtain their livelihood from the land they worked. The conclusion the author drew was

5 E. P. Thompson, "The Moral Economy of the English Crowd in the Eighteenth-Century," *Past and Present* (Feb. 1971) 50 (1), 76–136.

6 *Dialogo sopra le mancanze de' padroni, e contadini* (Faenza, 1785). [The editors would like to acknowledge their debt to the late Silvio Fronzoni for his help in identifying this text.]

that the "many vexations" the peasants suffered turned them into "thieves," and their "robberies" would be better defined as "just compensation."

While the Catholic Church offered theological justification for peasant robbery, short farces in rustic dialect from the beginning of the seventeenth century portrayed Bolognese peasants humorously congratulating themselves on their cleverness in stealing. The comedy by Giulio Cesare Croce, *Filippa combattuta da due villani* (*Filippa sought after by the love of two peasants...*), published in Bologna in 1612, was one of the most popular plays in the peasant theater (called *teatro di stalla*, "theater of the stable") and was performed by peasant actors until the Second World War. A clownish challenge takes place between the two suitors, Mingone and Gaspare, about the antiquity and nobility of their families. Mingone boasts about a grandfather "who at times robbed from the landowner, but this inclination was not a vice." In another comedy also by Croce, *Vanto di due villani cioè Sandron, e Burtlin sopra le astuzie tenute da essi nel vendere le cestellate quest'anno* (*The Self-Congratulations of two peasants about their astuteness in selling pressed grapes this year* – 1602), the peasants Sandrone and Burtlein are presented as two cheerful scoundrels. Burtlein says that he "came into the world only to pilfer" (*sgraffignare*). And Sandrone echoes him: "We peasants cannot live with so many compacts that weigh on our backs if we do not steal the grain." "No, no," answers Burtlein, almost offended by the word "to steal"; "they, the landowners want pigs, capons and money, and we go to the fair for hooks." And Sandrone cunningly responds: "Burtlein, the landowner tries as hard as he can, but no matter we will pay him back in his own coin." The two peasants brag that they steal everything: hemp, flax, grapes, beans. Burtlein says he uses "every skill" to avoid giving to the landowner "even one-third of his share." "But at least you give him a quarter," answers Sandrone ironically.

Peasants continued to fight their landowners with the weapons of agricultural tricks and thefts into the nineteenth century. But already towards the end of the eighteenth century the first signs of an epistemological transformation in agronomical discourse appeared. The scientific rules of agronomy began to change because the conditions of its creation changed, as did the criteria that connected and distinguished it from other forms of knowledge. New socio-linguistic connotations began to characterize its scientific structure. It became obligatory to refer, even if indirectly, to the new English and French agronomy and to the English agricultural revolution – the capitalistic transformation of agriculture. At the University of Bologna, a regular course in agronomy was introduced and the educational base created for a new profession, that of the agronomist. Professor Filippo Re, appointed to the new professorship in 1800, appears as the outstanding mediator-pioneer of this transformation. In his *Elementi di agricoltura* (*Elements of Agriculture* – 1815), the classification of land based on new soil chemistry replaced the old categories based on the dualities warm/cold, dry/humid, while the order of subjects follows the classification of Linnaeus. In these conditions of critical rethinking, the theme of peasant craftiness was expelled forever (together with cooking recipes) from agronomic discourse, but lived on, from the beginning of the nineteenth century and for fifty to sixty years after, in another minor literary genre, the almanacs. The thievery and tricks of peasants make their final appearance in the form of short dialogues, almost small theatrical scenes. The protagonists were the peasants Sandrone, Mongone or "Sgranfagnatutto" (pilferer), the landowner Liborio, the domestic servant "Sbagliatutto," ("blunderer") the steward and a mediator Dr. Trivellino. In these writings the peasant Sandrone defends himself, denounces the excessive contribution required by the compacts, and claims the right to live by his own labor. Responding to the landowner who accuses him of stealing, the peasant sometimes puts on the mask of the stupid servant, of one who knows nothing, at other times attacks, screams, and draws a knife.

In this same period, the first-half of the nineteenth century, the new agronomists came together in the Society of Agriculture and began to discuss the terms of the sharecropping contracts, which hindered the introduction of the cultivation of grasses in the system of rotation. This resulted, in the 1840s, in the reform assigning to the landowners half of the livestock so as to give them an interest in the cultivation of forage crops. In this manner the relations between peasants and landowners tended to change. This change was reinforced by experiments with the new agricultural machines – English, German and French – of the industrial revolution. By the mid-nineteenth century the thrust for innovation passed from the countryside to the city, from the peasants to the landowners. The agronomists, trained at the university, began to exalt the virtues of new machines – the iron plough, threshing machines, and reaper – while the peasants scorned the new and costly instruments that in principle they had to buy, which were often ill-suited to the physical and chemical nature of the land, and which they did not know how to use. It was the agronomist and the landowner living in the city who had to explain to the peasant how to use these machines. But the peasants particularly resented the new machines that reduced their possibility for maneuver and their technical autonomy. It was at this time that the city, and the landed proprietor residing in the city, discovered the "conservatism," the traditionalism of the peasant. The new progressive agriculture became a powerful arm against a peasantry that had become backward, tied to the past.

Among the practitioners of agricultural modernization were proprietors or large tenant farmers of Swiss origin, who wanted to promote livestock-raising. In their efforts they met with the opposition of impoverished peasant sharecroppers who had no livestock and were against the cultivation of forage crops. Not without self-pride Baron Crud, one of these Swiss tenant-farmers and a distinguished agronomist, recounts that only through persistent exercise of his authority did he succeed in compelling the peasants to sow clover – a work they did with tears and lamentations for fear they would have less to eat or starve. At this point the paradigm elaborated by the seventeenth-century agronomist seems clearly overturned. The good and true agriculture is no longer ancient agriculture, that of the "noble Romans." What is good and true is what is new and modern. The grave accusation of backwardness and conservatism directed against the peasantry becomes more intense during the nineteenth century and the first decades of the twentieth century – at the same time that cities and towns are being modernized.

The peasants could begin to escape from a condition of cultural subordination only in the early years of the twentieth century, when socialist proselytizers taught them that sharecropping was a feudal institution, and that the landowners were not only conservative but reactionary. The peasants, argued the socialists, must struggle for their emancipation – for the abolition of sharecropping, for collective property in the land, for freedom from superstition and religion, for a new society and for progress. This would no longer be a struggle employing cunning practices and petty crimes but an open struggle. One of these socialists, Zibordi, wrote in his *Nuovi dialoghi campagnuoli* (*New Peasant Dialogues*) in 1908:

> Look straight in the eyes of your landlord, respect him as another human being; loyally observe your contract with him; don't kneel before him, don't adulate him, don't trick him, don't sell with the labor of your hands your own conscience.

At another point in this dialogue the peasant is made to say: "It is only through our union that we can improve our conditions, and instead of competing among ourselves, be firm and never give in."

The cultural change of those years was notable and signifies a shift in morality. This occurred under the pressure of a socialist movement active among the agricultural day-laborers since late 1880, and particularly strong in the capitalist area of rice cultivation. These organizations in 1919 won over about eighty percent of the sharecroppers to a program whose long-range goal was the socialization of the land. But if we look closely at the demands framed during the difficult twelve-month strike in 1920 in the Bolognese countryside, which the peasants won (only temporarily), we discover that the socialist banner covered a number of goals that have deep roots in popular culture of centuries past: the abolition of all the contributions of fowls and pigs, an end to the rent for the house, the termination of free labor services, the right to cultivate a garden free of payments, and the right to minimal subsistence in time of dearth.

Five brief considerations may sum up this analysis.

First, the world of agricultural techniques before the industrial revolution belonged to a large extent to popular culture. The merit of Tanara was to have penetrated appearances and to have uncovered the clandestine process of labor, otherwise unknown beyond the world of peasants. The behavior of the Bolognese peasants reaches what we may call the extreme of duplicity. Yet duplicity is not the exception but the rule in the productive process, not only in the fields but also in the shops. Vernant demonstrated that in ancient Greek culture ability was always connected with deception, that "*techné*" (skill) was always tied to "*mètis*" (cunning).[7] It is the story of the weaker who defeats the stronger thanks to occult ability or tricks, as in the victory of Antiloch, the son of Nestor, over Menelaus. The popular world, the world of work, is lived with the help of deception. The secrets of artisans protected their patrimony of tricks and ruses, their "mysteries," which they stubbornly refused to reveal. Even Desaguiliers, secretary of the Royal Society, and Diderot and his collaborators on the *Encyclopédie* could not overcome the suspicions of workers in their effort to provide a scientific base to the techniques of crafts.[8]

Second, there was no clear separation between popular culture and the culture of the dominant classes. Rather there was a double circulation. The workers, in this case the peasants, played an important role in diversifying traditional techniques. This signifies also that popular culture is not necessarily the residue of a preceding culture elaborated by the dominant classes. But it would be wrong to describe the control by the landlord as always repressive; this control could even produce innovations.

Third, the contradiction between productive forces and relations of production operates within these same productive forces. At this level a permanent conflict is evident. And peasant technological culture can be seen as a continually changing response to the challenge by the landowning class.

Fourth, this challenge is connected to the increasingly closer relations between Bolognese agriculture and the international market. The hemp of

7 Marcel Detienne and Jean-Pierre Vernant, *Les ruses de l'intelligence: la mètis des Grecs* (Paris, [1974]).

8 See Part 3, Chapters 12 and 13 in this volume.

Bologna became the sails and ropes used in the ships of the fleet of the new mercantile powers. In 1748 a hemp merchant named Disraeli, grandfather of the future prime minister of Britain, followed the path of the hemp trade. He left Cento, a small center for hemp export near Bologna, to settle in London, the new trading center of the world. The peasants and landowners who remained in the area were equally affected.

The fifth and last consideration touches on the relations between innovation, transgression and camouflage. Mikhail Bakhtin, in his great work on Rabelais, describes the carnival as joyous parody of the official truth, as a grotesque disguise of the real, as the world turned upside down, as tolerated transgression of the rules of a life respecting hierarchy and order.[9] This research on the Bolognese peasantry demonstrates that the occult transgression of rules has profound roots in daily life, and that it is inscribed in the very practices of production and work. A truth largely ignored by historians but which Balzac attentively analyzed in *Les Paysans*, one of the novels of the *Comédie Humaine*.

9 Mikhail Bakhtin, *Rabelais and His World*. trans. Hélène Iswolsky (Cambridge, Mass. [1968]).

CHAPTER 2

Between Agriculture and the Manor: Structure, Strategy and Ambiguity in Agostino Gallo's *Dialogues*

Carlo Poni

The first edition of *Dieci Giornate della vera agricoltura e piaceri della villa* (*Ten Days of Real Agriculture and the Pleasures of the Manor*) was published in 1564. It was an immediate success. From 1565 to 1566 *Dieci Giornate* was reprinted in Venice three more times by two different printers, Domenico Farri and Giovanni Bariletto. Unique among the annals of Italian agronomy, its success continued. But for the author this was no cause for celebration, since these versions were in fact pirated ones and none of them had his approval. In a warning to readers, Gallo wrote of the *Tredici Giornate* (*Thirteen days* – the second edition, expanded from the *Dieci*)

> After I published the seven days of real agriculture with the three of the pleasures of the manor, I saw that the work had been reprinted in Venice three times in nine months, and it had not only been deformed and deprived of ornaments, but had been totally ruined with so many errors that I could hardly recognize it as my own (*Tredici Giornate*, "Ai lettori").[1]

Things were even worse on the legal front. The unfortunate result of Gallo's publishing the book so hastily, before the Senate of Venice had granted or communicated to him this privilege, was to encourage other potential pirate publishers. The decision to publish the book in Brescia was fatal, since the Senate's privileges covered only books printed in Venice.[2] It is no surprise that unscrupulous

1 I will always cite the first edition of the various *Giornate*. I did not want to gloss over the citations in the 1569 edition because I felt it was useful to at least give an idea of the subsequent additions and improvements to the *Dieci Giornate*. Obviously a systematic comparison of the various editions – which I feel is necessary – is beyond the scope of this essay. It would be useful to compare the Brescia version of the *Dieci Giornate* with the one printed in Venice. The printer Domenico Farri printed it twice in 1565 (using basically the same composition). Giovanni Bariletto published it a year later (1566).

2 In 1519 the privilege of printing was made conditional to publishing in Venice (H.G. Brown, *The Venetian Printing Press* [London, 1891], p. 55). It should be added that there were also

 | DOI:10.1163/9789004713277_004

printers with a keen editorial sense, such as both Domenico Farri and Giovanni Bariletto, reintroduced a work on the market which they knew would be a success. And so they reprinted it in small *ottavo* (pocket-size) form and in cursive for a wide audience, leaving out some prestigious ornaments such as the author's portrait, which in the Brescia edition was placed beside the frontispiece on the preceding page. In a second letter to the Senate of Venice requesting a new privilege – undated but certainly in 1566 – Gallo acknowledged that the decision to print in Brescia was a mistake, and complained about the Venetian printers' aggressive attack, writing that "they were assuming that the privilege of printing my book did not extend beyond Venice."[3]

In response to Farra and Bariletto's imprudent offense, which had defrauded him of "many years' work," Gallo responded with an effective counterattack. Practically denying ownership of a work that had been "dishonored" and "soiled," he decided to rewrite and extend it, adding "three working days, with the intent of having it printed in the city (Venice), so as to finally recover something useful from my long efforts at the practice of truly cultivating the soil and demonstrate more clearly how it was modern to the world and not stolen from the ancients."[4] This time (1566) Gallo waited patiently for the Senate's privilege for printing, which he placed at the beginning of the book, after the frontispiece, before handing over the manuscript to the Venetian publisher Nicolò Bevilacqua. In addition to the three new *giornate* which increased the book's length from seven to ten chapters dedicated to agriculture, he added an important inscription to Duke Emanuele Filiberto of Savoy, the notice *To readers*, a preface, and ten illustrations of rural tools (a precious resource for future historians).

To make the work less provincial he moved the inscription and tributes to Brescia from the beginning of *Dieci Giornate* to between the sections on agriculture and those on the manor. These features remained in the new edition of *Vinti Giornate* (*Twenty days*) (but between chapters seventeen and eighteen). It is likely that some of these changes had been suggested by the new entrepreneurial bookseller Nicolò Bevilacqua, who in 1573 moved to Turin with

---

other laws which prohibited Venetian printers from publishing books without the knowledge of the authors. The impression from reading Brown's book is that legal norms were violated fairly often and risk-free.

3 Archivio di Stato di Venezia, *Senato Terra*, Filza 46. Following this request the Senate granted a second privilege. See ibid., *Senato Terra*, Reg. 46 (1566–1567), March 23, 1566, c. 14'.

4 This harsh judgment may be directed at the versatile Francesco Sansovino who in 1560, under the pseudonym Giovanni Tatti, published *Dell'agricoltura* which was totally dependent on – almost a collage of – ancient agronomists. See M. Berengo, "Africo Clementi, agronomo padovano del Cinquecento," *Miscellanea Augusto Campana* (Padua, 1981), p. 59.

part of his family.[5] Still not satisfied with all these improvements, Gallo wrote brief introductions – about ten lines – to each of the old *Giornate* (with the exception of the first), added notes, mostly brief ones, in the chapters (indicated – but not always – by quotation marks), made some discrete deletions to pare down the discourse and rearranged the text with "a multitude of improvements in the language."[6]

Before discussing the work's contents, I would like to point out the improvements in language (not indicated by the author) because they lead us to one of the keys to this work and to the author's secret – but not so secret as to be invisible – dilemmas.

Agostino Gallo was a cultured person, a man of "good letters," and since 1563 an esteemed member of the Accademia degli Occulti (an academy of Petrarchian inspiration). Although for a few years he had operated a woollen cloth store, he was a member of the petty nobility and therefore belonged to the city's elite. He was also close to exponents of other elite movements for reform of the Church, such as Angela Merigi, founder of the Ursulines, and Girolamo Miani, founder of the Somasca Congregation.[7] But like all the urban elite he spoke a Paduan language (Brescian) different from courtly or Tuscan Italian, in which he had to and wanted to write. So Gallo experienced and suffered like all non-Tuscan intellectuals and literary figures from that burden that literary historians call the problem of language.[8]

---

5 On Bevilacqua's life and an account of the company he founded in Turin, cf. G. Vernazza, *Dizionario dei tipografi ... che operarono negli stati Sardi ... sino all'anno 1821*, eds. V. Armando and M. Bersano Begey (Turin, 1964), *ad vocem*. Bevilacqua moved to Turin in 1572 after extensive negotiations with the Duke of Savoy. His descendants, who remained in Turin after his death (1573), printed *Vinti Giornate* several times.

6 On the vocabulary of the *Giornate*, E. Pirro, "Il lessico delle *Giornate d'Agricoltura* di Agostino Gallo," *Lingua Nostra*, vol. XXX (1), 1969, 1–5; L. Dal Pane and C. Poni, "Le annotazioni manoscritte di Belisaria Bulgarini, alle Vinti Giornate dell'agricoltura e de' piaceri della villa di Agostino Gallo," *Ricerche storiche ed economiche in memoria di Corrado Barbagallo*, ed. L. De Rosa, vol. II (Naples, 1970), pp. 351–376.

7 Gussago, "Notizie istoriche intorno alla vita e alle opere di Agostino Gallo nobile bresciano," *Biblioteca Queriniana di Brescia*, ms. K.V. 49 (6).

8 M. Vitale, *La questione della lingua* (Palermo, 1984). This problem was also experienced by translators of Latin georgics. Thus Pietro Marino da Foligno in dedicating to Giulio Colonna his translation of Palladio asserted that he had to force himself to do it properly. If it is not "pure Tuscan – he continued – please pardon me, readers. Because due to the fact that I was born and raised in Umbria (today known as the Ducato), the established language has forced me to use the idiom that I have been used to since my childhood" (*Palladio degnissimo et antiquo scrittore della Agricoltura tradutto in vulgare acciò quelli che non sanno latina frutto e gran diletto ... acquistino* [Vineggia, 1538]).

In truth, in the *Protesti* to readers of *Dieci Giornate* he had sought to forestall criticism on the part of learned Tuscans or users-of-Tuscan, asking them not to scorn his "efforts ... due to poor style and the language of Lombardy," since he never had any intention of writing for them "but only for those who love manors and agriculture so that they can more easily understand the things appropriate for this delightful profession" (*Dieci Giornate*, p. 7).

To reiterate the limited and circumscribed character of his work, he emphasized that the *Giornate* were intended only to describe the practices and rites of "Brescian landowners and how to properly cultivate their fields ... and that apart from these [rites] ... I never thought to reason about the other ways used in other countries" (*Dieci Giornate*, p. 7^v).

These statements, however one wants to interpret them, reveal that Gallo was well aware of the formal problems his work hinted at but did not resolve. We should not necessarily believe that in his heart of hearts he felt that *Dieci Giornate* was so crude that it could not appear in the presence of learned people, and so limited that it could not be considered "modern" rather than "Brescian." His work, "even if it may be of some use to the world in terms of modern practices" could also be read by "simple persons who delight in agriculture" (*Tredici giornate*, pp. 351–352).

More than once in *Dieci Giornate* Gallo attempted to write in "illustrious" Italian. His descriptions of the landscape, of sunrises and sunsets (*Dieci Giornate*, pp. 152–153) show the clear literary influence of Petrarch, possibly filtered through Pietro Bembo's linguistic codifications. And it was precisely from Alberto Lollio, one of Bembo's most ardent supporters, that Gallo took the idea of the *Giornate*'s compositional structure: separating the pages on agriculture, i.e. on utility, from those dedicated to delight, i.e. the manor. Giovan Battista da Romano, in his oft cited letter of 1560, suggested to Gallo that he should write a work of the same value as the *Retorica* of the "most famous and celebrated Cavalcanti," with the goal of enriching "our language ... with a beautiful and useful book."[9] In his response Gallo did not take a position on this point. But I believe that in his heart of hearts he agreed, even though he was not able to write in "exquisite" Tuscan-Italian.

Three years after the *Tredici Giornate* was published Gallo added another seven days and reprinted it under the title *Vinti Giornate* (*Twenty Days*) with a new publisher, Antonio Percaccino (also Venetian). The newly added chapters

9 B. Cavalcanti, *La retorica* (Vinegia, 1558 [first edition, Pesaro, 1549]). Cavalcanti's initial problem was to express "the books on Rhetoric by Aristotle in the Tuscan language." Not that he wanted to write in a style that was "exquisitely composed and artificially adorned, but pure and clear" (*Dedication to the Cardinal of Ferrara*).

(a total of 82 pages added to the previous 180) were all on agriculture. These additions were important and rich with new information on beekeeping and raising silkworms. The organization of the text, however, remained essentially the same with regard to the 1566 edition.

To whom did Gallo direct his book? Questions like this are often difficult and intriguing. It seems clear that Gallo was writing for gentlemen and noblemen of the city, for those city dwellers who owned large and medium-sized properties in the countryside.[10] The leading character of the *Giornate*, the nobleman Giovan Battista Avogadro, had left Brescia to live at Poncarale in a beautiful house with an "undefined garden," a "beautiful vegetable garden," a large arbor and a small pond where he raised fish (*Dieci Giornate*, p. 1; *Tredici Giornate*, p. 38 passim). All the other characters in the dialogues are noble landowners from the city with the exception of Stranito, a herdsman originally from the mountains who appears for the first time in one of the *Giornate* added to the 1566 edition.

What Gallo proposed to this urban nobility, by then little engaged in military careers – even though noble names continued to appear among the *condottieri* of the Republic of Venice – was a new social and professional role: that of the gentleman-farmer.[11] Cultivating the soil could be more profitable than any other activity, mercantile or military. No profit was "more worthy of each noble person" than what came from the fields. Evidence for this were the lives of many ancient Romans: from Curtius Dentatus to Cincinnatus, from Cato to Scipio and to Emperor Diocletian. More than the most useful of all the arts, because "it gives life to the whole world," agriculture was also the "holiest" and most blessed, "because the man who delights in these matters is never idle." To this the name "Christian" fits, the cultivator of the soil praised by the saints "who always held that working the land was healthy for body and soul" (*Dieci Giornate*, pp. 192^{v}-193).[12]

---

10 We must bear in mind that the book – all books – could be read by an audience other than the one imagined by the author.

11 On the decline of the military role of the nobility on the mainland, see P. Pieri, *Il Rinascimento e la crisi militare in Italia* (Turin, 1951), pp. 261–269.

12 Following the work of A. Lollio and perhaps also B. Taegio (*La villa, Dialoghi* [Milan, 1559]), Gallo went beyond the still topical discussion of the essence of true nobility (genealogical trees, wealth, virtue) and indicates the exercise of agriculture as appropriate for the urban nobility. For humanistic discussions of nobility see. F. Tateo, *Tradizione e realtà nell'Umanesimo italiano* (Bari, 1967), pp. 355–421 and the systematic investigation of C. Donati, *L'idea di nobiltà in Italia, Secoli* XIV–XVIII (Bari, 1988); see also *Potere e Società negli Stati regionali italiani del '500 e '600*, ed. E. Fasano Guarini (Bologna, 1978). A few years before Gallo, the Brescian architect G. Lanteri, after praising the excellence and holiness of agriculture, recommended it to anyone "be they noble or ignoble" (*Della*

This complex discourse, which uses the humanistic and Christian traditions to promote the urban nobility's strong commitment to agriculture, is anything but naive. Even though it appears at the end of the dialogues, it can be interpreted as an opening to other arguments aimed at directing and orienting profound economic and social changes, precisely as they were occurring.

According to Avogadro (Gallo's alter ego) a "good gentleman-farmer," even if he spends some time in the city, should live out in the countryside, close to his property, especially at the time of planting, irrigating and seeding. Every evening like a "good father of the family" he should instruct his workers regarding the various jobs to do the following day. He should then get up "at the break of day" to see if they were carrying out the "tasks assigned to them, carefully distinguishing which of them work faithfully and which instead are careless, dealing with the latter wisely and when the circumstances allow. Just as he should never choose bad workers or servants if he can have good ones, even though they might cost more, in the same way he has to do the best he can putting up with those who are not good when ... it is not possible to have better." Most importantly the gentleman-farmer should not send them away "angrily" if he does not want to run the risk of remaining without workers. So a good father of the family should always be "kind, caring and open-minded towards those who serve him, especially showing affection to those who are loyal and have served for a long time, showing them kindness by making small gifts of goods or money, especially to those who are poor. ... In addition, paying them always in cash, and not in kind, so that they don't complain" that some things

---

Economica [Venice, 1560], pp. 70–71). On Lanteri see G. Barbieri, "Il trattatello della Economica di Giacomo Lanteri letterato e architetto bresciano del secolo XVI," *Studi in memoria del prof. Gino Zappa* (Milan, 1961), vol. I. pp. 153–166. There were, however, some who expressed doubts about the nobility of agriculture. If agriculture – P. Lauro asked – was an art so "delightful ... for what reason has the nobility not conserved it to practice it? And why have they let it fall to the lowest persons among the human race? This is a common doubt about many excellent practices of the ancients that now have been neglected" (*Lettere* [Venezia, 1553], p. 135). We owe the translation of Geoponici and Columella to Pietro Lauro. See Paola Lanaro Sartori, "Gli scrittori veneti d'agraria del Cinquecento e del primo Seicento tra realtà e utopia," *Atti del Convegno Venezia e la Terraferma attraverso le Relazioni dei Rettori,* ed. A. Tagliaferri (Milan, 1981), p. 275. On the subject of the nobility and agriculture see: O. Brunner. *Vita nobiliare e cultura europea* (Bologna, 1972), pp. 250–255 passim. (the first edition in German was published in 1949); G. Benzoni, *Gli affanni della cultura. Intellettuali e potere nell'Italia della Controriforma e Barocca* (Milano, 1978), pp. 134–143; F. Angiolini, "Le basi economiche del potere aristocratico nell'Italia centro-settentrionale dal XVI al XVIII secolo," *Patriziati e aristocrazie nobiliari*, eds. C. Mozzarelli and P. Schiera (Trento, 1978), pp. 37–63; P. Lanaro Sartori, pp. 284–288; E. Casali, *Il villano dirozzato* (Florence, 1982), pp. 85–99, passim.

are expensive or not good. To pay "liberally" salaried ("mercenary") workers was to be considered a point of honor, just like feeding them "at the proper hours." A "discrete father of the family" should not be upset if his workers eat a bit more than usual, nor should he send them outside in torrential rain or snow, or offend them with "rudeness." If he wants to get rid of servants "who are not well-intentioned" he should first pay them "for anything owed and then let them go with a generous payment" (*Dieci Giornate*, pp. 12–19^{v}).

It is easy to see in these pages the influence of the Biblical commandment to "pay workers their wages" which the fathers of the Council of Trent had reaffirmed by condemning payment in kind. A more personal touch in line with the spirit of the time is Gallo's additional exhortation to donate to the poor with "courteous" acts, to treat workers and servants with respect, and to be liberal and kind in providing generous payments when dismissed.[13]

After laying down these general principles Gallo turns to describing and evaluating "*massaria*" contracts (a form of sharecropping leaseholds common to the plains around Brescia) and landowners' management strategies. He urged them to make "honest contracts" with sharecroppers; to "be good company to them"; to forgive them if they stole something small "beyond what was theirs"; not to replace peasants too often; not to demand major gifts or gratuities from them which will cause the peasant to work less hard or perhaps even cheat him; to settle accounts with them "at least once a year"; to assist them with fodder in times of poor harvest; to give dowries to the daughters of poor sharecroppers "so that they may better have good fortune"; and "not to make any effort to enrich themselves on the misery of their peasants" (*Dieci Giornate*, pp. 19–20; 148^{v}-49). Landlords should not introduce into contracts clauses advantageous only to themselves and "damaging to the sharecropper," but only those "clauses advantageous to the estate" and to both contracting parties, such as "ploughing, harrowing, and thoroughly cleaning the fields," sowing "with good seeds," and hoeing legumes, millet and wheat in March (pruning). Contract clauses should not indicate these tasks generically, but should specify each work, how it should be done, how long it should take and "how many times a year." Gallo does not hesitate to emphasize more than once the importance of springtime pruning, because often "weeds suffocate the fodder crops and draw them down. … Then it is not surprising that most of the sheaves have no wheat." Landlords must require peasants on specified days to level the ground with an earth-scraper, dig ditches, and clean irrigation

13 In the city of Bologna "courtesy" was a sort of "generous gratuity" that silk merchants-entrepreneurs gave, spontaneously and without being asked "for being well-served," to workers who were good at spinning or weaving. [See ch. 7 in this volume.]

canals.[14] During the peak of the work season in the countryside – from May to October – landlords should not make sharecroppers transport their "stuff" (the landlords' share of the harvest) from the countryside to the city, "because of the damage that will result – especially when sowing must be done – by delaying one week to another or one day to another." He also urged landlords not to torment and not to criticize severely the peasants so as not to discourage and sadden them, and not induce them to leave the farm with the "chimera of a better prospect." To avoid future conflict he advised to choose peasants more carefully. Before taking on a new sharecropper he should find out about his habits – to ensure that he wasn't "a bad worker or had a bad character" – either from "the landlord whom he left or neighbors and others who know him." Once he made the choice, he suggested keeping him on, encouraging him to put down his roots on the farm, and to "persevere, cheerfully cultivating better all the time, so he may see that his kind master will treat him well." Indeed, no land will be "happier" than one that "is cultivated by workers born there, so that they love it like their own, and know very well from place to place the nature and quality of the land" (*Dieci Giornate*, pp. 19–21^{v}).

The author's close examination of "honest contract clauses," his criticism of those that were unjust, and the many expressions of solidarity with the peasants do not portray relations between landowners and sharecroppers as they actually were in real life. Rather they indicate the norms according to which the lords of the land, the *padroni*, should behave. No one knew better than Gallo that the ideal model was far from reality. He shared the opinion that the sharecroppers were mainly disloyal and bad. But in contrast to other detractors of peasants, he uses this conviction to launch an unexpected and hard attack on the old agricultural order and to those sharecropping contracts he sought to purge of the most unjust burdens.

The initial form of this attack is unusual. And it is expressed in the contrast – inspired by Columella – between the urban nobility's farming methods and those of the peasants. Abandoned to "wretched" and "crude peasants," the land became so "scorned" that it no longer yielded "good harvests." Only if it were returned to "sensible" citizens, who would cultivate it "with that purity and diligence of noble Romans," would it be able to produce "substantially more than it does" (*Dieci Giornate*, p. 22).[15] In practice Gallo proposed

14 On the digging of ditches and leveling of fields, see C. Poni, *Fosse e cavedagne benedicon le campagne* (Bologna, 1982), pp. 52–86 passim.

15 In his dedication to Emanuele Filiberto (*Tredici Giornate*, p.n.n.), Gallo says that the practice of agriculture, "this ancient and most generous mother," had become "too deficient and miserly" because it had been spurned by lords and noblemen. It would begin to thrive again when returned "to the grace of its noblest and generous children, as it was

replacing sharecropping with management "on one's own," already practiced in the Brescian plain, and what we may call "*boaria*" or "*biolcheria,*"[16] Returning in the tenth chapter to the topic of how to manage the land, the nobleman Avogadro – the protagonist of the *Giornate* – affirmed that "to farm more intelligently" he had bought "last year (1552?) bulls, horses, wagons, ploughs and all that is necessary to work this landed property, in the way that I want. And by God's grace, so far I have had the type of men in my house, that if they are not as good as I would like, they are at least willing to obey me in the day-to-day things I command them to do; which is rare to find among sharecroppers, some of whom take one's words in the worst way they can. But I decided never to give land to such ignorant people, so that they will not be able to tyrannize me every day as they did in the past." With this new form of management Avogadro harvested "just this last year more wheat than the sharecropper who just left had harvested in the last three years all together. This being the first [year] the yield will not be what it will be in other [years]. At the same time I am hopeful about the millet and the other crops that I am about to harvest." He would also have liked to cultivate the land that he owned (but rented out) at Ghierola "because I am sure that I will obtain at least twice as much" (*Dieci Giornate*, pp. 189^{v}-190^{v}).

What is the structure of this landed property where the landlord was the sole owner of the capital? From Gallo's work we can observe that the farm work was done by "men" paid "in cash every evening." The oxhand and cowhand lodged in the house where the sharecropper had formerly lived and were responsible for the care and use of the livestock (for ploughing, transport, etc.). The annual wage for these two workers was 10 and 15 *scudi* respectively, plus "for their food ... three sacks of flour, eight kegs of wine and as many *libre* of salted meat, cheese, oil, salt and wood as they need." Avogadro, enthusiastic proponent of agriculture at one's own expense, also insisted on the need to

---

during the happy Roman Empire." In short, city people should have exercised stronger control over cultivating the soil according to the model adopted from classical antiquity. On the *Führerprinzip* in Latin agronomists, see W. Kaltenstadler, *Arbeitsorganisation und Führungsystem bei den römischen Agrarschriftstellern* (Stuttgart-New York, 1978).

16 [The "*boaria*"and "*biolcheria*" contracts are mixed contracts. They differ from sharecropping contracts because the peasants earn wages in money and in crops, and they do not possess work instruments and animals for cultivating. Similar to the sharecroppers, they and their families live in a house on the farm owned by the proprietor, they work only for the landowner, and use the landowner's livestock in their work. *Biolcheria*, a traditional form of farming contract in which the farm is managed by a salaried foreman. derives from *biolca*, a unit of surface still used in northern Italy. The editors would like to thank Silvio Fronzoni for his assistance in explaining this terminology. – Eds.]

pay high wages to the oxhand and cowhand in order to obtain everything useful "that one can expect from agriculture" and to pay day workers punctually (*Dieci Giornate*, pp. 22–23).[17]

The scenarios for these new entrepreneurial strategies (a type of capitalism, one may say) were reinforced in the seventh and tenth *Giornate* by a sharp critique of sharecropping and the deceipts of sharecroppers. The seventh *giornata* contains a meticulous classification and analysis of these tricks, divided into three sub-groups: those that damage the *padrone* but not the sharecropper; those that damage the *padrone* to the advantage of the sharecropper; and those that damage the *padrone* and partly also the sharecropper (*Dieci Giornate*, pp. 124–127v).[18] In contrast, the tenth *giornata* contains a violent attack on one of Avogadro's interlocutors – Cornelio Ducco – on account of his "deceitful sharecroppers. … so rough and old fashioned in their crooked habits" that they always answer "unreasonably." It would be better to transform the lands into pastures than to "allow them to be worked by such vicious people" (*Dieci Giornate*, p. 190).

It would be difficult to overestimate the importance of Gallo's intense analysis of "independent" management. In contrast to all his predecessors, he carried out a profound revolution in the practice of agriculture. Gallo was the first agronomist to assert the superiority of the "capitalist form of farming" – described in terms of essential organizational tasks – over traditional

17 On these topics see also Carlo Poni, "Alcuni problemi di storia della mezzadria," *Agricoltura e sviluppo del capitalismo*, (proceedings of the conference organized by the Gramsci Institute, Rome 20-22 April 1968), (Rome, 1970), pp. 460–465, and Roberto Finzi, *Monsignore al suo fattore, Le "Istituzioni di Agricoltura" di Innocenzo Malvasia (1609)* (Bologna, 1979), pp. 79–85. During the 16th century, probably in the well-irrigated lowlands, the *aziende a boaria* began to spread. But the *massaria* form of sharecropping remained the most prevalent form in most areas. At the end of the 18th century Arthur Young wrote: "all the land on the Brescian and the Veronese territory are left at half produce, alla metà" (*Travels during the years 1787, 1788 and 1789*, vol. II [London, 1794], p. 154). This clear statement applies especially to the high-middle plains crossed by Young in his travels from Milan to Venice. About ten years later F. Ugoni confirmed that *biolcheria* were most common in the well-irrigated lowlands where flax and clover were cultivated in rotation with wheat (F. Ugoni, "Memoria sopra l'agricoltura di una porzione del dipartimento del Mella situata al mezzogiorno," *Annali dell'agricoltura del Regno d'Italia*, t. V [Milan, 1810], pp. 3–10).

18 On the technological trickery of Bolognese farmers, see Carlo Poni, *Gli aratri e l'economia agraria nel bolognese dal XVII al XIX secolo* (Bologna, 1963), pp. 43–70 and ibid., *Fossi e cavedagne*, pp. 52–57, 61–62 passim and ch. 1 in this volume. See also V. Hunecke, "Agronome und Bauern, Probleme bäuerlichen widerstands in Italien während des 16. Und 17. Jahrhundert," *Von Elend der Handarbeit, Beiträge zur historische Unterschichtenforschung* (Stuttgart, 1981), pp. 205 passim.

ones (sharing the yield from the land). He was the first to encourage city landowners to invest capital in tools and the means of production. And to promote, with his propaganda of the increase of gross product and earnings, the transformation of peasants into wage laborers, and thus transform the criticism of "sharecropping" production which favored the autonomy of peasants, into the prospect of a new estate structure founded on the decisions and commands of the proprietor, already an entrepreneur. No less important, from the point of view of the history of work culture, was his analysis of the tricks, also technological, of sharecroppers to reduce their contribution in the means of production and to gain for themselves a larger share of the earnings than their contract permitted. This was no longer a slanderous and strident accusation against peasants, who were never satisfied.[19] Rather it was a classification and analysis of the hidden and "almost hidden" work practices of peasants, and the negative consequences of these practices on the yield from the land and the division of the product. Without a doubt this represented a significant epistemological breakthrough.

Yet there is something more. Gallo's discourse defines, in addition to the strict subordination of peasants to city landowners, a new relationship between the city and the countryside. The domination of landlords over peasants becomes more intimate, penetrating the most closely guarded secrets of rural life, and claims to teach and impose on peasants the "true" way of working the land. The Brescian agronomist repeatedly asks for the establishment – based on the model created by the "most knowledgeable Romans" – of a new governing authority for the "wretched nation" of crude and ignorant peasants, with magistrates authorized to enforce good cultivation of the land to achieve abundant harvests (*Dieci Giornate*, pp. 22, 63^{v}). In the scenario envisioned by Gallo these magistrates would have enormous power, to the point of being able to seize through taxation half the harvest of poorly cultivated land, sell it at auction, and order the whipping and imprisonment of cheating peasants (Letter to Vincenzo Stella of 17 September 1563).[20]

---

19 On the satire of peasants, see D. Merlini, *Saggio di ricerche sulla satira contro il villano* (Torino, 1894); P. Camporesi, *La maschera di Bertoldo* (Torino, 1976); idem, *Il paese della fame* (Bologna, 1978). Gino Benzoni has shown that the satire of peasants flourished again in the life of the manor (*Gli affanni della cultura*, pp. 138–143). But see also Brunner, *Vita nobiliare*, pp. 88 ff.

20 The proposal to condemn bad farmers to prison in Venice returns in the pages about cultivating vines. Gallo writes that if the "poor vines" could denounce the offenses that peasants make against them "and find judges who will do justice to them– this is Avogadro speaking –there would be enough ignorant peasants to fill a hundred prisons. Punishment indeed appropriate for comparable generations who, not knowing, neither want to learn

Managing the land "on one's own account" called for new operating strategies. Forecasts of costs always had to be compared with forecasts of earnings in an attempt to achieve "low cost with greater benefit." Avogadro said: "I have no other aim than to reduce my farming to the least cost and the greatest possible profit" (*Dieci Giornate*, p. 128v).[21] To that end he advised to plough "with a pair of oxen and just one man" instead of using "four oxen and two men"; to reduce the quantity of wheat seed per unit of cultivated land, but to us the same refined techniques as in "planting flax";[22] to hoe millet when it had just sprouted to avoid the higher cost of hoeing it when it grew higher (*Dieci Giornate*, p. 128); to purchase medium-sized but solid oxen instead of the big and expensive Bolognese oxen (*Dieci Giornate*, p. 19); and to cultivate "dwarf" millet that "ripens in fifteen or twenty days, compared to other millets, and thus is less vulnerable to bad weather" (*Tredici Giornate*, p. 51). Like a true Brescian he also suggested buying "ploughshares of the finest steel there is," because the greater initial expense would be more than compensated by the longer duration of the metal (one year instead of six months), by the reduced fatigue of the oxen and improved ploughing of the soil (*Dieci Giornate*, p. 133). He also urged the purchase of undivided landed properties because "with one plough and wagon one can work forty *piò*[23] of connected land better than twenty five that are in different plots and far away in different districts" (*Dieci Giornate*, p. 14).

He also recommended – in the words of the herdsman Scaltrito – slaughtering 50–60 day-old calves when cheese was worth comparatively less than

nor admit their errors" (*Dieci Giornate*, p. 63). Taegio (*La villa*, p. 56) also wished for the institution of magistrates. So too, towards the end of the 17th century, would W.H. Von Hohberg (Brunner, *Vita nobiliare*, p. 281) as would L.A. Muratori (*Della pubblica Felicità* [Venezia, 1749], p. 20) around the middle of the 18th century. In the Duchy of Modena the Magistrate of Commerce and Agriculture was established and operated from 1762 to 1768 for the purpose of encouraging peasants to cultivate the land better. See Poni, *Fossi e cavedagne*, pp. 200–204.

21 Gallo did not have the conceptual tools to separate income from land from profit, even though he uses the word "profitto" from time to time.

22 According to Gallo the low productivity of fodder seeds was due to the (wrong) technique of seeding them with the plough. The plough, cutting through the soil and covering the seeds as they were planted, resulted in the seeds being crowded together and lined up in a heap. In place of this technique, which suffocated many seeds, Gallo proposed to substitute sowing with the harrow and rake (*Dieci Giornate*, pp. 41v-44). About 15 years later (in 1580) Taddeo Cavallini obtained his first patent for a mechanical seeder. See Poni, "Ricerche sugli inventori bolognesi della macchina seminatrice alla fine del secolo XVI," *Fossi e cavedagne*, pp. 153–172.

23 Unit of land (see note 25 below).

meat, and to slaughter calves 25–30 days earlier when the price of milk (and therefore of cheese) was comparatively higher. As long as hay cost only 5–6 *lire* per hundred weight – continued Scaltrito – it could be advantageous to keep calves for breeding. But once the price of hay more than doubled it was "total madness" to keep them for the first three years of life until their first calving (equal to the consumption of six-to-seven hundred weight of hay). It was more economical to buy four- or five-year old calves (already pregnant) in the Alpine valleys and in Switzerland where they could be raised for "little cost due to the great abundance of pastures and hay in those mountainous areas" (*Tredici Giornate*, pp. 216–217).[24]

The key to calculating the profitability of investments, in at least two cases, was the cost of land. With prices at around 100–200 ducats per *piò* it was not expedient to cultivate fields poorly which reduced its yield and earnings (*Dieci Giornate*, p. 51); nor was it worthwhile to plant walnut trees to obtain oil for lighting as done in the state of Milan and in Piedmont, where the fields "even though the most fertile in all of Italy" were of low value because they were poorly cultivated (*Tredici Giornate*, p. 182). Another key measure was the price of products. A new way of cultivating a grapevine nursery – suggested by Avogadro – could produce 1,500 plants in one *pertica* of land; sold for two *marchetti* each, they could bring in 25 ducats, for a total of 100 ducats per *piò* (*Dieci Giornate*, p. 62). From *ruso* which dyers used as a colorant, one could earn at least 25 Brescian *lire* per *jugero*. But it was not advisable to plant this in humid soil instead of flax which could yield more (*Tredici Giornate*, p. 177).[25]

Marketing practices also received Gallo's keen attention. Pears were preferable to apples because pears, sold by weight, brought comparatively higher prices than apples sold by "volume" (*Dieci Giornate*, p. 89). Hay cut when "tender," and therefore less bulky, was not to be sold by volume, but by weight. If you were buying it, it would be advantageous to price it by volume. Conversely, hay cut "too ripe," and thus artificially swollen, should not be bought by volume but by weight (*Dieci Giornate*, p. 146^v). Fodder accumulated for months or years should be measured for sale only after having been "thrown over with

24 On the export of Swiss livestock to the Po valley, see J.F. Bergier, *Genève et l'économie Européenne de la Renaissance* (Paris, 1963), pp. 58, 75–76.

25 I was not able to identify "ruso," not cited in Italian-Brescian dictionaries. The Lombardian term "*piò*" is replaced, from the *Tredici Giornate* onwards, with the cultured word *jugero*, which Gallo uses as an equivalent of *piò*. A Roman *jugero*, equal to 2,308 m², is smaller than a *piò*. Another unit of measure used by Gallo is "*possession.*" According to a metrological manual from the 1700s, a Brescian *possessione* could be considered approximately 35–40 *piò* (a single *possessione*) or approximately 70–80 *piò* (a double *possessione*). See C.F. Cristiani, *Delle misure d'ogni genere antiche e moderne* (Brescia, 1760), p. 77.

a shovel from one place to another," otherwise it would lose 6 to 7%. But in which month or season should grain be sold, given the high variation in price? Gallo recommended not to sell "when prices are down" (just after the harvest?), but to begin selling when the price starts to rise, "all the more when the others hold back." Another technique was to sell grain at three different times: at carnival time (January-February), Easter, "if the countryside is beautiful," and the rest in May. In short, "it's better to sell and regret it than keep it and then despair," as happened to "some who were so greedy and stubborn as to keep the fodder when it was in demand, and then when the price collapsed they nearly died of pain while others hung themselves by their throats" (*Dieci Giornate*, p. 146$^{r\text{-}v}$).[26]

The quest for profit, even guided by prudence and reason, had its limits. Gallo recognized that cultivating madder – the roots of which were used in the dyeing industry – was more profitable than woad or wheat.[27] But he did not recommend its cultivation because of the harmful effects on the health of workers of grinding its roots. It was essential "to hold dearer the body's health and to earn little than to earn much and lose health and life" (*Tredici Giornate*, pp. 175–176). For the same reason he advised against increasing the cultivation of rice; although "of great usefulness," rice contaminated the air because of the long time that water remained on the fields (*Dieci Giornate*, p. 41).

The sense of these complex strategies is reinforced and enriched by his analysis of crop rotation. In contrast to his contemporary Tarello (the other great Brescian agronomist) who proposed just one rotation with two variations, Gallo describes in a non-systematic way a rich array of rotations.[28] These have no beginning and no end; they are only parts of rotations. To understand this one has to bear in mind two things. First, "ordinarily" – at least in irrigated

26 One of the images from Shakespeare (*Macbeth*, Act 2, Scene 3) is that of "a farmer that hang'd himself on the expectation of plenty". It seems that Gallo provides a pertinent key to interpreting this verse. Torquato Tasso felt that the family father, always well informed about current prices in Turin, Milan, Lyon and Venice, would have been able to postpone sales of farm products according to the forecasts "that one makes of famine and abundance over the years and seasons" (T. Tasso, "Il padre di famiglia" [1582], *Prose*, ed. E. Mazzalibrescia. [Milan, 1959], pp. 108–110).

27 Madder is indicated by Gallo with the names *roza* and *pergolino*. See *ad vocem* E. Canevazzi and R. Marconi, *Dizionario di agricoltura*, 2 vols. Rocca San Casciano (Bologna, 1871–1892).

28 C. Tarello recommended a four-year rotation with two years of legumes (clover), one of rest and one of wheat. For pastures, which he would have wanted to cultivate, he suggested alternating a long foraging period (15 years) with five years of wheat. See M. Berengo, "Introduzione," C. Tarello, *Ricordo d'agricoltura* (Turin, 1975) and R. Baldoni, "Camillo Tarello e l'avvicendamento agrario," *Atti del Convegno su Camillo Tarello e la storia dell'agricoltura bresciana al tempo della Repubblica veneta* (Brescia, 1980), pp. 77–81.

areas – fields in Lombardy and Brescia never lay fallow (*Vinti Giornate*, p. 176). Second, there entered permanently in rotation leguminous plants – vetch and oats for dry soils, clover and alfalfa for wet and irrigated soils; as well as industrial plants, especially flax but also woad and madder.

All the rotations or fragments of rotations found in the *Giornate* are laid out in Table 2.1. Here I will focus on four aspects. 1) a legume (clover) planted along with cereal required two harvests a year; 2) alfalfa grown in irrigated fields could be cut six or seven times a year (*Tredici Giornate*, pp. 36–37); 3) in three of four rotations or fragments of rotations there was a commercial crop; 4) commercial crops, cultivated on irrigated land or at least on the humid land of the lower (or middle) plain, were always preceded by two years of clover. Gallo explicitly states that "typical of flax it becomes beautiful where there are clover roots" (*Dieci Giornate*, p. 49). Along the same lines he recommended buying irrigated land, "because with abundant watering (and with a good base, being level, of a regular size and well-cultivated) it is nearly impossible not to get double what you can get on other land" (*Dieci Giornate*, p. 14).

TABLE 2.1 *Crop Rotation in Gallo*, GIORNATE

I	II	III	IV	V	VI	VII
[clover]						
wheat	clover	flax				
clover	clover	flax	millet			
clover	clover	woad	wheat			
flax	alfalfa [for 10 or more years]					millet
wheat	wheat	millet	vetch and oats	beans	millet or wheat	

In short, Gallo describes rotations that are already those of the agricultural revolution.[29] The spread of leguminous plants had two effects. On the one hand it strengthened the raising of livestock (encouraged by the importation of calves already pregnant from nearby mountains) and increased the production of dairy products (*Tredici Giornate*, p. 221). On the other hand it enhanced the fertility of the soil, encouraging the introduction and cultivation over relatively large areas of industrial crops, particularly flax which supplied a profitable export market (*Dieci Giornate*, p. 192).[30]

---

29 See B.H. Slicher Van Bath, "Agriculture in the Low Country," *X Congresso Internazionale di Scienze Storiche*, vol. IV, *Relazioni, Storia Moderna* (Florence, 1955), pp. 169–203; M.J. Tits-Dienaide, "L'evolution des techniques agricoles en Flandre et en Brabant du XIV au XVIII siècle," *Annales E.S.C.*, vol. 36, no. 3 (1981), 362–381; J.D. Chambers and G.E. Mingay, *The Agricultural Revolution* (London, 1966); E. Kerridge, *The Agricultural Revolution* (London, 1967); J. Thirsk, "Agricultural Innovations and their Diffusion," *The Agrarian History of England and Wales*, vol. V, 1640–1759 (Cambridge, 1984). On the introduction of clover in Germany see G. Schröder-Lembke, *Die Einführung des Kleebaues in Deutschland von dem Auftreten Schubarts von dem KleefeThe lde* (Berlin, 1954). From B. Scaglia's first revelation of the Brescian estimates it turns out that in the 16th century in the Brescian lowlands, to which Gallo's work primarily refers, irrigated fields made up one third of the surface area of the *possessione*, wheat another third, and flax an eighth. In the other areas and on the small plots of independent peasants, there was no flax and cereal-growing was predominant (B. Scaglia, "Note sull'agricoltura bresciana nei secoli XV-XVI-XVII," *Atti del Convegno su Camillo Tarello*, pp. 123–132). In any case flax production had reached very high levels. According to the Venetian Captain Domenico Priuli, in around 1572 Brescia produced 29,000 quintals of flax, 80% of which was exported (*Relazioni dei rettori Veneti in Terraferma* XI, *Podesteria e Capitanato di Brescia,* ed. A. Tagliaferri [Milan, 1978], p. 122). On the relationship between irrigation and agriculture in the Veneto, see S. Ciriacono, "Irrigazione e produttività agraria nella Terraferma Veneta fra Cinque e Seicento," *Archivio Veneto*, series V, vol. CXI (1979), 73–135.

30 The cultivation of artificial grass also had another consequence. Instead of sending livestock out to pasture, it became more convenient to feed them hay in the stalls (*Tredici Giornate*, p. 19). Gallo also pays significant attention to the production of oil, both from olives and seeds (flax, grapes, camelina [*dradelle*], rapeseed and walnuts) used especially for lighting and industrial processes (treating wool, soap-making, etc.). The list also includes a plant with no name, indicated as a seed or grass of "Doctor Fioravanti," which Fioravanti himself distributed in Venice to "those who want it, free of charge" (*Tredici Giornate*, p. 181). This is Dr. Leonardo Fioravanti, who some months earlier had obtained a 20-year license from the Senate of Venice to produce "oil from material recently found by him" (A.S. V., Senato Terra, Reg. 45, 20 novembre 1565, c. 200). L. Fioravanti is the author of *Secreti medicinali* (Venice, 1562) and *Specchio di sapienza universale* (Venice, 1567). Cheeses from Brescia – exported to Rome, Venice and Germany – were supposed to be more highly prized than cheeses from Lodi or Piacenza which, because they were made

This high intensity of rotations was supported by an extraordinary development of the knowledge and practice of fertilizing the soil. In addition to manure, Gallo recommended using lime, the soil removed from the "field headlands," "diggings" from ditches and farmyards, household waste, dust from the road (pure or mixed with manure), ashes from ovens, horn filings, the residues of the production of saltpetre, waste from the processing of leather and skins, wheat chaff, fallow soil, green manure, and burnt field stubble (*Dieci Giornate*, pp. 34^{v}-35, 65^{r}, passim). In an important reconsideration contained in an addition to the *Tredici Giornate* (p. 36) he proposed replacing the burning of stubble with a practice introduced a few years previously. It was better to cut and use stubble as bedding for animals "then spreading that stubble soaked in cow dung on the fields." This was a practice in other areas of the Po valley in the 17th century.[31]

Rotations, fertilizing and working the land have to be adapted "to the diversity" of soils. Only by taking into account the diverse nature of the fields could "the most profitable income" be obtained. Thus on the worst soils (worth just 8–10 *scudi* per *piò*), instead of planting cereals or clover, it would be better to plant trees or vines, as the owners of "poor" land had successfully done in Gottolengo (*Tredici Giornate*, p. 21). More generally, vines should be planted in moderately warm, dry and sunny locations, thus "in the hills rather than the plains" (*Tredici Giornate*, pp. 69–70).[32] In contrast, rice had to be cultivated on irrigated lands on which there was a constant flow of water "two fingers"

in larger sizes, did not have "salt in the middle as was the case with other parts closer to the surface" (*Tredici Giornate*, p. 221).

31 A comparison of the origins, transformation and variations of this practice in the Po valley would be useful. On the burning of stubble see E. Sereni's important essay *Terra Nuova e buoi rossi* (Turin, 1981), pp. 3–100. The author, however, does not consider Gallo's criticism of this method when practiced "without the good intelligence of cultivating well that now one sees" (*Tredici Giornate*, p. 36). On the use in the Bolognese countryside of straw from the valleys as bedding for animals and then as manure in the fields (a method known by Gallo), see S. Fronzoni, "Sistema agrario ed equilibri idraulici tra XVIII e XIX secolo," *Problemi d'acque a Bologna in età moderna* (Bologna, 1983), pp. 112–122. An extensive investigation of burnt field stubble and its variations was done by F. Sigaut for nearly all of Europe with the exception of Italy (*L'agriculture et le feu. Rôle et place du feu dans les techniques de préparation du champ de l'ancienne agriculture européenne* [Paris, 1975]).

32 He also recommended pulling up vines from irrigated fields (where it was better to intensify the production of flax) and to plant vines on less good fields "that are never irrigated" (*Dieci Giornate*, p. 8). Not far from Brescia, in part of the Pavian plain within the triangle Pavia-Binasco-S. Angelo Lodigiano, in 1550 vineyards still occupied relatively large areas. C.M. Cipolla, "Ripartizione delle colture nel pavese secondo le 'Misure territoriali' della metà del 500", *Studi di Economia e Statistica della Facoltà di Economia e Commercio dell'Università di Catania*, 1 (1950–1951), 5–13.

in depth from April to July (*Vinti Giornate*, pp. 328–331). On dry land, oats and vetch should be planted as forage, not clover and alfalfa (*Dieci Giornate*, "Letter to G. B. from Romano"). Still, in certain cases it was possible artificially to modify the quality of the soil. Fields with too much clay ("strong") – which yielded little wheat during rainy years – could be corrected by mixing in "a large amount of sand ... as if it were a lot of manure" (*Tredici Giornate*, p. 21). In short, Gallo tended to promote the division of work on the land, specializing and diversifying cultivation according to the quality of the soil.

The advanced cultivating techniques in the *Giornate*, as stated explicitly by the author, derive from Brescian "rites" and practices. But they also document the high productive levels and agronomical progress achieved in the greater Lombard area, at the heart of which, not acknowledged by the Brescian Gallo, is the area of irrigated meadows of Milan and Lodi.[33] The "two fingers depth of water" that ran through the rice fields, the irrigation flows that covered the artificial meadows (and sometimes served to free the fields from snow), and the six or seven alfalfa harvests per year, are the signs of the impressive spread of agricultural practices beyond their origin in the area around Lodi.

References to farming practices in other areas are less frequent but still present: hemp was a characteristic of the Bologna countryside; the cultivation of silkworms could be found in the Venetian countryside; the cultivation of citrons and lemons on the Brescian shores of Lake Garda was compared to that of the Ligurian Riviera (*Tredici Giornate*, p. 167; *Vinti Giornate*, pp. 145 and 305). He also precisely describes the land reclamation methods for draining the Polesine swamps (*Vinti Giornate*, pp. 185–188). Apart from these references, which all relate to the Po valley (and bordering areas), Gallo constructs a significant comparison between "Italian" agriculture (actually only that of Lombardy) and that of the great plains of Germany. In northern Europe, with

33 According to Carlo Cipolla, during the course of the 15th century the uncultivated part of the Lombardy plain fell into neglect. Not all types of crops progressed proportionally. "Especially in the second half of the century grasslands extended over the area much more than other cultures" ("Per la storia delle terre della 'bassa' lombarda" [1957] reprinted in C. Cipolla, *Saggi di storia economica e sociale* [Bologna, 1988], pp. 133–138). See also A. De Maddalena, "Contributo alla storia dell'agricoltura della 'bassa' lombarda. Appunti sulla possessione di Belgioioso" (1958) reprinted in A. De Maddalena, *Dalla città al borgo* (Milan, 1982), pp. 179–198; G. Coppola, "L'agricoltura di alcune pievi della pianura irrigua milanese nei dati catastali della metà del secolo XV," *Contributi dell'Istituto di storia economica e sociale. Aspetti di vita agricola Lombarda* (*secoli XVI–XIX*), ed. M. Romani (Milan, 1973), pp. 185–286; G. Chittolini, "Avvicendamenti e paesaggio agrario nella pianura irrigua lombarda (secoli XV–XVI)," Istituto Internazionale di Storia Economica F. Datini di Prato, *Agricoltura e trasformazione dell'ambiente. Secoli XIII–XVIII*, ed. A. Guarducci,(Florence, 1984), pp. 555–575 including bibliography.

its abundance of "spacious" flat countryside and "light" soils, the cultivation of cereals and the practice of fallow permitted the use of horses "which plough twice as much" as oxen. In northern Italy where land was less abundant (relative to the population), less uniform "due to the diversity of land located in mountains, hills and valleys," and where land was normally not left fallow, it was more expedient to plough with oxen. The slower speed of ploughing would be compensated by the sale of well-fattened oxen to butchers after they had been used "for some time" to plough the fields (*Vinti Giornate*, pp. 175–176).[34]

This comparative approach induces him to imagine that "the ingenious" landowner should travel "at least all over Italy" to learn about the practices "that are better than ours, so as to introduce them in this ... area" (*Dieci Giornate*, p. 133). Here we see a profound cultural change. The ancient Romans remained a model because they provided an image of gentlemen-farmers from the city, but they were no longer a model for the excellence of their agricultural practices, as illustrated in georgic writing. The best practices are sought in the world of modern (contemporary) situations, not from the ancients. Travel takes the place of books. In the preface to *Tredici Giornate* Gallo states that his work deals with "real" agriculture "not from the ancients, but from modern inventions and justifiably so." Already in his 1564 edition he had written that every landowner should "strive to find profitable inventions" (*Dieci Giornate*, p. 133).

These assertions help to shed light on the relation between the infinite universe of available (existing) techniques and the process of selecting

34 Approximately two centuries after this comparison was made, Quesnay published his famous article on "Fermiers" (*Encyclopédie*) comparing two cultivation methods: the "petite culture," *labor intensive* and oriented towards subsistence (for the family), and "grande culture," *capital intensive* and oriented to the market. According to Quesnay the use of horses for ploughing, widespread in England, distinguished "grande culture" from "petite culture," which mainly used oxen. Quesnay's essay was extremely important for the history of economic thought because it pointed out the essential role of capital and "avances" (that is, credit) in operating large landholdings, which are also the most profitable. Quesnay's calculations are based on the assumption that cultivation with horses was connected to triennial rotation including one year of fallow. Gallo, on the other hand, associated cultivation with oxen with continuous rotation. It is known that Quesnay's calculations and his technical assumptions provoked lively debates and were rejected by French agronomists (see A. Bourde, *Agronomie et agronomes en France au XVIII siècle*, vol. I [Paris, 1967], pp. 476–485). But not even Gallo's assumptions are correct. Continuous rotation (without fallow years) was normally widespread in irrigated or humid areas, which covered only one part of the cultivated area of the Lombard plain. A similar phenomenon is found in irrigated areas in Catalonia, where irrigation eliminated fallow years. See P. Vilar, *La Catalogne dans l'Espagne moderne*, vol. II (Paris, 1962), pp. 272–280.

the necessarily limited number of those that are best. In his response of 4 February 1560 to da Romano's letter, Gallo states that the procedures of inclusion and exclusion he followed were based on the "actual experience of things." Often this was the result of empirical tests "either done with my own hands or done for me by others, or what I saw others do." A second criterion was verification by "trustworthy men whom I know to be truthful." At least in one case he describes an alternation (planting clover in September in fields that had already been planted with rye) which he assured would have good results based on "long practice" but that did not have many imitators (*Tredici Giornate*, p. 29).

The description, although brief, of the criteria for the selection of certain techniques shows that the ways in which *know how* was presented in the *Giornate* do not coincide, as we might expect, with how it was discussed among the urban nobility. On the contrary, his work superimposed on and tended to downplay the actual ways in which these processes were conceived. I refer here not only to the author's response to da Romano, but also to those operations centred on an intense inquisitorial look at landed proprietors (and their tenants, stewards and managers) who began to learn about, control and correct the working methods of sharecroppers. This was a tremendously important experience which began to take shape and develop during the 15th and 16th centuries, from the time sharecropping contracts became widespread in the countryside around Brescia.[35] It was this knowledge, born from the control of the land and the desire to make the property profitable, that set in motion Gallo's agronomy and economics. The distinctions between good and bad agricultural methods, between profit- or market-oriented agriculture and subsistence farming, and between the rationality of the landlords and the malicious ignorance of the sharecroppers, were the result of an immense individual and collective experience of a bitter social conflict, of an intense "dialogue" between landowners from the city and peasants.

How could landowners from the city become experts on agriculture if they had not observed and questioned the peasants? Gallo himself advises landlords who wish to become "good gentlemen-farmers" to learn the art and the means of exercising it by *conversing* "with the men of this profession," in other

35 Stefano Trevisan, a Venetian official, stated in 1460 that a form of sharecropping (*masseria*) had spread after local inhabitants and communities of the "territory" had lost ownership – beginning in 1430 – of much of the property of their land. See C. Pasero, "Il dominio veneto fino all'incendio della loggia (1426–1575)," in *Storia di Brescia*, vol. II (Brescia, 1963), p. 165. Excluded from this "territory" were Val Camonica, Val Sabbia, Riviera di Salò, and several feudal jurisdictions located in the lowlands.

words with the cultivators, to acquire the "secrets" not only from the "capable ones," but also from those "who pretend to be ignorant" (*Dieci Giornate,* p. 18^{rv}).

The condemnation of malicious and bad techniques produced centralizing effects, resulting from the accumulation of approved methods, as well as effects of marginalization and exclusion.[36] Yet despite being marginalized, the sharecroppers' cunning methods still had weight. To demonstrate their inferiority to the methods approved and recommended, Gallo is in a way forced to describe them. And in the act of describing them at times he acknowledges their intrinsic rationality.

Thus narrow ridge ploughing preferred by sharecroppers because it was less strenuous, faster and saved one third of the seed from use, was condemned by Gallo because it reduced the harvest by a third, to the disadvantage of the urban landowner. But he recognised that the "perfidious" sharecroppers would not suffer because "they would get fodder each time from the ploughing and other labors carried out." According to Gallo only wide-ridge ploughing (that is, *ad aiuola* or *a vaneggia*) would permit landowners to harvest more crops and obtain more profit, thus getting the best from the high value of the land. He does not say whether additional investments of the sharecroppers' labor force would produce additional earnings adequate for the peasant smallholder (*Dieci Giornate,* pp. 50^{v}-51 and 124). Other condemned practices included the tendency of "astute" sharecroppers to use manure for the cultivation of legumes, of which they ordinarily kept not one half (as in the case of wheat) but two thirds (*Dieci Giornate,* pp. 125^{v}-126). Gallo admits that even sharecroppers could propose some "innovation." But landlords should be wary especially on those matters "because almost all of them just say what could benefit themselves. But things will go well for the landlords as long as they diligently understand and observe their own affairs" (*Dieci Giornate,* p. 127^{v}).

Thus a "good gentleman-farmer" from the city, always gratified by flattering adjectives – able, expert, liberal, prudent, ingenious (*Dieci Giornate,* p. 46–64, 127^{v}, 128^{v}, 133) – is the true protagonist of good cultivation of the fields in the *Giornate*. To him we owe the progress of Brescian agriculture. Signore Herculano Cucco, "a very rare gentleman-farmer" was one of the most active in propagating cultivation of alfalfa; Count Giovan Battista Gambara introduced

36 The way social conflicts are resolved (similar or analogous to those investigated here) profoundly influences the direction of technical development. For such analytical procedures see footnotes 14 and 18, and ch. 11 in this volume.

it at the beginning of the century;[37] an unnamed Brescian noble found the "true way to plant flax"; the cavalier Ludovico Barighano, who had fought in the wars in the first half of the century, was an expert with horses; Cavalier Bonato grafted fruit trees with great competence and with his own hands; Sig. Vecellio Vecelli was an "expert gentleman-farmer"; Count Francesco Avogadro, a relative of Giovan Battista, had a "new type" of lemon seed sent to him from Genoa, which he cultivated in his "charming place" near the city (*Dieci Giornate,* pp. 49; *Tredici Giornate*, pp. 39, 281; *Vinti Giornate*, pp. 249, 251, 387.)

The fact that Cavalier Bonato worked with his own hands does not mean that this was common among gentlemen-farmers. On the contrary, city dwellers forced by poverty to work directly (with their own hands) on their own lands formally lost their status as citizens of the city.[38] In Gallo's mind however a good gentleman-farmer from the city is often presented as a new Cincinnatus – one who ploughs, plants and harvests, as if he no longer needed either sharecroppers or cattle-men ("bifolchi" or "boari"). But it is Gallo himself who warns that what a good gentleman-farmer did not or could not do himself – for example sleep next to the oxen "so that they won't be stolen" – could be done by cowherds (*Dieci Giornate,* pp. 128^{v}-129).

The title "good farmer" is also sometimes used to refer to "loyal sharecroppers," those peasants who worked according to the norms of "true" agriculture chosen and prescribed by landowners (*Dieci Giornate,* pp. 51–51^{v}).

The highly original way in which the *Giornate* formulates relations between urban landowners and peasants (therefore between the city and the country), and the deep intrusion of the landowning class on the practices, habits and economy of the peasants poses the problem of the relation between Gallo's discourse and the Brescian reality. No account portrays reality as it was in all its aspects. There is always a divergence between lived experience and

---

37 On the history of the spread of *erba medica* (alfalfa) see M. Ambrosoli, "Identificazione e riscoperta dell'erba medica nell'Italia centro-settentrionale 1400–1560," *Quaderni Storici*, vol. 19, no. 57 (1984), 883–905.

38 See A. Rossini, "Il territorio bresciano dopo la riconquista veneziana del 1516," in *Studi Bresciani*, 12 (1983), a. IV, p. 95. In contrast, the jurist G. Papa claimed that nobles who worked "in eorum propriis possessionibus ... propriis manibus" ("on their own property ... with their own hands") did not lose their status as citizens of the city (G. Papa, *Decisiones Parlamenti Delphinatus* (Lugduni, 1562), p. 518). A. Tiraqueau made the same claim citing Papa in an edition prior to that of 1562 (*Commentarii de nobilitate* [Lugduni, 1559], p. 487). Noblemen who worked for wages on the land belonging to others did lose their noble status (ibid., p. 491). Cavalier Bonato's work was actually in his garden rather than in the fields. The relationship between the nobility and gardening (in the broad sense) is an extremely important topic given the frequent role of gardens as experimental fields.

the discourse which represents it. The *Giornate* is no exception. Yet there is a relationship, which we may attempt to describe with the help of historical research.[39]

These studies provide evidence that Gallo was writing the *Giornate* during a phase of the consolidation (albeit not definitive) of an imposing transfer of land ownership from peasants and rural communities to city dwellers, noble and non-noble. From 1430 to 1486 Brescian city dwellers bought from rural people – individuals and communities – over 145,000 *piò* – (approximately 48,000 hectares) out of a total area of 400,000 *piò* (approximately 130,000 hectares). In 1623 Giovani Battista Cattanio, author of a *Relazione* in defense of rural landowners, calculated that rural inhabitants and communities owned two thirds of the land in 1440; by 1542 this had decreased to 35%.[40] This dispossession was the result of perverse effects of an unjust taxation system and other factors that ruthlessly extorted peasants. This was the source of a long sequence of bitter conflicts between local communities, represented by a single council, and the city, the communities often accusing the city of abusing its power before the judges and courts of the Venetian state. In short, in the not vast Brescian countryside forces and passions clashed, not unlike those that stirred up peasants in Germany before, during and after the great revolt of 1523–1525. Also similar were the judicial procedures of groups of German villages carried out (not during the years of the peasant war or other minor revolts) – to defend their lands and privileges from the demands of the noble lords.[41]

---

39 See Pasero, *Il dominio veneto*, pp. 85–88; 212–215, 385–389; idem., *Prefazione a Il catastico bresciano di G. Da Lezze (1609–1610)*, vol. I (Brescia, 1969); L. Mazzoldi, "L'economia dei secoli XVII e XVIII," *Storia di Brescia*, vol. III (Brescia, 1964), 132–133; C. Poni, "Accumulation primitive et agronomie capitaliste: le cas de Brescia," *Studia Historiae Oeconomicae*, 10 (1975), 17–28; Scaglia, *Note sull'agricoltura bresciana*; J.M. Ferraro, "Proprietà terriera e potere nello Stato Veneto: la nobiltà bresciana del '400-'500," *Dentro lo Stato Italico. Venezia e la Terraferma fra Quattro e Seicento*, eds. G. Cracco and M. Knapton. (Trento, 1984), pp. 159–182; A. Rossini, "Il territorio bresciano," and and D. Parzani, "Il territorio di Brescia intorno alla metà del Quattrocento," *Studi Bresciani*, 51–75. On the relationship between economic structures and the tax system in the Republic of Venice see *Il sistema fiscale Veneto. Problemi e aspetti (XV-XVIII secolo)*, eds. G. Borelli, P. Lanaro, F. Vecchiato (Verona, 1982).

40 This *Relazione* is cited in Poni, *Accumulation primitive*, p. 19 and is confirmed in other sources. On the extension of the territory see note 35.

41 Until some years ago the attention of German rural historians was on the great Peasants' War. Then research shifted to the legal forms normally employed in these conflicts between peasants and feudal lords. In short, there were disputes and then these disputes were brought to the courts. See W. Schulze, *Bauerlicher Widerstand und feudale Herrschaft in der frühen Neuzeit* (Stuttgart, 1980). The same happened in France. Obviously the court cases were costly. Thus rural communities had to accumulate the necessary funds

Gallo never discusses the disintegration of the property of peasants and of rural communities, nor the legal battles that set the city against the surrounding countryside over changes to the tax system. In effect he chose to leave unspoken a major issue that overturned and redefined traditional social relationships. But the absence of this theme is in some way present in his exaltation of the productiveness of agriculturists of urban origin obstructed by the practices of bad sharecroppers. It would be interesting to see if Gallo's arguments, though not addressing the merits of this conflict that were not solely fiscal, were used by city representatives against peasants and rural communities.

What of the economic and agricultural systems of independent peasants? Their properties, smaller and fragmented compared with those of city dwellers, covered nearly a third of the area until the end of the 16th century. These were in large part new lands they had laboriously and energetically conquered for farming, tilling uncultivated land bordering woods and grassland, or on the slopes of hills, or occupying abandoned ecclesiastic property such as at Ghedi and Bagnolo.[42] The soil on these lands was mostly of mediocre quality, far from fertile and irrigated fields. On the smallest peasant plots (2–3 *piò*) the "old" two-year and three-year rotations prevailed, while on the larger ones (6–7 *piò*) belonging to "principal peasants," rotations were longer. But grains continued to occupy two thirds of the land while only a sixth or seventh was pastureland.[43] How many impoverished peasant families emigrated? And how many were attracted to the nearby proto-industrial metalworking areas of Val Trompia and Val Sabbia? Or to the coastal area of Salò where linen spinning had developed? Other problems relate to the exact identification of social groups – peasants who were rich, middle-class and poor – who led the communities and the countryside during a hard centuries' long conflict that required heavy expenses.[44]

The last three *Giornate* of Gallo's work, those dedicated to the "pleasures of the manor," represent a significant change of direction only partly planned and expected given the dominant themes of the first seven *Giornate* or chapters (which become ten and then seventeen in the subsequent editions). In these

---

to send their own representatives to the cities where the courts were located and pay lawyers and legal expenses. For the eighteenth century, see H.L. Root, "Challenging the Seigneurie: Community and Contention on the Eve of the French Revolution," *Journal of Modern History*, 57 (1985), 652–668.

42 Pasero, *Il dominio veneto*, p. 213.

43 Scaglia, *Note sull'agricoltura bresciana*, The expression "principal peasants" is fairly frequent in G. Da Lezze's *Catastico*.

44 Recent literature on the conflicts between peasant communities and feudal lords emphasizes the leading role of rich and middle-class peasants rather than poor ones.

three *Giornate* he still mentions, on two or three pages, the malicious sharecroppers and the new business management of the property. But the focus of his attention shifts to the "delights of the manor," leaving behind the "economy of the manor," only cursorily addressed in terms of how to entertain friends who arrive unannounced for a visit (*Dieci Giornate,* pp. 197–202).[45]

The theme of the pleasures or delights of the manor is developed with great conviction and literary skill, re-elaborating well-tested bucolic forms. Life in the countryside means enjoying not just the beauty of nature – the dawns and sunsets. Here one finds "real peace, true liberty, assured peace of mind and pleasurable repose; one enjoys as well the fresh air, the leafy branches of trees, their exquisite fruits, clear water, the pleasantness of the valleys, the views of the mountains, the joy of the hills, and the delight of the forests." It is the very air of the countryside that reassures the mind, clears the intellect, calms the soul and reinvigorates the body (*Dieci Giornate,* pp. 155v-156v). Whereas peasants were "always healthy, robust and of vigorous appearance" city dwellers were "squalid, emaciated, lacked vigor and had shorter lives" (*Dieci Giornate,* p. 153). The moral aspect of the city dwellers was even more negative because they were at the mercy of people who were ambitious, envious, proud, disloyal – deceitful notaries, lying prosecutors, and unfaithful lawyers (*Dieci Giornate,* p. 155). While in the city it was easy to lose one's honor, in the countryside one could keep and even enhance it by hunting: whether individual and solitary hunting in the mountains and valleys that required "valiant" men, or hunting on the plains that often brought together large parties of friends and neighbors (*Dieci Giornate,* pp. 169v-170v). One also has to carry out religious and moral duties: attend mass, observe Lent, listen to the priest's sermons, visit the sick, aid the poor, advise the ignorant, resolve controversies, and read the sacred scriptures as well as Plato, Philo, and Seneca (*Dieci Giornate,* p. 186v).

In this context it was natural to praise "the simplicity of peasants, the sincere song of country girls, the rustic reed pipes of shepherds ..., the saintly profession of cultivators" (*Dieci Giornate,* p. 187). And yet again the theme of the deceitful and ignorant sharecroppers returns (*Dieci Giornate,* p. 190). But along with this appears something else: that of "our peasants," whom Avogadro views

45 Gallo knows – he read it in the tributes to A. Lollio's manor – the fundamental rules for the economy of the manor: a city dweller would never buy with money what he can produce "on his own land" (*Dieci Giornate,* p. 195v). M. Berengo rightly suggested that the *Giornate* belongs to the genre of *Oeconomicorum Libri.* See also on *Hausvaterliteratur* O. Brunner, *Vita nobiliare e cultura europea,* and my gratitude to Thorkild Kjaergaard for his *Farming Encyclopedics for the Western European Landowner. The "Hausvaterliteratur" 1550–1750,* presented at the European University Institute in Florence (1984).

kindly because "they do not fail to love and honor us with respect. And woe to anyone who dares to offend us ... because together we would chase them right off our land" (*Dieci Giornate,* pp. 148^{v}-149). Even the anxious, searching eye of city landowners turns into satisfied looks. Avogadro depicts himself as "being distracted" when he admires "an excellent cultivator" who, having put the field "in good order" ploughs it "with well-trained oxen." And in the same way he rejoices when he sees his steward directing a team of workers to "plant vines, to hoe, trim and prune them" or "straighten roads, square the fields, divide up land, maintain cart tracks, and level the meadows" (*Dieci Giornate,* p. 195^{r-v}).

After the troubled relations reported in the first *Giornate,* peace seems made with the world of the cultivators. Avogadro perhaps has won his battle? Has he delegated command and control of the work to the steward? Or do the "delights of the manor" distract him from the agricultural project described in the first part of the *Giornate*? And with this shift – not a simple turn – between the two parts of the *Giornate* perhaps there is greater discontinuity than Gallo would have liked to admit? Perhaps some truths slipped out that he would have liked to keep quiet?

This truth takes the form in the dialogues on the manor of an event, a story. In response to Cornelio Ducco, who asks him how he fills up his "time from month to month" Avogadro answers in a way that raises questions about his role as an urban gentleman-farmer. After stating that he normally gets up "at the break of day," he turns to describing (in July) a hunting party with a group of friends that lasts all morning. In the afternoon these same friends meet again "some to read, play cards, play table games, or chess," while others sing or play instruments. After dinner the group goes "to one friend's house, and then to another's to admire the beauty of their gardens, vegetable plots, fishponds or fountains." The conversation becomes livelier when the wives join the group. If someone starts to play the lute or viola, and if the master and mistress of the house start to dance, everyone joins in "gladly in all honesty and purity" (*Dieci Giornate,* pp. 157^{v}-158^{v}).

So it seems that all hours of the day were occupied by delightful and honest pleasures of sport, games, reading, conversation and dancing. Only the time between lunch and afternoon conversation (that most of them dedicated to a siesta) was left for "necessary business." Not much for a "diligent" and "knowledgeable" gentleman-farmer! And this in July! The harvest month! And in the other months? To this question there is no answer. Having reassured Ducco that what he said about dancing was the "simple truth," Avogadro starts talking about the jokes and pranks of a gentleman friend: Gavaccio. It is not difficult to explain this unexpected and abrupt mixing of cards. If Avogadro had continued in the same vein to describe his occupation from month to month, Gallo would have had to address explicitly the incompatibility between his agricultural project and the pleasures of the manor. The absence of reference to other months attenuates this contrast, makes it less visible, and maintains the ambiguity that one reads between the lines. But does not eliminate it. How time is spent in the manor is taken up again, but only in broad strokes, some pages later with the description of the hunt, for which no starting date is given but which lasts until Carnevale (*Dieci Giornate,* pp. 163^{v}-182). With the arrival of Lent these "amusements" stopped and one started to lead a more composed life. This meant reading holy books, listening to the parish priest's sermons, taking walks, making visits, riding horseback or playing ball. ... In May and June religious duties decreased and hunting started again, but only with birdlime and nets and not with an arquebus so as not to trample the "high fodder" in the fields. In describing how time was spent in the manor this is the *only* reference to farming.

We do not know how or whether Gallo was aware of the asymmetry and dualism between the two parts of the *Giornate*. Certainly he does not formulate or explain it. Nonetheless, he does try to correct it. In the last edition of the work he adds seven new days. In one of these (the seventeenth), in response to Vincenzo Maggio who asks what "makes an excellent agriculturist from month to month," Avogadro provides a real agronomic calendar divided into twelve months which takes up the entire chapter. Here things return to their rightful place. Instructions on how to cultivate the soil, scattered throughout the previous pages, are put in order for the farming year[46] in an organizational chart derived or transmitted from Latin agronomists, but reformulated and modified. By adding this new chapter Gallo perhaps intended to rebalance and correct Avogadro's one-sided response to Cornelio Duccio. But whereas the question of Cornelio Duccio is personal and direct (how Avogadro spends his time from month to month), that of Vincenzo Maggio addresses a *third person*: "the excellent agriculturist." And it is for him that Avogadro responds. But this person who hoes, ploughs, digs, sows and harvests with his own hands, and during the winter builds or repairs ploughs, harrows, rakes, bowls and cutting boards, is rather a peasant than a city-dweller. The peasant hunts, but only during the month of December. Absent are merry groups with their walks, conversations, visits, card games, chess, or ball games.

46 Instead of January, in accordance with the Latin agronomists' model, Gallo starts the farming year in November. His reasons for this are two-fold: 1) in that month, once harvests are over and winter cereals are planted, work starts "for the benefit of the following year," and 2) the sharecroppers who are dismissed leave the farm and new sharecroppers are taken on.

In sum, Gallo boldly depicts the conflicts between city landowners and sharecroppers, and with sharp frankness indicates "progressive" solutions to these conflicts. But he draws back undecided, and hesitates when the behavior of the character he has created, his dear Avogadro, would have required him to follow a similar path and represent clearly the internal conflicts between the landowners who lived in country manors and their relations with their stewards and managers. Certainly the issue is complex. Going to live in a manor implies an interest in agriculture and its income.[47] But if the "perfidious sharecroppers" are the enemies of "true" agriculture, is not the same true for those distracted by amusements that occupy the city dwellers in the manor from morning to night? I do not think I need to assist Gallo in resolving his contradictions. Rather than impoverishing the text by reducing it to an unambiguous interpretation, I prefer to highlight the complexity of the *Giornate*, its composite character, its complicated relationship with reality. But one could also say that the discourse of the Brescian agronomist shows profound tensions. Into the conceptual processes that organize the economy of the manor (*L'economia del Cittadino in villa* to use the same words as the title of the future work by the Bolognese Vincenzo Tanara) he weaves episodes, stories that, while potentially disruptive, are not able, beyond some unsettling effects, to disentangle the various jarring components.[48]

Gallo's work, in spite of its ambiguities and dualities, is decidedly optimistic. He places himself and his work without hesitation at the high point of a long phase of growth of Brescian agriculture, which began after the final destructive effects of the plague of 1477 had run their course. But what were the causes of the collapse and subsequent recovery? According to Gallo after the plague there were not enough workers to cultivate the land, nor to maintain the hydraulic works (canals, ditches, dikes and bridges). This caused the deterioration of agriculture and the transformation of many fields to pastures, woodlands and swamps. Over time the progressive increase in population brought a growth in the labor force. Thus the lands returned "to their earlier state ... with great industry, infinite expense and incredible ingenuity. Such that one

47 On the manor as the center of the organization of estates and properties, see A. Ventura, "Aspetti storici della villa veneta," in *Bollettino del CISA*, vol. XI (1969), 65–77; J. Ackerman, *Palladio* (Torino, 1974), pp. 19–37; L.H. Heydenrich, "La villa; genesi e sviluppo fino a Palladio," *Bollettino del CISA*, vol. XI (1969), 11–22; and the dense pages of G. Zalin, G. Borelli, L. Puppi, *La villa nel Veronese*, ed. G.F. Viviani (1975).

48 In Gallo's depiction the large noble families lived in harmony; according to Venetian governors, in contrast, they were divided by hostility and suspicion. See *Relazioni dei Rettori Veneti in Terraferma*, XI, pp. 40, 100 passim.

could say when a Brescian is born, and especially a nobleman, an agriculturist is also born, because one sees that Heaven generously instils us with the intelligence truly to cultivate the soil" (*Dieci Giornate,* p. 191^{v}).[49] Thanks to these factors – material, moral and technical – the countryside of Brescia became so productive that it was as fertile as the lands that God had given to the people of Israel. But whereas the fertility of the "Promised Land" was due to "Divine Providence," the lands of Brescia, "sterile by nature," could only be explained by the "greatest industry of good cultivation" (*Dieci Giornate,* pp. 192).[50]

Among the writers on agriculture in the early modern period, only a few, like Gallo, had the fortune to live in a period of such favorable economic expansion. This was the Indian summer (the summer of San Martino) of the Italian economy, to use Carlo Cipolla's apt and by now classic expression. And Gallo knew how to interpret it effectively when he constructed the provocative project of an agricultural economy owned and operated by city dwellers. It is in this context that all the new pages (and there are many) have their place in his agriculture.[51]

---

49 Gallo insists more than once on demographic increase as the cause of the growth of agricultural production. "The great multitude of people which nevertheless continues to grow" forced one to cultivate "as well as one can see, because otherwise the harvest would not yield enough to live on" (*Dieci Giornate,* pp. 190–191^{v}).

50 See the beautiful pages dedicated "to the Magnificent city of Brescia" (*Dieci Giornate,* pp. 2–6^{v}). These pages, while exalting the high levels of Brescia's agriculture and industry, also emphasize the fragility of its fundamental productive forces. The sophisticated hydraulic system, which forced some of the water "to flow hidden underground, some to pass through diverse channels under others, and some to pass higher through aqueducts above the largest ones," seemed to Gallo particularly exposed "to random Fortune, which, wanting to shatter similar enveloped, pillared and propped up reservoirs (as occurred several times in the calamitous times of plague and war) suddenly transforms you (Brescia) from rich into not much better than poor" (ibid., p. 6).

51 Gallo did not live long enough to see the rapid deterioration of economic conditions after the famine of 1569–1570 and the plague of 1576–1577, a prelude to new collapses such as the famine of 1590 and the plagues of the first decades of the 1600s. See Pasero, *Il dominio veneto,* pp. 361 and Mazzoldi, *L'economia dei secoli XVII e XVIII,* p. 3 passim.

CHAPTER 3

Environmental Crisis and the Shifting Practice of Property Rights: The Bolognese Marshlands, 17th to 19th Centuries

Carlo Poni and Roberto Scazzieri

1 Introduction

Work in economic theory and economic history has highlighted the endogenous character of property rights and the shifting balance between different patterns of appropriation and utilization. In particular, it has emphasized that self-sustained growth is often associated with the containment of common property domains (commons), either through the introduction of standard private property rights or the introduction of rules and institutions for the governance of open access commons.[1]

This chapter, the result of a collaboration between an economic historian (Carlo Poni) and an economist (Roberto Scazzieri), highlights the complex relationship between common property domains and private property rights by taking a different perspective, one which is suggested by the extraordinary environmental and institutional changes that took place in the Bolognese countryside at the beginning of the 17th century. A diversion in the course of the Reno River (induced by ill-conceived water management) brought about the flooding of an extended area between Bologna and Ferrara. This area, once rich agricultural countryside, turned into wetlands and became the site of a completely different type of economy. Traditional (private) property rights became uncertain and often impossible to enforce, cultivation switched from grain to rice, and sophisticated contractual arrangements that had been established in the area since the Middle Ages gave way to much more informal and flexible practices. The emergence of open access resources (open wetlands) was initially associated with the collapse of conventional property rights, but induced in its turn a search for new and flexible standards of private appropriation that could be used in the governance of wetland commons. In this

1 D. North, *Understanding the Process of Economic Change* (Princeton, 2005); E. Ostrom, *Governing the Commons. The Evolution of Institutions for Collective Action* (Cambridge, 1990), and idem., *Understanding Institutional Diversity* (Princeton, 2005).

 | DOI:10.1163/9789004713277_005

connection, the chapter also examines attempts by the Bolognese landlords and scientists to address explicitly the diversity of the "wetlands economy," and the multiplicity of standards that this diversity suggested as means to achieve a rational utilization of the marshlands.

The responsiveness of property rights to social and environmental constraints is often emphasized in economic theory.[2] In particular, it is acknowledged that, under many historical conditions, self-sustained growth is associated with the "containment" of commons. The aim of this study is to assess the dynamics of property rights within a complex field of institutional and environmental forces. The chapter is structured as follows.

Section 2 will reconstruct the emergence of the Bolognese commons as a consequence of environmental disaster. Particular attention will be paid to the process by which ancient (and considerably advanced) legal arrangements became impossible to enforce, once standard property signs (tenurial borders) became submerged and could no longer be visible. It will be emphasized that the emergence of the commons took place through a lengthy process, in the course of which a continuum of differentiated "liquid commons" began to appear. In areas with shallow waters (minor wetlands), certain types of regular cultivation were still possible; in areas with deeper water, regular cultivation throughout the year became impossible, even if, in summer, most of the water would dry up and the dried up wetlands could produce pasture; in even deeper waters cultivation was altogether impossible, and only marsh vegetation could be found. Finally, where waters reached the deepest level, even marsh vegetation disappeared and marsh commons gave way to real lakes and fisheries.

Section 3 attempts a systematic investigation of the relationship between the emergence of "liquid commons" and the dynamics of property rights. Here the core of the argument will be that, depending on the depth of marsh waters, the "visibility" of property signs (and of property rights) could vary significantly. At one extreme, standard appropriation rules could be followed; at the other, even the faintest traces of landed property rights could no longer be detected. In general, the "liquid commons" of the Bolognese wetlands allowed a complex interaction between the emergence of commons and the transformation of property rights. For example, in certain areas, landed property rights could still be enforced according to a classical pattern; in other areas landed property disappeared altogether; in yet other cases property rights could still be claimed but

2 R. Coase, "The Problem of Social Cost," *Journal of Law and Economics*, 3 (1960), 1–44; H. Demsetz, "Towards a Theory of Property Rights," *American Economic Review*, 57 (1967), 1–22; P. Young, *Individual Strategy and Social Structure: An Evolutionary Theory of Institutions* (Cambridge, 1998).

only on a seasonal basis. The last instance was one in which the depth of waters was significantly affected by seasonal climatic changes. Entitlements that could not be exerted under conditions of deep water in autumn or winter could again be claimed in the hot season, under conditions of shallow water or "dried up" countryside. This section suggests the notion of an institutional continuum, in which many intermediate situations can be seen as connecting the two poles of generalized commons and generalized private appropriation. The emergence of open access resources was associated with an initial collapse of conventional property rights, but induced in its turn a search for new standards that could be used in the governance of marsh commons.

Section 4 explores the taxonomy of the commons with attempts by Bolognese landlords and scientists (primarily in the 18th century) to address explicitly the internal diversity of the "wetlands economy." In particular, this section will examine contemporary proposals to recognize the variety of assets encompassed by the "wetlands economy," and the associated diversity of "rational" utilization criteria.

Section 5 addresses the general implications of the analysis presented for the economic theory of property regimes. In particular, the formation of specific property regimes should be seen as the outcome of interactions occurring within an already existing social domain. In this way, individual and collective property appear as opposing poles on a continuum, and any particular property regime may be considered as combining partial features of both. The historical case examined here points to property regimes as contested fields of interaction, and highlights that the weight of either component may result from the balance of opposing factors under particular circumstances. Section 6 concludes by addressing the methodological issue of "context" and its relevance for the understanding of the relationship between economic history and economic theory.

2 Open Access Resources: The Dynamics of Commons and Private Property

The economic analysis of open access resources has often focused on the institutional and technological characteristics of resources that are "held in common" (*commons*), either because private appropriation has not yet taken place, or because private property rights cannot be enforced.[3] The possibility

3 G. Hardin, "The Tragedy of the Commons," *Science*, (1971) 1243–1248.; Ostrom, *Governing the Commons*; see also H.S. Maine, *Ancient Law: its connection with the early history of society and its relation to modern ideas* (Oxford, 1959 [1st ed. 1861]).

that commons could substitute private appropriation at the "micro" level has seldom been investigated. Moreover, cycles in which phases of private appropriation are followed by phases of common utilization, and then again by the introduction of private property rights, have not attracted much scholarly attention. We could even say that, to this day, much historical information embedded in the economics of commons is associated with the consideration of agricultural commons, and with the view that such commons came to be gradually superseded by the "modernization" of cultivation practices and the enclosure of collective land.

We want to suggest that the relationship between commons and private appropriation can be a flexible one. As a matter of fact, a "common" utilization can both precede and follow phases of private appropriation. The dynamics of commons is often intertwined with the emergence and/or the disappearance of "limited" property rights, that is, of opportunities for private appropriation constrained to a narrow time interval or to specific crops.

The evolution of "liquid commons" in the Bolognese wetlands between the end of the 16th century and the mid-18th century suggests a flexible, shifting borderline between utilization of commons and private appropriation. It also calls attention to the possible co-existence of different modes of utilization for the same pool of resources, depending on the season or the "appropriation technique" in use. The evolution furthermore constitutes a remarkable historical process that seemed to reverse, for a relatively long period, the traditional pattern by which common access resources give way to private appropriation and utilization. Decisions taken around the close of the 16th century led to the attempt to alter the course of the Reno River and to divert it temporarily into the large marshland to the south of Ferrara (the "Valle San Martina"). This would have allowed the excavation of an alternative course for the Po River, so that eventually the Reno would return to its ancient course and would empty its water into the Po. This ambitious project eventually failed. The Reno was in fact "provisionally" diverted into the Valle San Martina, but the second stage of the hydraulic works could not be completed. Lack of adequate technology as well as financial resources made completion of the project impossible. At the same time, the conflict of interests between Bologna and Ferrara also made the ancient course of the Reno River no longer practicable. This left only the "provisional" outlet into the Valle San Martina for the Reno, and became the source of recurrent floods and submersion of agricultural land for a period of over 150 years. A first dramatic event took place in 1605 when a flood submerged various villages, bringing about the destruction of buildings and the complete loss of many fields.[4] The situation became increasingly worse in the following years. In 1621, a contemporary estimate identified the damage in terms of 217,000 *tornature* of agricultural land (45,208 hectares) completely or partially withdrawn from cultivation. In 1624, submerged agricultural land increased to an estimated 300,000 *corbe* (about 62,500 hectares). Around the end of the 17th and the early 18th century the Reno, after completely filling the marshlands of the Valle San Martina, started invading the "medium" Bolognese countryside, causing a more acute emergency.[5]

The water management crisis described above brought about a major overhaul in the structure of property rights and in the tenure arrangements associated with them. The main reason is that submerged, or partially submerged, areas became, to an increasing extent, areas in which property rights could no longer be exerted in the traditional way. A most striking outcome was that, in many instances, the standard "signs" of private appropriation (such as canals or footpaths separating one property from another) disappeared altogether from sight. In other cases property signs changed in character and ceased to be "signs of division," becoming mere focal points around which some property claim could be raised even if seldom enforced. This could happen, for example, when roofs, towers, and bell towers could still be identified and associated with former owners, in spite of the submersion of surrounding lands.

Thus a sequence of environmental shocks made the previous legal structure redundant and introduced a dramatic change in the natural and economic landscape. First, agricultural property rights switched back to a pre-contractual stage in which legal owners could exert only limited supervision, since it was often possible to identify the "centers of gravitation" of property entitlements but not the actual borderline between competing claims. Second, aristocratic and peasant households gave way to a combination of other social groups, such as vagrants, impoverished and homeless peasants, and jobless laborers. Third, the "mode of subsistence" of these social groups often drew upon the utilization of "liquid commons," that is, hunting, gathering and making artifacts such as straw boxes, hats, cages and similar objects.

This new framework suggests that the flooding of large areas of the Bolognese countryside was associated with the substitution of common for private property because exclusive utilization could be enforced at excessive cost. Steven Cheung maintains that "in a common property, there is no

4 C. Poni, "L'idraulica poderale, l'avanzata delle paludi, l'uso delle risorse palustri," *Bologna e l'invenzione delle acque*, ed. M. Tozzi Fontana (Bologna, 2001), pp. 128–132.

5 Ibid., 131–132.

delimitation or delineation of its use rights to any private party. No one has the right to exclude others from using it and all are free to compete for its use."[6]

While "delimitation" was often impossible, "delineation" was sometimes reduced to the identification of one or more focal points (as explained above). The economics of commons observed in the Bologna marshlands was characterized by a complex interplay of environmental constraints, "historical" property rights, and contemporary attempts to enforce property or utilization rights across a moving borderline between "closed" and "open" appropriation.

3 Commons, Appropriation and the Institutional Continuum: The *Agri Bononiensis Palustris Historia*

Appropriation is a common feature of most cases in which a stock of resources is put to use. But the characteristics of appropriation are subject to considerable variability. To illustrate this point, it may be useful to distinguish between "closed" and "open" patterns of appropriation. In the "closed" case, appropriation is associated with a definite spatial (and sometimes also temporal) horizon. This means that utilization rights are exclusive and contained within well-defined boundaries. Given resource endowment A, its partition into a set of "property domains" A_i implies that no property domain A_is may be used by an agent (or social group) $A_j \neq A_i$. In the "open" mode of appropriation, on the other hand, a given resource endowment Ω may be partitioned into a set of non-mutually exclusive utilization domains Ω_is. This means that appropriation of the utilization domain Ω_i by agent (or social group) A_i does not exclude that Ω_i could be appropriated by agent (or social group) A_j at some other time. In short, the "open" mode of appropriation is one in which multiple overlapping utilization domains are possible, so that the same individual (or social group) may be involved in appropriation activities associated with a variety of different domains, while the same domain could lead to a variety of appropriation activities.

The case of the Bolognese marshlands is an interesting "laboratory" for a theory of the institutional continuum between open and closed models of appropriation. The reason is that the environmental shock, or rather the sequence of shocks, that hit the rich agricultural plain to the north of Bologna

6 S. Cheung, "Common Property Rights," *The New Palgrave. A Dictionary of Economics*, eds. J. Eatwell, M. Milgate and P. Newman, vol. 1 (London, 1987), pp. 504–505.

brought about a variety of hydraulic and agronomic conditions, which in turn led to a diverse structure of appropriation and utilization criteria.

The situation is carefully described by the scientist Luigi Ferdinando Marsigli in his manuscript, *Agri Bononiensis Palustris Historia* [A History of Bolognese Marshes].[7] This work is based on a detailed investigation, promoted and organized by Marsigli in the second decade of the 18th century, of the environmental, technological and economic conditions of the Bolognese countryside since the water management crisis of the early 17th century. The first section of this "natural history" of the Bolognese marshes considers the variety of cases to be found in the "wet countryside" and introduces a taxonomy of marshes that suggests a multiplicity of utilization criteria.

In particular, Marsigli called attention to the manifold opportunities for appropriation by landlords that could be reintroduced (in spite of the environmental disaster) as soon as landlords realized that an irreversible structural change had taken place. This means that, in Marsigli's view, landlords could still exert some degree of control over the utilization of these emergent commons provided the environmental change was adequately assessed. For example, Marsigli was critical of many attempts by landlords to revert to the structural conditions prevailing before the environmental crisis by simply directing excess water into their neighbors' fields. Marsigli maintained that landlords should instead be cooperative and that their attitude to private appropriation should also change. In particular, landlords should turn their attention to the manifold economic opportunities associated with marshes once the "fine structure" of marshes was identified and the distinct modes of appropriation suitable to each micro-environment were implemented. In short, Marsigli argued that the peculiar situation of marshes did not make landlord appropriation impossible provided the appropriation mode was changed from traditional agriculture to innovative practices that combined the "risk culture" of rice with hunting, fishing, gathering and small craft production. This meant, according to Marsigli, that the appropriation of liquid commons by landlords would be an uncertain and unstable outcome of practices leading to the "partition" of commons not according to space, as with traditional enclosures of fields, but by environmental and seasonal conditions. In other words, conventional "delimitation" of property domains should generally be dropped due to the difficult identification of borders, and property

7 *Agri Bononiensis Palustris Historia* [A History of Bolognese Marshes], Ms. 139, Bologna University Library. An assessment of Marsigli's activity as a general in the Imperial army and a natural scientist in the Bolognese tradition of Malpighi and others is to be found in J. Stoye, *Marsigli's Europe 1680–1730* (New Haven, 1994).

"delineation" should instead be associated with the introduction of multiple foci around which a variety of utilization domains could be identified. Any given focal point would be a cluster of property and utilization entitlements that could only be enforced if landlords' claims successfully "fit" the environmental and seasonal structure of liquid commons.

It may be argued, from Marsigli's point of view, that reversion to common property is a contingent situation resulting from environmental shocks. In short, the specific conditions of the Bolognese wetlands would allow for new property rights to be identified and enforced provided that landlords were prepared to drop the old association between landed property and strict delimitation of property domains.

It could also be argued that the effective utilization of liquid commons by (former) landlords presupposed, according to Marsigli, a management of common resources that was at the same time exploratory and aggressive. This was because landlord appropriation of liquid commons entailed the "decomposition" of common resources and the identification of separate utilization domains. In this way it might be possible to discover that some delimitation was enforceable, in terms of seasonal use if not by property dimensions, and that property came to be delineated as a cluster of exclusive utilization entitlements of variable certainty and range. Marsigli's approach to the utilization of liquid commons was a complex blend of scientific methodology and self-interested rationality. It also revealed (we could say almost by default) that the emergent new commons could be appropriated by landlords only as a result of painstaking "delineation" and specific enforcement of claims associated with any remaining trace of private appropriation. This situation opened up a possible sphere of conflict with other social groups that might try to access liquid commons independently of traditional delimitation and other legal constraints.

The argument outlined above implies that the taxonomy of liquid commons delineated in Marsigli's *Palustris Historia* is not only a remarkable contribution to the natural history of marshes. It is also an important indication of the complex routes that appropriation may take if utilization domains cannot be separated in a clear and unambiguous way. There is here a fascinating field of inquiry that calls for additional research in archival and other primary sources.[8]

8 A possible source of information is archival material concerning litigation between landlords and local communities in the courts of Bologna.

4 A Taxonomy of Liquid Commons

Marsigli's *Palustris Historia* suggests the possibility of differentiating the liquid commons of the Bolognese wetlands according to a taxonomy that reflects a combination of hydraulic, environmental and socio-economic characteristics.

Marsigli's taxonomy is based on the four following general types: *acquitrino* (minor wetlands), *acqua* (deep-water wetlands), *palude* (marsh), *fondo di palude* (deep marsh). Minor wetlands are characterised by shallow water, so that "a very great number of plants normally grown outside water" could still be cultivated. The situation is different in deep-water wetlands, where water would reach the knee of the average person. In this case, terrestrial vegetation would not survive and only rushes or other marsh plants could be grown. However, most water would dry up in summer, and dried up wetlands could produce pasture or bedding for animals. The real marsh is where there is "enough water to nourish plants [...] that live completely underwater," or plants whose leaves and flowers "rest [in summer] on the surface of that same water." Finally, the deep marsh (*fondo di palude*) is where water never disappears even at the height of summer. The *fondo di palude* is "almost a lake" in which even canes or other marsh plants rot. In this case, fishing is the primary activity left for an economic utilization of the liquid commons.

Marsigli's taxonomy is at the same time a program for the "rational" utilization and appropriation of common resources. The core of Marsigli's strategy is differentiation and selective appropriation. This means that in certain areas (minor wetlands), traditional property rights could be enforced and cultivation attempted, often only the most risky type of rice cultivation. In other areas, Marsigli's analysis suggests the appearance of "seasonal" property rights: land submerged by water during the wet season would dry in summer and allow for the enforcement of landlords' claims to exclusive utilization. Finally, the *fondo di palude* entails a shift from landed property and the emergence of possibly more controversial claims to the exclusive utilization of the marsh as fishery.

To sum up, Marsigli suggests a subtle and flexible strategy by which landlords' collective action could at the same time reduce the size of the environmental damage and enhance the opportunities for the identification of exclusive domains in the appropriation and utilization of emergent commons.

5 Towards a Theoretical Framework

Property rights, then, had manifold dimensions, and those rights had specific structures in different contexts. In particular, the example of liquid and transient commons calls attention to the existence of a continuum of material rights associated with the specific conditions of people subject to changing environmental constraints. The extraordinary events that took place in the Bolognese countryside between the late-16th century and the mid-18th century highlight the persistence of this continuum long after the disappearance of "primitive" property types which allowed obsolete patterns of appropriation to resurface under suitable natural and institutional conditions. Such an outcome suggests that an economic theory of property should be general enough to encompass the variety of appropriation modes, thus avoiding reduction of the whole set of possible cases to any specific mode. The essential structure of an economic theory of property may therefore be based upon the following principles:

1. appropriation is associated with the identification of certain characteristics of objects;
2. such characteristics of objects have to be recognized across the social space;
3. alternative property domains may be compatible with the same conceptual and legal framework;
4. changing descriptions of the relevant objects may be associated with a radical transformation of property rights.

David Hume's philosophical theory of appropriation offers a foundation to an economic theory of property that is in principle compatible with a variety of appropriation modes. According to Hume, property presupposes possession, and the latter is identified as follows: "We are said to be in possession of anything, not only when we immediately touch it, but also when we are so situated with respect to it, as to have it in our power to use it."[9] For example, the owner of a deep-water wetlands (*acqua*, according to Marsigli's taxonomy) has power to use it for pasture and bedding only after it has dried up in summer, but that power disappears altogether in winter, when only marsh plants may be obtained. Indeed, the "power to use" material objects may be associated with a highly differentiated range of socially recognized rights of exclusion. Thus, in the case of a deep marsh (*fondo di palude*), rights of exclusion associated with relics of former ownership (for example, the roof top of a house surfacing above water) might co-exist (and conflict) with the right of exclusion associated with the actual ability to catch fish in the marsh. Hume's theory emphasizes the "practical" aspect of property and its necessary foundation in

9 D. Hume, *A Treatise of Human Nature*, ed. L.A. Selby-Bigge (Oxford, 1989 [1st edn. 1739]), p. 506.

possession. As a result, Hume's approach is conducive to a theory of property in which legal claims derive from contexts and *de facto* conditions rather than the other way round. This point of view is especially suitable when dealing with shifting environmental conditions such as those described in this chapter. For in such contexts "the power of using any object becomes more or less certain, according as the interruptions we may meet with are more or less probable," and "it is in many cases impossible to determine when possession begins or ends; nor is there any certain standard, by which we can decide such controversies."[10] Contested property domains highlight the flexible character of property rights and the association between possession, ownership and "declarative speech acts," that is, speech acts whose successful performance brings about a particular state of affairs.[11] However, as noted by Dick Ruiter, "[S]tates of affairs resulting from successful performances of declarative speech acts exist in a world of utterance as parts of some institution."[12] This means that speech acts associated with property (typically, speech acts of the declarative type) presuppose an already existing domain of established rules and social norms. The latter domain includes socially recognized appropriation rules and is not circumscribed by the rules for the introduction and exchange of exclusive ownership entitlements (private property rights). As a result, identification of property rights presupposes a social space in which modes of appropriation are subject to constraints associated with more general social norms. Entitlements of individuals belonging to the same social group are not always sharply differentiated, and under many historical conditions appropriation rights over "external" objects are closely intertwined with the framework in which interactions among agents takes place. This situation led Henry Sumner Maine to argue that:

> there is a strong improbability of our obtaining any clue to the early history of property, if we confine our notice to the proprietary rights of individuals. It is more than likely that joint-ownership, and not separate ownership, is the really archaic institution, and that the form of property

10 Ibid.

11 J. Searle, *Speech Acts* (Cambridge, 1969); J. Searle and D. Vanderveken, *Foundations of Illocutionary Acts* (Cambridge 1985).

12 D.W.P. Ruiter, *Institutional Legal Facts. Legal Powers and Their Effects* (Dordrecht, 1993), p. 52.

> which will afford us instruction will be those which are associated with the rights of families and of groups of kindred.[13]

The property domain is a characteristic social interaction domain in which agents relate with one another as subjects belonging to a plurality of partially overlapping groups. In practice, this makes property arrangements highly context-dependent: patterns of possession and utilization may be very different under similar contractual arrangements, and different contractual arrangements may be associated with similar patterns of possession and utilization. This argument entails that "real" property regimes are often different from "formal" property regimes: the former derive from a complex web of influences that is not always apparent when the purely legal features of property are considered. One important consequence is that property regimes are inherently relational, so that the "law of persons" (*jus personarum*) and the "law of things" (*jus rerum*) should be considered as mutually determining one another rather than being artificially separated from each other and divorced from the intersubjective structure of society. This point of view turns property regimes into sophisticated relational arrangements whose understanding both in economic and legal terms requires that characteristic elements of the law of things, such as the analysis of contract, should be investigated by addressing "the original condition of Persons."[14]

This argument calls attention to the structure of the social domain in which property rights are determined. In particular, we may conjecture that social domains associated with a highly nested structure of relational

---

13 *Maine, Ancient Law*, p. 215. Similar attention to multiple forms of property entitlements (individual, collective and mixed) is common in late-19th century reconstructions of the emergence of "modern" property rights. See, for instance, E. de Laveleye, *De la propriété et de ses formes primitives* (Paris,1874); M. Kovalevsky, *Modern Customs and Ancient Laws of Rússia* (London, 1891); O. Gierke, *Community in Historical Perspective: A Translation of Selections from Das deutsche Genossenschaftsrecht* (The German Law of Fellowship), principally from vol. 1, trans. Mary Fischer, ed. Antony Black (Cambridge, 1990), originally published in German as *Das Deutsche Genossenchaftsrecht, v. 1, Rechtsgeschichte der Deutschen Genossenschaft* (The legal and moral history of the German Fellowship),[Berlin, 1868]. Paolo Grossi, has provided a comprehensive assessment of this literature and noted that awareness of the wide range of historical property forms is essential to the understanding of the evolution of property rights in contemporary society; see Grossi, "Un altro modo di possedere," *L'emersione di forme alternative di proprietà alla coscienza giuridica postunitaria* (Milan, 1977), translated as Grossi, *An Alternative to Private Property: Collective Property in the Juridical Consciousness of the Nineteenth Century* (Chicago, 1981).

14 Maine, *Ancient Law*, p. 214.

arrangements would generally allow a more flexible adjustment to external shocks (such as the environmental disaster described in this chapter) relative to social domains characterized by lower nesting, and thus by a more immediate exposure of formal arrangements to external shocks.[15] Nesting allows alternative "interpretations" of basic principles, as the same principles may be embedded in distant and seemingly incompatible institutional arrangements, such as individual and common property. For this reason, a nested social structure may be able to switch from one property regime to another more easily than a social structure in which the relational setup is less clearly developed. Here we find an instance of the "folding back" of institutional domains investigated by Masahiko Aoki in his theory of institutional variety and institutional change.[16] According to Aoki, institutions are generated within a set of nested interaction domains, and the possibilities of choice within any given domain are influenced by cognitive frames and beliefs associated with more encompassing domains. In our case, possession and ownership were framed by beliefs in which the continuum of property regimes clearly played a part. Roman law and its clear-cut distinction between "right of persons" and "right of things" came to be interpreted in terms of a multi-layered conception, a point of view induced by the environmental disaster we have described.

6 Economic History and Economic Theory

This chapter has considered a historical case in which the collapse of standard criteria for the delineation and delimitation of property rights was associated with the emergence of open access resources. The new structural conditions had a far-reaching influence in the economic and social sphere: established patterns of land tenure could no longer be sustained, and new patterns of resource utilization began to emerge. This framework was inherently unstable and conducive to social tensions, if not to open social conflict. The attempt by

15 This conjecture is consistent with Herbert Simon's view that complex systems characterized by a sufficient number of "intermediate structures" are generally more capable of absorbing gradual changes than systems characterized by a simpler internal structure; see Simon, "The Architecture of Complexity," *Proceedings of the American Philosophical Society*, 106, 1962, 467–482.

16 M. Aoki, *Toward a Comparative Institutional Analysis* (Cambridge, Mass., 2001).

lower social strata, such as homeless peasants, vagrants and poor laborers, to make use of the open resources made available through water disasters inevitably clashed with the attempt by former landlords to enforce the claims associated with the remaining signs of property, and to advance new claims over the utilization of the emergent commons.

Marsigli's *Palustris Historia* provided the historical and conceptual background of our reconstruction. It is worth recalling that Marsigli's piece is primarily a contribution to the "natural history" of open-access resources, and to the possibilities that could be envisaged in order to reduce once again such resources into the economic rationality associated with the standard individualistic conception of property. One important outcome of Marsigli's *Palustris Historia* is to show that open access and closed access often co-exist side by side and that the shift from one resource category to the other could reflect a subtle balance between external shocks and the dynamics of social conflict. In particular, Marsigli's treatment of liquid commons calls attention to the link between the emergence of exclusive claims and the differentiation of a common stock into a variety of specific resources. This type of argument is noteworthy, as it calls attention to the contingent nature of property regimes. In particular, Marsigli emphasizes the specific conditions, environmental and institutional, associated with any such regime, and the transitory character of property entitlements which appear, in his investigation, to be extremely sensitive to external shocks. This is especially true when property delineation is uncertain, as minor parametric changes – for example, changing weather conditions – could tip the balance against a certain property regime and make an altogether different regime dominant.

Context is essential to the activation of property rights under conditions of uncertain entitlements.[17] Our reconstruction has shown that environmental collapse followed by parametric uncertainty may be associated with a transformation of property rights: landed property based upon Roman law receded into the background and was substituted by a contested domain, in which new and competing rights were asserted and sometimes successfully enforced by claimants. Changing context was fundamental both in determining the

17 This is a special instance of the relationship between context and the epistemic process by which certain characteristics of any given object of attention may acquire salience while other characteristics of the same object recede to the background; see R. Scazzieri, "Context, Congruence and Co-ordination," *Reasoning, Rationality and Probability*, eds. M. C. Galavotti, R. Scazzieri and P. Suppes (Stanford, 2007), pp. 187–207.

general evolution of the property regime – away from the Roman landed property model – and in influencing the balance between different property types under specific circumstances. In another article Carlo Ginzburg and Carlo Poni argued that:

> it would not be going too far out on a limb to suggest that the growing fortunes of microhistorical reconstruction are tied to growing doubts about the established procedures of macrohistory. Precisely because we are no longer so sure that the game is worth the candle, we are persuaded to reanalyze the rules of the game.[18]

It has also been pointed out that microhistorians "have concentrated on the contradictions of normative systems and therefore on the fragmentation, contradictions and plurality of viewpoints which make all systems fluid and open."[19] Our analysis has illustrated a specific aspect of the rules of the game, such as the emergence and transformation of property claims under the specific environmental conditions of liquid commons by emphasizing the interdependence of economic theory and economic history. Economic theory provides the general conceptual background and the awareness that agents could advance competing claims within a common domain of social interactions; it also highlights the critical role of changing context under conditions of uncertainty. Economic history supplies the general background information and the specific knowledge of environmental contexts that could influence the shift from one property regime to another.[20] We may conjecture that economic history derives from theory its specific relevance for economic causality, as historical reconstruction allows identification of the set of conditions determining the emergence of a particular regime from within the continuum of property entitlements that could be envisaged in theory. To conclude, our research suggests that the "theory" of economic history[21] is not a distinct body

18 See in this volume part IV, ch. 14, C. Ginzburg and C. Poni, "The Name and the Game," pp. 3–4.

19 G. Levi, "On Microhistory," *New Perspectives on Historical Writing*, ed. P. Burke (Oxford, 1991), pp. 93–113.

20 This shift sometimes has the nature of a one-off change, as with traditional landed property made obsolete by environmental disaster, and has sometimes the character of an oscillation between different property regimes, as with the competing claims on Marsigli's deep-water wetlands.

21 J.R. Hicks, *The Theory of Economic History* (Oxford, 1969).

of knowledge, but a particular approach to the analytical reconstruction of contexts and circumstances: one in which contingent factors take on causal relevance within a range of possibilities, provided the latter is large enough to encompass a sufficient number of alternative outcomes.

CHAPTER 4

Family and *Podere* in Emilia-Romagna: Peasant Sharecroppers

Carlo Poni

Anyone who skims the pages of the *Inchiesta Agraria* of 1881 will come across frequent descriptions of the "patriarchal" peasant household, which, it is said, could be found everywhere in the countryside of Rimini and Forlì and throughout Romagna. The peasant households in the province of Bologna are also "patriarchal," and it is the "usual patriarchal type" of household which one finds in the rural areas of what were once the Emilian duchies of Modena and Parma.[1]

As to the internal structure of these households, the *Inchiesta* tells us that, "they are always of the same type ... the head of the household, or its most competent member, has authority over all aspects of household life, and is given the title of *reggitore* in recognition of the fact that he controls not only the agricultural but also the financial aspects of the household's affairs. His wife, who is given the title of *reggitrice,* is in charge of domestic matters, of the poultry and of the sale of retail products: eggs, cheese, fruit, etc." She was subject to the *reggitore*, while all the women of the household—sisters-in-law, daughters, and daughters-in-law—took orders from her. Only the *reggitore* had dealings with the landlord "over the division of the produce, the settlement of

1 [In preparing this article, Carlo Poni consulted this very extensive collection of reports and data on the system of sharecropping in Emilia-Romagna: *Atti della Giunta per la inchiesta agraria e sulle condizioni della classe agricola*, vol. II, *Relazione del Commissario Marchese Luigi Tanari sulla Sesta Circoscrizione* (Rome, 1881), hereafter *Inchiesta Agraria*. These pages in the *Inchiesta Agraria* inform his comments on the following material (editors' addition): the patriarchal peasant household: pp. 221–23, 237–38, 304, 338, 361, 396, 444, 505, 528, 604, 610–611, 624, 630, 668, 674; the ratio of peasant per hectare: p. 297 (Parma), p. 434 (Bologna); the impact of military service on sharecropping families: pp. 228, 238, 246–247, 324–325, 338, 361, 381, 398, 423, 447, 472, 508, 527, 530, 558, 586–587, 607–608, 613–614, 632, 640, 646, 654, 669, 675, 722, 756; the effect of the tax on milling, pp. 240–241, 304–305, 338, 361–362, 379, 396, 410, 422, 444, 459, 556, 585, 605, 611, 624, 630, 639, 645, 674, 721, 755; impoverishment of *mezzadria* in the Bologna area, pp. 243, 434, 445, 662; "trebb," p. 604. The period covered is mainly the nineteenth century. For more extensive bibliographical references to sharecroppers, see Carlo Poni, "La famiglia contadina e il podere in Emilia-Romagna," *Fossi e cavedagne benedicon le campagne. Studi di storia rurale* (Bologna, 1982). – Eds.]

 | DOI:10.1163/9789004713277_006

accounts, and the management of the farm." He oversaw the work of the *bifolco* (one of his sons), who was responsible for the livestock, and the *campagnolo* (the eldest son), who was in charge of cultivation of the fields. The *campagnolo* was also in charge of all the other members of the family—brothers, sons and nephews—and supervised the women, apart from the *reggitrice*, when they worked in the fields. The relative autonomy of the *reggitrice* was also shown by the fact that she managed a cash fund of her own, which consisted of income from retail sales, and was separate from that of the *reggitore*. With this cash, which was significant only in the well-off families, the *reggitrice* would buy a few things from travelling haberdashers or at the fairs, such as needles, sewing-cotton, "Genoa blue" (for dyeing her home-woven hemp cloth), and a few articles of clothing (headscarves, veils and so on) for the women of the family.

When the girls married they left their father's household and joined their husband's, taking their dowries with them, while the men brought into the household their brides with their dowries. Here we touch on the central mechanism that determines the structure of the peasant household, which thus contains within itself several nuclear families (conjugal family units). The married sons lived under the authority of their father together with their sisters and their unmarried brothers (the patrilocal family), and they all inhabited the same farmhouse. Thus they formed, in Peter Laslett's terminology, a (single) multiple family household.[2] But there were also other types of multiple family households to be found, such as the *frérèches* (cohabiting families of married brothers), in which the head of the household was one of the brothers.

When the father died the task of guiding the family would fall to the oldest or the ablest of the sons. Sometimes this choice, which could give rise to bitter tensions, involved the intervention of an external mediator, who might according to circumstances be the parish priest, the landowner, the *partitore* (who supervised property divisions among peasants) or an influential neighbor (a well-known member of the peasant "aristocracy" of the village). But a *reggitore* who was chosen could hardly ever concentrate in his own person that undisputed authority which was characteristic of the father, the natural head of the family. In certain areas, such as the countryside of Faenza, the wife of a chosen *reggitore* could not be the *reggitrice* "if there are other women ... so that the concentration of all power into one married couple may not damage the interests of the others." I consider this rule applicable only for the *frérèches*.

2 For the terminology employed in this article see P. Laslett, "Introduction: The History of the Family," *Household and Family in Past Time* (Cambridge, 1972). The Emilian sources commonly use the term *stirpe* to refer to the conjugal family units (nuclear families) within the household.

A source relating to the nearby area of Cesena says this explicitly: "When there are two married brothers who have attained the age of majority, the *reggitrice* shall not be the wife of the *reggitore*, but of the other." In the region around Parma, "when the *reggitore* died his place was taken by the oldest married man, and that of the *reggitrice* by the oldest married woman." But if there was no married woman and the family was still united "one of the brothers would marry soon. The rest of the family, even the older members, were then answerable to the new couple."[3] Here death seems to decide the moment of marriage. This was necessary above all because the family system seems to have excluded the sister (and also the widow) from the position of *reggitrice*.

We do not know when this type of household organization became established. But we can be sure that in the plain on the right bank of the Po river its origins are closely linked to the origins and diffusion of sharecropping. This economic structure spread and became preponderant between the fourteenth and sixteenth centuries and lasted for centuries in spite of periods of partial and temporary setbacks.[4] By sharecropping I refer not so much to the contract in its legal form but to the material expression of that contract in the countryside: the farmhouse, the cowshed, the fields. The basis of this agrarian system was a subsistence economy for the peasant household, and its guiding principle was the production of rent for the landowner, almost always a nobleman, a city-dweller or an ecclesiastical body.

The landowner provided the land with the house, the barn, the well, the oven etc.—the agricultural holding, the *podere*—as well as half the seed and half the oxen. The peasant provided all the labor power, of himself and his family, as well as all the implements (the plough, the four-wheeled cart, the hand-cart, spades, hoes and so on), half the seed and half the oxen (in the countryside of Bologna the peasant had to provide all the oxen). The peasants committed themselves to employing all their energies in the cultivation of the land, hence they could do no work for other people. Certain activities

---

3 *Monografia sulle condizioni dell'agricoltura e della classe agricola del Circondario di Faenza*, 1879, pp. 84–85; F. Masi, *L'agricoltura nel Circondario di Cesena*, 1879; (F. Barbuti), *Monografia dell'agricoltura parmense* (Parma, 1880), pp. 127–128. The *Monografia* and Masi's work are preserved in manuscript in the Archivio Centrale dello Stato in Rome (A.C.S.R.). Status symbols of the *reggitore*, around the beginning of the nineteenth century, were "shoes, cloak, umbrella ... and he alone wore them" (L. Biffi, *Memoria intorno alle condizioni dell'agricoltura e della classe agricola nel circondario di Faenza* [Faenza, 1880], p. 151). In the special case where the wife had no brothers, the husband went to live in the wife's house. This arrangement has a special name: *ardot* (in the dialect of Romagna).

4 G. L. Basini, "L'azienda agraria del monastero di S. Pietro e Prospero di Reggio-Emilia, XVII–XVIII secoli," *Quaderni Storici*, vol. 13, no. 39 (1978), 955–975.

(spinning, weaving, and so on) which directly satisfied the needs of the family were tolerated, especially in the winter season. As recompense for his contribution to production the landowner appropriated half the gross product, while the sharecropper retained the other half. In addition, sharecroppers had to make supplementary contributions to the landowner: *in kind*, capons for Christmas, hens at Carnival time, eggs at Easter, chickens for the Feast of St. Peter, geese for All Saints' Day; *as free services*, transport and a few other jobs; and *in cash*, house-rent. Thus the "master's share," according to some sources, came near to two-thirds, including an important proportion of the funds required for the subsistence of the peasant family. The latter was often forced to run up debts with the landowner. The sharecropper, burdened by debts and incapable of producing an average level of returns, was often threatened with dismissal, because the sharecropping contract was a tacitly renewable annual contract.

Vincenzo Tanara, a Bolognese agronomist of the seventeenth century, provides us with the earliest analysis of the resulting division of labor which we have already encountered within the peasant household. He describes how "among country people the tasks are divided up by the eldest, the head of the household: to one is assigned the task of ploughing and of caring for the oxen, and he is known as the *bifolco*; to another is assigned the task of working the land by hand, so he is known as the *bracciante* (or *campagnolo*)." Even prior to Tanara, in 1609, Celio Malespini had depicted an old Bolognese *reggitore* in his *Duecento Novelle*. He showed him in the evening with the family, assigning to "both men and women all the tasks which they had to do the following day."[5]

This type of peasant household could reach a considerable size. Enzo Carretti, director of the *Museum of Agriculture* in San Martino in Rio (Reggio Emilia), cited for the period around the First World War extreme cases of "large peasant households ... having as many as fifty members (for example the Morini of San Donnino di Casalgrande)." The interviews carried out by the *Museo della Civilta Contadina* (Museum of Peasant Culture) of San Marino di Bentivoglio (Bologna) suggest an average of fifteen to twenty individuals per household. However, the demographic research of the 1847 census of the Papal states by Athos Bellettini established that in the Bolognese plain the average number of individuals in the sharecropping household was 9.9, while in some villages—Crevalcore, Santa Maria in Duno, Castel Maggiore, and

---

5 V. Tanara, *Economia del cittadino in villa* (Bologna, 1644), p. 125; C. Malespini, *Duecento Novelle* (Venice, 1609), part II. Malespini's *reggitore* assigned to the men (Pirino, Menghinazzo and Simone) the jobs of fertilizing the field, woodcutting, and transporting the wheat to the mill; to the women (Orsolina, Agnolina and Simona) the care of the animals: cows, pigs and sheep.

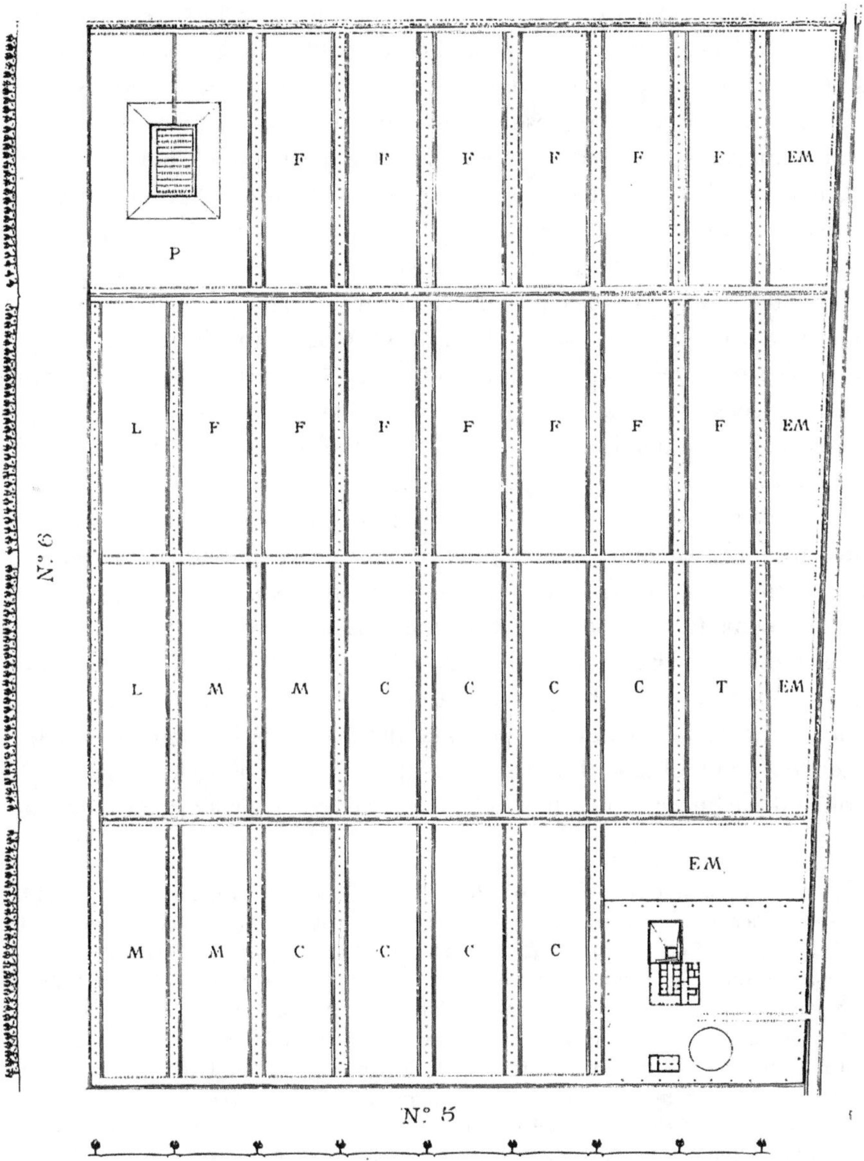

FIGURE 4.1 Model sharecropping farm divided into four sections. The strips—from six to nine in each section—are separated by rows of trees planted between two ditches in each strip of earth called "cavaletto". Below, right: the house, the cowshed, the oven, the threshing-ground. Above, left: the hemp retting pool. F = grain; EM = lucerne; C = hemp; M = maize; T = clover; L = sainfoin; P = pastures. The farm consists of 15.80 hectares; the family includes 12 people—4 men, 4 women, and 4 children.
SOURCE: *MONOGRAFIA DEL PODERE BOLOGNESE* (BOLOGNA, 1881)

Borgo Panigale—the average came close to twelve (see Table 4.1). But these averages, although significant, mask the inequalities in size among different families. They provide only a very approximate picture of the real state of affairs. A more accurate representation could be obtained by classifying separately small, medium and large households. Such a scheme, however, would still have the disadvantage of providing a static picture of households which were constantly changing over time, for we would need to know in addition how many of the small households were destined to grow until they became large, and how many of the large households were on the point of fragmenting. The answers to such questions will only be obtained through a careful study of parish records—registers of baptism, marriage, funerals and *stati delle anime* (periodic censuses of families carried out at Easter time)—as well as of the archives of the General Register Office. Nevertheless, the very idea of a family cycle implicit in the above suggests another dimension of the problem which must be discussed. The small family that grows into a larger one is usually a nuclear family which becomes extended or multiple and grows by means of the marriages of the adult sons. The reverse process is a tendency to return to the original family size. Aspects of this disaggregation are the splitting-up of the family, the dispersion of the sons and daughters, a prevalence of deaths over births, and so on. This means that in the course of their individual lives a large number of peasants experience different types of family—nuclear, extended, and multiple.[6] But if the size of the family changes, the size of the farm and the house where the family lives and works must also change. Thus

6 On the cyclical development of households see L. K. Berkner, "The Stem Family and the Developmental Cycle of the Peasant Household. An Eighteenth-Century Austrian Example," *American Historical Review*, LXXVII (1972), 398–418; D. I. Kertzer, "European Peasant Household Structure: some implications from a nineteenth-century Italian community," *Journal of Family History*, vol 2, n. 4 (1977), 333–349. See also the important article, C. Klapish-E. Demonet, " 'A uno pane e uno vino', la famille rurale toscane au début du XVe siècle," *Annales E.S C.*, vol. 27, no. 4 (1972), 873–901. According to A. Bellettini and A. Angeli (*Primi risultati di una ricerca sulla struttura delle famiglie della campagna Bolognese nel 1847*, Colloquium "Strutture economico-sociali e sistemi familiari," Corciano, Perugia, 5–7 June 1978), in the twenty-eight parishes of the Bologna "suburbio" 1) "among the sharecroppers [9,177] there is a clear preponderance of nuclear families and multiple families in almost comparable measure, while extended families are much reduced in importance"; 2) "the absolutely typical structure of the wage-laborer's family is ... nuclear" (there were 5,507 wage-laborers, or *braccianti*); 3) the "other families" also are fundamentally of the nuclear type (totaling 6,808 members). Of the total number of families (3,622) living in the area, there were 807 multiple families (about 22%) while the individuals who live in multiple families amounted to 8,045 out of a total of 21,492 (about 37%). See C. Corsimi, and G. B. Sgritta. "Il Convegno di Corciano: un incontro a piu' voci sulla famiglia," *Quaderni Storici*, vol. 13, no. 39 (1978), 1193–1198. [The author supplied no page references for the quotations in this note .- Eds.]

the conclusions reached by the demographic analysis of changing household size should coincide with evidence for geographical mobility. The small household lives and works on a small *podere*. If it becomes large it must move to a larger *podere*.[7]

The adaptation of family size to space touches upon a profound structure in agrarian society. The demographic structure of the family seems to be inscribed in the productive organization of the land—its division into small, medium and large farms. An almost "unconscious" control sets the base and the ceiling to its size. The structure of the landscape may have the potential to "program" the dimension of the family, to regulate its reproduction. But if the demography of the sharecropping family is linked to the productive form given to the land, the form of the land is connected in turn to the centers that govern the countryside: to the political power of the towns expressed and interpreted by those urban groups—nobles, non-nobles, ecclesiastical institutions—who possess almost all the land. This political and economic power determined the framework of the area, created the basic productive structures in the plain, and built the extensive agricultural drainage system. Estates and farms lay within this vast network. The basic unit of production, the peasant family and the *podere*, held a central place in this pattern. This system, developed over time, isolated the families in their individual houses on scattered farms, but it reduced to a minimum the distance between home and work, between unit of production and unit of consumption.

Unfortunately we know very little about the size of peasant holdings. The historians of landownership have transcribed from the property registers

---

7 Obviously I am referring to a tendential process. Within certain limits the family could respond to its own expansion by increasing the intensity of its work. One can suppose that this process, caused essentially by an increase in the number of children, tends to alter for the worse the ratio within the household of individuals who only consume (in this case the children) to individuals who work as well as consume (the adult men and women). The result must be a reduction in the yield per head, unless there is a corresponding increase in the productivity of labor (as a result of mechanization, more intensive use of manure, etc.). This model, developed by the Russian scholar A.V. Chayanov (*The Theory of Peasant Economy*, ed. D. Thorner [Homewood, 1966,] originally published in Moscow in the 1920s), is based on the assumption that we are dealing in the first place with a nuclear family, in which the couple must first support the children, who are born—on average one every three years—as pure consumers, until they reach an age when they can take part in productive labor (around twelve or fourteen years old). From this point on the ratio of consumers to producers tends to improve progressively. See also G. Levi, "Famiglie contadine nella Liguria del Settecento," *Miscellanea storica Ligure*, vol. v (1975), no. 2, 208–290. The ratio between consumers and producers is, according to Chayanov, of foremost importance in assessing decisions made by households to break up or join together. I will return to this problem below.

TABLE 4.1 Household members in agricultural work, communes of the Bolognese plain, 1847

Communes	Landowners (cultivators and non-cultivators)	Tenants (cultivators and non-cultivators)	Sharecroppers	Daylaborers and "salariati"	Other
S. Agata	4.4	7.7	9.0	4.4	4.1
S. Agostino	7.1	5.5	7.1	4.4	
Anzola	4.1		11.1	4.0	8.2
Argelato	6.7	1.0	10.3	4.6	5.0
Argile	4.0		8.6	4.5	10.0
Baricella	5.4		8.2	4.1	8.5
Bondeno	7.0		9.2	4.1	3.5
Borgo Panigale	14.5		11.8	5.3	
Budrio	5.6	3.8	9.7	4.3	6.4
Calderara	5.1	11.2	10.3	4.1	2.3
Castenaso	4.7	10.2	11.2	4.7	5.4
Castelfranco	6.1	8.0	9.6	4.3	5.8
Castel Maggiore	5.2		11.7	4.7	1.0
Cento	5.4	5.4	7.2	4.1	4.7
Crespellano	6.6	3.5	11.2	4.0	4.8
Crevalcore	5.9	14.7	11.9	4.8	6.8
Galliera	5.6	4.8	10.2	4.4	5.6
S. Giovanni in Persiceto	5.5	6.3	9.8	4.4	6.3
Malalbergo	4.0		10.8	4.4	5.3
S. Maria in Dono	8.0	1.0	11.8	4.6	5.4
Medicina	5.3	6.9	8.1	4.0	5.4
Minerbio	5.5		11.5	4.4	6.2
Molinella	5.7	6.3	8.8	4.0	6.2
S. Pietro in Casale	6.1	5.5	9.7	4.1	5.5
Pieve Terra	5.7	6.0	6.4	4.4	6.0
Poggio Renatico	5.4	5.8	10.8	4.6	7.0
Sala	13.0	6.0	11.0	4.1	5.2
Viadagola	10.0	5.0	11.1	4.2	5.7

SOURCE: A. BELLETTINI, *LA POPOLAZIONE DELLE CAMPAGNE BOLOGNESI ALLA META' DEL SECOLO XIX* (BOLOGNA, 1971) (*catasti*) hundreds of thousands of pieces of information onto tens of thousands of filing-cards, and have then added them together to construct a picture of the way in which the land was distributed among landlords. The individual units of land tied to the organization of labor and the demography of the labor-force, the *podere*, that are embedded in the landlords' records documented in the *catasti* await similar analysis. Yet as early as 1573 the municipal council of Faenza was called upon to decide on a resolution prohibiting the construction of houses ("domum seu tugurium") on sites of less than 10 *tornature* (about 2 hectares) of arable land or meadow.[8] Unfortunately we know nothing of the reasons behind this proposal, and we do not even know whether it was effectively put into practice. In which other towns were similar provisions discussed? And what were the consequences? What does the minimum size of 2 hectares suggest? The lowest size the law permitted for a sharecropper's *podere*? Or the minimum allocation of land leased with a house to the *salariati*, that is agricultural wage laborers on fixed contracts (who worked for the sharecroppers on a casual basis as *avventizi*)?

We cannot answer these questions. But other analytical approaches are possible. Around the middle of the nineteenth century the Bolognese agronomist Carlo Berti Pichat wrote an important article: "Intorno ad alcuni rapporti della popolazione coll'estensione dei poderi" ("On certain connections between the agricultural population and the size of *poderi*"), which deals with some of the questions we have been considering. Only one part of his study need concern us here, and that is his research into the units of production—both *poderi* and household labor-forces—of a number of districts near Bologna: Borgo Panigale, Spirito Santo, Meldola, Rigosa, Zola and Gesso.

Table 4.2 shows all the farms of these districts broken down into five categories according to their size, and relates the total area of land in each of these categories (ranging from *poderi* of below four *corbe* to *poderi* of more than sixteen) to the number of peasant households farming the land and the total number of individuals contained in these households. Unfortunately the use of old-style units of measurement—baskets of seed-corn (*corbe*) rather than hectares—makes the table a little less self-explanatory than it might have been. But even if it is impossible to translate numbers of *corbe* directly into units of surface area, it is nevertheless possible to say that on average 17.50 *corbe* represented about 20 hectares of farmland.[9]

8 Archivio Comunale di Faenza, *Acta Conciliaria*, vol. 11, 5 February 1573.

9 G. Astolfi, "Del bestiame tenuto alla stalla e del confronto tra il modo attualmente praticato nel coltivare le terre e nell'educare il bestiame ed un nuovo metodo qui proposto," *Il fattore di campagna* (Bologna, 1826), vol. 1, pp. 327 passim.

TABLE 4.2 Size of *poderi* and members per household in six districts of the province of Bologna, mid-19th century

Districts	I Up to 4 *Corbe*			II Between 4 and 8 *Corbe*			III Between 8 and 12 *Corbe*			IV Between 12 and 16 *Corbe*			V More than 16 *Corbe*		
	Total area sown	House holds	Individuals	Total area sown	House holds	Individuals	Total area sown	House holds	Individuals	Total area sown	House holds	Individuals	Total area sown	House holds	Individuals
Borgo Panigale	22	7	39	202	30	233	211	20	218	62	4	63	258	13	230
Spirito Santo	31	10	44	74	1	86	166	16	151	103	7	85	206	9	158
Meldola	31	10	53	46	8	65	78	8	80	87	6	74	168	8	140
Rigosa	4	1	6	16	3	29	19	2	16	59	4	55	—	—	—
Zola 1	51	18	87	178	27	203	192	18	182	169	11	144	512	22	451
Zola 2	22	8	37	114	17	107	171	16	147	28	2	21	36	2	28
Gesso 1	13	4	24	68	10	76	109	10	105	102	7	108	215	10	191
Gesso 2	12	5	15	89	14	112	21	2	23	—	—	—	—	—	—
Totals	186	63	305	787	120	911	967	92	922	610	41	550	1395	64	1198

Land areas expressed in terms of baskets of seedcorn (1 corba = hl 0.78).

SOURCE: C. BERTI PICHAT, "INTORNO AD ALCUNI RAPPORTI DELLA POPOLAZIONE AGRICOLA COLL'ESTENSIONE DEI PODERI", *FELSINEO*, VOL. V, NO. 33, 14 JANUARY 1845

TABLE 4.3 Size of labor force and size of *podere* in six districts of the province of Bologna, mid- 19th century

		Productive workers	
Size of *podere*	**Size of household**	**Male**	**Female**
For a *poderi* of 8 *Corbe*	11	3	2
For a *poderi* of 12 *Corbe*	14	4	3
For a *poderi* of 16 *Corbe*	18	6	4
For a *poderi* of 18 *Corbe*	19	6	5

SOURCE: BERTI PICHAT, "INTORNO AD ALCUNI RAPPORTI DELLA POPOLAZIONE AGRICOLA"

If we now turn to an analysis of the data, we can see that in Borgo Panigale seventy-four households, consisting on average of ten individuals, cultivated seventy-four *poderi* with an average size of ten *corbe*. Much more important, however, are the results obtained when these figures are broken down according to the different sizes of farms. Of these seventy-four households seven, composed on average of five individuals, cultivated small *poderi* of less than four *corbe*. At the other extreme thirteen households, composed on average of eighteen individuals, cultivated holdings of more than fifteen hectares.

From this table, using additional information provided by an inquiry into the composition of the sharecropping population according to age and sex, Berti Pichat drew up another table (Table 4.3) which isolates, within each household, the nucleus of the labor force (male and female) engaged in the cultivation of the land. His research indicated that on the small *poderi* the average size of the family was greater (as was the density of population per hectare), and Berti Pichat used this to argue in favor of the breaking up of the larger *poderi*, those exceeding twelve *corbe*, in order to increase the population of sharecroppers and to reduce the number of poverty-stricken and socially dangerous *salariati*. This argument arose out of social and political preoccupations, which prevented Berti Pichat from recognizing that the relationship between adult workers and individuals who were only consumers (children) within each household tended to improve, that is to increase, as one went from the smaller *poderi* to the larger ones, and that this fact was connected to the greater availability of land for cultivation by each individual (and therefore, *ceteris paribus*, to a higher productivity of labor). Table 4.2 indicates that on the smaller farms, up to 4 *corbe*, 305 individuals (including children) cultivated a total of 186 *corbe* (one individual for roughly half a *corba*), while on the larger farms 1,198 individuals (including children) cultivated a total of 1,395 *corbe* (less than one individual per *corba*). It is possible to state that almost all the large families took the form of a multiple family household.[10] This may mean that the multiple *ménages* (in which among other things it is possible to practice a more rational cooperation which allows a higher productivity of labor) were more likely to achieve the status of well-off peasants than the (small) nuclear families who cultivated smaller *poderi*. If this were true, one could advance the hypothesis that certain features of the productive system tended to discourage the splitting-up of large (multiple) families and to favor their formation. This is a hypothesis which only future research may be able to confirm.[11]

But countertendencies were also at work, with varying degrees of effectiveness. Other rules affecting the hereditary system in fact applied when the sharecroppers were (as in certain areas around Bologna and Modena) members of *partecipanze agrarie*, that is to say ancient collective properties which still exist today. Every 12–20 years these *partecipanze* proceeded to redistribute by lot small parcels of land, the *parti*, among those who were eligible. It is worth citing an example. In the *Partecipanza* of San Giovanni in Persiceto (Bologna), which dates back to the twelfth century, that is to say a few centuries before the formation and spread of sharecropping, it was established at least from the seventeenth century onwards that heirs would have to separate from each other in order to be able to take part, after 14 years, in the redistribution of the *parti intere* (reserved for heads of families). For this reason, when the father died, speedy measures were taken to divide the family and set up separate households, and in contrast to traditional sharecropping families the terms of the division were registered before a notary.[12]

10 These same families, consisting on average of 12 individuals, composed about 75% of the sharecropping population in the parish of St. Nicolo—St. Agata (Zola).

11 See A. Balugani and S. Fronzoni, "Poderi e mezzadri di una 'impresa' bolognese, 1720–1770," *Quaderni Storici*, vol. 14, no. 40 (1979), 105–129; Opera Pia dei Poveri Vergognosi, *Regole statutarie, patrimonio amministrato e tavole statistiche* (Bologna, 1883). This last publication contains tables which link the size of the *podere*, the crop-rotation, "man-power," "animal-power" and "machines and tools". See also C. Klapish-E. Demonet, " 'A uno pane e uno vino'," p. 886.

12 See the *Capitoli sopra la division de' Beni Comunali della Comunita di* S. *Giovanni in Persiceto del 1733 ristampati il 1814* (Bologna, 1883), pp. 12–14. In 1733 the interval of 14 years was lengthened to 24 years, because the splitting-up of families increased the number of people with legitimate claims, consequently reducing the size of the *parti*, "which cannot be of sufficient benefit to the families of the participants for their own support," ibid., p. 13. See also P. Lodi, 'Famiglia e regime fondiario: l'area di una Partecipanza', a degree thesis supervised by Prof. C. Poni at the University of Bologna, 1977–78. The phenomenon, here

The case is interesting because it shows how archaic property structures tended to promote the formation of small families, unlike the agrarian structures of the later sharecropping system. A quick glance at Table 4.1 tells us that where *partecipanze* existed, as at S. Agata, Cento, S. Giovanni, Medicina and Pieve, the average membership of sharecropping families varied from 6.4 in Pieve to 9.8 in S. Giovanni. These are smaller than average figures for families in the area of the plain.

The relationship of family to *podere* is also considered in the preliminary proceedings of the *Inchiesta Agraria.* Thus Filippo Ghini wrote that the peasants of Cesena "constitute as many sharecropping families as there are farms into which the district is divided, therefore those persons who live in a single house and cultivate the same piece of land are known as a family." Federico Masi specified, once again for the Cesena area, that "the size of the lowland *podere* varies from 3 to 35 hectares," and that the size of the farming families grew in proportion "from 2 to 18 or an absolute maximum of 20 individuals including women and children, living-in farmhands and also the serving-woman, if there are any." The farmhouse, too, had to be "in proportion to the size of the farm and the composition of the family." In the Report of the *Comizio Agrario* of Lugo a *podere* was said to be "big" if it was greater than 12 hectares, "medium" if its size varied between 7 and 12, and "small" if it fell below these specifications. The "many plots, each with a house on it, of three, or two hectares, or less," were thought of as very small *poderi.* It would not be difficult to extend the list.[13]

Until now, I have assumed that family size and family cycle were a variable which depended on the productive organization of space. But this dependency was an ideal model rather than an objective fact. Such empirical soundings as have been taken so far seem to show marked differences in the relationship between size of *podere* and size of family.[14] It would also be useful to complicate

---

scarcely touched upon, may prompt a little theoretical reflection. It contradicts unilinear, evolutionist conceptions, while it confirms the importance of exhaustive analytical research into economic and social structures. For the relationship between family, land tenure and systems of inheritance see *Family and Inheritance. Rural Society in Western Europe 1200–1800*, eds. J. Goody, J. Thirsk and E. P. Thompson (Cambridge, 1976); see in particular L. K. Berkner, "Inheritance, Land Tenure and Peasant Family Structure: a German Regional Comparison," pp. 71–95, and D. Sabean, "Aspects of Kinship in Rural Western Europe before 1800," pp. 96–111.

13 F. Ghini, *Inchiesta Agraria. Memoria sul Circondario di Cesena*, 1879; F. Masi, *L'agricoltura … di Cesena; Relazione sulle condizioni agrarie del Circondario di Lugo*, 1879, p. 62. All these works are in Archivio Centrale dello Stato in Rome (A.C.S.R.).

14 See the articles of R. Bissoli, "Lavoro e rendita di un'azienda Bolognese del XVIII secolo," *Quaderni Storici*, vol. 14, no. 40 (1979), 130–154, and A. Balugani and S. Fronzoni, "Poderi

the model by introducing other variables, such as overall population movement, fluctuations in agricultural production, and so on. Furthermore, one should pay attention to the small demographic changes within the family, of little importance as far as numerical size is concerned, but which nevertheless, by changing its internal structure, have a definite effect on the utilization of the internal space of the house.

The *reggitore*, especially if he was the natural head of the family, had the right to the biggest bedroom, situated like the other bedrooms on the first floor (at least in the nineteenth century). But if the *reggitore* died, the *reggitrice* had to change bedrooms. She moved her own furniture into a smaller room and surrendered the big room to the new *reggitore*. Almost always the former *reggitrice* had to accept into her own room other people, one or more grandchildren or an unmarried daughter. In general one can say that those widowed had to surrender space—always scarce—to married couples. Unmarried men often slept, at least until around the end of the nineteenth century, "in winter in the cowsheds, in summer in the haylofts."[15] But when they married they acquired the right to a bedroom. I am referring only to the nineteenth century and to the areas of the plain. In the absence of preliminary research into the history of the farmhouse it is not possible to examine earlier periods, when perhaps all the family's beds were crowded into one bedroom.[16] Let us bear in mind that in the peasants' wretched homes space was often insufficient, the windows small and unglazed, the ground-floor of beaten earth, the external walls falling away. This situation began to change only in the nineteenth century, although sometimes earlier depending on the area.

As Berti Pichat realized, the relationship family/*podere* can also be expressed in terms of unit of labor/average area cultivated. According to the *Inchiesta Agraria*, in Romagna and in the province of Bologna there was generally one laborer per hectare, while in the ex-duchy of Parma there was only one for every two hectares. These rather imprecise averages would be confirmed in broad outline if they were expressed in terms not of laborers per hectare but overall

e mezzadri". See also C. Poni, "Azienda agraria e microstoria," *Quaderni Storici*, vol. 13, no. 39 (1978), 801–805. According to the author of the *Monografia sulle condizioni dell'agricoltura ... di Faenza*, "the greater or smaller number of persons is in proportion to the productivity of the *podere*, so that while there is sometimes, on the most fertile land, the relationship of one person to each hectare, on poor land, by contrast, there is one person to every two or three [hectares]."

15 C. Rognoni, *Sull'antica agricoltura parmense. Saggi storici* (Parma, 1897), p. 53.

16 In the mountains around Parma, even towards the end of the nineteenth century, all the members of the peasant family used to sleep "always in one bed" (*Monografia dell'agricoltura parmense*, p. 136).

numbers of days of work per hectare, for this varied considerably according to the intensity and sophistication of the system of rotation and of the agricultural methods employed. For example, the biennial rotation of wheat and fallow required at least three times less labor-time for a given area than the biennial rotation of wheat and hemp, the form of rotation that prevailed in the countryside north of Bologna. The smaller amount of labor per unit of cultivated land in the Ducati area (where Parmesan cheese is produced) must also be explained by the form of the rotation which prevailed and which included the cultivation of grass. It is evident that our analysis needs to be based not just on information regarding the size of farms but also on information regarding crop-rotation and methods of cultivation, since only on the basis of such data is it possible to build up a picture of the underlying economic realities. At the same time, the work of the agrarian economists of the Bologna school gave rise to the proposal (which was not new) to substitute the formula one adult person = one unit of labor with a more articulated table (see Table 4.4). This was taken up in numerous important works, especially in the years between the two wars.

However, not even with the help of these new research approaches can we conceive of the relationship between the household (as a team of workers) and the land (as requiring a certain quantity of labor-time for its cultivation) as a ratio between two fixed quantities. We need to take account of the fact

TABLE 4.4 Reduction of male and female working hours to a common unit

	Age Groups					
Categories	**10 to 18 years**		**18 to 68 years**		**Over 68 years**	
	Men	**Women**	**Men**	**Women**	**Men**	**Women**
1. Adults			1	0.6		
2. a) old people still able to undertake less arduous rural work					0.5	0.3
b) healthy young people	0.5	0.3				

SOURCE: A. SERPIERI, *GUIDA A RICERCHE DI ECONOMIA AGRARIA*, 3rd ED. (BOLOGNA, 1969), P. 20

that the amount of overall labor-time expended in farming varies from month to month with the annual cycle of production. Thus the gross annual labor-time needs to be broken down in order to establish the distribution of the total quantity of labor-time expended over the months of the year, the ratio between the labor-time expended by men and by women in agricultural work, and the ratio between the labor-time expended by members of the household and that expended by *avventizi*, that is day laborers.

Graphs 4.1, 4.2, 4.3 and 4.4 present the essential results of the research carried out around 1930 by Aldo Pagani on two sharecropping *poderi* of the Bolognese plain. On both *poderi*, situated in the low-lying flatlands on the left bank of the river Reno, the same triennial system of rotation was in operation: wheat, hemp and meadow. The cattle were principally destined for meat, as well as being used for work. On farm A, which had an area of 15.75 hectares, there lived and worked a sharecropping household made up as follows:

	M	F
more than 60 years old	1	1
between 40 and 60	1	-
between 20 and 40	2	2
between 10 and 20	1	1
less than 10	3	2

In total there were fourteen individuals in the household, of whom eight were male (five of them fit for work) and six female (four of them fit for work). Farm B, which had an area of 25.32 hectares, was worked by a household of eighteen individuals, made up as follows:

	M	F
more than 60 years old	-	-
between 40 and 60	-	-
between 20 and 40	4	4
between 10 and 20	2	1
less than 10	5	2

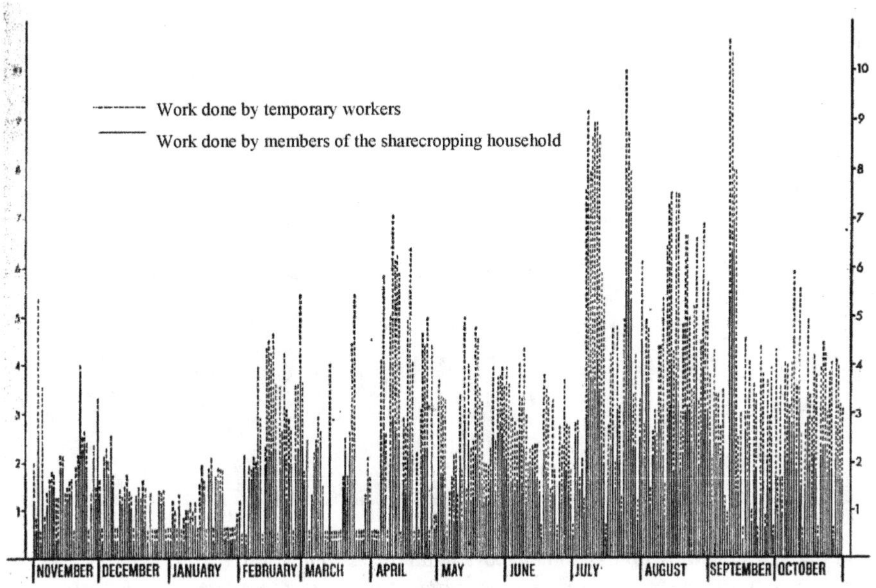

GRAPH 4.1 Daily work hours: temporary workers and sharecroppers, hemp farm A. In this *podere* as in *podere* B the crop-rotation was: 1/3 wheat; 1/3 hemp; 1/3 clover.
SOURCE: A. PAGANI, *LA DISTRIBUZIONE DEL LAVORO UMANO NELL'AZIENDA AGRARIA*

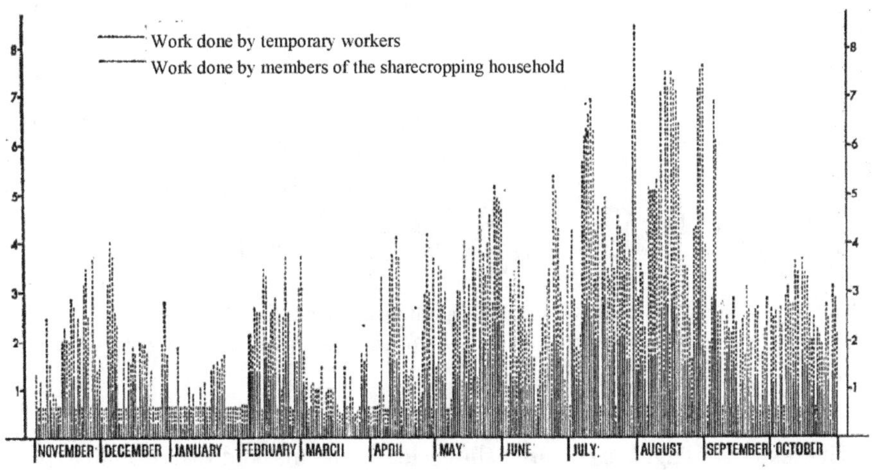

GRAPH 4.2 Daily work hours: temporary workers and sharecroppers, hemp farm B.
SOURCE: A. PAGANI, *LA DISTRIBUZIONE DEL LAVORO UMANO NELL'AZIENDA AGRARIA*

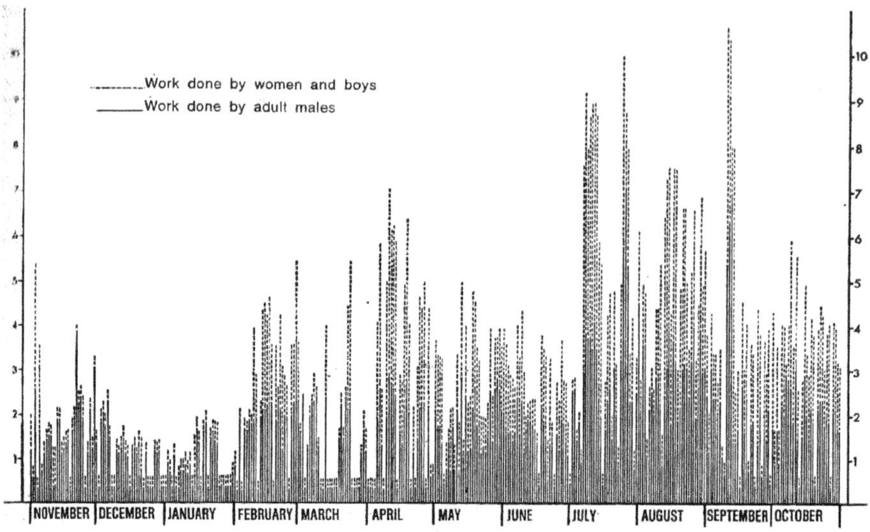

GRAPH 4.3 Daily work hours: women, boys, adult males, hemp farm A.
SOURCE: A. PAGANI, *LA DISTRIBUZIONE DEL LAVORO UMANO NELL'AZIENDA AGRARIA*

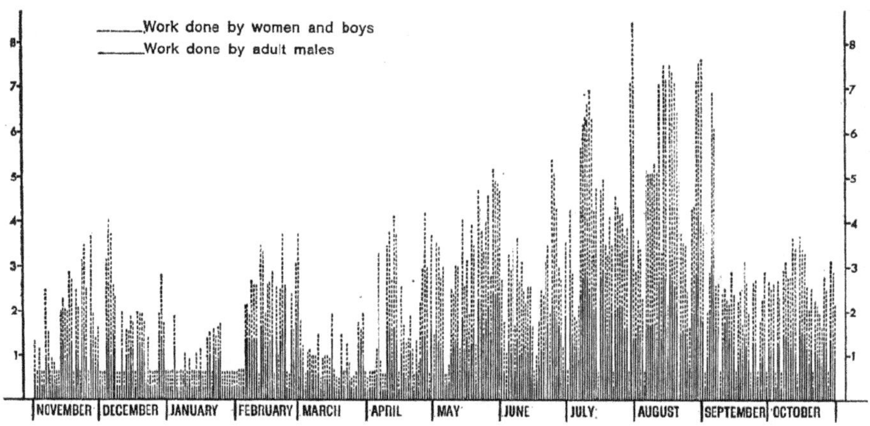

GRAPH 4.4 Daily work hours: women, boys, adult males, hemp farm B.
SOURCE: A. PAGANI, *LA DISTRIBUZIONE DEL LAVORO UMANO NELL'AZIENDA AGRARIA*

The results of Pagani's research show clearly the marked variation in expenditure of labor-time from one season to another. During the so-called "dead-season," from mid-December to the end of January, and during the month of March and the first days of April almost no work was done except in the outhouses. The months of greatest activity were July and August when the harvest was brought in and the hemp was worked. We can see that the women and children of the household represented an important part of the labor-power, and that their contribution was greater than that of the *avventizi*.[17] As early as 1890, *I Risultati dell'Inchiesta sulle condizioni sanitarie dei lavoratori della terra* (The Results of the Enquiry into the Sanitary Conditions of Farmworkers) reported that women and children were subjected to "excessive toil," which caused in the women "uterus displacement, abortions, premature births," in the children "development deficiency and frailness," and in all of them premature aging.[18]

To return to the labor-pattern, it is also noteworthy that the difference in the size of the two farms had little effect on the distribution of labor through the year, and that in the smaller farm there were fewer hectares per laborer. Graphs 4.5 and 4.6 show in addition the labor-time of the women between farmwork in the fields and housework: in the winter, spinning; in the spring, weaving; and throughout the year care of the poultry, cleaning of implements, preparation of food, and so on. It would be interesting to have similar information for the men, who repaired implements in the home, plaited reeds and straw in the winter, and so on.

These few examples of cottage industry, however, could not develop into a putting-out system, and therefore did not initiate a broadly-based process of protoindustrialization, because the sharecropping agreement made it difficult for the peasant to commit himself to work off the *podere*. Artisan work was permitted only in so far as it fulfilled the immediate needs of the family.[19]

The graphs show that the monthly distribution of work through the year is clearly tied to the nature of the agrarian system and its historical evolution. It could not be the same on *poderi* where, instead of hemp, which was widely cultivated in the countryside of Bologna and Ferrara, different crops were cultivated, and in different proportions. This is illustrated by the research carried out by Luigi Perdisa in the mid-1930s, the conclusions of which are reproduced here only in part. On farm C, ten hectares in size and situated in the region of Lugo (Ravenna), 43% of arable land was given over to meadow, 28% to wheat, 7% to beet, 6% to maize, and the remaining 15% to various other crops. The most common fruit-trees were vines, which were planted in rows, followed by

17 The women did all the jobs except the heaviest such as digging, ploughing, and transporting sacks of wheat.

18 See M. Panizza, *Risultati dell'inchiesta istituita da A. Bertani sulle condizioni sanitarie dei lavoratori della terra in Italia. Riassunto e considerazioni* (Rome, 1890), pp. 278–281. See also L. Cortesi, "Agostino Bertani e l'Inchiesta Jacini," *Societa*, XV, no. 3 (1959), 587–609.

19 The problems posed by proto-industrialization can only with difficulty be applied to sharecropping agriculture. But see by way of contrast P. Kriedte, H. Medick, J. Schlumbohn, *Industrialisierung vor der Industrialisierung, Gewerblich Warenproduktion auf dem Land, in der Formtionsperiode des Kapitalismus* (Göttingen, 1977), and in particular Medick, "Die proto-industrielle Familienwirtschaft," pp. 90–193.

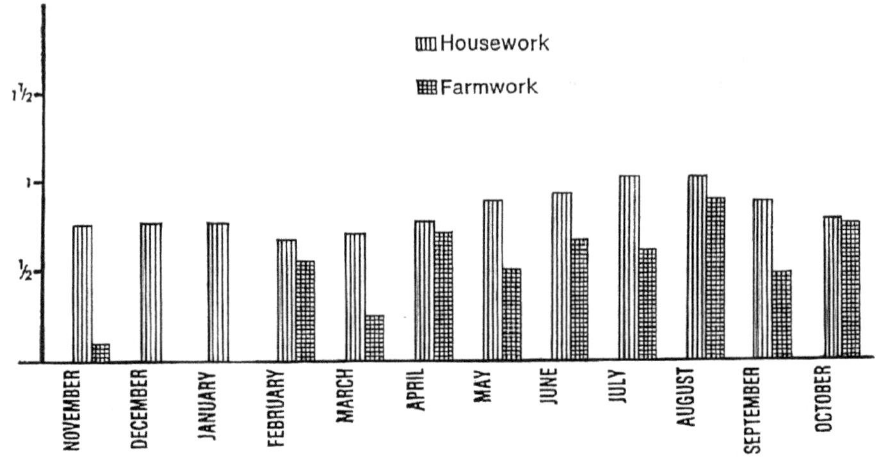

GRAPH 4.5 The distribution of female household labor between farmwork and housework, (farm A)
SOURCE: A. PAGANI, "LAVORI AGRICOLI E LAVORI DOMESTICI DELLE DONNE NELLE CONDIZIONI FAMILIARE", *PROBLEMI DEMOGRAFICI* (PIACENZA, 1931)

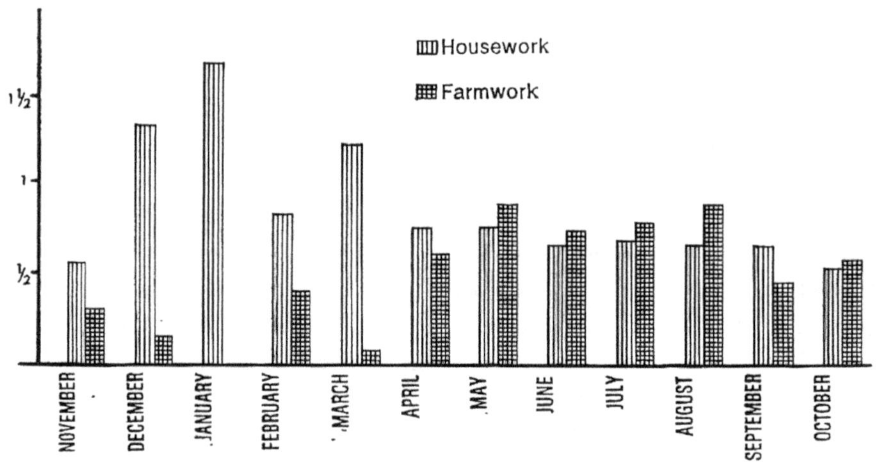

GRAPH 4.6 The distribution of female household labor between farmwork and housework, (farm B)
SOURCE: A. PAGANI, "LAVORI AGRICOLI E LAVORI DOMESTICI DELLE DONNE NELLE CONDIZIONI FAMILIARE", *PROBLEMI DEMOGRAFICI* (PIACENZA, 1931)

peaches, which accounted for one hectare. Graph 4.7 shows that most work was done in June and October, the months for the wheat harvest, the haymaking and the grape harvest. On *poderi* mainly, even if not exclusively, engaged in

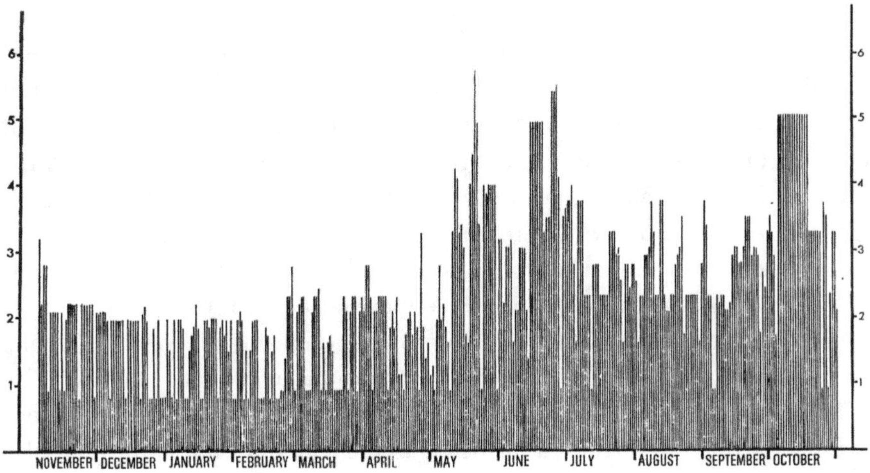

GRAPH 4.7 Daily work hours, farm C for one hectare
SOURCE: L. PERDISA, *LA DISTRIBUZIONE DEL LAVORO MANUALE IN PODERI A MEZZADRIA DELLA ROMAGNA* (FAENZA, 1935)

dairy farming, such as in the areas of the provinces of Reggio and Parma where Parmesan cheese was produced, the time spent working in the cowshed and dairy was of greater relative importance.

During the busy season few sharecropping farms could have managed without the assistance of *avventizi*. These workers, more commonly known as *braccianti,* formed a large agrarian proletariat who lived in precarious conditions. They rented miserable lodgings of one or two rooms. Their families, which were fairly unstable, tended to be nuclear, and in any case smaller than the sharecropping households. The sharecroppers were unwilling to take on laborers who would have to be paid and, whenever possible, preferred to help each other ("scambio delle opere"), for example, with the mowing of fodder. These exchanges strengthened the ties of marriage and friendship between peasant households. They represented "the stitches in a fabric of reciprocal loans" which has yet to be reconstructed.[20] The loan of oxen for farm-work, for example, was called *zerla*—the *zerla* is literally the beam which serves to attach extra pairs of oxen in front of the pair yoked to the shaft of the wagon or plough.

Up to now I have only put forward the simple picture of small sharecropping households growing into large ones, and the reverse process of large ones breaking up and becoming small. The reality however was more complicated. When a household became too large for its *podere* the problem was sometimes

20 For this quotation see S. Fronzoni, "Fonti orali e ricerche sul lavoro contadino: l'esperienza di un museo," *Quaderni Storici,* vol. 12, no. 35 (1977), 454.

solved by one of the secondary conjugal family units leaving the household and setting itself up on another *podere*. Such divisions probably became common during the nineteenth century, a period of demographic expansion. But it must have been much more common for the secondary conjugal family unit to obtain lodgings and sink into the ranks of the day laborers (*braccianti*). If a household was too small to cultivate its *podere* it could take in one or two farmhands (*garzoni*), who were also referred to as servants. In certain regions there actually existed an annual fair for the sale of adolescents and young boys. This was the case at San Giovanni in Persiceto and at Borello (Cesena) where, on the Feast of the Annunciation (25 March), called locally "Madona di garzon," the *braccianti* and poor peasants brought their sons to market.

These processes of growth and fragmentation depended on numerous factors: not only on the size and social circumstances of the family, but also on its internal composition, and especially on the ratio between adults—the workers—and mere consumers—the children and the elderly (see note 7 above). The addition of one or two hands could correct the balance in households where there was a predominance of old people, or where there were a number of children who were not yet old enough to work. According to a short work by Girolamo Cirelli, *Il villano smascherato* (*The Peasant Unmasked*), the live-in farmhands ate "at the same table" as their peasant employers, from whom they received a meager salary and a few clothes. Yet the peasants, out of a kind of "stubborn pride," would never have consented to "give their daughters in marriage" to a former live-in farmhand.[21] We find this refusal again two centuries later. Luigi Biffi wrote: "Among the existing categories of sharecroppers one notices a hierarchical order, I would say almost a kind of aristocracy, so that if the daughter of a sharecropper is united in matrimony with a live-in farm hand it is with the same condescension as the young Marchesa who concedes her small white hand to an obscure bourgeois."[22] The situation of the live-in farmhands was temporary anyway. In the great majority of cases they became *braccianti*.

A move from one farm to another was not easy for a sharecropping family to arrange. Notice of a decision not to renew the lease, which always terminated

21 This short work attributed to by Cirelli was published by G. L. Masetti Zannini, "Un trattato inedito e sconosciuto sulle tradizioni dei contadini romagnoli," *Rivista di Storia dell'Agricoltura*, vol. 7, no. 1 (1967), 37–72. According to Masetti Zannini, this writing should be attributed to Giovanni Antonio Battarra, the well-known author of *Pratica Agraria* (1778).

22 L. Biffi, *Memoria … di Faenza.*, p. 137. For the "aristocracy of the landless rural population" see also F. Masi, *L'agricoltura … di Cesena* … Among live-in farmhands and serving women, foundlings, the "figli dell'ospedale," were relatively numerous. Wet-nursing was common in numerous areas.

after twelve months had elapsed, usually in November but sometimes in May unless it was tacitly renewed, had to be given at least five months in advance. The outgoing tenant had a right to his half of the produce of the agricultural year. Together with the landlord, but frequently in disagreement with him, he balanced up debits and credits. Then it was necessary to value the winter stores (*scorte morte*), such as straw and hay, so that the outgoing peasant left in the barn (when customs did not differ) equivalent quantity or value to what he had himself received on taking over the *podere.* These negotiations, together with the valuation of the cattle (*scorte vive*) gave rise to numerous conflicts and led to the practice of hidden "compensations" which the outgoing sharecropper would take from the produce or from the "capital" belonging to the landowner. The transport of the household's furniture and goods was arranged with the help of neighbors. In the province of Reggio (for example at San Martino in Rio) the miller, if the household had an account with him, took charge of the transport of their stocks of grain. The *reggitrice* was the last to leave the house. Her final act was to remove the chain from the fireplace and to take the andirons, and it was she who was the first to enter the new house where she immediately set about lighting the fire. In some areas of Romagna the *reggitrice* on first entering the house put the salt and the oil on the mantle-piece in order to ensure good fortune.

The separation from the old *podere* did not end with the move from one house to another. The outgoing sharecropper had sown wheat in the month of October, before leaving the *podere,* and had, at least in the countryside of Bologna, Rimini, Parma and Imola, the right to harvest it. So he would return with his family to his old *podere* for the spring weeding and the harvest, which he shared half and half with his former landlord.

This custom disappeared after the Second World War, but it remains important as an example of the reciprocal exchange of roles. Every peasant household was, in the agrarian year after it moved from one *podere* to another, both incoming and outgoing, both new and old. As the incoming household it was host to the old tenants when they came to work in the wheat fields. As the outgoing household it went to carry out the same tasks on its old *podere,* where another household was already established. This custom, together with that of exchanging labor with neighbors and relatives, provided opportunities for sharecroppers to meet together in the workplace.

In the winter months relations among households were at their closest. It was then, in the evenings, when a number of households or family groups would gather in the cowsheds, where the animals (cows and oxen) provided warmth, for the *trebb.* On these occasions people would stay up for four or five hours, the women spinning, the men playing cards. They would gossip about goings-on in the village and discuss the crops, and in the twentieth century, politics. Riddles and ghost stories were told, and it was still the custom in the nineteenth century for prayers to be said. Sometimes there was a special occasion to celebrate. There would be music, singing and recitations within the "cow-shed theatre." The young men would flirt with the girls and begin to form attachments. Perhaps because of this, diocesan synods from the beginning of the seventeenth century condemned "that diabolical practice among some peasants of spending the night at assemblies where the young men are in the company of or in close proximity to the young girls." One ecclesiastical *Constitutio* threatened outright excommunication ("lata sententia") for the disobedient. But it was defending a lost cause. As early as 1659 the bishop of Modena, Ettore Molza, had to permit the "coetus nocturnos" (night-time gatherings) of the peasantry. He insisted however that men and women should meet separately, "ut peccata, quae alioquin contingere possunt, et vero contingunt non raro, quantum fieri potest, impediantur" ("in order that sins, which otherwise might defile, and truly they defile not seldom, might be prevented, as much as possible"). In the Napoleonic period some Modenese parishes still condemned the *"trebbi"* as a "danger to the soul."[23]

It would not be difficult to extend the documentation to other areas and to more recent periods. The preliminary reports of the *Inchiesta Agraria* repeat the condemnation of the *trebb*, on the grounds that they were a school of moral corruption and were occasions for playing cards for money. But other censures, of a hygienic nature, were added to the traditional ones: in the cowsheds the air was thick with noxious fumes, so that "when spring arrives, the faces which had gone in with the tanned color of the fields are seen coming out pale and yellow and almost jaundiced."[24]

The underlying structure governing the relations of members of the peasant household with each other only becomes fully apparent at times when the household's goods were divided up, whether as a result of death or because some members of the household planned to leave. This question of the division of property deserves further study. The sharecropping household, whether

23 The *trebb* was an institution to be found throughout Emilia-Romagna, and has often been referred to in literature. The prohibitions may be found in *Constitutiones et decreta in Secunda Diocesana Synodo Mutinensi ... ab A. Rangono Mutinae Episcopo Promulgata* (Mutine, 1637); and *Constitutiones in Prima Diocesana Synodo Decretae ... ab H. Molza Episcopo Mutinensi*(Mutinae, 1660). Municipal councils, for example that of Bologna, issued prohibitions against the *trebb*.

24 *Inchiesta Agraria*, p. 604; F. Barbuti, *Monografia dell'agricultura parmense*, p. 128. To the condemnation of the *trebb* are added those of the inn, the tavern and the café, which

large or small, was not held together by an understanding that the patrimony should be transmitted to a single heir. According to the Consultazione Legale of 1709, written by the Bolognese lawyer Girolamo Calzolari, there existed among the members of any particular peasant household "a truly universal community of all goods."[25]

What happened if, on the death of the *reggitore*, the household split up? As a first task, an inventory was made of the family goods under two broad headings: the fixed family assets (agricultural tools, cattle, and other movables), and the stored goods (the harvests of wheat, minor cereals, wine, hemp etc.). The patrimony was supposed to be divided in equal shares among the sons, that is to say among the different conjugal family units within the household. The women, including the daughters, were all excluded from the inheritance because "they are not members of the community." Even the goods acquired "through the industry of brothers who have remained within the community of all goods" were owned in common. The only exception made was for earnings which were "military or quasi-military" ("castrensi or quasi-castrensi"), such as a soldier's pay, for they "do not entirely fall within the said community of goods ... being considered rewards for valor and not just for industry." This point is developed by Calzolari to imply, although he does not say so explicitly, that brothers who live outside the community, that is outside the household, have a right to participate in the division of property provided they have paid to the community at least "that part of their earnings which corresponds to what the other brothers, who have not acquired military or quasi-military sources of income, are able to earn through their labor and industry, so that equality is preserved among them." The equal status of the heirs was thus based not only on ties of blood, but on their common participation in this community of life and labor. If one failed to participate in this community of life and labor, it was only possible to preserve the rights of a member of the community by making adequate financial compensation. This was a matter on which there was room for dispute, but in the provinces of Modena and Reggio sons who had left the household had no choice of preserving their membership but were automatically barred from inheriting.

---

became, towards the end of the nineteenth century, places where democratic and socialist ideas were spread.

25 G. Calzolari, *Consultationes Legales Materiam Usu Frequenter Concernente* (Bononaie [Bologna] 1709), pp. 31–69. Citations in this chapter come from the Italian edition: *Consultazione legale sopra il modo in cui si debba la divisione di' beni in commune esistenti specialemente fra i contadini* (Modena, 1768).

While the "patrimonial goods" were divided among the conjugal family units, the "fruits," that is to say the crops harvested "at the time of the division and in the future," were divided *per capita*.[26] Participating in this division were all the members of the household "who have worked, the division being in proportion to their work and based on the judgment of a man of good will." In practice children, both male and female, under twelve years of age were excluded from the division of the crops, "for they must be content with having received, until the day of the division, food and clothing." Those between twelve and eighteen years old received two-thirds of that given to the adults, while women received two-thirds of the amount given to the men. While everyday clothes were left to those who wore them, the best clothes, if paid for with the money from the "patrimony," had to be divided among the conjugal family units. But they were divided *per capita* if made of "remnants of cloth produced by communal labor."

Before proceeding to the division of the communal property, the expenses and debts incurred by the community had to be deducted. But how was this deduction made? From the "patrimonial goods" and therefore at the expense of the conjugal families, or from the "fruits" and therefore at the expense of the individuals? The question is difficult to answer. In 1787 the "agricultural experts" of the Reggio area found themselves in general agreement that the deduction should be made according to the nature of the debt. Debts incurred "in order to buy cereals or other foods which are divided among individuals" had to be repaid out of the stored goods (and therefore *per capita* and not out of the fixed assets). Otherwise the family "which has fewer members would be paying for the cereals which the more numerous families enjoyed the previous year." On the other hand, debts incurred in order to buy "wagons, casks, vats" had to be deducted from the "patrimony."[27] Among these debts were included the dowries which still had to be paid to women who had left the household during the lifetime of the community of goods, along with those to be repaid to women who had brought dowries into the household during the same period. After the division, the dowries to be given in the future to the daughters of the male heirs were solely the responsibility of their fathers. Thus women were never heirs of the fixed assets, except in the absence of brothers or sons within the household, and in other cases, for there were some which still need to be identified and studied.

---

26 "The future" refers only to the year following the division, when the winter cereals sown by the household were harvested in June.

27 Archivio di Stato di Reggio Emilia, *Archivio dei Collegi, Collegio dei Periti Agrimensori, Atti*, 1787–1807.

Females were not heirs in the households into which they were born because they were destined to leave and join another household, and it was necessary to prevent the patrimony of the household, or part of it, from passing out of the community's control. Nor were they heirs in the households they joined, where they became wives and mothers; when these households broke up their dowries were returned to them. Significantly, the Statutes of the city of Bologna laid down that all the members of a sharecropping family, except the wives, were "obligati in solidum" (each is liable for the whole) to repay all debts contracted with the landowner.[28]

In short, the dowry could not be touched, and this rule remained in the *Codice Civile* until dowries were legally abolished in 1960. But how much could dowries amount to? We find some replies to this question in the preliminary reports of the *Inchiesta Agraria*. We read there that the dowry was "in proportion to the family's means." In general, the woman brought into the house she was entering as a bride a few pieces of furniture for the bedroom (such as the married couple's chest), the trousseau (a few sheets, linen and personal effects), a little jewelry (in Romagna a coral necklace), and a small sum of money. This sum normally varied between 100 and 200 lire, the maximum being 500 lire in well-off families.[29] Certainly this influenced the strategy of choosing a spouse, favoring matrimonial exchanges between families of the same "rank." We know that sharecroppers represented a kind of aristocracy with respect to other categories of workers. But inside this "aristocracy" there existed strong

28 *Sanctionum ad causas criminales spectantium Inclytae Civitatis ... Bononiae,* with a commentary by A. Monterentii, tome II, bk. VI (Bononiae [Bologna], 1577), pp. 76–78. The birth of a girl child was received with disappointment by the men of the house. And the present which was given in Romagna to a woman who had given birth to a female—a basket containing an odd number of eggs—served as a charm to ensure that she would "have a boy child when she next gave birth" (M. Placucci, "Usi e pregiudizi dei contadini della Romagna" [Forli, 1818], reprinted in *Romagna Tradizionale. Usi e costumi, credenze e pregiudizi,* ed. P. Toschi [Bologna, 1952], p. 61). The "grief" of the father had to be expressed in public. See G. Tassoni, *Arti e tradizioni popolari. Le inchieste napoleoniche sui costumi e le tradizioni nel Regno Italico* (Bellinzona, 1973), p. 291. According to the author of *Monografia sulle condizioni dell'agricoltura ... di Faenza,* "the families which are most frequently found to be in the worst economic conditions are those in which there are many young women who, while they are of limited use in the work of the *podere,* require heavy expenses for their needs" and for luxury (p. 84). What happened to widows who remarried? They went to live in the house of the new husband. But they were not allowed to take with them the children of the first marriage who stayed in their father's home.

29 *Monografia sulle condizioni dell'agricoltura ... di Faenza,* p. 85. Oreste Trebbi and Gaspare Ungarelli (*Costumanze e tradizoni del popolo Bolognese* [Bologna, 1932], pp. 53–54) rightly note that the dowry obligations "imposed by long tradition" were not "identical in all

social differences. And a more exclusive "aristocracy" was formed by the well-off sharecroppers.

The exclusion of women from the community of goods, and so from inheritance, and the equal division of the "patrimonial goods" among co-habiting sons seem therefore to be, at least in modern times, the essential characteristics of a system of inheritance which is entirely different from that prevalent among the nobility, where the transmission of much of the patrimony to the eldest son was generally guaranteed. The equality of the different conjugal family units within the peasant household meant that there was rarely a sole heir. This was one of the obstacles, although not the only, and perhaps not even the most important, preventing rich sharecroppers from becoming small freeholders.

This brief conclusion may serve as a point of reference, but one should be careful not to view it as a complete account. For one thing, it is largely based on a "learned" source (Calzolari's *Consultazione*) which tends to translate customs and practices into juridical language whose objectivity cannot be ascertained. Yet it would be even more misleading to separate categorically popular customs from official law, for "legal" provisions may also embody customary practices. For an example, we need only look at the regulations governing "the division of property among peasants" in the *Codice di Leggi e Costituzioni* promulgated in 1771 for the Duchy of the House of Este (Modena and Reggio), which corroborates the views of Calzolari. These regulations were reproduced in the civil code of the Duchy in 1851 and remained in force into the mid-twentieth century. As late as 1952 the Chamber of Commerce of Reggio Emilia wrote that "the provisions confirmed by the ducal code of 1771, in the light of many years of satisfactory experience, and then reconfirmed and reproduced verbatim in article 974 of the code of Parma and article 1064 of the ducal code, were not annulled by the introduction of the Italian code [1864]. Consequently they continue to govern the division among peasants ... and are in force throughout the province."[30] Here we have an example of a code of law, abolished in

---

places." It is worth noting here that while the trousseau and the furniture remained in the bride's hands, the dowry (in the proper sense of the word) became part of the accumulated communal goods, to all intents and purposes in the hands of the *padre-reggitore*. Trebbi and Ungarelli observe that marriage used to be preceded and accompanied by gifts (in the form of headscarves, aprons, shirts) which the bride-to-be gave to her mother-in-law, to the other members of her new family, and to her own older sisters who were still unmarried.

30 Camera di Commercio, Industria e Agricoltura di Reggio Emilia, *Usi e consuetudine vigenti in Provincia di Reggio Emilia* (Reggio Emilia, 1952), p. 156.

principle but some parts of which remain accepted as "custom" within a later and different legal system. This in itself is a valuable indication of the weight of social practices.

It is worth noting, moreover, that article 1067 of the ducal code of 1851 aimed to provide a simple rule governing an issue which we have seen was potentially contentious: it excluded from the community of goods, and so from succession, anyone who "had left the household and lived elsewhere for a period of six years."

Just as the legal code of the house of Este embodies customs, so too did the code of the Duchy of Parma and Piacenza promulgated in 1820. This latter code, however, included an important innovation: it distinguished between the hereditary patrimony, which it called the "old" patrimony, and the "new" patrimony—those goods acquired through "the common industry" of all the members of the household.[31] This distinction had already been made in the second edition of Calzolari's *Consultazione legale* (Modena, 1768) in the context of a particular situation: the one in which the division was made not after the death of the father, but after the death of the father and his sons (the first two generations), the heirs thus being the members of the third generation, who were the grandchildren of the former and the children for the latter.[32] In this case, the old patrimony was divided into equal portions for each group of descendants of the fathers in the second generation (regardless of differences in the numbers of sons of each father). The new patrimony, on the other hand, was apportioned directly to each individual member of the third generation in equal amounts. Women and children were to be excluded from the inheritance, according to Calzolari; but on this point the code of Parma introduced a modification of historic importance, for it permitted women to inherit a share of the new patrimony equal to two-thirds that of the men. Thus half of the household, excluded for centuries from the community of goods, finally acquired (in 1820) a right over that part of the patrimony which it had personally helped to create.

This democratic modification of the law, along with the distinction between old and new patrimonies on which it was based, applied only to the territories of the ex-duchy of Parma. And in other places where the distinction between

31 *Codice Civile per li Stati Parmensi*, 5th ed. (Parma, 1858), p. 297, art. 978 and 979; this code does not use explicitly the terms "old" and "new" assets.

32 This particular case is also a critical one, if it is true that the divisions of families took place at the third generation, according to C. Klapish-E. Demonet, "'A uno pane e uno vino'," p. 881.

old and new patrimonies was adopted, women often continued to be excluded from the inheritance, as in the countryside of Faenza. In the countryside of Lugo, at least after the First World War, women also participated in the *per capita* division of the new patrimony.

The situation in the province of Bologna is still wrapped in mystery. There, despite the distinction between "old" and "new" patrimony which Calzolari indicates in the Modenese edition, the practice seems to have diverged from that indicated in the Parma code. It was not until after the Second World War, according to the testimony of the *partitori*—peasants or parish priests who supervised the property divisions and administered the law among the peasants – that the distinction between "old" and "new" patrimony was introduced in the Bolognese area.[33]

The admission of women into the community of goods and the establishment of absolute equality (even *per capita*) between men and women were, in any event, the result of a relatively recent transformation. These changes took place at different dates in different areas, but they began between 1920 and 1950, depending on the area, and continued even after 1964, when it became illegal to stipulate new sharecropping contracts.[34]

In the course of this evolution in the division of the sharecropping patrimony, the presence of men and women of marriageable age introduced other significant modifications in inheritance practices. Popular customs in the Bolognese area, periodically written down by the Chamber of Commerce of Bologna, prescribed (as stated in a publication of 1935) that when the household divided the communal property, only those men and women who had reached the age of 25 were considered to have the right to "that sum which, according to custom and the means of the family, is necessary to provide for marriage." In another collection of customs ten years later, it is stated: "A young man or girl who at the moment of the family division is less than 25 years old but more than twenty has the right to so many fifths of necessary marriage expenses" depending on "how many years have been completed after the twentieth."[35] Similar practices appear in the same period also in other or nearby areas, such as Romagna. These customs pose other questions. Are they

33 For the testimony of the *partitori* see S. Mignani, "Storia local e fonti orali: material per una ricerca," thesis supervised by Prof. Carlo Poni at the University of Bologna, 1975–1976.

34 In the provinces of Ravenna and Bologna it was already the custom in the 1930s to assign to children under the age of fourteen a fraction of an adult's share, each child receiving as many fourteenths of an adult's share as he was years old. Infants under the age of one received nothing.

35 *Usi e consuetudini mercantili dalla provincia di Bologna* (Bologna, 1935), pp. 116–117.

the result of recent tendencies, or are they rooted in the past? Do they apply only at the moment of division of the patrimony? Or are they general practices which may influence the marriage decisions of the younger members of the household, and thus even postpone the age of marriage?[36]

Certainly the study of customary law, the reality of the practices and their geographical extension, is still an untapped but fruitful subject of research. Was it, we may ask ourselves, the women—wives, sisters and daughters—who threatened the ancient structure of the sharecropping household? Or, as in the account of the *Inchiesta Agraria*, did the decay of the institution date back to around 1880 with the effects of military service on the men? Conscription, introduced immediately after the unification of Italy, had a number of positive effects. It civilized the young peasants, awakened their intellects, improved their education and introduced them to new ideas. But, according to the *Inchiesta*, it also had negative results. The young men returned from military service to find they had no taste for agricultural labor and often resolved to leave and seek their fortune elsewhere. They disseminated "ideas and tendencies many of which are neither useful nor deserving approbation"; they were less tied to traditional customs and, because they had "the presumption to believe they have learned all they need to know," claimed the right "to give orders in the household, undermining the authority of their elders."[37] A few

36 According to the preparatory reports of the *Inchiesta Agraria*, the age of marriage was relatively late. Roughly speaking, and only for Romagna, men married between the ages of 25 and 30 and women between 20 and 25. See G. Gaspari, *Della stato attuale dell'agricoltura e delle classi agricole nel Circondario di Imola* (1879), p. 135; *Monografia sulle condizioni dell'agricoltura ... di Faenza*, p. 91; *Relazione sulle condizioni agrarie del circondario di Lugo*, p. 92; Curio, *Memoria intorno alle condizioni dell'agricoltura e della classe agricola nel circondario di Rimini* (1879); Ghini, *Inchiesta Agraria. Memoria.di Cesena*. Age at marriage, age gap between spouses, duration of marriage, length of widowhood, birth-spacing: all these and other similar topics must be studied. In at least one area (the countryside around Faenza) "the convention that only firstborn children should marry" had recently (1881) been abandoned; see *Atti della Giunta per l'Inchiesta Agraria e sulle Condizioni della Classe Agricola* (Rome, 1881), vol. II, p. 605 (see also vol. III). This "convention" and its abandonment pose numerous problems. Another source, also relating to the countryside around Faenza, states that "to get married one asks for the permission of the head of the family and anyone choosing to follow his own fancy may be forced to leave the house" (*Monografia sulle condizioni dell'agricoltura.di Faenza*, p. 85). This custom was probably spread over a wider area. An interesting set of themes can be found in P. Bourdieu, "Célibat et condition paysanne," *Etudes Rurales*, nos. 5–6, (1962), 32–131.

37 On the crisis in the sharecropping family, in addition to the *Inchiesta Agraria* see G. Goretti, "Sulle mutate condizioni agricole del territorio Bolognese. Relazione e proposte," *Annali della Società Agraria Provinciale di Bologna*, vol. XXII (Bologna, 1883), pp. 54–64 and the debate in the following pages.

decades later Aldo Spallicci, a poet from Romagna, wrote a moving lament for the *reggitore* whose authority had been rejected by his sons.[38] Unfortunately we lack sources or accounts which would tell us how the women responded to these changes. We do not know if they supported the young men in their rebellious attitudes, and if they did so, in what way and to what extent.[39]

The crisis of authority within the sharecropping family is bound up with a more general process of change within the complex agrarian structures of Emilia and Romagna at the end of the nineteenth century. Huge capital sums were being invested in land reclamation. Tens of thousands of laborers transformed through their efforts vast territories, making them suitable for cultivation. In the province of Ravenna one-third of the area which is now farmed was reclaimed at this time. The market for *salariati* was as a result greatly expanded. Especially on the "new" land, but not only there, farms worked by *salariati* became more common. Emilio Sereni has described how "the extensive demand for labor caused by the spread of projects for land reclamation made it possible for the younger members of the sharecropping household to find independent employment, which they almost always preferred to working on the family farm in conditions of semi-servitude under the authority both of the head of the household and of the landlord."[40]

Even in areas given over entirely to sharecropping cultivation a process of social differentiation was taking place among the peasantry. A few were becoming comparatively well-off, while many were growing poorer. The *Inchiesta Agraria* expressed grave concern about the damaging effects of the tax on the

38 A. Spallicci, *La Madune Poesie in Dialetto Romagnolo* (Milan, 1926, p. 161): "*Little Giuseppe.* Who is the *reggitore* of the household, who gives the orders? / One can see that I can no longer say a word / That I cannot open my mouth to ask a question / That everyone snaps at me: "Keep quiet Finöla / You don't understand a thing! Have you turned into wood?" / And every day they go on like this / That now this old man isn't worth a penny / The andirons in the hearth are of more account. When I was a boy it was my elders / who made the decisions. Now the youngsters give commands, / and those who have brought them into the world—isn't it true?—are of no account. / Finöla, though, isn't going to beg. / He has his own old-fashioned ideas and what is he to do / if they still seem good to him and he doesn't want to change?"

39 The complex cultural transformation of farm-workers has not yet attracted sufficient attention. Among the few studies see L. Arbizzani, "Ideali ed istituti nuovi nella cultura contadina post-unitaria (1859–1945)," *Cultura popolare nell'Emilia-Romagna. Strutture rurali e vita contadina* (Milan 1977), pp. 219–241, and the accompanying bibliography.

40 E. Sereni, *Il capitalismo nelle campagne (1860–1900)*, (Turin, 1947), p. 341. Sereni probably exaggerated the results of capitalist transformation and the desire of young sharecroppers to become wage-laborers. More realistic are the reflections of Countess Pasolini (see below and note 42).

milling of grain and of peasant indebtedness. During the same years the demographic transition intensified. The decline in infant mortality, and the increase in life expectancy after the age of twenty, combined to increase the size of the conjugal family units which made up the peasant household. This process was made possible by an intensification of cultivation, which required a larger labor force.[41] It was at this time, I believe, that those extraordinarily large peasant households which contemporaries took to be a survival from a long-forgotten past first appeared. Something which was comparatively recent—the formation of large households with dozens of members—appeared to be ancient. This curious inversion of historical perspective itself demands an historical explanation.

Not enough research has yet been done for it to be possible to measure the resulting growth in the number of multiple family households. Still it is worth noting an article by the Countess Maria Pasolini, written at the end of the nineteenth century. She describes how, on a farm of eighteen hectares in Coccolia (Ravenna), a sharecropping household grew from having six members in 1859 to having nineteen in 1889. During the same period what had been a nuclear family became a multiple family household: after 1881, it became a *frérèche* made up of three conjugal family units. The author emphasizes on several occasions that this expansion was based upon important capital investment, a partial reorganisation of the system of drainage, and an improved course of rotation, all of which made possible an increased yield. But other forces also emerged, working against the expansion of the household. Indeed where the growth in household size was "excessive" one or more of the conjugal family units would be forced to leave, often to sink into the army of *braccianti*.[42]

The large patriarchal family was destabilized by the growth in the size and number of the conjugal families of which it was composed. As a result sharecroppers and *braccianti*, or at least households on the margins of these groups, often came to be linked by ties of kinship. But the households of *braccianti* never grew into multiple family households, nor did the father of such a family ever become *reggitore*. Thus in the same countryside two distinct systems of

41 The slow introduction of mechanization in part limited the process of increased labor productivity.

42 As Countess Pasolini wrote: "When a household could no longer feed itself on the land assigned to it, it divided up. A member will leave, either to set up another sharecropping household on another farm, or to become a member of the class of *braccianti*, which was always regarded as the worst of the alternatives, and seen as the prelude to a yet further decline in living standards" (M. Pasolini, "Una famiglia di mezzadri romagnoli nel comune di Ravenna," *Giornale degli Economisti*, vol. 11, pt. 1 (1890), 248).

household organization were to be found, or rather two distinct subsystems, for, despite their differences, they were linked together by the fact that both sharecroppers and *braccianti* lived off the produce of the land. Sometimes the land was the same: that of the *poderi* where the *braccianti* worked for the sharecroppers as day-laborers. More often the *braccianti* had to combine seasonal work on "old" land with work found on the capitalist holdings on the recently reclaimed land, digging ditches, planting rice, and so on.

In addition to households dividing as a result of rapid demographic growth, the introduction of new, more intensive courses of rotation often also led to the division of the larger *poderi*, as some landowners preferred to let out small farms that now required greater work.[43] This was more common in some areas than in others but was nevertheless a widespread and significant tendency. The combination of demographic growth with reductions in the size of holdings may serve to explain the appearance of another relatively novel phenomenon: the large nuclear sharecropping family, whose size was based not on the number of conjugal family units, but on the number of (unmarried) children.

So far I have presumed that the peasant household was reasonably free to stay on a farm or leave for another, to continue as a community or break up. But this was not in fact the case. Landowners often played a decisive role. They paid close attention to the size of their sharecroppers' households to ensure that the family's labor-power was large enough to cultivate the land, and became alarmed if the number of unproductive consumers—children—became too great.[44] The disproportion in sharecropping families between producers—those who worked—and consumers—children and elderly who ate— was one feature of the crisis in the system of sharecropping, the Inchiesta Agraria suggested, that initiated efforts by landowners to reduce the size of such families, especially of those with many "useless mouths". Such a policy could not be systematically enforced, but it explains the behavior of those peasants who, when the landlord was visiting, would hide their children in cupboards.

It is safe to assume that as a general rule landlords gave notice to households which were, either as units of production or consumption, the "wrong size" for their farm and which were at the same time indebted, impoverished, insubordinate and unable to produce the average level of income. When it came to

---

43 See note 40.

44 The idea of the landowner's control over the demography of the peasant family has been developed for the Polish countryside by W. Kula, "La seigneurie et la famille paysanne dans la Pologne du XVIII siècle," *Annales E.S.C.*, vol. 39, nos. 4-5 (1972), 949–958. See also M. Cattini, "In Emilia orientale: mezzadria cinquecentesca e mezzadria settecentesca. Continuità o frattura?" *Quaderni Storici*, vol. 13, no. 39 (1978), 864–879.

choosing their successors the landlord would assess the available households according to the following criteria:

1) their size had to be "well-suited" to the demands of the *podere*, and they had to have few "useless mouths";
2) they had to be free of debt;
3) they had to own cattle and "capital goods" (a wagon, agricultural tools, household furnishings, etc.);
4) they had to have reserves of food for a year;
5) they had to be of good moral character, not given to drinking, and good workers under the effective control of a *reggitore* who in turn was submissive to the authority of the landlord.

Similarly, failure to meet any of these criteria might provide grounds for eviction, although it is important to recognize that the system was a flexible one. If a household was on the whole a "good" one, but was too large for its *podere*, the landlord could make it possible for it to move to a larger one, or could offer a small *podere* to one of the secondary conjugal family units.[45] In this case the head of the conjugal family unit which was gaining its independence would normally become the *reggitore* of the new household, but he could also choose to retain communal rights in the original household. In that case the head of the old household extended his authority beyond his house to include the branch of the family which had moved elsewhere (even if nearby). At this point it is worth emphasizing that the landlord did not only make all the basic strategic decisions connected with the organization of productive agricultural space, which in the long run determined the fate of sharecropping households. He also, time after time, selected or excluded the families, introducing them to or expelling them from the process of production. Each sharecropping household was thus the end-product of an age-old process of differentiation, advancement and rejection.[46]

The dependence of the peasantry upon their landlords, which in the early decades of the twentieth century still expressed itself in many humiliating ways—the landlord's right for example to visit the farmhouse at any hour of the day or night, or the control he exercised over household size—was in some

45 The proprietors of large and medium-sized holdings could resort to "pruning" more easily than could the proprietors of small-holdings. That is, they could cut out from an over-sized *podere* that area beyond the tenant's capacity to cultivate and lease it either to another sharecropping household or to a family of wage-workers.

46 St. Martin's day, when leases terminated, was a day of celebration in Bologna for peasants who had not been given notice. Two or three families would gather together "to spend an evening rejoicing, playing cards, eating roast chestnuts, celebrating with the new wine which was scarcely out of the vat. This ... gathering, which cemented friendships and

degree counterbalanced by the protection the landlord was able to give them. It was also normal for him to be their advocate if they had trouble with the law and to guide them in all their dealings with the state. Above all they turned to him if they had occasion to put anything in writing. The relationship between landlord and sharecropper was decisively transformed only during the Second World War by the resistance to the fascist regime, by the great struggles in the 1950s to reform the agrarian contracts, and by the transformation in the social attitudes of the peasantry through their militancy within trade unions, agricultural cooperatives and political parties. All of these experiences enabled peasants to win an ever-greater degree of autonomy.

In the second half of the twentieth century sharecropping and the traditional peasant household was fast disappearing. A rapidly spreading process of industrialization after 1955 profoundly altered the social composition of the population. The percentage of workers employed in agriculture in Emilia-Romagna declined from 44% to 18% in the years 1955 to 1965. And the area covered by the sharecropping farms, equal to 34% of the cultivated area in 1961, fell to 14.1% of the cultivated area by 1970 (see Maps 4.1 and 4.2).[47] That percentage continued to fall. The average size of the households of peasant farmers and sharecroppers which, in the region we are concerned with, was 5.8 in 1951 had shrunk to 4.2 by 1971. The *reggitore*, as authoritarian head of the household, is a figure who no longer exists: social roles have become more flexible. The new working class has close links to the countryside, and the children of the peasantry now generally work in industry or in the tertiary sector. Even when they continue to live in their parents' farmhouse they help out in the fields only on a part-time basis or very occasionally. In addition, the widespread opportunities for peasants to buy land have freed them from their old personal subordination to the town-dwelling landlord.

---

bonds of affection among families, was called 'metter zapp'" (F. Cervellati, 'La Parrocchia di Sabbiuno di Piano. Uno Studio sulla religiosita popolare (1880–1913)', thesis supervised by Professor R. Ruffilli at the University of Bologna, 1976–77). Good families were probably the ones that endeavored not to divide the patrimony and to preserve a strong position in dealing with the landowner.

47 On the process of industrialization see A. Bellettini, "Aspetti del quadro economico dell'Emilia-Romagna negli anni della Ricostruzione e del primo sviluppo," *Statistica*, 1978, no. 1; R. Zangheri, "Caratteri dell'economia emiliano-romagnola," off-print, *Atti della Accademia delle Scienze dell'Istituto de Bologna*, Classe di scienze Morali, Rendiconti, vol. LXVI, 1977–78 (1978).

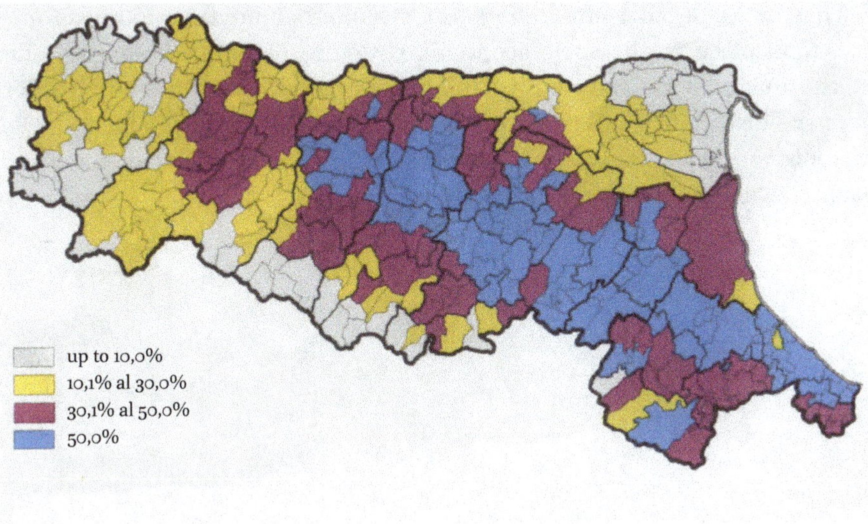

MAP 4.1 Distribution of sharecropping farms in Emilia Romagna, 1961
SOURCE: F. TASSINARI, *UOMO E LAVORO IN EMILIA ROMAGNA: ANALISI E PROSPETTIVE* (MODENA, 1977), FIG. 20

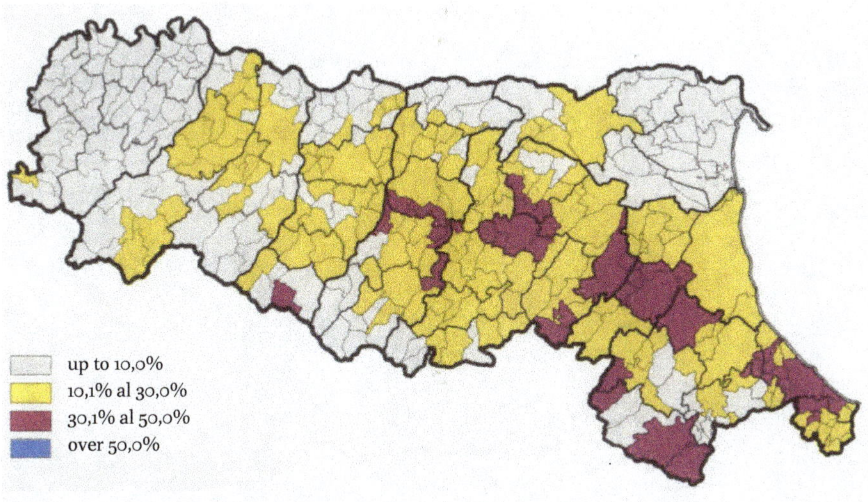

MAP 4.2 Distribution of sharecropping farms in Emilia Romagna, 1970
SOURCE: TASSINARI, *UOMO E LAVORO IN EMILIA*, FIG. 21

Thus in the decades after the 1950s a profound and extensive transformation took place in the socio-economic structure of Emilia-Romagna. This transformation destroyed many of the characteristics of the old agrarian order, from the distribution of landed property to the relations of production. Old customs, too, began to disappear, and the old relationship between town and country evolved or was being reshaped.

PART 2

Artisans, Workers, Merchants

SECTION 1

Crafting Shoes

CHAPTER 5

Norms and Disputes: The Shoemakers' Guild in Eighteenth-Century Bologna

Carlo Poni

Historians examining popular culture have come to express different, even conflicting views. Some maintain that popular culture was extraneous to that of the élite. Others stress the relationship between high culture and low culture. For some, popular culture is a collection of texts and customs; for others, it is neither an artifact nor a document but a way of reading and appropriating a text. For some historians, the alliance between throne and altar suffocated popular culture; for others, popular culture is, like a phoenix, always capable of being reborn.[1]

Among these schools of thought may also be found points of contact and common themes. The terms "people" and "popular" often refer to an indistinct "romantic" collectivity lacking internal differentiation, while the word "culture" occupies a space which many identify with rituals, festivals and religious practices. Often excluded from these analyses is the role of work as a component of popular culture. Yet in the vast majority of the cities of the *ancien régime* the people were workers: carpenters, tailors, weavers, masons, spinners, tanners, barbers, hatters, bakers, porters, blacksmiths and others. In each craft and trade there were different tools, raw materials, techniques, different movements of the body and the hands, different ways of buying and selling. Accordingly each trade and each craft had different traditions and social practices, a different identity and status in society and a different culture of work.[2]

Some years ago I suggested that research be conducted into the work culture of different groups of artisans in order to widen and enrich the history of

1 On the terms "popular" and "culture" see P. Burke, "Popular Culture between History and Ethnology," *Ethnologia Europaea* xiv (1984), 5–13, who offers a less superficial analysis of the terms "popular" and "culture." See also S. Clark, "French Historians and Early Modern Popular Culture," *Past and Present,* vol. 100, no. 1 (1983), 62–99.

2 See P. Burke, *Popular Culture in Early Modem Europe* (London, 1978), pp. 36–42; H. U. Thamer, "On the Use and Abuse of Handicraft: Journeyman Culture and Enlightened Public Opinion in 18th and 19th Century Germany,," in *Understanding Popular Culture,* ed. S. Kaplan (Berlin, 1984), p. 276.

 | DOI:10.1163/9789004713277_007

popular culture.[3] This investigation into the internal conflicts and disputes of the shoemakers' craft and guild in a large urban center is an attempt in that direction.[4]

In eighteenth-century Bologna shoemakers were probably the fifth largest group of craftsmen, behind silk-weavers (mainly women), silk-spinners, carpenters and hemp-workers.[5] In 1752 the number of rural and urban shoemakers called *obbedienti* – the lowest and most numerous category of master shopkeepers – was four hundred, of whom approximately a third were in the city. To this number must be added the members of the guild council, an oligarchy of fewer than twenty people, from whom the head and other officials of the guild were annually chosen by lot. Subject to the shoemakers' guild were the urban and rural cobblers who numbered five hundred in 1752.[6] Completing the members of the craft were the journeymen and the apprentices, whose exact number is unknown. This particular structure was a result of a transformation which began in the fourteenth century, and was consolidated during the sixteenth century, when the municipal aristocracy succeeded in stabilizing

3 [See Chapter 7 in this volume.]

4 There has been a revival of interest in the history of craftsmen and guilds. See the *International Handwerkgeschichtliches Symposium* organized in 1978, 1982 and 1986 by the Hungarian Academy of Science.

5 Shoemakers were one of the most numerous groups of craftsmen. According to evidence Eric Hobsbawm and Joan Wallach Scott published, shoemakers in eighteenth-century Seville exceeded in number all other categories of artisans. The same was true in Prussia in 1800, where the other large groups of artisans were tailors and blacksmiths. In Bavaria in 1771 shoemakers were second in number to weavers, while in market villages they were the largest group. In rural Friesland there were six shoemakers per thousand inhabitants, as compared to four weavers, four carpenters, and two bakers and two smiths. See E. J. Hobsbawm and J. W. Scott, "Political Shoemakers," *Past and Present,* vol. 89, no. 1 (1980), 86–114; A. Griessinger, *Das symbolische Kapital der Ehre: Streikbewegungen und kollektives Bewusstsein deutscher Handwerksgesellen im 18. Jahrhundert* (Frankfurt-on-Main, 1981), pp. 87–94.

6 These figures are given in the *Riposta alle negative che danno gli huomini del Consiglio dei calzolai alli loro obbedienti.* This petition is attached to the report entitled *Sentimento del consultor Piella ... sopra diversi ricorsi degli obbidienti dell'Arte dei Calzolai contro detta Arte,* 17 Apr. 1752, Archivio di Stato di Bologna (hereafter A.S.B.), Assunteria d'Arti (hereafter Arti), Miscellanea (hereafter Misc.), xv, no. 25. The figures refer to shoemakers and cobblers who paid the annual *obbedienza* fee to the guild council. But some shoemakers – just like other artisans – often did not pay the annual fee, thanks to patents granted by certain noble families, the archbishop, the Holy Office, some university colleges (such as the Collegio di Spagna), or because they were members of military corps or lived in privileged rural communities. A source which I consider trustworthy, dated 1745, puts the number of the urban shoemakers at 117: Biblioteca Apostolica Vaticana, MS. Patetta 3041, "Arte dei callegari di Bologna: atti e documenti, 1745–1798.". In 1766, according to a calculation made by the master Giuseppe Mingardi, the urban shoemakers numbered 140 (see

its political power. Until the end of the fifteenth century the majority of the masters were full members of the guild, and only a few were *obbedienti*. By the middle of the eighteenth century those who were full members had been reduced to a handful, while the vast majority of master cobblers and shoemakers were included among the *obbedienti* who had to pay an annual fee to the guild council, the shoemakers 4 lire and the cobblers 2 lire. This oligarchical transformation involved almost all the guilds and went hand in hand with a steady loss of autonomy as the guilds were increasingly subjected to the authority of the aristocratic city government.[7]

The shoemaker's trade as traditionally practiced called for a wide range of technical know-how and skills but a limited division of labor. In the workshop the master first cut the leather, and then later sewed it together with the help of his apprentices and journeymen. The master shoemaker was more than a worker who possessed the exclusive right to make shoes; he was also a small trader who purchased the raw material and sold the finished product on the local market.[8] Above the master shoemaker was the guild council, which was empowered to select new masters; to regulate or rather to decide status and grades inside the guild, from *obbedienti* to council member; to guarantee the

---

note 73). An investigation by Fabio Giusberti, "Le botteghe di una città pre-industriale: un paesaggio regolato," in *Mercati e consumi: organizzazione e qualificazione del commercio in Italia dal* xii *al xx secolo* (Bologna, 1984), pp. 847–78 shows there were 91 cobblers' and 109 shoemakers' shops in Bologna in 1758; the sources however give no indication of shops located in the city center. It is not known what proportion of the rural shoemakers and cobblers was itinerant. The population of the diocese of Bologna increased during the eighteenth century from 220,000 to 295,000. The population of the city – approximately 65,000 – remained virtually unchanged right through the century (A. Bellettini, *La popolazione di Bologna dal xv secolo all'unificazione nazionale* [Bologna, 1961], p. 48).

7 On the oligarchical transformation of the Bolognese guilds, see R. Greci, "Il contratto di apprendistato nelle corporazioni Bolognesi, xiii-xiv sec.,," pt. 2, *Atti e memorie della Deputazione di Storia Patria per le Province di Romagna*, xxviii, (1977), 61–106; G. Tamba, "Da socio ad 'obbediente': la Società dei Muratori dall'età comunale al 1796," *Muratori in Bologna dalle origini al secolo xviii* (Bologna, 1981), pp. 53–146; M. Fanti, *I macellai di Bologna: mestiere, politica e vita civile* (Bologna, 1980), pp. 123–127, 170–181, 199–200; and L. Gheza Fabbri, "Per lo studio delle corporazioni Bolognesi fra il xvi e il xviii secolo: i libri matricularum," *Economia* e *storia*, iii, (1983), 1–15. In some crafts even the journeymen and apprentices paid the *obbedienza* fee. In practice the master paid the *obbedienza* of the employees and deducted it from their wages.

8 It would appear that the Bolognese shoemakers tended to work to order rather than to supply a market. One seventeenth-century Bolognese author wrote that the shoemakers made "new shoes to the exact measurements of a person's foot, in just the same way as tailors cut and sew new clothes to measure"; see O. Montalbani, *L'honore dei Collegi dell'Arti*

quality of the product; and to act as a tribunal in civil lawsuits affecting members of the guild and involving an amount of no more than 60 lire.[9]

This essay is divided into three parts. The first analyzes the disputes between urban and rural shoemakers; the second those between shoemakers and cobblers; and the third part describes the struggle of masters (*obbedienti*) against the guild council. The first two sections examine the strategies evolved by groups of artisans in their efforts to extend or reinforce the technical monopolies and practices of their craft to the detriment of other artisans, by prohibiting the latter from making use of particular types of raw material and from practicing specific skills. These "attacking" strategies were countered with strategies of defense and counter-attack developed by those groups threatened with the expropriation of their know-how. At stake were not only the economic livelihood of the groups but also ancient statutory norms, the defense of a culture of work that had been inherited and that had to be handed down to subsequent generations, the safeguarding of an identity, and the conservation of a status. In these conflicts the various craft groups – whether in attack or defense – appear to be solidly and compactly ranged. The third section of the article, which investigates conflicts between the "bottom" and the "top" of the shoemaker's craft, reveals the existence of processes of socio-economic differentiation and of major strains within the single craft.

Common to all these disputes is the continual, albeit at times inconsistent, intervention of the authorities: from the city Senate – and its *pro tempore* head, the Gonfaloniere – to the Cardinal Legate (a political representative of the Pope in Bologna, not the archbishop), from the Assunteria al Sollievo delle Arti (a Senate committee authorized to control trade corporations and industrial activity) to the Magistrato dei Tribuni delle Plebe e Collegi delle Arti, whose main responsibility was to keep watch over the quality and price of foodstuffs.[10]

---

della città di Bologna (Bologna, 1670), p. 63. This assertion seems to be belied by the fact that a number of itinerant shoemakers sold shoes in the city and that some shoemakers' shops contained as many as twenty-five to forty-five pairs of shoes (A.S.B., Tribuni della Plebe [hereafter Tribuni], Atti, Libro BiancoRosso, xi [1730–2], fos.55^{v}, 58); see also Table 5.2. We do not know if the large workshops supplied the export trade.

9 *Statuti et ordini della Onoranda Compagnia et Arte dei Calzolai della città di Bologna* (Bologna, 1721), pp. 43–64.

10 For the institutional structure of the "governo misto" of Bologna, see "L'ordinamento Bolognese dei secoli xvi-xvii: lo stato, il governo e i magistrati di Bologna del Cavalier Ciro Spontone: edizione del MS. B. 1114 della Biblioteca dell'Archiginnasio," 2 vols., ed. S. Verardi Ventura, *Archiginnasio*, nos. 74 (1979) and 75 (1981).

1 Urban Shoemakers versus Rural Shoemakers

Shoemakers in Bologna feared the competition of those in the countryside. Rural shoemakers could sell shoes at low prices because, as the guild council explained, rent for shops and the cost of living were lower in the countryside, as were the excise taxes. To escape competition from rural shoemakers, the city shoemakers tried to limit the supply of tanned skins and leathers to the countryside, where fewer animals were slaughtered than in the city, and to discourage the sale in Bologna of shoes made in the countryside. Numerous orders, issued during the eighteenth century, stipulated that shoes could only be sold in the shops of master shoemakers. Itinerant shoemakers who sold shoes in the city market had to obtain a special license granted by one of the members of the guild council. When the license was granted each pair of shoes was stamped, different stamps indicating different qualities and prices.[11]

The need to protect their urban market was only one of the concerns of the Bolognese shoemakers. Beginning in 1734, the guild council, as the organ of the interests of the urban members, complained through its legal adviser to the Senate of the loss of the peasant shoe market, which had been almost completely taken over by the rural shoemakers.[12] To ward off competition in the countryside, the city shoemakers, aided and counselled by the Assunteria al Solievo delle Arti, began to elaborate more effective administrative measures.

Some of the steps considered were extreme. In early 1735 the guild council proposed to the Assunteria to prohibit the opening of new shoemakers' shops in rural areas.[13] A few weeks later the Assunteria debated the proposal to grant no more lifelong permits to "those opening shoe-shops in the countryside" and instead to issue three or four-year permits.[14] These plans were abandoned in favor of a more moderate proposal. The purpose was to divide the trade into two parts so as to limit the market for rural shoemakers. The latter would be prohibited from making shoes of fine workmanship, that is, with the upper parts made of calfskin for city wear; instead they would only

11 *Statuti et ordini della Onoranda Compagnia et Arte de' Calzolai*, pp. 65–7. These regulations were often redrafted. See *Notificazione generale e bando sopra l'Arte dei Calzolai e suoi obbedienli della città e contado di Bologna* of 1 Feb. 1741, republished with amendments in 1744, 1745, 1756 and 1770 (A.S.B., Archivio del Legato, Bandi).

12 A.S.B., Arti, Atti, Reg. 4 (1733–4), 13 Sept. 1734, fo. 141r-v.

13 A.S.B., Arti, Misc., i, no. 79, *Memoriale dell'Arte dei Calzolai all'Assunteria d'Arti perché sia proibito di aprire bottega da calzolaio in campagna* (n.d., but early Jan. 1735). The pamphlets of the Miscellanea volumes are only numbered up to 1776.

14 A.S.B., Arti, Atti, Reg. 5 (1735–6), 17 Jan. 1735, fo. 11.

make sturdy shoes of cowhide, which were more useful for the peasants.[15] Only the city shoemakers, who had virtually stopped producing shoes of cowhide some decades earlier, would make the finer shoes.[16] Each group was to have its own monopoly: rural shoemakers in the countryside, city shoemakers in the city. This proposal was accepted by the Cardinal Legate and the Gonfaloniere and, without any consultation with the country shoemakers, a new order was issued on 17 October 1735.[17]

A balance between the interests of the urban and rural shoemakers seemed to have been introduced, but in practice the city shoemakers gained an important advantage. The new rules presupposed that only cowhide shoes were used in the countryside. In fact a variety of social groups living there – priests, doctors, shopkeepers, estate managers, and others who were well off – wore calfskin shoes; but even the peasants, who went barefoot during the summer months, wore calfskin shoes on Sundays, holidays, to go to market, and on other occasions. While the sales of country shoemakers were restricted, the market for urban shoemakers expanded as they obtained at least a part of the rural market – that for good-quality shoes.

This outcome, not surprisingly, aroused opposition among country shoemakers. In early 1736 they expressed their views in a long petition (entitled *Repliche*), probably written by a lawyer, Dr. Ferrari. They claimed that they had always enjoyed the right to make calfskin shoes, whose use was widespread in the countryside, even among peasants. They should not have to bear the burden of the economic difficulties of the city shoemakers. In conclusion, they offered a compromise requesting that the order be revised to permit them to produce at least coarse calfskin shoes, leaving the urban shoemakers with a monopoly only over fine calfskin shoe production.[18] The country shoemakers

15 A.S.B., Arti, Atti, Reg. 5, 14 Mar. 1735, fo. 40; 3 Oct. 1735, fos. 79–80.

16 According to the shoemakers' guild, "of the eighty former city workshops which used to manufacture sturdy [cowhide] shoes, there are barely three left" (*Memoriale dell'Arte dei Calzolai*). In Modena shoemakers were in principle prohibited from making both sturdy shoes and fine shoes in the same shop. See *Artigianato e oggetti di artigianato a Modena dal 1650 al 1800: catalogo di una mostra impossibile*, ed. F. Valenti (Modena, 1986), p. 83.

17 A.S.B., Arti, Misc., viii, no. 34, *Bando sopra i lavori delle scarpe ed altro che si fanno* in *campagna*, Bologna, 17 Oct. 1735. Research undertaken by Alberto Guenzi has shown that 1735 and 1736, when the price of bread rose quite sharply, were years of poverty (A. Guenzi, *Pane e fornai a Bologna in età moderna* [Venice, 1982]). If one accepts E. Labrousse's thesis regarding crises "de type ancient," it is reasonable to suppose that the increase in the price of bread went hand in hand with a drop in the demand for manufactured goods – including shoes. This too could have persuaded the political authorities to issue the order.

18 A.S.B., Art i, Misc., viii, no. 51, *Ragioni dell'Arte dei Calzolai contro li calzolai di campagna … e Repliche dei nominati calzolai di campagna*, 1736. The pages of this manuscript are

reformulated the dichotomy – coarse work / fine work – differently, shifting the terms of reciprocal obligation in their favor, and defending their economic interests and their culture of work. Yet their requests were rejected by both the guild council and the Assunteria. According to Lorenzo Piella, professor of civil law at the university and official legal adviser to the Assunteria, "the distinction between coarse calfskin and fine calfskin ... has no foundation ... because calf hides are of one kind only, and only one part of the hide is coarser than the rest. The country shoemakers, preparing the coarse part of the hides, would be required not to work with the finer parts, and the magistrates would encounter a thousand controversies on their inspections to establish which was fine calfskin and which was coarse ... making the order unworkable."[19]

For its part, the shoemakers' guild council asserted that if shoes of calfskin were widely worn by peasants, the Legate's order would finally put a stop to such an "abuse," to the advantage of the city shoemakers, many of whom were without work because of a scarcity of calfskin.[20]

In this debate the Bolognese shoemakers clearly expressed an urban mentality that was hostile to the spread of industrial (and protoindustrial) activities in the countryside. The order prohibiting fine leatherwork in the countryside was, in their view, inspired by the "just and economic principle" that "the crafts must be carried out in the city and not in the countryside, except for those without which one cannot exist even in rural areas."[21] This same argument, also put forward by the lawyer Piella, was rejected by the country shoemakers. In their petition they defended "the natural freedom" of all persons – including peasants – "to wear the shoes that are most pleasing or most advantageous to them." In particular they criticized as "totally mistaken and unreasonable" the

---

divided into two parts, with the *Ragioni* on the left and the *Repliche* on the right. From now on I shall cite the two sources separately to avoid confusion.

19 A.S.B., Atti Misc., I, [L. Piella], *Relazione e voto al legato sopra il ricorso fattogli da alcuni calzolai di campagna* (n.d., but 1736). Piella taught at the university from 1717 (when he discussed his doctoral thesis) until 1762; see U. Dallari, *I notuli dei lettori legisti e artisti dello Studio di Bologna dal 1384 al 1789*, 4 vols. (Bologna, 1888–1924), iv. As a lawyer he published at least two legal reports for his clients. Laudatory poems were addressed to him on two different occasions: see *Raccolta di varii poetici componimenti in occasione di conferirsi la laurea dottorale in ambo le leggi al signor Lorenzo Piella Bolognese*, ed. V. Corbelletti (Bologna, 1717); *All'illustrissimo ... Lorenzo Piella ... ricevendo la laurea dottorale in Sacra Teologia nella celebre Università di Bologna D. Paolo Ignazio Piella di lui degnissimo figlio* (Bologna, 1758).

20 *Ragioni dell'Arte dei Calzolai.*

21 Ibid. On city opposition to the spread of industrial activity in rural areas, see S. Fronzoni and C. Poni, "L'economia di sussistenza della famiglia contadina," *Cultura popolare nell'Emilia Romagna: mestieri della terra e delle acque* (Milan, 1979), pp. 11–49.

proposition "that the guilds should be active in the city and not in the countryside." The rural shoemakers did not deny that the guilds should have their main base in the city, but they argued against any exclusive privilege of shoemaking, an activity which should be common to both city and countryside.[22]

This debate lasted throughout 1736. Its dramatic climax came with a trial initiated at the end of April 1736 by San Giovanni in Persiceto, a small urban-rural community that came under Bolognese jurisdiction. The trial was in defense of two local shoemakers who had been sued by the Tribuni della Plebe "for manufacturing shoes ... of fine workmanship, in violation of the rules laid down by the order published on 17 October 1735."[23] The intervention of the municipal government of San Giovanni in Persiceto changed the character of the dispute. No longer a corporate conflict between. two groups within the same craft, it became a confrontation between the vertical organization of a craft and a territorial body. The lawyer Giuseppe Taruffi, who represented the municipality of San Giovanni in Persiceto before the Tribuni, argued that the privileges granted by Pope Eugene IV and the "agreement between the pope and the town authorities" gave all inhabitants of San Giovanni "the right to exercise any art or craft of any kind whatsoever, without being hindered by the community of Bologna." This led to the request that "unwarranted" seizures be suspended and that the Tribuni confirm the privilege of the shoemakers of San Giovanni in Persiceto to "make shoes of fine workmanship, notwithstanding the said order."[24] The lawsuit was rapidly settled. Without making the declaration of principle that had been requested of them, the Tribuni acquitted the two shoemakers and ordered that the confiscated shoes be returned to them.[25]

---

22 *Repliche dei nominati calzolai di campagna.* On the power relationship between Bologna and its territory, see A. de Benedictis, *Patrizi e comunità: il governo del contado bolognese nel 1700* (Bologna, 1984).

23 A.S.B., Tribuni, Atti, Libro Bianco-Rosso, xii (1732–6), 30 April 1736, fo. 286^{v}.

24 A.S.B., Tribuni, Atti, Libro Bianco-Rosso, xii, 30 April 1736. The papal privileges of the small country towns were granted in the fifteenth cenrury, before the consolidation of firm control by Bologna over its territory. The conflicts between city and rural towns involved the two major authorities (the Senate and the Legate) of the "governo misto." The Legate was the natural defender of the privileges granted by the papacy. See G. Forni, *Persiceto e S. Giovanni in Persiceto, dalle origini a tutto il secolo xix: storia di un comune rurale* (Bologna and Rocca S. Casciano, 1921); de Benedictis, *Patrizi e comunità.*

25 A.S.B., Tribuni, Atti, Libro Bianco-Rosso, xii, 4 May 1736, fo. 288. Some years later the community of San Giovanni in Persiceto began legal proceedings against the shoemakers' guild of Bologna in defense of local shoemakers who refused to accept guild inspections

The decision of the Tribuni was more than a passing incident. There were more than ten other rural communities with privileges which could, with some hope of success, claim the same exemption granted to San Giovanni in Persiceto. Among them were such important towns as Budrio, Castel S. Pietro and Medicina, which were very active in the defense of their privileges against Bologna and had frequent recourse to the final appeal courts in Rome. Indeed, immediately after the decision, inspections and lawsuits in the small, privileged centers ceased almost completely, while the various organs of the government in Bologna began to draft an amendment to the order. In March 1737 a first version of a modified order began to circulate between the Senate and the Legate.[26] It allowed the shoemakers of the small, privileged centers to continue the production of fine-quality shoes undisturbed. To which communities would this apply and to how many? The Cardinal Legate, Giovan Battista Spinola, refused to name them in advance, wishing to retain the right, "in case of doubt," to decide which "towns were to enjoy the privilege of making shoes of fine workmanship."[27] The Assunteria, arguing that "such a reservation was prejudicial to the public advantage," insisted that all the privileged communities be indicated by name in the reform.[28]

This disagreement, which set the Senate against the Legate in a struggle for power, continued for several years. A solution satisfying the Senate could not be found during the term of the new Legate, the authoritarian Cardinal Giulio Alberoni.[29] It only became possible to reach an agreement upon the appointment of Cardinal Giorgio Doria (1744–54). In 1746 a new order was published prohibiting the production of fine-quality shoes in the countryside, with the addition of a list specifying the eleven privileged communities exempted from the order.[30]

---

and to pay the *obbedienza*. On 3 February 1749 the dispute was officially suspended by a Senate committee who judged it inopportune (A.S.B., Congregazione di Governo, Reg. 13 [1748–50], fo. 25).

26 A.S.B., Arti, Misc., ix, *Notificazione sopra il bando circa i lavori delle scarpe ed altro che si fanno in campagna*, 26 Mar. 1737. According to a survey carried out by the Senate in 1732, there were (privileged areas excluded) about 116 shoemakers and 121 cobblers in the countryside (A.S.B., Arti, Notizie sopra le Arti, Artefici del contado, 1732).

27 A.S.B., Arti, Reg. 6, 8 April 1737, fo. 21.

28 Ibid.

29 On Alberoni's adverse feelings towards the Bolognese aristocracy, see P. Castagnoli, *Il Cardinale Giulio Alberoni*, 3 vols. (Piacenza and Rome, 1932), iii, pp. 175–176.

30 A.S.B., Archivio del Legato, Bandi, *Bando sopra i lavori delle scarpe ed altro che si fanno in campagna*, 12 October 1746. The eleven privileged communities were: Budrio, Castelfranco, Crevalcore, Castelbolognese, Casal Fiuminese, Castel San Pietro, San

The Senate of Bologna in effect had foiled the attempt of the Legate to extend his power, but its victory was paid for by the limitation of the area over which the order was to be enforced. The effectiveness of the order began to weaken after only a few months, when the Legate started to issue free licenses to a certain number of shoemakers, almost all of whom were inhabitants of the "suburbio" of the city, so that they could work with coarse calfskin.[31] In the last seven years of his tenure Cardinal Giorgio Doria granted at least twenty-three licenses (see Table 5.1.). His successor, Legate Fabrizio Serbelloni, also continued to grant licenses to rural shoemakers, but only after payment of a fee of 10 *soldi*. Hereafter payment of a fee for the licenses became standard practice, and was extended to the non-privileged areas of the territory outside the "suburbia." After 1781 a growing number of rural shoemakers began to ask for and to obtain licenses for both coarse and fine calfskin, costing them 20 *soldi*. However, the number of licenses, granted in principle for an unspecified period, remained relatively limited until August 1785. They grew rapidly during the tenure of Cardinal Giovanni A. Archetti, who began to impose annual renewal requirements. In the nine years of his legation he issued 518 licenses, more than all of his predecessors put together (see Table 5.1.) From then on, as many country shoemakers living outside the privileged areas requested and obtained the necessary exemption, the old order became completely useless.[32]

The real victor in this conflict was the Legate. While it was not "to the public advantage" for the Legate to decide which should be the privileged

Giovanni in Persiceto, San Giorgio, Molinella, Medicina and Vergato. To this list the community of Piumazzo was added in the second half of the century.

31 The Legate's chancellery stipulated that only calfskins weighing more than five pounds could be described as coarse. All the quantitative data to which I make reference (see also Table 5.1) have been taken from the *Expeditiones* of the Legate. These data are put forth here in a preliminary way. On the size of the "suburbio," see A. Bellettini, *L'evoluzione demografica del suburbio bolognese durante l'età moderna e contemporanea* (Bologna, 1977).

32 It would be interesting to know how many rural shoemakers continued to work coarse and fine calfskin clandestinely and how many emigrated to the eleven small privileged towns and to Bologna in order to be able to carry on their work. The reports of the inspections that the officials of the shoemakers' guild conducted periodically in the countryside to uncover those shoemakers who disobeyed the rules are unfortunately lost. But the reports of the inspections of the Tribuni have survived. These reports were intended to enforce the regulations relating to the prices and quality of consumer goods which were of interest to the provisioning authorities (flour, bread, oil, lard, caviar, chickens, pasta, fresh and salted pork, etc.), but they also contain denunciations against tanners, candlemakers, weavers and shoemakers. The reports for the years 1737–43, the six years following the publication of the order against the rural shoemakers, provide evidence of only nine denunciations. One example is that of the shoemaker Bernardo Brighenti of

TABLE 5.1 Licences granted to the rural shoemakers, 1747–1796[a]

Legate	Fine calfskin	Coarse calfskin	Total licenses
G. Doria (Jan. 1747–July 1754)	2	2	21
F. Serbelloni (July 1754–Oct. 1761)		68	68
G. Spinola (Nov. 1761–June 1768)		85	85
L. Pallavicino (June 1768–Nov. 1769)		55	55
A. Branciforti (Nov. 1769–Feb. 1777)	1	106	107
M. D'Aquino (Feb. 1777–Dec. 1777)		39	39
I. Boncompagni Lodovisi (Jan. 1778–Aug. 1785)[b]	15	63	78
G. A. Archetti (Sept. 1785–Oct. 1794)	253	265	518
I. Vincenzi (Jan. 1795–June 1796)	74	85	159

a These data are taken from the following registers: nos. 238 (1747–50), 239 (1750–2), 240 (1752–3), 242 (1753–4), 243 (1754–7), 245 (1757–61), 246 (1761–5), 248 (1765–8), 249 (1768–9), 251 (1769–74), 253 (1774–7), 254 (1777), 256 (1781–3), 258 (1783–4), 259 (1784–5), 261 (1785–6), 263 (1787–8), 264 (1789–90), 265 (1791–2), 266 (1793–4). Payment for the licences began in 1755.

b There is no information regarding the first years (1778, 1779 and 1780) of Boncompagni Lodovisi's term in office.

SOURCE: ARCHIVIO DI STATO DI BOLOGNA, ARCHIVIO DEL LEGATO, EXPEDITIONES

communities, it was even more prejudicial to the city's autonomy for him to grant hundreds of licenses. The fact that it was the Legate and his chancellery that distinguished coarse from fine calfskin represented another humiliation

Arcoveggio, from whom nine pounds of calfskin and thirteen pairs of "finely made" shoes were seized. From Giuseppe Serra, "pork-butcher and shoemaker" of Sasso, seven pairs of calfskin shoes were seized on 7 April 1742: A.S.B., Tribuni, Atti, Libro Bianco-Rosso, xiii (1737–43), fos. 248, 267–268.

for the Assunteria and its learned legal adviser. The Bolognese Senate, which had incautiously raised the issue in the first place, was the real loser in terms of both prestige and power.[33]

Those who gained, on the other hand, at least for a few decades, were the rural shoemakers who obtained licenses for an unspecified period (especially those who paid no fee). The picture changed towards the middle of the 1790s when the licenses began to be limited to one year and a fee was charged for them. This change did not escape the attention of the shoemakers who had previously benefited, as is revealed in a petition of 1792 from a group of country shoemakers asking the Senate to reduce the "heavy burdens" which weighed on them: they were forced to pay not only the annual fee of the *obbedienza* and for the licenses, but also other duties to the "detriment" of their families. Country shoemakers had had some of their property "unjustly" sequestered by the collector for the guild council because they were late in paying the annual *obbedienza,* but, the petitioners pleaded, their delay was due to their being "poor and burdened with large families."[34]

The Assunteria, to whom the Senate transmitted the petition, received the shoemakers' complaints with sympathy and understanding. Since they considered a reduction of the annual fee (the *obbedienza*) and other duties inopportune, an alternative was to abolish the licenses. This course of action was probably encouraged by hopes of healing an old wound, and became more likely when the city shoemakers (and in their name the guild council), under pressure from the Senate, recognized the need to abolish a by now ineffectual order and to accept the right of country shoemakers to use calfskins.[35] The problem then was how to formulate a proposal for abolition that would both appear just and be accepted by the Legate, who had the final word. The

33 Along with the Senate, the Assunteria al Sollievo delle Arti – to which the task of combating and limiting abuses and privileges had been assigned in 1730 – also suffered defeat. On the origin and role of this Assunteria, see A. Giacomelli, "Carlo Grassi e le riforme bolognesi del settecento. 1. L'età Lambertiniana," *Quaderni culturali bolognesi,* no. 10, 1979, 18–19; A. Guenzi, *La "fabbrica" delle tele tra città e campagna: gruppi professionali e governo dell'economia a Bologna nel secolo* XVIII (Ancona, 1988).

34 A.S.B., Arti, Misc., 1, *Memoriale di diversi calzolai del contado ... per ottenere diminuzione delle gravezze pagate annualmente,* 15 December 1792.

35 The existence of a negotiation between the guild council and the Assunteria becomes apparent if one compares A.S.B., Arti, Misc., liii, *Promemoria e progetto dell'Arte dei Calzolai all'Assunteria Arti sopra il ricorso delli calzolai di campagna,* 18 Feb. 1793, and A.S.B., Arti, Misc., liii, *Sentimento del consultore Gavazzi all'Assunteria d'Arti sopra li due affari dell'Arte dei Calzolai,* 28 February 1793. See also A.S.B., Arti, Misc., liii, *Promemoria dell'Assunieria d'Arti al legato a favore dei calzolai del contado,* 13 March 1793. In favor of the abolition of licenses was the fact that "despite the order of 1735, the amount of calfskins

Assunteria resorted to an argument that emphasized the balance between "burden" (obligations) and "faculties" (rewards). Giuseppe Gavazzi, the legal consultant of the Assunteria – who was, like Lorenzo Piella, professor of law at the university – stated that the country shoemakers paid an annual *obbedienza* "equal to that of the city shoemakers." Where the burdens were equal, "so also should be the advantages and ability to work."[36]

Supported by this legal argument, the proposal was submitted to Legate Archetti for approval. He rejected it "absolutely." In his opinion there was no need to abolish the order, since "he already granted the licenses whenever they were requested." At most he was ready to come to an agreement to make the fees "less burdensome"[37] – a half-promise that he did not keep.

This conflict, like the others I shall describe, reveals that the shoemakers' guild had lost part of its autonomy. It could no longer redefine, on its sole authority, the craft status of rural shoemakers. Municipal authorities also demonstrated a lack of capacity to make or enforce decisions. The case also demonstrates how conflicts between groups of low status were used by different segments of the élite in order to enhance their power.

2 Cobblers versus Shoemakers

The conflict between shoemakers and cobblers concerned the shoemakers' exclusive right to produce new shoes and the consequent restriction of the cobblers' activity to the repairing of old shoes. This division was reinterpreted in 1688, when the Bolognese Senate decided that cobblers could sell "remade" shoes in which "the buyers could easily see the inclusion of old material."[38] In short, the cobblers were permitted to rework used goods and to sell them on the market. This concession was an important victory for the cobblers, who could now learn the craft of shoemaker, that is, to make shoes. Despite this, in

---

which left the city was almost the same as if the order did not exist" (*Promemoria e progetto*).

36 *Sentimento del consultore Gavazzi.* Giuseppe Gavazzi taught at the university from 1772 until 1800 (see Dallari, *Notuli dei lettori legisti,* iv). He participated in the debates on the "economic plan" of the city of Bologna with the pamphlet *Alla Sacra Congregazione particolare deputata … all'esame del piano economico della città di Bologna* (Rome, 1792).

37 A.S.B., Arti, Atti, Reg. 16 (1793–4), 13 March 1793, fo. 36.

38 The order was incorporated in the shoemakers' statutes: *Statuti et ordini della Onoranda Compagnia et Arte de' Calzolai,* pp. 71–2. Moreover the regulation stated that if the sole

Bologna, as in other towns and cities, cobblers constituted an inferior craft and, though members of the shoemakers' guild, they had no say in how it was run.

However, the demarcation between the two crafts was not respected, since the shoemakers continued to repair old shoes, especially those which they had sold as new merchandise to their clients. To defend themselves against such encroachments, the cobblers began to petition the Senate, requesting a reinforcement in the regulations in order to safeguard the exclusive rights of each craft. According to the cobblers, if those who repaired and remade old shoes could not make new ones, then those who produced new goods could not repair old ones.[39] This principle, which the Senate then made its own, was unanimously approved by the shoemakers' guild council on 11 November 1736. The eight members present at the meeting affirmed that "since the cobblers are prohibited from producing new shoes, which is the exclusive right of shoemakers, so the shoemakers are prohibited from repairing old shoes, which is the exclusive right of cobblers."[40] The regulation was solemnly approved by the Senate of Bologna, in a Senato Consulto.[41] But the rule was not applied in an even-handed manner. In a petition to the Senate, of an unknown date after 1741, a group of cobblers maintained that the council of the shoemakers' guild, responsible for seeing that the rules were observed, "every day" sent groups of inspectors, from which the cobblers were excluded, "to arrest the cobblers who disobeyed," but they never arrested any shoemakers, "whom we see doing daily what is within our competence."[42] Further protests led the Assunteria in 1752 to ask the Tribuni to implement the Senato Consulto "especially in response to complaints from the cobblers."[43]

A new phase in the dispute between the cobblers and the shoemakers started in 1784 with the intervention of the Cardinal Legate and the Gonfaloniere as mediators. The cobbler Vincenzo Tabellini was twice charged

---

was new the uppers should be old, and that if the uppers were new, then the sole should be old.

39 A.S.B., Arti, Atti, Reg. 5 (1735–6), 31 October 1735, fo. 91; 7 November 1735, fo. 93.

40 A.S.B., Arti, Misc., viii, no. 37, *Relazione al senato … e congregazione qui unita tenuta dell'Arte dei Calzolai*, 14 November 1735.

41 A.S.B., Senato, Partitorum, Reg. 49 (1731–7), 17 March 1736, fos. 138^{v}-9. See also A.S.B., Senato, Filza 62, the *Relazione* of the *Assunteria* to the Senate, 16 January 1736, fos. 107–9.

42 A.S.B., Arti, Misc., ii, no. 31, *Memoriale dei ciabattini di città … acciò siano mantenute le leggi proibitive ai calzolai di rapezza re scarpe use, giacché essi non possono lavorare di nuovo* (n.d.).

43 A.S.B., Arti, Atti, Reg. 8 (1749–53), 29 May 1752, fo. 143. See also the petition sent to the *Tribuni* by the cobbler Antonio Rubbi (A.S.B., Tribuni, Atti, Libro Bianco Rosso, xv [1749–56], 15 June 1752, fo. 165^{v}). Towards the end of June 1752 the cobblers delivered a list to

by the guild council with having new leather in his shop and manufacturing new shoes. The Legate declared him innocent on the first occasion. After the second charge Tabellini presented to the Assunteria a petition signed by forty-seven cobblers which accused the shoemakers of repairing old shoes and at the same time of "searching for cobblers who, having little work, might make new shoes on occasion." The petition concluded with a request that the order of 1736 be enforced and the "exclusive rights of each craft be respected."[44] The Assunteria's discussion went beyond the issues raised by the petition. The Gonfaloniere, Giovanni Lambertini, who attended the meeting, found the cobblers' demand for the strict enforcement of the order "reasonable." but he considered it difficult to apply. In his view it was impossible to prohibit the shoemakers "from repairing used shoes, since they are obliged to do so by their regular customers who are unwilling to make use of the cobblers." He proposed instead that the cobblers also be allowed to make new shoes, provided they passed the prescribed examination for shoemakers and did not employ their workers or apprentices in the task.[45]

A few days later the Assunteria's legal consultant submitted a detailed plan for the approval of the guild council. The cobblers – but not their workers or apprentices – would be permitted to make new shoes once they had passed the guild examination and paid a mastership fee of 5 lire (while continuing to pay the cobblers' annual *obbedienza* of 2 lire). The shoemakers would be permitted to repair old shoes, on condition that they did not employ cobblers.[46]

The proposal attempted to establish a new equilibrium between the two still distinct crafts, bringing the rules closer to actual practice. But the guild council rejected it. They feared that this concession to the cobblers would lead to an excessive increase in the number of those making new shoes, thereby reducing the income that was "necessary to the sustenance of men's families." They also considered it unfair to lower the examination fee to a mere 5 lire, when the statute granted the guild 10 lire "in compensation for the inconvenience and time"

---

the *Tribuni* of those shoemakers making new shoes and repairing old ones (fo. 167ᵛ). Unfortunately, this list has not been preserved.

44 A.S.B., Arti, Misc., xxxv, no. 64, *Memoriale di Vincenzo Tabellini scarpinello*, 2 August 1784.

45 A.S.B., Arti, Atti, Reg. 13 (1784–6), 2 August 1784, fos. 40–1. From the legal point of view, the Gonfaloniere was also the "natural" judge of disputes among the guilds. His action as a mediator did not coincide with his functions as a judge. In the cases here examined he intervenes as head of the Senate and not as a judge. The Archive of the Gonfaloniere was being reorganized and could not be used for this research.

46 A.S.B., Arti, Misc., xxxv, no. 72, *Progetto fatto per provedere all'instanza fatta dai ciabattini*, 16 Aug. 1784.

spent in conducting the examination. In addition, they called for an increase in the cobblers' annual *obbedienza,* to make it equal to the shoemakers' fee of 4 lire. The guild council also predicted that the "promiscuousness" of the two crafts would pave the way to every kind of fraud injurious to the consumers.[47]

After this reply, the Assunteria, with the encouragement of the Legate, redrafted the plan to satisfy the guild's demands for an examination fee of 10 lire and an annual *obbedienza* fee of 4 lire. If the two crafts were to remain separate, the Assunteria led the shoemakers to understand that the alternative was to include cobblers among the inspectors sent to the workshops. To ward off that danger the shoemakers' guild accepted the reform in January 1785.[48]

Obstacles preventing the "promiscuousness" of the two crafts now seemed to have been overcome. At this point the cobblers, through their spokesman Tabellini, rejected the agreement, which would have required them to pay the same mastership fee and yearly fee as the shoemakers, while denying them the right to teach shoemaking to their apprentices and sons.[49] Although the cobblers' opposition gained the sympathy of the Cardinal Legate, it seems that the plan the shoemakers had accepted was approved by a Senato Consulto. Its effectiveness remains doubtful.[50] Disputes and negotiations between cobblers and shoemakers continued in the following year, after which the historical record is silent for almost a decade. At least in theory the cobblers could have appealed to a tribunal to defend their rights. But to do this they needed funds and therefore an autonomous organization of their own supplied with

---

47 A.S.B. Arti, Misc., xxxv, no. 82, *Risposta e opposizione dell'Arte dei Calzolai,* 8 November 1784.

48 A.S.B., Arti, Atti, Reg. 13 (1784–6), 8 November 1784, fo. 49^{r-v}; 17 January 1785, fo. 62^{v}; 24 January 1785, fo. 65.

49 A.S.B., Arti, Misc., xxxvi, no. 48, *Memoriale … di Vincenzo Tabellini,* 6 June 1785. See also A.S.B., Arti, Atti, Reg. 13, 6 June 1785, fo. 93.

50 In their letters to the Assunteria, Tabellini and another cobbler, Girolamo Sandri, refer to a Senato Consulto of 19 July 1785 in favor of the "promiscuousness" of the two crafts: see A.S.B., Arti, Misc., xxxvii, no. 9, *Suppliche di Vincenzo Tabellini e Girolamo Sandri ciabattini con cui domandano … l'esecuzione del Senato consulto dei 19 luglio 1785 … o che sia rinnovata la proibizione di tale promiscuità,* 23 January 1786. I have not been able to find any trace of this decision in the Partitorum of the Senate. Searches for a draft of this resolution (perhaps not approved or suspended) so far have been in vain. In the early 1790s Tabellini led a lively protest by forty shoemakers against the poor quality of the leather produced by the tanners (A.S.B., Arti, Misc., liv, *Ricorso di Vincenzo Tabellini ed altri entroscritti calzolai … contro li calegari,* 9 September 1793). On 1 November 1788 the shoemakers of Minerbio accused the itinerant cobblers of the countryside of making new shoes (A.S.B., Arti, Atti, Reg. 14 [1787–8], fo. 173).

revenues. It was perhaps the absence of such an organization that prevented them – and probably also the dispersed rural shoemakers – from bringing charges against their adversaries before a judge.[51] When in 1794 the shoemakers' guild accused the cobbler G. Tinarelli of making new shoes, the issue seems to have been resolved through a new form of compromise. The Assunteria ruled that the cobbler should take the examination to become a master shoemaker, while the guild should permit him to delay paying the examination fee.[52]

The reaction of the political authorities to guild disputes was not uniform. In the conflict between cobblers and shoemakers the government seemed committed to devising proposals capable of winning the agreement of both parties. Despite concessions exacted from the shoemakers, this effort failed when the cobblers rejected the proposed solution. In contrast, the concurrent conflict setting city shoemakers against country shoemakers found the government supporting one of the sides. Each case touched different interests and convictions of municipal officials. The city authorities were on the side of the urban shoemakers with whom they shared the same ideology, the belief that cities should be devoted to industry and the countryside to agriculture. They were also concerned that the crisis in urban industry would further reduce employment in the city. Moreover the noble senators, all of whom were landowners, feared a loss of labor for agriculture with the spread of industrial activities into rural areas, and opposed the consumption of luxury goods (such as calfskin shoes) among the peasants. The conflict between shoemakers and cobblers, in contrast, affected no broad interests, only those of the two groups involved. The relative impartiality of the city authorities mirrored the scant interest they had in this dispute.

3 Master Shoemakers versus the Guild Council

The conflict which opposed the shoemakers who were masters – *obbedienti* – to the guild council was directed against the hierarchical power structure within the guild. It began in July 1749 with the request that the masters (shopkeepers who employed apprentices and journeymen) addressed to the

51 See the interesting analysis by H. L. Root, "Challenging the Seigneurie: Community and Contention on the Eve of the French Revolution," *Journal of Modern History,* lvii, no. 4 (1985) 652–681.

52 A.S.B., *Arti,* Atti, Reg. 16 (1793–4), 28 April 1794, fo. 176^{v}.

Assunteria to reduce their annual *obbedienza* to the guild council.[53] They justified this demand by their poverty and by the fact that the annual payment of 4 lire, which had been fair in the past when "there were not so many shoemakers' shops ... and as a result [every shop] had a lot of work," was no longer equitable now that there were "a multitude of shops all without work and the masters without the means to make a living."[54] In later petitions, from 1749 to 1754, this attack assumed a more complex and acute form. The masters questioned the policy and the role of the members of the council who, they charged, were guilty of boosting the number of shoemakers by setting easy and even fraudulent examinations. This uncontrolled increase, the masters claimed, yielded greater revenues for the guild council members who pocketed the examination fees, but also produced greater poverty for the masters. Easier examinations – the only test granting the right to practice the trade – also permitted the guild council members to nominate as masters relatives and clients who lacked technical ability and who were later destined, thanks to further favoritism, to climb the hierarchy of the guild.[55] The council members, the masters charged, "were concerned only with their own interest and not with that of the entire body of the guild and the public."[56] Furthermore they had neglected to create dowries for the shoemakers' daughters, as laid down in the guild statutes.

The masters made proposals designed to remedy such abuses. They asked: (1) that one of their representatives be admitted to the guild council "when meetings were held that related to the public interest"; (2) that applicants who had not "practiced the profession for a minimum of ten years" be excluded from examination for the mastership; and (3) that the annual fee (the *obbedienza*)

53 This petition (hereafter Petition no. 1), untitled and undated but drafted in July 1749, is an annex to the report (A.S.B., Arti, Misc., xv, no. 25, *Sentimento del consultor Piella ... sopra diversi ricorsi degli obbidienti dell'Arte dei calzolai contro detta Arte,* 17 April 1752). See also A.S.B., Arti, Atti, Reg. 8 (1749–53), 22 July 1749, fo. 44; 5 August 1749, fo. 48^v; 12 August 1749, fo. 50^v.

54 Petition no. 1.

55 See the *Risposta alle negative che danno gli huomini del Consiglio dei Calzolai* (1749) and the continuation, undated and untitled, of this *Risposta* (hereafter Petition no. 4). Both reports are annexes to the *Sentimento del consultor Piella.* See also A.S.B., Arti, Misc.,iii, *Memoriale degli obbedienti dell'Arte dei Calzolai ... con informazione e voto sopra le domande accennate* (n.d.). The masters also complained that they had to bear all the participation expenses in the August Fair, from which council members were exempt, and wrongly accused the guild council of having encouraged the spread of fine work in the countryside.

56 Petition no. 4.

be set at an amount proportional to the size of the shops, some of which had no apprentices or journeymen while others employed ten to twelve hands.[57] Was this last perception correct? It would appear to be, judging by Tables 5.2 and 5.3, based on two official surveys carried out by the guild council itself in 1697 and 1745.

The masters looked to history as a support for their arguments. The existing oligarchical structure of the guild was contrary to its ancient fifteenth-century form. In those days there had been fewer masters and they had been more skilled at their work. The majority were full members – only a few were *obbedienti* – and shops were widely dispersed, less vulnerable to competition and all of approximately the same size. This argument, and the request that the amount of the *obbedienza* be proportionate to the size of the shop, seems to express the vision of impoverished artisans, threatened by the expansion of larger shops.

With the exception of the first petition in 1749, which carried thirty-eight signatures, none of the other memoranda and requests from the masters was ever signed.[58] We do know, however, that in 1749, at a meeting held in the Church of Santa Maria della Morte, the masters elected two representatives, Giuseppe Mingardi and Giuseppe Pignoni, the latter regarded as an "expert in law." These two leaders acted as the strategists of the attack on the guild council.

The petitions of the masters, probably conceived and written by Pignoni or by a lawyer, and then "reproduced in not unpleasing verse" by Mingardi,[59] received a favorable hearing from the Assunteria. In April 1752 the legal adviser to the Assunteria, Lorenzo Piella, supported some of the master shoemakers' requests, such as the appointment of a master to assist the council deputies in administering the tests. Professor Piella also pleaded for tougher examinations, with precise guidelines as to the skills to be tested, so as to guarantee

57 Ibid. See also the *Risposta alle negative che danno gli huomini del Consiglio dei Calzolai* and the *Memoriale degli obbedienti dell'Arte dei Calzolai*. Only the masters of the largest shops should have to pay a 4 lire *obbedienza* fee. The dispute about the excessive cost of the *obbedienza* fee, although not a mere pretext, was used to air more important issues.

58 We have evidence regarding the size of the shops of eighteen of the thirty-eight signatories. Eleven of these eighteen handled fewer than 100 calfskins per year, five handled between 101 and 150 skins and two handled between 151 and 200 skins. This information can be gathered by comparing the thirty-eight names of the signatories with the list of shop-owners accounted for in the 1745 investigation (see Table 5.3). The twenty missing names are those of masters licensed to practice after 1745.

59 This is Piella's evaluation of Mingardi's poetic abilities (*Sentimento del consultor Piella*). Unfortunately, only one of Mingardi's three compositions has survived. Pignoni handled 100 calfskins in 1745, Mingardi 104: see Biblioteca Apostolica Vaticana, MS. Patetta 3041.

TABLE 5.2 Urban shoemakers' shops and journeymen employed, 1697[a]

Journeymen per shop	Shops	Journeymen	Pair of shoes produced monthly	Monthly average no. of pairs of shoes per shop
2	13	26	1,020	78.5
3	8	24	983	122.8
4	9	36	1,660	184.5
5	6	30	1,190	198.3
6	2	12	600	300.0
7	2	14	630	315.0
8	1	8	450	450.0
9	3	27	1,400	466.6
10	1	10	500	500.0
11				
12	3	36	1,875	625.0
13	1	13	550	550.0
Total	49	236	10,858	221.6

a These figures refer to only 49 shops, those with more than one Journeyman. The *Tribuni* calculated that 5,429 pieces of leather were necessary to produce 65,148 pairs of shoes every six months. In 1745 the shoe makers' guild calculated that the 117 shops in the city consumed annually 11,379 pieces of leather. (See Source to Table 5.3.) The annual production of shoes – more than 120,000 pairs – seems high. Unfortunately we have no knowledge of what the general term "shoes" implied, regarding either the categories of goods, the social groups for which they were intended, or the production techniques employed.

SOURCE: ARCHIVIO DI STATO DI BOLOGNA, TRIBUNI ATTI, LIBRO RECENTIORE VI (1688–1701), 23 SEPT. 1697, FO. 199[R-V].

better workmanship. On the question of the annual fee, he opened the way to a possible reduction since, he wrote, "the laws governing the imposition of charges should be moderated when a change in the state of affairs is such that the charges become excessive."[60]

60 *Sentimento del consultor Piella.* I shall not give a summary of Piella's second legal report, since it is not very different from the first one (A.S.B., Arti, Misc., xvi, no. 3, *Informazione*

TABLE 5.3 Urban shoemakers' shops and number of calfskins worked, 1745[a]

No of skins consumed	No. of shops	Total no. of skins	Average no. of skins per shop
0–50	20	670	33.5
51–100	49	3,606	73.5
101–150	22	2,697	122.5
151–200	14	2,558	182.5
201–250	7	1,588	227.0
251–300	2	570	285.0
301–350	1	320	320.0
351+	2	780	390.0
	117	12,789	

a The Survey was carried out by the guild council. The tendency towards economic disparities is confirmed by another anonymous source with no date (Probably early eighteenth century) which – if I read it correctly – attributes the largest workshop with a daily production of between twenty and fifty pairs of shoes: Biblioteca dell'Archiginnasio di Bologna, MS. Malvezzi, Cart.312, no.3, "Relazione delle scarpe che si fabricano giornalmente per l'ordinario nelle botteghe de' calzolai di Bologna in ordine a' tacchi et altre cose bisognevoli per adoprar li fianchi".

SOURCE: BIBLIOTECA APOSTOLICA VATICANA MS PATETTA 3041, "ARTE DEI CALLEGARI DI BOLOGNA: ATTI E DOCUMENTI, 1745–1798"

Most of these suggestions were in large measure accepted by the Assunteria. Within a few days this committee decided to compare the guild's present and past income so that "any evidence of an increase in income might permit a reduction in the masters' annual fee."[61] The Assunteria also undertook to ask the masters to provide "a list of the most able subjects" to select as monitors of the examinations.[62] On some vital points it seemed the conflict had been resolved in the masters' favor.

But after this decision the Assunteria did not show any particular haste in concluding the affair. In January 1754, two years later, it decided to consult

e voto del consultor Piella ... sopra diversi ricorsi degli obbedienti dell'Arte dei Calzolai, 14 January 1754).

61 A.S.B., Arti, Atti, Reg. 8, 24 April 1752, fo. 139v.

62 Ibid.

expert masters "who are not of the guild council, to see if they can draw up tests which are less easy" than those currently held.[63] In the same month it opened an inquiry to discover "at what age an apprentice normally becomes a journeyman, and at what age he demonstrates sufficient ability so that he may be said to have learned the shoemaker's craft."[64] It was not until May 1754 that the Assunteria openly criticized the guild council, accusing it of having accepted as masters those who were not "well instructed and expert" in the craft. On the same day, to limit the "excessive liberty" of entry into the guild, the Assunteria finally ordered the guild council "not to pass any candidate in the future ... without the Assunteria's participation and consent."[65] The following month, in a reply to an appeal by the guild council, the Assunteria reaffirmed its decision, in practical terms equivalent to a suspension of the examinations, until new regulations could be issued "regarding the quality of the tests ... and the way of conducting them."[66]

The sharp clash with the Assunteria (and therefore with the Senate) brought into the open tensions within the guild council that previously had been repressed. In June 1756 seven of its "young" members denounced to the Assunteria those council officers (the head, Giuseppe Tempesta, and three other "old" members) who had admitted Antonio Leoni as master without requiring him to perform "the test for cutting and forming a shoe," and who had promoted him rapidly into the council so that he might fill the place left vacant after the recent death of his father Lorenzo.[67] The Assunteria authorized the lawyer Angelo Panelli to conduct a speedy and rigorous inquiry into the matter. The investigation, completed within a month, revealed that Leoni, who had been promoted to the rank of master on 14 February 1755, became a member of the council two weeks later: a truly lightning career!

---

63 Ibid., Reg. 9 (1754–65), 14 January 1754, fo^{v}.

64 Ibid., 21 January 1754, fo. 4^{v}.

65 Ibid., 6 May 1754, fo. 14^{v}.

66 Ibid., 10 June 1754, fos. 16' -17.

67 A.S.B., Arti, Misc., xvii, no. 40, *Ricorso di alcuni novizzi dell'Arte dei Calzolai ... contro detta Arte*, 14 June 1756. The principle that not only the trade but also the position on the guild council was hereditary was strongly rooted in corporate culture. lt was, however, subject to precise rules. The son or brother of a deceased council member could only succeed him providing he satisfied certain conditions. He had to be at least twenty-five years of age; to be born of a legitimate rnarriage; to have carried on the profession as a master for at least five years (later reduced to three); to be able to read and write; to have a good reputation, etc.. The shop of Lorenzo Leoni, the biggest in the city, handled 368 calfskins (Biblioteca Apostolica Vaticana, MS. Patetta).

Dr. Panelli recommended nullifying Leoni's admission as master and his appointment to the council on the grounds of errors and falsehood. The "practical" test had been performed "by the hand of the shoemaker Domenico Spisani and his apprentice" at the home of Tempesta, the guild's head, clearly an accomplice. Furthermore Antonio Leoni, as two of his father's journeymen testified, had never practiced the craft "in any shop whatsoever."[68] These events, embarrassing to the council officers, came to an unpredictable end on 30 July 1757, when Leoni fired two pistol shots at a real or supposed "opponent" (and missed).[69] Arrested, tried and condemned, he was expelled from the guild by decree of the head of the Senate.[70]

The time now seemed ripe to reform the abuses of the shoemakers' guild. The senators and the Assunteria, however, were turning to a more ambitious and comprehensive strategy. Instead of reforming one guild and then another, in response to pressure from the masters, these two municipal bodies planned to reform all the guilds at the same time. The scheme, put forward in its entirety in 1761, dealt with four main issues: (1) a reduction in the number of guilds; (2) the appointment of "assistants" from the Senate to take part in guild meetings; (3) the pooling of all guild revenues; and (4) a reform of relations between the masters (*obbedienti*) and their respective guilds.[71] The project, which was similar to plans for the reform of guilds in various states of enlightened Europe, dragged on for a number of years and was eventually abandoned.

The master shoemakers, disillusioned with the turn of events and dissatisfied with the leadership of Mingardi and Pignoni, decided to convene a meeting in 1766, in the Church of Santa Maria della Morte, in order to ask Mingardi (Pignoni having died) for an explanation "of what he had done." In requesting permission from the Senate to hold the meeting, the shoemakers asserted that since 1749, the year of their first meeting, malpractices had multiplied rather than diminished, "because since that time until the present day" there had

68 Ibid., xvii, no. 45, *Informazione del Dott. Angelo Panelli ... sopra il ricorso fatto*, 5 July 1756. See also ibid., *Risposta a giustificazione dell'Arte dei Calzolai ... circa la legittimità dell'aggregazione di Antonio Leoni*, 2 September 1756.

69 A.S.B., Tribunale del Torrone, Filza no. 8187 (1756–7), fasc. 66, pt. 2, deposition of Sante Negrini, 30 July 1757. The shots were fired in the leather shop of Giuseppe Tomba, who had denounced Leoni for not settling a debt of 900 lire. As the proprietor was not there, Leoni fired his pistol at Tomba's helper, Sante Negrini.

70 A.S.B., Arti, Misc., xix, no. 74, *Memoriale di Antonio Leoni calzolaio al Senato per ottenere di essere mantenuto e reintegrato*, 5 June 1764.

71 A.S.B., Arti, Atti, Reg. 9, 10 February 1761, fo. 124^{r-v}.

been a considerable increase in the number of unqualified masters, "causing notable damage to the rest of them, because given the number of masters, they were unable to bear the burden of 4 lire for the annual *obbedienza* fee."[72]

What happened at the meeting is not known. In defense of his leadership, Giuseppe Mingardi wrote a short poem of 202 verses in *terza rima* which was sent to the Assunteria on behalf of the masters.[73] The poem repeated the accusations against the council members, who were guilty:

> of accepting masters
> Who know not how to use either awl or cutting knife;
>
> of considering:
>
> Two paper models, and a gold coin
> ... a sufficient test
> To obtain a master's license;
>
> of having used their power:
>
> ... to cultivate the vice
> Of living only from the sweat of others
> And not for common decency or advantage.
>
> Justice and charity required that the annual fee, deemed "insufferable," be reduced and that only those with an adequate apprenticeship be allowed to take the mastership test:
>
> Ten years should be the time
> That apprentices spend as journeymen
> And to these the license should not be denied.

In his poem Mingardi did not request that the masters be represented on the guild council. Instead he voiced an even bolder political aspiration: an alliance between masters and senators against the corrupt and incompetent oligarchy,

72 A.S.B., Arti, Misc., xx, no. 54, *Memoriale degli obbedienti calzolai all'Assunteria d'Arti*, 14 April 1766.

73 Ibid., no. 56, *Giuseppe Mingardi assonto degli obbedienti calzolai a piè di Felsina di lui madre: canzone*, 21 April 1766. Mingardi had probably read some passages from the Divine Comedy.

the guild council. Praising the Senate as a judicial body, Mingardi expressed his desire for a judgment in favor of the masters. This hope was sustained by the idea that there still survived among members of the urban elite:

> The love to preserve the just laws
> That are embodied in statutes.

The poem then depicted the Senate assembled as a tribunal in the "invisible" presence of "the king of kings." This tribunal, Mingardi maintained:

> To the shame of the guilty, exalts the just;
> Here they follow in the footsteps of Augustus Caesar …
> Here, in the end, they carry out what God commands.

This apologetic exhortation then underwent a sudden change in tone and concluded with the assertion, amounting to a warning, that God requires of princes and judges that "justice be rendered rapidly to the poor, who with reason request it against the powerful and the unjust."[74]

The Assunteria's reply was not long in coming; the masters were asked to present their arguments "in prose rather than in verse."[75] This cutting and sarcastic answer was uncalled for, especially if we consider the intense debate of the previous years. The shoemakers (*obbedienti*) did not respond, and they apparently disappeared from the public scene.

One of the masters' earliest demands reappeared about seventeen years later, although in a more restricted form, now significantly presented by the head of the guild. In an application dated January 1782 to the Assunteria, he called for a ruling against those masters who managed more than one shop.[76] After a discussion lasting several months, a Senato Consulto ordered that any master shoemaker "who had several shoemaking shops" had to place at the head of each "a master approved by the guild."[77] This regulation, which applied only to shops that were physically separate, increased the burden of the *obbedienza* on the larger producers and helped to guarantee the employment of masters willing to work as wage employees. We do not know the circumstances that led the guild council to raise this issue. Nevertheless, the council's

74 Ibid.

75 A.S.B., Arti, Atti, Reg. 10 (1766–77), 28 April 1766, fo. 6^v.

76 Ibid., Reg. 12 (1782–4), Jan. 1782, fo. 3; 18 February 1782, fo. 13.

77 A. S. B., Archivio del Legato, Bandi, *Notificazione sopra le botteghe di calzolaio*, 8 July 1782.

application is evidence of a process of concentration of production, the intensity and character of which we cannot yet judge, given the limited amount of documentation so far available for the second half of the eighteenth century. A later and isolated attempt to revive another demand, made at the beginning of the conflict, occurred in 1787, in the petition of a master shoemaker, A. Tabarini. Complaining of the continued "disorders" in the guild, Tabarini asked the Assunteria if he might be appointed "assistant" to the guild council (following the pattern of the silk-weaving guild) in order to represent the interests of the masters. His request was not heeded.[78]

The discourse which the masters used to attack the guild council, as indeed that which the guild oligarchy employed in its defense, was constructed in such a way as to pass over in silence a significant and perhaps fundamental part of the issue under discussion. This silence, which the Assunteria also observed, enabled these two groups of shoemakers – masters and guild council – to dominate the conflict. The actual situation, however, was more complex. The demands that the masters made to the guild council – tougher examinations, a lengthy apprenticeship, membership on the examining board – pursued an objective which, while absent from their explicit discourse, was of primary importance: to reinforce their control over apprentices and journeymen in the workplace. More difficult tests as well as lengthier and more demanding periods of apprenticeship would bolster the master's authority, restoring to him a role that the guild council's loose practices had weakened.

Steven Kaplan has perceptively shown all the difficulties that beset apprentice bakers in Paris on their "Road to Mastership."[79] It would appear that for apprentice shoemakers in Bologna this "road" was not quite so arduous. The defeat of the masters – and hence the weakening of corporate privilege – may have dampened frictions in a strategic area of social conflict. The prospect of a short apprenticeship and the lowering of entrance requirements may have taken the sting out of relations between masters and those under their charge, even if it created other tensions.

Regrettably, the sources I have used do not permit me to reconstruct the ways in which apprentices and journeymen perceived and took part in this conflict, and how they reacted to the concentration of production in large workshops. Like their French counterparts, the journeymen of Bologna formed

---

78 A.S.B., Arti, Atti, Reg. 14 (1787–9), 26 November 1787, fo. 73^{r-v}.

79 S. Kaplan, *The Bakers of Paris and the Bread Question, 1700–1775* (Durham, 1996), pp. 271–301 and *La fin des corporations* (Paris, 2001), pp. 241–250.

a "cabal," and held clandestine meetings against the masters.[80] The little evidence that we have of these meetings does not, however, relate to shoemakers. It would doubtless be valuable to see how apprentices and journeymen, especially those working in larger workshops, voiced their needs and interests in response to the arguments of the masters.

4 Conclusion

The disputes between the various craft groups examined in this article were settled by applying existing rules (statutes, orders, proclamations) or by drafting new rules to address new problems. These rules, unlike the norms of "good manners," were binding. Yet they were sufficiently flexible and inconsistent to allow for a variety of interpretations, and they could be bent and distorted in the defense of the interests in dispute.[81] Initially the principle of reciprocal obligations, for example, was used to the detriment of the rural shoemakers, who then adopted its terms in a compromise designed to ward off the attack against them.

Amid all the strategies of defense and attack, the jurists played a vital role. The craft groups involved in disputes frequently turned to the legal profession for assistance. The Assunteria also employed lawyers as consultants. These intellectuals, who were numerous in Bologna owing to the reputation of the city's university for the study of law, were entrusted with the task of giving legal form to the rights of the parties in conflict while following procedures that had evolved from past practice.[82]

80 S. Kaplan, "Réflexions sur la police du monde du travail, 1700–1815," *Revue historique*, cclxi (1979), 30–43. On the conflicts between master shoemakers and their journeymen in eighteenth-century Germany, see A. Griessinger and R. Reith, "Obrigkeitliche Ordnungskonzeptionen und Handwerkliches Konfliktverhalten im18. Jahrhundert: Nürnberg und Würzburg im Vergleich," *Deutsches Handwerk* in *Spätmittelalter und Früher Neuzeit*, ed. R. S. Elkar (Göttingen,1987), pp. 117–180.

81 These formulations are close to those of R. Chartier, "Culture as Appropriation: Popular Culture Uses in Early Modern France," *Understanding Popular Culture*, ed. Kaplan, pp. 230–53; and of J. Revel, "Forms of Expertise: Popular Culture in France, 1650–1800," *ibid.*, pp. 255–273. But there is one qualification. In my opinion the reading of a text constitutes a further text. The dialogue is not therefore between one text and its reading but between one text and another.

82 Anthropologists, political scientists and sociologists have greatly contributed to the development of a corpus of literature on conflicts and their settlement. See,

Did lawyers act as the spokesmen for their clients? Or did they tend to impose their own categories of thought, their own discourse on those of the shoemakers? Ever since the statutes had been compiled, legal language had penetrated the world of work; crafts and guilds had learned how to manipulate this language. Against this background of cultural contacts between artisans and legal experts, the lawyers wrote their reports for the political authorities and drafted the shoemakers' petitions, endowing the artisans' demands with the clarity and order characteristic of legal discourse. Of course, jurists also pursued their own interests, both as individuals and as a social group. The question which remains unanswered is how far they succeeded in exploiting social and work conflicts to perpetuate and increase the power of legal practices, and thus to supplement their own prestige and wealth. The sources, and their interpretations, do not reveal any friction or rifts between the groups in conflict and their legal representatives. They suggest that jurists did not in fact alter the character of the disputes they were called upon to translate into legal language.[83] Their discourse was straightforward and free from erudite quotations. They brought a practical frame of mind to real-life situations. The artisans, in turn, appropriated legal arguments for their own defense. This transfer of discourse was facilitated by the fact that the artisans could hear in the lawyers' legal language the echo of their own voice – of their rights, their demand for justice. The identity and the culture of work of the different groups of shoemakers, as well as their awareness of their respective status, were continually shaped through intense dialogues that were at once horizontal and vertical. The disputes between city and rural shoemakers, between shoemakers and cobblers, and between the masters and the guild leaders had the effect of strengthening and sharpening their group and individual identities. And their relations with learned legal circles reinforced their sense of their rights.[84]

---

for example: P. H. Gulliver, *Disputes and Negotiations: A Cross Cultural Perspective* (New York, 1979); S. Roberts, *Order and Dispute* (Harmondsworth, 1979); idem., "The Study of Dispute: Anthropological Perspectives," *Disputes and Settlements: Law and Human Relations in the West*, ed. J. Bossy, (Cambridge, 1983), pp. 1–24; *Private Interest Government: Beyond Market and State*, eds. W. Streek and P. C. Schmitter (London, 1985).

83 On relations between work and law, see M. Sonenscher, "Journeymen, the Courts and the French Trades, 1781–1791," *Past and Present*, vol. 114, no. 1 (1987), 77–109. I agree with Sonenscher on a number of essential points. But there are various differences. In particular I do not accept the separation between high legal culture and the culture of work.

84 In a recent discussion on the political militancy of the artisans in the first half of the nineteenth century, J. Rancière stressed that the shoemakers' trade was seen as a "maligned"

Doubtless not every individual shoemaker was aware of the privileges of the trade. It is probably reasonable to suppose that members of the guild council had greater knowledge than the simple masters, that master shoemakers knew more than the cobblers, and that city shoemakers were better informed than those in rural areas. But they all possessed some degree of knowledge, all defended themselves, attacked, invoked rules, and engaged in struggle. They all knew how to secure the assistance of a lawyer, provided they had the money to pay for his services.[85] Clashes were preceded or followed by genuine compromises or fake reconciliations. Open conflicts were interlaced with clandestine activities or concealed patterns of behavior that infringed various norms. But these infringements were often felt to be morally justified. Shoemakers repaired old shoes, cobblers manufactured new ones, rural shoemakers undertook fine

---

one, both "within the literate as well as the popular tradition"; J. Rancière, "A Reply," *International Labor and Working-Class History,* no. 25, 1984, p. 46. Bolognese sources do not confirm this impression. In 1453 when all the heads of the twenty-four guilds were invited to approve and confirm the new statutes of the city, the head of the shoemakers' guild, Jacobo Bartolomeo, signed thirteenth after notaries and money-changers but before carpenters, painters, tailors and masons (*Statuta civilia civitatis Bononiae* [Bologna, 1532], fo. 95v). According to the lawyer Alessandro Machiavelli (in the second half of the eighteenth century), the shoemakers, who had shown their political ability more than once, were "honorable" and "valuable" (Biblioteca dell'Archivio di Stato di Bologna, MS. D.b.vii.3, A. Machiavelli, "Discorso sopra le Arti Collegiate della città di Bologna, del loro pregio e valore e del modo di esercitarle senza denigrare la nobiltà dei natali"). The view of Tommaso Garzoni (from Bagnacavallo) was more realistic and more complex. He condemned the tricks of shoemakers who, he alleged, sold sheepskin as calfskin and passed off reworked down-at-heel shoes for brand-new ones! But he acknowledged that the shoemakers' swindling, like their poverty, was "common ... to all the sorts of people who serve others." He recognized that they were "upright men and honorable because they are Christians like everybody else, excepting when a cobbler seeks to discourse on holy writ – which suits his mouth as well as a beret suits a donkey's head" (T. Garzoni, *La piazza universale di tutte le professioni del mondo* [Venice, 1589]), p. 824. In other words, the accusation was that cobblers strayed beyond the realms of their craft and that they passed judgment on things about which they knew nothing. This amounted to a version of the proverb "Ne sutor ultra crepidam judicet" ("a shoemaker should not judge beyond the shoe"), a charge that could also have been levelled at the militant shoemakers of the nineteenth century.

85 Those historians who analyze the ways in which rural communities turned to civil tribunals to defend their privileges and rights are engaged in the same current of rediscovery of legal sources. Until now this ground has been neglected in favor of investigation into more dramatic events such as peasant revolts and wars.

work. It is in this dense texture of social experience, in this thick "plurivocality" that the cultures of work took shape.[86]

86 M. Bakhtin, "Discourse in the Novel," *The Dialogic Imagination: Four Essays*, ed. M. Holquist, trans. C. Emerson, M. Holquist (Austin, 1981), pp. 259–422. The notion of "plurivocality" – which does not exclude the concept of domination – seems to me the most effective conceptual instrument for an understanding of the exchanges between different social groups.

CHAPTER 6

Local Market Rules and Practices: Three Guilds in the Same Line of Production in Early Modern Bologna

Carlo Poni

This study proposes to reconstruct the relations between butchers, tanners and shoemakers (three trades which were also guilds) in early modern Bologna, a relatively large city of around 60,000 inhabitants.[1] The three guilds were linked together by the trading of skins. The tanners bought the already flayed ox, cow and calf hides from the butchers and tanned them to make leathers that were then sold to the shoemakers to make shoes.

While the flayed hides deteriorated rapidly in quality, the leathers lasted longer, although they too lost their value quickly once they became too dry. Both the hides and the leathers were intermediate products in the same line of production. This peculiarity, common to many goods, creates special relationships between individual firms in the different phases of the production process. These production relationships are essentially mediated by the market: semi-manufactured goods are bought, transformed and resold, and are then subject to other transformations and transactions before finally reaching the consumer market. Such an organization of these relationships can be replaced by the verticalization of several phases in the production process within a single firm or conglomerate (internal organization).

1 In 1569, the population of Bologna was over 60,000 and in the period 1581–87 levelled out at between 70,000 and 72,000. It then dropped in the years of scarcity from 1591 to 1594 and fell in 1595 to 58,900, to rise again above the 60,000 mark in 1597. It then maintained this level until the plague year of 1630 when it collapsed to around 45,000. It was only in 1660 that it reached 60,000 again. In the course of the eighteenth century the population rose slowly to reach around 70,000 inhabitants and remained at this level from 1771 to 1791, to fall again during the years of French domination (A. Bellettini, *La Popolazione di Bologna dal secolo XV all'unificazione italiana* [Bologna, 1961], pp. 24–32).Weights and measures: the Bolognese *libbra* was equal to 0.369 kg. The Bolognese *lira* was made up of 20 *soldi*, each of 12 *denari*; or 20 *bolognini* of 7 *quattrini* each. *Soldi* and *bolognini* were equal in value, the *denaro* being valued at only 58 per cent of the *quattrino*.

 | DOI:10.1163/9789004713277_008

But these organizational modes of production have specific costs, as has been pointed out in the work of some economists.[2] There are, for example, particular costs regarding internal management – the monitoring and assessment of the performance of the sectors and phases operating within a single firm. Choosing a "spot" market (a market for immediate delivery) also has costs, those of market research and the negotiation of prices, quality and the desired flow of goods. These potentially high costs can be reduced by recourse to long-term contracts with clauses guaranteeing quality, quantity, price and delivery times, to be negotiated periodically. If the goods are perishable, there is even more reason to make use of such contracts in order to decrease risks and costs, the alternative being the internalization of production within a single firm. With the help of these analytical tools, rather summarily outlined above, I will attempt to examine the market relationship among the three guilds, butchers, tanners and shoemakers, in seventeenth- and eighteenth-century Bologna, in light of certain questions which the new institutional economists have raised with regard to the dilemmas and strategic choices facing the contemporary business world.[3]

Obviously the attempt to apply such notions in a context very different from that in which they were produced must be viewed with some caution. I have used them with discretion and only when I have wanted to provide particular conceptual precision. Nevertheless, words are not stones, and those used here are also conditioned by the context in which they appear. The initial inspiration for this research came from a long and passionate familiarity with the work of Marcel Mauss and Karl Polanyi, and in particular with concepts such as "reciprocal obligations" and "market embedded in society."[4] The archival

2 Studies on the different forms of production organization ("new institutional economics") are closely tied to the work of O.E. Williamson. See *Market and Hierarchies: Analysis and Antitrust Implications* (New York, 1975); *The Economic Institutions of Capitalism: Firms, Markets, Relational Contracting* (New York, 1985); *Economic Organization: Firms, Markets and Policy Control* (Brighton, 1986). See also *Power, Efficiency and Institutions. A Critical Appraisal of the Markets and Hierarchies Paradigm*, eds. A. Francis, J. Turk and P. Willman (London, 1983); *The Economics of the Firm*, eds. R. Clarke and T. McGuinness (Oxford, 1987). A good review of this literature is provided by E. Rullani, "Economia delle Transazioni e Informazioni: Saggio sulla Nuova Teoria Economica dell'Organizzazione," *Annali dell'Impresa*, no. 2 (1986), 9–17.

3 A similar operation, although with larger interpretative ambitions, was carried out by D.C. North in his *Structure and Change in Economic History* (New York, 1981). See also by the same author, "Markets and Other Allocation Systems in History: the Challenge of Karl Polanyi," *Journal of European Economic History*, 6 (1977), 703–716, and "Transaction Costs in History," *Journal of European Economic History*, 14 (1985), 557–576.

4 M. Mauss, "Essai sur le Don," *L'Année Sociologique* (Paris, 1924–5) (reprinted in M. Mauss, *Sociologie et anthropologie* [Paris, 1960]); K. Polanyi, *The Great Transformation* (New York 1957); *Trade and Market in the Early Empires,* eds. K. Polanyi, C.M. Arensberg and H.W.

sources which I have examined would have remained silent had it not been for their insights and hypotheses. The final text is thus a compromise between different methodologies. This has resulted in some ambiguities and imbalances – but perhaps also in a certain creative tension. The history of trades and guilds in the early modern period has been enriched by scholarly research and may provide a key to understanding whole sets of institutions, rules and behavior in the Ancien Regime.[5]

Pearson 19834 (Glencoe, 1957). It is almost superfluous to refer to E. P. Thompson's seminal article, "The Moral Economy of the English Crowd in the Eighteenth Century," *Past and Present,* vol. 50, no. 1 (1971), 76–136.

5 S. Kaplan, "Réflexions sur la Police du Monde du Travail, 1700–1815," *Revue Historique,* 263, 1979, 17–77; W. H. Sewell, *Work and Revolution* in *France* (Cambridge 1980); A. Griessinger, *Das symbolische Kapital der Ehre: Streikbewegungen und Kollektives Bewusstsein deutscher Handwerksgesellen im18. Jahrhundert* (Frankfurt-on-Main, Berlin and Vienna, 1981); *Deutsches Handwerk* in *Spätmittelalter und Früher Neuzeit,* ed. Rainer S. Elkar (Göttingen, 1983); A. Black, *Guilds and Civil Society in European Political Thought from the Twelfth Century to the Present* (Ithaca, 1984); M. Sonenscher, "Journeymen, the Courts and the French Trades, 1781–1791," *Past and Present,* vol. 114, no. 1 (1987), 77–109; *Economia e corporazioni. II governo degli interessi nella storia d'Italia dal Medioevo all'età contemporanea,* ed. C. Mozzarelli (Milan, 1988); "Corps et Communautés d'Ancien Régime," a collection of articles introduced by J. Revel, in *Annales E.S.C.,* vol. 43, no. 2 (1988), 295–451; R. Reith, "Zur beruflichen Sozialisation im Handwerk vom 18. bis ins frühe 20. Jahrhundert," *Vierteljahrschrift für Social- und Wirtschaftsgeschichte,* 76 (1), 1989, 1-27, and the important German bibliography listed in that work. On the Bolognese guilds in the early modern period see L. Gheza Fabbri, "Le Adunanze Segrete dei Carpentieri Bolognesi (1573–1574)," *Atti della Accademia delle Scienze dell'lstituto di Bologna. Classe di scienze morali. Rendiconti,* 1978–9, 32–44, "Drappieri, Strazzaroli e Zavagli: una Compagnia Bolognese tra il XVI e il XVIII Secolo," *Il Carrobbio,* 4 (1980), 163–180, and *L'Organizzazione del lavoro* in *una economia urbana. Le Società d'Arti a Bologna nei secoli XVI e XVII* (Bologna, 1988); M. Fanti, *I Macellai bolognesi. Mestiere, politica e vita civile nella storia di una categoria attraverso i secoli* (Bologna, 1980); G. Tamba, "Da Socio a Obbediente. La Società dei Muratori dall'Età Comunale al 1796," *Muratori a Bologna. Arte e società dalle origini al secolo XVII I* (Bologna, 1981), pp. 43–156; A. Guenzi, *Pane e fornai a Bologna in età moderna* (Venice, 1982), "La Carne Bovina: Consumi, Prezzi e Controllo Sociale nella Citta di Bologna (Sec. XVII e XVIII)," *Popolazione ed economia dei territori bolognesi durante il Settecento* (Bologna, 1985), pp. 537–51, *La Fabbrica delle tele tra città e campagna. Gruppi professionali e governo dell' economia a Bologna nel secolo XVII,* (Ancona, 1988) and *La Tessitura femminile tra città e campagna a Bologna nei secoli XVII e XVIII* (Bologna, 1988); F. Giusberti, "La 'Ruga delle Pescherie' de Bologne au XVIIIème Siècle: Conflits et Transactions," *Annales E.S.C.,* no. 2, 1983, 401–408; M. Fornasari, "II Padre della Fame è la Fatica: l'Ascesa Sociale di un Notaio Bolognese nel '500," *Il Carrobbio,* 13 (1976). [See also in this volume, chaps. 5 and 7.]

1 Transactions between Tanners and Shoemakers

Shoemakers in Bologna did not have the right to tan the leather they needed. The leather that they cut and sewed could be tanned only by members of the tanners' guild.[6] The tanners, in turn, did not have the right to make shoes.[7] While the tanners' guild possessed a monopoly of the preparation and sale of hides, the shoemakers had no absolute monopoly over demand to match the tanners' monopoly of supply. Yet they were the most significant buyers of tanned hides (the other buyers being coach makers, glove makers and saddlers) and were able to make use of certain juridical devices in order to control the market and thus guarantee the supply of raw material that they required. In principle at least, each shoemaker had to limit his purchases, calculating them on the basis of his shop's requirements. All the leather he purchased had to be used to make shoes. He did not have the right to resell leather, a measure which prevented the speculative resale of the finest leather, the poorest quality leathers remaining for shoe production.[8]

This network of dependence and compensation guaranteed a system of reciprocal obligation, although it neither set nor indicated the prices at which goods were to be sold. The prices of tanned hides and leather were negotiated from time to time according to procedures established during the sixteenth century, if not earlier. In principle, the rates for tanned hides were negotiated by representatives of the two guilds. If no agreement could be reached, as in

6 The Bolognese tanners were in fact divided into three guilds: the *pellacani,* the *callegari* and the *cartolai.* In principle only the *pellacani* – the richest guild with most members – had the right to tan ox, cow and calf hides; I use the word "tanners" to refer to this group alone. The *callegari* had the right to tan the hides of small animals (goats, sheep, etc.) and on request also a small number of calf hides. The *cartolai* also only had the right to finish those hides which were the monopoly of the *callegari.* There were frequent conflicts between these three guilds, despite the fact that some of the members of the *pellacani* were also members of the *callegari* and/or the *cartolai.* This conflict will not be considered here. At the end of the eighteenth century the three guilds were combined, after protracted negotiations, to form a single guild of *callegari.* Unless otherwise specified, I use the word "tanners" to indicate the master-shopkeepers and not journeymen, and "leathers" to indicate both types of leather produced: sole leather made from ox and cow hides and upper leather made from calf hides.

7 See the *Statuti dei Pellacani,* in the Archivio di Stato di Bologna (hereafter A.S.B.), *Assunteria Arti* (hereafter Arti), *Notizie attinenti a l'Arte dei Pellacani,* vol. I. The reciprocal exclusion, already present in the statutes of the sixteenth century, was confirmed in the statutes of the shoemakers' guild. See *Statuti et Ordini della onoranda Compagnia et Arte de' Calzolai della città di Bologna* (Bologna 1721), p. 64.

8 Ibid.

1612, 1654 and 1659, the two sides requested the intervention of the authorities.[9] They appealed directly to the Cardinal Legate, the representative of the papal government, who would then appoint one of the judges of his court to act as arbitrator.[10] The talks between representatives of tanners and shoemakers would be granted a hearing before the judge. After listening to both sides, crossexamining the consulting experts and accountants, the judge would close the debate with a decree fixing the new price list. This decision, although it took the form of a decree, was not final. If one of the parties was not satisfied with the decision, it had the right to appeal and to present new arguments in its favor.

In March 1659, for example, the representatives of the shoemakers' guild called for a reduction in the price of leathers in the light of the decrease in the "price of materials [principally gall] used to tan and perfect leather."[11] The tanners opposed this request, claiming that "the prices of hides from which leather is made" had risen greatly and outweighed the reduction in the price of the materials. The judge, Giuliano Laureti, appointed by the Cardinal Legate to arbitrate in the dispute, presented his decision on 15 March 1659 in favor of the shoemakers. He rejected the arguments of the tanners on the grounds that all previous decisions on the matter had been based on the price of the materials used for tanning, and that the price of leather must increase or decrease

---

9 *Decretum differentiarum in causa et materia pretii coraminum facta per Excellentiss. Dom. Herculem Rangonem Judicem, die 14 januarii 1612* (Bologna, 1634); A. Papinio, *Decreto in data 19 ottobre 1654 che stabilisce li prezzi dei corami in sequito di lite insorta fra le Società dei Pellacani e quella dei Calzolai* (Bologna, n.d.); G. Laureti, *Decreto in data 17 marzo 1659 che stabilisce li prezzi dei corami in sequito di vertenza insorta fra la Compagnia de' Calzolai e l'altra dei Pellacani* (Bologna, n.d.); G. Laureti, *Decreto in data 15 maggio 1659 che modifica l'altro del 17 marzo ... del prezzo dei corami e in ciò ad istanza della Compagnia dei Pellacani contro quella dei Calzolari* (Bologna, n.d.). The decree of Ercole Rangone can be found in A.S.B., Arti, *Notizie attinenti l'Arte ... dei Pellacani,* vol. I. The other three decrees are preserved in the Bibliotcca Comunale del'Archiginnasio (hereafter BCAB) and are cited with the title indicated in the catalogue of the library. Between 1600 and 1660, the price of leather had been fixed by decree on at least two other occasions, once by Judge Scipione Beneduccio (sometime before 1612 according to Judge G. Rangone), and once by Judge Francesco Panighi on 14 September 1634 (cited by G. Laureti).

10 The Cardinal Legate represented the sovereign, the Pope. The head of the diocese was the archbishop. On the institutional structure of the *governo misto* of Bologna, see "L'Ordinamento Bolognese dei secoli XVI–XVII: lo stato, il governo e i magistrate di Bologna del Cavalier Ciro Spontone, edizione del MS. B. 1114 della Biblioteca dell'Archiginnasio," 2 vols., *Archiginnasio,* ed. S. Verardi Ventura, nos. 74, 1979 and 75, 1981.

11 The story which follows comes from G. Laureti, *Decreto in data 17 marzo 1659* (no page numbers).

in relation to fluctuations in the price of the materials.[12] Because the price of the materials had fallen from "110 *lire* per thousand *libbre*" to "80 lire· per thousand *libbre*" since the price of leather had been set in 1654, the judge ordered a reduction in the price of various types of leather by nine *quattrini* per *libbra*. This decrease applied to all the fourteen different types of skins and leather, regardless of variations in the quantity of materials used and their incidence on the costs of production, the assumption being that the prices (and thus the gains and losses) would balance out. The decree not only fixed the new prices, it also reproduced, almost to the letter, the regulations governing relations between shoemakers and tanners that had been incorporated into the 1612 price agreement (decreed by Judge Ercole Rangone). These regulations stipulated the quality of the product and set out punctilious procedures for ensuring the supply of leather, something which naturally favored the interests of the shoemakers.

In particular, the tanners were required to produce leather that was "dry, seasoned and properly conditioned ... experience having shown that leather is often sold damp and sodden to the detriment of shoemakers and of the public." The head of the tanners' guild had to supply the head of the shoemakers' guild with a precise list of "all the quantities of fresh hides" that the tanners had bought from the butchers, as well as of all the leathers "heated up" (that is, prepared) daily, with the name of the tanner who had processed the skins. The tanners could cut only half of each tanned hide, leaving the other half intact throughout "the whole of the following day," so that it might be sold "in one piece at the pleasure of the shoemakers and distributed in accordance with the orders of the heads of the said shoemakers." Lastly, tanners were prohibited from hoarding skins "in a way prejudicial to the shoemakers' guild."

The tanners' guild, dissatisfied with the decree, immediately appealed to the Cardinal Legate, arguing that the decrease of nine *quattrini* was out of proportion to the drop in the price of the materials. They asked for a "revised calculation." The Cardinal Legate accepted their request because, he declared, everyone is entitled to have "his just due."[13] Judge Laureti then reconvened the representatives of the two guilds and together with them appointed two accountants. The calculations were reviewed and after several meetings "a common consensus" was reached on 15 May 1659: the price would be lowered by eight *quattrini* instead of nine. The difference of one *quattrino* was a

---

12 This principle was reaffirmed in an agreement signed by the two guilds in 1647, mentioned in A.S.B., Tribuni della Plebe e Collegio delle Arti (hereafter Tribuni), Atti, Libra Giallo, IV, 1647–70, 6 May 1648, fo. 76.

13 G. Laureti, *Decreto in data 15 maggio che modifica l'altro del 17 marzo* (no page numbers).

miniscule gain for the tanners. More important for them was the elimination of all the punctilious rules in favor of the shoemakers, leaving only the one that guaranteed the quality of leather.

This brief sequence of events highlights the existence of a decision-making process aimed at obtaining the agreement of the parties concerned. In principle the corporations set the price of leather, and the political authorities intervened to arbitrate only when the two sides failed to reach agreement.

Another body which in some cases acted as arbitrator between the shoemakers and the tanners was the Tribuni della Plebe e Collegio della Arti, a magistrates' court whose responsibility was to check the quality and prices of foodstuffs and other consumer goods such as leathers and shoes.[14] One such intervention took place in 1648 when, with the two guilds in conflict, the magistrates advised them to nominate two experts who would be responsible for fixing the price of the leathers.[15] In 1671 these same Tribuni, adopting a decision that was better suited to their institutional role, claimed, apparently for the first time, the right to fix the price of leather in the name of a political and moral principle: the "public good" and the "benefit of the poor."[16] According to the Tribuni, those judges charged by the Cardinal Legate with the settling of disputes "between shoemakers and tanners with regard to the price of leather" had to conform to earlier procedures. But the Tribuni could intervene on their own initiative to lower the price of leather, and consequently of shoes, in favor of the poor (a concept not openly expressed in the preceding negotiations). Neither Judge Laureti nor any other judge could impose rules on the Tribuni, who had to act according to their own norms. The Tribuni alone, free from outside interference, could decide whether or not to examine production costs before fixing new prices, and whether or not to accept objections from a contesting guild.

With these assertions the Tribuni intended to introduce new norms that contrasted with traditional practices and that would justify their intervention,

---

14 The Tribuni were made up of representatives of the twenty-one official guilds and eight citizens representing the four sections of the city, nominated every two months and serving on a rotating basis. They were secondary courts attended only by one judge and a notary. See V. Sacco, *Istruzione per li Signori Gonfalonieri del Popolo o Tribuni della Plebe ed onorandi Massari delle Arti* (Bologna 1740).

15 A.S.B., Tribuni, Atti, Libro Giallo.

16 For the arguments used by the Tribuni to justify their interventions, see A.S.B., Tribuni, Atti, Libro Rosso, V, 21 July 1671, fo. 39^{v} and 21 August 1671, fos. 40–1. According to the jurist Vincenzo Sacco, the Tribuni should not have "only the relief of the poor at heart" but also the "earnings of the artisan-shopkeeper which must serve to maintain his ... family" (V. Sacco, *Istruzione,* p. 48).

unsolicited by either the tanners or the shoemakers. In practice, however, they applied rules similar to those used by previous arbitrators, which Judge Laureti had confirmed. In the first few months of 1671, the price of gall fell from eighty to sixty-two lire per thousand *libbre*. In consequence of this decrease in price, the Tribuni authorized new rates that also reduced the price of leather by eight *quattrini* per *libbra*. The price of "black lustrous leather" alone was left unchanged in response to the tanners' request. Why was the shoemakers' guild silent on this occasion? According to Giacomo de Cavalariis, a former tanner turned informant for the Tribuni against his own guild, "the reason the shoemakers don't appeal to the magistracy to lower the price of leather … is that, if they did, the tanners would stop giving them credit."[17] This information sheds light on the economic relations between the tanners and the shoemakers. The procedures to set quality and prices may be looked upon as devices for defending a weak and poor craft against one that was richer and more powerful. The tanners, not more than twenty in number, also enjoyed a strong oligopolistic position in supplying the market in comparison to the demand that arose from several hundred shoemakers and cobblers.[18]

How the tanners responded to this second price reduction is not known. They may have lowered the quality of the materials they used, and hence of the end product, in order to reduce production costs, as some sources seem to indicate. On 12 April 1703, the Tribuni gave their support to the "many complaints and protests of the poor purchasers [the shoemakers] who buy … leather that is of such low quality that before long it is worn out, and this is because the tanners have been processing the fresh hides with bark and not with the gall that has been used since time immemorial, bark being very harmful." The Tribuni seemed inclined to prohibit, "in the name of the public good and for the benefit of the poor," the production of "similar goods that are harmful to all persons and of profit only to those who make them." They appointed a commission of inquiry that included representatives of the tanners' and shoemakers' guilds. Its task was to gather information about the "quality of … leathers tanned with bark and of that tanned using gall, and the differences between them." But the

17 De Cavalariis' testimony was given on 13 August 1671 (A.S.B., Tribuni fos. 42–42v). De Cavalariis also gave the Tribuni calculations on the production costs of tanning, which were unfavorable to the tanners but which could not be used as they were inconclusive.

18 It could hardly be said, however, that the tanners were in a flourishing condition in 1671. They were just beginning to climb out of a deep crisis which had begun in 1637 when they lost their near-exclusive monopoly of the right to tan the coarse hides. According to the Tribuni, in 1671 "numerous butchers" were also tanning hides (A.S.B., Tribuni, Atti, Libro Rosso, v, 21 August 1671,fo. 41).

commission not only inquired into the quality of goods but also paid particular attention to the cost of production.[19]

The cost of bark, the commission found out, was twenty *lire* per thousand *libbre*, barely a third of that of gall, so that bark had in part replaced gall and lowered the cost of the materials used in tanning by approximately 50 per cent. On 4 May, after hearing the tanners' representatives and considering their calculations, the Tribuni were granted an audience with the Cardinal Legate who praised the "vigilance and zeal" with which they had worked for the "poor and the public." In his presence and with his consent, a new price list was issued set out in two tables. The first of these confirmed the prices fixed in 1671 for skins tanned with gall alone; the second set lower prices for the majority of the leathers, treated with a mixture of bark and gall.[20]

The tanners' guild protested against this decision, claiming that their representatives had not been adequately heard. To broaden the conflict they addressed their pleas to the Cardinal Legate and the Assunteria del Pavaglione, a committee of the city Senate. The hand of their legal advisor may be seen in the language of their petition, which drew on the principles the Tribuni themselves had previously expressed. The tanners argued that the new price rates "rested on causes that were groundless, far removed from justice or equity, and very prejudicial to the public and to private persons." The tanners' guild did not deny that bark cost less than gall, but stated that "when you work with bark and gall, over twice as much is required ... and so there is little difference in cost between the two kinds of materials. Furthermore, since more than twice as much time is needed to treat leather with bark and gall combined than with gall alone, more money is spent on wages for more journeymen and on rent for larger workshops, and capital is left idle for a longer time." They argued that the two ways of treating hides incurred the same costs and also resulted in "the same quality, so that they could scarcely be distinguished, having the same appearance, the same color, the same excellence ... the same degree of perfection, as is well known to the shoemakers, whose job it is to have a proper knowledge of the intrinsic quality of different kinds of leather." Having demonstrated the inconsistency of what they called the "prime causes" for the new rates, they demanded, in conclusion, that the two types of leather should be sold at the same price (that of 1671). The tanners not only highlighted what they saw as the incompetence of the Tribuni; they further charged the court with subordinating the public to the private interest. According to the petition, the

19 A.S.B., Tribuni, Atti, Libro Bianco, VII, fo. 78^{v}.

20 Ibid., 4 May 1703, fos. 85^{v} -86^{v}.

magistrates had been deceived by some of the Tribuni "who favored the rates in question, but who themselves are interested parties because they hoard and speculate in foreign gall [gall was imported from the Levant], and are suspected of promoting their particular interests." The tanners in contrast identified themselves with the public interest. By using bark, the tanners brought profit "to the economy of this city," because those monies that would have been transferred to foreign countries for the purchase of Levantine gall were spent in the territory of Bologna on bark that accumulates in the woods of the region, benefiting the owners of the woods and the workers thus employed.[21]

The tanners' statement, a copy of which the Tribuni obtained from Abbot Buzzetti, "an auditor of the Chamber" of Cardinal Legate d'Adda, struck a hard blow at the honor of the Tribuni. They had good reason to fear that the prices set on 4 May would be withdrawn without their knowledge. They felt they were being accused when Abbot Buzzetti asked them to reply to the tanners' criticisms and to state "their reasons and motives so that the most appropriate and needful resolutions might be reached."[22] But they were reassured by the solidarity of the Assunteria del Pavaglione and the Gonfaloniere (the head of the Senate). Some backstage mediation must have led the tanners to send a conciliatory letter to the Tribuni on 30 May 1703, which entreated them "reverently ... to deign to listen" to their arguments, so that the price of leather might "be lowered by an equitable degree ... without harming the trade."[23] Representatives of the two sides resumed talks, and after a few minor disputes they reached an agreement – with the help of the Cardinal Legate and the Assunteria del Pavaglione. A formal public investigation (*scandaglio*) would be made of the process of production to determine the costs of producing skins tanned with different materials.[24]

This investigation began on 18 August 1703, with a solemn ritual designed to instil trust in public authority among the participants. In the presence of five

21 The tanners' protest is recorded in the registers of the Tribuni (VII, 24 May 1703, fos. 93ᵛ-94). They apparently had already presented a protest to the Assunteria del Pavaglione, although I have not been able to find it. The Assunteria del Pavaglione had authority over the silk-worm cocoon market (called *Pavaglione*), but also had some degree of jurisdiction over the tanners.

22 A.S.B., Tribuni, VII, 22 May 1703, fo. 92ᵛ.

23 Ibid., 30 May 1703, fo. 95ᵛ.

24 During the first meeting with the Tribuni (1 June 1703) the tanners' representatives had promised that they would not use bark in the future so long as they were allowed, as a transitory measure, to sell the leathers already prepared with bark and gall. This request was implicitly rejected, however, by the Gonfaloniere and by the Assunteria del Pavaglione (ibid., fos. 97–97ᵛ). On 3 July 1703, the tariffs of 4 May were suspended.

members of the Tribuni, representatives of the tanners and of the shoemakers, and a notary who recorded the event, six hides (two of good quality, two of medium and two of low quality) were weighed, washed, cleaned, stamped and cut into two parts. The twelve pieces of hide were then passed to three tanners. Six pieces (two of each quality) were given to the tanner Francesco Carlini, who swore on the Bible to process the skins "faithfully and honestly" with gall and bark. The same ritual was repeated on the same day with two other tanners, Tadeo Corticelli and Francesco Pignoni, each of whom was given three pieces of the same qualities as those worked by Carlini. Both took an oath on the Bible that they would process the pieces faithfully, Corticelli with gall alone and Pignoni with gall and myrtle leaves. The investigation ended in March 1704 with a conclusion in favor of the tanners. Several weeks earlier the Tribuni had anticipated this outcome and abolished the rates they had previously introduced.[25]

Some time later, with the creation in the 1730s of the Assunteria al Sollievo delle Arti – a new Senate committee that was granted wide powers of control over the guilds and industrial activities – the Tribuni had to give up a part at least of their right to intervene. On 18 September 1747 the Assunteria al Sollievo delle Arti took the decision to raise the price of leathers, at that time in short supply, because, "having examined the issue ... we think that since leathers are sold in the neighboring towns and villages at higher prices than in Bologna, it is impossible that all the leathers produced in the city remain here, or that one should place hopes in foreign imports."[26]

In the cases examined so far, the interventions by public bodies to fix the price of leather appear to have been motivated by three factors: the desire to solve the conflicts between the two guilds; the wish to defend the needs of the poor, and the need to match the prices of neighboring markets, the reason behind the variations in price being, in at least three cases, a decrease in the

25 The "soundings" ritual (*scandaglio*) is described in ibid., fos. 113–113^{v}. From this source it appears that the *scandaglio* was suspended after six months. From other sources we know that the tanning process lasted a longer period, from twelve to twenty-four months. After being treated with chalk, the hides were unhaired, fleshed and stretched. After this, the real work of tanning began, which ended with the hides being laid in ditches in distinct layers, each layer separated from the others by gall and tanning bark. See F. Griselini, *Dizionario delle Arti e dei Mestieri*, vol. v (Venice, 1769), pp. 179–92. The "soundings" were a normal practice in Bologna and were frequently used to decide upon the cost of making bread and thus the price of bread on sale. See Guenzi, *Pane e fornai a Bologna*, pp. 77–136 and "La Carne-Bovina," pp. 537–551.

26 A.S.B., Arti, Atti, VII, 18 September 1747, fo. 64. This Assunteria was presided over by the Gonfaloniere.

price of the materials. But the shifts in the price scale of leather were also connected to changes in the price of fresh hides, something which is clear from the negotiations that took place from 1771 to 1772, when shoemakers and tanners were initially allied against the butchers.

In late 1770 a rise in the cost of livestock had forced the butchers to demand from the Tribuni a sharp increase in meat prices. Instead, they had to put up with what the Tribuni described as "a very modest" (*discretissimo*) price increase. To make up for their loss, at least to some extent, the butchers had no alternative but to ask for an increase in the price of hides. They faced opposition on this issue from the tanners and shoemakers but were supported by the Tribuni and by the authorities in general. In the course of the discussions between butchers, tanners and shoemakers, the latter were in the weakest position. At first the shoemakers sided with the tanners in an attempt to prevent or limit, in the name of the "just price," the increase requested by the butchers. Once the higher price came into effect, however, the shoemakers were abandoned by the tanners, who tried to pass the increase on to the shoemakers by raising the price of the leathers. The Tribuni conceded this second increase, justifying it with an even-handed argument that sought to take account of the interests of both guilds. In their decision of 26 March 1771 the Tribuni declared: "If the price of leather was fair when the hides cost less, an increase in the price of the said hides, in the absence of a decrease in the other costs involved in tanning, must have as a consequence an increase in the price of leather, provided that it is kept within narrow limits and that it constitutes as slight a burden as possible on the shoemakers and the public, and that the shoemakers obtain satisfaction for their complaints about the poor quality of the leather."[27]

The shoemakers were the only guild that did not accept either price increase. On the day of the decision, the Council of the shoemakers' guild informed the Tribuni that they had further arguments to present, a statement that at least served to postpone the immediate approval of the decision. Invited on several occasions to present their arguments, the shoemakers' guild resorted to delaying tactics.[28] Meanwhile, with a further increase in the cost of materials,

27 A.S.B., Tribuni, Atti, Libro Rosso, XVIII, 26 March 1771, fos. 132-132^{v}. The opposition to raising the price of hides which began on 6 October 1770 continued on 14 and 26 March 1771, when a rise was decided. In short, the prices of the hides could also vary in relation to the price of meat. If meat prices rose, guaranteeing the butchers high earnings, then the price of hides could decrease, as the income of the butchers was based above all on the sale of meat. But if meat prices did not rise to offset increases in the price of livestock, the butchers would attempt to compensate for their loss of earnings (although this compensation could not be adequate) by raising the price of the hides.

28 Ibid., 19 April 1771 (fo. 138); 8 June 1771 (fo. 145); 21 June 1771 (fo. 150).

the prices fixed in March could no longer be maintained. In December 1771, the Tribuni conceded a new "tacit" increase of six *quattrini* per *libbra* on the price of leather (a "tacit" increase did not require the publication of a new list, but only that the written permission be displayed in the shop).[29] On 4 May 1772 the Tribuni set the new rates, explicitly sanctioning the previous increase. The minutes of this final meeting indicate that the shoemakers' arguments were heard several times, but that they had "nothing relevant to add," except to make a request "for the lowest price increase possible."[30]

During these complex negotiations the authorities, it appears, tended to arbitrate patiently between the conflicting parties rather than to impose their own solutions. According to a 1772 report by the tanners, after 1671 there were neither "increases nor decreases in the price of leathers, neither gross nor retail, as the price of the materials and the other costs involved varied only slightly."[31]

The sources consulted contain few distinctive traces of direct negotiations between tanners and shoemakers,[32] The (hopefully) temporary absence of these sources makes it impossible to complete the analysis of the negotiations between the tanners and the shoemakers. But this absence should not affect our understanding of the framework within which the two guilds operated. This can be defined as an institutional bilateral monopoly with a barrier to entry constituted by the rules and practices of guild membership, the necessary requisites being Bolognese citizenship, a three-to-five-year apprenticeship, adulthood, passing the entrance examination and paying a membership fee.[33] Only the tanners had the right to tan ox and cow hides; only the shoemakers (and a few other small groups) had the right to buy the leathers. The price and quality of the goods, on the other hand, were periodically negotiated by the representatives of the two guilds, often in the presence of the authorities, or directly by the authorities themselves who were substitutes, in certain situations, for the transactional autonomy of the guilds.

---

29 Ibid., 23 Dec. 1771, fo. 191^{v}- 192.

30 Ibid ., 4 May 1772, fo. 221. In 1775, the shoemakers tried again to obtain a price reduction (ibid., 23 and 30 March 1775, fos. 440 and 443).

31 A.S.B., Arti, Misc. Arti, XXIII, no. 60, 20 January 1772.

32 All the decrees issued between 1612 and 1659 (see note 9) referred back, more or less explicitly, to direct negotiations which had failed. The notaries had an important role in the life of the guilds, writing and signing the minutes of the councils, as well as all official documents and contracts. Random soundings carried out in the notarial archives – on the assumption the contracts were registered by notaries – have not yet borne fruit.

33 On the difficulties bilateral monopolies may have in operating smoothly, see Williamson, *Economic Organization*, pp. 106–107.

2 Transactions between Butchers and Tanners

From 1581, negotiations between the tanners and the butchers over the price and quality of the flayed skins took place according to the same principle of reciprocal exclusion.

The contracts between the tanners and the butchers also included precise regulations regarding sales procedures. After flaying the skins, the butchers had to put them "on show" without wetting them, "in a dry place and not rolled up together," which in practice meant not in the shop but in an open space, usually nearby. It was here that the tanners had to come to buy the hides, either the day they were flayed or the following morning (if this was not a holiday, in which case they had to come a day later).[34] This regulation gave a guarantee to the tanners that they would not be buying water-sodden hides. The butchers, in turn, were sure of the sale of their hides before they lost all their natural humidity. If the buyer did not pay for the hides, the tanners' guild had to take responsibility for the debt. Later, a ban was issued by which no tanner could be admitted to the market unless he provided adequate financial guarantees.[35] In principle, these contracts were renewed every three to five years, either during Easter or immediately afterwards, and were valid from Good Friday, when (after Lent) the "butchers' year" started.

Unlike the direct agreements between the shoemakers and the tanners, I have found a considerable number of long-term contracts between the tanners and the butchers: in the notarial archive and in some files of the Senate, three contracts for the 1582–1600 period, three for the period from 1601–1700 and three for the years between 1701 and 1731.[36]

---

34 These contracts also established that the hides should be free from bone, noses, lips and pieces of meat, and that the butchers should not wash the hides until they had been flayed. These clauses and those cited in the text were found in the contract registered by the notary Giovan Battista Taccone on 28 February 1581 (A.S.B., Notarile, vol. 1574–1608, fos. 55^{v}-57). The same clauses are present in other contracts from the end of the sixteenth and throughout the seventeenth centuries. In the eighteenth century they were replaced by a more general expression which obliged the butchers to sell the hides "in a good condition."

35 A.S.B., Arti, *Notizie attinenti l'Arte ... dei Pellacani*, vol. I, *Statutorum Artis Pellacanarum*, 15 April 1600, fo. 27.

36 The first four contracts were registered by the notary Giovan Battista Taccone on 28 February 1581, 23 March 1584, 13 April 1594 and 17 April 1601 (A.S.B., Notarile, vol. 1571–1608). The next two were registered on 14 April 1609 by the notary Stefano Tacconi (ibid., Notarile, vol. 1596–1610) and on 20 March I624 by Vincenzo Vaselli (ibid., Notarile, vol. 1621–4). The three contracts stipulated in the eighteenth century were registered by Camillo Bartolotti on 10 June 1720 and on 21 March 1721 (ibid., Notarile, vol. 1719–22) and by Casimiro N. Minelli on 28 March 1731 (ibid., Notarile, vol. 1730–2). I was able to trace

If direct negotiations failed, the authorities intervened, either on request or on their own initiative. Thus on 23 April 1604, 5 June 1604, 27 March 1619 and 14 September 1634, the prices of the hides were fixed by the Cardinal Legate and a Senatorial commission working together.[37] In 1587 and 1637, with no agreement between the two parties, the same authorities conceded to the butchers – despite opposition from the tanners – the right to tan the hides themselves, or to sell the skins at whatever price they wished. On 6 April 1709, on 4 May 1715 and during the period from 1770 to 1772, it was the Tribuni who arbitrated between the representatives of the two guilds.[38] To these seven interventions we may add nine others, between 1610 and 1725, which confirmed decisions already taken or which affected other important aspects of the negotiations.[39]

We need not enter into the details of all these interventions. The unsuccessful negotiations of 1637 deserve attention as they throw light on the negotiating strategies of the two guilds.[40] In that year, with warehouses full of unsold leathers due to competition from imported leathers (which were cheaper, although of lower quality), the tanners refused to grant the butchers the rise in the price of hides they were requesting. But the failure to reach an agreement was also due to the intransigence of the butchers, who in fact wanted to break with the tanners, having already bought some workshops in which hides could be tanned. The tanners, not having immediate access to information as to the butchers' intentions, put up what they saw as a sufficient defense of their interests by agreeing that the butchers should have the right to sell the hides at whatever price they wished, as long as they sold them only to the authorized buyers (that is, only to the members of the tanners' guild). But the butchers cleverly sidestepped this restrictive clause by raising the question of market size directly with the authorities. After obtaining the agreement of the Cardinal Legate and the Senate, they offered their hides, by means of a "printed edict," to all who wished to buy them, even if they were not members of the

these documents with the help of a *Sommario delle scritture ritrovate nelli libri dell'Archivio dell'Arte dei Pellacani* of 19 July 1732 (ibid.), generously pointed out to me by Maria Gioia Tavoni.

37 *Statutorum Artis Pellacanarum*, fos. 32^v-33, 33^v-34, 47^v-48 and 58–58^v. But see also *Sommario delle scritture ... dell'Arte dei Pellacani.*

38 For the decisions of 6 April 1709 and 4 May 1715, see *Sommario delle scritture ... dell'Arte dei Pellacani.*.

39 Ibid.

40 What follows can be found in the dossier *Beccai contro Pellacani*, in A.S.B., Arti, *Notizie attinenti l'Arte ... dei Pellacani*, vol. II. See also the printed pamphlet *Informazione ai Signori di Reggimento per il Massaro et huomini della Compagnia dei Pellacani* (Bologna, 1637), in ibid.

tanners' guild.[41] To those who proposed to buy "in large numbers," the butchers granted the use of tanning workshops. But they were also prepared to sell small quantities to tanners' journeymen, a provocative move aimed at opening up a breach in the solidarity of their adversary. Once confusion and disagreement reigned in the ranks of the tanners, it would be easier for the butchers to enlist the deserters and fugitives needed in order to set up their own tanning workshops, intended to internalize and verticalize production.

In effect, the butchers broke with the bilateral institutional monopoly over at least two strategic issues. They bought the right to tan hides (recognized by the Cardinal Legate with the concession of patents indicating names and not specifying time limits) and they drastically lowered the barriers to entry and exit, thus transforming a monopolistic market controlled institutionally into a "contestable market."[42] Both these breaks were bound to put the tanners in an impossible position, as in fact happened. But what advantage did the butchers draw from this? If we start from the hypothesis that the fixed prices were too low with respect to production costs, the butchers followed their interests in working towards and obtaining the concession of the right to tan the hides. Their aim was to capture, in the medium term, if not all at least a part of the income that the tanners earned from the low price of the raw materials. By putting themselves on the demand side as well as that of supply, they would have gained as tanners what they lost as butchers. In addition, by expanding the multiproduct aspect of their firms (producing meat and hides for two different markets, one for consumption and one for intermediate goods), they would be able to obtain economies of scale and also economies of scope, adding another sector to the one in which they traditionally worked. In particular, operating within a multiproduct firm (or seventeenth-century "conglomerate") they would also be able to shorten the transaction times for the transfer of the hides to the tanners, avoiding one of the burdens of transaction costs.[43]

The second move – the offer of tanning workshops to those who wished to enter the market – had the aim of raising demand and thus the price of the hides. But it would have another, unintended effect. It would reduce the sunk costs (the costs for new entrants) and thus create conditions which were favorable also to pirate entry ("eat and run entry"), damaging both the guilds

41 The "printed edict" can be found in *Notizie attinenti l'Arte ... dei Pellacani*, vol. I.

42 On contestable markets, multiproduct firms and economies of scope, see W. J. Baumol, J. C. Panzer and R. Willig, *Contestable Markets and the Theory of Industry Structure*, foreword by E.E. Bayley (New York, 1982).

43 The joint production of beef and leathers is considered by the authors of *Contestable Markets*, pp. 75–76, as an intuitive case of a multiproduct firm.

in conflict.[44] In short, at least on paper, the two measures were contradictory, although it is not known how this contradiction was managed in practice.

Having lost their monopoly over the hides and facing defeat in the leather market, the tanners were hit and nearly wiped out by a severe and long-lasting crisis. The decision of the Legate, in 1656, to force the butchers to sell the hides only to tanners with their own workshops does not seem to have had any lasting effects.[45] It was only in 1665 that the tanners began to win back their monopolistic privileges. By around 1690, when the traditional negotiations over price, quality and transaction procedures began again regularly, they appear to have regained their privileges in their entirety. Not even the butchers were able to gain sufficient advantage from the difficulties of their adversary. According to the tanners, in order to run their new tanning workshops the butchers had to employ artisans who lacked the necessary skills, with consequent losses in quality, price and earnings.[46]

After this episode, a bitter experience particularly for the tanners, the antagonistic cooperation between the two guilds was kept at acceptable levels of conflict with no further outbreaks of head-on warfare. The tradition of long-term contracts was resumed and with it the negotiations over prices, quality and selling procedures.

3 Rules and Practices

What was the real effect of the prices and the levels of quality that were legally set? Were the agreements actually respected and carried out by all the members of the guilds involved? And were the guilds able to convince or compel their members to adhere to the settlements? Analogous problems have been examined by students of contemporary industrial relations. Agreements between the representatives of labor and business lose credibility if either side fails to gain the full consent of its members. "Obligation of influence" is the term in Italy to designate the practice of conferring responsibility on representatives of labor and business in order to ensure the consent of their members to agreements they have negotiated.[47] The same problem exists with the long-term

44 *Contestable Markets*, pp. 6–7, 349–351.

45 This ban has not been found, but it is summarized very briefly in *Sommario delle ... scritture ... dell'Arte dei Pellacani.*

46 See an undated letter (post-1637) sent by the tanners' guild to the Gonfaloniere in the dossier *Beccai contra Pellacani.*

47 G. Ghczzi, *La Responsabilità contrattuale delle associazioni sindacali* (Milano, 1963), pp. 65–76.

contracts between the guilds that were full of clauses aiming to avoid or limit damage resulting from "opportunistic" behavior. How, then, was this problem resolved in eighteenth-century Bologna? How were those who violated the rules punished and to which tribunal were appeals made? We know that the guilds themselves could, on certain occasions and within certain limits, act as tribunals (as was the case with a considerable number of the Bolognese guilds). Unfortunately, however, the archives of these guilds have been lost. Yet evidence does indicate that when the guilds failed to enforce the agreements, the authorities – the Tribuni and the Assunteria Arti – would intervene.

In 1752, the Tribuni imposed harsh punishments on those tanners who refused to pay the butchers the agreed price, suspending their right to buy hides. In the magistrates' view, there could be no individual deviation from the price agreed by the guilds. If the tanners believed that the price of the hides was too high, they had to present written objections to the magistrates and, following an inquiry, "if they were held to be right, justice would take its due course."[48]

The year after, in February 1753, the butchers tried to sell the hides at a price higher than the legal rate. The Tribuni requested that the butchers also follow the appropriate procedures, "if they have a complaint against the price."[49] The real price, as these examples indicate, had to conform to the legally established rates.

Nevertheless, the prices that the artisans paid were pegged to the quality of the goods, and could vary somewhat from the official rates. Fresh hides that were not of equal weight were not considered to be of equal quality. From a Senatorial source of 1730, we learn that the agreed prices were applied to hides weighing over eighty *libbre*, while the prices of lighter hides tended to be lower (see Table 6.1).

The price of the hides did not depend on their weight alone. It was calculated that "dry" hides – above all those arriving from slaughterhouses in the countryside – might lose up to 60 to 70 per cent of their original weight. A fresh hide weighing 80 *libbre*, once it had been dried, would weigh only 30 *libbre*; a hide weighing 75 *libbre* when fresh would weigh only 25 *libbre* when dry; and

48 A.S.B., Tribuni, Atti, Libro Bianco-Rosso, vol. XV, 14 June 1752, fo. 165. Most of the tanners considered that the price fixed (14 lire 5 *soldi* for a hundred *libbre* of hides) was too high and should be lowered.

49 Ibid., fo. 250. In 1742, the Assunteria al sollievo delle Arti, "in view of the continuing controversy between tanners and butchers over the price of hides," decided to leave "each side in liberty this year to act in the way that best suits its business" (A.S.B. Arti, Atti, VI, 9 April 1742, fo. 277^{v}).

TABLE 6.1 Weight and price variations of fresh and dry hides

Fresh hides		Dry hides	
Weight libbre	Price per 100 libbre	Weight libbre	Price per 100 libbre
80	12.15	30	30.0
75	11.15	25	28.0
65	11.0	20	20.0

The graduated prices were mainly applied to hides from rural areas.
SOURCE: *SECONDA PARTE D'INFORMAZIONE AL LEGATO SOPRA IL REGOLAMENTO DELLE TRE ARTI PELLACANI, CALIEGARI E CARTOLARI*, ATTACHED TO THE *RELAZIONI, REFLESSI, MEMORIE…SOPRA IL REGOLAMENTO PER LE TRE ARTI* (ASB, Arti, Misc. 1, no 88, probably 1737)

one weighing 65 *libbre* when fresh would weigh a mere 20 *libbre* when dry. Graduated prices were drawn up, taking account of such variations and establishing proportions between different weights of fresh and dry (but not desiccated) hides.

The larger, dry (but flexible) skins tended to rise in price, while fresh skins saturated with water or damp tended to decrease in price. In 1746, the tanners obtained from the city government an order that recognized their right to obtain a reduction in the price of hides that had been excessively soaked by the butchers or damaged by cuts when the animals were skinned.[50] In 1770, this right was confirmed but at the same time limited: the tanners could only contest the excessive dampness or poor quality of a hide at the moment of purchase.[51] Again, in 1783, the tanners complained that they had to pay for "water, blood, and filth" at the same price as the skins. These complaints, which on

50 See the Order, *Bando sopra le pelli delle macellerie,* Bologna, 21 April 1746 (A.S.B., Archivio del Legato, Bandi).

51 See the Order, *Bando sopra le pelli si grosse che minute che cadono in comparto,* Bologna, 22 August I770 (A.S.B., Archivio del Legato, Bandi). In 1771, the butchers complained that the tanners, instead of fetching the hides on the days agreed upon, left them "in the butchers' shops for two or three days to·the grave detriment and prejudice of the butchers" (A.S.B., Tribuni, Atti, Libro Rosso, 24 July 1771, fo. 163). When the hides became dry, they could be refreshed by certain procedures which, however, could not restore their original pliability.

occasions developed into real disputes, were only kept within limits by the fear the tanners had of the butchers, "intractable and blood-thirsty people."[52] The butchers had a long-standing tradition in Bologna of being the most militant of the guilds and of playing leading roles in political agitation.[53]

The tanners, then, complained that the fresh hides were excessively damp, but the shoemakers, in turn, protested that the leathers were too oily. In other words, the tanners, in spite of the technical regulations laid down in the statutes of their guild and confirmed by judicial decrees, apparently behaved in the same "opportunistic" way as the butchers. Having soaked the hides in tallow, they saturated them "craftily" in chalk powder "in order to dry out and conceal the tallow and the excess oiliness." The shoemakers therefore paid for "tallow and skin chalk" and made shoes that were of poor quality, "thus incurring the complaints of the general public."[54] In August 1745, the Assunteria al Sollievo delle Arti ordered that the "shoemakers who had bought material of poor quality" from the tanners should bring it to the Assunteria so that appropriate steps might be taken.[55] According to the shoemakers, the tanners obliged those who wished to purchase "good-quality leathers" to buy a certain percentage of third-rate leathers as well. New negotiations ensued, against the wishes of the tanners, in an attempt to bring prices into line with the actual quality of the leathers.[56] In short, the prices legally declared and agreed to were not the same as the prices that were actually paid. The legal rates were a reference point, a yardstick, alongside which a series of "private" transactions took place.

As already stated, a large percentage of the leathers the tanners produced were sold to the shoemakers. But they were not obliged to buy all the leathers they were offered. This situation gave rise to considerable tensions between the two guilds, especially when the unsold leathers began to dry out and to lose weight and quality. At such times, when local demand was weak, the tanners

52 See the report, *Sentimento del Consultore Gavazzi sopra l'instanza dell'Arte delle tre Arti dei conciapelli*, 10 September 1783 (A.S.B., Arti, Misc. XXXIV, no. 50) and *Risposta dei Tribuni ... per ovviare li abusi che si commettono dai macellai* (ibid. no. 65, 17 November 1783).

53 M. Fanti, *I macellai bolognesi*.

54 See the report, *Riflessioni sopra i capi di ricorsi avanzati dai pellacani, callegari e cartolari*, attached to the *Memoriale delli pellacani, callegari e cartolari all'Assunteria d' Arti* (A.S.B., Arti, Misc. II, no 64, years uncertain). See also *Ricorso e ragioni dell'Arte dei calzolari al Vicelegato contra l'Arte dei pellacani e callegari ... per gli abusi introdotti*, 23 November 1768 (A.S.B., Arti, Misc. XXI, no. 36).

55 A.S.B., Arti, Atti, VII, 17 August 1745, fo. 23.

56 A.S.B., Arti, Atti, VI, 9 May 1737, fo. 99. See also *Promemoria dell' Assunteria d' Arti al legato sopra li qui annessi ricorsi dell' Arte dei calzolari contro li callegari*, 4 November 1793 (A.S.B., Arti, Misc. LIV).

tried to export at least some part of their unsold leathers. But they could not do so without the permission of the shoemakers' guild, which had to indicate its consent by stamping the leathers to be exported from the city, even those sold in the countryside around Bologna. The shoemakers' guild, fearing that its members might be left without sufficient supplies of leather, would not agree easily to apply the stamp, and would do so only for small amounts not exceeding fifty *libbre*.[57]

When tanned hides and leathers were in poor supply, the shoemakers' guild would request the right to import. They too had first to obtain the permission of the tanners' guild, which then stamped the imported leathers (a permission equally difficult to obtain).[58] This perfect reciprocity of control over import and export (at least in principle) forced the conflicting parties to turn once again in the second half of the eighteenth century, to the authorities (the Assunteria al Sollievo delle Arti), who had the final say. A decision in favor of one of the parties was reached after careful consultations and thorough investigations of the quantity and quality of the leathers on sale, stored in the warehouses, or in the process of being tanned. The records of these investigations, although not preserved in their entirety, are a precious source for reconstructing the scale of artisan activities as well as tanning techniques.[59]

Not all the export and import trade, however, was open and above board. Whenever prices of leathers were higher in Bologna than in neighboring areas, a clandestine import business sprang up. The effect of this was to depress legal prices. On 27 July 1730, for example, the head of the shoemakers' guild stated that "good quality leather" could be purchased "at 11 *soldi* per *libbra*," even though the official price was "higher, that is to say 14 *soldi* per *libbra*."[60] A few weeks later, the head of the tanners' guild explained that they had been

---

57 Control of exports was provided for by the *Statuti et ordini della onoranda Compagnia*.

58 In 1756 the tanners declared that they were ready to supply the city with a constant flow of leather, in order to obtain the right to export their goods. But the proposal was not accepted. See the report, *Informazione dell' Assunteria d' Arti, ... sopra il memoriale dei pellacani e callegari dove dimostrano che l'incaglio che hanno dei corami da essi fabbricati deriva per colpa dei calzolai*, 6 December 1756 (A.S.B., Arti, Misc. XVIII, no. 60). The shoemakers in the second half of the eighteenth century, in order to lower the price of leathers, produced a printed manifesto to start up a cooperative that would look after the sale of imported hides on their behalf. The shop was actually opened and operated for a few years, but with little success. The Assunteria Arti considered ordering its closure, but in the end decided not to take action; the shop was never made legal.

59 See for example, *Visita dei Tribuni ... col massaro dell'Arte dei calzolari a varie pellacanerie e botteghe*, 23 July 1738 (A.S.B., Arti, Misc. X, no 24); *Relazione dei Tribuni ... sopra la visita fatta alle Pellacanerie*, 16 January 1769 (ibid., Misc. XXI, no. 41).

60 A.S.B., Tribuni, Atti, Libro Bianco-Rossi, XI, 27 July 1730, fo. 20^{v}.

obliged to reduce prices "below those fixed by the official list" in order to combat the "continual import ... at lower prices of leathers produced in the countryside."[61] The tanners then made the characteristic move of requesting more stringent controls on imports, so that they might raise the prices once again instead of undercutting official prices. As previously noted, on 18 September 1747, the Assunteria al Sollievo delle Arti granted a price increase for those leathers in short supply, so as to compensate for the price of such goods produced in Bologna with those of the surrounding areas.

The attempt to make use of the market as a means of sustaining the whole elaborate system of corporatist relations seems evident. However, the exchanges between butchers and tanners and between tanners and shoemakers cannot be accounted for by market forces alone. On the contrary, they were founded on the rights and duties that derived from guild membership. The rules and regulations of the corporate bodies provided a sense of security. The fixing of price guidelines protected the interested parties from sudden, uncontrolled leaps in price levels caused by monopolistic practices and short-term disturbances in the market. Through the daily exchanges, the butchers, tanners and shoemakers experienced the freedom of negotiating quality and prices while buffered against excess risk. The political authorities intervened from time to time to mediate between the interests involved or to defend the "common good" (as they perceived it).

4 Selling by Quota

Butchers and tanners were also linked by relations which went deeper than those indicated in the price list. The tanners, in accordance with a practice called *comparto* (quota), were obliged by law as well as by custom to buy all the hides provided by the butchers at the agreed price, and to buy them only from designated butchers. When the price was negotiated, the head of the tanners' guild established the number of hides each tanner had the right to buy. Another operation followed (of which only few traces survive), giving precise indications as to the particular tanners to whom each butcher or group of butchers had to sell their hides in order that each buyer received the correct quota assigned to him.

In principle, these personalized reciprocal obligations, if formulated by the guild officials, had then to be approved by the Senate and/or the Cardinal

61 Ibid., 26 August 1730, fo. 33^{v}.

Legate. Previously, in the early stages – the long period between 1517 and 1629 – when these obligations were established, it was the Legate and/or the Gonfaloniere, at least formally, who decided these quotas.

This form of social obligation was constructed according to specific rules. Neither the officials of the tanners' guild nor the authorities could establish equal or arbitrary quotas. The hides were divided among the tanners according to their wealth and their hierarchical rank within the guild.

What were the origins of these transactional constraints set up around the middle of the sixteenth century? They can be considered as a delayed response to certain monopolistic practices of the "richer and more powerful" of the tanners, accused by the guild itself in a report to the Vice Legate (14 December 1510) of buying all or nearly all the hides from the butchers to the detriment of the "poor" tanners, who were virtually forced out of business. Once all or nearly all the hides had been bought up, the richer tanners sold the leathers to the shoemakers at inflated prices and on credit, thus capitalizing on their advantage.[62]

These harmful practices could only take place by going flatly against fundamental transactional norms. According to the old statute of the guild, if a tanner was engaged in negotiations concerning more than ten hides, he would have to concede a part of the sale to any other tanner who arrived subsequently. The same statute, in order to prevent secret agreements between monopolists, forbade the tanners to buy hides until they had been flayed and put on display in a place open to the public.[63] The report sent to the Vice Legate accused the rich tanners of buying in a covert manner, inside the butchers' workshops in private rooms, in order to get around the ten-skin rule and to negotiate the price of the hides "by weight" (*a peso*), as if they had already agreed upon "a certain price per *libbra*," rather than coming to an agreement based on a calculation of their value carried out "by sight" (*a occhio*), as was the tradition.[64] According to the tanners' guild, these two new practices had to be severely forbidden, and should be liable to a fine of ten gold *scudi*. This proposal was given immediate effect in a ban issued by the Vice Legate. We do not know, however, how the ban was applied in practice and with what success. Thirty years later, on 1 December 1541, the ban was abolished and replaced by a new set of regulations, according to which each tanner could buy hides from the same butcher only in alternate weeks and as long as he bought them "publicly

62 Letter to the Vice-Legate (14 December 1510) reported in *Statuti Pellacani*, pages unnumbered, in *Notizie attinenti l'Arte … dei Pellacani*, vol. I.

63 *Statuti Pellacani*, pages unnumbered.

64 Letter to the Vice-Legate.

and openly," the penalty of non-compliance being again a fine of ten gold *scudi* and exclusion from the guild.[65]

These procedures had the conscious and explicit objective of preventing hoarding and offering reasonable access to the market to the poorer tanners. At that time (1541), the price of the hides was left to private negotiations. However, if agreement could not be reached by making an "on the spot" evaluation, negotiations could be continued on the basis of weight.[66]

On 7 August 1554, these regulations were replaced by new norms that the Gonfaloniere introduced and imposed on the guilds. For the first time, quota sales were established. The new regulations, which came into force only on 7 May 1557, had the aim of resolving the disputes between "rich and poor tanners," the Gonfaloniere being moved solely by considerations of "justice, tranquility and peace." The members of the guild were divided into three "classes," among which 550 hides were distributed every month. The first class (six tanners, including the head of the guild and the Council officials) had the right to buy 215 hides; the second class (eight members) were allotted 191 hides; and the third class (fourteen tanners, probably including some journeymen) were allowed to buy 149 hides. The number of hides bought by individual tanners within each class could vary. From this point on, quotas were established for periods which varied from one to five years with the exception of 1578 and the long gap between 1637 and 1690 (see Tables 6.2 and 6.3).[67]

---

65 *Statutorum Artis Pellacanorum*, fos. 1^{v}-4.

66 Ibid. On 25 March 1551 a new agreement was made between tanners and butchers over the manner of selling the hides, which prohibited not only monopolistic practices but also sale by weight (so correcting the decision of 1541), with the exception of hides from the countryside (A.S.B., *Statuti Pellacani*, pages unnumbered). It is clear from this agreement that both buyers and sellers of hides, forced to "spot" buying, also bet on the weight of the hides while they negotiated the price. This practice was severely condemned. The *Statuti Pellacani* contain the official decisions until 1551, the *Statutorum Artis Pellacanorum* the acts and decisions from 1541 to 1643.

67 *Statutorum Artis Pellacanorum*, fos. 1 7^{v}–22^{v}. In 1546, at a time of a shortage of leather and with the growing danger of monopolistic practices, the authorities had already made a step towards the quota system "in order that the poor men of the trade of tanners can support themselves and their families by their labor and industry ... and also for the public utility of everyone." According to the new rules, the tanners would have been divided into three groups: that of the "rich men," that of the "not so rich men" and that of "the poorest men". Every week the category which would have the right (and obligation) to buy all the hides the butchers put on sale would be established by lottery. But this lottery had to serve another purpose as well. It had to be done in such a way that half of the-hides would go to the rich tanners, a third to the "middle" tanners, and the rest to the poorest (about 17 per cent) (order of the Gonfaloniere, 30 September, 1546, in *Notizie attinenti l'Arte ... dei Pellacani*, vol. 1).

We can consider these quota assignments as true drawing rights, although they were subjected to numerous conditions. In particular, the complex regulations of 15 April and 8 May 1600 established by the Vice Legate Orazio Spinola (together with the Senate) included a series of specific requirements: that those who were included in the quotas had to give a guarantee of security; that anyone who did not buy the quota assigned to him for two consecutive months would be suspended from the right to buy hides for the whole year; that the hides which were not bought or which were "free" should be "distributed among those of the same class" until new quotas were drawn up; that when the new quotas were decided upon, two representatives from each of the three "classes" should be present; and that those who had drawing rights should work with their own hands, the penalty for non-observance being termination of their privilege. The provisions also forbade, as previous legislation had done, the commercialization of these rights (as happened with the formation of tanners' companies, which freed one or more member from the need to work with his own hands), the penalty being expulsion from the guild. The "poor tanners of the third class" were forbidden from buying hides in the country, something which was thus implicitly allowed to the other two classes. To prevent the accumulation of drawing rights in the hands of individual families, another stipulation excluded from the quota system sons who could not show that they had been independent of their fathers in terms of "habitation, food and clothing" for at least five years. When the father died (especially if he had been a member of the guild council), the drawing rights would be passed on to the heir following the normal rules of inheritance – first the eldest son, then the other sons and the brothers and finally the other relatives. The condition for this inheritance was that the heir should be male, that he should be over twenty and that he should belong to the guild.[68] Subsequent rules (13 May 1609) laid down by the Cardinal Legate Giustiniani in accordance with the Senate, decreed that those who already had a right to a quota could not inherit that of the father unless their quota had originally been subtracted from that of the father, and as long as no one ended up with a monthly quota of more than fifty hides (excepting rights which had been acquired previously). This clause, disadvantageous to the richer tanners, was to some extent compensated by

68 *Statutorum Artis Pellacanorum*, fos. 27–32. In principle hides from the countryside were not included in the quotas. In 1753, the Tribuni stated that the cattle hides of Poggio Renatico and of Samoggia, the estate belonging to the Lambertini noble family, were excluded from the *comparto*.

another which exempted the tanners from manual work as long as they at least bought and sold the skins personally.[69]

This set of regulations, although based upon a hierarchy of privileges (the three classes), seems to be dominated by a concern to safeguard the rights of the weaker social groups. While they permitted the realization of profits, they also tended to favor the survival of independent producers. However, it would be naive to believe that rules established at the end of the sixteenth century continued to operate unchanged for decades or indeed centuries. The rich tanners, all council members and officers of the guild, exercised what may be called an effective political lobby. They exploited their position of power to increase their drawing rights, to decrease or at any rate keep within limits the quotas of the "poor," to capture the quotas that remained "free," and to gain control over eventual increases in the total number of hides. This lobbying, an activity carried out more or less openly, gave rise to protests especially from the "poor" tanners. They came not only from those who really were in a state of poverty, but also from those who, out of ability or ambition, hoped to climb rapidly up the social scale and whose low quotas operated as a brake.

In fact, the 1609 clause which set a ceiling to the number of hides was aimed at correcting abuses which by this time had become common practice. In 1595, the four most powerful tanners (Antonio Pedrini, Giovanni Andrea Volpara, Battista Gappi and another Giovanni Andrea Volpara) had managed somehow to accumulate an average of eighty hides a head, completely upsetting the quotas fixed in 1586. In 1600, the same tanners, although they had lost some of their power, still bought seventy hides each. Between 1604 and 1612, their quotas decreased slowly, but it was only in 1632 that no tanner – "not even the richest ones and the oldest members of the guild" – bought more than fifty hides.[70]

Table 6.2 shows that the drawing rights of the rich tanners jumped from 38–39 per cent on the first two occasions when quotas were set (1577–1586) to over 50 per cent in the years between 1600 and 1604.

Unfortunately, for 1595 and for the years after 1604 it has not been possible to find the division of the quotas into classes, but only the quotas assigned to each tanner. This is important quantitative data, but it does not enable us to reconstitute the classes. In 1600, for example, two tanners were assigned to the first class, even though they were only allowed 14 hides, while others in the same year, with 20 hides, remained in the second class. Those whose quota increased, then, sometimes rose to the class above and sometimes did

69 Ibid., fos. 37–37^{v}.

70 Ibid., fos. 25–57^{v}.

TABLE 6.2 Distribution of hides among three classes of tanners

Year		Class I	Class II	Class III	Total	Undivided total
1577	T	6	8	14	28	
	H	212	191	149	552[a]	—
	%	38.41	34.60	26.99	100	
1586	T	5	8	15	28	
	H	238	200	172	610[a]	
	%	39.02	32.79	28.20	100.01	
1595	T					12
	H					499
	%					
1600	T	7	6	7	20	
	H	337	100	92	529	
	%	63.77	18.90	17.39	100.06	
1604	T	6	6	8	20	
	H	328	128	114	570	—
	%	57.54	22.46	20.00	100	—
1609	T	—	—	—	—	30
	H	—	—	—	—	620
	%	—	—	—	—	
1612	T					29
	H					585
	%					
1613	T					30
	H					640
	%					
1614	T					32
	H					640
	%					
1619	T					29
	H					632
	%					
1627	T					21
	H					562
	%					

TABLE 6.2 Distribution of hides among three classes of tanners (*cont.*)

		Class				
Year		I	II	III	**Total**	**Undivided total**
1632	T					23
	H					578
	%					

Notes:
a according to the source: 555
T = Tanners; H = Hides
SOURCE: ARCHIVIO DI STATO DI BOLOGNA, ARTI, NOTIZIE ATTINENTI L'ARTE ... DEI PELLACANI, VOL. I, STATUTORUM ARTIS PELLACANORUM

TABLE 6.3 Purchases of hides among three classes of tanners, 1577–1604

Class	1577		1586		1600		1604	
	Min.	**Max.**	**Min.**	**Max.**	**Min.**	**Max.**	**Min.**	**Max.**
I	27	50	39	62	14	82	20	80
II	20	25	20	30	12	23	14	25
III	6	8	4	20	13[a]		17.50[a]	

Notes:
a Average number given in the source.
SOURCE: ARCHIVIO DI STATO DI BOLOGNA, ARTI, NOTIZIE ATTINENTI L'ARTE ... DEI PELLACANI, VOL. I, STATUTORUM ARTIS PELLACANORUM

not. Without wishing to deny that there were economic differences among the three classes, they would appear to be differences of orders rather than of groups based exclusively on wealth.

The tendencies towards accumulation, particularly noticeable around the turn of the century, gave rise to strong protests.[71] Thus on 6 March 1596, the shoemakers' guild accused "four or five" tanners – arrogant rather than

71 The stories which follow come from the dossier *Ricorsi e Proteste*, in *Notizie attinenti l'Arte ... dei Pellacani*, vol. II.

powerful – of undertaking the division "to the great damage of the tanners' guild and the general public," but also to the shoemakers who were forced to submit to their monopoly and to pay high prices for "bad quality" leathers. Another protest, the date of which is not certain but which probably occurred around the same period, accused the same group of four or five tanners of setting quotas contrary to the statutes and gaining control of the hides of dead tanners "without the authorization of the Senate." Those who increased the number of their own hides necessarily decreased the number that went to the "poor." On 11 April 1615, the five heirs of Daniele Dell'Arosto protested against a quota which gave them only sixteen hides (little more than three per person), when even to newcomers at least "six per person" were allotted. Given their "poverty and difficult family situation," they asked for considerable increases and two separate quotas, as only three of them lived together. Even quotas already in force were open to corruption. Thus Paolo Vocieri paid for his admission by renouncing, for three years, the quota to which he had a right. In 1624, Giovan Battista degli Alemanni, a "very poor tanner," protested because his quota of "eight hides every month had not been raised in twelve years," even though he had "always worked with his own hands." He asked to be allowed to participate in the division of the forty spare hides in order "to sustain his family with his own industry" and to pay the rent of his workshop (200 *lire* a year). On 25 June 1625 Domenico Maria Salomoni, who had been turned down on more than one occasion from the guild council onto which he wanted to be co-opted, accused the members of the council of "grave malignity" in preferring to give quota rights to "gentlemen who, neither they themselves nor their predecessors, have ever worked as tanners." Of particular interest is the complaint of a group of poor tanners. Their complaint gave voice to basic legal and political principles. On 12 February 1627, in the lead-up to the new quotas, they asked the Senate that the "good rules and healthy regulations" should be enforced as they were by now seriously disregarded, "with damage to the public and to private individuals." In particular, they invoked the principle of "distributive justice" so that the poor people could have what was due to them and "the rich do not rule the guild with arrogance and tyranny."

Complaints and protests were made to the Senate and the Cardinal Legate, but it was often with these authorities that abuses originated. The quotas the poor considered to be unjust were countersigned by the Cardinal Legate and/or the Gonfaloniere . The legates were greeted with grumblings and protests each time they used their authority to have civil or military members of their court co-opted onto the guild. Over the years, colonels, captains and artisans of other guilds appointed by the legates appear among the members of the tanners' guild.

The best-documented case is that of the barber Domenico Ruinetti, made a member of the guild "by the grace of" the Cardinal Legate Matteo Barberini (later Pope Urban VIII), who had served the Cardinal "with great fidelity in France" at the time when the latter was the Apostolic Nuncio.[72] The Cardinal Legate's heavy-handedness is apparent from the threatening tone of his letter to the head of the tanners' guild, dated 26 August 1614, demanding the immediate cooption with full quota rights of Ruinetti to the post left vacant by the death of Cristoforo Salomoni, on pain of depriving him of quota rights and threatening "punishments." The council, "after long discussions" (*post multa colloquia*), approved the co-option unanimously, but recorded in the minutes that the decision had been taken "to avoid threatened punishment," thereby contesting its legitimacy.

Later, on 9 November, the council met again and, in an attempt to defend the rights of Domenico Maria Salomoni, brother of the dead tanner, confirmed (again emphasizing the illegality of the imposition) the full validity of all the statutory regulations relating to hereditary transmission of quotas by which brothers were the legitimate successors in the absence of sons. The guild then took Ruinetti to court to exclude him from the quota. After various appeals, the case ended up before the Tribunale della Rota of Rome, which issued an ambiguous judgment. The barber was given guild membership but not quota rights. During the trial, the guild stressed the need to respect the rules regarding hereditary transmission and the professional qualification laid down in their statutes. They feared that co-opted members, unable to work the hides "with their own hands," would "enter into trade," selling them to tanners at double the price negotiated with the butchers. This is the first (and up to this point the only) evaluation of the price of drawing rights. The evaluation is perhaps exaggerated, but it does shed light on the aggressive strategies of the butchers during the failed negotiations of 1637. Domenico Ruinetti's lawyers, on the other hand, argued that the membership rules of the guild were not usually respected, as was demonstrated by at least seven irregular applications for membership granted since 1595, and that quota rights could not be passed on "from one heir to the next ... but were subject to the decisions of the higher authorities." They pointed out that the authorities, in fact, were responsible for lowering quota rights that were too high and raising those that were too low, referring clearly to the rules laid down by Cardinal Legate Benedetto Giustiniani in 1609 and to their initial application.

---

72 See the dossier *Domenico Ruinetti Processo*, in *Notizie attinenti l'Arte ... dei Pellacani*, vol. II.

Later the two parties reached a compromise. When the quotas were renewed in 1619, the Gonfaloniere and the Cardinal Legate Ubaldini allocated ten hides a month to Ruinetti on condition that he learn the tanners' trade within four months.[73] It was in this year too, probably for the first time, that seven tanners were expelled from the guild because they had been selling their quotas in a way that "was contrary to the statutes."[74] This severe decision, affecting about a quarter of the members, left an extra seventy hides to be divided among the remaining tanners.

The question of the influence of hereditary systems on the distribution of the skins is a fascinating one. But the series of surnames (set down only for the quotas from 1577 to 1627) is not sufficient to allow us to reconstruct horizontal or vertical lines. It is also necessary to bear in mind descent via the female line (above all through widows and daughters). The long-term reconstruction of families and relatives must also be linked to that of property, not just inherited property but also property which was accumulated, bought or sold. Above all, in the eighteenth century social mobility existed not only downwards but also upwards, as tanners' sons become lawyers and notaries while still continuing to demand their quota rights.

Around the year 1730 the Assunteria Arti formulated an ideal quota model which, while respecting the established hierarchy, aimed to introduce or reintroduce principles of justice in an area in which abuses had become common.[75]

73 *Statutorum Artis Pellacanorum*, fo. 49.

74 Ibid., fos. 54–5. The authorities made sure that the "consignments" of hides took place smoothly. In the eighteenth century at least, in cases of disagreement between individual tanners and butchers, it was possible to request an alternative distribution of the assigned quotas. Thus, for example, on 22 April 1768 the butcher Giacomo Bedini informed the Tribuni that "he no longer wanted to deliver his hides" to the tanner Giuseppe Capurri because of "difficulties with him regarding weight and money". He therefore asked "that the said Signor Capurri be substituted and that the hides be delivered to another tanner." Twenty years earlier the Assunteria al Sollievo delle Arti had already suggested that the butchers be granted the right to request the substitution of tanners who failed to pay for hides delivered to them.

75 *Seconda parte d'informazione al Legato sopra il regolamento delle tre Arti.* The system was practiced at least until 1793. In Bologna the division by quota applied only, but not always, to intermediate goods. We know, for example, that the corn-reed makers bought ox horns by quota. In any case, this way of buying and selling was part of the urban transactional culture. In 1665 the shoemakers had to buy by quota all the unsold leathers, by order of the authorities. In 1770, the silk merchants were obliged to buy by quota, again by the authorities (in an order which, however, was not formalized as a decree), all the unsold raw silk of the cocoon merchants, who did not have the right to organize weaving (a privilege held exclusively by the silk merchants). It could be said, then, that the damaged parties (and the authorities) had recourse to selling by quota each time the bilateral institutional monopolies of the guilds situated in the same productive line ran into difficulties,

According to this project, ordinary members of the guild would receive an annual quota of 200 hides, while members of the guild council would be given 300. The head of the guild would receive 450 hides, over and above the 300 to which he was entitled as an ordinary member of the guild council, and 150 additional hides would be given to the guild officials. Furthermore, the eight most senior members of the council would receive an extra 1,450 hides to divide among themselves. In short, the quotas were calculated on the basis of two principles: position in the guild hierarchy and seniority in terms of length of guild membership. But the income scale, to which the size of the quotas corresponded, was conceived of according to the principles of distributive justice, so as to ensure to everyone, even those who received the smallest quotas, a "decent livelihood." Ordinary guild members, with quotas of 200 hides, would earn 680 lire a year (slightly more than the cost of their labor), which was less, but not much less, than the tanners who received larger quotas but who had to hire one, two or more journeymen. According to some calculations, members of the guild council with quotas of 300 hides would earn 1,020 lire a year, whereas the head of the guild, with 750 hides, would earn 1,635 lire a year.

This mode of exchange, embedded in the fabric of social relations, offers close analogies with well-known anthropological models concerning primitive societies. But the reciprocal obligations of primitive societies were based on unwritten customs, were non-monetary (with the exception of the exchange of shells), had no formal punitive enforcement, and concerned goods destined for immediate consumption. In contrast, exchange by quota in early modern Bologna was sanctioned by written rules, concerned only intermediate goods, required monetary payments and, in principle at least, sanctioned the punishment of violators by the authorities. Moreover, these rules were deeply imbued with principles of moral economy: the just price, the common good, distributive justice, the right to life. These values came from Thomist-scholastic culture but had deeper roots in the Bible and the Gospels. If we use other conceptual parameters, however, the complex transactions between the tanners and the butchers can also be "read" with the help of the modern notion of the bilateral institutional monopoly, with division by quota and the recovery of the residual increases, an extraordinarily modern structure.

---

the alternative being the abolition of the bilateral monopolies and the freedom to expand the size of the firms vertically. See the exploration of "market principle" and "marketplace" in S. Kaplan, *Provisioning Paris. Merchants and Millers in the Grain and Flour Trade during the Eighteenth Century* (Ithaca, N.Y.) 1984, pp. 23–40.

TABLE 6.4 Skin quotas (*comparti*) and (attributed) incomes within the hierarchy of the tanners guild

Position in the hierarchy	No of skins attributed	Income
		In Bolognese lire
Matter	200	680
Council member	300	1020
Senior council member	400	–
Head of the guild	750	1635
Senior head of the guild	930	–

SOURCE: ARCHIVIO DI STATO DI BOLOGNA, ARTI, SECONDA PARTE D'INFORMAZIONE AL LEGATO SOPRA IL REGOLAMENTO DELLE TRE ARTI

SECTION 2

Manufacturing Silk

CHAPTER 7

'Measure for Measure': From Fine Thread to Rigid Labor Control. Changing Conditions of Work in Silk Factories

Carlo Poni

Over the course of the seventeenth and eighteenth centuries, a relatively large and increasing number of workers in the silk industry experienced two important developments. The first was the transition from piece-work to daily wages; the second, the introduction of a factory system.

Although these two experiences are interrelated and connected, they cannot be considered to be a single process or to coincide. Of all the workers in the silk industry, only the workers in the mechanical spinning sector were involved in the factory system in the form of the silk mills "alla bolognese" powered by water wheels, which spread rapidly from the second half of the seventeenth century onwards.[1]

The move from piece-work to daily wages in the silk industry, on the other hand, took place at the beginning only for reeling, an operation carried out directly by hand by women workers using two instruments: the tank full of boiling water into which the silk cocoons were thrown before being unwound; and the bobbin on which the thread was collected in skeins.[2] It is not possible to indicate exactly when the change in payment for labor in the reeling process took place. The first indication, to be found in a source from Piedmont, dates from 1667.[3] But it is difficult, at the present stage of research, to establish what

1 See Carlo Poni, *La seta in Italia: una grande industria prima della rivoluzione industriale* (Bologna, 2009), ch. 1. In the silk mills "alla bolognese" which produced organzine, a high quality thread, almost all the phases of production – winding, spinning and twisting – were mechanized, with the exception of doubling. The task of the worker was to feed the machines and to knot the thread when it broke. The technical term for "twisting" was "throwing". In this essay, I will use the term "spinning" to indicate the overall operation of the silk mills.

2 Reeling was seasonal work which traditionally took place over three months, from mid-June to September. The first description of the work of the reelers, to my knowledge, appears in the small poem by G.C. Croce, *Lodi delle pulite e leggiadre caldirane* (Bologna, 1624).

3 *Regole per I filatori e lavorante da seta et altri venditori d'essa del 14 maggio 1667*, G.B. Borelli, *Editti antichi e nuovi de' Sovrani Principi della Real Casa di Savoia* (Turin, 1681), Part III, Book X, pp. 1088–1089. A Bolognese source of the 17th century (1667) suggests that in Bologna too the reelers (*caldierane*) were paid by the day. According to this source, "every time the master

 | DOI:10.1163/9789004713277_009

this date represents. The beginning of a process which would continue (but with what speed and regularity and in what area) in the following decades? Or the documentation of a practice which was already widespread? Perhaps both. This date, which it will be necessary both to fix and flesh out, in any case cannot be taken to indicate the beginning of a new way of paying labor. Daily payment was already to be found in agriculture centuries before it was introduced into silk reeling. And some categories of urban workers such as bricklayers, masons and roofers and such like were already traditionally paid by the day.[4]

If it did not indicate a turning point in the way of paying for labor, the introduction of daily wages is tied up, at least in the case of the Piedmontese mode of reeling, with a "modest" but decisive technological innovation which permitted the production of a new type of thread: fine, regular and round. This was a qualitatively new product, which constituted an important leap forward with respect to the traditional thread that was thick, irregular and flat. In this way, the basis was laid for the production of an entire new range of textiles.

The structural differences between mechanical spinning and reeling – respectively the concentration of production without daily wages and daily wages without the concentration of production – did not remain unaltered over the long term. A process of imperfect convergence between the two sectors began, in different stages which still have to be discovered, with the concentration (but without mechanization) of tens of boilers for the reeling process under the same roof. Towards the middle of the eighteenth century, this concentration, although relatively rare, strengthened the tendency to construct large firms bringing together reeling and spinning, although in different buildings, and amassing hundreds of male and female workers in the same

---

reeler (*caldirano*) stops his work, his expenses also stop, as they consist of the wood, food and wages of the reelers who are paid by the day" (Archivio di Stato di Bologna, hereafter A.S.B., *Reggimento, Assunteria Arti, Misc. Arti*, vol. V, 1667–1715, *Per rispondere alli Assunti dell'Arte di seta. Considerazioni e stabilimenti per bando de' caldierani*, 25 April 1667). Given the context, I think that we should infer that the reelers were paid only on the days that they worked. From an eighteenth-century source it appears clear that the reelers were paid by the piece (*Senato Consulto a regolamento dell'Arte della Seta e di veli e delle sue maestranze* [Bologna 1770], p. 8). In Bologna, of all the workers in the silk mills only the crêpe workers, a few hundred, were paid by the day.

4 It is not by chance that the analyses and the trends of the history of wages are generally based on data from the construction industry. See F.P. Braudel and F. Spooner, "Prices in Europe from 1450 to 1750," *The Economy of Expanding Europe in the Sixteenth and Seventeenth Centuries*, eds. E.E. Rich and C.H. Wilson (Cambridge, 1967), p. 426. The wages of builders form the basis for the important work on the history of wages published in Italian, D. Sella, *Salari e lavoro nell'edilizia lombarda durante il secolo XVII* (Pavia, 1968).

or nearby areas.[5] Here we encounter the high point of a process of vertical integration in which techniques for the control of labor were reinforced and refined on the basis of an already clear separation of labor from the means of production and the product of this labor.

These sequences appear reassuring and convincing, not least because they are rooted in a strong theoretical tradition. But real life can be more complicated. How did worker behavior change over the course of these transformations? Exactly how did the worker paid by piece-work differ from the worker who received a daily wage? What changed in terms of working practices and in work culture? To answer these questions we cannot be content with an external analysis of the world of production. It is necessary to attempt to understand from within the materiality of social behavior, to delve into the methods of the productive processes and the organization, control and remuneration of work.[6]

This essay will try to provide some answers to these questions. But it will succeed only partially, both because of the difficulty of the topic, which as yet has no tried methodology, and because it uses sources which have not been collected systematically on the basis of a specific project. This explains the provisional and partial nature of the conclusions I have drawn, to be tested further with other research which has a greater awareness of the problems to be faced. The numerous archives and libraries in which I have worked (in particular in Bologna but also in Bergamo, Milan, Turin and Paris), however, do provide a breadth of scope and a wealth of perspectives which are often not available when you work in a single archive or in a single area.

The first topic, that of the relation between piece-work and the quality of the product, can be found in a collection of Bolognese sources. The first of

5 For some cases of the concentration of reeling and spinning in the same workplace, see Poni, *La seta in Italia,* ch. 1. Within the space of the "large silk mill" of Piacenza a spinning factory with 109 boilers was built (see ibid., ch. 5).

6 The topic of the behavior of the worker in the factory or workshop can be found in a large number of books and articles. See for example *Movimento operaio e socialista,* CXI (1980), n.s., no. 1 devoted to "Cultura operaia e disciplina industriale." See also M.R. Smith, *Harpers Ferry Armory and the New Technology* (Ithaca, N.Y. – London, 1977); J. W. Scott, *The Glassworkers of Carmaux* (Cambridge, Mass., 1974); *Case Studies on the Labor Process,* ed. A. Zimbalist (New York – London, 1979); H. Gutman, *Work Culture and Society in Industrializing America* (New York, 1977); D. Montgomery, *Workers' Control in America* (Cambridge, 1979); D. Bigazzi, "'Fierezza del mestiere' e organizzazione di classe: gli operai meccanici milanesi (1880–1900)," *Società e Storia,* I (1978), no. 1, 87–108; R. Edwards, *Contested Terrain. The Transformation of the Workplace in the Twentieth Century* (New York, 1978); W.M. Reddy, "Skeins, Scales, Discounts, Steam and Other Objects of Crowd Justice in Early French Textile Mills," *Comparative Studies in Society and History,* April 1979, no. 21, 204–215.

these is dated 1737. This was a crisis year for the voile industry, which produced a smooth fine cloth for a huge international market which included head veils.[7] If the voile could not be sold, the silk mills which twisted the local raw silk reeled in Bologna also went into crisis. Some of these mills actually closed, such as the one run by the master silk spinner Antonio Marchetti, which handled a total of 3,500 *libbre* of silk a year and employed around 20–30 workers.[8] As a consequence of the decrease in production, employment levels fell along with wages.

How did the silk mill workers (the *velamaroli*) try to account for the decline in earnings and seek an increase? In a *Memoriale* sent in 1737 to the Senate of the city, they claimed that "the great poverty they found themselves in" was due to the fact that the merchants had:

> ordered silk which was excessively and unusually fine, while the poor claimants could not produce more than one *libbra* of silk a day, earning only nine or ten *baiocchi*, but when the silk was made of the usual thread they would produce two *libbre* a day and sometimes even more.

As they had suffered "because of this change, a decrease amounting to half their earnings," they requested the Senate to ask the merchants to give them an increase in pay, being unable to maintain "their poor and miserable families with such a small income."[9]

The *Memoriale* breaks a deafening silence on work conditions and resonates with connections and unexplored implications. The request for the increase in

---

7 In this essay the term "crisis" is used exclusively to mean a drop in sales due to changes in fashion, competition, war or epidemics. Their duration could vary from less than a year to two or three years, according to research carried out with my colleague Alberto Guenzi on the relation between these economic crises and the subsistence crises. In 1727 it was calculated that there were a total of 4,946 voile weavers in Bologna (see Poni, *La seta in Italia,* ch. 4). Exports of voile varied between 40,000 and 50,000 *libbre.*

8 *Memoriale* of Antonio Marchesi, *filatogliere* (master spinner), A.S.B., *Reggimento, Assunteria Arti, Misc. Arti,* vol. IX (1737). The calculation of the number of workers employed is indicative. I have not been able to reconstruct the differences between the organzine mills and the voile mills. It is likely that in the latter only winding and spinning were carried out (see note 1). In 1727, a total of around 600 workers were employed in the voile mills, a number which can be considered reasonable for most of the 18th century.

9 *Memoriale de' velamaroli che supplicano acciò da mercanti sia loro accresciuta la mercede de' loro lavori ne' filatoi in grazia del filo delle sete troppo sottile,* A.S.B., *Reggimento, Assunteria Arti, Misc. Arti,* vol. IX (1737). The Bolognese *libbra* was equal to 0.361 kg. The *baiocco* was a roman coin worth roughly 1/21 of the Bolognese *lira.* On the issue of measurement from an economic and social perspective, see W. Kula, *Miary i Ludzie* (Warsaw, 1970).

pay emerges from the analysis of the quality of the product and connects this to different levels of earnings. The meaning of these claims can be found in the context of specific economic relations. The *velamaroli* were paid by the piece, and the piece-work was calculated in terms of the quantity (in weight) of the thrown silk: 8–9 *baiocchi* per *libbra*. The introduction by the merchants of a finer thread more or less halved the productivity of labor: from two *libbre* to one *libbra* per day, with a proportional drop in the earnings of the workers which decreased from 18 to 9–10 *baiocchi*. Here it is necessary to specify that the thickness of the thread – particularly that used for voile, was not decided at the moment of spinning but in the immediately preceding operation: that of reeling. This operation, although it was conditioned and guided by the voile merchants, who were the only ones authorized to buy raw silk, was overseen by another category of merchant-entrepreneurs, the master reelers (*caldierani*). These entrepreneurs, who together with the voile merchants had the almost exclusive right to buy the silk cocoons from the landowners, employed women and children to do the reeling.[10] The wealthier master reelers, who worked their own cocoons, were called "free reelers" (*caldierani arbitranti*); those who worked the cocoons of the merchants were called "piece-work reelers" (*caldierani fatturanti*),[11] a distinction which we will return to later. At present it is enough to note that the merchants tended to penetrate the sector and manage the reeling directly. In 1770, they owned 86 out of the 295 boilers in the city.[12]

The petition of the spinners for an increase in wages was unsuccessful. On 5 August and 16 September of the same year, 1737, the Guild Committee (*Assunteria d'Arti*) of the Senate examined the "blind" (anonymous) petition of the *velamaroli* and spinners, considered the request for an increase in the "payment for spinning voile in view of the greater fineness with respect to the past," and met the head of the Spinners Guild, Pietro Ratti, with two master spinners Francesco Boni and Paolo Belvederi, to examine the question.[13] During the

10 The silk worms were bred by peasants (sharecroppers) along with their landowners. Only a small percentage of the production was concentrated in the city. In the eighteenth century, the women and girls employed in the seasonal task of reeling came mostly from the countryside and from the hills above Modena.

11 The (not rigid) distinction between "free" (*arbitranti*) and "piece-work" (*fatturanti*) master reelers can be found in a number of sources. Here I will mention only the *Memoriale delli caldirani aribtranti e fatturanti per provedimento all'incaglio delle sete*, A.S.B., Reggimento, Assunteria Arti, Misc. Arti, vol. XXII (1770).

12 *Nota delle caldiere fatte nell'anno 1770*, 29 December 1771, A.S.B., Reggimento, Assunteria Arti, Misc. Arti, vol. XXIII (1771–1772). The "free reelers" ran 68 boilers in one year and the "piece-work reelers" 141.

13 A.S.B., Reggimento, Assunteria Arti, Decreti e Atti, reg. 6 (1737–1743), cc. 47 and 57.

meeting, which was held on 30 September 1737, the head of the Guild argued that although the thread used for voile was "finer, there had been no increase in payment [from the merchants], and no increase had been passed on to the workers," and this was confirmed by Francesco Boni. The other master spinner, Paolo Belvederi, who only made organzine from raw silk, said that "as the payment made to him by the merchants had not increased, he had not increased that of his workmen."[14]

The declarations of the two master spinners and of the head of the guild have a series of important implications which require explanation. It is clear that in conditions of pay not dissimilar from those of the *velamaroli*, it was the spinners in the silk mills called "alla bolognese" who produced the *orsoglio*, a spun thread better known on the international market as organzine. For both the thread for organzine, produced in principle with raw silk imported from Romagna and the Marches and sold by specialized merchants, and the thread for voile, their thickness was decided during the reeling process at the place of production. It is important to bear in mind that local spun thread could be exported only as a finished product, as the fabric voile, whereas the organzine that could be exported was produced by twisting ("throwing") two threads of raw silk – twisted singly and then doubled and retwisted together. It was for this reason that the thread for organzine was finer (in the eighteenth century) than the thread used for voile. In all, the Bolognese silk mills constituted a complex structure.[15]

From the minutes of the meeting it is also appears that the master spinners of the two types of silk mills (of the thread for organzine and the voile fabric) were paid by the piece by the merchants, and that they in turn paid their workers in proportion to how much they were given. The master spinners, in other words, which the sources always present as the renters of the mills they ran (or as agents for others, but never as owners), were in some ways closer to their workers (numbering from a minimum of 10–20 to a maximum of 40–60 per mill) and were intermediate figures between the mass of spinners and

14 Idem., c. 59. The number of workers employed in the organzine mills reached around 2,000 in 1670. Towards the end of the 18th century, after alternating periods of decline and partial recovery, this number dropped to a few hundred (see Graph 7.1 for this decline).

15 On the complex structure of the Bolognese silk mills, see N. Morini, "L'arte della seta in Bologna. Contributo per una storia delle antiche corporazioni bolognesi di arti e mestieri," *La provincia di Bologna nell'anno Decimo* (Bologna, 1932), pp. 1939–1969; L. Dal Pane, *Economia e società a Bologna nell'età del Risorgimento* (Bologna, 1969); see Poni, *La seta in Italia*, ch. 4.

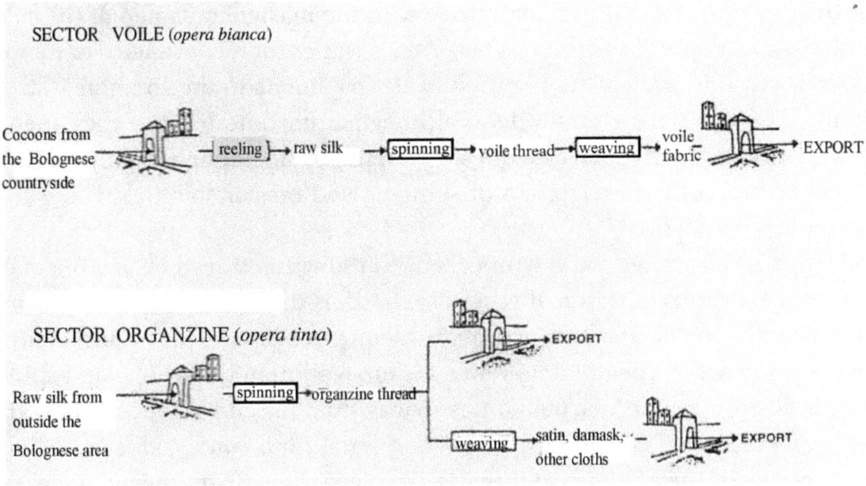

FIGURE 7.1 Silk imported and exported from the city of Bologna
SOURCE: THIS FIGURE WAS ELABORATED BY THE AUTHOR ON THE BASIS OF THE MATERIAL PRESENTED IN THIS CHAPTER

the merchants who owned the raw silk.[16] Proximity, however, does not mean equality. The master spinners made a contract with the merchants which led them to behave as "piece-work setters": they received a "generous" piece-work payment which they passed to their workers. The spinners instead were paid on the basis of a relationship which could be described as "piece-work subordinates." In other words they were subject to fixed working conditions which we could call firm organization, and were subject to the rule of the master spinner.[17]

16 Among the few silk mills in Bologna which had more than 60 employees we may note the one owned by the Monastery of Santa Maria Maggiore which employed 80 workers and that of the Becadelli family which employed 100 (*Nota delli filatogli che sono stati disfatti dall'anno 1730 sino al presente*, 15 September 1792, A.S.B., Reggimento, Assunteria Arti, Buste Gialle, vol. LXXXII). On the social and personal relations between master spinners and spinners we know little. Lucia Ferrante has shown that the master spinners protected those employees involved in the bread riots at the end of the 17th century (L. Ferrante, "Tumulti di più persone oer causa del calo del pane... Saccheggi e represssioni a Bologna, 1671, 1677," *Rivista Storica Italiana*, XC, 1978, no. 4, p. 806).

17 On piece work, see G. Giugni, "Organizzazione dell'impresa ed evoluzione dei rapporti giuridici. La retribuzione a cottimo," *Impresa e Società*, II, 813–888; V. Foa, *La struttura del salario* (Rome, 1976); B. Mottez, *Systèmes de salaire et politiques patronales* (Paris, 1966); L. Barrassi, *Il contratto di lavoro nel diritto positivo italiano* (Milan, 1901). See also the articles by S. Ortaggi, "Cottimo e produttività nell'industria italiana del primo Novecento,"

The meeting of the Guild Committee with the master craftsmen of the silk mills was not definitive in its outcome. And it was never reconvened. For many years afterwards, there is no mention of the payments to the spinners in the minutes of the Senate committees, although from time to time they mention particular events such as requests for relief by unemployed spinners and action to prevent the emigration of spinners and master spinners who were unemployed or in debt.[18]

Why, how and when did the process of thinning the thread begin? It is not easy to answer this question. It is certain that this thinning was not the result of innovation in Bologna, but instead an attempt to adapt "to the requirements of the customer."[19] The dominant area for innovation in the reeling and spinning of silk (organzine "alla piemontese") was, from the end of the seventeenth century, Piedmont, in northern Italy. The partial (and contested, as we shall see) success of the attempts at imitation allowed the Bolognese merchants to gain from the temporary profits of innovation.[20] The new "practice of making the threads for voile much finer than before" had as a consequence that "the *libbra* of silk that once, for example, was made up of 10 *braccia* (lengths) of silk was now made up of 15."[21] Connected with this change in length, the Bolognese merchants (certainly not alone) began to sell the cloth (the voile) by the *braccia* and not by the *libbra* in order to capitalize on the new differential between the weight and the length of the thread.[22] According to a *Memoriale*

Rivista di Storia Contemporanea, 1978, no. 1, 15–58; and idem., "Cottimo e organizzazione operaia nell'industria del primo Novecento," *Rivista di Storia Contemporanea*, 1978, no. 2, 161–199. I would like to thank S. Ortaggi for allowing me to read the typescript of her insightful work *Il pensiero di Frederick W. Taylor tra empiria e sistema*, in *Teoria Politiche e Storia Sociale* (Saggi, I, 1974–1986), pp. 137–184.

18 See for example, A.S.B., Reggimento, Assunteria Arti, Decreti e Atti, reg. 6 (1737–1743), cc. 117 and 141; idem., Decreti e Atti, reg. 10 (1766–1777), c. 1.

19 *Lettera degli Assunti delle Arti al Cardinal Legato*, 1738, A.S.B., Reggimento, Assunteria, Arti, Misc. Arti, vol. X (1738–1741). The letter can be found in the file entitled *Editto di revoca di alcune rinovazioni sopra la fabbrica delle sete.*

20 The language of the time used the expression "benefizio all'utile dei primi che s'adattarono a questo nuovo metodo" ("participation in the profits by the first to adapt to this new method") (*Foglio al Reggimento sopra diversi dubbi riguardanti l'approvazione e stabilimento dell'Unione dei Mercanti da velo* and *Riflessioni,* 20 April 1770). The quotation is taken from the *Riflessioni.*

21 See *Lettera degli Assunti delle Arti..*

22 The city officials responsible for the guilds wrote in 1736: "Finally, bargaining for voile today by length and not weight is accepted because the same length of voile is bargained for as in the past but using less silk, which principally reflects the fact that modern voile weighs a third less than old voile" (Relazione delle Assunterie di Camera de d'Arti al Senato per sostenere la negoziazione delle sete nostrane, 18 June 1736, A.S.B., Assunteria

of 1770, "the fatal innovation which those living well remember, of selling voile no longer by weight but by length," had started an unstoppable process of the thinning of the thread. But the more the merchants wanted the "thread of their silk" to be fine, the more they brought to:

> poverty all the workers employed in the very noble activity which in the past provided amply for them and their families, because the work carried out on thick silk thread used to be done with less expenditure of time and as a consequence today they are not able to earn in a month what they once earned in a week.[23]

As well as making their workers poor, the thinning of the thread would produce a crisis of overproduction as "the thread for the voile [had become] excessively abundant, because the length came to exceed the use and the consumption that it could have."[24] This accusation, made in 1738, was repeated a number of times at moments of crisis, at least until 1770. In that year the merchants replied that the thinning of the thread, instead of shrinking the market, actually enlarged it because the new voile, "lasting less," allowed the sale of larger quantities "which would not be sold if the thread had been strong as before."[25] The argument was shrewd, but risky, given the sharp drop in sales and exports of voile in 1769 and 1770, when they fell to the lowest level of the period 1745–1795.[26]

It would in any case be wrong to present the thickness of the thread as an area of conflict restricted to the spinners and the silk merchants. It was instead a site of negotiations and conflicts among a number of complex social groups.

The landowners, who had a half share in the breeding of the silk worms with their sharecroppers, feared that excessive thinning of the thread would intensify and multiply the crises of overproduction. And they were alarmed by the negative influence that the fall in demand for voile had on the price of

---

Arti, Misc. Arti, vol. VIII, 1736). The phrase "contrattandosi a nostri giorni il velo" (selling voile today) is crossed out in the text and substituted with "adoprandosi il velo dalle persone e comprandosi" (using and buying voile from individuals).

23 See *Foglio al Reggimento sopra diversi dubbi.*

24 *Lettera degli Assunti delle Arti.*

25 *Riflessioni* [...] *lette in Senato*, 20 April 1770. These *Riflessioni* are an appendix to the *Foglio di Reggimento sopra diversi dubbi* (see above note 20). The author recognizes that the use of voile had decreased both in England and in France.

26 At the end of June 1769, there were 8,374 *libbre* of unsold silk; in February of the following year the figure was 5,064 *libbre* (*Rimanenza delle sete*, A.S.B., *Reggimento, Assunteria Arti, Misc. Arti*, vol. XXII, 1970). Around 2,000 workers were unemployed. See *Memoriale dei capi maestri filatoglieri*, 29 November 1769, A.S.B., Misc. Arti, vol. XXI (1768–1769).

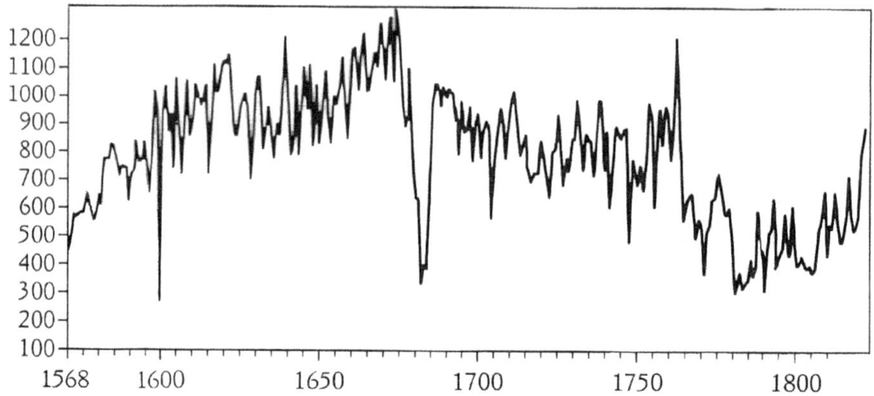

GRAPH 7.1 Cocoons brought into Bologna (calculated in thousands of *libbre*) 1568–1840
SOURCE: TAVOLA DIMOSTRATIVA LA QUANTITÀ DI FOTICELLO DI SETA INTRODOTTO E PESATO NELLE FIERA DEL PAVAGLIONE IN BOLOGNA (1568–1806) [BOLOGNA, NO DATE]

cocoons and thus on their yields. The "piece-work reelers" who transformed the silk of the merchants, were also in favor of thicker thread which required less care and attention. On the other hand, the "free reelers," who made raw silk from the cocoons which they bought from the landowners, wanted to produce the finest thread possible in order to sell their thread both for the production of voile and of organzine. In that way they could subtract themselves from the monopsony of the voile merchants.[27] This objective was a difficult one because of the modest technical level of Bolognese reeling. But it found some support, at least from 1737 onwards, in the interests of the landowners and their political representatives, the Senate. The latter agreed, on the suggestion of the Guild Committee, that the sale of thread on two markets would lead to a better "placing" of both the cocoons and the local raw silk with "an increase in the prices of the fair" (the Pavaglione), of "customs yields" and of employment.[28]

27 "The master reelers who manufacture silk for themselves," says a *Memoriale* of 1737, "are those who ask for the freedom to reel their silk in the mills into thread which can be useful to them, that is, for voile or for organzine, thus avoiding the subjugation of their materials when they remain unsold and in the control of the voile merchants," A.S.B., Reggimento, Assunteria Arti, Misc. Arti, vol. IX (1737), *Proposizioni per un facilito del Dazio del Pavaglioni* [...] *e Relazione.*

28 See ibid. The term *Pavaglione* was used to refer to the cocoon market.

It was not easy for these opposing and shifting interests to reach a lasting agreement. In general, we may say that in "good" years the landowners and the voile merchants would reach a compromise favorable to the reeling of a medium-thick thread (called "half thread"), but different from "fine" thread. This compromise, which also established particular wage levels, would be formalized in a decree published by the highest political authority, the Cardinal Legate. The "Decree concerning the reeling and manufacture of silk of the Bologna reelers" often repeated from the 1730s onwards, laid down:

> So that the silk [...] will be as far as possible of the desired quality, we demand of the reelers that the thread should be what is termed "half thread" (*mezzo filo*) so it cannot be fine silk, and that they should make sure that the silk is well spun and of the same thickness.[29]

In years of overproduction or in which voile was unable to find a suitable market, all the landed interests and some of the merchants came together to release both "free" and "piece-work" reelers from these constraints and to permit the reeling of the thread to the thickness the reelers desired, with a resulting temporary fall in pay for the silk workers. In these periods, the Cardinal Legate together with the city authorities, published an "Edict of revocation of some decrees concerning the production of silk" which suspended the monopsony of the voile merchants over local raw silk and the law which imposed the production of "half thread":

> leaving [...], in the interests of trade and the sale of silk, the liberty to anyone to convert our silk into organzine or weft and to use it in dyed cloth (*opera tinta*) or to export it wherever he likes as is the case for the organzine made from imported raw silk. [...] And moreover that everyone should reel or have reeled by others the silk thread which is best for him and that best responds to the needs of the market.[30]

---

29 *Bando e provisione sopra il trarre e fabbricare le sete de' calderani in Bologna*, 14 giugno 1730 (A.S.B., Reggimento, Raccolta Bandi, ad annum). I have not been able to find earlier proclamations. Already in 1728, a decree forbade, in line with a long tradition, the use of "the raw materials used to make voile [...] for making organzine and weft" unless "the officials and men of the [Silk] Guild decided that the harvest was abundant beyond all needs" (*Bando sopra la fabbrica de' veli ed altro*, 30 April 1721, A.S.B., Reggimento, Assunteria Arti, Misc. Arti, vol. VI, 1715–1734).

30 *Editto di revocazione di alcune ordinazioni sopra la fabbrica delle sete*, 12 June 1738, A.S.B., *Reggimento, Assunteria Arti, Bandi ed Editti*, Book III. More often, without having recourse to this or other edicts, such as the *Notificazione sopra la facoltà di tirar in caldiera serta da*

To understand better the overall dynamics of the conflict it should be kept in mind that all the cocoons produced in the countryside around Bologna had to be sold by law in the Pavaglione, the city market, and that the raw materials, once brought into the city, could only leave it as voile. This meant that normally it was forbidden to use local silk to produce organzine which, as we know, could be exported.[31]

At this point it is not difficult to construct a system of binary opposition with on the one hand the good years, those of the "half thread" and "normal" wages, and on the other the bad years of "fine thread" and a fall in wages. This opposition helps us understand the characteristics of the crisis of 1737 and the resistance to the demands of spinners for a wage increase. The fluctuations in wages during lean years was one of the means by which the crisis was governed, and one which the merchants could not and would not give up. With the return of good years and the "half thread," wages would rise again.[32]

These considerations need further precision through analyses of the trends of the economic cycle. But we need to remember that the compromise over the "half thread" was really only about terminology. The count of this thread, like the "fine" variety, was never defined in terms of the relation between a given length and its weight.[33] In the absence of an adequate technical definition, the

---

orsoglio e trame, 18 March 1735, A.S.B. Reggimento, Assunteria Arti, Misc. Arti, vol. VII (1750–1753) – the Silk Guild conceded permits at its discretion. See note 29. Sometimes these concessions were given too late, when the reeling was nearing its end. The voile merchants were not always compact. Each merchant acted according to the stock of voile that had not been sold, the number of cocoons bought, etc.

31 Only a small part of the organzine was used to weave satin, damasks, etc. This sector, which produced only a few thousand *libbre* of fabric, was known by the name *opera tinta* (dyed cloth). In general, it was forbidden to use silk from outside Bologna for voile, except in years in which the production of local silk was insufficient.

32 Another means of mitigating the cyclical and seasonal crises, from 1692 onwards, were the loans with guarantees in the form of silk bales in which the Monte della Seta (the Silk Bank) specialized. See M. Margi, *I cinquecento anni del Monte di Bologna* (Bologna, 1973), p. 107.

33 The history of the concept of count, its spread and its use in trade is still to be written. Its definition can be found in the *Encylopédie* in the entry *Fil* (thread). The indeterminacy of the "half thread" should have been resolved by the Silk Guild by distributing "to all the master reelers a sample [...] for each one to keep as a model to which all could conform as regards the thickness of the thread" (*Senato Consulto a regolamento dell'Arte della seta*, p. 6). The rule was applied only sporadically because it was too costly. In 1772, two "samples" of half thread were sent out, "one of which showed the [ideal] thickness, the other the size that could not be exceeded" (*Bando a provisione sopra il trarre e fabbricare le sete de' caldierani di Bologna*, 23 June 1772, A.S.B., Reggimento, Assunteria Arti, Bandi ed Editti, Book IX).

thickness of this "half thread" was to a great extent subject to the interpretation of the merchants. In fact, the thinning of the thread, drastic but temporary and *reversible* in the years of crisis, happened as a normal and long-term *irreversible* trend in the good years and went under the name of "half thread."

This two-level process tended to undergo modifications in the second half of the eighteenth century. In 1750, thanks to the efforts of the merchant Bernardo Giovanardi and the Senate, "Piedmontese" reeling (whose technical characteristics will be analyzed below) was introduced in Bologna. Along with the new technology came a new organization of work, with the construction of a large mill able to house forty boilers and to employ at the same time at least a hundred women, counting both workers and winders.[34] This was a major novelty for Bologna, where traditional reeling factories usually had between one and four boilers. The new factories produced a more homogeneous and finer thread than that usually reeled in Bologna (both in the years of "half thread" and in those of fine thread), which was used for the production of ultra-fine organzine called "alla piemontese." The innovation was a response to the need to train the Bolognese women weavers in this new technique, in the excessively pessimistic expectation that the production of voile would completely collapse. But the novelty was not strong enough to spread.[35] The setting up of a "public" factory for the production of raw silk for ultra-fine organzine, however, did redraw the map of traditional conflicts, also through the gradual reduction of the gap between "half thread" and fine thread.

Around 1770, the anonymous author of an important pamphlet distinguished between "the real half thread" and the half-thread currently in use. He denounced the fact that the latter had become so fine, because of pressure by the merchants, that piece-work reelers were not able to get their workers to produce it.[36]

In these conditions, the thread having now reached a new and irreversible limit of fineness, it was no longer possible to maintain the pay of the spinners at traditional levels. The renewed protests of the master spinners and their workers against the ultra-fine thread (in 1739 and in 1770) were linked with the

---

34 See the many files on "Piedmontese" reeling in A.S.B., Reggimento, Assunteria Arti, Misc. Arti, vol. XV (1750–1753), and the two boxes on the *Caldierini alla Piemontese* to be found A.S.B., Assunteria, Arti, Notizie attinenti alle Arti. Giovanardi had set up his firm on his own in 1746.

35 The cocoons bought by the Società dei Calderini (the Reelers' Society) for Piedmontese organzine, in the period between 1773 and 1790, always amounted to less than 5% of the total production sold on the Pavaglione market (see Poni, *La seta in Italia*, ch. 4).

36 Biblioteca Comunale dell'Archiginnasio di Bologna (hereafter B.C.A.B.), *Osservazioni e comment dei capitol de' mercanti*, c. 7 and 12, ms. B 2460.

decision of the silk merchants, who were forming an association characterized by strong monopolistic tendencies – the Merchants' Union – to raise the piece-work rates.[37] "This," said the merchants, "is in order to help the workers" because "the pay in the past, *fair* with regard to former times and the silk of the past" had become "*unfair* in relation to the times and the silk of today."[38] The wages of the master spinners were raised from 26 to 30 *baiocchi* a *libbra*, those of the workers (*garzoni*) from 9 to 12 *baiocchi*.[39] The argument for the increase, in the shrewd wording of the Merchants' Union, suggested that it was 7 *baiocchi* overall: 4 for the master spinners and 3 for the workers. In fact, the proposed increase was only of 4 *baiocchi* to the master spinners, who would have to pay the workers 3 *baiocchi* more.[40]

The Merchants' Union also promised to pay these wages to the master spinners and the workers "at whatever time, whether the mill was full of silk as it should be or whether it was not because of greater or lesser work."[41] This would appear to be a commitment to pay the wages "to all whether working or not working."[42] But the promise, as is clear from the Senate Decree of 1770, had a more limited effect. It meant a stop to labor mobility and thus also to the dismissal of workers – "with the exception of workers who were clearly

37 According to the master spinners, in 1769, a crisis year (see Graph 7.1 and note 26), high unemployment was accompanied by a decrease in wages "due to the excessive thinness of the silk this year demanded by the merchants in contravention of the law." The small increases in pay conceded by the merchants did not compensate for the "thinness of the silk which was so pernicious to work and the cause of so much trouble and suffering to the workers that for the work of four days, six [days] were certainly not enough" (*Memoriale de' capi maestri filatoglieri*, 25 November 1769, A.S.B., Reggimento, Assunteria Arti, Misc. Arti, vol. XXI, 1768–1769). About a year later, the apprentices said that the organzine thread had "become so thin that we were completely unable to earn a living, even though some merchants paid eight, nine or ten *baiocchi* for each *libbra*" (*Memoriale dei lavoranti filatoglieri da orsoglio* [...] *per ottenere aumento di mercede*, 7 November 1770, A.S.B., Reggimento, Assunteria Arti, Misc. Arti, vol. XXII, 1770). Despite the unemployment, it was not easy to find spinners because the workers, "given over to laziness and to begging, preferred to live like this rather than return to work" (*Memoriale de' Mercanti da velo*, 21 December 1769, A.S.B., Reggimento, Assunteria Arti, Misc. Arti, vol. XXI, 1768–1769).

38 *Foglio de' Mercanti da velo* [...] *per giustificare che li capitoli fra di loro stabiliti hanno per oggetto il bene delle loro maestranze*, 22 November 1769, A.S.B., Reggimento, Assunteria Arti, Misc. Arti, vol. XXI (1768–69) (italics in the original). See also the *Addizioni e riforme della Convenzione Generale tra le fabbricanti da velo*, 31 July 1769, ibid.. On this occasion the wages of the weavers of "low" voile were also increased.

39 See *Addizioni e riforme della Convenzione Generale*.

40 See *Osservazioni e commento*, c. 3.

41 *Foglio de' mercanti da velo*.

42 *Osservazioni e commento*.

incompetent" – if only for the period of the "employment agreement (*condotta*), for a month, or for a year." A temporary block, in other words, regulated by an employment agreement and valid only in normal years. "If the issue gets complicated" the right to lay off was accepted, although not indiscriminately. Merchants and master spinners would have to divide the "available work" above all in favor of those workers who were "the oldest in the craft and the most faithful [...] and in the proportion necessary to let everyone earn something."[43] I am unable to say how this "social pact" was managed or what influence it had on the employment agreements (were they shortened?). According to the ironical author of the *Osservazioni*, the promise to respect the pact of the employment agreement was made by the merchants after they had carried out massive dismissals "according to the nice principle of the Union."[44] The merchants, instead, argued that they had undertaken "considerable expense" for the "maintenance of many underemployed workers," and this argument was accepted by the Papal courts.[45]

In any case, the new "production prices" were essentially inadequate. They indicated not only a new phase in the manufacture of fine thread but also the contractual weakness of the spinners, particularly those employed in the production of organzine, who were inexorably driven out of the productive process by a long-term structural crisis reflecting a long-lasting decline in the export of organzine. (Graph 7.1 represents, with a sharply falling line, that long-lasting decline in the exports.)

The finenesss of the thread, the value of piece-work, and access to work were not the only issues for negotiations and tensions between the merchants and the spinners. Another element played a significant role in the remuneration and the autonomy of work, one which had an impact on productivity, prices and profits: the *cascami*, the waste of material from the productive process.

The first impression of anyone who begins to study this topic, which is still neglected in historical analysis, is that the percentage of waste varied from city to city according to the different phases of work and the quality of the raw materials. In Florence, for example, during the 15th century, the waste produced from spinning varied on average from 3% to 20%.[46] Gabriella Sivori has calculated that in Genoa, towards the end of the 17th century, spinning waste

43 *Senato Consulto a regolamento dell'Arte della seta*, pp. 10–11.

44 *Osservazioni e commento*, c. 4.

45 A.S.B., Reggimento, Assunteria Arti, Misc. Arti, vol. XXIII (1772). *Motu proprio di Clemente XIV con cui si approva la Società dei Mercanti da velo.*

46 See *L'Arte della seta in Firenze. Trattato del secolo XV* [...] *e dialoghi*, collected by G. Gagiolli (Florence, 1868), p. 77.

amounted to 8%, while that of dyeing and weaving varied from 8% for "black flat velvets with one thread" to 25% for "colored damasks."[47] In Piedmont, as in other areas, the "consuming" from producing organzine was the object of negotiation between the parties involved. It was only in 1784 that Vittorio Amadeo III published a decree which fixed the percentage of waste between 4.5% and 10% according to the type of organzine.[48] In Lyon, at the beginning of the 18th century, the *maîtres ouvriers* asked the Consulat (a craft and trade tribunal) to fix the level of waste (*déchet*) at one ounce per *libbra*.[49] Later, an *Arrêt du Conseil d'Etat du Roi* of 19 June 1744 for Lyon fixed the *déchet* of material "fabriqués à la tire ou au bouton" at 12 *deniers* per *libbra*.[50]

These percentages provide some basic information. But in everyday work situations what forms of cultural and social behavior took the place of these figures? A trial held in Bologna towards the end of the 17th century gives us a number of insights into the social context of waste.[51]

In 1681 the voile merchant Giovan Battista Neri gave to the master spinner Antonio Montanari, agent or tenant of Francesco Pedini,[52] 431 *libbre* and 4 *once* of raw silk "laborandas pro fabricandis velaminibus" (to be worked to make voile), agreeing to a price of 1.8 *lire* (28 *soldi*) per *libbra*. Having completed the work, Montanari gave back to the merchant 445 *libbre* and 1 *oncia* of "damp" spun silk along with 15 *libbre* and 4 *once* of short or broken silk threads (*sfilzini*).[53] In all, then, 460 *libbre* and 5 *once*, around 29 *libbre* more than the raw silk which he had received. Apparently, the merchant should have been happy with the extraordinary success of his silk. But this was not the case. He

47 G. Sivori, "Il tramonto dell'industria serica genovese," *Rivista Storica Italiana*, LXXXIV (1972), no. 4, 921–925.

48 G.I. Ghiliossi, *Setificio nazionale*, Part One, 1786, p. 142, Biblioteca Reale di Torino (BRT), *Storia Patria*, ms. 556.

49 J. Godart, *L'ouvrier en soie. Monographie du tisseur Lyonnais. Étude historique économique et sociale* (Lyon-Paris, 1899), p. 464. A careful analysis of waste should distinguish between synchronic and diachronic variations.

50 *Arrêt du Conseil d'État du Roy qui ordonne l'exécution des Status et Règlement pour les fabriques de Lyon*, 19 June, 1744, p. 60, Archives Municipales de Lyon (AML), hh, *Arts et Métiers, Ouvriers en étoffes* [...] *de soie*, no. 132.

51 The quotations from the trial are taken from *Informazione nella causa insorta fra G.B. De Nigris e Fr. De Pedini per calo di seta nel lavorarla nel filatoio* (Bologna, 1690). The title of this short pamphlet is taken from the catalogue of the BUB (University of Bologna library) but does not appear in the original text.

52 Pedini owned a silk mill with a water wheel with two machines with 44 rods and 40 bobbins (A.S.B., Reggimento, Assunteria d'Ornato, Chiaviche del Canale di Reno e filatoglieri 1653–1785, *Descrizione di tutti li filatogli* [...] *esistenti nella città di Bologna*, 18 July 1683).

53 In dialect dictionaries there is no entry for *sfilzino*. We may take these to be short and broken threads tied together.

turned in fact to the Trades Tribunal (*Foro dei Mercanti*), accusing the master Montanari of fraud for having returned to him only 353 *libbre* and 2 *once* of thread, the other 91 *libbre* and 11 *once* being the weight of the water. He thus demanded to be given back a further 35 *libbre* of silk and 90 *lire*, 5 *soldi* and 10 *denari* as a discount for the additional amount that he had paid for the spinning ... of the "damp thread." With the appeals and counter-appeals five judgments were given. The last laid down first that Neri was entitled to only 389 *libbre* and 2 *once* of thread as at least 42 *libbre* and 2 *once* had to be taken off for "natural decrease," and second, that the 445 *libbre* and 1 *oncia* that were given back – minus the 55 *libbre* and 10 *once* due as "decrementum" of the water – included around 390 *libbre* of thread, one more than he had a right to.[54]

To whom did the "natural decrease" belong? The judgment does not deal with the problem directly. The answer is that the waste did not belong to the owner of the raw silk (with the exception of the short and broken threads – the *sfilzini*) but to the person who had worked the silk, in this case the master spinner. In practice, all those who worked the silk kept some small part as waste, including the spinners of organzine and of voile thread, and with them the dyers, the weavers and the winders – all in all between 7,000 and 8,000 women, men and children.[55]

The waste, sold in small quantities outside the legal market, was reworked in a more or less hidden fashion and sold either as a semi-finished or finished product. In Bologna this activity produced floss (fine silk thread produced from the outside of the cocoons), gloves and stockings.[56] The waste of the productive process, then, along with ownership rights deriving from medieval artisan traditions, created the conditions, necessarily fragile and small but nevertheless not without substance, for a simple commercial production. The silk workers, then, were not only wage-earners paid by the piece but also, on a more or less ad hoc basis, independent workers of the silk which they were able to appropriate as waste.

There was, however, a strong relation between these two social figures. The right to waste was in a sense the extension of piecework. Karl Marx, after stating that "the piece-wage is nothing but a converted form of the time-wage, just

54 According to other sources, in the water-driven silk mills of organzine, the silk was not dampened (see Poni, *La seta in Italia*, ch. 1). Evidently water was part of the production process of thread for voile.

55 This figure is obviously approximate, and does not take account of yearly trends. According to other calculations, towards the end of the 18th century, but before the acute crisis of the 1790s, there were around 10,000 silk workers. See ibid., ch. 4.

56 *Senato Consulto a regolamento dell'Arte della seta*, p. 19.

as the time-wage is a converted form of the value or price of labour-power," admitted, almost in self-contradiction, that the worker "takes the outward appearance of piece-wages seriously" and believes that "his product" is being paid for, that is, his work already made objective in the product, and not his "labour power."[57]

It is highly likely that the Bolognese silk workers, whether spinners in a factory or domestic workers like the weavers, took very seriously this real "appearance." Just as sellers of their labor already incorporated into the product, they appropriated, almost like independent workers, that part of the raw material which became waste in the productive process. This thought process denoted a rich tradition of "workers' know-how" which can be linked to a very old but still lively cultural legacy: that of the artisan workshop which continued to provide behavioral models and to lay down the rules of the game. These rules could not be avoided even by the merchants. They fought them, but they were obliged to come to terms with them. They did not deny the workers the right to the waste but demanded that *all* the waste, without exception, should be given back to the merchants who would "pay them for its real value."[58] In order to take the raw materials from the hands of their workers or master artisans, and stop their transformation into independent producers, the merchants claimed the exclusive right to buy the waste of their own silk. They knew that the very existence of a "free" trade in waste tended to multiply the waste, "encouraging the women weavers to tear silk with serious damage" as well as "workers' theft."[59] The struggle of the merchants to buy and control the waste and to combat the independent production of the workers (spinners, winders and weavers) reveals social behavior in transformation, an example of a less aggressive method of forcing the workers, at least to some extent, to bow to the needs of capital.

Similar trends can be found in all the silk cities. In Lyon, as in Bologna, the merchants (*maîtres marchands*) recognized that the master craftsmen (*maîtres ouvriers*) had a right to the waste, but they demanded the exclusive right to buy it "at current prices."[60] In the same way the merchants tried to abolish, with the decrees of 1731 and 1744, the figure of the worker-merchants

57 K. Marx, *Capital. A Critique of Political Economy,* vol. 1, ed. Ernest Mandel, trans. Ben Fowkes, trans. (London, 1976), part 6, ch. 21, pp. 692 and 700.

58 *Bando ed editto pubblico intorno a più cose per conservatione del vero e legittimo modo di fabricare velami di seta in questa città*, Bologna, 19 and 20 March 1587, A.S.B., *Reggimento, Assunteria Arti, Misc. Arti*, vol. v. The same order can be found, as we will see, in the *Senato Consulto a regolamento dell'Arte della seta*, pp. 9 and 19.

59 *Bando ed editto public intorno a più cose.*

60 *Arrêt du Conseil*, 19 June 1744, idem. On the "theft" of silk from the merchants, see P. Metzger, "Étude Historique et Juridique sur le piquage d'once à Lyon au XVIIIe siècle,"

(*ouvriers marchands*) – independent weavers – accusing them all of receiving stolen silk from the master craftsmen. In both cases, however, the merchants were defeated, at least temporarily. The new regulations of 1737, favorable to the worker-merchants, abolished the rules of 1731, and the application of the *Règlement* of 1744, which reintroduced in a more stringent manner the prescriptions of 1731, was blocked by a riot which was supported by a majority of the people of Lyon, by the Jesuits and by the canon accountants (*comptes chanoines*) of the city.[61]

The Bolognese silk workers were not content with "natural decrease." They tended to appropriate a part, even a small part, of the finished or semi-finished product. Doing this they transgressed an important maxim of the legal system. But they did not position themselves entirely outside the law. It is important to remember that in the practice of everyday life the workers and merchants would sometimes negotiate a fixed percentage of waste, agreed *ex ante*, after a careful examination of the raw material. But these agreements, on the face of it a variation within the system, actually opened up new spaces for negotiation. What were the positions of the parties in the negotiations if the "real" waste was less than the "agreed" waste? According to the workers, the difference between the two wastes was due to the particular ability of a worker which was not taken into account in his or her wage. Thus if the agreed waste amounted to 9% and the real waste to 5%, the spinner claimed the right to appropriate the difference, in this case 4%. On the basis of this practice, interpreted extensively, the silk workers had complicated and deformed the legal system of waste, introducing the notion of "fixed" decrease, that is, one not negotiated but tacitly tolerated or established by custom. "With the specious pretext," wrote the Silk Guild on 27 July 1731, "of appropriating a certain and fixed decrease, although the work in itself did not lead to this decrease," the workers appropriated "that which remained after this favorable concession, cheating themselves and their consciences because they led their spiritual fathers (their confessors) to think that the waste is the result of their own work and care."[62]

Here we can observe the main lines of the workers' argument over waste: from the right to a tacitly tolerated fixed decrease, to the appropriation of any surplus as an extra (*regalia*) – over and above the natural waste – in

---

Revue d'Histoire de Lyon, XIII (1914), no. 1, 241–270 and its continuation in another issue of the same year.

61 M. Garden, *Lyon et les Lyonnais au XVIIIe siècle* (Paris, 1970), pp. 574–579, *passim*; P. Bonnassieux, *La question des grèves sous l'Ancien Régime* (Paris, 1882).

62 *Memorie alli Assunti di Pavaglione per l'Università dell'Arte della seta della città di Bologna*, 27 July 1731, A.S.B., Corporazione Arti, Arte seta, vol. XX, fasc. 18.

the name of a particular ability not taken into account in their wages. It is not improbable that this complex mechanism, carefully set out in the language of the moral theology of the Catholic church, saw the contribution of the same priests who were inclined to let themselves be "cheated" by their parishioners and to absolve them of their sins without demanding the restitution of what had been taken from their bosses.

The merchants rejected all the claims of the workers to the point of denying, at least implicitly, the right of the worker to the "natural decrease." Their position on this dates from 1666, when in a printed Declaration they denounced "the very serious damages they had received [...] from the excessive decreases" and the "withholding" of their silk on the part of workers "on various pretexts [...] in an entirely illegal manner." According to this Declaration all the silk workers, including the master-spinners and the workers in the silk mills, should have given back all the silk they received "to the merchants, simply and without any malicious artifice" and be content with "the agreed remuneration." They rejected, then, all "abuses, regardless of all pretexts: hard work, increases, exertion or diligence in calculation." And they accused of theft all those who kept the waste.[63]

But how effective could these accusations be, alongside the warning to give back what had been stolen, if they were not supported by the moral authority of the Church? A *Declaration* [...] *to correct the abuses introduced in waste* printed in 1751 as a poster placed in all the silk workshops and firms in the city was perhaps the strongest public effort of the merchants to get the support of the priests. This Declaration, which repeated the doctrine of "natural waste," and repeated many of the points of the Declaration of 1666, preached morality to the spinners and to all the silk workers, but with a clear attempt to influence the priests and the confessors. The merchants warned that "it is not possible to enjoy eternal life if first you do not give back what belongs to others." The poster concluded with an explicit invitation to the clergy and the parish priests, "asked in the proper and right way," to read the same Declaration "on feast days" in the squares and in the churches during the sermon, and to warn the faithful "to do and carry out what is expressed and declared in it."[64]

63 *Dichiaratione fatta da tutti li Mercanti dell'Arte della seta di Bologna sopra li pregiuditiali abusi praticati da gran parte degl'operarii di dett'Arti in danno di detti Mercanti*, 16 April 1666, A.S.B., *Reggimento, Assunteria Arti, Bandi e Stampe*, Book VII. Another *Dichiaratione* before this one had been published in 1612 but I have not been able to trace it.

64 *Dichiarazione de' mercanti dell'Università dell'Arte di seta della città di Bologna per correggere gli abusi introdotti sopra i calli ed altre de' lavorieri*, 20 December 1751, B.C.A.B., *Raccolta Gozzadini*.

It might appear strange that it was the merchants, and not the bishops, who sent instructions to the parish priests on delicate moral questions regarding confession. But it is perhaps more important to observe that the moral content of the Declaration differed on a number of issues from traditional doctrine. The Catholic Church tended, in fact, to justify small theft by servants of the belongings of their employers when the remuneration for their work was below the "just wage." These thefts were considered to be, or could be considered to be, "legitimate compensation," even if hidden and occult, if certain conditions were present. In particular, the right to a higher wage had to be "certain and evident" and no legal means should be available to obtain a "just wage."[65]

The intervention of the silk merchants "to correct the abuses in the matter of waste" and to restrict the area of hidden compensation (and clandestine production) should be seen, then, as part of a cultural change which involved the Church as well.[66] But the merchants were not able to separate their arguments from those of the workers even on this aspect. In another Declaration, an undated manuscript, after repeating the condemnation of "excessive waste through negligence and fraud," they asserted that it should be up to their own "spontaneous generosity [...] to know when and in what circumstances they should give to their workers an extra gratuity in proportion to their good service, and this done voluntarily, not as an obligation, habit or custom found in the law."[67]

The issue of waste was regulated by the Senate Decree of 1770 which confirmed, with one or two explicit restrictions, the doctrine of natural waste. The master-spinner of the silk mill should give back all the silk waste to the merchants "with an obligation on the part of the merchant to pay this waste at the current prices of that year." In turn, the master-spinner should "demand of the workers, both male and female, all the waste [...] with a commitment to proceed against all those who contravened the law with an accusation of theft."

65 The literature on this subject is extensive; see for example L. Gutiérrez de la Huerta, *Tractatus de compensiationibus*, vol. III (Naples, 1700), pp. 274–293, which has a large bibliography.

66 The right to hidden compensation had already undergone a restrictive interpretation in 1679 with a decree from Pope Innocent XI. The Pope denied the right to hidden compensation to servants who estimated their work to be greater than the wage received (Gutiérrez de la Huerta, ibid., p. 275). Over the course of the 18th century the restrictive interpretation tended to become more established.

67 *Dichiaratione fatta da tutti li Mercanti dell'Arte di seta di Bologna circa gl'operarii di dett'Arte*, B.C.A.B., b. 2420 (nos. 5 and 6). There are two distinct editions of this *Dichiaratione*. The quotation is taken from ms. 6.

How could the workers be forced to abide by this injunction? The Senate Decree answered this question by demanding that the master-spinners and the workers report all those who "either in the silk mill or outside of it [...] appropriated even the slightest amount of silk or waste" if they were to avoid being accused of complicity.[68] Was this rule effective? I have my doubts. An effective control would have required other sorts of rules, such as the definition of working hours specifying when the workers entered and left the mills, the setting up of checks with guards and porters, and the preparation of a factory rule-book. There are no traces of such decrees in the Bolognese sources (to my knowledge), while there are a large number of complaints against workers seen to be lazy or insubordinate, sometimes presented as fearing "neither men nor even God, choosing to work when they wanted, how they wanted, and never giving back what was entrusted to them."[69]

The nature and the management of waste, in other words, gave rise to conflicts, adjustments, and even counterproposals (such as "favors") and legal interventions. These were, in any case, affected by specific economic circumstances. In bad years, those in which wages were halved, the waste increased. In response to the hated fine thread, with its sad message of suffering and poverty, the spinners were unable to carry out their work with the greater attention and care that were required. The waste, and in general theft on the part of the workforce, had an inverse trend compared with wages, the former increasing when the latter decreased.[70] This increase in clandestine waste even if it did not compensate for a decrease in wages, gave rise to small additions in incomes, encouraging clandestine work and the hidden economy.

The rights of workers to a part of the raw materials and the implicit negotiation of the rules which regulated it are part of what we might call the "moral economy of work" in the pre-industrial age.[71] These constituted a set of rules

68 *Senato Consulto a regolamento dell'Arte della seta*, pp. 9–10. The right to waste was guaranteed to the weavers at the same conditions as the master spinners. In Florence the right of the workers to waste was abolished, at least formally, in around 1730–1740 (Archivio di Stato di Lucca, Arte della Seta, no. 41).

69 *Memorie alli Assunti di Pavaglione per l'Università dell'Arte della seta.*

70 See P. Massa, *L'arte genovese della seta nella normativa del XV e del XVI secolo* (Genoa, 1979), pp. 147–148, *passim*; B. Buffoni, 'Il problema del controllo del lavoro nell'industria della seta a Genoa tra il '500 e il '600', thesis supervised by E. Grendi, University of Genoa, 1973–74.

71 The expression "moral economy of work" is adapted from E.P. Thompson, "The Moral Economy of the English crowd in the Eighteenth Century," *Past and Present*, 1971, no. 50, 76–136. While the "moral economy of the crowd" refers principally to bread riots, the moral economy of work refers to the behavior of workers in the workplace.

both strict and flexible. In Bologna these norms were unchanging, as immobile as the structures of the silk factories fenced in by guild restrictions. At the same time silk manufacturing was also pliable and permeable to the efforts of merchant capital to penetrate, yet still resistant to major changes. The silk merchants were never able to relocate the early phases of production (reeling, for example) to the countryside, as they would have liked, nor break the mediation of the master reelers and master spinners in order to modernize and make more competitive structures that had become outdated.[72]

While the Bolognese merchants, prisoners of a long-established urban culture of work and production, were unsuccessful, the entrepreneurs of Turin and Piedmont were instead able to triumph. They operated in a marginal and "new" area of silk mills in the Po valley, free from ties to the guilds. Starting from a position of relative backwardness, these "late comers" were able to reach a number of quantitative objectives, becoming the second largest producers of raw silk and organzine in Italy after the Veneto and improving the quality of the product, overtaking all other competitors.[73]

The analysis so far presented of the complicated process in Bologna of making the silk thread finer was interpreted as a complex response to an external challenge that came mainly from the Piedmont area. This interpretation applies to a particular period, more or less between the end of the 17th century and the beginning of the 18th century, and not to any earlier period. The water-driven silk mills of Bologna, a radical labor-saving innovation compared to the traditional hand-spinning plants and which were a near monopoly of the city until around 1660–1680, were for the whole Po valley area the greatest stimulus to carrying out upstream modifications to the productive process, that is to unwind from the cocoons, through reeling, a thread which was substantially more resistant than the traditional one. How did this process come about? It is necessary to remember here that labor-saving machines sometimes give rise to enormous waste of raw materials. This seems to be a particular characteristic of the early American innovations relating to the cutting and shaping of wood, for example. These machines wasted huge quantities of wood and were able

72 There were some changes, however. For reeling, see above pp. 165–176. The penetration of the merchants in the spinning sector was stronger. But at least until the middle of the 18th century, with a few exceptions such as the Pizzardi firm, they limited themselves to renting silk mills and not buying them.

73 For quantitative data on the production of silk in Italy and in Europe, see Poni, *La seta in Italia*, ch. 1. While in Bologna the production of cocoons tended to decrease from the 17th century to the 18th century, in Piedmont the production of organzine increased considerably during the same period. Imported materials should be subtracted from these figures, however.

to spread only in areas in which the price of wood, as in the United States, was extremely low. In the field of silk spinning (a very expensive raw material) the drive towards mechanization could be successful only by containing within tolerable limits the quantity of waste. In practice, the introduction of the silk mills "alla bolognese" into the productive process required a restructuring of the method of reeling and the production of a thread prepared for the traction of a mechanized instrument with an important improvement in the quality of the product.

In short, it was necessary to reel thread that was more resistant. But how? By making it thicker? Not necessarily. The problem was resolved by reducing the limit of variability for the thickness of the thread, thus producing a more homogeneous thread. Following this solution it was then possible to produce thread which was not only more resistant but also finer. The result was obtained by selecting and pulling separately cocoons with diverse characteristics, regulating the number of the floss silk filaments to join to form the thread, reducing the number of threads twisted contemporaneously for each (which in Romagna decreased from six to four), perfecting the technical instruments, improving the professional capacities of the workers and intensifying the control on their work.[74] The Bolognese mills were not only a cost-reducing innovation. They were designed to work with and produce a new and different thread, one which was more resistant and finer compared to the one commonly used. Even the thread for the voile, seen as "thick" in the 18th century, was already the result of a process of thinning and uniformity, but one which had been forgotten and which was no longer apparent to contemporaries. Even more radical was the process of the thinning and standardization of the raw silk for the production of Bolognese organzine, which was reeled where it was produced in Romagna and the Marches but sent to mills in Bologna.

The interdependence of high-level technologies and high quality silk was reinforced by the high prices of the most resistant and finest thread: prohibitively high for merchants whose reference point was the traditional hand-spun silk. An anonymous Bolognese pamphleteer wrote around 1600 that in Naples, Venice, Florence, Lucca and Genoa, where the silk mills (usually hand mills) did not have mechanical winders, unlike the Bolognese ones, "only with difficulty can they make large quantities [..] of fine silk and they run up heavy

74 This process has not yet been reconstructed. It has some constant elements but also important differences. In the second half of the 17th century the bobbins used in reeling in Bologna still wound 8 skeins (*Bando e provisione sopra il fabricare e tirare le sete in Bologna*, 1667). For a comparison between reeling in Romagna and in Bologna, see *Relazione delle Assunterie di Camera e d'Arti al Senato*.

expenses for the wages of the silk workers [who carry out the winding by hand], meaning that they operate at a loss."[75] The price variations, then, increased the variations in thread, changing more and more the nature of the market.[76]

These processes can be understood relatively easily in the areas in which the introduction of Bolognese silk mills *ex novo* tended to modify old equilibria. The sudden spread of the quasi-Bolognese water-powered mills in the area around Bergamo in the second half of the 17th century is strongly linked to a notable improvement and thinning of local raw silk.[77] According to a calculation made in 1679, raw Bergamo silk cost 1.5–2 *lire* more than the that of Brescia, Mantua and Milan (where there were as yet no water-powered mills).[78]

In Piedmont, too, modifications and improvements in reeling were connected to the widespread introduction of Bolognese silk mills, first seen in Turin in 1667, introduced by Giovan Francesco Galleani.[79] In fact, there was no region in which the improvement of raw silk was so noticeable. The "Rules for the Spinners and Silk Workers" (*Regole per i filatori e lavoranti da seta*) promulgated by Duke Carlo Emanuele II on 14 May 1667 and later rewritten and republished in 1720 and 1724, document with some precision the innovations which had been introduced.[80] They specify that the number of threads reeled at the same time per boiler and per reeler were reduced to two, and that the two threads, instead of being strengthened and joined by rolling on a cylinder, which was discarded, were crossed (from six to twelve times) before being wound onto the bobbin. The results were extraordinary.[81] The attention of the worker, concentrated on just two threads, permitted the radical reduction in the thickness of the thread, thus making it finer and more uniform. The twisting together of the two threads

75 *Ragioni per le quali si dimostra non essere a questa città espediente che fuora di essa vadano orsogli di sete reali fatti a questi nostri filatugli*, A.S.B., Corporazione Arti, Arte Seta, box 20.

76 See Poni *La seta in Italia*, ch. 1.

77 The first water-powered silk mill in Bergamo was set up by Andrea Tasca in 1651.

78 *Deposizione giurata di Pasino Locatello*, 21 May 1679, Biblioteca Civica A. Mai di Bergamo, ms. MMB 776 (9), 44–65.

79 The official negotiations between Galleani and the city of Turin began on 16 January 1664, Archivio Civico di Torino, *Ordinati*, vol. 195 (1664–1666).

80 See the *Regole per i filatori e lavoranti da seta*; the "Manifesto del Consolato di Torino [...] per la filatura delle sete" of 29 May 1720 and the second "Manifesto del Consolato di Torino" of 8 April 1724, both published in *Raccolta per ordine di materia delle leggi emanate dai Sovrani della Real Casa di Savoia*, ed. F.A. Duboin, t. XVI, vol. XVIII (Turin, 1849), pp. 163–191.

81 In April 1728, an English salesman from Hamburg wrote: "It is impossible that any other silk can be made use of in lieu of piemontese silk for making alamode, lustring, pourdesway [...] because there is no silk in the world so apt, so clean and so fine," Public Record Office, *Board of Trade*, C.O. 388, *Correspondence*, vol. XXVII, c. 110.

produced a thread that was very different from all previous threads: wound onto the cylinders the thread became flat, but after twisting it became round.[82] The *Regole* further laid down that the reelers were not to be paid "according to the *libbra* of silk which they had worked but by the day and at rates which would give them good reason to use all the necessary diligence."

These technical and economic innovations were reinforced with the threat of fines and warnings by the city authorities, who consciously took on the task of defending the general interests of commerce against "the maliciousness [...] of many who, leaving aside the substance and chasing after the shadows of an apparent gain, neglect the diligence which is needed for the production [...] of silk."[83] With these new techniques productivity declined, if calculated by the *libbre* of silk worked. But productivity increased in terms of the value produced. According to a group of French merchants, the silk reeled in the "Piedmontese" factory set up in La Sône (in the Dauphine) by the brothers François and Fleury Jubié was sold in 1745 at up to 16 *francs* per *libbra* as against the 9–10 *francs* per *libbra* of the silk produced by traditional methods, which they criticized as "coarse and full of imperfections."[84]

In Italy, as in France, the Piedmont rules were frequently reprinted, summarized, translated and to a greater or lesser extent partially assimilated, applied and discussed. In 1765, the *Encyclopédie* dedicated no small number of pages to a penetrating comment on them. The author(s) of the entry *Soie* revealed a profound knowledge of the consequences produced by the substitution of piece-work with daily wages. When work was paid by the piece "so much for each pound" ("à raison de tant chaque livre") the reelers neglected quality and aimed at quantity:

> letting the waste pass [...] so as to advance the work and go on and earn more as a consequence; instead, when the spinner is paid by the day, one takes care to watch over her and she takes care to work better.[85]

---

82 The comment on the roundness of Piedmontese thread was made by J. Vaucanson, "Construction d'un nouveau tour à filer la soie," *Histoire de l'Académie Royale des Sciences ... avec les Mémoires de Mathématique et de Physique* (Paris, 1753), p. 147. This paper, which can be found in *Mémoires de Mathématique*, proposes an improvement of the Piedmontese techniques with the introduction of "double crossing". See also F. Griselini, *Il setificio*, vol, II (Verona, 1783). Naturally the Piedmontese reelers knew how to produce thread of the required thickness, and thus also thick thread, according to the demands of the market. In any case, we are talking here of extraordinarily uniform thread.

83 *Regole per i filatori e lavoranti da seta*, p. 1088.

84 *Registre du Bureau du Commerce*, Archives Nationales de Paris (hereafter A.N.P.), F[12], 92, pp. 178–180.

85 *Encyclopédie, ou Dictionnaire raisonné des sciences, des arts et des métiers*, eds. Diderot and d'Alembert, (Paris, 1751-1771) in the entry *Soie* (silk). According to J. Proust, the

Here we have an early analysis of the waste resulting from piece-work and the advantages of daily wages in order to produce a better (and more uniform) product under adequate surveillance.

Whether discussions on the Piedmontese proposals on wages led to the idea of linking daily wages to a minimum level of production is uncertain, though there is one such example. In 1751, the Intendent of Languedoc, Jean Emmanuel de Saint Priest, in an "Ordinance concerning the Spinning of Silk" (*Ordonnance concernant la filature de soyes*) inspired by the Piedmont rules, directed that the reelers should be paid "their wages by the day"; furthermore, he expressly prohibited piece-work ("so much per pound of silk") and setting "as a daily task a fixed weight of cocoons to reel or a fixed weight of silk to be spun."[86]

The disadvantages of piece-work in reeling were also analyzed by the great French technician, Jacques de Vaucanson. Although appreciating the Piedmont rules as "the best and the most extensive," he argued that their success could be effective only when reeling and spinning were concentrated in the same factory. The entrepreneurs, owners of the factory and of the cocoons, would then be able to verify the quality (uniformity, fineness etc.) of the raw silk during the successive operations of winding and spinning.[87] This observation, which corresponded both to Vaucanson's project to construct large factories where reeling could be controlled, and to the examples of Piedmontese spinning and silk mills introduced into France, precisely capture the direction of the trend.[88] This is amply documented also in Italian and particularly Piedmontese sources.[89] In this area, in fact, we find the high point of the increase in the size

entries *Damas* (damask) and *Soie* "are entirely conceived to show the superiority of the Piedmontese machines compared to the French ones" (J. Proust, *Diderot et l'Encyclopédie* [Paris, 1967], p. 204). We owe to Diderot the compilation of at least two entries on silk: *Asple* and *Bobine* (both types of bobbin). The entry *Soie* is by the editors. On the attempts by Diderot to improve the Piedmontese technology and on his criticisms of Vaucanson, see Proust, ibid, pp. 203–204.

86 *Ordonnance concernant la filature des soyes*, A.N.P., F^{12}, 439.

87 J. Vaucanson, *Second Mémoire sur la filature des soies, Histoire de l'Académie Royales des Sciences* [...] *avec les Mémoires de Mathématique et de Physique* (Paris, 1773), pp. 449, 452, *passim*.

88 Ibid., p. 451, *passim*. In 1763, Vaucanson had built a large silk reeling factory at Aubenas (Ardèche) and defended "the large silk mills" on the Piedmontese model against the attacks of the "modern economists" (ibid., pp. 450 ff). On the introduction of the art of "reeling and spinning silk to produce organzine" in France in the Piedmontese style, see *Mémoire de frère Jubié sur la nécessité de corriger les abus de tirages de soye dans la Province du Dauphiné* (1749), A.N.P., F^{12}, 1435.

89 The advantages of vertical concentration are well analyzed by a Piedmontese author. The merchants who, having bought the cocoons, could process them in their own factories, had four advantages: "The first is that making the reeled silk immediately into organzine

of spinning mills (up to 100 boilers for reeling) and of mechanical spinning (as many as 200 or more workers) and their vertical integration within the same firm, one which worked only occasionally or partially for third parties.[90] In the new large factories the distance between the capitalist entrepreneurs and the workers increased. Discipline in the Piedmontese mills appears with clarity in the work of Dubet, who describes "supervisors" and "commissioned" experts whose eyes were constantly and severely "fixed on the spinners and who were each asked only to oversee a small number of tasks." While in France, continued the writer, "we are usually content to have in our reeling rooms a sort of Argus [...] in one place who can oversee the tasks, from which he observes only the use of time and the faithfulness of the [female] workers, but not their precision in reeling."[91]

The spread of "bureaucratic" control, which imposed silence, order and subordination, is connected to a more careful analysis of the different phases of the productive process. In addition to the controls on reeling, the rules in the silk mills also aimed at standardizing the size, weight and proportions of the machines in order to produce more homogeneous thread.[92] However, the technical improvements were effected not only by means of political or administrative decrees, nor did they relate only to the machinery. Proposals for innovation on the part of inventors from different walks of life appear with a certain frequency in the archives of the Consulat in Turin.[93] One of the most interesting innovations was that analyzed by the architect Giovan Battista Borra. He calculated in a report on the silk mills of Racconigi that the spinning

---

in the mill leads to less waste. Second, the merchant, having the mill ready, can undertake his experiments there in order to proceed with caution with the rest of his spun silk, both in terms of the quality of the cocoons, and in terms of their price. Third, the silk which is produced according to demand can be ready for immediate sale. Fourth, and finally, the merchant who has quickly transformed part of his silk into organzine can more easily obtain cash or continue his business" (*Memoria* no. 87, BRT, *Storia Patria*, ms. 865[1], pp. 1675–1676). This is a memo presented at the competition launched in 1798 by the Academy of Sciences of Turin on the topic: "What are the means to provide for the sustenance of the workers usually laboring in silk throwing in the mills."

90 On the size of the large Piedmontese mills, see G. Prato, *La vita economica in Piemonte a mezzo il secolo XVIII*, (Turin, 1908), pp. 218–225; G. Arese, *L'industria serica piemontese dal secolo XVII alla metà del secolo XIX*, (Turin, 1922); see Poni, *La seta in Italia,* ch. 1.

91 A. Dubet, *La muriometrie. Instruction nouvelle sur le ver à soie* (Lausanne, 1770), pp. 257–258. In a recent article, M. Perrot has argued that in the silk mill of Aubenas, set up by Vaucanson, relatively little control was exercised (M. Perrot, "The Three Ages of Industrial Discipline in Nineteenth-Century France," *Consciousness and Class Experience in Nineteenth-Century Europe* [New York-London, 1979], p. 152).

92 "Manifesto del Consolato di Torino," 8 April 1724, see pp. 1734 ff.

93 See Arese, *L'industria serica piemontese*, pp. 54–55.

machines, which carried out the second operation for the production of organzine, should do "approximately three revolutions a minute" because revolving "more quickly would break the thread; if the movement were slower less work would be carried out" while the throwing machines (the fourth and last operation), "in order that the work should be most perfect," should carry out "four revolutions every minute."[94] This mathematical calculation, already in operation in the mills of Racconigi, permitted a more efficient technical control of the productive process and of the behavior of the workers, reducing idle time and increasing labor productivity. Even the organization of work was formally quantified in a system of fixed relations which identified the lowest indivisible work unit, made up of eight children on the reeler, four workers at spinning, eight women doublers and one thrower.[95]

In this situation, with the appearance of an apparatus of control and technical innovations capable of guaranteeing the uniformity of the productive process, the conditions were created in the silk mills for the definition of a wage corresponding to a specific period of time. In 1777, Antonio Dell'Acqua, in a report which was highly critical of the "silk factories" of Como, Lecco and Malgrate, where the Piedmontese rules were not applied, argued that:

> the workers in the silk mills should be paid by the day and not by the *libbra*, as happens at present everywhere; when the owners of the mills pay for silk by the *libbra*, they oblige these same workers to defraud this manufacture buy using all sorts of tricks and means, such as putting garlic on the silk reels [...] and the reason appears clear: the more *libbre* of silk they work, the more they earn in a day.

According to the advice of Dell'Acqua it was necessary for workers to be "paid by the day and that the day should be regulated with specific hours," in the same way "as seen everywhere." The introduction of specific hours, differing according to whether someone worked only by day or whether by day and by night and rigorously applied, would prevent the workers from leaving the building "during the day whenever they felt like it" and sleeping at home, while "all night long the spinners worked [...] without the slightest supervision." Dell'Acqua proposed three types of working hours. For the mills which operated only by day he suggested a shift of 17 hours, "that is, 15 hours of work,

94 *Relazione del Signor architetto Giovanni Battista Borra nella causa di* S.A.S. *il Signor Principe di Carignano contro li signori filatoristi di Racconigi*, p. 54. The quotation is from a typescript copy which can be found in Archivio Storico di Racconigi, cat. XIV, mazzo 283.

95 See Poni, *La seta in Italia*, ch. 1.

one hour of rest and one hour split between the morning and the evening for meals." For the mills which operated "day and night without stopping" he suggested shifts of 12 hours or, "with an increase in the number of workers," alternating four-hour shifts.[96]

Although Dell'Acqua argued that the silk mill workers were everywhere paid by the day, I think this practice in reality was not widespread.[97] Nevertheless, even the analysis of a daily wage and its connection to the definition of days in terms of hours of work opened up new horizons to entrepreneurs and "directors" in their search to obtain more efficient disciplining of the workforce and their productive capacity.[98] The programming of this greater discipline had already appeared in 1726 in the *Regole* of the large silk mill in Farra (Gorizia).[99] This laid down 14 working hours (with an hour break at midday), fines for lateness calculated "according to the length of time," procedures for hiring and firing, and weekly payment of wages (by piece-work). The *Regole* also demanded obedience on the part of the workers to the foremen and under-foremen, restricted the right to enter or leave the area of the fenced-in mill encircled by high walls with only one door, and threatened with prison those who sowed discord or those "who stole silk or waste or anything else." Here the right of the worker to the waste was not only legally denied but was reinforced by severe instruments of repression. Around half a century later, the Abbé Turbini laid down a plan for an architectural model of a silk mill in which the surrounding

96 Letter from Antonio Dell'Acqua of 25 September 1777, Archivio di Stato di Milano, Commerico, Parte Antica, box 234. Dell'Acqua, who came originally from Messina, aspired to the public post of Inspector of Manufacture. On the greater autonomy of the workers paid by piece work, see the authors cited by Mottez, *Systèmes de salaire et politiques padronales*, pp. 53–57.

97 Piece-work was still widespread in Lombardy in the 19th century. See S. Merli, *Proletariato di fabbrica e capitalismo industriale. Il caso italiano (1880–1900)* (Florence, 1972). According to another study on the textile industry in Piedmont, piece-work was "not widespread [...] in the silk sector". The authors, however, do not distinguish between reeling and spinning. See G. Chicco, M. Marchetti and S. Mobiglia, "Conflittualità operaia e organizzazione produttiva nell'industria tessile piemontese dalla fase post-unitaria al periodo giolittiana," *Quaderni di Sociologia*, XXV (1976), n.s., nos. 2–3, p. 137.

98 According to Karl Marx, while piece-work served to measure the productivity of labor, the introduction of daily wages could serve to break the workers' resistance to the reduction in piece-work rates (Marx, *Capital*, p. 697. The examples examined here of the passage from payment by the piece to payment by the day can be explained by the need to improve the quality of the product and to discipline the behavior of the workers. On the different types of piece-work, see Foa, *La struttura del salario*, pp. 79–87, and Mottez, *Systèmes de salaires et politiques padronales*, pp. 69–76, *passim*.

99 In addition see the *Regole da essere osservate dalla maestranza che pro tempore lavorerà nel Cesareo filatoglio di Farra d'Isonzo* published by R. M. Cossar, *Storia dell'arte e*

wall would include, as well as housing for the workers, an infirmary, a small church and a bell tower with a clock. In his plan, the silk mill was to have a horizontal rather than vertical structure as in a traditional construction model, in order to allow the "director to see at one glance the whole building and to look after his interests."[100]

Only more extensive and thorough research will allow us to date and locate the spread of these and other similar architectural structures and factory rules, research which will have to extend also to the 19th century. But there is also much more that needs to be done. We should try to reconstruct how the spinners perceived the overall changes in their working conditions, how they negotiated the relinquishing of waste, what forms the arguments and the behavior of the workers took where piece-work was replaced by daily wages or by a mixed wage, how the culture and thinking of the workers changed as they participated in and reacted to changes in working and living practices.

The life of the spinners and of other categories of silk workers certainly was and remained a poor one. Research into poverty in Bologna by Fabio Giusberti has brought to light models of family structures in which the "poor beggar" would often be the brother or father of a spinner.[101] Sources from Turin describe old spinners, made blind by their work, begging in the streets of the city.[102]

• • •

This study is a contribution to the history of the culture of work. The analysis presented here of the silk workers (spinners and reelers) could be extended to other categories of workers. Research could be carried out on working practices, habits, traditions, statutes, forms of organization, methods of struggle, relations with the market, the working capacities of weaving families, blacksmiths, printers, shoemakers, bakers, builders ... all of which have to

dell'artigianato in Gorizia (Pordenone, 1948), pp. 246–249. See the detailed comment in Poni, *La seta in Italia*, ch. 1, and the reflections of M. Fatica, "Potere, intellettuali, società e poveri tra accumulazione originaria e accumulazione capitalistica," *Democrazia Industriale*, I (1980), no. 1, p. 23. The whole of this interesting article should be read.

100 G. A. Turbini, *L'economia per la filatura delle sete* (Brescia, 1778), pp. XCIV–XCV, CVI–CXIII, CXXIII–CXXV. For more on Turbini and the relationship between the architecture of factories and rules for the control of labor, see Poni, *La seta in Italia*, ch. 1, pp. 52–59.

101 F. Giusberti, "Poveri bolognesi, poveri forestieri e poveri inventati: un progetto di 'rinchiudimento' nel XVIII secolo," *Storia Urbana*, IV (1980) no. 13, p. 52. See also Ferrante, "Tumulto di più persone," p. 806 *passim*.

102 I am referring to the manuscripts of BRT, indicated in note 89.

be contextualized within a system of relations with other classes and social groups.[103] The culture of work understood in this way can contribute to widening and enriching the history of popular culture. A closer look could even suggest the possibility of linking popular culture in the sense of work to popular culture according to traditional definitions, such as the history of the imaginary, of religions and of popular ideologies, of festivals, of annual rites or rites of passage. It is necessary, in short, to explore paths and tracks which lead us to other routes farther off, analyzing and rethinking the relations between the everyday and the exceptional, between working days and days of rest, between the role of artisans and that of workers in the workplace and in the productive process, in the same way as has been done for in the religious processions and the dressing up of carnival.

Looked at through the lens of work culture, popular culture is not an imitation or derivation of the culture of the élite. Instead, a more complex system of relations emerges, a continual process of negotiation between competing or opposing interests which include dependence and conflict. Struggling to defend their "privileges" (such as the right to waste) the workers and artisans were aware that they could find justification in customary practices and in the compassion of the highest moral authorities.

103 See the introduction to W.H. Sewell Jr., *Work and Revolution in France. The Language of Labor from the Old Regime to 1848* (Cambridge, 1980), and the article by S. Kaplan, "Réflexions sur la police du monde du travail (1700–1815)," *Revue historique*, 1979, no. 261, pp. 17–77.

Sharecroppers' house, "House and household. The women are all indoors standing by the windows, while the men are all outside standing near the front door." (Canolo di Correggio, Reggio Emilia, c. 1880)
SOURCE: LA BIBLIOTECA PANIZZI, REGGIO EMILIA, ITALY

Ploughing a field with oxen
SOURCE: MUSEO DELL'AGRICOLTURA E DEL MONDO RURALE, COMUNE SAN MARTINO IN RIO (CATERINA FERRARI)

Threshing wheat and machine baling of straw
SOURCE: ARCHIVIO FOTOGRAFICO, FONDAZIONE CINETECA DI BOLOGNA (GIULIANA CERABONA)

Model of the silk mill machine "alla bolognese" (mulino da seta). The *mulino da seta* twists the threads; the mechanical winder (in the foreground) provides the threads to the *mulino*. Exhibit in the Museo del Patrimonio Industriale of Bologna.
SOURCE: MUSEO DEL PATRIMONIO INDUSTRIALE DI BOLOGNA, ARCHIVIO FOTOGRAFICO.

Silk factories, Bologna. A. Basoli (1774–1848). Factories of the Cavadizzo (in Bologna)
SOURCE: COLLEZIONI D'ARTE E DI STORIA, FONDAZIONE CASSA DI RISPARMIO, BOLOGNA

Silk mill, Bergamo. Ronzoni, Pietro (1781–1862). Textile mill in Bergamo. Oil on canvas
SOURCE: MUSEUM: GALLERIA DI PIAZZA SCALA, MILANO. PHOTO CREDIT: ALBUM / ART RESOURCE, NY

CHAPTER 8

Technology, Organization of Production, and the Gender Division of Labor

Carlo Poni

1 Twisters and Winders

Towards the second half of the 19th century the workforce employed in silk processing (excluding weaving and dyeing) in northern Italy was almost totally female. Peasant women and their daughters raised silkworms: men carried out some auxiliary tasks such as gathering mulberry leaves, but only cooperated with the women during the final phase of raising the silkworms. The workforce in the spinning mills where the threads were reeled into skeins was also exclusively female – with the exception of mechanics, porters, supervisors and stokers. The subsequent processes of winding and mechanical "throwing"[1] or twisting for the production of weft and organzine for the warp were also increasingly done by women and girls.

The history of the gender division of labor in these three sectors is, however, not the same. In the first two – raising silkworms and reeling – the absolute prevalence of women and girls seems to coincide with the mediaeval and modern forms of the silk industry. In all the drawings depicting silk worm raising and thread reeling (as in all the descriptions) men carry out only auxiliary roles compared to women.[2]

Winding and twisting were different and more complex operations. In these sectors women's roles developed in different ways. According to a widely shared opinion, the principal innovation in silk production, and one which was the basis for all the others, occurred in Lucca at the beginning of the

1 ["Throwing" is the industrial process in which silk which has been reeled into skeins is twisted and wound onto bobbins or spools. -Eds.].

2 According to Bernardino Ramazzini silk reeling was done only by women, as if nature had produced silk "quasi solum in illarum gratiam" (*De morbis artificium*, 1700, p. 200). But in Calabria and Sicily, where reeling was done with mangles ("*caldiera alta*"), silk was traditionally reeled by "Master reelers" assisted by apprentices and errand boys (see C. Capalbo, "Mercato esterno e tradizione di mestiere. La produzione della seta a Cosenza tra Sette e Ottocento," *Meridiana*, no. 3 (1988), 87–89; S. Laudani, "'Li posti delle mangani'. Note sulla seta siciliana fra Sette e Ottocento," *Meridiana*, no. 6 (1985), 109–114.

 | DOI:10.1163/9789004713277_010

14th century. It was then that the hand-operated circular spindle – a twisting mechanism – was introduced. This machine was able to simultaneously twist dozens of threads, thus replacing dozens of hands.[3] This was an extraordinary machine for the epoch in which it was built. Probably no more than four or five people (including the two who provided the power) could work at this spindle, invented in Lucca, while several dozen more women winders worked from home. These numbers were greater in areas where a new source of power was added to the original machine: the water wheel.[4] Due to this innovation, introduced in Bologna in 1341, small spindles operating in rooms not much bigger than 10 square meters were replaced over time by silk mills distributed over several "plants," located on two or three floors, the largest of which occupied hundreds of square meters. By the mid-1500s these operations were packed with dozens of workers working with thousands of threads.[5] The numbers of home-based winders also increased proportionately when they were supplying medium-sized or large mills.

In Bologna in 1371 there were twelve silk mills with water wheels, and their numbers continued to grow during the 1400s.[6] In these industrial plants the entire workforce was male. This was also the case in those plants that Bolognese entrepreneurs and "machinists" built, challenging the laws of the cities, in Modena (1501), Trento (1538), Faenza (1559–1561), and Reggio Emilia (towards the end of the 16th century). It was the workers' task to supply the machines with raw material, tie the threads when they broke, take down the reels to place the twisted skeins in baskets (an operation called *cavatura*), oil the transmission parts and operate the mechanisms that regulated the number of twists of the thread per unit of length.

Since women generally were not allowed in silk mills, they worked at home winding silk thread for the mechanical twisting. To understand the role and importance of winding one should bear in mind that while water- or hand-powered spindles could only process yarn wound onto spools, the reeled silk came off in skeins. So before starting to twist the silk, it had to be unwound from the skeins and wound onto spools. This operation was done at home by hand by winders, generally called *maestre* (the most experienced). To produce weft, each thread of silk – once wound – was given a single twist in the form of

---

3 T. Bini, *I lucchesi a Venezia* (Lucca, 1853), p. 54, passim.

4 G. Livi, *I mercanti di seta lucchesi in Bologna nei secoli XIII e XIV* (Florence, 1881), pp. 28–29.

5 For information on the spread and technological evolution of silk mills see C. Poni, *La seta in Italia, una grande industria prima della rivoluzione industriale* (Bologna, 2009), ch. 1.

6 G.N.P. Alidosi, *Instruttione delle cose notabili della città di Bologna* (Bologna, 1621), p. 37–38.

a Z (counter clockwise). To produce organzine for the warp, on the other hand, the two threads (already separately Z-twisted) had to be wound again onto the same spool (doubling) and – remounted onto the silk mill – given a second S-twist (clockwise). This second winding, like the first, was done by hand by the women called *maestre* or "doublers."

What was the reason for this division of labor? The literature on the subject gives no explanation. According to one theory (perhaps inadequate), assigning men the task of mechanical twisting and women the hand winding could be explained by the fact that men got the more skilled work and women the less skilled. Indeed, simple hand-winding without twisting appears to require fewer skills than the complex tasks of twisting, which also entailed a certain level of mechanical knowledge.

That men were assigned the more qualified work outside the home can also be explained by the fact that only men were allowed to become apprentices at workshops under the supervision of a master. Women, on the other hand, while generally but not always excluded from corporate organizations, learned and practiced skills (such as sewing, spinning and winding) in their own homes or in those of neighbors. These skills were perceived as fundamentally feminine and in any case less incompatible with other tasks such as housework and child care, as they were performed at home.

While these perceptions were apparently based on common sense, they actually stand on rather shaky ground. Certainly every epoch and every geographical area features specific divisions of labor between men and women. But these divisions do not always follow the same logic; they change over time and do not exclude the mixing of tasks. In short, the segmentation of the labor market and the segregation of women do not derive from primitive archetypes nor do they follow timeless constants. Furthermore, until we know in which phase of their lives women (girls, married women with or without children, and widows) were involved in wage work – in our case winding was a form of piece-work – it is impossible to establish the sense of connection with housework, which in turn should be defined with analytical accuracy (and not described by superficially projecting our own experience back in time). Nor is the distinction between skilled and unskilled labor based on solid evaluations. We can say for certain that in the silk industry women were always paid less than men. As long as the tasks were different one can hypothesize, albeit with caution, that wage differences corresponded to different skill levels. This explanation however does not help when women were paid less than men for the same tasks.[7]

One of the theories to consider in explaining women's exclusion from the work of twisting is as follows: in silk mills, where dozens of men gathered, the work was done in semi-darkness lit only by oil lamps because of an ancient belief (not entirely unfounded) that silk's extended exposure to sunlight would negatively affect its color. Could the preoccupation with avoiding sexual promiscuity have influenced the policy of excluding women from access to permanently dark places? Another theory focuses on handling the heavy wooden reels after taking off the skeins of twisted thread (at the end of each processing cycle) and resetting the production cycle. This work required physical strength more fitting for men than women, whose long, wide skirts could also be dangerous as they could easily get caught in the mill machinery. In any case, female labor was the most vulnerable part of the workforce, and the least protected from market fluctuations. Sources from Bologna repeatedly cite that in the years of crisis in the silk industry, thousands of unemployed "old maids" ran the risk of turning to prostitution to have enough to eat.[8] These factors reveal the existence of a vast supply of poorly paid female labor with a lack of alternative work.

2 *Tavellari,* Women Weavers and Children

Towards the middle of the 15th century a new technological innovation, the mechanization of the first winding process, also originally from Bologna, led to a restructuring of the gender division of labor. This new machine, operated by the same water wheel that propelled the twisting machine, had important socio-economic consequences for the areas in which it spread. It concentrated winding under the same roof as the mill, drastically reduced the volume of labor required, improved the quality control of the product, shortened production times, and decreased capital and production costs. Alongside these profound changes (which were capital-saving and labor-saving) female labor replaced that of men.

The employment of hundreds and/or thousands of women who wound more or less intermittently at home, was replaced, in relation to the first

---

7 I discussed these problems with Angela Groppi, whom I thank for her generous collaboration.

8 *Memoriale ai Senatori dell'Arte dei tessitori di seta* (Bologna, n. d.), unnumbered pages; L. Ferrante, "La sessualità come risorsa. Donne davanti al foro arcivescovile di Bologna (sec. XVIII)," *Mélanges de l'École Française de Rome* (1987), 989–1016.

winding, by a much smaller number of children who worked on the top floor of the mill (or in adjacent rooms) under the supervision of one or more adults, called *tavellari*. The children's task was to clean the threads and tie them when they broke. In addition to supervising, the *tavellari* helped mount the skeins and did small repairs when the machines got blocked or broke down.[9] This innovation was adopted in Bologna on a large scale, where it was introduced in the period of the expansion of the silk industry. Excluded now from the first winding, women were given the possibility of working on the second winding (doubling), which continued to be done by hand at home, as well as voile weaving, which was also in expansion.[10]

This move of female labor from a less skilled job (the first winding by hand) to another more highly skilled one (weaving voile) deserves some attention. It reinforces the theory that in the 16th century there was no general decrease in the use of female labor, and specifically that this decrease did not occur in weaving.[11]

Nevertheless, we should bear in mind that in Bologna women were only allowed to work at the lower levels of weaving: that of the production of voile, which in 1591 employed around 12,000 weavers. Men, on the other hand, entrenched themselves in luxury weaving (damasks, brocades, etc.), where the work was more skilled and the wages were higher. Thus it seems that the classic relationship was re-established: men had the skilled and better paid work, while women had the less skilled work. Over the long term, however, women also invaded this second sector. Between 1680 and 1796 there were more women registered in the silk weaving guild than men (591 women versus 196 men), although by now the sector was already in profound decline.[12]

The fact that thousands of women were employed as weavers should not be taken for granted or perceived as natural or obvious. Even in 18th century Gorizia, silk taffeta weavers opposed the admission of women "to the weaving trade" both for formal reasons – because they had not been apprentices under a master "something that is not practiced anywhere," – and because they feared competition from a labor force that would accept lower wages. According to the weavers of Gorizia, women should be employed only "in the most basic

9 See Poni, *La seta in Italia*, ch. 1., pp. 4–19, 42–44.

10 Ibid., ch. 4, pp. 156–157.

11 J.C. Brown and J. Goodman, "Women and Industry in Florence," *The Journal of Economic History*, LX, no. 1 (1980), 73–80.

12 A. Guenzi, "La tessitura femminile tra città e campagna. Bologna, secoli XVII–XVIII," *La donna nell'economia, secc. XIII–XVIII*, ed. S. Cavaciocchi, Istituto internazionale di storia economica "F. Datini" di Prato (Florence, 1990), pp. 247–260.

tasks – such as winding, doubling, or reeling silk – tasks which require more patience, more precision, and less pay, jobs which would be difficult for men to take on [...]. If women were free to toil over the looms, they would all give up the other more bothersome and poorly paid tasks and snatch up the easier and more lucrative ones."[13]

According to this patriarchal conception, which appears to dictate the segmentation of the labor market, women were supposed to have the "more bothersome" and less well-paid jobs, whereas men were to have the easier and better paid tasks.[14]

The sources gathered so far do not enable the reconstruction of the strategic reasoning for the introduction of mechanical winding – why and how it was pursued by the Bolognese entrepreneurs who invented it. It could be that mechanical winding was introduced precisely to free up female labor to employ in weaving. Or we could consider the spread of mechanical winding as an entrepreneurial response to the risks of the excessive spread of hand winding, and hence almost a preventive (and protective) reaction to rising wages and the "danger" of hand winding moving to the countryside when the available urban labor force became exhausted. This potential spread to rural areas, which occurred in the 17th century in many cities which were either unable to adopt mechanical winding (such as Como) or were hostile to it (such as Bergamo), was opposed in Bologna by entrepreneurial strategies that aimed at high quality, and therefore required efficient control of production and labor "naturally" identified with the urban area. Above all rural manufacture was profoundly rejected by Bologna's urban culture and political institutions, which explicitly prohibited all sectors of silk manufacturing apart from raising silkworms from moving to the countryside.[15]

In the 16th century the activity of women winding at home was replaced by child labor (in factories) not only in Bologna but also in Trento and possibly

13 *Lettera al Cesareo Regio Consiglio* from 1760, Magistrato degli Stati Provinciali, Magistrato Commerciale, Archivio Storico Provinciale di Gorizia, no. 327/II, pp. 191–198. On the segmentation of the labor market, see *Labor Market Segmentation*, eds. R. Edwards, D. Gordon and M. Reich (Lexington, MA., 1975); *The Dynamics of Labour Market Segmentation*, ed. F. Wilkinson (London, 1982).

14 On the notion of patriarchal society and "patriarchal capitalism," see G. Lerner, *The Creation of Patriarchy* (Oxford, 1986); S. Walby, *Patriarchy at Work* (Minneapolis, MN., 1986); and idem., *Theorising Patriarchy* (Oxford, 1991). On the Venetian corporations' fight to keep women out of the silk factories, see W. Panciera, "Emarginazione femminile tra politica salariale e modelli di organizzazione del lavoro nell'industria tessile veneta nel XVIII secolo," *La donna nell'economia, secc. XIII–XVIII*, pp. 585–596.

15 See Poni, *La seta in Italia*, ch. 4.

in those cities in Emilia where Bologna-type silk mills were set up, with water wheels (and probably mechanical winders). The same assumption applies to those mills with water wheels (and probably also with mechanical winding) often built by experts from Bologna in the first decades of the 17th century in Padua, Treviso, Feltre, Mantua and Pescia. Unfortunately we know practically nothing about the organization of work in these mills. Some of them were not very successful or only partially functioning around 1630. In any case, they could not successfully compete with the industrial plants in Bologna which continued to increase in number and size.

The situation changed radically in the second half of the 1600s when in just a few decades at least a hundred water-powered silk mills with mechanical winding – some of them colossal in size and the result of enormous investments – were constructed in the hilly rural areas south of the Alps, especially in Piedmont and in the Venetian hinterlands. There were powerful factors motivating this move to the countryside or small urban-rural centers: abundant waterways, cheap rural labor, a massive increase in the local production of raw silk induced by growing international demand, the proximity of rich northern and west European markets, and the absence of corporate obstacles that in the cities still restricted merchants' and entrepreneurs' strategic choices. Where high quality production was the goal, the problem of controlling labor was resolved by concentrating reeling in spinning mills encircled by walls that separated the plant from the surrounding countryside. With the verticalization of production, especially in Piedmont, spinning mills (with the reeling operation) were built inside the same walls as the silk mill. Other measures included increasing the number of overseers, housing labor in dormitories adjacent or connected to the industrial plants, and introducing and applying meticulous general and/or factory regulations.

In these rural areas the introduction of mechanical winders had social consequences similar to those which had already occurred in Bologna. The new machines drastically reduced the female labor employed at home. But not everywhere did boys of different ages replace women: for the first time girls too appeared at the mechanical winders. Moreover, the advantages of concentrating and verticalizing production induced numerous entrepreneurs, particularly in Piedmont and Bergamo, to concentrate the second winding (doubling), carried out by hand, within the walls of the silk mills, or in adjacent or connected rooms. This process was not mechanized until the 19th century.[16]

16 Ibid., chs. 1 and 4.

3 Different Reasons for the Gender Division of Labor

In the year 1700, 31 of the 48 silk mills "exactly like those in Bologna" were concentrated in areas north of Vicenza, the most important industrial district in the Venetian hinterlands. The 13 mills for which I found numbers of employees, divided by task, gender and age, show a significant change in the gender division of labor.[17]

Not only boys but also girls were working at the mechanical winders. Only in four cases did the presence of girls exclude that of boys and only in one case did the presence of boys exclude that of girls. In all other cases boys and girls worked together at winding under the same roof. In at least five cases there was a *maestra* watching over them. In the Stroppari family's biggest mill (they owned two in the area of Marostica) a woman supervised the work of 48 boys and girls. These mixed gender situations hint at a lessening of the conflict between female and male roles. Even the darkness of the work areas tended to become less of a cause for segregation and exclusion.

This plant, employing 128 male and female workers and 34 doublers at home, was 3 stories high with 15 windows along the front of the building, and was separated from the surrounding space by an irrigation ditch and an unfinished wall that encircled a large courtyard. In Bologna, walls separated small courtyards between silk mills and residential homes, often in spaces remaining between houses built next to each other. In contrast, the new silk mills at the end of the 17th century located in hill areas took on a new form. Here the mills were surrounded by a large courtyard or field, fenced in by high walls or waterways. This space not only separated the industrial activity (the workers and the precious raw materials) from the surrounding countryside and from robbers, it also showed the importance of controlled spaces (like the courtyards of convents) which could also be used as areas for young bodies, exhausted from work, to relax and refresh themselves. But these spaces were sometimes taken over by another production phase: that of reeling, which took place under porticos (open on one side) filled with dozens of women and girls.

These forms of aggregation, which began to emerge at the end of the 1600s, were fully developed by 1720 in the form of the great imperial silk mill at Farra (Austrian Friuli), which employed over 150 workers: men, women, boys and girls. Most of the labor force had migrated from bordering Venetian Friuli and Rovereto (at that time part of the Austrian empire). Inside the great wall that

17 Archivio di Stato di Venezia (hereafter A.S.V.), *Cinque Savi alla Mercanzia*, envelope 495, *Nota degl'edifitii da seta che lavorano* […] *alla bolognese in Marostega e Villa Nova* (September 24, 1700).

isolated the factory from the surrounding countryside were various blocks of buildings: in addition to the mill with four twisting machines there was a spinning factory under a portico with several boilers for reeling, living quarters for families of the workers, and the house of the director and his helpers and supervisors. In the industrial plant with its mechanical winders, men did the usual tasks of the first and second twisting or "doubling", whereas boys/girls and women did the winding and doubling by hand. Thus in the Farra mill, or rather within its walls, we also find the doublers, mostly the wives and children of the workers. But the novelties do not end here. Again, there was a group of supervisors with different levels of authority who watched over the large labor force which worked, lived, ate and slept within the factory walls.

But the families living within the mill's walls were not large enough to provide the number of girls and boys needed for the mechanical winding. Indeed, "boys and girls from the village"[18] also worked there. This fact might suggest a connection between girls starting to work in the silk industry and the rural location of the industrial plants. It is not surprising that poor peasant families would send excess labor and "hungry mouths" to the work in the factories while the adult males (fathers and sons) worked in the fields. This strategy could also apply to peasants in the Alto Vicentino (the hilly area north of Vicenza). In the 19th century the strategy was followed much more closely by impoverished peasants in the hill area of Lecco. In short, whereas technological innovation in urban centers led to the replacement of women by children and adolescents doing the first winding, in the countryside something different happened: not only boys but also girls worked at the mechanical winders.

The original aspects of the Farra mill are markedly illustrated in its "Rules" (published in 1726): a real set of factory regulations, in some parts not unlike those of the 1800s. It envisaged fourteen hours of work a day (with a one-hour break at noon), a communal morning prayer, fines for being late, hiring and firing procedures, and weekly pay for piece-work. The "Rules" also obliged workers to obey and be "faithful" to bosses and supervisors; restricted the right to enter and exit the walls to one day a week (Sunday); prohibited men and women from having "suspicious practices, or love affairs, under pain of being castigated or thrown out, and men from daring to go out either by night or by

18 "Regole da essere osservate dalla maestranza che pro tempore lavorerà nel Cesareo filatoglio espresse ne' seguenti capitoli," R.M. Cossar, *Storia dell'arte e dell'artigianato in Gorizia* (Pordenone, 1948), p. 247. It is wise to bear in mind that the factory at Farra was a state-owned company run by private entrepreneurs. It would be interesting to compare the "Rules" of this "Cesareo filatoio" (imperial silk mill) with those issued by Colbert for the state-owned Manufactures Royales.

day to talk secretly with any young women"; and threatened prison to rabble rousers and those who had committed "theft of silk, rags or other things." In addition, workers could not carry knives or firearms under threat of imprisonment and losing their job.[19]

The fact that the first set of factory rules I am aware of refer to a production space where men and women work together provokes reflection. Indeed years later the writings of the abbot and architect Turbini compared the order that reigned in the spinning – and silk mills to that of a "cloistered convent."[20]

In Piedmont the first silk mills "alla bolognese" also appeared only in the second half of the 1600s. The first of these mills was built in 1664–65 in Turin by Giovan Francesco Galleani. In just over ten years numerous mills of this type were built in the villages around Turin as well as in Racconigi. According to statistics from 1725–30 there were 70 silk mills with water wheels in the Kingdom of Savoy, 19 of which were concentrated in Racconigi. These mills employed on average 100 workers (men, women and children). The largest of these mills, belonging to G. Peyron, already in 1708 employed no fewer than 300 workers (again including men, women and children), nearly a third more than the largest of Count Galleani's mills, which also in 1708 employed 200 workers.[21]

This staggering size and the rapid expansion of mills, which continued throughout the 18th century, can be explained by the precipitous growth of raw material production, which in Piedmont went in one century from a few thousand pounds to over 1.2 million (or 1.5 million) pounds in the decade 1778–1788. Along with this enviable quantitative record – unique in the annals of the history of the silk industry for its overwhelming dynamism – there is another even more important record. As early as the last decades of the 1600s the "mellow,

19 Ibid., pp. 246–248.

20 G. A. Turbini, *L'economia per la filatura delle sete* (Brescia, 1778), pp. CXII–CXIII.

21 On the size and number of silk mills in Piedmont, see G. Prato, *La vita economica in Piemonte a mezzo il secolo XVIII* (Turin, 1908), pp. 212, 216–235. G. Arese, *L'industria serica piemontese dal secolo XVII alla metà del XIX* (Turin, 1922), p. 64, table XIX. For additional writings on Piedmontese silk mills see P. Chierici, "Da Torino tutt'intorno: le "fabbriche da seta" dell'antico regime," *Torino sul filo della seta*, ed. G. Bracco (Turin, 1992); P. Chierici, "L'architettura delle fabbriche magnifiche: procedure e tempi della concentrazione produttiva fra Sei e Settecento nel Piemonte meridionale," *Le fabbriche magnifiche. La seta in provincia di Cuneo tra Sei e Ottocento* (Cuneo, 1993); L. Palmucci Quaglino, "Lo spazio del lavoro: filatoi, filanda e manifatture di seta a Torino tra Settecento e Ottocento," *Torino sul filo della seta*, ed. G. Bracco; G. Chicco, "L'industria della seta in Piemonte da metà Seicento a metà Ottocento," *Le fabbriche magnifiche*, and idem., *La seta in Piemonte (1650–1800)* (Milan, 1995). See also Poni, *La seta in Italia*, ch. 1.

soft and light"[22] Piedmontese organzas earned higher prices at the market in Lyon than the best organzas from Bologna, which until then had dominated the international market. This was an exceptional achievement, deriving also from the technical improvements that Galleani and others after him had introduced with the active support of local politicians, who had imposed new, highly innovative reeling methods in the entire state (Letters patent, May 14, 1667). By the first decades of the 1700s Piedmontese silk mills, with their superior technology, had surpassed the Bolognese silk mills, the technology of which they had adopted and refined. This phenomenon was consecrated by Denis Diderot in the pages and drawings of the *Encyclopédie*.

In 1788, responding to a competition promoted by the Turin Academy of Science, silk mill entrepreneur Gasparo I. Tempia calculated that due to the "intimate correlation" between the various mill operations, 3 "workers" on the first twisting, 7 "doublers" (by hand) and 1 twister on the second twisting corresponded to 6 children working on the mechanical winder, making up in total one working unit of 17 people of whom 7 were women.[23] Recent research shows that in 1727, in the 26 silk mills at Racconigi, approximately 40% of the labor force consisted of young women ("daughters"), while boys made up 38%. These proportions are fairly close to those of 1788, which suggests an equal division of labor: the "daughters" did the doubling, and the boys the winding.[24]

The gender division of labor in Piedmont thus appears more rigid than in the countryside north of Vicenza. In Piedmont there were no girls working at winding (at least until 1788) but the women doublers, albeit with traditional hand tools, worked under the same roof or within the walls of the mill, where there was often a silk mill for reeling.[25]

The fact that women worked under the same roof or within the walls of the silk mill, deserves some attention. Women's roles in the manufacturing process

---

22 Thus wrote an anonymous English merchant in his travel diary preserved in *Mss. Rawlinsoniani*, Bodleian Library, Oxford, D. 1510. This source is a real investigative account of the industry and the silk yarn market in the Po Valley (excluding Veneto). Not until the last stage of his journey (Florence) did the anonymous author shift the focus of his investigation from yarn to fabric. Since the pages of the manuscript are not numbered, the stage of the journey with location and date are given as a reference: in this case Turin, January 5–6, 1678.

23 See Poni, *La seta in Italia*, ch. 1.

24 See Chicco, *La seta in Piemonte (1650–1800)*. For a precise analysis of the organization of production spaces on maps and in the field, see Chierici, "Da Torino tutt'intorno: le "fabbriche da seta" dell'antico regime;" Palmucci Quaglino, "Lo spazio del lavoro nei setifici ottocenteschi," *Torino sul filo della seta*, ed. G. Bracco.

25 See Poni, *La seta in Italia*, ch. 1.

were still separated physically from those of men. Doubling and even more so reeling were conducted in different spaces from the twisting operations. But it is significant that the doublers were "forced" to leave their homes or neighbors' small workshops to work in a space where dozens of men were concentrated. Wages, calculated by one of the participants of the Turin Academy competition, strongly penalized women. The twisters earned 23.9 *soldi* a day, the male workers 15.6 *soldi*, and boys, for a job that required (according to the source) neither dexterity nor skill received the "miserable wage" of 9 *soldi*. The doublers, for "a nauseating but at the same time delicate task" had to be satisfied with 8.5 *soldi*. In short, for a job that required some skill women earned less than children and just one third of wages of the twisters.[26] The slow advance of women workers in mills did not significantly affect their separation, isolated as they were in the tasks of reeling and doubling. Only adult males worked at twisting. In contrast, the presence of girls at the mechanical winders in the areas of Vicenza and Piacenza showed that their centuries-long exclusion had been overcome.

Whereas in Piedmont the political authorities encouraged and obliged entrepreneurs to choose the most advanced manufacturing combinations, in other areas entrepreneurs had to deal with a governing culture that was preoccupied with employment levels. Thus on 18 April 1671 the municipal council of Bergamo, with a deed granting Paolo Chiesa the use of a publicly owned "portion of water" for his silk mill, expressly prohibited the introduction of mechanical winders "so that this work will not be taken away from the poor and they can continue to get by."[27] The council of Bergamo continued this prohibition in the 17th and 18th centuries in the name of the "public interest" in order not to deprive women from the countryside of work "which provides many peasant families with food, thus supplementing the sterility of the land."[28] These political and social norms were rigorously applied. In the mid-1700s in Bergamo and its surrounding villages, not one of the 51 silk mills had a mechanical winder. This gave rise to an extensive network of home-based women winders in the city and surrounding countryside.

Prevented by the city's political authorities from using mechanical winders, entrepreneurs from Bergamo had made organizational choices similar to those in Piedmont, bringing doubling and thus also the *maestra* doublers under the

26 Ibid.

27 Archivio Civico di Bergamo, *Azioni*, reg. 72 (1670–1675), Resolution of April 18, 1671, cc 43–44.

28 Biblioteca Civica di Bergamo, "Deposizione giurata di Pasino Locatello," 21 May 1679, *Per l'Arte de' Filatoglieri contro la città di Bergamo*, Ms. MMB 776(9), 44–65.

same roof as the mill. According to state statistics from 1765 compiled by the Venetian board of trade, in Bergamo's 69 mills there were a total of 570 men working at the first and second twisting operations and 1,057 women doublers, whereas 13,010 women winders worked at home.[29]

These aggregate data hide a highly differentiated reality. Next to the large mills were small and medium-sized mills. Whereas Andrea Ostani's mill (which was relatively large for Bergamo) employed 19 men at the first and second twisting, 32 women doubling and 400 home-based winders, in Alessio Silvestri's medium-sized mill 7 men worked at the first and second twisting, 13 women at doubling and there were 50 home-based winders. Antonio Fornovi's small mill employed 3 men, 6 women and 150 home-based winders.[30]

The number of home-based winders in these three mills seems quite disproportionate (although this is not an isolated case) compared to the size of the operation (which can be calculated by adding up twisters and doublers). There is a reason for this: there were no set working hours for home-based working units. Each winder's working time, however calculated, depended upon many variables linked to a woman's life cycle (age, marital status, number of small children, and the family's overall income ...). Another obstacle for peasant women was the seasonal demands of farm work. These women could dedicate most of their labor to winding during the late autumn and winter months. Their availability decreased in summer when entire farming families were working in the fields. These, however, were precisely the months of greatest and most intense work in the mills — twisting began in the month of July.

We should also consider that each single winder could work for more than one mill owner. Giuseppe Tiolo, owner of a small silk mill in Udine, stated that he had "about 30 women continuously occupied with winding," and acknowledged that "these women are not only working for me, but also for others."[31] This also applied to Bergamo, and suggests that the number of 13,010 winders taken from the sum of partial data from the 69 mills should be treated with some caution.

The reasons for the absence of mechanical winders in areas with hydraulic-powered silk mills varied according to geographical area. Como-based entrepreneurs Molo and Lavizari could not make them work profitably because of excess waste due to the lack of a local supply of raw silk strong or uniform

---

29 This provisional data is taken from A.S.V., *Cinque Savi alla Mercanzia*, envelope 479. For an explanation of the data contained in this important source see Poni, *La seta in Italia*, chap. 8.

30 A.S.V., *Cinque Savi alla Mercanzia*, envelope 479.

31 Ibid.

enough not to break when it was reeled mechanically. But they also rejected innovation and destroyed the mechanical winders "for the scarcities of boyes to attend to ye tavelle," according to the careful English observer mentioned previously.[32] It is not hard to believe that families opposed this innovation because it took away from the women their jobs and their children. In other cities such as Bologna, where women were offered new work possibilities, employing child labor had encountered less opposition.

Even where mechanical winders had been successfully introduced, the demand for child labor and its "free" supply (on the part of parents) did not always meet the requirements of the market. This was especially so when the pay for hiring children (generally for three years) was considered too low. In 1770 silk mill owners in Modena, complaining about the scarcity of child labor, asked the Grande Albergo dei Poveri (Great Hotel for the Poor) to provide their mills with "the necessary girls" but only after having educated and disciplined them, taking away their "freedom." Silk mill owners in Bologna asked the Senate to force idle girls to work at the winders.[33] In short, neither in Bologna nor Modena did they consider hiring adult female labor for the mechanical winders, in response to the "scarcity" of children. The multiplicity and variety of situations underlines the different geographical and regional (or sub-regional) contexts in which these issues were not strictly technological but also political, social and cultural. In none of the cases examined were women allowed to work at the better paid job of mechanical twisting, monopolized by men.

This persistent exclusion cannot be considered an indication of women's supposed technological incompetence, nor their lack of physical strength. Research on the functioning of female charitable institutions shows that women and girls at least temporarily separated from men could do all the tasks normally done by men, and could participate as workers in advanced types of manufacturing. In hospices, hospitals for the poor and convent schools, women and girls who had been taken in because they were poor, without families, orphans, "badly married," or "unsafe," were generally subjected to rigid collective discipline and learned a trade (sewing, mending, embroidering, spinning, and twisting, or weaving).[34]

---

32 See *Mss. Rawlinsoniani,* Como, February 10–11, 1678.

33 Archivio Storico Comunale di Modena, *Camera Segreta*, Parts IV and XV, *Arte della Seta*, no. 3, t. I. See also the attached Promemoria and A.S.B., *Reggimento, Pavaglione*, Atti (1620–1745).

34 See L. Ciammitti, "Quanto costa essere normali. La dote nel "conservatorio" femminile di Santa Maria del Baraccano (1630–1680)," *Quaderni Storici*, vol. 18, no. 53 (1983), 469–497; D. Lombardi, *Povertà maschile, povertà femminile. L'ospedale dei Mendicanti nella Firenze dei Medici* (Bologna, 1988); *Ragnatele di rapporti. Patronage e reti di relazioni nella storia*

According to Daniela Lombardi, at the Ospedale dei Mendicanti (the Beggar's Hospital) in Florence the separation between the roles of men and women in manual twisting had been completely superseded. Women were no longer confined to winding and doubling but worked for the first time on the twisting machines. And they were still the ones who provided the manual power to operate the twisting machines.[35] At the end of the 16th century in Venice this latter task was considered to be particularly difficult. The Venetian twisters – all men – claimed to suffer "seriously" from the efforts required to operate the city's 500 twisting machines, so seriously that at least during the summer some of the machines stood idle.[36]

In Florence the effort required to power the twisting machines was perceived differently. These machines were operated not only by women from the Ospedale dei Mendicanti, but also by other women "of low conditions" living in the Santa Croce and San Giovanni neighborhoods.[37] A beautiful drawing done in Lucca by the German naturalist Georg Christopher Martin towards the middle of the 18th century depicts a girl working at a hand-operated twisting machine.[38] In short, what was perceived in Venice as a particularly painful and stressful masculine "effort" is portrayed in Florence and Lucca as a task that could normally be done by a woman. This is a good example of cultural relativism in contrast to "natural" binary opposition that would have men doing heavy work and women light work.

delle donne, eds. L. Ferrante, M. Palazzi and G. Pomata (Turin, 1988); A. Kelikian "Convitti operai cattolici e forza lavoro femminile," *Donna lombarda (1860–1965)*, eds. A. Giglio Marchetti and N. Torcellan (Milan, 1992), pp. 180–186; A. Groppi, *Conservatori della virtù. Donne recluse nella Roma dei papi* (Rome-Bari, 1994).

35 See Lombardi, *Povertà maschile, povertà femminile*.

36 C. Poni, "Piccole innovazioni e filatoi a mano: Venezia (1550–1600)," *Studi in memoria di Luigi Dal Pane* (Bologna, 1982), pp. 371–389.

37 See the 1632 census in Biblioteca Nazionale di Firenze, Mss Magliabechiani, EB, 15, 2, and Archivio di Stato di Firenze, *Registro di tutti li sottoposti dell'Arte della Seta di questa Città l'anno 1663, Misc. Medicea*, f. 994. This last source was studied by M. Carmon, "Sull'economia toscana del Cinquecento e del Seicento," *Archivio Storico Italiano*, 1962, no. 433, 32–46, and by M.T. Bettarini and R. Ciappetti, "L'arte della seta a Firenze. Un Censimento del 1663," *Ricerche storiche*, 1 (1982), 35–48.

38 The drawing by G.C. Martin, which is in the Archivio di Stato di Lucca was published in 1969; G.C. Martin, *Viaggio in Toscana (1725–1745)*, ed. O. Trumpy (Modena, 1969).

4 Women Taking Men's Places

The disintegration of traditional roles, particularly evident in certain situations, took place as a general trend during the course of the nineteenth century when a new and dense network of silk mills began to emerge in the foothills above the plains of Lombardy just south of the Alps. There are at least three areas to consider: the provinces of Bergamo, Como and Milan. In 1891 these three provinces contained over two thirds of Italy's total production capacity, calculated in numbers of spindles. Here the focus is on the hilly area around Como, Varese and Lecco (in the province of Como), the most important manufacturing region with 551,949 active spindles in 1891, around a third of Italy's entire production capacity.[39]

The beginnings were modest. In this countryside north of Milan some hand twisting had already been established at the end of the 1500s.[40] But it began to appear more frequently in the economic and political history of the Duchy of Milan only towards the second half of the 17th century, when dozens and then hundreds of hand twisting plants were built in the countryside – particularly in the area north of Milan and near Varese – whereas their numbers in Milan itself (around 600 in 1654) decreased. This trend accelerated over the course of the next century, with the collapse of the twisting industry in Milan (130 operations in 1709 and no more than 81 in 1760) alongside its rapid development in the countryside and other minor centers in the Duchy. The drastic decline of silk twisting in the city can be explained in part by the decline of the Lombard metropolis as the center of high-quality textile production destined for international markets, and in part by an unfair tax system that hit yarn exports once they entered the city to be twisted. This radical shift also allowed entrepreneurs to hire cheaper workers who earned at least a part of their subsistence from working in the fields.[41]

As early as 1677 Como appeared to the attentive English merchant cited above to be the most favorable market in Lombardy for exporting twisted yarn

39 Ministry of Agriculture, Industry and Commerce (MAIC), *Annali di Statistica, Statistica Industriale. L'industria della seta in Italia*, fasc. XXVII, 1981, p. 91. There were 44,869 inactive spindles.

40 See L. Trezzi, "A Case-Study of De-industrialization of the City. The Silk Mills of the City and Duchy of Milan from the Seventeenth to the Eighteenth Century," *The Rise and Decline of Urban Industries in Italy and in the Low Countries. Late Middle Age and Early Modern Times*, ed. H. Van der Wee (Leuven, 1988), pp. 139–152.

41 See Poni, *La seta in Italia*, ch. 1. The city corporations, which opposed the move of doubling to the countryside, complained that silk work took peasants away from their work in the fields.

to England, for three good reasons: the better quality of yarn compared to that from Milan (because it was produced in mills powered by water wheels), better prices, and incomparably lower export duties. However, the Englishman recognized that the organzas from Como and Lecco were of lower quality than those from Bologna and Piedmont.[42]

The inferior quality of the product came alongside significant technological backwardness. As we have already seen, the silk entrepreneurs Molo and Lavizari, who first introduced the silk mills "alla bolognese" in Como, could not use mechanical winders (which were destroyed) due to the inferior quality of raw silk from the Duchy of Milan, which would break if it was subjected to mechanical reeling. The lack of a solution to this problem, which could have been resolved by improving reeling techniques, was transmitted from one generation of entrepreneurs to the next like a fatal inheritance. Towards the end of the second half of the 1700s various attempts to introduce mechanical winding failed "because the mostly poorly spun silk contributed to a ruinous decline."[43]

In 1810 a total of 1,744 workers (of whom 926 were winders) were still working in the 118 mills in the area of Lake Como (which included Como, Lecco and Varese). In addition about 18,000 "women and girls" were occupied for most of the year winding silk at home.[44] How should these figures be interpreted? We may hypothesize that the winders worked on the mechanical winders whereas the 18,000 women working at home not only did doubling but also winding, which was only partially mechanized. Nevertheless, unlike nearby Bergamo, women were still not working in factories either as doublers, or as winders. In Lecco, on the other hand, by 1844 women and girls made up 64% of the workforce for twisting.[45] A few decades later, according to statistics published in 1879 by Alberto Errera for the province of Como, women and girls made up 87% of the labor force in silk-spinning and winding.[46] They were by far the

42 See *Mss. Rawlinsoniani*, Como, February 10–11, 1678; see also R. Merzario, *Il capitalismo nelle montagne, Strategie familiari nella prima fase dell'industrializzazione del Comasco* (Bologna, 1989).

43 "Relazione del 'visitatore' comte Odescalchi," M.V. Ballestrero and R. Levrero, *Genocidio perfetto. Industrializzazione e forza lavoro nel lecchese 1840–1870* (Milan, 1979), p. 17. Other attempts were more successful; see Merzario, *Il capitalismo nelle montagne*, p. 111.

44 A. Cova, "L'alternativa manifatturiera," *Annali dell'Economia Comasca. Da un sistema agricolo a un sistema industriale. Il Comasco dal Settecento al Novecento*. I: *Il difficile equilibrio agricolo-manifatturiero (1780–1814)*, ed. S. Zaninelli (Como, 1987), p. 172.

45 This data from 1844 was compiled by a medical doctor from the province of Como cited in Ballestrero and Levrero, *Genocidio perfetto*, pp. 22–23.

46 A. Errera, "Inchiesta sulle condizioni degli operai nelle fabbriche," *Archivio di statistica*, (1879), 115–185.

majority not only in spinning mills, but also in the silk mills and in mechanical winding, whereas there were no more winders at home. Doubling, not mentioned explicitly, was probably included either in the figures for spinning or for winding.

Women replacing men and the extensive employment of boys and girls in the same factory occurred simultaneously with other converging entrepreneurial decisions, aimed at introducing new technology and also in response to the challenges of international competition. After 1850, alongside the spread of mechanical winding, mechanical doubling was introduced. In the same decades entrepreneurs began to replace the round wooden mills, by then perceived as slow, heavy and cumbersome ("gothic"), with new lighter rectangular frames, more manageable and better suited to women's work.[47]

By 1904, 72% of the province's spindles were in rectangular frames.[48] However, at least until the 1880s different technological levels remained typical of the silk district of Como and Lecco. The district brought together technologies that featured centuries of adjustments, improvements and sudden jumps in quality. These differences in technological levels can also be interpreted in terms of the composition of labor by gender, task and wage level. Thus where workers at doubling [lavoranti al binatoio] – all women – earned 20–50% less than the twisters who were all men, this probably represents an old round mill with manual doubling in which a mechanical doubling machine (and winder) had been added.[49]

In contrast, in places where women made up the entire labor force, including those doing the first and second twisting, such as Alberto Keller's silk mill at Mandello sul Lario, we have a plant equipped with rectangular twisting frames. But the female "conquest" of this last male technological fortress coincided with the unfavorable restructuring of wage differences. Women twisters earned about one *lira*, just a few cents more than doublers, while men's wages for the same task ranged from 1.30 to 2.00 *lira*. In Keller's company men only

47 B. De Simone, *Lettera ad un suo amico sul commercio delle sete in Milano*, Supplemento de "L'Ape delle cognizioni utili," 1834, fasc. II, p. 5; F. Gera, *Il trattore da seta ossia l'arte di svolgere i bozzoli* (Venice, 1844), pp. 181–196; C. Semenza, "L'evoluzione delle macchine," *Associazione serica italiana. Il primo cinquantenario di vita sociale (1877–1927)* (n.p., 1928), pp. 133–134.

48 Trezzi, "A Case-Study of De-industrialization of the City."

49 P. Rota, "Notizie circa i salari degli operai addetti ad alcune delle principali industrie della Lombardia negli anni 1847, 1859, 1866, 1874," *Annali di statica*, III s., vol. XIV, parte II, (1885), 18. The wage figures refer to a silk mill in Bergamo belonging to Mr. Berizzi.

continued to work as loaders and steam engine managers and were paid a daily wage of 2.50 *lira*.[50] In short, the admission of women to those highly skilled jobs brought a decline, in terms of wages, of the professional status that previously had been attributed to men. Thus new forms of "segregation" emerged. Nevertheless, over the long term the difference between the wages of men and women actually became more favorable for women compared to the silk mills in Piedmont, when (at the end of the 18th century) male twisters earned three times as much as women doublers.

However, the relationship between the composition of the labor force by gender, task, wage level and underlying technological structure is not always so clear. This is the case for certain mills in Lecco where a new task appeared, that of *cavatura*, whose main task was to take the skeins off the reels – after reeling – and put them in baskets. This new specialization, done exclusively by men and rewarded with a significant wage increase, promoted women doublers, winders and the *maestre* to being twisters, but de-skilled the role of twisters by subtracting the work of the *cavatura* and perhaps other tasks, such as manoeuvring the mechanisms that regulated the number of twists. These women, apparently promoted to a higher job level, were paid barely 1 *lira* a day in 1874, whereas the (few) *cavatori* who took advantage of the new division of tasks received over 3 *lira* a day.[51] This type of restructuring was probably carried out in old-type mills, replacing men in the twisting operation with women and thus lowering the total wage bill. These strategic changes brought back the 1 to 3 ratio between women's and men's wages.

Peasant families provided the female labor, adapting to the pressures of economic conditions and to the complex innovations of capitalist entrepreneurs aiming to reduce production costs. Until the second half of the 18th century – as Maria Vittoria Ballestrero and Roberto Levrero have written – peasants impoverished by the imposition of new harsh agrarian contracts – so-called "rent for grain" – encouraged their women and daughters to work in the silk industry.[52]

---

50 Ibid., p. 51. Alberto Keller had "de facto excluded men from the silk mills," partly for moral reasons, to avoid "a certain violation of custom," and partly because he was convinced that women were "better than men at the precise and patient work required to process silk." On the third floor of the silk mill was a dormitory for the girls who came from "far away towns." In other living spaces "workers' families lived in the cleanest dormitories" (L. Magrini, *Setifici del nobile signor Alberto Keller in Mandello e Villanovetta* [Milan 1859], pp. 20, 23, 51). On the industrial archeology of the Lecco silk industry, see B. Attaneo, *Archeologia industriale nel lecchese. Le filande* (Lecco, 1982).

51 Rota, *Notizie circa i salari degli operai*, p. 17.

52 Ballestrero and Levrero, *Genocidio perfetto*, pp. 10–14. Merzario, *Il capitalismo nelle montagne*, pp. 93–107, dates the impoverishment of peasants earlier, to the beginning of the 18th century.

In the first phase, when mills but not mechanical winding began to expand, women and daughters worked at home raising silk worms, reeling and winding. With the change in technical and market conditions a growing number of women were employed at mechanical winding, in the spinning mills and silk mills. Thus a new division of labor was created, already occurring in other rural areas but different from what had dominated the older silk cities. In Bologna the women worked in their homes, while men (and boys) went to work in the mills. In the hilly countryside around Lecco and Como men stayed at home to cultivate the land, and women were sent to work in the factories. If the journey from home to factory was too far to go every day, girls stayed in housing and dormitories built within the walls of the silk mills or in adjacent buildings.

The feminization of the workforce for "almost" all tasks enables us to delineate "career" stages in the factories. Young girls, having spent a certain number of years at the simplest tasks (turning, brushing, or winding) subsequently became doublers and finally twisters or *maestre* in the spinning mills. Each of these tasks could entail various skills. Very few women ended their careers as supervisors.[53] Normally factory work (or manufacturing) ended at the ages of 20–23, when the girls got married or had their first child. The return to farming was often definitive, although some women probably returned to the silk factory or spinning mill at around the age of 30.[54]

These forms of hiring female labor occurred where peasant families still had a relationship to the land. But some entrepreneurs (although in reality not many) sought to employ whole families, already completely proletarianized who had migrated from poor mountainous areas, and who were sometimes lodged inside the factory walls.[55] Whether still tied to the land or uprooted from it, these were mainly poor peasant families who offered an unlimited flow of cheap labor to the industry.

---

53 See Rota, *Notizie circa i salari degli operai*, p. 51.

54 The age of 20–23 years is indicated by the entrepreneur Antonio Nessi in response to the questions from the Como Chamber of Commerce (1872) (Archivio di Stato di Como, *Camera di Commercio*, 36). Yet in Nessi's silk mill, located on the periphery of Como, fourteen women worked as doublers and rewinders, ranging in age from twenty to forty years old. This data probably refers to women who now lived permanently in the urban area and would not return to the farms. According to Errera (*Inchiesta sulle condizioni degli operai*, p. 150), "usually peasant women left the factory at twenty years of age to get married [...]. By the age of 30, physically and spiritually exhausted, they die in the furrows."

55 In Berizzi's silk mill "the workers lived with their families" (C. Correnti, "Voto della Commissione nominata nel Congresso degli scienziati italiani sul lavoro dei fanciulli negli opifici italiani," *Annali universali di statistica*, (1884), II series, vol. I, 321–322).

These social and economic transformations recall the rural protoindustrial model developed by Franklin Mendels in his famous research on Flanders. The thousands of rural, home-based winders (18,000 at the beginning of the 1800s) and the low wages of originally peasant labor are examples of similarities. But there are also profound differences. Whereas in the hilly areas of Como and Lecco the growth and expansion of home-based work was a direct consequence of the expansion of production plants which, albeit small, were already examples of manufacturing or a factory system, in the Flemish protoindustrial area the expansion of the *Kaufsystem* (purchasing system) preceded and prepared for the phase of factory production.[56] When, between the 18th and 19th centuries, entrepreneurs from Como and Lecco introduced mechanical winders, all they did was to use reserves of technical expertise already acquired over time.

Other differences can be traced back to the particular features of the silk production cycle. In Mendels' rural protoindustrial model (conceived basically in reference to the spinning and weaving of linen in the form of the *Kaufsystem*), the "industrial" work was done during the "idle" winter months, harmoniously supplementing work in the fields. In these areas, the bobbins did not spin and the looms were silent as long as peasant families were working in the fields.

The productive cycle of the silk industry was different, and not as easy to integrate with other work. Its season started in the spring, with the raising of silkworms, and reached its peak of activity (with reeling and twisting) in the summer, coinciding with the height of agricultural work. Peasant families – actually the family head – often had to make important strategic decisions. They had to choose between investing in competing and chronologically overlapping jobs: either working in the fields or working in the factories. We already know that young women, and even girls and boys from the ages of seven to nine, were sent to the spinning factories or silk mills. Most of the others, married men and women, remained on the land or were sent to do better paid work (for men in the expanding mechanical engineering industry), even though some continued to work in the silk industry.

Certainly the conceptual parameters of the expression "rural protoindustry" should not be considered definitive. It can be redefined. This was done by Louis Bergeron, who introduced the concept of "formes tardives" (late

56 F. Mendels, "Proto-Industrialization. The First Phase of an Industrialization Process," *Journal of Economic History*, XXXII (1972), 241–261. In contrast to Mendels, H. Medick emphasized the rural protoindustrial role of the putting-out system. See H. Medick, "The Protoindustrial Family during the Transition from Peasant Society to Industrial Capitalism," *Social History*, 1 (1976), 291–315.

forms) of protoindustry during the 19th and 20th centuries, otherwise known as parcelled-out artisan production. Or it can be replaced with the Marshallian concept of "industrial district," as I applied it to the Bolognese silk industry.[57] This is a flexible analytical tool which can also be effectively used to study industrialization in the areas of Como and Lecco (more in general Lombardy) in the 19th century, and takes into account all sectors of production: agriculture, silk, cotton, mechanical engineering (in the Lecco district) and silk weaving (in Como).

As long as the various production phases of the silk industry retained their traditional features of chronological succession (silk worm cultivation in May-June, reeling in June-October and then twisting, which began in July and continued into the fall and winter months) women could work on the various segments of production or even just certain phases, counting on some discontinuity in production to help work out the conflict between silk and farm work. This flexibility decreased with the construction of large, steam-powered spinning mills, which operated all the year (except for a winter break of one to three months), adapting their production times to those still longer times of the silk mills and winding operations.

The convergence between the companies' demand for female labor and its (low cost) supply from impoverished peasant families continued in the province of Como at least until 1880. This process went through stages of stalling and regression caused by declines in the production of silk worms, hit hard by epidemics of pébrine (protozoa) and calcino (fungus), and only partially compensated for by imports of raw silk from other Italian and Asian sources.

A significant turning point occurred in 1891 when the number of men and women working in twisting dropped to about 14,000 from the 24,316 in 1879. The number of active spindles dropped to 551,949 in the same year compared with 698,733 in 1878. In 1900 the number of employees rose to around 16,000, working 797,000 active spindles.[58] In these years the industrial processing of silk waste began to acquire importance, becoming a rapidly expanding sector. To comprehend the potential size of this sector one should bear in mind that from reeling to weaving, silk yarn could lose up to 40% of its weight, which was then regained in the (final) dyeing phase.[59]

---

57 See Poni, *La seta in Italia*, ch. 4. This pluralistic approach was used successfully by P.R. Corner, *Contadini e industrializzazione. Società rurale e impresa in Italia dal 1840 al 1940* (Rome, 1993).

58 See Errera, "Inchiesta sulla condizione degli operai," pp. 14–21; MAIC, *Annali di Statistica. Statistica Industriale. L'industria della seta in Italia*, p. 91; ibid., *Statistica Industriale in Lombardia*, pp. 191–199.

59 On the carding of waste, see ibid., *Statistica Industriale in Lombardia*, p. 200.

Between workers and merchant-entrepreneurs there was the traditional battle for the possession of silk waste, which according to an ancient tradition was the property of the workers (winders, doublers, twisters, dyers, etc.). To control the level of waste and prevent workers from producing independently (making gloves and stockings, possibly in competition with their employers) merchant-entrepreneurs claimed the exclusive right to purchase silk waste from their workers, promising to pay them the current price.[60] Only in factories which had developed all or part of their institutional potential (as for example in the case of the Farra silk mill) did the practice of workers appropriating silk waste disappear, as it was directly equated with theft. The development of factory rules in the 1800s – up to now a little studied topic with the exception of Stefano Merli's pioneering research – also served to eliminate this ancient "privilege" rooted in the distant past.[61]

Nevertheless, home processing of silk waste continued in the countryside around Como and Lecco. A perceptive observer of "peasant industry" in Brianza, the Englishman Charles Beldam, confirmed that peasant families with women who raised silk worms kept the waste (deformed cocoons, "scraps," etc.) and then sold them after carding them or boiling them with soap or salt. At least some peasant women continued to use their "odd time in spinning, generally in the winter time." Very few did this "as a recognized industry." These women spun only during the long winter evenings or when bad weather prevented them from working the land. Some peasant homes also had a small hand twister. Rural proto-industry still survived, albeit "almost obsolete," partly because it served families (if they had a loom) and partly because of sales to small local businesses (*Kaufsystem*).[62]

Obviously most women (and girls) worked in the factories. But the inclusion of women in factories went alongside important changes in attitudes towards work and work tasks. We know that the winders brought their knitting into the factory and continued to knit during working hours. They did not interrupt their own personal work if one thread broke, or if one *tavella* stopped, in contrast to men and boys who tied up the broken threads by hand.

Only when a certain number of threads had broken would women stop to tie them up. An expert silk mill director, Cavalier Giovan Battista de Bernardi, confirmed that the *tavellaro* (the supervisor) who "loudly called for workers to tie up the broken threads [...] had to take them away from their knitting [...]

60 See Poni, ch. 7 in this volume for an analysis of the "battle" for the possession of silk waste.

61 S. Merli, *Proletariato di fabbrica e capitalismo industriale. Il caso italiano* 1880–1900 (Florence, 1972).

62 See C. Beldam, *Raw Silk. A Peasant Industry in the Brianza* (London, 1898), pp. 39–40.

if they had three blocked *tavelle* in a row, or three broken threads."[63] In short, women came to work in factories but continued to do individual work that competed with the collective work of the factory.

How can this behavior be explained? As a reaction to low wages? As an expression of ties to the family that were not interrupted by the factory walls? I have no answer to these questions. Tasks have long been treated as opaque objects I am pleased to be able to shed at least a little light on their actual content.

---

63 G.B. de Bernardi, *Come si fila la buona seta* (n.p., n.d.) pp. 78–79; see also Merli, *Proletariato di fabbrica e capitalism industriale*, p. 156.

CHAPTER 9

Fashion as Flexible Production: Strategies of the Lyon Silk Merchants in the Eighteenth Century

Carlo Poni

Historians of the industrial revolution and capitalism have emphasized the importance of mass production, a concept almost invariably associated with a series of related notions such as "low prices," "modest or inferior quality" and "extensive market." These notions come together towards the end of the eighteenth century with cotton, which has been recognized as playing a fundamental role in the early phase of the Industrial Revolution in Britain. Competition over prices and the meeting of supply and demand in a free competitive market are the most widely-held conceptual parameters of an interpretative model tied to the categories of classical economics.[1]

To a large extent ignored, or at least underestimated and underused by historians, are the concepts of competition over product quality and differentiation, monopolistic competition, barriers to entry, flexible production, market segmentation and transaction costs. This is due perhaps to the view that these concepts have validity only for contemporary capitalist societies and that they are irrelevant with respect to the economies of the past.[2]

In this chapter I want to show that these concepts can be used to throw light on a variety of phenomena which have hitherto remained obscure and whose importance in terms of the formation of the capitalist market and of entrepreneurial strategies has still to be fully appreciated.

1 According to E. L. Jones, economic historians of the industrial revolution, with only a few exceptions, have seen market and demand as a reflection of "the rising tide of mechanical production." See "The Fashion Manipulators: Consumer Tastes and British Industries (1660–1800)," in L. P. Cairn and P. J. Uselding, eds., *Business and Enterprise* (Kent, OH., 1973), pp. 198–226.

2 See P. Sraffa, "The Laws of Return under Competitive Conditions," *Economic Journal*, 36, 1926, 535–550; H. Chamberlain, *A Theory of Monopolistic Competition* (Cambridge, 1933); M. J. Piore and C. Sabel, *The Second Industrial Divide* (New York, 1984); C. Sabel and J. Zeitlin, "Historical Alternatives to Mass Production: Politics, Market and Technology in Nineteenth-Century Industrialization," *Past and Present*, 108, August, 1985, 133–176; O. E. Williamson, *Markets and Hierarchies* (New York, 1983); idem, *The Economic Institution of Capitalism* (New York, 1985).

 | DOI:10.1163/9789004713277_011

It is within this framework that I will examine silk fabrics and fashion in eighteenth-century Europe. The silk industry is distinctive in the contrasts it offers to the cotton industry. Prices are high rather than low, markets are small rather than extensive. Changes in fashion can best be understood using the concepts of flexible production, monopolistic competition and barriers to entry. Towards the end of the seventeenth century the combination of silk and fashion led to a fundamental shift in the mercantile practices of the textile industry. These new practices were based on the annual or seasonal differentiation of production planned in advance and carried out according to deliberate and systematic strategies.[3]

Fashion has often been associated with luxury. A certain interrelation between the two does exist, but it is nevertheless important to make some fundamental methodological distinctions. The luxury of official court ritual and the ceremonies of the ecclesiastical world were often archaic and old-fashioned, and a piece of clothing considered to be luxurious might also have been old-fashioned.[4] Perhaps it is also true that a fashionable piece of clothing

3 Fashion has been the object of historical interest for some decades. See D. E. Robinson, "The Styling and the Transmission of Fashions Historically Considered," *Journal of Economic History*, vol. 20 (1960), 576–687; idem, "The Importance of Fashion in Taste to Business History. An Introductory Essay," *Business History Review*, vol. 37 (1963), 5–36; E. Robinson," Eighteenth-Century Commerce and Fashion: Matthew Boulton's Marketing Techniques," *Economic History Review*, 16 (1963), 39–60; D. C. Coleman, "An Innovation and its Diffusion: The New Draperies," *Economic History Review*, vol. 22 (1969), 417–429; N. B. Harte and G. Ponting, eds., *Textile History and Economic History* (Manchester, 1973); J. Thirsk, *Economic Policy and Projects. The Development of a Consumer Society in Early Modern England* (Oxford, 1978); N. McKendrick, J. Brewer and J. H. Plumb, *The Birth of a Consumer Society. The Commercialization of Eighteenth-Century England* (Bloomington, IN., 1985); U. C. Pallach, *Materielle Kultur und Mentalitaten in 18 Jahrhundert* (Munich, 1987); D. Roche, *La culture de l'apparence. Une histoire du vêtement* (*XVII–XVIII siècle*) (Paris, 1989); T. Kusamitsu, "Novelty, Give Us Novelty: London Agents and Northern Manufacturers," *Markets and Manufacture in Early Industrial Europe*, ed. M. Berg (London, 1991), pp. 114–138.

4 Thus the "mantille de Cour," an old, black ceremonial cloak with white decorations which the French ladies of the court wore on the day they were presented to the king, was almost immediately discarded "le jour passé" ("the day after") and "tout ce qui était noir se change en étoffes de couleurs ou d'or" ("everything that was black changes into fabrics of color or of gold") (M. de Garsault, "Art du Tailleur," in *Description des Arts et métiers faites ou approvées par Messieurs de l'Académie Royale des Sciences de Paris*, 2nd ed., vol. IX [Neuchatel, 1780], pp. 107–108). This means that the role of the court at Versailles in launching new fashions must be clearly distinguished from the rules of ceremony. From the Regency onwards, the "Société de Cour" increasingly became a cultural and social space which included Versailles and Paris, with Paris in a dominant role. It was not by chance that the ladies of the court hurried to Paris for their wardrobe. See N. Elias, *The Court Society* (Oxford, 1983). The court of the King of Prussia, renowned for an etiquette that required simple, spartan

was not necessarily a sign of luxury.[5] Unfortunately, the centuries-old polemic against luxury has constituted a major epistemological block to the analysis of the complex phenomena which come together under the name of fashion.

A great deal has been written about fashion. Psychologists, psychoanalysts, sociologists, linguists and historians have asked themselves and continue to ask themselves about the nature of fashion. Is it an expression of the spirit or the taste of a certain historical epoch? Is it the desire for pleasure, a means of communication and symbolic distinction? Or a symptom of the instability of human nature?[6] There is no lack of complex, rich and meaningful definitions,

---

clothing above all for the men, offered little scope for the new fashions from France. See A. Ribeiro, *Dress in Eighteenth Century Europe (1715–1789)* (London, 1984), pp. 66–67.

5 The compulsive need to enlarge existing markets and conquer new ones led entrepreneurs to replace high quality fabrics with less costly ones. Thus in 1750, the Sieur Delasalle, one of the major manufacturers and designers of silk fabrics in Lyons, asked the Paris Conseil de Commerce to be allowed to manufacture fabric "en grand et petit dessein avec du trait faux doré et surdoré ... file sur soie" ("in large and small design with lines of imitation gold and "surdoré" spun onto the silk") instead of with an entirely golden thread. According to Veron de Forbonnais, who supported Delasalle's request, the legislators should be concerned above all with preventing the "faux fil" ("fake thread") from being fraudulently sold as golden thread, and should not prohibit its production altogether. It was important to avoid producing "une perfection chimérique" ("a chimerical perfection"). It was enough to protect the consumer with the help of appropriate markings so that "le faux et le fin" ("the fake and the fine") could not be confused. Veron de Forbonnais predicted that once the "fabrication en faux" ("false manufacture") had been perfected, the "fabrication en fin" ("fine manufacture"), much dearer, would decline (Veron de Forbonnais, *Lettre à M+ + + Négociant de Lyon sur l'usage du trait faux filé sur soie dans les étoffes* [n.p., 1759], pp. 18–22, 30). A few years earlier, in 1756, Forbonnais had declared himself against solid gold snuffboxes in favor of those which, although they had not an ounce of gold in them, were perfect imitations. According to Forbonnais, gold snuffboxes were bought by "l'homme de luxe ... prodigue sans égard" ("the man of wealth, spendthrift with little concern") while the "goût générale" ("general taste") was instead by now in favor of "commodité" ("usefuless") and "au bon marché" ("inexpensive") (*Lettre de M. du T. ... négociant à Paris à M. Rissch, négociant à Francfort sur les ouvrages et les bijoux d'or et argent* [n.p., 1756]). The Venetian silk merchant and writer Antonio Zanon thought that fashion was "necessary to the Arts and useful for commerce when based on its own [national] products." He thus proposed that a distinction should always be made between "luxury and fashion and between indifferent and damaging luxury" (where the adjective "damaging" should be understood as "imported"), (A. Zanon, *Dell'agricoltura*, vol. III [Venice, 1764], pp. 153–154).

6 See, for example, A. L. Kroeber, "On the Principle of Order in Civilization as Exemplified by Changes in Fashion," *American Anthropologist*, vol. 21 (1919), 235–263; P. N. Nystrom, *Economics of Fashion* (New York, 1928); idem, *Fashion Merchandising* (New York, 1932); E. B. Hurlock, *Motivation in Fashion* (New York, 1929); I. Brennikmeyer, *The Sociology of Fashion* (Winterthus, 1962); K. Gibbins and T.K. Gwinn, "A New Theory of Fashion Change: A Test of Some Predictions," *British Journal of Social and Clinical Psychology* (1975),

but they rarely explain why fashion (as rapid change) should have triumphed exclusively in Western European countries and not, for example, in the Middle or Far East. This problem was posed by Fernand Braudel in the early 1960s. According to Braudel, as long ago as 1609 an official of the Shogun at Yedo complained to the Spanish of "la variété de leurs costumes, domaine dans lequel il sont si peu constants que tous le deux ans ils sont vêtu de façon différente" ("the variety of their clothing, about which they are so inconstant that every two years they dress in a different way"), while in Japan "il y a plus de mille ans que cette nation n'a pas changé de costume" ("for more than one thousand years this nation has not changed its form of dress").[7]

How can this difference be explained? It may be said, as an initial hypothesis, that fashion as short-term, periodic, programmed change exists in societies characterized by a certain degree of social mobility, in which hierarchical structures are flexible enough to allow for the imitation of the behavior of the higher social groups by those lower on the social scale. *Vivere more nobilium* ("to live like a nobleman") did not only mean buying land and living off the income from it. It also meant living and dressing as the nobility did. But as soon as the visible distinctions of the social orders are no longer regulated and established by custom or religion, and when sumptuary laws fall into disuse, the conditions which tend to modify the behavior of the elite are created. According to the well-known theory of Georg Simmel, in reply to efforts at imitation on the part of the rising classes, the elite formulates new fashions and new models of consumption, preparing the ground for new efforts at imitation, each of which are destined to be periodically frustrated. A specific process is thus set in motion: a limitless and endless chase in which the social level of a given social group or class can be measured by the number of years it lags behind the fashion.[8] This mechanism, in time, tends to restructure and confuse the traditional

1–9; M. R. Solomon, ed., *The Psychology of Fashion* (Lexington, MA. 1985); R. Konig, *Menscheit auf dem Laufsteg. Die Mode im Zivilizationprozess* (Munich, 1983).

7 F. Braudel, *Civilisation materielle et capitalisme*, vol. 1, *Les Structures du quotidien* (Paris, 1967), pp. 240–250.

8 G. Simmel, *Die Mode* (1895), in *Gesammelte Essais mit einem Vorwart von Jürgen Habermas* (Berlin, 1986), pp. 38–63. Even those who have criticized Simmel's approach for its stark dualism, which leaves no space for action on the part of intermediate social groups, and for its inability to explain the dynamics of present-day fashion, nevertheless recognize its validity for the study of changes in fashion in Europe in the period between the sixteenth and eighteenth centuries. See G. D. McGracken, "The Trickle-Down Theory Rehabilitated," Solomon, ed., *Psychology of Fashion*, pp. 42–43. This author has refined Simmel's theory, taking account of the results of new research on topics such as recent changes in women's fashions, now aimed at expressing social or professional roles, and the influence of the mass media in the launching of new fashions. On anti-sumptuary legislation, see G. Bistort, *Il magistrato alle pompe nella Repubblica di Venezia. Studio storico* (Venice,

distinctions between social groups. Impoverished nobles are unable to follow the changes in fashion in the same way that well-off merchants and tax farmers do. Fashion, in short, is a symptom, albeit an ambiguous one, of the slow passage from a society based on status to another based on wealth. It frees the individual from sumptuary and corporate laws, proclaims its own sovereignty over dress (but only for the wealthy urban classes), and changes visibly and irreparably the forms of civil society, creating new forms of sociability. It is not surprising, then, to discover that fashion was seen as an insidious agent of social change.[9]

But what is the precise relationship between the "well-off" and those who create fashion? Here we must challenge those interpretations which see fashion as being created by poor, humble artisans of the lower classes.[10] Fashion, seen in the context of silk manufacture, is the product of relatively centralized strategic decision-making, of choices made by powerful economic interests already integrated into the elites of power and taste. These interests, which exercised considerable influence far beyond the borders of a national market,

1912); V. Baur, *Kleiderordnung in Bayern von 14 bis zum 17 Jahrhundert* (Munich, 1975); L. C. Eisenhart, *Kleiderordnung der deutschen Städte zwischen 1350 und 1700* (Göttingen, 1962); H. Freudenberger, "Fashion, Sumptuary Laws and Business," *Business History Review*, vol. 37 (1963), 37–48; N. B. Harte, "State Control of Dress and Social Change in Pre-Industrial England," D. C. Coleman and A. H. John, eds., *Trade, Government and Economy in Pre-Industrial England ... Essays Presented to F. J. Fischer* (London, 1976), pp. 132–165 and bibliography. Changes of clothing, even on a daily basis, already practiced although only exceptionally in the sixteenth century, must be distinguished from annual and programmed change in fashion. I refer to that Milanese noble woman who, according to a French jurist, wore new and different dresses every day. And so had 365 dresses. See B. Cassaneus, *Catalogues glorial mundi* [Venice, 1769], pp. 25–26, 324. In Cassaneus's writing, the colors were more or less noble according to their closeness to white or to black. On noble coats of arms the noble colors had to be placed "in nobilioci loco" ("in a noble place"). The theme of "Mediolani matronam" ("Milanese lady") is taken up by S. Kobierzycki, *De luxu romanorum* (Leuven, 1628), p.112.

9 Luxury, too, as an ostentation of wealth on the part of high finance and as a bourgeois imitation of the nobility and of the Court of Versailles, could be seen as an attack on the social hierarchy to be re-established with new sumptuary laws. See A. J. Chevalier du Coudray, *Le luxe, Poème* (Paris, 1773), pp. 10–14, 21, 39 passim. In fact, in the eighteenth century imitation of the luxury of the upper classes is nothing other than fashion. Erasmus Jones wrote that "people, where they are not known, are generally honored according to their clothes." For this reason in a "large and populous city" many people wear clothes "above their ranks" (E. Jones, *Luxury, Pride and Vanity. The Bond of the British Nation* [n. p., 1736], p. 36).

10 T. Veblen, *The Theory of the Leisure Class* (1899; reprinted New York, 1975), and idem, *The Instinct of Workmanship and the State of the Industrial Arts*, J. Dorfman, intro. (New York, 1964), pp. 180–186, passim.

engaged in a dialogue with the taste of consumers, who became increasingly refined and demanding, in turn influencing the strategies of the producers.

The Lyon silk merchants were the first, as far back as the closing years of the seventeenth century, to use annual product differentiation as a strategic weapon to create barriers to entry, to capture important shares of the international market, and to outmaneuver firms in competition with them. This change in the rules of production heightened competition and gave a new dynamism to both production and the market. Quoting Adam Smith, we may say that at the beginning of every year, the "work to be done" would no longer be the same as the "work done."[11] This in turn led to the consolidation of new power on the market which was destined to upset old equilibria. This cluster of changes constituted a real turning point. The introduction of annual fashions in the production of fabric, planned and programmed in advance, delivered a sharp blow to old market practices which were "embedded in society" and regulated, at least formally, by the sumptuary laws. The introduction of short-life products had another consequence as well. It split production volumes, distributing the new fashions over an increasingly diversified demand. The entrepreneurs were now obliged to work in the short term, to interiorize uncertainty as a structural factor. They were no longer conditioned by long-term expectations. Lyon, in short, was a protagonist of the "great transformation" proposed by Karl Polanyi, even if its role in the "modern world system" as promoter of profound social changes has as yet gone unrecognized.

The anonymous author of the report presented to the British parliament in 1713, entitled *The Case of the Silk Weavers Humbly Offered to the Consideration of both Houses of Parliament*, wrote that French silk fabrics were preferred to the English ones because "the fashions are or are likely to be taken from France." The result was that the British merchants "cannot make provision for a Spring Trade for fear that a New Fashion should come from France, and render ours despicable." In order not to incur a defeat on the market at the hands of a differentiated product, the English merchants preferred to imitate the French products, with the result that they were left with the residual share of the market (a certain amount of time was needed in order to examine the fabrics which were to be copied, prepare the looms, imitate the dyes, train the weavers and so on). But as soon as the British entrepreneur began to reproduce the new fabric, "another fashion comes from France," and so the game began again. The result was that the French products conquered "the first of the market, and the

11 A. Smith, *An Inquiry into the Nature and Causes of the Wealth of Nations,* E. Canaan, ed. (London, 1961,) I, ch. VII. See the comments made by Patrizio Bianchi in his *Produzione e potere di mercato* (Rome, 1991), pp. 29–32.

English the Fag-End" and thus the latter had to be content with selling at much lower prices.[12]

In short, competition over quality and product differentiation rather than price enabled the French merchants to capture the most profitable share of the market, with high prices protected by high barriers to entry, while the English products sold only on the residual share of the market, with low prices. This is a clear case of "time-based" monopolistic competition, each operator with a product in some degree different from his rivals. Innovations had to be not only rapid but also appealing. They had to anticipate and satisfy immediately a demand which was often hesitant but in search of new products. It was by means of this intelligent innovation that Lyon was able to make a victorious exit from the crisis of the seventeenth century.[13]

"French fashions pernicious to England" is the appeal we hear in the pages of Joshua Gee. According to him, the new fashions were cleverly invented by the French merchants in order to prevent the sale of English goods.[14] For Defoe, such was the unpatriotic passion of the English ladies for the French products that the London merchants were forced to pretend that the Spitalfields products had been imported from France.[15]

---

12 This pamphlet should be seen in the context of the fierce struggle of the English commercial interests against the eighth and ninth articles of the Peace Treaty of Utrecht which reduced duties and removed the prohibition of French commodities. See also *The State of the Silk and Woolen Manufacture considered in Relation to a French Trade* (London, 1713). The anonymous author of this broadsheet recognized that the French "excel in the inventing of patterns, and their skill is so great ... that by the great esteem they have got in the world will sell 20 or 25 percent above those of any other nation in Europe. For this reason we in England are obliged, for the most part, to copy their pattern." Already in 1679, an anonymous English writer had denounced imports from France of enormous quantities of silk fabrics (velvets and satins) "made in Lyon" (J. B., *An Account of the French Usurpation upon the Trade of England* [London, 1679], pp. 2, 5, 10). A century later A. Goudar (*L'espion francois à Londres* [London, 1779], p. 92) wrote ironically about the clothes worn at a ball at the court of London: "En générale les robes étaient superbes et d'un grand goût. Mais ce goût n'étoit pas du cru du pays. Il était copié de la poupée de Paris" ("In general the clothes were superb and in very good taste. But this taste was not of their country. It was copied from the fashion dolls of Paris").

13 Supply and demand, rather than being considered in opposition to each other, must be explained within a single discourse, without pretending that they are always in harmony with each other.

14 J. Gee, *Trade and Navigation of Great Britain* (London 1729), pp. 30–32.

15 D. Defoe, *The Compleat English Tradesman*, II, Part II (London, 1727), pp. 154–161. Some decades later, Ludovico Muratori wrote that in several Italian cities, "fabrics ingeniously made there only ceased being the object of disdain, and were considered to have been made with the necessary dignity for the clothing of noble persons, when people were led

Something similar happened in the Po Valley. In 1755, a group of Bolognese merchants, having begun to produce fabrics in imitation of French ones (lustring, taffetas, *façonnés* and *péruviennes*) had to suspend production because their products, not having "that shiny and bright quality found in French fabrics, are rejected by almost everyone and end up on the back shelves of the shops." But even if the imitations were successful, there was still the problem of overcoming "the considerable disorder caused by the fact that the French change their designs ... from one season to another which is, in fact, what attracts the buyer." As there were no "designers capable of these new creations" in Bologna, the manufacturers had to take "the same French designs" and then set up the looms for the market of the following year. But at that precise moment, a "new creation" with new material and new designs would arrive from France and all the imitation Bolognese products would remain unsold (despite being protected, as were the British ones, by laws which forbade the introduction of foreign fabrics).[16]

In 1764, the silk merchant and writer Antonio Zanon, with somewhat greater analytical rigor, voiced the angry disappointment of the Venetian silk merchants at the fanaticism of the Italians for all things foreign – and especially French – and their "contempt for their own manufactures." The Venetian merchants, defeated in the struggle for leadership in the fashion sector (an area which according to Zanon had been abandoned after "painful experiences"), were now resigned to the inferior role of imitating French fashions. But this very choice, open to them says Zanon because the Italian artisans "have a talent for imitation," forced the merchants to dance to a tune they did not know. Like the Bolognese merchants, Zanon notes that "the Italians will struggle to imitate French fashion, but before one suit can be finished another completely different one comes out and ... all the new Italian fabrics become old junk in just a few weeks." Moreover, immediately before the introduction of a new fashion the French merchants drastically lowered the price of the remaining stock, forcing the imitator firms to keep pace with an economic situation of ruthless (and perhaps predatory) competition that tended not so much to

to believe that they had been brought across the mountains from Lyon" (*Della Pubblica Felicità* [Lucca, 1749], pp. 218–219).

16 *Memoriale di G. Canevoli e T. Mattioli all'Assunteria d'Arti per ottenere la moderazione del bando ... rispetto ai lustrini o sieno taffetà, façonné e péruviennes che non possono fabbricarsi in Bologna,* May 5, 1755 (Archivio di Stato di Bologna, *Arti,* "Miscellanea," vol. XVI, fasc. 68). Around ten years later, Bologna had become "the French warehouse, given that the French adventurers collect there the out-of-fashion fabrics or those which will shortly become unfashionable, and send them from there to Venice. Indeed, some Venetians actually go there to collect stocks" (Zanon, *Dell'agricoltura, dell'arti e del commercio,* III, pp. 333–334).

beat their competitors as to crush them. Zanon concluded that "this very word 'fashion' is an enormous and long-lasting treasure for France, and is considered by the French as a reputation which amounts to a highly-precious capital."[17] On another occasion he declared, echoing a phrase attributed to Colbert, that the "empire of fashion" was for France what the Potosi mines were for Spain.[18]

According to Zanon, the strategies of the Venice merchants, of little success at home, fared better "in countries too far away to have strong connections with France," such as the countries of the Ottoman empire where French and Dutch attempts to compete with Venetian damask had failed. Zanon attributed this failure to two factors: "one derives from the unchangeability of Oriental fashions and ways of dressing; the other from the fact that the Turks are unable to free themselves from their preference for Venetian cloth."[19]

---

17 Ibid., III, pp. 342, 334–339, 363–364. The Lyonnaise producer started lowering prices "while he was about to produce a new fashion. Other price decreases followed after the new fashions had begun to circulate" (p. 364). Muratori (*Della pubblica felicità,* p. 277) observed that the rapid changes in fashion and the fact that fabric and clothes quickly became obsolete led to an increase in the second-hand market. He wrote: "The fairs of a large city are a curious spectacle where the second-hand clothes dealers make a great display of their wealth in various shops with their *andrienne,* their tunics, their robes, their clothes embroidered with Spanish stitching and other sumptuous laces. Clothes and garments that seem to have come straight from the hands of the tailors can also be seen." On this subject, and also on the theft of clothes, see the excellent descriptions in Roche, *La culture de l'apparence,* pp. 313–346; and Ribeiro, *Dress in Eighteenth-Century Europe,* pp. 60–62, passim. Goudar worried that every year the warehouses filled up with unsold items from "de vieilles modes" ("old fashions"), and that they were joined each year by "d'autres qui augmentent continuellement les nombres des anciens" ("others which continually increase the number of old ones") (*Les intérêts de la France mal entendus* [Amsterdam, 1761], pp. 217–218). These leftovers were eventually sold in northern Europe, and "le plus souvent au dessous du prix de la valeur intrinsique de la première matière" ("most often below the price of the intrinsic value of the raw material").

18 The Venetian merchant Zanon was aware that the harshest competition was by now coming from across the English Channel. He wrote: "The English and French genii battle even over the invention of new designs. And armies will perhaps decide the fate of the fashions. But the French will always be superior in their sales, because their inventions are prolific, their work is more skillful and their prices are lower" (*Dell'agricoltura, dell'arti e del commercio,* II [Venice, 1763], pp. 123–124).

19 Ibid., vol. V (Venice, 1765), pp. 124–125. The Turkish preference for Venetian silks is confirmed by numerous sources. The Lyons merchant Bonnafous had little success when he tried to enter the Constantinople market with imitation Venetian damask produced in Lyon. See the letter of May 25, 1755 in Archives Nationales de Paris (hereafter A.N.P.), F12, 1443. J. B. Labat wrote in 1735: "Les modes changeantes n'ont point gâté l'esprit ni les usages des orientaux" ("changing fashions have not spoiled the spirit nor the customs of the orientals") (*Mémoires du Chevalier d'Arvieu,* t. III [1735], p. 209). For Accarias de Serionne too, in the Levant – where the new European fashions had not taken root – Venetian fabrics

Not even the Dutch silk industry was able to stand up to the competition of the Lyon fashions. The manufacturers of Amsterdam had enjoyed considerable prestige in the seventeenth century. An example can be found in the story commonly told of "velours à ramage fabriqués à Milan, envoyés en Hollande et de là renvoyés et vendu ensuite à Milan pour velours d'Hollande" ("velvets 'à ramage' made in Milan, sent to Holland and from then sent back to Milan where they were sold as velvet of Holland") together with a sure profit for the commissioners. The word "Dutch" was enough to add "une valeur nouvelle" ("a new value") to the Milanese material which could cover the transport costs from and to Milan via Amsterdam.[20] However, around 1720, the great materials of Amsterdam (damask and velvet) began to lose ground on the international market.[21] The Haarlem products fared better as they specialized in imitating:

> différents desseins d'étoffes de Lyon, car on n'a jamais possedé dans ces manufactures l'art du dessein qui embellit, qui enrichi tous les ans celles de Tours et surtout et principalement celles de Lyon, par une extrême variété, par les grâces du goût et de la nouveauté.[22]

The differentiation of fashion in Lyon, then, gave rise to strong market dynamism, established new hierarchies of power and, around the end of the seventeenth century or at the beginning of the eighteenth, brought about an important process of general restructuring in the new and old silk centers and in the international silk fabric market. In Europe, three different sectors can be

---

dominated (*Le Commerce de la Hollande ou Tableau du commerce des Hollandois*, vol. II [Amsterdam, 1768], pp. 146–147).

20 Accarias de Serionne, *Le Commerce de la Hollande*, I, p. 294.

21 J. G. Van Dillen, "Economic Fluctuations and Trade in the Netherlands (1650–1750)," in P. Earle, ed., *Essays in European Economic History (1500–1800)* (Oxford, 1974,) p. 205. From a letter sent by Esaie Gillot, a silk fabric merchant from Amsterdam, to the firm Caret et Cie of Lyon, it would appear that the Haarlem manufacturers were still active towards the middle of the eighteenth century and that they continued to copy the "nouveaux desseins" ("new designs") as they arrived from Lyon (Archives Départementales du Rhone, Procédure de la Conservation, Livres de commerce (faillites), Caret et Cie, Liasse VII, Provinces Unies, 1). On this source, see *Papiers d'industrie et de commerçants Lyonnais. Lyon et le grand commerce au XVIIIe*, under the direction of P. Léon (Lyon, 1976), and the bibliography.

22 ("different designs of fabrics of Lyon, because one never possessed in these manufactures the art of design which made more beautiful and enriched every year those of Tours and especially and principally those of Lyon, by their great variety, gracefulness of taste and of originality"), Accarias de Serionne, *Le Commerce de la Hollande*, I, p. 293. According to Veron de Forbonnais, "l'habilité et l'invention des nos dessinatuers sont tout le mystère di nos succès" ("the ability and the creativity of our designers are the entire mystery of our success"), (*Lettre à M.+++Négociant de Lyon…*, p. 24).

distinguished. The first, in the vanguard, was the Lyon area itself which dictated the annual fashions in flowered silks (*façonné* and *grand façonné*). Its productive system, based essentially on putting-out, released on the market each year a wide range of fabrics manufactured contemporaneously.[23] The second was that of the areas and industries that imitated the Lyon fabrics, above all in color and design. These often included firms benefiting from extensive help from their governments (following mercantilist policies) to produce import substitutes. This sector, encouraged in England and Holland by the Huguenot emigration, included at different times and with varying success Valencia, Berlin, Venice, Haarlem, Spitalfields and others.[24] The third sector consisted of areas that had abandoned or avoided the market for fashion fabrics and occupied sectors in the market with products that were often traditional, not subject to rapid change or in any case not "fashionable." For this sector, after the shock of the initial impact, the annual fashions did not constitute direct competition. This was the case of the Venetian damask exported to the Ottoman empire; of Genoese velvet used in many countries of Europe by the higher public officials, judges and magistrates; of Bolognese crêpe, which adapted itself as decoration to all fashions, sales of which would rise during the frequent periods of court mourning; and of the damask and velvet of Amsterdam, which held on the Paris market "pendant un tres grand nombre d'années ... à cause de leur solidité et surtout parce qu'ils ne changent point de mode" ("over a great number of years ... because of their sturdiness and especially because they do not go out of fashion"). According to Accarias de Serionne:

23 Each entrepreneur presented each year a range of new products, taking account also of the economic possibilities of their particular clientele.

24 On Valencia, see. S. Rodriguez Garcia, *El arte de las sedas valencianas en el siglo XVIII* (Valencia, 1959); M. Garzon Pereira, *La industria sedera en Espana* (Granada, 1972), pp. 89–92; A. Domingo Ortiz, *Sociedada y Estado en el siglo XVIII espanol* (Barcelona, 1976), p. 271; V. M. Santos Isern, *Cara y cruz de la sederia valenciana* (*siglos XVIII–XIX*) (Valencia, 1981); V. Ribes, *Los valencianos y America. El commercio valenciano con Indias en el siglo XVIII* (Valencia, 1985), pp. 61–92. On Berlin, see. *Acta Borussica. Denkmaler der Preussischen Staatsverwaltung im 18. Jahrhundert, Die Preussische Seidenindustrie im 18. Jahrhundert und ihre Begrundung durch Friedrich der Grossen im 18. Jahrhundert*, 1–3 (Berlin, 1892). Volumes 1 and 2 contain a collection of documents edited by G. Schmoller and O. Hintze. The third volume, written by Hintze, is instead a historical monograph. On the limits of Prussian silk mercantilism, see the extensive survey of H. Kisch, "Prussian Mercantilism and the Rise of the Krefeld Industry," *Transactions of the American Philosophical Society*, vol. 58, Part 7, Philadelphia, 1968, pp. 3–15, and the bibliography. For Spitalfields, see. F. Warner, *The Silk Industry of the United Kingdom. Its Origins and Development* (London, 1921), pp. 53–63 passim.

> telle a été sur cet article la bizzarerie de la mode, qu'on la fait consister dans l'uniformité permanente de l'étoffe, pendant que la mode exige tous les ans impérieusement, des fabriques de Lyon, un goût nouveau et des nouveaux desseins.[25]

Apart from these three major groups, which together cover almost all the forms of the international market, we should also consider those materials (not from Lyon) which suddenly became fashionable because they were able, largely though not exclusively through their low cost, to stimulate the capricious taste of the public. This was the case of a "strong taffeta," also called "nobilata" produced in Rome around 1780 which had notable success on the market. Roland de la Platière bought a piece while travelling in Italy, spending the modest sum of 110 livres "de France" for a suit which was "très jolis, plus que complet ... en couleur, doublé de blanc" ("very good-looking, a three-piece suit ... in color and lined in white").[26] The success of the "nobilata" was probably short-lived, but it is evidence of a new sector which would benefit from further research.[27] Another sector which would have considerable success in the future was that of the *mélangés* fabrics (mixtures of silk with wool, cotton or

---

25 ("such has been on this matter the bizarreness of fashion, that one makes it consist of the permanent uniformity of the fabric, while fashion demands imperiously every year of the fabrics of Lyon a new taste and new designs"), Accarias de Serionne, *Le Commerce de la Hollande,* I, pp. 294–295.

26 Roland de la Platière, *Lettres écrites de Suisse, d'Italie et de Malte,* vol. V (Amsterdam, 1780), p.100. According to Roland, the "nobilata," like the other Italian fabrics "a le défaut d'être composée de matières écrus ou mal écrués, d'où le corps, qui paroît en résulter, n'est que la roideur qui empêche les fils de s'approcher assez en rend les plis tranchants, fait qu'elle s'éraille et se coup" ("has the defect of being composed of material that is raw or poorly bleached, so that the body of the fabric that results is stiff, preventing the threads from being close and makes the wrinkles sharp, so the fabric is coarse and tears"). In any case, Roland notes, "le goût français est toujours le goût dominant à Rome, comme à Turin, à Parme, à Modene. On n'y a pas, ainsi qu'à Naples, la ridicule manie de singer les anglois" ("the French taste is the dominant taste in Rome, as in Turin, Parma, Modena. One doesn't have, as in Naples, the ridiculous fixation of 'aping' the English") (p. 101). But it was only the gentlemen, not the ladies, who followed the London fashions. Roland de la Platière, later to be a leader of the Girondin faction, was involved in commerce in Lyon before becoming "inspecteur des manufactures" ("inspector of manufacturers") (F. Bacquier, *Les inspecteurs des manufactures sous l'Ancien Régime* [Paris, 1927], p. 384). On the interest of Lyon in the scouring ("décreusage") of silk, see "Observation sur le sujet suivant proposé par l'Académie des Sciences ... de Lyon: Trouver une manière nouvelle de décreuser la soie sans altérer ni la qualité ni son lustre," *Journal de Commerce* (November 1760), 134–135.

27 In 1777 the *failles* of Anvers (silk fabric "à grosgrain") became fashionable in France. Orders were so numerous that "les fabricants avaient de la peine à y suffir" ("the manufacturers had difficulty to supply enough") (C. Van Cauwenberghs, "L'industrie de la soye

linen), in the right price range for the urban middle classes who tended to imitate the clothes of the elite but with inferior fabrics. The analysis offered here is a first attempt to classify silk manufacturing and weaving in the era which saw the hegemony of Lyon, an attempt which, however, must be refined and developed. It is necessary in particular to reconstruct the importance of the various imitation industries in relation to Lyon, explain the growing success of *mélangé* and account for the greater or lesser resistance of the "traditional" sectors. The latter continued to sell the same fabrics which, although probably not insensitive to changes in fashion and taste, registered these changes on a different time scale.[28]

Up to now, Lyon has been considered as a homogeneous industrial center, but this was not the case. In fact, the imitation industry was of considerable importance here too. Indeed, it had actually originated in Lyon. As far back as 1711, the city authorities ordered all the members and employees of the Communauté des Marchands et Maîtres Ouvriers en Soye (Community of Merchants and Master Workers in Silk) not to use designs made by others, nor to sell or lend their own.[29] This order also had the effect of hindering the social and professional mobility of the *maîtres ouvriers,* the large majority of the weavers (hereafter referred to simply as *ouvriers*) who worked on piece rates for the *marchands fabricants* (hereafter *fabricants*), from whom they received the designs and the raw material. If they wanted to begin "à travailler ou faire travailler ... pour leur compte" ("to work or to employ someone independently") they would have had to be enrolled on the register of the Communauté, paying 300 livres (reduced to 200 livres for their sons). This rule, introduced, it was said, to revive the financial fortunes of the Communauté, constituted a crucial turning point. It reinforced and formalized a process of social differentiation tied to the introduction of annual change in fashion and the growing importance of the *fabricants.* As can be seen from Table 9.1, in 1732 the members

---

à Anvers depuis 1532 jusqu'à nos jours," *Bulletin de la Société royale de géografie d'Anvers*, 1887, p. 119).

28 For the history of the Lyon silk industry, see E. Pariset, *La Chambre de Commerce de Lyon* (*1702–1791*) (Lyon, 1886); J. Godart, *L'ouvrier en soie: monographie du tisseur Lyonnais: étude historique, économique et sociale* (Lyon, 1899); E. Pariset, *Histoire de la fabrique lyonnaise: étude sur le régime sociale et économique de l'industrie de la soie à Lyon depuis le* XVIe *siècle* (Lyon, 1901); and the more recent analysis by M. Garden, *Lyon et le Lyonnais au* XVIII *siècle* (Paris, 1970). The work of J. Godart continues to be a fundamental guide to any research on the Lyon silk industry.

29 *Lettres patentes portant homologation de l'Ordonnance Consulaire du 25 Octobre 1711 servant de Règlement pour le Communauté des Marchands et Maîtres Ouvriers en Soie de la ville de Lyon* (Lyon, 1717), pp. 5–9.

of the Communauté, also called the Grande Fabrique, were grouped into three categories: the *fabricants* (in all fewer than 100 rich entrepreneurs), real putter-outers; the *ouvriers* (around 8,000 in 1732) who carried out the weaving at home on piece rates for the *fabricants* from whom they received the thread and the designs; and the *maîtres* (around 700 in 1732), small independent weavers working on their own who, like the *fabricants*, had a direct relationship with the market, one denied in principle to the *ouvriers*.[30] In the same year 1732, the 1711 proposal was represented by the *maîtres gardes* (the heads of the Communauté) with the aim of striking a blow at the independent weavers (the *maîtres*), accused of maintaining their place on the market through fraud, cornering silk and designs stolen by the *ouvriers* from the large merchants who claimed to make up the Grande Fabrique.

According to the *maitres gardes*, the independent weavers of the Petite Fabrique, unable to employ "bons dessinateurs" ("good designers"), paid as much as 8–10 thousand livres a year by the larger merchants, used "la plus part du temps des desseins volés au bonnes fabriques" ("most of the time designs stolen from good manufactories"). This double theft (of the design and the silk) had distorting effects. It pushed up enormously the cloth production costs of the large merchants, who employed weavers working at home. On the other hand, it encouraged opportunistic behavior on the part of the independent weavers who were able to offer at low cost their imitation cloth, which was necessarily of inferior quality as it was produced with a mixture of different types of silk found here and there.[31] These accusations were hotly contested

30 The term *Grande Fabrique* does not indicate centralized manufacture but rather the network of putting-out firms which gave work to thousands of weavers at home and constituted an economic structure. Each *ouvrier* might have from two to four looms on which apprentices, *compagnons* and members of his family, would work. These social and professional classifications were not constant. The meaning of the words changed according to who used them and the more or less conflictual nature of the context in which they were uttered. The case of Lyon, like that of other old industrial centers, shows the importance of studying urban as well as rural putting-out systems. See C. Poni, "Protoindustrialization: Rural and Urban," *Review* (*Fernand Braudel Center*), vol. 9 (1985), 305–314, and idem, "Per la storia del distretto industriale serico di Bologna (secoli XVI–XIX)," *Quaderni Storici*, vol. 25, no. 73 (1991), 93–167. It should be remembered that every year thousands of women arrived in Lyon from the surrounding countryside to work as "tireuses de cordes" (rope-pullers), an operation necessary in order to transfer the design onto the cloth. The introduction of perforated cards (the Jacquard loom) freed the women from this burdensome task. For the gender division of labor see ch. 8 in this volume as well as D. M. Hafter, "Women Who Wove in the Eighteenth-Century Silk Industry of Lyon," in *European Women and Preindustrial Craft*, D. M. Hafter, ed. (Bloomington, IN), 1995, pp. 42–64.

31 *Mémoire des Maîtres Gardes de la Communauté des maîtres ouvriers et marchands d'étoffes d'or, d'argent et de soie servant de réponse aux requêtes présentées au Roi ... par quelqu'un*

TABLE 9.1 Organization of the *Communauté des Marchands* and the *Maîtres Ouvriers* (1732)

Grande fabrique	
Putting out system	***Kaufsystem* (*petite fabrique*)**
Marchands fabricants (putting out entrepreneurs) circa 70 *Maîtres ouvriers* (dependent weavers) circa 8,000	*Maîtres marchands* (independent weavers) circa 700

Access to the market was permitted only for marchands fabricants and maîtres marchands, and was prohibited for maîtres ouvriers.
SOURCE: *MÉMOIRE DES MAÎTRES GARDES DE LA COMMUNAUTÉ DES MAÎTRES OUVRIERS ET MARCHANDS D'ÉTOFFES D'OR, D'ARGENT ET DE SOIE SERVANT DE RÉPONSE AUX REQUÊTES PRÉSENTÉES AU ROI … PAR QUELQU'UN DES MAÎTRES OUVRIERS ET MARCHANDS DE LA MÊME COMMUNAUTÉ OPPOSANS À I'ARRÊT DU 8 MAI 1731* (LYON, 1732) ARCHIVES MUNICIPALES DE LYON, HEREAFTER A.M.L., CHAPPE, HH. 132

by the independent weavers, who claimed that the international success of the Grande Fabrique, from which the *maîtres gardes* would have liked to exclude

des maîtres ouvriers et marchands de la même Communauté opposans à l'Arrêt du 8 mai 1731 (Lyon, 1732), Archives Municipales de Lyon, Chappe, HH. 132. This memoire includes a "Mémoire préliminaire" (pp. 9–26), two "Requêtes" (first and second) presented to the king by the *maîtres marchands* with the "Réponses des Maîtres Gardes" printed opposite (pp. 27–48 and 49–64), and a "Mémoire des négocians de la ville de Lyon" also with the "Réponse des Maîtres Gardes" printed opposite (pp. 65–90). The order of May 8, 1732 forced the *maîtres marchands* (independent weavers) to choose between the profession of *maître ouvrier* and that of *marchand fabricant*. Whoever opted for the latter would have to enroll on the register of the Communauté, paying 200 livres (and 100 livres for his sons). This repeated attempt to abolish the independent weavers as a separate group, carried out because they were considered receivers of the silk and designs stolen by the *maîtres ouvriers*, failed, however. The quotations are taken from the "Mémoire préliminaire" (pp. 12–16, 18–19) and from the "Réponse des Maîtres Gardes … à la Mémoire des négocians de la ville de Lyon" (p. 75 and passim). The majority of the *Maîtres Gardes* were always, or nearly always, on the side of the *marchands fabricants*. The best designers worked for the *fabricants* on a contractual basis, but there were also freelance designers who sold their designs to the highest bidder.

them, was due to the high professional quality of their work and that of the *maîtres ouvriers*.[32]

The weavers (*maîtres* and *ouvriers*) often proudly attributed the commercial success of Lyon to their own professional excellence. The *fabricants* tended to downplay these declarations. While claiming not to want to minimize the merits of the weavers, they declared that all the weavers did was set out "sur le dessein de manière qu'ils n'ont qu'à lire et suivre exactement ce que leur est présent" ("on the design in such a way that they only have to read and follow exactly what is before them"). The perfection of the *façonnées* ("patterned weaves") was essentially due to the intelligence of the entrepreneur. It was he who chose and decided upon "la qualité des soyes, la beauté de la dorure, la delicatesse du dessein, la sage distribution des nuances, le bon goût" ("the quality of the silks, the beauty of the gilding, the delicacy of the design, the sensitive distribution of tones, the good taste"). These were capacities, knowledge and sensitivities which could not be acquired "ny en travaillant sur le métier ny restant dans la boutique d'un ouvrier à façon" ("neither by working on the loom nor staying in the shop of an out-sourced worker"). The professional training of the *fabricant* merchant could not be limited to weaving. He had to take care of correspondence with foreign merchants; obtain orders from them; encourage them to visit the warehouses of Lyon; induce them to send "par anticipation ses commissions pour avoir les loisirs de les effectuer" ("to send their orders in advance so they have the time to carry them out"); entice them with the prospect of large profits so as to persuade them to prefer "notre manufacture aux étrangères" ("our manufacture to those of foreigners"); take advantage of the moment at which the exchange rate was favorable to foreign correspondents and ask them to pay their debts, "adoucissant par un moyen si simple le prix d'une marchandise" ("sweetening by such a simple means the price of the goods"). It was only this type of knowledge that could ensure "une consommation plus considerable pour l'avenir" ("more sales in the future"). But these special skills could only be achieved working alongside the *fabricants* in their warehouses as apprentices.[33]

32 "Première Requętte," pp. 33–39. See also the "Mémoire des négocians de la ville de Lyon," pp. 83 ff.

33 *Mémoire pour les Maîtres Marchands d'étoffes de soye, d'or et d'argent de la ville de Lyon* (n.d. [post. 1737]) pp. 19–20 (Archives Municipales de Lyon, Chappe HH 133). The major *fabricants* were active not only in Lyon. They also operated as entrepreneurs in southern France where they owned reeling plants and silk mills. Out of the many cases of such merchants, I will cite just two examples: Joubier and Montessuy.

In another pamphlet, the *maîtres gardes* (after defending in similar terms the *fabricants* from the accusations of the *ouvriers* who depicted them as wholesale merchants "inutils à la manufacture" ("useless to manufacture"), came up with an original analogy, comparing the *fabricants* to the architect, seen as "le chef, l'âme, le créateur perpetual des différens ouvrages qu'il fait construire" ("the head, the soul, the perpetual creator of the different works that they have constructed"), and the *ouvriers* to the mason who carries out "son travail purement méchanique" ("his purely mechanical work") with no idea of the beauty produced by his work.[34]

Returning to the theft or circulation of stolen designs, it should be added that some Paris merchants were also involved in this illicit traffic. Having bought "les premières pièces d'un assortiment d'étoffes" ("the first pieces of a selection of fabrics"), they had the designs copied and then sent them to those independent weavers of Lyon who were willing to supply them. In this way they were able to get hold of the cloth "bon marché" ("cheaply") and resell at a price which was perhaps no different from that of the original cloth.[35] Unfaithful traders ("commissioners") did likewise. If a certain type of cloth began to be successful, they would have the design copied and then secretly pass it on to the weavers. Once they had the cloth, the traders would sell these imitations instead of the original, cheating both their clients and the "bonnes fabriques" ("good manufacturers") whose trust they had betrayed.[36]

34 *Réponse des Maîtres Gardes et Adjoints Marchands aux observations … sur 43 articles du Règlement arrêté … le 19 juin 1744 pour la fabrique de Lyon* (Lyon), n.d. [but 1759]), pp. 7–8 (Bibliothèque Municipale de Lyon, *Catalogue Coste,* 10 594). M. Paulet pointed out other aspects: "J[ai] toujours vu une différence sensible entre les étoffes fabriquées par *un bel ouvrier,* et celles fabriquées par un ouvrier médiocre. On nomme *bel ouvrier* celui qui prende soin de régler tous les mouvements de son métier et non pas celui qui ne cherche qu'à faire une grande quantité d'ouvrage" ("I always saw a considerable difference between the fabrics produced by 'a good worker' and those produced by a mediocre worker. One calls a 'good worker' one who takes care to regulate all the movements of his loom, and not one who only seeks to make a large quantity of fabrics" (*L'art du fabriquant de d'étoffes de soie,* VII section, I partie [Paris, 1776], p. 91).

35 "Mémoire préliminaire," pp. 14–18. The Conseil d'Etat du Roi only approved the law protecting property in designs on July 14, 1787. See *Arrêt du Conseil d'Etat du Roi portant Règlement pour les nouveaux dessins que les fabricants d'étoffes, de soieries et de dorure du Royaume auront composés ou fait composer.* This *arrêt* made explicit reference to requests coming from the *fabricants* of Lyon and Tours.

36 "Mémoire préliminaire". Jacques Savary, *Le parfait négociant,* II [Paris, 1675], pp. 143–144 identified five types of commissioner. The commissioners referred to in *Mémoire préliminaire* could be the "négociants qui demeurent aux lieux des manufactures ou dans les villes où il se fait grand commerce, qui achètent de marchandises pour le compte de négocians demeurant d'autres lieux" or else "négocians à qui d'autres envoyent des marchandises pour vendre pour leur compte, suivant les ordres qu'ils en reçoivent" ("businessmen

This traffic, forbidden by the 1737 Statutes, was not limited to the Paris-Lyon axis. Merchants and traders, encouraged by the profits to be made, also sold designs to foreign competitors, thus encouraging imitations. Even though they were contested, these practices were relatively unharmful as long as foreigners copied the designs and fabrics of the previous year. Indeed, the imitations were predicted and anticipated by the challenge-response mechanism upon which the very success of the Grand Fabrique was based. An anonymous *marchand fabricant* wrote in 1761:

> La concurrence ... nous a forcé de chercher la préférence. ... Le goût a du se perfectionner plus rapidement, se renouveller entièrement et varier toutes les fois que nous avons pu être imité. ... Que l'étranger nous copie encore cent ans, il ne formera pas des dessinateurs. C'est notre goût, c'est notre imagination que lui manquent: l'imitation éteint l'un et ne donne pas l'autre. Eh, comment donneroit-elle ce goût qui règne cette année, et que la mode, une convention générale et le caprice anéantiront l'année prochaine?[37]

---

who live in the place of manufacture or in the cities where they have considerable trade, who buy merchandise on behalf of other businessmen living in other places" or else "businessmen to whom others send their merchandise to sell on their behalf, following the orders that they receive").

37 ("Competition forced us to seek a preference. ... Taste must perfect itself more rapidly, renew and vary itself entirely every time that we can be imitated. ... Even if the foreigner still copies us for a hundred years, he will not produce designers. It is our taste, our imagination that he lacks: imitation eliminates the one and does not produce the other. How to produce this taste which dominates this year, and which fashion, a general accord and caprice will obliterate the next year?"), "Mémoire sur l'envoie des échantillons de la fabrique de Lyon," *Journal de Commerce*, 1761, 108, 128–129. The article was published in serial form. The founder and editor of the journal, printed in Brussels, was Accarias de Serionne. See H. Hasquin, "Jacques Accarias de Serionne, économiste et publiciste français au service des Pays-Bas Autrichiens," *Études sur le XVIIIe siècle*, 1 (1974), 159–169. For a long time it was wrongly thought that the editors of the *Journal de Commerce* were the merchant, Camus, and the Abbé Roubaud. The "Mémoire sur l'envoie des échantillons," the importance of which it would be hard to overestimate despite the fact that it has remained more or less unknown, was reprinted as a pamphlet with the same title in Turin in 1761. This text, as will become clear later, shows how the major silk merchants of Lyon were fully aware of the peculiarities of their practices. From this point on, I will quote from the Turin edition. On the "goût" ("taste") of Lyon fabrics see also P. Bertholon, *Du commerce et des manufactures distinctives de la ville de Lyon* (Montpellier, 1787), pp. 25–26, 46–49. In a rich and stimulating article, J. M. Jones has dated the supremacy of taste over luxury as late as 1787, although in fact, taste had been dictating changes in fashion from the first half of the eighteenth century. Jones's dating can be explained by her sources: the fashion journals published in the last decades of the century. See J. M. Jones, "Repackaging

After 1730, busy with fierce corporative conflicts and engaged in limiting the illegal commerce in designs and stolen silk, the Lyon entrepreneurs did not recognize the damage that new trading practices, seemingly advantageous, had begun to inflict. The rapidly spreading practice of sale by *échantillons* (by sending out collections of pre-production samples) had enabled the trade network of the Grande Fabrique to thicken and spread. This new sales method permitted the large merchants to customize their fabric in accordance with the taste of their buyers with only minimal costs and to start the looms working only after receiving the order. The advantages were clear: a reduction in end of season warehousing, "just in time" production, personalized products, decrease in capital employed compared with the size of sales, and profit increases.

However, this practice could also be seriously damaging. The three months between the sending of the *échantillons* and the arrival of the fabric ordered gave a considerable advantage to the imitation industries. The author of the pamphlet *Sur l'envoie des échantillons* (1761) told how a Viennese merchant, having received the *échantillons* from Lyon, sent them to Venice to have them copied. He was thus able to sell imitation cloth in Vienna even before the original arrived from Lyon. In cases such as these, the original French fabric (and we should remember the talent for imitation on the part of the Venetian weavers) "n'étoit plus ... qu'un article passé, ou du moins un article soumis à la concurrence et exposé au rabais" ("was nothing more ... than an item out of fashion, or at least an item subject to competition and exposed to price-cutting").[38]

The anonymous author did not limit himself to describing this perverse mechanism. At the end of his pamphlet, he also formulated a twenty-article

Rousseau: Femininity and Fashion in Old Regime France," *French Historical Studies*, vol. 18, no. 4 (1994), 939–968.

38 "Mémoire sur l'envoie des échantillons," pp. 82–83. In order to send the *échantillons* the entrepreneurs had to finish the manufacture of at least one piece and then cut it up. If no orders arrived, the loom was dismantled. Often the *fabricants* made mistakes in their predictions. A fabric on which they had "conçus les plus belles espérances" ("conceived the highest hopes") might not meet with "aucun succès" ("any success"). On the other hand, "ses pressentiments contre les desseins d'un goût hazarde et fantastique" ("his forebodings against designs of a daring and fanciful taste") were sometimes contradicted with "la plus heureuse réussite" ("the happiest success"), (Adamoli fils, "Lettre à M. Vial marchand fabricant à Lyon beau-frère de l'auteur," *Journal de Commerce*, December 1761, p. 70). Production times varied considerably according to the quality of the design and the lengths ordered. The *péruviennes* were woven at the length usual for men's clothing, in four days. To produce fifteen *aunes* (the length for women's clothing) of the simplest *broché* (*"nué"*) (brocade), four or five weeks were necessary. *Broché,* used for women's clothing with complex and rich design, could only be produced "dans l'espace de deux mois et plus" ("in a period of two months or more") (ibid., p. 74. 1 *aune* = 1.18 metres).

proposal for a set of rules prohibiting trade by means of *échantillons* (and thus also their expedition). This project was integrated in the nine-article *Règlement* approved a few years later. Not all the spokesmen, however, found themselves in agreement. Adamoli fils, in favor of the *échantillons,* was of the opinion that the new imitation industries would find difficulty in reaching the size that enabled the Lyon industries to carry out a high division of labor with consequent reductions in costs. He wrote: "Les manufactures compliquées, telles que sont celles des étoffes de goût demandent ... la réunion d'une grande quantité de métiers" ("complicated manufactures, such as those of tasteful fabrics require ... bringing together a large number of looms") so that all the workers with their different jobs could be employed throughout the year. The speed and perfection of the assembly of the loom was dependent precisely on the specialization of workers and on the division of labor. "Si l'ouvrier qui doit fabriquer la pièce vouloit aussi monter le métier, il y employeroit beaucoup de temps et le monteroit mal" ("If the worker who has to produce the piece wants also to assemble the loom, he would employ much time and assemble it poorly"). Thus it would not have been easy quickly to achieve the critical mass and competitive level that the Grande Fabrique had acquired "par une longue pratique" ("through long experience"). No European ruler had so far managed to defend successfully the internal market in favor of local industry and give satisfactory support to the flow of exports through incentives. Finally, in the field of fashion fabrics, with or without *échantillons*, foreign firms would continue to flounder "dans la nuit de l'obscurité" ("in total darkness").[39]

This analysis, which emphasized what we would now call barriers to entry and the competitive advantages of Lyon, was not enough to counter the arguments against sending the *échantillons*, which was prohibited on March 15, 1765 by the assembly of the Communauté. On this occasion, one of the *maîtres gardes,* Jean Marie Duperrel, reported to the assembly that of the thousands of *échantillons* sent every year to foreign merchants, only relatively few orders were obtained, sometimes only from one *échantillon* out of ten sent out, while the other nine were passed on to be copied by the local weavers.

These abuses were widespread. In Hamburg, one so-called merchant had received from a Lyon trader several cases of *échantillons* and had not placed a single order. In Naples, a Lyon merchant who had taken with him a complete assortment of *échantillons,* gave them to the supervisor of the local "Royal Manufacture" to be copied, getting in exchange "quelques commissions légères" ("some small orders"). In London, another Lyon trader, when he was leaving to

39 Ibid., pp. 76–77, 93.

return to France, sold a collection of *échantillons* whose value amounted to 1,800 livres for only 13.10 livres. This was probably an exaggeration, but *maître garde* Duperrel was stressing, also on behalf of his colleagues, how it was much less dangerous to send designs than to send *échantillons*:

> dans les quels on voit non seulement la composition du dessin, mais encore son effet, les nuances, le tissu de l'étoffe, l'armure du métier, la qualité des matières, la quantité des portées, cette art enfin du mélange et cette gradation des couleurs qui produisent les belles nuances et qui donnent prix aux étoffes.[40]

If the sending of *échantillons* were prohibited, would it be possible to stop foreign firms copying material after buying a single item? J. M. Duperrel replied to this objection that as foreign firms had to buy at the beginning of the season, they would be at a disadvantage of several months with their copied material and would in any case have to buy two *aunes* of fabric. Beaten in terms of timing, they would be forced to carry out their imitations with a delay of one season or one year. "Mais alors les desseins de l'année précédente seroit tombés, et ne soutendrons pas la concurrence avec nos étoffes nouvelles" ("but then the design of the previous year would be outdated, and would not support the competition from new fabrics").[41]

---

40 ("in which one sees not only the composition of the design, but also its impression, the tones, the form of the fabric, the weave of the loom, the quality of the material, the measure of its range, and last that art of blending and that gradation of colors that produces the beautiful tones and sets the price of the fabrics").

41 *Arrêt d la Cour de Parlement qui homologue la délibération de la Communauté des Maîtres Marchands et Maîtres Ouvriers fabricants en étoffes d'or, d'argent et de soie de la ville de Lyon du 15 Mars 1765 concernant la prohibition de l'envoie des échantillons des mêmes étoffes hors la dite ville, 14 mai* (1765), pp. 5–10. In this text, the term *maîtres marchands* indicates also the *marchands fabricants*. *Échantillon* trading had been practiced at least from the seventeenth century. Immediately after the publication of this *Arrêt* prohibiting the sending of *échantillons*, some Lyon merchants proposed to send short pieces of fabric (from 2 to 3 aunes long), in return for payment, to their foreign correspondents; the latter refused to pay and rejected the offer. See the letter sent by Fabre and Defez from The Hague to M. Carret of October 3, 1764. They wrote: "La deffence du Parlement sur l'exportation des échantillons nous a fait de la peine. Nous nous étions flattés de prendre plusieurs commissions … nous ne pouvons pas nous charger des échantillons de trois aunes que vous nous offrez, et qu'il vous est permis d'envoyer" ("The prohibition by Parlement of the export of samples has created difficulties for us. We were flattered to take several orders … we cannot be responsible for samples of three *aunes* that you offer us and which you are permitted to send"), ("Carret et Cie," Liasse VIII, in Archives Départementales du Rhône, Procedure de la Conservation, Livres de commerce).

However, the trade by *échantillons* (from this point onwards prohibited but never entirely eradicated) gave way to other manipulations favorable to the Grand Fabrique. In countries where French cloth was banned (as in Britain and Ireland) some merchants were able to bring in real pieces of cloth under the name of samples imported for the production of imitations. In 1763, for example, Mr. Cottingham, a large Dublin silk merchant, imported, in his words, "a number of new patterns in pieces in order to serve the kingdom with the newest fashions from his own looms." The Dublin weavers contested this, claiming that he had imported cloth to sell directly on the market. Frightened and embittered at the prospect of losing their jobs, the weavers massed in front of Mr. Cottingham's house and attacked it twice. The imported fabric was cut up, his looms were destroyed and he was burned in effigy. According to the reporter who narrated the episode, the rebellious weavers "would have assassinated him, if he had fallen into their hands." The crowd dispersed only after having extorted a promise from Mr. Cottingham "that he would never import any more silks" and after he had given over a bond of "1,000 pounds for performing the covenant."[42] Other merchants used the *échantillons* for other purposes. Those of Frankfurt, for example, who did not buy fabric "de la première fraîcheur" ("of the first freshness") as they traded in "vieux desseins" ("old designs") cleverly used the new samples as benchmarks to devalue the year-old fabrics.[43]

The feverish and worried discussion over the theft of and trade in designs and *échantillons* did not stop the entrepreneurs of the Lyon fashions or rather, as one of them put it, of the "modes de Paris faites à Lyon" ("fashions of Paris made in Lyon") from celebrating taste in highly poetic language. In the words of the already-mentioned anonymous merchant:

> Le gout, comme la beauté fragile n'a qu'une saison, commes les grâces il n'est soumis à aucune règle, et ne s'acquiert point avec une froide

42 *The Gentleman's Magazine*, 33, 1763, 410–411. During the riot, the weavers wounded "several soldiers. ... Their leader, with an astonishing intrepidity, when a loaded musket was at this breast, called to the mob to fire, saying: 'I desire nothing more than to die in this cause.'" In the same year, an anonymous author published a harsh, sarcastic pamphlet against Mr. Cottingham, *The Weaver's Address to the Citizens of Dublin or Dean Swift's Advice to the good People of Ireland together with his Apparition occasioned by the Importation of Wrought Silk from France* (Dublin, 1763.). The author sets up an imaginary trial of Mr. Cottingham, although he is never mentioned by name.

43 Adamoli fils, "Lettre à M. Vial," pp. 78–79.

> imitation. ... Dans le façonné, le succès de notre fabrique est fondé uniquement sur le goût. C'est par lui qu'elle se soutient malgré l'envie et la rivalité.[44]

But copying material by designs and *échantillons* was not sufficient if the colors were not imitated as well. This was a difficult task, given the technologies available which did not permit the isolation of the ingredients. It would not even have been enough to use the same materials (mordants and colorings) in the same proportions, as the physical and chemical properties of the water used also made a difference. For their blacks, the Lyon merchants used the water of the Rhône mixed with that of the Saône. For the colors such as crimson, deep red, violet and purple, the water of the Saône alone was used. For all the other colors (white, green, grey, yellow and so on), the water of the Rhone was used.[45] But apart from the inimitable (and perhaps imaginary) dyeing virtues of the rivers of Lyon, how could foreign merchants get hold quickly of the dyeing formulas and the additives used to produce not only the new combinations but also those delicate shades for which the Lyon materials were justly famous? There was one short cut: to buy thread already dyed in Lyon, as the Tours merchants did, although this export was explicitly forbidden by the Communauté.[46]

---

44 ("Taste, like fragile beauty has only one season, like elegance it does not submit to any rule, and is acquired only through cold imitation. ... With patterned weaves (*façonné*), the success of our fabrics is based uniquely on taste. It is what sustains us despite envy and rivalry"), "Memoire sur l'envoi des échantillons," pp. 34–37.

45 The history of dyeing techniques in France and especially in Lyon was based on a vast information network stretching from India to Europe. On the importance of the "Art of Dyeing," an anonymous English author wrote in the "Preface" to the translation of French treatises on coloring: "Few people can estimate the intrinsic value of manufactured woolens, silks or cottons. But men, women and children can judge of their colors, on the beauty of which therefore the first sale of a new manufacturer must depend. And the continuance of that sale will also depend more on the permanency of their colour than of their stuff" (*Art of Dying Wool Silk and Cotton*, by M. Hellot, M. Macquer and M. le Pileur d'Apligny [London, 1789], p. v).

46 The prohibition "d'envoyer ou de favoriser la sortie hors du Royaume des soyes teintes propres à fabriquer des étoffes" ("of sending or favoring the sending out of the Kingdom of colored silks ready to be made into fabrics") was issued on July 13, 1725 by the Prévôt des Marchands on the request of the Maîtres Gardes (AML Chappe HH, no. 147). According to an anonymous author, the prohibition of the export of dyed silk had forced foreigners to "s'appliquer aux teintures" ("to work at dyeing"). And they had succeeded so well in this that they had reached the "même degré de perfection, si l'on excepte la couleur de rose, qui est encore inférieur à celle de Lyon, mais qui aura sans doute à son tour le même sort que les autres couleurs" ("same degree of perfection, if one excepts the color rose, which is still inferior to that of Lyon, but which without doubt will have in its turn the same fate

More pernicious than the illegal trade in designs, *échantillons* and dyed yarn was the emigration of weavers, designers and entrepreneurs, often enticed to move to other states or foreign cities with promises of rich bonuses on employment, or of generous financing and high profits and wages. Sometimes waves of emigration were sparked by economic crisis and unemployment, as in 1752 and 1759. On other occasions, religious persecution and the desire to follow the Protestant religion prompted emigration to freer and more secure countries. In England and Holland, silk manufacturing benefited enormously from the flight of religious minorities after the Revocation of the Edict of Nantes in 1685. In Spain, and in particular in Valencia, the extensive and highly-qualified French emigration was encouraged by the prospect of high wages and profits.

Lyon replied to what it saw as dangerous desertion in several different ways, ranging from the exclusion of those professing Protestantism from apprenticeships to the imprisonment and punishment for criminal activity of those who were discovered making preparations for emigration or already on their way to the frontier. The news that entrepreneurs, designers and technicians were getting ready to open workshops in foreign countries to reproduce the fashions of their home country was looked on with preoccupation by Lyon and gave rise to opposition. In 1755, the Chamber of Commerce denounced the entrepreneurs Bachelard and Parisien, accused of setting up a silk manufacture in Naples, and retaliated by forcing the "corps de fabricants ... à envoyer aux négocians qui sont à Naples plusieurs assortissemens de belles étoffes avec ordres de les vendre à bas prix au danger d'y perdre quelque chose" ("the corps of manufacturers ... to send to the businessmen who are in Naples several collections of beautiful fabrics with orders to sell them at a low price because of the danger of loss"). The profit which was lost would be small in comparison with the benefits "qui en resulteroit pour tous" ("which will result for all"). As well as the dumping of fabric, it was decided to order all the creditors of Bachelard and Parisien (including Soubay de Combes, Daude, Nicolas, Guerignon and others) to form a consortium and demand together that the two black sheep pay for their misdeeds. This threat, it was thought, would be enough to make them abandon "promptement leur entreprise qui les oblige à une grande dépense" ("promptly their enterprise which necessitates a great expense"). Similar threats and rulings had been issued on previous occasions "lors de

as the other colors"), ("Consideration sur la finance et sur le commerce de France," *Journal de Commerce*, January 1762, 21–23). In fact, smuggling ensured the continuation of the trade in dyed yarn. But the growth of the Lyon chemical sector was hindered by this prohibition. New dye works were set up in the countryside as a reaction to the mercantilist policy of the city.

l'établissement de la manufacture de Hollande" ("since the establishment of the manufacture in Holland").[47] This shows that the Grande Fabrique kept up an effective control over a large area and was able to benefit from a good information and command service capable of functioning even over long distances.

It is by no means certain, however, that the emigration of weavers and entrepreneurs had the results that were feared. Vincent de Gournay, the *Intendent de commerce* who visited Lyon in the 1750s as the official responsible for the French silk industry for the Bureau de Commerce of Paris, smiled "bitterly" when some merchants told him of the efforts that were made to stop the emigration of weavers and merchants. His views in favor of "laisser faire" and hostile to corporate restraints, even after his death in 1759, were caricatured and ridiculed by an anonymous author who claimed he had proposed "d'amener l'étranger sur nos métiers ou les leur envoyer tout montés avec nos ouvriers" ("to bring the foreigner to our looms or to send looms already assembled with our workers"), offering in return only "son system favori de la concurrences sur le prix" ("his favored system of price competition"). According to this author, competition over prices was not always possible and it should only be resorted to "quand on n'a plus autres ressources" ("when one no longer has other resources")[48] – when it was not possible to have recourse to product differentiation. A defender of de Gournay made the criticism that the suppression of corporative restraints would not annul all the competitive advantages. There were certain structures and values that could not be transferred, such as "l'ensemble d'une manufacture, le goût, les desseins, l'économie, l'amour du travail"

47 See *Moyen qu' il paroît que l'on pourroit employer pour empescher le succès de l'établissement que se fait à Naples d'une manufacture d'ètoffes à l'imitation de celle de Lyon. L'Avis de la Chambre de Commerce* (n.d. [but 1755]), in Bibliothéque Municipale de Lyon, Cotte, no. 10428 or 1002. See also the *Mémoire* of the designer Jean Renard of Lyon to the King of Naples in ASN, "Pandetta comune," fascio 73, fasc. 1380/bis. Renard promised to teach the "composition et la lecture des desseins" ("composition and the reading of designs") and the procedure "pour le blanc, cremoise et ponceau de Lyon" ("for white, cream-color and dark red of Lyon") (pp. 1, 13–14). Roland de la Platière met a Lyonnais in Rome who managed an "entreprise" which produced, although with little success, fabric "de soie brochés et en dorure" ("silk brocade with gold decoration") (*Lettres*). The imitating manufactures of southern Italy never substantially developed. Ange Goudar, who was in Naples in 1767 for the wedding of the Bourbon King Ferdinando IV with Maria Carolina of Habsburg, was quick to notice the huge expenditure on clothes and jewelry, which amounted to "une grande portion des richesses générales, qui passeroient en France de manière que le mariage se feroit à Naples et les noces à Lyon" ("a great portion of the general wealth passes to France in the sense that the marriage takes place in Naples and the celebration in Lyon") (*Naples. Ce qu'il faut faire pour rendre ce Royaume florissant*, [Amsterdam, 1771], pp. 111–112).

48 "Mémoire sur l'envoie des échantillons," *Journal de Commerce*, pp . 125–136. I do not quote from the Turin edition because it does not include the attack on Germany.

("the entire system of manufacture, the taste, the designs, the economy, the love of work").[49] These ideas, similar to those of Adamoli fils, are evidence that with the lively industrial atmosphere of Lyon, some merchant entrepreneurs began to move beyond the defense of corporative restraints to see the possibility of new protective barriers that were compatible with "laissez faire."

To thwart the setting up of import-substitute industries in foreign countries, the merchant-entrepreneurs of Lyon began to use other methods (which we would now call horizontal product differentiation), adapting designs and colors to the different national tastes. For the German and English markets, light colors were used; for the Spanish, some black threads were added. Some decoration necessary for specific markets was sometimes added to the French designs.[50] The correspondence between merchants, preserved in the Archives Départmentales de Lyon, documents the "open" orders, those based on *échantillons* and the variations in colors and designs asked for by foreign traders.

The information system was used in the same way that contemporary entrepreneurs prepare the launch of new products. Absolute secrecy surrounded the

---

49 "Observations sur un article du *Journal de Commerce* … concernant feu M. de Gournay Intendant du Commerce," *Journal de Commerce*, April 1761, 71–85. On the ideas of de Gournay, see G. Schelle, *Vincent de Gournay. Laisser faire, laisser passer* (Paris, 1897); G. Senestat-Escande, *Les idées économiques de Vincent de Gournay* (Bordeaux, 1911); S. Meyssonier, *La balance et l'horloge. La genèse de la pensée libérale en France au XVIII siècle* (Paris, 1989), pp. 167–200, 232–239. In 1786 M. Mayet recognized that it was easy "aux Fabriques étrangers de contrefaire nos étoffes et de copier nos dessins. Le bas prix de notre main d'oeuvre est le seul avantage qu'ils ne peuvent nous dérober" ("for foreign manufactures to imitate our fabrics and to copy our designs. The low price of our labor force is the sole advantage that they cannot steal from us"), (M. Mayet, *Mémoire sur les manufactures de Lyon* [London, 1786], pp. 37–38). In a previous statement, he considered "Le bas prix des étoffes" ("the low price of fabrics") as one of the advantages of Lyon. The others were: "la qualité de leurs fonds, le goût qui règne dans leur dessins" ("the quality of their collections, the taste that reigns in their designs") (p. 18).

50 "Mémoire sur l'envoie des échantillons," p. 75. According to Abbé Morellet, "quoique nos modes et notre goût dans les étoffes de soie ayent beaucoup d'empire sur les étrangers, il faut cependant convenir qu'ils ont leur goût auquel nous nous conformons en partie, et auquel nous continuerions de nous conformer, quand même nous ne ferions pas autant des étoffes de soie" ("although our fashions and our taste in silk fabrics have much influence on foreigners, nevertheless it must be admitted that they have their own taste to which we conform in part, and to which we may continue to conform, even though we may not make as many silk fabrics") (*Réflexions sur les avantages de la libre fabrication et de l'usage des toiles peintes en France* [n.p., 1758], p. 50). See also Veron de Forbonnais, *Elémens du Commerce*, Premiere Partie (Leiden, 1754), p. 252. For criticisms of the obsession with French fashion, harmful to trade and to the morals of the Spanish, see B. G. Feijoo, *Theatro critico universal o discoursos varios en todo genero de materias para desengano des errores communes* (Madrid, 1728), II, pp. 139–149 passim.

phase in which the new annual fashion was conceived and chosen. Once the new fashion had been launched, maximum publicity was given immediately using all possible channels of communication: the *échantillons,* the network of traders, mercantile correspondence, *poupées* (dolls) and, from 1781 onwards, the fashion journals. Even the foreign travelers who had themselves made one or more suits in the latest fashion became, once they returned to their country of origin, unconscious bearers of the new Lyonnaise or Parisian tastes.

According to some, the wholesale buyers were better served if they bought directly from the shops of warehouses in Lyon. Negotiating directly with the *marchand fabricant,* the buyer could ask to "réduire le dessein de trois quarts ..., changer les nuances ..., donner plus de contrast à ce groupe, plus de jeu à cette guirlande ..., substituer ici un fond cannelé léger, passer cette fleur de cette manière" ("reduce the design by three quarters ..., change the tones, give more contrast to this group, more play to that garland ..., substitute here a light fluted background, alter that flower in that manner"). A third party would then enter the discussion when a designer was called upon to make a design out of ideas that were still uncertain and confused. The *ouvrier* (the weaver) would then join the group and try to imagine the difficulties of putting the new design into concrete form. "Et s'il ne peut exécuter d'une manière, il en propose une autre" ("and if he cannot do it in one way, he proposes another").[51] But the opposition between the two types of sale was not total. The merchants who bought by *échantillons* went more or less regularly to Lyon and to Paris to make the most important purchases and to get a feel of the market.

The press too tried to influence the taste of the public, exalting the superiority of the Grande Fabrique. "En Espagne," wrote the anonymous merchant, "où la concurrance est si rare et le goût si borné on copie très lentement et très exactement chaque année nos desseins de l'année précédente." In London, "l'on conserve dans l'étoffe le plat, massive et le bizarre goût chinoise. On ne songe guère à nous copier. Si on le fait quelque fois, on voudrait se déguiser à soi même. On nous défigure en nous copiant."[52]

51 "Mémoire sur l'envoie des échantillons," pp. 78–79. These sales methods, practiced on an international market, indicate a type of flexibility that was personalized and original. We should keep in mind that on local markets goods were often bought to order. I am thinking here of the sale of shoes, for example.

52 ("In Spain," wrote the anonymous merchant, "where the competition is so rare and taste so limited, they copy very slowly and very exactly each year our designs of the previous year." In London, "the fabrics retain dullness, heaviness and the bizarre Chinese taste. They hardly think of copying us. If someone does it sometimes, one wants to disguise it to oneself. They disfigure us in copying us.") Ibid., pp. 57–58. When necessary, the Grande Fabrique worked also "sur des desseins d'Angleterre" ("on the designs of

The same author confirms the practice of lowering by up to 50 percent the price of fabrics that went out of fashion, and informs us that a large part of these fabrics was sent to the provinces, to the West Indies, to the fairs of Leipzig and Frankfurt on the Oder where "les grossiers" ("the wholesalers") opened their emporia to a picturesque crowd of Poles, Danes, Russians, Swedes, Hungarians, Wallachians and Turks. Those two fairs were a frontier world, in direct contact with countries whose customs were more or less immobile, characterized by "différents goûts" ("different tastes") little influenced by the fashions and tastes of Paris. In this area, where there was little sensitivity to the "quality" of the product, it was easy to do good business with products that were either in or out of fashion. It would seem almost as if fashion had fixed the Oder (or somewhere not far to the east of it, with the exception of the court of St. Petersburg and Moscow) as the frontier of a certain kind of Europe whose capital was Paris.[53]

But while taste and fashion triumphed, the quality of the material declined. The rapid differentiation of the product and the annual appearance of new fashions led to a decrease in quality. There was, in fact, no reason to produce long-lasting materials. Daniel Defoe wrote in 1728: "French cloth, with all its superficial French gloss upon it is fine, but thin and spongy and will do the weaver neither credit nor service. While the English cloth wears to the last like a board, firm and strong, and has a kind of beauty even in its rags."[54] Towards

England") as happened in 1759 (*Réponses des Maîtres Gardes et Adjoints-Marchands aux Observations particuliers et intéressantes des Maîtres Gardes et Adjoint Ouvriers .sur 43 articles du Règlement ... arrêteé le 19 Juin 1744* [Lyon, 1759], pp. 28–29). On fashion reviews, see A. Kleinert, *Die frühen Modejournale in Frankreich. Studien zur Literatur der Mode von den Anfangen bis 1848* (Berlin, 1980). Right from the beginning of the eighteenth century, dolls dressed in the latest fashions were sent annually from Paris to the principal cities of Europe.

53 "Mémoire sur l'envoie des échantillons," pp. 69–71. As L.-A. Caraccioli wrote, "Les seigneurs moscovites sont devenus presques parisiens à force de les copier" ("the Moscovite nobles have become almost Parisian by copying them") (*Paris, Le modèle des nations étrangères ou l'Europe française* [Venice, Paris, 1777], p. 44).

54 D. Defoe, *A Plan of the English Commerce* (London, 1728), pp. 178–179. According to Veron de Forbonnais, the production of fabric was "plus parfait en Angleterre qu'à Lyon" ("more perfect in England than in Lyon") (*Lettre à M+ + + Négociant de Lyon ...*, p. 25). M. Paulet, *maître ouvrier* in Lyon until 1752, also recognized that the British had taken silk weaving "à un très haut degré de perfection" ("to a very high degree of perfection") and attributed this to the high specialization of looms and weavers. In Spitalfields, he wrote, "les métiers une fois consacrés à telle ou telle étoffe ne sont jamais monté pour une autre. Ainsi tel ouvrier qui fait du satin ne fera jamais de taffetas ou de velours. ... Par ce moyen chacun d'eux acquiert dans son genre une precision à laquelle nul autre ne peut attendre, parceque le fabricant ne change jamais la qualité de la soie" ("the looms, once assembled for one type of fabric are never reassembled for another. Thus a worker who makes satin will never

the end of the century, an anonymous Bolognese nobleman wrote sarcastically: "Today an *andrienne* lasts, apart from the honor of the fashion, for just three years. Then [at the beginning of the eighteenth century] it lasted forty without dishonor."[55]

A look through the *Règlements* of the Communauté also testifies to the decline in the quality of the fabrics. The 1737 *Règlements,* which the *maîtres* and the *ouvriers* managed to impose on the *fabricants,* established the precise width, density and length of the fabric, and sometimes even the weight each type of fabric should have per *aune,* conforming to the spirit of the *Règlements et Statuts* of 1720. This policy came up against the stiff opposition of the *fabricants,* who, overturning the policy approved in 1737, managed to get a new set

make taffetas or velvets. … By this means each of them acquires a precision in his work which no one else can attain, because the manufacturer never changes the quality of the silk") (M. Paulet, *L'art du fabricant d'étoffes de soie,* 1st and 2nd eds. [Paris, 1793], p. xv). Unlike M. Paulet, M. Mayet criticized foreign manufacturers "où les ouvriers passent tous les jours d'un genre à un autre, par caprice ou par necessité," ("where the workers change every day from one line of work to another, by caprice or by necessity") while in Lyon no one would have asked a weaver of "gros de Tours" to begin work "à la gaze ou au taffetas" ("on gauze or taffeta") because he would not have been able to give to either of these fabrics "cette légèreté, cette délicatesse, ce brillant qui en constituent la perfection" ("that lightness, that delicateness, that brilliance which constitutes perfection"), (*Mémoire sur la manufacture de Lyon,* pp. 19–20). The contrast between these two texts gives rise to some intriguing questions.

55 *Opusculi quatro sopra il lusso* (Bologna, 1787), p. 239. The author regretted "those rich swirling gold and silver fabrics which adorned the shoulders of our ancestors and which from the first days of marriage onwards promised immortality." Today instead, "the flowers to be found on the lightest of silk are so fragile and ephemeral that they seem to be about to lose their leaves" (ibid.). Abbé Jacquet's astute judgment was that fashion had removed "à la richesse sa pesanteur naturelle" ("from sumptousness its natural heaviness") to give it instead "avec la variété de la nature la simplicité des grâces" ("with the variey of nature the simplicity of gracefulness") (*Sur les moyens de faire refleurir les manufactures de Lyon,* December 22, 1784, in Académie des Sciences de Lyon, Ms. 110, p. 52). Zanon also pointed out the fragility of the fashion fabrics: "The French fabrics can be worn only for a few hours and in good weather. As soon as they are taken off, they are folded up carefully in white, clean linen and put away in the wardrobe with the utmost prudence. They are only rarely shown and, like illustrious relics, are only touched with great delicacy. Quite the opposite is the case with our fabrics. They are worn without care in all weathers and on all occasions, they are hung up on old nails" (*Dell'agricoltura, dell'arti e del commercio,* v, 251–252). Around 1740, an anonymous Venetian attacked the "inventors of fashion," who one year imposed "fabrics covered with flowers, woven with an art that was more apparent than real," and the following year took away "all the merits of the previous fashion" with fabrics "of a different form and design" on which appeared "natural fruits" (*Saggio di una nuova filosofia con cui insegna il modo di far denari* [Venice, 1740], pp. 158–159).

of *Reglements* adopted in 1744 reducing the width, length and weight of several types of fabric.

The counterattack of the *ouvriers* was spirited. They complained that the density of the *taffetas brochés* (taffeta brocade) had been reduced by 40 percent, with the result that it was impossible to make them "passablement bons" ("passably good"), while the density of the "simpletés et doubletés" ("simple and double") taffetas had been lowered by around 20 percent. For velvet, the decline in quality was justified and encouraged by the introduction of new (conventional) ways of counting the warp, which resulted in making the fabrics thinner by a third. All fabrics, then, as regards the thickness (and weight) of the warp, were by now "au dessous de tout ce qu'il y a de moindre" ("below everything that is the least") and only sold because of "l'apprêt qu'on leur donnent" ("the embellishment that is given to them").[56]

Particularly stiff opposition among the dependent weavers (the *maîtres ouvriers*) was provoked by an operation called *lustrage* which they had renamed *étirage* (stretching). *Lustrage,* carried out by a polishing machine, probably introduced in the second half of the seventeenth century by *fabricants,* was intended to make the warp smoother (before handing it over to the weavers to set on the looms), but it also had an important side effect – that of lengthening the warp by around 8–10 percent. This enabled the entrepreneurs also to draw distinct advantage from the new weight/length ratio, the practice of selling by weight having already been substituted by selling by length.[57] This certain profit for the merchants corresponded to a considerable inverse loss for the weavers. The thread, subject to excessive tension and thus losing much of its natural strength, was easily broken when working with it on the loom. The increase in the number of breakages led to more frequent interruptions (to tie

56 *Mémoire pour les maîtres ouvriers à façon des étoffes d'or, d'argent et de soye de la ville de Lyon* (1749), pp. 65–69. In this text, the term *maîtres marchands* indicates *marchands fabricants*. There are a number of reports for and against the *Règlements* of 1744. I have made use of this *Mémoire* because it is the most important for the aims of this paper. For the history of the conflicts and negotiations between the various sides in the struggle see J. Godart, *L'ouvrier en soie*, pp. 276–296 passim. The decrease in the number of threads in the warp is related to the thinning of the thread thanks to progress made in reeling and twisting techniques in Piedmont. In Bologna (whose reeling and twisting techniques were in the eighteenth century some way behind those of Piedmont), it was calculated that with the new thinner threads it was possible to produce fabrics up to 50 percent longer; on the spinning of silk in Bologna see in this volume, ch. 7. Nearly all the Piedmontese production of organzine (yarn used for the warp) was exported to Lyon where it was used in the production of high-quality fabric.

57 In France, sale by length was a characteristic of Lyonnais fashion fabrics. In the more conservative Tours, sale by weight continued for much longer.

up the broken threads) and thus to an increase in drudgery and a decrease in pay (the weavers being paid on piece rates). This was the reason behind the defense of the quality of the product by the weavers, who accused the merchants of a doubly illicit profit, selling bad quality fabric under the pretense that it was good quality, and increasing demand by trading in products which did not last and thus had to be replaced after only short periods.[58]

After 1744 no new *Règlement général* was approved. A new phase got underway: that of the pressure of the large merchants on the Bureau de Commerce de Paris to obtain exemption from the rules and practices that had been approved. One example was the prohibition in the 1744 *Règlements* of mixing different quality silks. There was a practice, however, not entirely new, of mixing "raw" silk (made up of leftover silk, useful only for sewing) with "cooked" silk (the best quality silk obtained from the cocoons by means of boiling water). This mixing of different quality silks was practiced, for example, in the production of "petits velours" but was not allowed in the production of golden or silver materials "figuré à la tire ou au bouton," known also under the name of "étoffes façonnées (patterned fabrics) et grandes façonnées." The request to use raw silk in these fabrics – supported by the great designer Jacques Revel – led to a deep division in the ranks of the merchant entrepreneurs. Some feared that excessive (and perhaps fraudulent) lowering of the physical quality of the product might disgust the buyer. The *maîtres gardes* thought likewise, and it

58 *Mémoire pour les maîtres ouvriers*. pp. 52–58 passim. The *maîtres ouvriers* calculated that with bad quality warp, the time necessary to weave a given quantity of fabric would be multiplied five times (ibid., p. 71) with a consequent decrease in wages paid according to piece rates. M. Paulet also opposed the use of *lustrage* because its high waste ratio, due to the breaking of the thread, was damaging to the *fabricant* (*L'art du fabricant d'étoffes de soie*, VII section, I partie [Paris, 1776], pp. 416–418). On the other hand, Bertholon praised this practice invented by Octavio May in 1665 (*Du commerce et des manufactures*, p. 40). According to Veron de Forbonnais, if the Lyon *fabricants* had tried to use the "traits faux" ("fake thread") in the luxury fabrics rather than the "traits fins," ("fine threads") they would have been reported by their own *ouvriers*. It is the workers who thus appear as the guarantors of quality (*Lettre à M +++ Negoçiant de Lyon*, pp. 6–11). Among the various contributors to the *Règlement* of 1744, the *maîtres ouvriers'* hostility was particularly directed towards the entrepreneur J. Claude Montessuy and the engineer Jacques Vaucanson. The first was accused of having produced bad quality fabric (later confiscated), the second for having declared on several occasions that the Lyon fabrics were too good, and that if "[ils] ne dureroient que trois mois ce seroit toujours assez" ("they only last three months that would still be enough") (ibid., pp. 30–31). On the business relationship between Vaucanson and Montessuy, see A. Doyon and L. Liagre, *Jacques Vaucanson, mécanicien de génie* (Paris, 1966), pp. 175–203, 256–261 passim.

was only after a long and protracted struggle that, with certain conditions, they authorized the use of these mixed silks in the *façonné*.[59]

According to the merchant Raymond Vial, the use of "raw" silk in *façonnées* (patterned) gold and silver fabric, "demandé par le consommateur et autorisé par quelques permissions" ("asked by the consumer and authorized by some official permits") should have been left to the responsibility of the individual entrepreneur. "Il est si fort," he wrote:

> notre intérêt à bien faire que la plus grande perfection de l'étoffes auroit été la suite naturelle de cette liberté. C'est au génie seul à prescrire les règles de l'art. Mais on a voulu l'assujeter à des lois gênantes aux quelles il a fallu déroger lorsque des productions nouvelles et imprévues en ont fait reconnaître l'inutilité.[60]

This claim for liberty of production was not only theoretical. Vial had on his looms a large number of articles to be sold on the Paris market to which he would not have been able to "donner la légèreté et la main que l'acheteur désire" ("give the lighteness and the touch that the buyer desires") without using the prohibited silk.[61]

According to another note, signed by a large group of merchants and addressed to the *Intendant du commerce* De Cotte, the "raw" silk made the golden and silver materials stronger and lighter, while it also made the job of the weavers easier. The perfection of the materials and the ease with which they could be worked would thus coincide with lower production costs and higher profits. The innovation, then, would be to the advantage of everyone,

---

59 The use of raw silk (*filoselle*) was justified because it gave both softness and *fermeté* (firmness) to the fabric. In order to manufacture cheap fabrics for export, the entrepreneurs successfully asked for over 145 special permits granting exemption from the *Règlements* of 1744 in the period 1754–62 (Godart, *L'ouvrier en soie*, p. 85).

60 ("It is so strongly," he wrote, "our interest to do what is right that the greatest perfection of our fabrics would be the natural result of that liberty. It is to genius alone to prescribe the rules of the art. But one wanted to subject it to bothersome laws which it would be necessary to contravene when new and unexpected productions would make their uselessness known").

61 Letter from Raymond Vial of 1763, in Archives Nationales de Paris (A.N.P.), Bureau du Commerce, F12, 1446. The language of Vial demanding "liberté" from the "lois gênantes" ("bothersome laws") incorporated the discourse of de Gournay, who had declared himself to be in favor of the use of raw silk. Vial was the brother-in-law of Adamoli fils. It was only in 1779, after the abolition of the corporations by Turgot in 1776 (later revised to a certain extent), that merchants and weavers were allowed to weave fabrics of whatever quality they wanted, despite the fierce opposition of the *Maîtres Gardes*.

even if it would lead to envy on the part of those who were tied to customs and rules which were both out of date and which gave smaller profits.[62] According to the *maitres gardes*, on the other hand, stern measures should be taken against those merchants who seemed not to have "d'autre but que de vendre une chose pour une autre" ("any other aim but to sell one thing for another").[63] They opposed those who argued in favor of the "raw" silk on the grounds that it was a "spécieux prétexte" ("specious pretext") in order to cheat the consumer. How was it possible otherwise to explain the behavior of those merchants who ordered their weavers "de fabriquer les deux premières aunes de la tête des pièces et les deux dernières de la queue avec de la soie cuite et d'en mélanger le corps avec de la soie crue sans aucune lizière distinctive" ("to make the first two *aunes* of the head of the piece and the two at the end with boiled silk and to mix the rest piece with raw silk without any distinctive border?"). This was the origin of the order to give mixed fabrics a special "lizière," a label specifying that it was "étoffe en soie cru" ("a raw silk fabric") in order to protect the consumers.[64]

It was not wholly true, however, to imply that the decline in the quality of the fabrics was due solely to the immorality of the merchants. Merchants of this type had always existed. At the end of the eighteenth century, the decline in quality was rather the result of the way in which the fashion market had come to be structured. In 1771, Isaac de Pinto, comparing French and English material, wrote:

> Les manufactures angloises sont trop étoffées, trop riches ... durent trop long tems, on les trouve trop chères. Le luxe et la mode veulent

62 1763 letter, in A.N.P., Bureau du Commerce, Fl2, 1441.

63 Letter of January 17, 1764, in idem.

64 Letter of December 1764, in idem. On August 12, 1766, the *Maîtres Gardes,* in reply to a letter from the Intendant De Cotte, made heavy accusations against the entrepreneur Buisson, "le quel a debuté par la fraude en tramant de galette dans une étoffe précieuse. ... Une anecdote capable de détruire la reputation du fabricant le mieux établi" ("who began with fraud by 'weaving dough' in a precious fabric....An anecdote capable of destroying the reputation of the best established manufacturer."), ("Réponse des Syndics et *Maîtres Gardes* de la Communauté ... de Lyon," in A.N.P., Bureau du Commerce, Fl2, 1443). A few years earlier, the merchants had denounced "les manoeuvres que pratique le nommé Buisson, actuellement à la tête des manufactures de Naples, pour avoir les desseins avant qu'ils ayent paru et débaucher les ouvriers de toute espèce pour en rendre l'exécution aussi exacte qu'à Lyon" ("the maneuvers practiced by a certain Buisson, currently head of the manufactures in Naples, who obtained the designs before they appeared in public and hired workers of all kinds to carry out the work as exact as in Lyon"), (*Réplique des Maîtres Marchands aux observations des Maîtres Ouvriers*, A.M.L., Chappe HH 133).

> du changement. On a trouvé le secret en France de faire des étoffes de soie à grand marché. Il est vrai qu'elles n'ont point de corps, elles s'usent dans peu temps, mais on n'en veut presque que pour une saison. La mode change et pour le même argent on est bien aisé d'avoir deux robes ou deux habits neufs. Ce qui favorise beaucoup plus les manufactures françaises.[65]

Nevertheless, the decrease in quality should not be seen as an absolute decline but rather as a process of vertical differentiation which involved not so much abandoning high quality production as paying greater attention to market segmentation. An observant commentator on the relationship between quality and fashion, Veron de Forbonnais, wrote: "Dans chaque pays il est différentes classes de peuple et de facultés. Pour les séduire et les contenter, il convient de leur offrir dans chaque espèce particulière des assortimens proportionnés aux différentes facultés" ("in each country there are different classes of people and abilities. To attract and to please them, it is appropriate to offer them in each particular case an assortment proportioned to their different means"). This strategy, aimed at producing "assortiments de divers prix dans une même étoffe" ("assorments of the same fabric at different prices"), would be appreciated by the shopkeepers as it would lead to increased profits. Fabrics of different qualities, ranging from the best to the worst, would be perfect if they were all worth the price asked.[66]

The relative decline in physical quality was in some ways compensated for by the uniformity of the fabric. The Lyon *fabricants* bought the organzine for the warp from Piedmont, the best in Europe, which conformed to a commercial technique probably invented by the silk merchants of Turin and which guaranteed the quality of the product by means of a quality indicator called

---

65 ("The English manufactures are too full, too rich ... last for too long, and one finds them too expensive. Luxury and fashion want change. The secret was found in France to make silk fabrics for a large market. It is true they [those fabrics] lack body, they wear out in a short time, but one wants them for only about one season. Fashion changes and for the same money one is pleased to have two new dresses or two new garments. This favors much more the French manufactures.") I. de Pinto, *Traité de la circulation et du credit* (Amsterdam, 1771), p. 26. The English too should have learned to produce "des étoffes voyantes et moins chères" ("eye-catching fabrics and less expensive") (ibid.).

66 Veron de Forbonnais, *Elémens de commerce, Première Partie* (Leiden, 1754), pp. 254–255, 260–261. According to Forbonnais, women from the middle and lower ranks of society gave little thought to quality as long as they were dressed "d'une manière aussi éclatante qu'une femme de plus haut étage ou plus riche" ("in a manner as dazzling as a woman of a higher station or richer").

the *titolo* (count). The *titolo* indicated the weight of a given length of thread (400 *aunes*) in *deniers* (1 *denier* = 1/20 of a gramme). This sales technique signaled a decisive reduction in transaction costs. Merchants identified the thickness of the thread by its number. The count 24 (that is 24 *deniers*) indicated the thinnest organzine. Thicker fabric was indicated with numbers from 24 to 60. However, these numbers were only approximate. The number 27, in fact, when referring to a *ballot* (about 50–60 livres), was used to indicate thread between 24 and 30 *deniers*. Once the variation rate was identified (with the help of specialized consultants paid in Lyon by the *livres* or *ballot*) the threads (in skeins) of different thicknesses were separated and used for different types of fabric. Alternatively, they were separated in such a way that on the looms the thinner threads were always next to the thicker ones. This meant that the streaks which lowered the quality and the price of the fabric could be avoided.[67]

The Lyon silk industry, although Lyonnaise, was also Parisian. Many of the Lyon merchants had a shop or workshop in Paris.[68] The capital was also the most important outlet market for the Lyon material, and it was in Paris that the shipment of goods to foreign markets often took place.[69] The expression "modes de Paris faites à Lyon," quoted above almost in passing, would seem to indicate an even stronger tie, even though it would imply relegating Lyon to a purely executive role. The social practices underlying the Paris-Lyon relationship, though, need some explaining. One of these practices was the mediating role of the merchants and traders who operated on two markets at once. Even more decisive was the role of the over 100 designers, often merchants or partners of merchants. This double professional and social role is proof of the high reputation the designers enjoyed both in Lyon and in France as a whole. This reputation, along with the high number of designers, is something which cannot be found in any other European silk city. In Italy, the fabric designers, when they existed, do not seem to have occupied a position of prestige with respect to the merchants.[70] In England the importance of having first-class designers

67 Paulet, *L'art du fabricant d'étoffes de soie*, VII section, I partie, pp. 413–416. According to M. Mayet, this technique – "mettage en main" ("handover") – was practiced only in Lyon (*Mémoire sur les manufactures de Lyon*, pp. 20–21).

68 Claude Louis Couchard, for example, *marchand fabricant* in Lyon, was at the same time "maître des six corps" ("master in the six corps") in Paris (L. Gueneau, "Paris. Les industries et le commerce de la soie," *Revue d'Histoire Moderne*, 4, 1926, p. 293). Philippe de Lasalle also lived part of the time in Lyon and part of the time in Paris.

69 Idem.. pp. 288–289. According to Gueneau's estimate, of the 9,000 pieces of silk which came into Paris in January 1779, 7,500 came from Lyon, 500 from Tours and 300 from Avignon.

70 This subject has so far gone unexamined. In 1764, F. Griselini started working on a manual for the training of fabric designers, although it seems to have been left unfinished.. See F.

was never fully appreciated by the silk entrepreneurs engaged in a continual effort to imitate the French patterns.[71]

In Lyon, the studies to be completed before becoming a designer were long and costly. After learning the rudiments of design, the prospective designer was sent to a workshop of a flower painter. Training usually finished in Paris, sometimes in the workshop of one of the Gobelins painters. After returning to Lyon and finding employment in one of the merchant firms, the young designer would continue to spend long periods in Paris every year, where he would make visits, in the company of older and more experienced colleagues, to various print and art collections, the Gobelins and porcelain factories, the Versailles gardens, the Jardin des Plantes, the Cabinet du Roi, the most famous churches, the royal palaces, theatrical performances and so on. This immersion in the atmosphere of the capital of elegance, of luxury and of refinement, where he would converse with fabric sellers, *couturiers*, *faiseuses de modes* ("fashion-makers"), tailors, goldsmiths and embroiderers, refined his taste and civilized his art. But the inspiration and crucial information necessary for the design of the fabrics for the following year would be gained visiting the most famous silk warehouses, those of the famous silk traders Bourjol, Barbier, Saurozat, Nau, Despignes, de Courcy, David, Le Roux, Dore, Mercier, Buffault, Martin and so on, all to be found in the same area of the city around Châtelet and the Palais Royal. It was here that the most important customers of the Grande Fabrique, together with the designers, could see "chaque jour ce que la Fabrique de Lyon produit de merveilleux toutes les années." ("every day what marvels the Manufacture of Lyon produces every year").[72] These visits gave rise to substantial interaction between the producer firms and the needs and expectations of the market, something which would not have been possible if the firms had been represented by salesmen or by commissioners, not always

Griselini, "I principi dell'arte del disegno per ogni genere di stoffa di seta," *Giornale d'ltalia attinente le scienze, lettere e arti*, December 1756, 178ff. The Venetian Pietro D'Avanzo, silk fabric designer, had written some years earlier (sometime around 1753) his *Regole per la meccanica del telaio da seta*, which remained unpublished. It has now been published with a brief introduction by I. Chiappini di Sorio (I. Chiappini di Sorio, Pietro D'Avanzo, *Regole per la meccanica del telaio da seta* [Bologna, 1981]).

71 P. Thornton, *Baroque and Rococo Silk* (London, 1965), p. 57. This work is highly recommended for anyone researching into silk and silk manufacture.

72 See Joubert de l'Hiberderie, *Le dessinateur pour les fabriques d'étoffes d'or, d'argent et de soie* (Paris, 1765), pp. 86–113. See also E. Leroudier, *Les dessinateurs de la fabrique Lyonnaise au XVIII siècle* (Lyon, 1908), and *Le livre de Raison de Jacques Charles Dutillieu publie ... par F. Breghot du Luc* (Lyon, 1886). Since the age of Louis XIV, France had dictated styles of dress to the other courts and cities of Europe. It could be said that the fashion in fabrics, with new designs and colors every year, developed alongside an adjacent sector that had already consolidated a leading position.

able to relay the right information to the designers at the critical moment at which the designs and colors were invented.

In a recent article entitled "Implementing the Marketing Concept through a Program of Customer Visits," two American scholars have emphasized that the firm as a unit is always on the brink of losing contact with its customers, and that similarly the marketing functions are always on the brink of losing contact with other fundamental sectors of the firm (the Research and Development functions and the organization of the actual production). The solution to this problem, the authors Edward F. McQuarrie and Shelby H. McIntyre argue, is that the firm should make a deliberate decision to send at regular intervals a team of "decision makers" (including designers) to visit the customers. According to the authors, "face to face communication has a unique capacity to transfer complex and ambiguous information among parties."[73] This information procedure is presented as an original phenomenon, which is in a certain sense true. However, even in the eighteenth century it was an international practice among the entrepreneurs of the Grande Fabrique, who correctly entrusted the designers with the task of drawing up the new fashions in collaboration with the most important customers.

Each year hundreds of designers returned from Paris to Lyon with thousands of designs. Although this was costly and, in a sense, redundant, it was nonetheless functional in terms of the sophisticated and pressing requirements of the market. The final choice of design and color for the year – the bouquets of flowers arranged in elegant garlands, the harmonious combinations of different brightly colored stripes, the exotic chinoiserie – was made in Lyon in collaboration with the merchants.[74]

---

73 E. F. McQuarrie, Sh. H. McIntyre, *Implementing the Marketing Concept through a Program of Customer Visits* (Cambridge, Mass.), 1990. The two authors make reference to a "technology company."

74 According to L. E. Miller, the overall number of designers in Lyon oscillated between 180 and 270 in 1758–59. They were divided into three categories: freelance, salaried, and partners of the large merchants. See "Design, Technique and the Division of Labor in the Lyon Silk Industry," paper presented to the "Workshop on Design, Commerce and the Luxury Trade in the Eighteenth Century" (1988). On April 27, 1749, journeying from Paris to Lyons, a Lyon fabric designer remarked to his companion, Abbé Nollet, that "les fabricants de Lyon se cachent les uns aux autres les desseins qu'ils font faire, et qu'ils ne font jamais voir leurs nouvelles étoffes avant d'avoir fait leur principaux envoies à Paris et ailleurs. Et la plus part des dessinateurs passent deux ou trois mois à Paris pour avoir connaissance des desseins des autres et pour savoir ceux qui ont les mieux réussi" ("the manufacturers of Lyon hide from each other the designs that they will have made, and they never let the new fabrics be seen before having made their major shipments to Paris and elsewhere. And most of the designers spend two or three months in Paris to gain knowledge of the

Sometimes, when the new fashion had already been launched, the designers returned to Paris to check how the market was reacting. It should be remembered that each individual entrepreneur was in competition with all the others and that the fabric designs, even if they came from the same cultural and industrial matrix, were of varying qualities. There were, for example, differences in color, decoration and taste, degrees of perfection in the design and of precision in the weaving, not to mention the names of the firm or designer.

These innovative practices made a clear separation between the designing of the fabrics and their actual production. But as soon as the decision to set up a new design on a loom was made, the conditions for creative cooperation were established. The designer copied the design onto squared paper; working sometimes with the help of a second designer, he began to prepare and organize warp and weft and to arrange *maillons*, *lacs* and *aiguilles*. In this he had help from a trusted technician, from a *liseuse* with the specific task of transposing the design from paper to loom, and from a weaver. The problem was how to transpose the artistic innovation onto the loom; how to reconcile the design, and its imitation of "la belle nature ... avec les règles austères de la mécanique" ("beautiful nature ... with the austere rules of mechanics"); how to overcome the obstacles "que la mécanique oppose au génie de l'artiste." ("that mechanics oppose to the genius of the artist").[75] In fact, to overcome these obstacles, the designer should have acquired as part of his training at least "une teinture du métier" ("a rudimentary knowledge of the craft") which could have been intensified later with innovative experiments. According to Joubert de l'Hiberderie, writing in 1765, the designers were the first to create order out of "le chaos dans le quel l'art de fabriques des étoffes étoit encore plongé au commencement du siècle" ("the chaos in which the art of manufacturing fabrics was still immersed at the beginning of the century").[76]

designs of others and to know those that have the most success"), (J. A. Nollet, *Journal du voyage de Piedmont et d'Italie en 1749*, Bibliothèque Municipale de Soissons, ms. 150).

75 Joubert de l'Hiberderie, *Le dessinateur*, pp . XVII, XXII, 15, 21, 28.

76 Idem, p. x. According to M. Paulet, the transposition of a design should be left to a "monteur de métier. Cet artiste doit ... être le conducteur du dessinateur, parceque sur cent dessinateurs, à peine en est-il un qui conoisse le métier; et c'est cependant ce que tous devroient connoître. C'est la base du métier" ("an assembler of looms. This artist must ... be the conductor of the designer, because of one hundred designers, hardly one knows how the loom operates; and it is however what all must know. It is the base of the craft"). Paulet, self-taught weaver and designer, emphasized his own ability to combine "les effets des dessins avec la possibilité de les rendre en travailland l'étoffe" ("the results of designs with the possibility of depicting them in working on the fabric"), (Paulet, *L'art du fabricant d'étoffes du soie,* VII section, II partie [1789], p. 884).

Without doubt the designers also contributed to the intellectual and industrial atmosphere which influenced the great Lyon technological innovators who transformed the machinery of the loom. Here I will mention only a few: Baptiste Falcon who, using an idea of Basile Bouchon, introduced perforated cards into the loom, by means of which designs could be memorized and mechanical impulses could be sent, transferring the designs onto the material; Jacques Vaucanson, to whom the invention of the automatic loom is attributed; and Joseph-Marie Jacquard, who, at the beginning of the nineteenth century, concluded a series of long and laborious innovations by inventing the loom which bears his name and which, along with the invention of the Falcon loom, was the precursor of the machine with the numerical controls and the robots which characterize flexible production today.[77]

Designers also played important, direct roles in innovation, above all making possible product differentiation through the support of the necessary technological flexibility. In 1770 Philippe Delasalle, well-known designer and entrepreneur, constructed a mechanism, based on perforated cards, by which one design could be substituted with another without resetting the loom so that orders from clients could be met as quickly as possible. A costly, difficult and time-consuming operation (the previous design had to be destroyed in order to set up another) became, if we can believe Delasalle, something which could be done in an instant. He wrote:

77 C. Ballot, "L'évolution du métier Lyonnais au XVIIIe siècle et invention de la mécanique Jacquard," *L'introduction du machinisme dans l'industrie française* (Paris-Lille, 1923). These new looms were intended to substitute the "tireuses de cordes" with a mechanical device and to discipline the work of the weavers. See H.Clouzot, *Le métier de la soie en France (1466–1815)* (Paris, 1914), and Bianchi, *Produzione e potere di mercato*, pp. 83–84. Insufficient attention has been paid to the extent to which the general development of methods of production is dependent on inventions and innovations originally aimed at improving the production of luxury goods. See Robinson, *The Importance of Fashion*, pp. 9–11. Following the practice which developed under Colbert, the inventors received bonuses and compensation for their innovations. The funds for this compensation were financed by the duty on foreign silk (collected in Lyon). Abbé Bertholon wrote: "Il est juste que celui qui enrichit la société par d'utiles découvertes, jouisse du fruit de ses labeurs, recouvre ses avances et partage un profit que d'autres ne manqueront pas de faire. … Le Souverain doit donner des récompenses: des titres d'honneur à ceux qui ont de la fortune, et des richesses à ceux qui en ont besoin. Tel est l'usage des revenus de l'Etat" ("it is right that whoever enriches society by useful discoveries should enjoy the fruits of his labors, recover his financial outlay, and share a profit that others will not fail to make. … The Sovereign must give some reward: titles of honor to those who are wealthy and wealth to those in need. Such is the practice for the revenues of the state"), (*Du commerce et des manufactures*, p. 94). See also Ballot, "L'évolution du métier," pp. 340–359 passim.

> Souvent le terme pour le quel on veut l'étoffe étant très court, on est obligé de renoncer la commission parce qu'une partie de ce temps nécessaire pour la fabrication seroit employé à remonter le dessin, ce qui n'arrivera point avec le nouveau mécanisme puisqu'au moment même qu'on reçoit la commission on peut le faire travailler.[78]

This problem was solved satisfactorily only by Jacquard. The words of Philippe Delasalle, however, suggest that the innovations in Lyon in the eighteenth century should be seen also as a reply to the challenge of annual product differentiation and the simultaneous supply of a large number of designs.

During the eighteenth century these technological innovations probably did not have a wide diffusion, but it is certain that the Lyon merchants (and the designers) were the very first to exploit fully and systematically the flexibility offered by the artisan or putting-out organization of production. In the past, this (potential) flexibility had been exploited only partially. It is true that each textile center produced contemporaneously tens of different types of fabric. For example, in 1544 the "sayetteurs" and the "bourgeteurs" of Lille were authorized to produce more than ten different fabrics (without counting sub-types) as well as fabrics that were "inventés présentement ou à inventer ci-après" ("created at the moment or created afterwards").[79]

Even in the most important of the old silk cities there was considerable variety of product. But this multiplicity often hid high specialization of production in the few sectors or types of fabric which had good access to and a well-established reputation on the international market. This was the case

78 ("Since the time for providing the fabric is very limited, one is obliged to give up the order because part of the time necessary for the manufacture would be employed to reassemble the design. With the new mechanism this doesn't happen any more. because the same moment one receives the order one can begin to work on it"). See the bundle of letters in the A.N.P., Bureau du Commerce, Fl 2, 1444A (1772–75). Claude Millet, a turner and mechanic, accused Lasalle of having stolen the invention from him. See *Mémoire pour Claude Millet maître tourneur et machiniste de la ville de Lyon, pour justifier qu'il est l'inventeur du métier pour la fabrique en soie contre le Sieur Lassalle*, [1769], in A.N.P., Bureau du Commerce, Fl 2, 1444A, 1769–70. The new frame took the name "réversible". See also Belle M. Borlan, *Philippe de Lasalle* (Chicago, n.d.). The Jacquard loom was also "reversible," it being possible to change the pattern in a short time. See N. Rothstein, "The Introduction of the Jacquard Loom to Great Britain," *Studies in Textile History*, V. Gervers, ed. (Toronto, 1977), p. 282. The introduction of perforated cards encouraged large firms to set up archives to stock the patterns created so that they could be recalled when needed. In this way quick access to past experience could enable the rapid construction and production of new patterns.

79 See M. Vanhaeck, *Histoire de la sayetterie à Lille* (Lille, 1910), vol. II, pp. 58, 102–103, 106–107.

of Genoese velvets, Venetian damasks, Bolognese crêpes, Florentine satins, Milanese gold and silver fabrics and so on. These names, however, rarely corresponded to a single, unchanged and unchanging pattern. The merchant entrepreneurs had known for centuries that supply could be differentiated in order to defend their market share from a dangerous competitor or when entering a mature market. Neither, of course, was demand stable. At the end of the sixteenth century the Bolognese crêpe merchants realized with alarm that German buyers were beginning to require heavier crêpe than that which was being offered. In the eighteenth century, the Italian merchants who sold silk fabrics in Poland tried to satisfy the oriental tastes which predominated among the Polish nobility, offering fabric "ben lustri" ("with a high sheen"), the largest possible gold and silver flowers and Persian patterns or Arabic designs.[80] It would not be difficult to cite other examples. But it was only in Lyon, or Lyon and Paris, that the strategy of annual programmed fashions in design and color were discovered, that the opportunities of product and process differentiation and flexibility were explored to the full and used consciously as an annual market strategy.

In 1764, Antonio Zanon, certainly not someone who was sympathetic towards the much envied French competitors, praised highly their superior skills. He wrote: "To do justice to the French [for French read 'Lyonnaise'] it should be admitted that they have brought more perfection and charm to silk fabrics in fifty years than the Greeks and the Venetians have in seven hundred."[81] Nevertheless, these extraordinary results and their enduring superiority were never sufficient to protect the second city of France from the ups and downs of economic conjuncture. Wars which shut off access to external markets, mourning at court, instability in the production and price of raw materials, mercantilist policies of governments aimed at bolstering national

80 A. Manikowski, "Il commercio di tessuti di seta in Polonia nella seconda metà de XVII secolo," *Fasciculi Historici*, vol. 10 (1982), 160–161. The history of the new draperies can also be considered in the light of differentiation processes. See M. Malowist, "Les changements dans la structure de la production et du commerce du drap au cours du XIVᵉ et du XVᵉ siècle," in *Croissance et régression en Europe, XIVᵉ–XVIIᵉ siècle*, (Paris, 1972). See also E. Coornaert, *Un centre industriel d'autrefois. La draperie-sayetrerie d'Hoondschoore (XIV'–XVIIIᵉ siècles)* (Paris, 1930); J. Craeybeckx, "L'industrie de la laine dans les anciens Pays-Bas méridionaux de la fin du XVIᵉ au début du XVIIIᵉ siècle," in *Produzione, commercio e consumo dei panni di lana (nei secoli XII–XVIII), Atti della Seconda settimana di studio (1970) dell'Istituto internazionale di storia economica "F. Datini" di Prato*, Florence, 1976; and D. C. Coleman, "An Innovation and its Diffusion: The 'New Draperies'," *Economic History Review*, vol. 22, no. 3 (1969), 417–429.

81 Zanon, *Dell'agricoltura, dell'arti e del commercio*, III, p. 160.

imitation industries all struck cruel blows to Grande Fabrique employment, wages and profits. Count d'Albon wrote in 1789:

> Avec vos fabriques de luxe vous ne pouvez pas répondre aux ouvriers de deux jours de vie. Aujourd'hui vous les occupez, demain une récolte manque, le goût des consommateurs change, un deuil de Cour de quelque durée interdit l'usage de vos fabrication, une autre manufacture vous enlève la préférence, une guerre s'élève, vos métiers s'arrêtent, vos ouvriers n'ont plus du pain.[82]

It might be asked when the production of the "modes de Paris faites à Lyon" began. This question cannot be answered with any precision. Economic, social and technological transformations, particularly the complex ones which involve mentalities, deep-rooted practices and modes of production, have no precise beginnings, no immaculate birth, and do not spring from intellectual creative impulses deprived of concrete roots. We might be tempted to indicate the year 1713. But *The Case of the Silk Weavers,* printed in that year, describes mercantile practices which had already become established by this date. For how long? Since the second half of the seventeenth century? Since the late seventeenth or early eighteenth century? I have no definitive reply to this question, but research into this point should probably start from a letter sent on January 6, 1665 from the Prévôt des Marchands (Provost of the Merchants) of Lyon to Colbert. This letter included a brief report on the progress made by Lyon weaving, which had by this time almost completely replaced the imported Italian fabrics previously sold on the Paris market. But these new fabrics did not circulate under their own name, as Lyonnais fabrics. The preference of the French consumers for rich Italian fabrics (from Genoa, Milan, Florence, Venice) was still so strong that, in the words of the Prévôt, "les marchands de Paris ... obligent nos ouvriers à mettre sur leur étoffes les planches et les marques des pays étrangers" ("the Paris merchants ... require our workers to put on their fabrics the signs and marks of foreign countries"). In a later letter of November 3, 1665, the Prévôt was even more explicit, stating that "tout ce

82 ("With our luxury manufactures, you cannot assure workers even two days of life. Today they are employed, tomorrow the harvest fails, the taste of consumers changes, mourning at Court for a length of time prohibits the use of our manufactures, another manufacture takes away your preference, a war breaks out, your looms stop, your workers no longer have bread"), Comte d'Albon, *Lettre sur le commerce, les fabrications et les consummations des objets de luxe* (Lyon, 1789).

qui s'envoie de cette ville à Paris s'y vend sous le nom des fabricants d'Italie" ("everything this is sent from this city to Paris is sold under the name of Italian manufacturers").[83]

Italy and the Italian textile centers, then, were still the reference point, the crucial yardstick. Just ten years later, however, a significant novelty appears. In the work of Jacques Savary there is an explicit mention of "étoffes façonnées et de couleurs dont les modes changent d'une année à l'autre" ("patterned fabrics and colors whose fashion change from one year to the next"). Unfortunately, this reference is nowhere elaborated upon, apart from a comment that with this fabric "l'on y peut gagner considérablement parce que il y a quelques fois à perdre la moitié de ce qui reste" ("one can earn considerably even though sometimes the half of what remains is lost"). Nor is there any reference either to Lyon or to the silk sector. Despite these limits, the importance of Savary's note should not be underestimated, and may be taken as a profitable starting point for future research.[84]

83 These two letters are quoted in E. Pariset, *Histoire de la fabrique Lyonnaise,* pp. 82–84. In the letter of January 6, 1665, the Prévôt declared with pride: "Il n'y a point d'ouvrage de soie, d'or et d'argent de quelque endroit d'Italie qu'il vienne que nos ouvriers n'égalent (à la reserve des velours noirs de Gênes ...) et que même ils ne surpassent" ("there is no work in silk, gold or silver, from whatever place in Italy they come, that our workers do not equal [except for the black velvets of Genoa...] and which they even surpass"). For an introductory comparison between the Italian and French silk industries see S. Ciriacono, "Silk Manufacturing in France and Italy in the Seventeenth Century," *Journal of European Economic History* (1981), 167–199.

84 Savary, *Le parfait négociant,* I, pp. 15–23. Savary made a sharp distinction between the entrepreneurs who imitated and those who created. After listing the many difficulties encountered by those who tried to imitate foreign or local fabrics, he weighed the advantages and disadvantages of creating new fabrics. The buyers would have hesitated before buying because their quality would only become clear after they had been worn for some time. This disadvantage was balanced out by the fact that little money would be lost "sur un ouvrage nouvellement inventé parceque les Français, qui aiment naturellement le changement, ne manquent jamais à l'acheter, quelque méchant qu'il soit, pour paroître à la mode" ("on a work newly created because the French, who naturally love change, never fail to buy it, however bad it may be, so as to appear 'à la mode'".) Besides this, he advised the merchants who had "trouvé l'invention de quelque marchandise" ("created some merchandise") to produce small quantities "jusqu'à ce qu'ils ayent reconnu qu'elle puisse avoir le débit" ("until they know that they can make the sale") in order to avoid the danger of heavy losses. Savary was not writing out of hearsay. He himself had previously launched three new invented fabrics, and these had met with various degrees of success. Without going into too much detail, the first fabric was in fashion "seulement pour cinque ou six ans" ("only for five or six years"); the second was "un droguet façonné" ("a patterned fabric") (imitated also in Rouen), in fashion for three or four years; and the third was a gold and silver "droguet," sold in Paris for only a few months because it had imperfections despite being very attractive. It seems clear that none of these creations involved annual

That the Lyon merchants had a considerable degree of awareness of their own commercial practices emerges from the way in which they managed and manipulated the rules of the Communauté at the beginning of the eighteenth century (as regards the protection of design copyright, for example). It was only towards the middle of the eighteenth century, though, that this awareness matured sufficiently to be aired publicly. This took place during the often highly conflictual debates over strategic choices, debates which were often backed up with arguments that were highly original and stimulating, including at times views that foreshadow later theories. Yet in their own day these ideas did not generate an analytical school, also because from the mid-eighteenth century onwards, the attention of the public and of the principal economic thinkers was captured by the physiocratic model that was hostile to luxury and fashion, seen as taking work away from agriculture and depressing population growth.

It might be asked whether the production of traditional textiles and fabrics came to an end in Lyon after the invention of annual fashions. The answer would be no. The production of imitation fabrics continued in Lyon throughout the entire eighteenth century: "fake" Venetian brocade, Bolognese crêpes, Genoese velvets. The same was true for plain fabrics (whether traditional or not), whose production increased from 1770 onwards in relation to the *façonnés* (patterned fabrics). These sectors (the traditional and plain fabrics) probably supported employment in the months between the spring and winter fashions, or when, because of court mournings, there was little or no demand for annual fashions. Perhaps this was another reason why the production of fabric with a short life cycle, although in expansion, was not able to take over the entire silk sector, even in Lyon.[85]

---

change or innovation in either design or color. These were isolated attempts, different from the fashion system of Lyon (ibid.). Nevertheless, before Savary no one, as far as I know, had described and understood better the rules to follow for creating new products and new processes. According to Agnes Geijer, in 1667 Colbert ordered the manufacturers "to produce new patterns every year" (*A History of Textile Art* [Stockholm, 1979], p. 154). Unfortunately, the author does not cite a source for this information, nor have I been able to find one.

85 Ibid. In 1739, out of 8,289 looms, 4,874 (around 58 percent) were being used to weave *façonné*. In 1769, 5,500 of the 11,000 looms produced *façonné*. See Clouzot, *Le métier de la soie en France*, p. 76. See also the statistics of Abbé Jacquet, *Sur les moyens de faire refleurir les manufactures de Lyon*. The number of looms does not appear to be compatible with the number of weavers, around 8,000 in 1731, each of whom had the right to use up to four looms. All these statistics require further analysis.

Up to this point, I have assumed that fashion fabrics had a short life, as is maintained by the French, English and Italian sources which reveal the commercial strategies of the Grande Fabrique. But the important research of Peter Thornton, Donald King and Natalie Rothstein have shown that annual fashions can also be considered as part of a longer cycle, following the dominance of particular styles or tastes. According to Rothstein, between 1700 and 1825 some ten distinct periods can be identified: the "bizarre" style of the years 1700–1712; the "luxuriant phase" of 1713–1719; the "lace patterns" of 1720–1732; the quest for three dimensional form of the years 1733–1742; the rococo of 1743–53; the retreat from naturalism of the period 1754–1770; the advent of neo-Classicism of 1770–1780; stripes and dots in 1780–1790; the dark stripes of 1790–1795; the eclipse of woven design (1796–1810); and the revival of woven design (1810–1825).[86] These authors, and Natalie Rothstein in particular, present these medium-term phases, the result of careful and meticulous research, with some caution. But these periods do lengthen the life of the fabrics. As long as one style or taste had not completed its own life-cycle, it was no doubt easy to adapt materials, but above all clothes, to the new annual fashions, using trimming, embroidery, frills and flounces.[87]

The success of the strategies elaborated by the Lyon merchants in the eighteenth century was dependent on the presence of two fundamental conditions. The first was the preference for *façonné* (patterned silk), the second the preference for silk in fabrics and in fashionable clothing. The latter was based on the mercantilist exclusion (although this exclusion was challenged and never absolute) of calicoes and *indiennes,* cotton with bright colors and designs imported from Asia. The conflict for control of the home market was particularly harsh in England and France, where the vested interests of wool and silk feared the competition of these exotic, attractive, resistant and washable fabrics, very popular because of their low price and used both for clothing and for decorating furniture and walls. In both countries, the battle against calicoes was won (at least in legal terms). In 1721, the English Parliament prohibited their import and consumption, although not their production, as this was aimed at foreign markets. France went one step further, prohibiting the

---

86 N. Rothstein, *Silk Designs of the Eighteenth Century* (London, 1990), pp. 32–62.

87 See Ribeiro, *Dress in Eighteenth-Century Europe,* pp. 60 passim. With embroidering, it became possible to transform plain into *façonné* fabrics without having to use complicated looms. This technique was first developed in Lyon. As it was easy to imitate, it spread to other countries in Europe which used it in competition with the Grande Fabrique. See also M. de Saint-Aubin, "Art du brodeur," in *Descriptions des arts et métiers,* XIV, pp. 175–176.

production as well as the consumption of *indiennes,* at least up to 1759 when the restrictive legislation was removed.[88]

These were ambiguous victories, though. The same vested interests that managed to exclude calicoes and *indiennes* nevertheless used them, re-elaborating their designs and exotic colors especially in silk fabrics, in a successful campaign against the conservative taste that characterized Italian silks.[89] It may have been this unexpected blow, repeated later by means of recourse to other "folkloric" tastes, which revealed the weakness of the Italian products in a crucial phase for the formation of the new fashions.

The preference for silk and *façonné* began to weaken towards the end of the 1770s when a sharp change of taste towards the simple, the natural and the spontaneous began to favor plain silks and cotton. The work of Jean-Jacques Rousseau is both the highest expression of this new sensibility and a crucial element in its growth and diffusion. The greatest refinement became the exhibition of simplicity. In the 1780s, cotton conquered Versailles. Marie-Antoinette began to dress in cotton, and with her the ladies of the court.

In 1789 the brilliant pamphleteer L.-A. Caraccioli wrote that by now all the Parisians were wearing white *indiennes*:

> Une assemblée de françoises étoit autrefois un magnifique parterre où l'on voyoit l'émail de toutes les couleurs. Ce n'est maintenant que le tableau le plus monoton, et qui n'offre aux yeux que du blancs et du blanc.[90]

---

88 See for France, E. Depitre, *La toile peinte en France au XVIIe et au XVIIIe siècle* (Paris, 1912); H. Clouzot, *Histoire de la manufacture de Jouy et de la toile imprimé en France* (Paris-Brussels, 1928) vols. 1–2; S. Chassagne and S. D. Chapman, *European Textile Printers in the Eighteenth Century. A Study of Peel and Oberkampf* (London, 1981); S. Chassagne, *Le coton et ses patrons (France 1760–1840)* (Paris, 1991). For an analysis of the literature on this subject, see J. K. J. Thomson, "State Intervention in the Catalan Calico-Printing Industry in the Eighteenth Century," in Berg, ed., *Markets and Manufacture in Early Industrial Europe*, pp. 57–59. Along with the calicoes, imports of Indian silk fabrics were also prohibited.

89 R. Gronwoldt has shown that there was a certain innovative activity also in Italy; see "Notes on Italian and Spanish Textiles of the Seventeenth Century," *Studies in Textile History*, V. Gervers, ed., 126–132. On the influence of far eastern products on English taste in the seventeenth and eighteenth centuries, see Jones, *The Fashion Manipulators*, pp. 204–207.

90 ("An assembly of French women in the past was a magnificent flowerbed where one could see an array of colors. Now it is only a monotonous scene which offers to your eyes only white and white"). L.-A. Caraccioli, *Lettres d'un indien à Paris,* vol. I (Amsterdam, 1789), pp. 235–236 passim. The preference for white *indiennes* (not produced in France) gave rise to a crisis not only for silk fabrics but also for "les toiles peintes et imprimées" ("the colored and printed cloths") which had fallen to "un point qui est à peine concevable: point de demandes, point de consommations" ("a point that is hardly conceivable: no demand,

In the same year, a number of French newspapers reproached French ladies for being "tributaire de l'industrie angloise, par l'usage immoderé des étoffes de coton blanc" ("dependents of English industry, by the immoderate use of white cotton fabrics"). Cotton had become the fashion.[91] French newspapers were making the same criticism of their ladies, of being unpatriotic, that from Addison and Defoe onwards had been made of the British ladies, overly fond of French fashions.[92]

The defeat of silk and *façonné* and the victory of plain fabrics and cotton led to a major crisis in Lyon where, in the late 1780s, also due to the collapse of the production of raw silk, unemployment and poverty reigned, only partly mitigated by the activity of several generous (but insufficient) charities. This deep crisis, much longer and more destructive than those preceding it, reveals the extent of the presumption of the great Lyon silk merchants. They had believed that they dominated the market for fashion fabrics, but this dominion was tied to a certain taste, a certain style. As soon as there was an abrupt and unexpected change in taste, when Paris (and Versailles) "betrayed" Lyon, the great city on the Saône found to its dismay that it had its own vulnerability. Already unable to maintain its place on the market, the coming Revolution was to strike another severe blow at a fabric now seen as aristocratic and unpatriotic.

---

no purchases") (*Réflexions d'un négociant électeur de 1790*, [n.p., n.d.], pp. 2–4). See also E. Leroudier, "La décadence de la fabrique Lyonnaise à la fin du XVIIIe siècle," *Revue d'histoire de Lyon*, 10, 1911, 343–361, 415–444. Abbé Jacquet wrote that even for *façonnés* competition had become fiercer. "A peine une belle étoffe sort-elle de notres manufactures, qu'elle est contrafaite par les fabriques rivales, et il ne leur coûte presque rien pour s'approprier les plus beaux fruits de notre génie" ("barely does a beautiful fabric leave our manufactures than it is imitated by rival factories, and it costs almost nothing to appropriate the most beautiful fruits of our genius"). This led to the reduction of outlets "qui empêchent à l'inventeur de se récompenser de ses travaux et qui l'obligent de partager avec le plagiare le moisson qu'il devroit recueillir seul" ("which prevents the creator from being compensated for his work and which obliges him to share with the plagiarist the harvest of wealth which he should reap alone"). This in turn resulted in a major reduction of gains for the *fabricants*, fabric designers and workers of the Grande Fabrique (Abbé Jacquet, *Sur les moyens de faire refleurir* ..., f. 54).

91 *Affiches de Dauphiné*, June 20, 1788, p. 38. According to Abbé Jacquet, the worst blow to the Lyon manufactures came from fashion itself, "qu'elle avoit si bien servi, la mode qui leur devoit son plus belle éclat, ses plus brillantes parures, oui la mode, le tyran capricieux leur a porté le coup le plus mortel" ("which had so well served, fashion to which they owe their most beautiful splendor, their brightest adornment, yes fashion, the capricious tyrant dealt them the most mortal blow"), (Jacquet, *Sur les moyens de faire refleurir*, f. 57).

92 At the same time the market for silk fabrics for wall coverings and interior decoration diminished due to competition from wallpaper. See H. Clouzot, Ch. Follot, *Histoire du Papier peint en France* (Paris, 1935).

The beginning of this chapter proposed a sharp opposition between silk and cotton. The conclusion suggests a different relationship. When the annual fashions moved into cotton, as Abbé Morellet had predicted, cotton fabrics were subjected to similar product and process strategies already applied with success to silk fabrics.[93] At the same time, through cotton, fashions became popular with larger and lower social groups. The victory of cotton over silk, at least in the late eighteenth century, was also a victory of fashion over luxury.

It was only after the Revolution that silk fabrics came back into fashion. But they were unable, in a market that was by now in enormous expansion, to regain the dominance they had enjoyed in the early modern period. Silk fabrics had to share the field with wool and cotton, which had conquered what was now a bourgeois (English-dominated) market for men, while silk, expelled from jackets and trousers, was forced to limit itself to women's clothing.

I hope I have succeeded in giving a satisfactory and detailed explanation of the reasons behind the extraordinary and long-lasting success of Lyon, with its unique combination of complex elements that made it so difficult to imitate. In more general terms, this combination can be said to have brought together a rich and intricate superstructure; a marked dominance of software over hardware; seemingly endless creative capacities; rapid decision-making; systematic management of information (at times withheld, at others divulged); and a high degree of culture, taste and imagination. It was made up, too, of technological innovations such as the Jacquard loom which memorized designs and transferred them to the cloth in ways which were already, in some sense, "computerized." As Jonathan Zeitlin and Charles Sabel have already suggested, Lyon can be seen as a unique instance of an industrial district linking a "pre-industrial" past with a "post-industrial" future.[94]

---

93 Abbé Morellet, *Réflexions sur les avantages de la libre fabrication*, p. 111.

94 Sabel and Zeitlin, "Historical Alternatives," pp. 133–176.

PART 3

Engineers and Theorists

CHAPTER 10

The Synergy between Two Innovations: Canals and Silk Mills in Bologna

Alberto Guenzi and Carlo Poni

At the end of the 15th century in his *De Bononiae laudibus oratio* the humanist Benedetto Morandi outlined what was to become the canonical image of Bologna. He not only exalted Bologna's nobility, antiquity and wealth according to the Aristotelian rules.[1] Immediately after proclaiming its pre-Roman origins (although it was associated with the foundation of Rome) and before describing the fertility of its countryside and the excellence of its university, the learned humanist dedicated a dense paragraph to the city's production and manufacturing structure.

After a brief description of Bologna's geographical position at the foot of the Apennines, on a broad plain between the Reno and Savena rivers, Morandi turned to describing the giant artificial barrier constructed on the riverbed of the Reno, forming an artificial canal: the Reno canal, which led "per manufactam foveam" ("by a man-made canal") inside the walls of the city. This waterway served many useful purposes, and was like "a continuous flow of gold." No city – continued Morandi – had profited as much, in terms of public and private benefit from the natural course of a river, as Bologna had from the artificial course of this canal. Its waters provided power for numerous production sites: silk mills, fulling mills, paper mills, flour mills, water-powered saws and metal workshops were established where iron and bronze weapons as well as blacksmiths' tools were polished and sharpened.

In this description the comparison of artificial and natural waterways was important, and concluded in favor of the former due to the economic advantages it provided. But even more striking is Morandi's keen attention to the abundant variety of processing machines, rather than simply focusing on the quantity of power sources, i.e. water wheels. This attention is then transformed into a description, in Virgilian style, of the main characteristics of a mode of production that had already evolved into a factory system. In his

1 B. Morandi, *De Bononiae laudibus oratio* (Bologna, 1481). All the citations, translated from Latin, follow the numbering in pen from the exemplar held in the Biblioteca comunale dell'archiginnasio (hereafter B.C.A.B.) in Bologna and are contained in pp. 11–113.

 | DOI:10.1163/9789004713277_012

analysis of silk mills he asserts that in each of them 1500 reels wound simultaneously "with no human labor, apart from loading the silk and replacing the full reels with empty ones." Here the man-made aspect of production no longer refers to man in opposition to nature, but to machines which have taken the place of manual labor and reduced man almost to a spectator of the production process.

The artificial canal served multiple purposes within the city. But once it was outside the city walls it became a navigable canal, which joined the cities on the Po River and the sea, enabling export and import. Even though Morandi does not say it explicitly, the sea meant Venice, with which Bologna had close ties, as did other cities in the Po valley. From the 16th century onwards, inside Bologna's city walls there was a port area with a custom house, warehouses, docks and hoists.[2]

In addition to the Reno canal, another smaller canal flowed through Bologna deriving from blockage of the Savena riverbed and thus called the Savena canal. According to Morandi, the waters of this canal were used in tanneries, in cleaning fabrics, and especially in the city's dye-works for wool and silk fabrics, giving the water an "admirable color."[3] These same waters were then also used to collect and carry, through underground channels, the city's sewage.[4]

The description of the two artificial canals permits us to see features of a productive organization that suggests diversified use and specialization of urban space. While the Reno canal powered the city's water wheels, the waters of the Savena canal entered directly and immediately into the final step of the production process of the clothing industries (fabrics and leather).[5]

After Morandi's work – which was reprinted many times – the image of the Reno and Savena canals and the industries connected to them became a common part of writing on the city for the next three centuries, whether the writer was a traveller, a scholar or a political analyst.[6] But when were the two canals built? And what was their innovative effect?

The process of building hydraulic macro-structures in Bologna can now be described with more precision based on new analysis of original documents. The most recent research indicates that the locks and canals were constructed

2 E. Rosa, "L'ultimo porto di Bologna," *Atti e memorie della Deputazione di storia patria per le province di Romagna*, 9, XXV–XXVI (1974–75), 137–186.

3 Morandi, *De Bononiae laudibus*, p. 12.

4 A. Guenzi, "L'area protoindustriale del canale di Reno in città nel secolo XVIII," *Problemi d'acque a Bologna in età moderna* (Bologna, 1983), pp. 173–210.

5 L. Dal Pane, *Economia e società a Bologna nell'età del Risorgimento* (Bologna, 1969), pp. 245–308.

6 Cf. A. Sorbelli, *Bologna negli scrittori stranieri*, ed. G. Roversi (Bologna 1973).

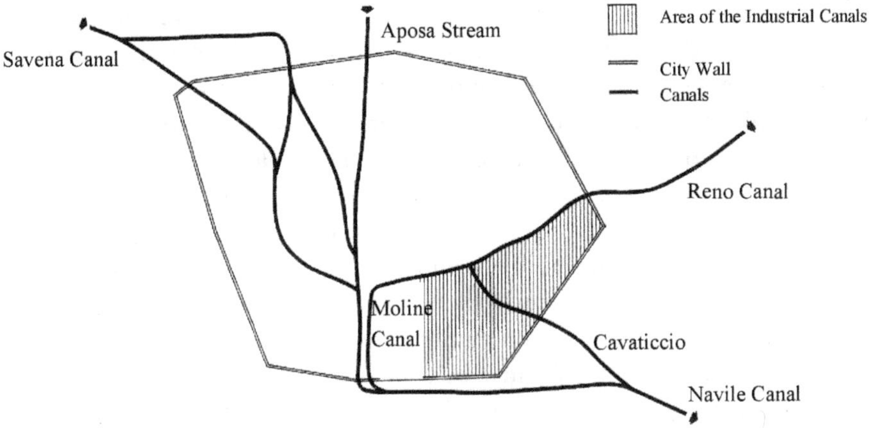

FIGURE 10.1 Hydraulic macrosystem of Bologna (16th–19th centuries)
SOURCE: DRAWING MADE BY THE AUTHORS

in the second half of the 12th century.[7] Initially these works served to channel water into the defensive moats around the city and power the water wheels of the grain mills. Around 1250, after the introduction of 11 fulling mills and other industrial plants, new canal works (for example, the restructuring of the Reno canal) and a different use of the urban space resulted in relocating all the flour mills to the north-eastern part of the city, on a section of the Reno canal which took the name Canale delle Moline (mill canal). Other industrial activities located in different parts of city then came to be concentrated around the first nucleus of water-powered factories (mainly fulling mills) on the Cavaticcio canal. In this same area, about a century later, all the water-powered silk mills were built with the exception of the three oldest ones located to the south near the current Porta Castiglione.[8]

At the end of the 14th century, when Bologna's industrial hydraulic system seemed well-established, a series of innovations relaunched and upgraded it. We refer to the construction of numerous small underground conduits (*chiaviche*), which by extracting water from the main canals – principally the Reno canal – distributed it in a capillary fashion throughout the city, exploiting the natural slope of the terrain.[9] Initially these small conduits – real civil engineering

7 A.I. Pini, "Energia e industria tra Savena e Reno: i mulini idraulici bolognesi tra XI e XV secolo," unpublished paper presented at the conference *Tecnica e società nell'Italia dei secoli XII–XIII*, Pistoia, 28–31 October 1984.

8 G. N. Alidosi Pasquali, *Instruttione delle cose notabili della città di Bologna* (Bologna 1621), pp. 37–38.

9 Guenzi, *L'area protoindustriale*, p. 177.

projects – were used to collect urban solid and liquid sewage. Subsequently conduits flowing through the cellars were equipped with dozens and then hundreds of water wheels. At the end of the 17th century there were nearly 400 of these, the highest urban concentration of water wheels in Europe.[10]

The transition from drainage conduits to industrial conduits most likely took place during the 15th century. This assertion is supported by two facts: in 1393 all the water wheels were still located along the canals; only at the end of the 15th century did the city government begin to grant rights for diverting water from the Reno canal exclusively for industrial purposes.[11]

This loose chronology hides a number of questions. When were the conduits first introduced? In particular, by what means were they installed? Were they introduced in pre-existing cellars? Or were the cellars built to contain the conduits? Were water wheels built where the conduit-cellar connection had already been made? Or was this type of connection not yet in practice? Apart from the construction of the conduits, when did cellars become widespread? Here we face problems that until now have been largely ignored.

In any case, the introduction of the conduits and the exploitation of their flows for industrial purposes produced a revolution in the relation between water and water-powered plants. The water wheels were moved from the course of the canals to the cellars of buildings sometimes hundreds of meters away from the water-supply points; thus the possibilities of establishing production sites multiplied without modifying the complex equilibrium of the system, since after long detours and having powered several water wheels, the conduits returned the water to a common collector. The topography of the Bologna area – the slope of the city located at the foot of hills, and within the urban area significant inclines producing differences in elevation – all facilitated the flow of water.

Favorable geomorphological conditions along with the progressive adaptation of infrastructure resulted in the consolidation of the urban hydraulic system as it appears in documents from the 17th century. In the northern part of the city, between the Reno canal in the city and the wall, there was an exceptional concentration of plants and water wheels on the underground conduits. In this area the water-powered plants along the canal had water wheels in their

10 C. Poni, "Espansione e declino di una grade industria: le filature di seta a Bologna fra XVII e XVIII secolo," *Problemi d'acque*, p. 241.

11 The date 1393 (see Table 1) is from the Archivio di Stato di Bologna (hereafter A.S.B.), *Difensori dell'avere per i diritti di Camera. Amministrazione dei beni del Comune*, reg. 39 (1393–1422). For water concessions see *Raccolta di leggi intorno al canale di Reno di Bologna* (Bologna 1838), Appendix, pp. 80–81.

cellars. Even the *sega dell'acqua* ("water saw"), a building located over the Reno canal, obtained its water from an underground conduit.[12]

By the 17th century, when the underground conduit system was fully developed, the idea of a *subterranean Bologna* emerged as an expression used in the title of one of numerous urban maps that described, between the 17th and 19th centuries, the city's hidden waterways. But today the reader's eye can easily get lost in the inextricable maze of these drawings without being able to understand the hierarchy of the conduits. We were able to obtain a more detailed understanding by cross-checking the maps of *subterranean Bologna* with those of the *Partimenti di Ornato*.[13] Using as classifying criterion the ownership of conduits and water rights, we managed to construct a typological chart which identifies three different systems for distributing motive power (and therefore three different forms of industrial localization). If the underground conduit belonged solely to one private owner, it supplied one single user, and normally powered plants that lined the canal; if it was publicly owned (a neighbourhood underground conduit) it primarily served to drain waste water (*acque bianche*) and sewage water (*acque nere*); private users could also divert these waters for productive uses. The third type of underground conduit (the large conduit – *chiavica grossa*) belonged to consortiums of private owners which obtained water from communal conduits. Figure 10.2 shows three types of industrial plants and their respective underground conduits provided by the Reno canal in the city. It should be noted that some plants were supplied by "runoff" water already used by other water wheels.[14]

This localization had some consequences for the technology of water wheels (all with horizontal axles): on the canals the wheels were turned by water flowing under it, and in the cellars the wheels were turned by water falling onto it from an overhead source. We know very little about the form and the size of the wheels (probably with containers to catch the water) located on the underground conduits. These "secret" wheels, in contrast to those on the

12 Guenzi, *L'area protoindustriale*, p. 183.

13 The iconography of subterranean Bologna is extraordinarily rich and covers a timespan of about three centuries. Here we limit ourselves to citing the most important comprehensive maps: C. Saccenti, *Disegno nel quale si vede descritte le chiaviche che pigliano l'acqua dal canale di Reno con le sue misure (1643)*, A.S.B., *Gabella Grossa, Atlanti di mappe e stampe*, Arm. B- Cass. 3, c. 2 r.; *Bologna sotteranea* (18th century), B.C.A.B., mss. Malvezzi, cart. 81, 39; [map of the *chiaviche* of the Reno canal in the city] drawn by Alfonso Saccenti in 1902 and kept at the Consorzio della Chiusa di Casalecchio e del canale di Reno (Consortium of the Casalecchio locks and the Reno Canal) in Bologna. The *descrittioni di filatogli* and *I partimenti d'Ornato* have been analysed respectively by Poni, *Espansione e decline*, pp. 227–228 and Guenzi, *L'area protoindustriale*, pp. 198–210.

14 In the middle of the 17th century 40% of the plants located along the underground conduits used "runoff" water.

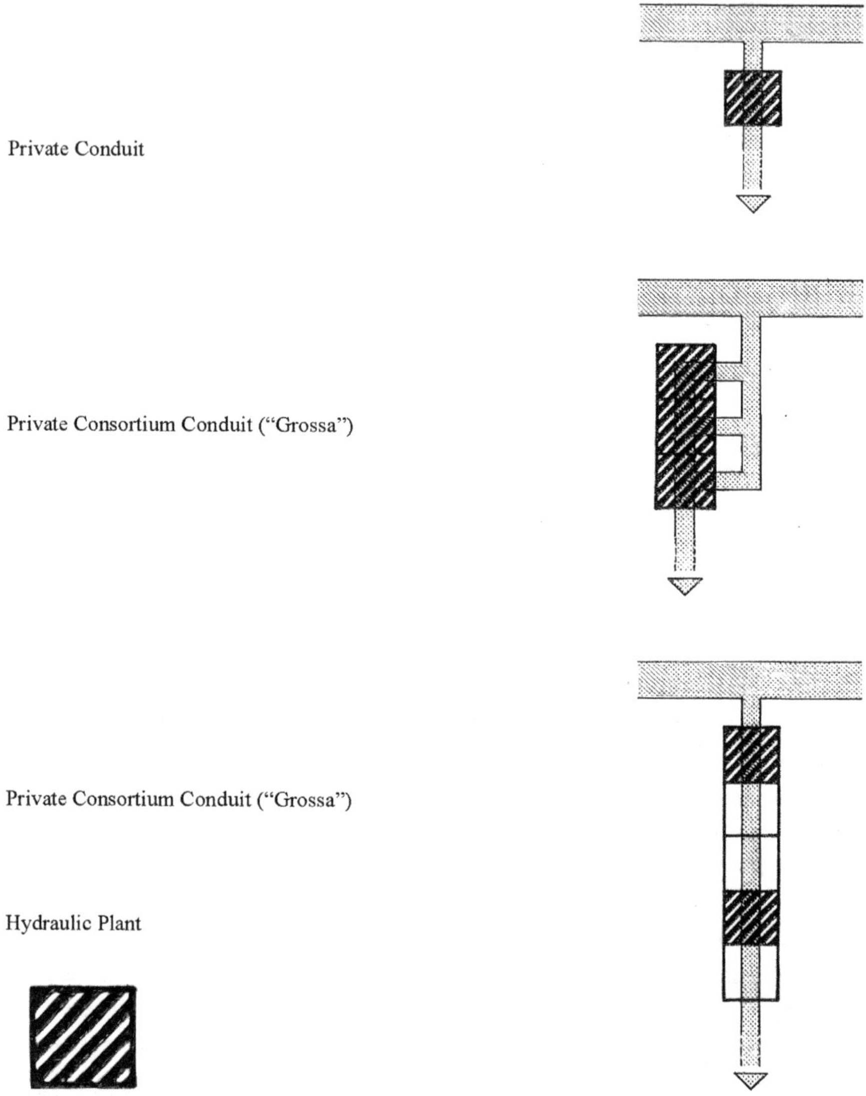

FIGURE 10.2 Typology of underground conduits supplied by the Reno canal in the city (Bologna, 17th–18th centuries)
SOURCE: DRAWING MADE BY THE AUTHORS

canals, were never portrayed by landscape painters, nor were they accurately drawn until the end of the 19th century.[15]

15 See A. Guenzi, "Il frumento e la città: il caso di Bologna in età moderna," *Quaderni storici*, vol. 16, no. 46 (1981), 153–167; L. Ferrante, S. Fronzoni, F. Giusberti, A. Guenzi, C. Poni, "Paesaggio e strutture produttive: la città di Bologna e il suo contado in età moderna," *Paesaggio: immagine e realtà* (Milan, 1981), pp. 179–191.

The two stages or periods of hydraulic innovation – first the construction of the canals and then the underground conduits – could be described (using an original analysis of Rondo Cameron)[16] with a logistic curve. As is well known, a logistic curve, derived from a mathematical formula, is similar to an elongated S. This curve is called a growth curve by biologists because it represents the increase in a population of small insects in a container that is isolated but constantly supplied with food. It is characterised by an initial phase of accelerated growth, followed by a second phase of deceleration which tends to take an asymptotic character on the Cartesian plane.

As an analogy one could say that the first phase of production and organization of Bologna's macro-hydraulic system could be represented by an S curve, tending upwards before reaching the asymptotic trend, and then driven by a second innovation which corresponds to the phase of construction and utilization of the underground conduits for industrial purposes.

While the first phase or first innovation is common to many cities in the Po valley (including, for example, Modena, Reggio Emilia, Parma, Padua, Treviso, and Udine), the second phase or second innovation rarely supported the processes of growth and diversification of industrial plants. As far as we know and with the exception of cases yet to be identified and studied, in no other Italian or European city did the construction and industrial utilisation of underground conduits reach the intensity of those of Bologna. And there is a reason. The disaggregation of the kinetic energy of a waterway into many small underground conduits with small capacities and therefore small amounts of energy would not be justified – even with favorable geographic conditions such as significant natural inclines – without the contemporaneous existence of machines requiring limited flows of energy to operate them.[17]

In Bologna this machine was the spinning mill or silk mill.[18] At least this is the answer we have deduced *ex post facto* since in the medium time period all the city's silk mills were gradually moved or re-moved to the underground conduits, and by the end of the 17th century these mills made up 90% of all the water-powered factories in the city.[19] Nonetheless we have not found any documents indicating this connection as the goal of a conscious strategy. One can only cautiously state that this relationship and the knowledge behind it were

16 R. Cameron, "The Logistics of European Economic Growth: A Note on Historical Periodization," *Journal of European Economic History*, 2 (1973), 145–148.

17 R. Gordon, "Hydrological Science and the Development of Waterpower for Manufacturing," *Technology and Culture*, 26 (1985), 204–235.

18 C. Poni, "All'origine del sistema di fabbrica: tecnologia e organizzazione produttiva dei mulini da seta nell'Italia settentrionale (sec. XVII–XVIII)," *Rivista Storica Italiana*, LXXXVIII (1973), 444–497.

19 Guenzi, *L'area protoindustriale*, pp. 174–175.

constructed – either consciously or perhaps only subconsciously – over the course of a long period in which small groups of workshops began to aggregate and then function as parts of a complex mechanism.

The silk mills introduced in Bologna by immigrant artisans from Lucca were hand-powered and therefore had no connection to waterways as a source of power. It was in Bologna that the mills were equipped with water wheels and mechanical connections for the transmission of movement.[20] For centuries this innovation in Bologna was considered a secret to be jealously guarded – hidden as we know in cellars and called "the water system" (*ragione dell'acqua*). Master spinners or "machinists" who took this "know-how" to other cities were considered to have committed a serious crime, a true betrayal of the "patria," and should be punished by death.[21]

The use of water wheels in silk mills, beginning in the 14th century, enabled the transition from small, hand-powered silk mills to larger ones, liberating the labor force and concentrating more operating machines – the multi-level spinning machines (*piante a più valichi*) – under the same roof. This increase in size then expanded vertically with the introduction of the mechanical winder, powered by the same wheel that moved the spinning machine. Before the mechanical winder, winding had been donc by women (*maestre*) who worked at home. Mechanical winding replaced the female workforce with that of children who worked, under the surveillance of one or more adult workers, on the top floor of the mill or somewhere near.

Replacing the *maestre* with child labor was highly labor-saving. In a medium-sized mill, a few dozen children could replace the work of several hundred home-based women workers. The increase in the average size of mills enabled significant improvements in the quality of the product. This new organization of work and production required a restructuring of the reeling process, to produce a thread stronger and more uniform, therefore better suited for mechanical traction (of winding and twisting).[22] Thus mechanical winding was also *capital saving*. It cut production times, reduced the tying up of capital, and enabled better control of labor and product quality. This was already in the 15th and 16th centuries a factory system, as was the silk mill constructed by John Lombe in England in 1717 after a year of industrial espionage in Italy.[23]

---

20 See G. Livi, "I mercanti da seta lucchesi in Bologna nei secoli XIII e XIV," *Archivio storico italiano*, vol. VII, series IV, no. 121 (1881), 25–28.

21 C. Poni, "Archéologie de la fabrique: la diffusion des moulins à soie 'alla bolognese' dans les États vénitiens du XV au XVIII siècle," *Annales. E.S.C.*, 6 (1972), 1475–1496, reprinted in *La seta in Italia*, ch. 1, pp. 3–69.

22 See ch. 7 in this volume.

23 P. Mantoux, *La révolution industrielle au XVIII siécle* (Paris, 1959), pp. 189–192.

But the Bologna silk mills – later called "alla bolognese" to differentiate them from others without water wheels, without mechanical winding and smaller in size, the so-called mills "alla milanese" or "alla genovese" – should not be seen solely from the perspective of the hydraulic system. This was the heart of Bologna's most important industrial sector: the silk industry. It was an entirely urban industry – at least from the 15th century on – from reeling and spinning to weaving, dyeing and "pleating." A unique example in Italy and in Europe of vertical concentration.[24]

Only silkworm cultivation was done in the countryside by peasants. But the entire rural production of cocoons had to be brought into the city and sold at the *Fiera del Pavaglione* to authorised buyers.[25] Once inside the city walls, the silk could leave only as the finished product: voile. This was a fine fabric exported in great quantities to markets near and far: from Venice to the Levant, from France to Germany. In addition to this production based on local silk, enormous and increasing quantities of "foreign" raw silk arrived in Bologna from Veneto and the Marches, to be twisted in its mills, increasingly renowned for the high value added that transformed the thread into organzine. Organzine was partly used by Bologna's weavers[26] and partly re-exported as a semi-finished product to the great textile centers (especially Venice and later England) where it was used as warp for the production of luxury textiles. According to a Bologna source, at the end of the 16th century "about 20,000 people" lived from silk manufacturing – representing a third or a quarter of Bologna's population, distributed among various subsectors.[27]

This unique concentration in Bologna would not have been possible without the construction of water powered silk mills with mechanical winders. Without this innovation it would have been necessary to rely on the home-based work of thousands of women for winding, with at least part of them spread out across the countryside. Likewise, a large percentage of weavers

---

24 C. Poni, "A Proto-industrial City: Bologna XVI–XVIII Century," *La Protoindustrialisation: théorie et Réalité: rapports / VIIIe Congrès international d'histoire économique* (Budapest 16–22 August), 2 vols., ed. P. Deyon and F. Mendels (Lille, 1982).

25 Silk worms were also raised within the city walls. The "city" cocoons were sold at a special market called Pavaglioncino. See F. Piro, "Sistema fiscal, struttura e congiuntura in una economia 'preindustriale'. Il caso di Bologna, 1564–1666," *Annali dell'Istituto Storico Italo-Germanico in Trento*, 2 (1976), 117–182. See G. Baldi, *Per una storia dei prezzi: le "vacchette" della fiera del Pavaglione di Bologna*, in *Studi in memoria di Luigi Dal Pane*, Bologna 1982, pp. 557–573.

26 L. Grossi, 'L'arte dei tessitori da seta cotta nella città di Bologna in età moderna', Master's thesis discussed at the Faculty of Literature and Philosophy of the University of Bologna (A. Guenzi, supervisor) 1985–86.

27 Poni, 'A Proto-industrial City'.

TABLE 10.1 Hydraulic plants in Bologna (1393–1797/98)

	1393	1653	1683	1705	1747	1785	1797/8
Silk mills	16	95	119	74	53	35	18
Other plants	19	19	20	16	18	23	33
Grain plants	–	15	15	15	15	15	15

SOURCE: A. GUENZI, "L'AREA PROTOINDUSTRIALE DEL CANALE DI RENO"

TABLE 10.2 Water wheels in the hydraulic plants in Bologna (1393–1797/98)

	1393	1653	1683	1705	1747	1785	1797/8
Silk mills	16	260	353	247	180	123	–
Other plants	21	20	20	30	46	51	–
Grain plants	–	30	30	30	30	30	30

SOURCE: A. GUENZI, "L'AREA PROTOINDUSTRIALE DEL CANALE DI RENO"

would have had to move to the countryside. Thus it was technological innovation – mills with mechanical winding – that made possible the concentration of the silk industry. But we could also formulate an entirely different sequence, attributing to the city's institutions and culture, profoundly hostile to the ruralisation of the "mechanical arts" (*arti mechaniche*), the main stimulus for the innovation that perpetuated the urban centre's monopoly for centuries. This result could not have been achieved by keeping the water wheels of the silk mills on the Reno canal. The system of conduits ensured the conditions for the radical urban expansion of an industry that in other areas was more decentralised and segmented.

The current image of Bologna is that of the city of the "two towers," or "one hundred towers." This is an image full of meaning. The towers, built at the beginning of the 13th century by a landowning nobility residing in the city, symbolize the political power that the city exercised for centuries over a vast rural area, providing it with cultural, religious, administrative and military services. Thus the towers and city walls identify Bologna as a *città-centrale* ("central city plan") in relation to the surrounding countryside. But Bologna was not

TABLE 10.3 Licenses for water to power silk mills in Bologna (1491–1620)

Year	Licenses	Year	Licenses
1491	1	1557	1
1493	3	1558	1
1499	2	1566	1
1516	1	1582	5
1525	5	1583	2
1526	1	1584	1
1528	1	1585	1
1531	1	1595	1
1533	1	1600	1
1535	1	1620	1
1545	1		

SOURCE: A. GUENZI, "L'AREA PROTOINDUSTRIALE DEL CANALE DI RENO"

TABLE 10.4 Groups who made their living from the silk industry in Bologna (1591)

Boiler workers and women who work at the boilers	1,600
Spinners and boy assistants	2,600
Winders	4,000
Warp workers	300
Weavers of veils	12,000
Ruffle and pleat makers and boy assistants	150
Varied workers	1,000
Cloth weavers	3,000
Dyers and boy assistants	250
TOTAL	*24,000*

SOURCE: A. GUENZI, "L'AREA PROTOINDUSTRIALE DEL CANALE DI RENO"

only this. Its industry, its commerce, the *Canale Navile*, and the university (at least in certain periods) gave it, from an early age, another significant identity as part of a network of cities connected across long distances through the international trade of goods and ideas. This second characteristic (the city as part of a "network system") is strongly connected to but is not identified with the first (the "central city plan").[28] The city of towers did not represent but actually hid the industrial and commercial city. If we were to construct a metaphor for this other city, we would seek it out in the subterranean conduits, the water wheels and the silk mills.

Yet the oft noted flexibility of Bologna's hydraulic system and its creative combination with silk mills have to be placed in a context that was insuperably rigid: the walls encircling the industrial area were also the limits of a culture of silk that did not succeed in projecting its own development beyond the city into the nearby countryside. This "economic dogma" played in Bologna's favor as long as the *know-how* of the silk mills remained firmly within the city. The breach that opened up when Bolognese machinists and master spinners emigrated to Modena, Trento and then Mantua and Reggio raised acute alarm in Bologna.[29] At least in the medium term this did not produce the feared consequences for two good reasons. The production of raw silk in the Po valley grew between the 16th and 17th centuries more rapidly than the spread of silk mills "alla bolognese"; and the construction of improved water-powered mills in other cities, close or distant, was limited and therefore not dangerous.

Widespread diffusion of these mills could only occur by transforming urban hydraulic systems into the Bologna model. In other words, until a dense and sophisticated system of underground conduits was constructed in which tens or hundreds of water wheels could be installed, the spread of mills "alla bolognese" would be inevitably limited, even in cities that already had an industrial canal. And so it happened. As far as we know, no city wanted or could imitate Bologna's intricate hydraulic system, nor find an effective substitute. Of the few urban centers that managed to construct a dense system of waterways, Bergamo alone succeeded. Starting in 1640, in little more than fifty years the city succeeded in constructing a few dozen mills which were almost all "alla bolognese." In 1720 there were fifty of them. But the effect of this massive innovation (which perhaps also spread to villages near the city) was partially lost because the city authorities, worried about reducing the level of women's employment, did not permit the construction of mechanical winders. In Como, on the other hand, mechanical winders could not function "due to the scarcity of boys," according to an anonymous English traveler.[30]

28 On the concepts of "central city plan" and "network system" see P.M. Hohenberg and L.H. Lees, *The Making of Urban Europe (1000–1950)*, (Cambridge, Mass. and London, 1985).

29 Poni, "All'origine del sistema di fabbrica".

30 See the diary of a journey to Italy (1677–78) by an anonymous English silk merchant. Bodleian Library, Oxford, mss. *Rawlinsoniani*, D. 1510, cc. n. n.

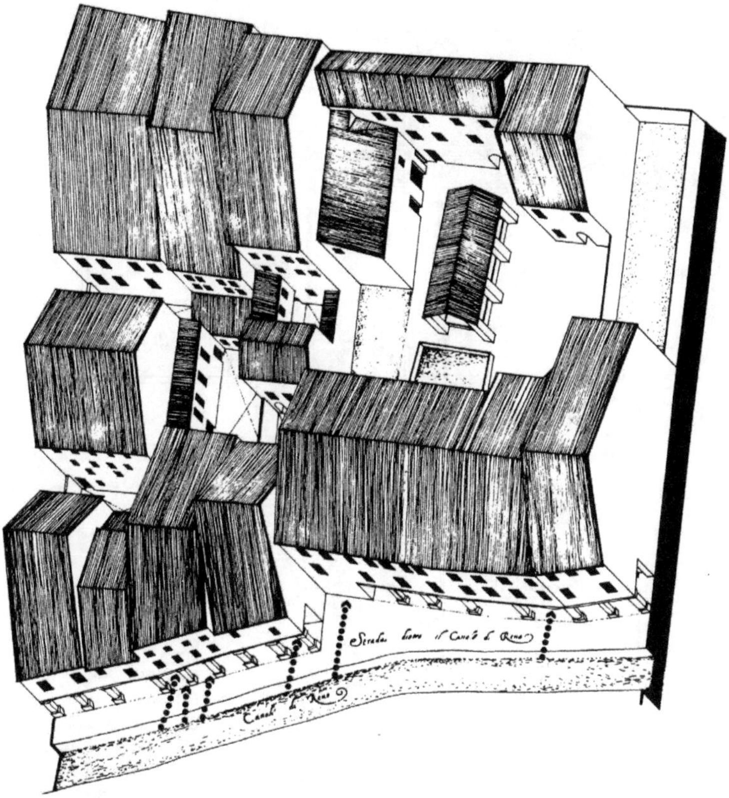

FIGURE 10.3 Silk mill "alla Bolognese" (external)
SOURCE: THREE-DIMENSIONAL RECONSTRUCTION OF THE RIZZARDI SILK MILL (17TH–18TH CENTURIES). VERSION PREPARED BY RAFFAELA BRUNI. MUSEO DEL PATRIMONIO INDUSTRIALE, BOLOGNA, ARCHIVIO FOTOGRAFICO

The situation changed drastically in the last decades of the 17th century when large and improved silk mills began to be built in the Piedmont countryside, and subsequently (in the 18th century) in rural Veneto and Lombardy. These large structures arose near small urban-rural centers, destined to grow rapidly (as in Racconigi), located at the mouth of pre-Alpine valleys such as Rovereto, or in the hilly area between Lake Maggiore and Lake Garda (Varese, Erba, and Garlate).[31] In these areas of the upper Po valley waterways were numerous and abundant, the protoindustrial labor force from the countryside

31 D. Sella, *Contributo alla storia delle fonti di energia: i filatoi idraulici della valle Padana durante il seconolo* XVII, in *Studi in onore di Amintore Fanfani*, vol. V (Milan, 1962), pp. 621–631.

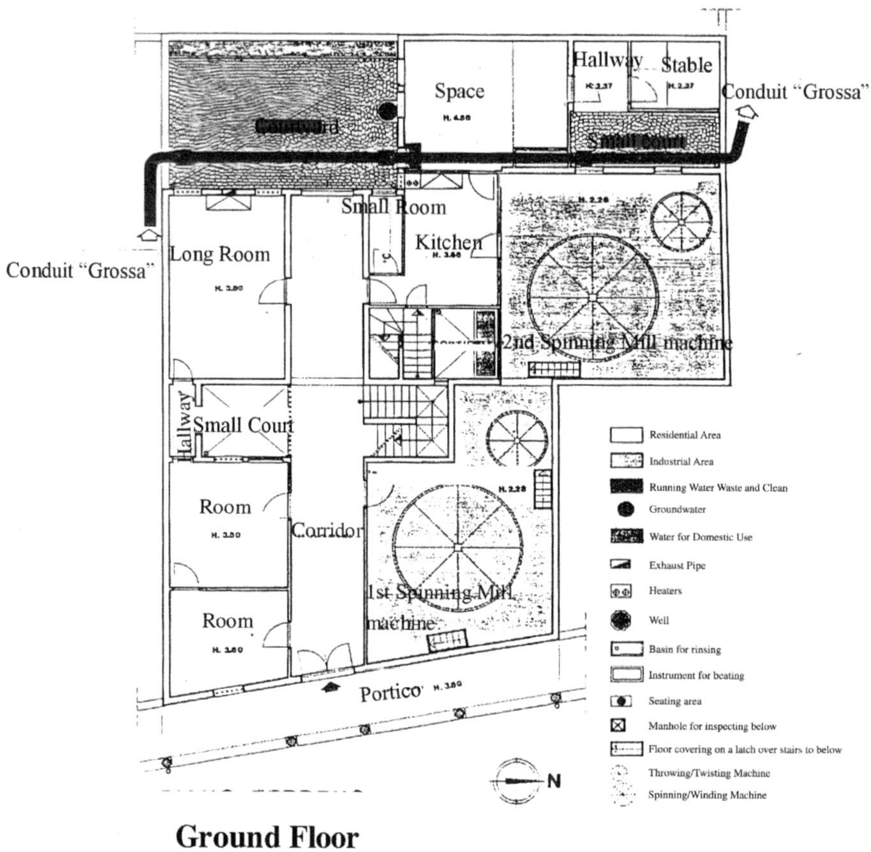

FIGURE 10.4 Pedini silk mill (internal)
SOURCE: HISTORICAL DIAGRAM OF THE PEDINI SILK MILL, BASED ON A MAP OF 1759. VERSION PREPARED BY BARBARA MONTEVECCHI. MUSEO DEL PATRIMONIO INDUSTRIALE, BOLOGNA

was available for low pay, trade was easier with European markets, and the flow of foreign capital was more intense. Here over the course of two centuries, starting from these roots, a new, original production system evolved characterized by numerous manufacturing plants spread across vast areas, which we can consider the first "long wave" of Italian industrialization.[32] The economic decline of the Bolognese hydraulic industrial system – so preponderantly

32 L. Cafagna, "Protoindustria o transizione in bilico? (A proposito della prima onda della industrializzazione italiana), in *Quaderni storici*, vol. 18, no. 54 (1983), 971–984. Cf. A. Dewerpe's recent contribution, *L'industrie aux champs. Essai sur la protoindustrialisation en Italie du nord (1800–1880)* (Rome, 1985).

urban – was also connected to the success of the new "regional" system, a nebula fed by the unprecedented growth of raw silk production.

This transformation, which took place in the 19th century, almost completely by-passed the area south of the Po (with a few minor exceptions). In Bologna the close relationship between "threads" of water and "threads" of silk, already weakening over the course of the 18th century, finally broke at the turn of the century. With the disappearance of the silk mills and the collapse of the silk industry, a rich patrimony of entrepreneurial and artisanal knowledge was lost forever. It was from the depths of this irreparable crisis that Bologna found itself confronted with new times and the challenge of the industrial revolution.

CHAPTER 11

Behind the Scenes: The Staging of a Theater of Machines

Carlo Poni

Novo teatro di machine et edificii (*New Theatre of Machines and Buildings*), perhaps the most important book on machines of the late Renaissance, was printed in Padua in 1607, after Vittorio Zonca's death at a young age a few years before. It was almost as an epigraph that the publisher Pietro Bertelli placed on the frontispiece next to the author's name the words "Architect of the Magnificent Community of Padua," a title that Zonca had received by "public decree" ten years earlier, on 12 February 1597, from the Padua city council.[1] This appointment involved neither employment nor compensation. Nor did it establish a monopoly position similar to those of modern professional associations.[2] Public decrees were one way of gaining professional qualification, albeit with uncertain legal effect, not obtained by completing a university course of study or through years of apprenticeship under a master of one of the city's craft guilds.[3]

What was an architect's professional profile? According to Zonca's letter to the city council requesting the post, an architect's job was to "supervise those works which derive their perfect being and embellishment from the mathematical disciplines, such as the drawing up of designs for construction; their application according to their proportions; the levelling and regulating of water and terrain, including in the designs not only flat surfaces but relief as well as concave features; in addition, formulating views regarding contentious

1 *Archivio di Stato di Padova* (hereafter A.S.P.), *Archivio Civico Antico, Atti di Consiglio del Comune (1597–1600)*, Reg. XVII (20), cc. 18–9. This source had already been noted by T. Beck, *Beiträge zur Geschichte des Machinenbaues* (Berlin, 1899), pp. 293–4. By what means the publisher Bertelli obtained the manuscript we do not know (see *Novo teatro*. pp. XXXVIII).

2 A.S.P., ibid. Once the resolution was voted on (105 in favor, 31 against) some councilors asked to specify that this did not take away "libertas ciucumque particulari quin etiam ab aliis possit serviri" ("from any individual the liberty to be served by others" [i.e., to hire another architect]). This post-script was voted almost unanimously.

3 Little is known about the professional training of architects in the 15th and 16th centuries. See C. Wilkinson, "The New Professionalism in the Renaissance," *The Architect. Chapters in the History of the Profession*, ed. S. Kostof (New York, 1977), pp. 124–160 and bibliography.

 | DOI:10.1163/9789004713277_013

sites, both in civil and criminal cases, and taking into account both private and public benefit."[4]

It is not difficult to detect the influence of the Latin architect Vitruvio Pollione[5] in this profile. It is evident, for example, in the pre-eminent role of the "mathematical disciplines," which architects had to master at a much higher level than surveyors, "who" – wrote Zonca repeatedly – "due to their profession and responsibility, have only to demonstrate the amount of flat surface area of land, measuring it by pacing it out."[6] Along with the influence of Vitruvio – and the tradition Vitruvio inspired – the other decisive influence on Zonca was his practical experience as a hydraulic engineer: "levelling and regulating water and terrain." These surveying practices had a rich tradition in the Po valley, and were at the heart of a profession that had formed and developed with the rapid advance of large-scale canalisation and land reclamation.[7]

Unfortunately little is known of Zonca's professional work. Giuseppe Lazara – an erudite Paduan – wrote in 1650 that he had been "painter, master of mathematics, sculptor and senior engineer of the city."[8] Research, particularly in the libraries and archives of Padua and Venice, provides evidence of an event which illuminates one sector of activity of Zonca's work while stimulating the desire for further information. In the autumn of 1599 Vittorio Zonca, already 30 years old, was working as an expert consultant (*perito straordinario*)

4 "sovraintendere a quelle opera che dalle discipline matematiche hanno il loro perfetto essere et abelimento, come ... l'invenzione delle piante, l'elevationi di quelle con la perfetta disposizione degli ordeni loro, il livellare et regolare l'acque et terreni, pigliare in disegno non solo le superficie piane, ma li rilievi – et per concavo ancora – oltre il formare le posizioni de' siti contentiosi, così nelle cause civili come nelle criminali, moderando per interesse de' privati et sì per benefitio pubblico" (A.S.P., ibid.). The letter is basically incorporated in the resolution. [In this chapter, given the complexity of Zonca's text, the original Italian has been included in the footnotes. - Eds.]

5 In addition to Vitruvio's text (book X) I also refer to Daniele Barbaro's comment on Vitruvio. See *I dieci libri dell'Architettura di Vitruvio*, ed. and trans. Daniele Barbaro (Venice, 1556). See also V. P. Zoubov, "Vitruve et ses commentaires du XVI siècle," *La science au seizième siècle: Colloque international de Royaumont, 1–4 juillet 1957* (Paris, 1969), pp. 67–90, and the more recent L.A. Chiapponi, "Fra Giocondo da Verona and his edition of Vitruvius," *Journal of the Warburg and Courtauld Institutes*, 47 (1984), 72–90.

6 "che hanno per professione et carico di dimostrar col passo le quantità sole delle superficie piane de' terreni" (A.S.P., ibid.). The professions of architect and surveyor are treated separately by T. Garzoni, *La piazza universale di tutte le professioni del mondo*, reprint (Venice, 1589), pp. 191–197 and 756–764.

7 S. Ciriacono, "Scrittori d'idraulica e politica delle acque," *Storia della cultura veneta. Dal primo Quattrocento al Concilio di Trento*, 3/II, eds. G. Arnaldi and M.P. Stocchi (Vicenza, 1980), pp. 491–512, and bibliography.

8 Biblioteca Civica di Padova (hereafter B.C.P.), Ms. B.P. 15.1363, G. Lazara, "Memorie certe di tutte le famiglie di nobili e cittadini quali per l'addietro furono ammesse al Consiglio nella nostra città di Padova," [1650] (see index).

in the service of the "Magistrates and Deputies for the waters of the Tartaro River" of the Republic of Venice.[9] In this role, in 1599 he drew a map attached to an interstate agreement between the Duchy of Mantua and the Republic of Venice to regulate the waters at their borders. The original map was not found, but in its place are three eighteenth-century copies.[10] This map is significant, not only because it documents professional dedication and skill. Drawn to scale, this map contains certain instructions on how to read the drawing that not all cartographers believed needed to be explicit. "With this scale," noted Zonca, "one can show all the distances from one point to another between the two bridges," but the rest, he cautions, "the area outside this line between the two bridges, represents approximately the positions but not the true proportions, as they were drawn simply by sight and not measured."[11] This instruction with one stroke separates the central area between the "two bridges" measured and drawn to scale, from the peripheral areas measured "by sight," and reveals a specific sense of the difference between approximate space and exact space. Drawn with different instruments, the two spaces should be read in different ways.[12] Understanding the map is therefore prefigured and guided by the author's critical and scientific awareness.

---

9 The expert's reports, which covered the period September 23 – November 16, 1599, are in the Archivio di Stato di Venezia (hereafter A.S.V.), *Archivio Secreta, Archivio Zendrini*, Reg. 30. See also the collection *Decreti e scritture sopra il fiume Tartaro*, in the Biblioteca Universitaria di Padova (hereafter B.U.P.), Ms. 246. Zonca's name also appears in the file of the interstate agreement at the Archivio di Stato di Mantova, *Archivio Gonzaga*, b. 180. I am grateful to Marco Belfante who kindly drew it to my attention.

10 Two of the three maps are in the collection *Disegni a mano delle acque delle provincie venete per i lavori idraulici* (B.U.P., 26 b 7). The first copy (ibid., no. 17) was by Tomaso Scalfurato from a previous copy drawn by Bernardino Zendrini on March 6, 1728, which in turn was a copy of another map made on April 24, 1725 by the engineer Pietro Zambelli. Zendrini had reduced the map by a half. The second map (ibid., no. 18) was drawn by the surveyor and engineer Domenico Piccoli on February 1, 1740. This copy is on a much smaller scale than the previous one. The third map is at the Archivio di Stato di Verona, *Fondo Prefettura, Disegni*.

11 "Con la scala si ritroveranno tutte le distanzie da loro a loco dentro le due linee di ponti, [avvertendo che il resto] che si trova fuori delle dette linee di ponti, rappresenta l'essere circa le positura, ma non la vera quantità delle proporzioni, essendo quello stato tolto con l'occhio semplicemente e non con le misure." This text has been taken from Scalfurato's map from the Padua State Archives, corrected in several places by comparing it with the map from the Verona State Archives.

12 On this topic see A. Koyré, *Dal mondo del pressappoco all'universo della precisione*, introd. and trans. P. Zambelli (Turin, 1961). For a history of drawing machines see P.J. Booker, *A History of Engineering Drawing* (London, 1963,) and Y. Deforge, *Le graphisme technique. Son histoire et son enseignement* (Macon, 1981).

This awareness also serves in reading the *Novo teatro,* to see the representation in scale of a number of machines (which escaped almost all scholars), and to understand why in one of his drawings Zonca separates the space meticulously measured – an enlargement with various views of a machine "for making grooves in lead for glass windows" – from the rest of the image roughly proportioned to reduced-size human figures (*Novo teatro*, p. 79).[13] In so doing, he carried out an operation that implicitly broke with the existing mode of representing machines. He decontextualized the scale from its original – the drawing of maps – and with an innovative gesture transported it to a completely different field – the drawing of machines. The consequences of this transposition also affect the way it was read. While it separates drawings which were measured only approximately from those which were measured precisely, the scale immediately makes possible an accurate comparative and transversal reading of the machines depicted.

Yet this innovation passed unobserved and had few followers among contemporaries. Not even Zonca's "plagiarizers" in the seventeenth century faithfully reproduced the drawings that they copied. Thus Heinrich Ziesing, when he reproduced the "Mill moved by animal power," left the scale out and replaced it with a flowering bush.[14]

Georg A. Boeckler also eliminated the scale each time (only twice) that he found it in the drawings he copied from Zonca.[15] Of the few architects and

13 Vittorio Zonca, *Novo teatro di machine et edificii* [1607], ed. Carlo Poni (Milan, 1985). For the few scholars who "saw" the scale in Zonca's work see Deforge, *Le graphisme technique*, p. 62, note 20, and also the entry "Zonca Vittorio," ed. G. Tabarroni, *Annali della Scienza e della tecnica dalle origini al 1900. Scienziati e tecnologi dalle origini al 1875*, vol. III (Milan, 1975), (see index). At the beginning of the 17th century measuring to scale was not an absolute novelty in drawings of machines. In a manuscript from the 1500s belonging to a group of machine drawings by Francesco di Giorgio Martini, the scale is indicated at least once in the same way as in *Novo teatro* and explained by Martini with the words: "This is the foot used to make the drawing" (see Figure 11.1). Zonca too normally uses feet (the Paduan foot = 0.357 m) as a unit of measure, and only once the inch (the Paduan inch = 0.029 m) on page 79. In the *Novo teatro* in one case (p. 43) the measurement is explicitly indicated by encoding the "semi-diameter of the wheel of the drawn figure" which measured 7 feet. In another comment (p. 87) length is indicated as "the height of a common man, which is five feet" (= 1.78 m).

14 H. Zeising, *Theatri machinarum* (Leipzig, 1612–1614). This work is divided into six parts. The third was attributed to Henning Gross and the last three to Hieronymus Mesiger. The "Mill made with animal power" (*Novo teatro*, p. 25) is partially reproduced in part III, fig. 6 (Figure 11.2 in this volume). In other examples Zeising correctly reproduced the scale.

15 G.A. Boeckler, *Theatrum machinarum novum* (Cologne, 1661). See drawing numbers 38 and 39 which correspond to those on pp. 33 and 36 in *Novo teatro*.

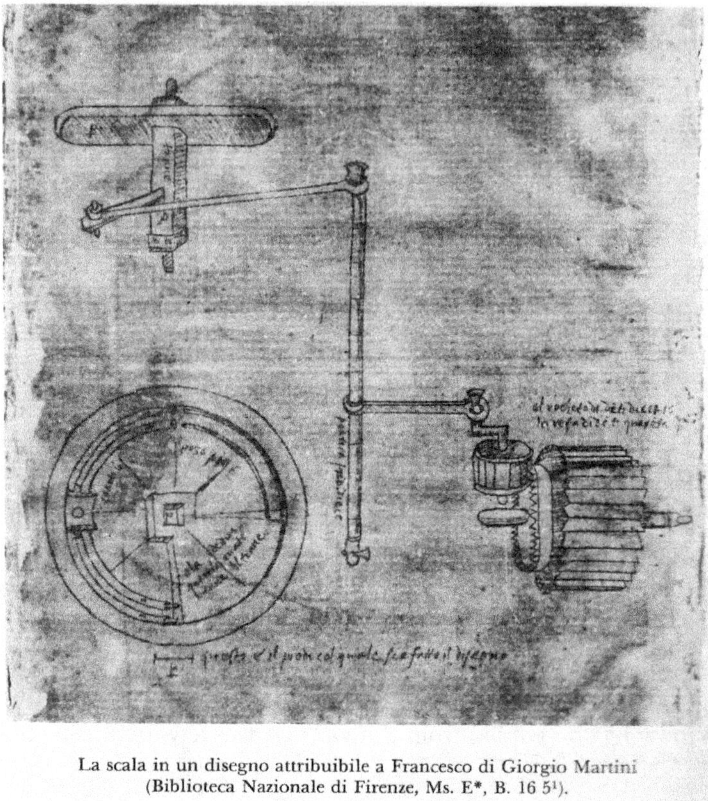

FIGURE 11.1 The scale in a sketch. This drawing is attributed to Francesco di Giorgio Martini. At the bottom is written "This is the foot used to make the drawing".
SOURCE: PALAT. E.B.16.5, VOL. I (STR. 1416), F. 51V. ON PERMISSION OF THE MINISTRY OF HERITAGE AND CULTURAL ACTIVITY, BIBLIOTECA NAZIONALE CENTRALE, FLORENCE

engineers before 1740 who systematically used scale in drawing machines before 1740, I can cite only two Germans, Leonhard C. Sturm and Jacob Leupold,[16]

16 L.C. Sturm, *Vollständige Mühlen Baukunst* (Augusta, 1718); J. Leupold, *Theatrum machinarum molarium oder Schau-Platz der Mühlen-Bau Kunst* (Leipzig, 1735). Other volumes of *Theatrum* may be found in the work by Leupold. For a survey of numerous publications by Leupold see U. Troitzch, "Zum Stande über Jacob Leupold (1674–1727)," *Technik Geschichte*, vol. 42, 1975, no. 1, 268–86. The use of scale in drawing machines also appeared

FIGURE 11.2 "Mill moved by animal power"
A drawing by Zonca. Note the scale in the bottom right.
SOURCE: ZONCA, *NOVO TEATRO*, P. 25

a Swede, Pehr Linpergh,[17] and a Dutchman, Jacob Polley.[18] These authors, well known to Denis Diderot, probably inspired the use of scale in the *planches* of the *Encyclopédie*.[19] Yet Zonca's name does not appear among them. Though Diderot was aware of some books on machines from the late Renaissance – such as Agostino Ramelli's work – it seems he never read the *Novo teatro*.

This relatively minor influence of Zonca's precise technical representations can be explained in part by the weakness evident in the contemporary technical graphics, which did not succeed in producing a perceptible visual distinction between drawings done to scale and those done by sight; and in part due to the lack of visual effect of the scale, often small, given minor importance,

in A. Bosse, *Traité des manières de graver en taille-douce* (Paris, 1645) and B.F. Belidor, *Architecture hydraulique ou l'Art de conduire ... les eaux*, 2 vols. (Paris, 1737–1739).

17 P. Linpergh, *Architectura mechanica, Moel Boek* (Amsterdam, 1725).

18 J. Polley, *Groot Volkommen Moelenboek* (Amsterdam, 1734). Along with Polley, the work was signed by L. Van Natrus and C. Van Wuuren. The scale also appears in other Dutch works depicting locks and dikes. See, for example, *Theatrum machinarum of Keurige Verzameling*, tomes I–II (Amsterdam, 1736–1737); the first volume is edited by T. Van der Horst and the second by J. Polley. On the use of scale in architectural drawing see Deforge, *Le graphisme technique*, pp. 33–6, 57–61 and passim.

19 See J. Proust, *Diderot et l'Encyclopédie* (Paris, 1962).

FIGURE 11.3 "Mill moved by animal power"
A copy based on Zonca (see Figure 11.2), but instead of a scale (bottom right) there is a small plant.
SOURCE: H. ZEISING, *THEATRI MACHINARUM* (LEIPZIG, 1612–1614,) PART, III, NO. 6, PRINT COLLECTION, MIRIAM AND IRA D. WALLACH DIVISION OF ART, PRINTS AND PHOTOGRAPHS, THE NEW YORK PUBLIC LIBRARY, ASTOR, LENOX AND TILDEN FOUNDATIONS

incomplete and not applied consistently (in only eleven out of forty-two drawings).

In addition to scale, the *Novo teatro* contains two other interpretive tools for the comparative and transversal reading of graphics. The first appears directly in the drawings and applies to certain objects – gears, wheels, shields (*timpani*) and bobbins – identified as parts of a common series. These objects were sometimes drawn in an abstract space, separate from the drawings which depicted their assemblage.[20] The intention to demonstrate, through these

20 See for example, *Novo teatro*, pp. 30, 33, 36, 45, 68, 82 and 85. These analytical details, which do not appear in all drawings, are not new. Leonardo had already done that, with more detailed and clear drawings. But we must always remember that Leonardo's works remained unpublished for four centuries. These techniques of representation went from *Novo teatro* to H. Zeising's *Theatri machinarum*. Zonca had seen examples of analytical deconstruction in the works of Giorgio Agricola whom he cites (pp. 86 and 92) and perhaps read in the Italian translation (G. Agricola, *L'arte de' metalli*, translated into Tuscan by the Florentine M. Florio [Basel, 1563], and the Latin edition, *De re metallica* [Basel, 1561]). Rarely in Zonca's drawings do instruments complimentary to mechanical work appear (such as "Pestrino's" shovel, *Novo teatro*, p. 30). More frequently he depicts the material or objects that are produced, such as swords, knives and sickles in "Mola d'aguzzar" (*Novo teatro*, p. 36). In "machina per pestar il carbon" (p. 82) the pistol and gunpowder container indicate the ultimate use of the product. For the history of machine drawings and books on machines we should keep in mind the works of V. Biringuccio (*Pirotechnia* [Venice, 1540], lithographic edition with notes [Milan, 1978]); A. Ramelli (*Le*

analytical studies, the identical or nearly identical parts of different machines seems obvious. This intention is reinforced and deepened by brief technical glossaries for the illustrations, so that the single elements stand apart from the whole.[21] These studies emphasize the elements that transmit motion and seem to be directed towards a technology for the construction of machines starting from their components.

A second indication of transversal reading appears in the captions and consists of a proposal – borrowed from Vitruvio and the pseudo-Aristotelian *Meccaniche* – to disassemble each machine into its parts and arrange them into "six classes" (*ragioni*) of which "all the various types of machines are composed."[22] Thus the need to distinguish the basic parts used in assembling the machine: screw, lever, weight scales, wedge, wheel axle, and pulley. Only someone who knew how to disassemble every machine in "two, or three, or more of the above-mentioned classes" would be able "by himself to construct marvellous works, with the help of judgment and drawings" (*Novo teatro*, p. 1). In the captions Zonca often exemplifies these instructions for decoding the apparent multiplicity of mechanisms by reducing them to the six invariable classes (*ragioni*). A press "for polishing" is placed in the class of the screw, as are other types of machines such as those for lifting weights, and oil and wine presses (*Novo teatro*, pp. 1, 46–52). Other analyses are interwoven with this one, deriving directly from theory and intended to reduce the six classes of mechanics to one common class. The screw is connected to the lever, and the lever to the wheel axle (*Novo teatro*, pp. 4, 31, 41–8).

---

diverse et artificiose machine [Paris, 1588]); and the Pseudo-Juanelo Turriano (*Los veintun libros de los ingenios y de las maquinas*, vols. I and II, introd. J.A. Garcia-Diego [Madrid, 1984]). This last and important text remained for centuries in manuscript form and virtually unknown in the Biblioteca Nacional de España.

21 I believe that Zonca was one of the first, after Agricola, to compile these technical glossaries. The names of the "parts" of machines, explained "methodically," were supposed to help read the drawing (see *Novo teatro*, pp. 95 and 109), though Zonca's glossaries are not adequate for the modern reader. The problem of the vocabulary of the *Novo teatro* should be investigated in the larger context of the formation of Italian technical language, a problem that cannot be addressed in this work. For a general overview of books on machines see A.G. Keller, *A Theatre of Machines* (London, 1964).

22 Zonca cites more than once both Vitruvio, the "noble Writer" (*Novo teatro*, p. 15), and the *Questiones mechanicae*. Although he knew Latin – in fact he cites a passage by Vitruvio in Latin (p. 66) – it is likely that he read both authors in Italian translations. On the printed editions of Vitruvio and the pseudo-Aristotelian *Meccaniche* see S. Drake and P.L. Rose, "The Pseudo-Aristotelian Questions of Mechanics in Renaissance Culture," *Studies in the Renaissance*, XVIII (1971), 65–104; P. Galluzzi, *Momento. Studi Galileani* (Rome, 1979), pp. 63, 74–89. It is not improbable that Zonca had read Aristotle in the *Parafrasi di Monsignor Alessandro Piccolomini sopra le Mecaniche d'Aristotele*, trans. O.V. Biringucci (Rome, 1582), or the Latin text of *Paraphrasis* printed in Venice in 1565.

But Zonca did not stop at formally deconstructing the process of assemblage – the grammar of machines – nor at repeating exercises for reducing the number of classes to wheel axles or levers. In *Novo teatro* the principles of mechanics were directly applied to production techniques to improve the efficiency of machines. Thus to construct hydraulic mills one would need to start by "knowing the weight [to move], which is the millstone compared to the proportion of half the diameter of the wheel with half the diameter of the shaft. Hence theoreticians affirm that the proportion of the diameter of the wheel to the proportion of the diameter of the shaft is like that of the moving weight to the weight and force of water" (*Novo teatro*, p. 19). Here a calculation appears that cannot be solely explained with the pseudo-Aristotelian *Meccaniche*, the only work on mechanics explicitly cited by Zonca. The focus on the relation between the "radius of the wheel, and the radius of the shaft" can be traced back to other figures such as the mathematician Guidobaldo Del Monte. Guidobaldo – never cited by Zonca –analyzing the axle of a wheel, wrote in 1577 that in this instrument "the power sustaining the weight ... has the same proportion to the weight as the radius of the axle to the radius of the wheel."[23] A few years later Galileo (not even he is cited) asserted in his *Mecaniche* that in the axle of a wheel "the proportion of the force to the weight will always be the same as the radius of the axle to the radius of the wheel."[24]

Zonca did not limit himself to defining the dynamics of proportions according to the formulations of Guidobaldo and Galileo. He also commented on and clarified these with concrete examples. He wrote:

> to put it more practically, if you want to know, for example, how much weight can be lifted above its shaft per the size of a wheel, do as follows: measure the diameter of the shaft, and let's imagine it is the thickness of

23 "la possanza sostenente il peso ... ha la proporzione medesima al peso che il mezzo diametro dell'asse al mezzo diametro della ruota" (Guidobaldo del Monte, *Le mechaniche*, Italian trans. Filippo Pigafetta [Venice, 1581], p. 103). The Latin edition – *Mechanicorum libri* – was printed in 1577 in Pesaro. This demonstration was already done by Erone Alessandrino, whose works were not known to mediaeval and Renaissance authors. Zonca's mechanical analyses are elementary compared to the detailed calculations on wind mills developed in those years by S. Stevin, "Van de Molens, gereviseert door den' Professor Golius 1634," *The Principal Works of Simon Stevin*, eds. Committee of Dutch Scientists (Amsterdam, 1955–1966), vol. v, pp. 335–379.

24 "la forza al peso [doveva] avere sempre l'istessa proporzione, che il semidiametro dell'asse al semidiametro della ruota" (G. Galilei, *Le mecaniche*, in *Le opere di Galileo Galilei*, new reprint of the Edizione Nazionale, vol. II [Florence, 1932], p. 169). For the English translation, see *On Motion and on Mechanics*. Comprising *De Motu* (ca. 1590). Translated with introduction and notes by I.E. Drabkin, and *Le Meccaniche* (ca. 1600), translated with introduction and notes by Stillman Drake (Madison, 1960, p. 161).

> an arm, and suppose that the wheel is six arms in diameter. Divide the shaft's thickness in half [which] would be half an arm, and this will be the lever of the shaft. Then divide the diameter of the wheel, which will be three arms, and this will be the lever of the wheel. Now as many times as the lever of the shaft fits into the lever of the wheel, that many *libre* can be lifted per *libra* above its shaft. The half arm, or lever of the shaft, fits six times into three arms, the lever of the wheel; therefore one can say that if one *libre* of weight is placed on the circumference of the wheel, six *libre* can be lifted above the shaft. As a result, if the Architect knows the weight of the millstones in advance, he can build the right size wheels for the weight of the millstones (*Novo teatro*, pp. 19–20)[25].

Here the professional profile of an architect of machines emerges, one who is neither a theoretician of mechanics nor a simple transmitter of empirical knowledge incorporated in popular technology. His task is to apply theoretical speculation on the method of constructing machines and improve their functioning by providing elements of calculation and cross sections, all of which are to be grafted onto the body of repeated and accumulated practice. "The shorter the shaft, the faster the millstones will move," warned Zonca, but this would also increase the tension on the timbers and the transmission mechanisms with the risk of breaking. To avoid this danger it would be necessary to replace the wood with "very strong iron bars" and employ "expert Masters to adjust them and repair them" (*Novo teatro*, p. 20). Other problems could arise if the circumference of the wheel were too small, as was the case with the "machine for fulling woollen cloth" (raising the nap) in the city of Padua – "a very old machine" – which had a diameter of just 7–8 feet (*Novo teatro*, p. 43),[26]

25 "per dirla più pratticalmente, se vuoi sapere v<erbi> g<gratia> quanto peso possi levare sopra il suo fuso la grandezza d'alcuna ruota, fa in questa maniera: misura il diametro del fuso, et ponilo come sarebbe a dire di grossezza d'un braccio, et la ruota presupponi c'habbia sei braccia di diametro. Dividi per metà la grossezza del fuso [che] sarà mezo braccio, et questa sarà la sua lieva; dividi poi il diametro della ruota, che sarà braccia tre, et questa sarà la sua lieva. Hora quante volte la lieva del fuso entra nella lieva della ruota, tante libre leverà per libra sopra il suo fuso. Il mezo braccio, dunque lieva del fuso, entra sei volte nelle tre braccia, lieva della ruota; dunque si dirà che se sarà posta una libra di peso sula circonferenza della ruota, leverà per sei libre di peso sopra il fuso. Per la qual cosa se l'Architetto haverà conoscimento di tai cose saprà proportionatamente fabricar le ruote di tai machine, di quella misura che giudicherà convenevole alla gravezza che potessero importar le macini."

26 The first documents proving the existence of water-powered fulling mills in Padua date back to the end of the 13th century. See L. Rizzoli, *L'Università dell'Arte della lana a Padova* (Padua, 1930), p. 14.

"for which, when the water rises and the river swells, the wheel is completely covered with water and becomes immobile because the shaft can no longer turn around its center, hence the fuller stops working."[27] The machine also had another problem. In the shaft there were "too few *ascole* – that is, the [levers] that raise the hammers – hence they move very slowly and as a consequence do little work in a day." To improve the functioning of the fuller and make it "much better and correct," it would be enough to double "the diameter of the wheel," increasing it from 7 to 14 feet "or actually even more, so that in the event of flooding the machine will not stop working; but also to increase the speed of the hammers and make them work better," the number of levers (*ascole del melo*) should be doubled, "what were four would be eight, and well fixed."[28] With this comment, Zonca was concerned to provide a theoretical explanation. The enlarged wheel would acquire more power but lose speed (literally: it would have spun "more easily" but "with slower movement"). Hence his advice to speed up the machine so that it could "work very fast and well," increasing the number of levers (*ascole*).

The idea of an inverse relationship between power and speed – albeit expressed in a confused way – and the other theoretical *excursus* brought to light on the preceding pages, suggests a brief inquiry of the mechanical culture of Padua and Venice in the 16th century. This culture was active and lively, even though not the product of independent thought. At its base was the problem of the correct reading and translation in Latin and then in vulgate [Italian] of Aristotle's *Meccaniche*, printed for the first time in Venice at the end of the 15th century in Greek by Aldo Manuzio. For the entire 16th century the scientific communities of Padua and Venice were engaged in this task more actively than any other Italian or European university community.[29]

27 "per la qual cosa, quando crescono l'acque, et si gonfia il fiume, la ruota viene coperta dall'acqua, et diventa immobile, perché il melo, o fuso, non si può più raggirare nel suo centro, onde il follo s'arresta di di lavorare" (*Novo teatro*, p. 43). Some documents from Padua note the opposite: insufficient functioning of the fullers (as in 1628) due to lack of water. See ibid, p. 148.

28 "over più, perché nel tempo dell'acque // grosse la Machina non si astenghi di lavorare; ma perché anco il moto de' martelli … sia più veloce, et lavori meglio"… "ascole del melo, le quali erano quattro et saranno otto, et bene assicurate" (*Novo teatro*, p. 43).

29 I took information on mechanical research and thought in the Padua-Venice area from the following works: Drake, "Introduction," in *Mechanics in Sixteenth-Century Italy. Selection from Tartaglia, Benedetti, Guidobaldo and Galileo*, trans. and annotated by S. Drake and I.E. Drabkin (Madison, Wisconsin, 1969), pp. 3–60; Drake and Rose, "The Pseudo-Aristotelian Questions of Mechanics"; P.L. Rose, *The Italian Renaissance of Mathematics. Studies on Humanists and Mathematicians from Petrarch to Galileo* (Geneva, 1975); Galluzzi, *Momento*, pp. 74–89. Some topics fundamental to the research framework are still lacking,

The first printed Latin translation of *Meccaniche* (Paris, 1517) was compiled by the Venetian humanist Vittore Fausto, notable also for his technical knowledge of shipbuilding. In 1525 Niccolò Leonico Tomeo, celebrated professor of philosophy at the University of Padua, had the second Latin translation printed in Venice. This translation, which was highly successful and went through numerous editions, may have been the text used in the lessons on mechanics at the University of Padua taught by the mathematician Pietro Catena (from 1547 to 1576) and his successor Giuseppe Moletti (1577–1588).

In addition to this dense interpretative and didactic activity in academic circles in Padua was the work of Alessandro Piccolomini, who lived in Padua as a student from 1538 to 1542, as well as Diego Hurtado de Mendoza, imperial ambassador to Venice (from 1539 to 1546). To Piccolomini we owe the Latin *Paraphrasis* of *Meccaniche* (Rome, 1547), subsequently translated into Italian by Oreste Vannocci Biringucci (Rome, 1582); to the second – a friend of Piccolomini and student of [Niccolò] Tartaglia – the first Spanish translation of *Meccaniche*.

Guidobaldo Del Monte and Bernardino Baldi, both leaders of the rediscovery of Archimedes and exponents of the school of mathematics at Urbino linked to the name Federico Commandino, belonged to the next generation of students (pupils of Pietro Catena). In 1577 Guidobaldo (later friend and protector of Galileo) published *Mechanicorum liber*, "the most authoritative and systematic work on statics since the time of the Greeks" according to P. Lawrence Rose.[30] This work featured a new approach compared to the pseudo-Aristotelian *Meccaniche*: the quest for the mathematically expressed relationships on the Archimedes model. By comparing Aristotle's and Archimedes' analyses of levers, Guidobaldo wrote in 1588 that whereas Aristotle had limited himself to saying that the weights farthest from the fulcrum had greater power, Archimedes had gone beyond this, asserting that the weights in the lever were in an inverse relationship to the distance from the fulcrum. "Without this knowledge – continued Guidobaldo – the *res mechanicae* would not have been

---

such as the works of medieval *de ponderibus* (on weights) writers and the dissemination of Archimedes in the Middle Ages. On these topics I refer readers to M. Glagget's fundamental works on Archimedes (*Archimedes in the Middle Ages*, vol. I; *The Arabo-Latin Tradition* [Madison, 1964]; *Archimedes in the Middle Ages*, vol. II: *The Translation from the Greek by William of Moerbeke*, 2 vols. [Philadephia, 1976]; *Archimedes in the Middle Ages*, vol. III: *The Fate of the Mediaeval Archimedes, 1300–1565*, 3 vols. [Philadelphia, 1978]). By the same author see also "Leonardo da Vinci and the Mediaeval Archimedes," *Physis*, XI (1969), 100–151, and *La scienza della meccanica nel medioevo* (Milan, 1972).

30 Rose, *The Italian Renaissance of Mathematics*, p. 222.

able to progress because all mechanical science [*facultas*] depends on this unique and essential foundation."[31]

This was the complex context of elaboration and reinterpretation (not only in Padua) faced by the last professor of mathematics appointed in Padua before the end of the 16th century – Galileo Galilei. In the autumn of 1592 Galileo, not yet thirty years old, was appointed to succeed Giuseppe Moletti.[32] Already in his first year in Padua (1593) the young scientist from Pisa was giving private lessons on mechanics and circulating handwritten lecture notes on the topic for students' use. A second, handwritten edition of the course on mechanics appeared in 1594. But it was only around 1599 (or 1601) that Galilei gave the treatise *Le mecaniche* its definitive form (but only published in 1634 by Mersenne paraphrased very freely in French). In this work Galileo followed Guidobaldo in his approach, based on Archimedes, but tended to go beyond the distinct separation of statics and dynamics made by his friend from Urbino. As early as 1593 Galileo asserted that since even a small amount of force could alter the equilibrium of the lever or scale, no difference should be made between the power required to hold the weight and that required to move it.

In short, towards the end of the 16th century the cultural milieu in Padua was saturated with rich reflections on mechanics. The young Vittorio Zonca, who in 1597 made a defense of mathematics in a letter to the City Council, had probably attended (private?) lessons in which both the pseudo-Aristotelian *Meccaniche* as well as Vitruvio's *Architectura* were discussed. In any case the 1590s, the last decade of the century, marked the period in which he read, made notes on, and assimilated his authors, and in which he reached whatever level of maturity could be granted to one whose life was too short. In the *Novo teatro* he refers explicitly to Vitruvio and the *Meccaniche*. But as already shown, at least some citations do not derive from Aristotle. They belong to his "return to Archimedes" and can be attributed to either Guidobaldo or Galileo, or both. His nearly literal citations would support Guidobaldo; in Galileo's favor is the fact that he lived in Padua.

From the autumn of 1592 to the autumn of 1602 (when Zonca died), Galileo and Zonca lived in the same city, both taught mathematics and had common acquaintances.[33] Vittorio's paternal uncle, the canonist Antonio, was professor

---

31 Guidobaldo del Monte, *In duos Archimedis aeque ponderantium libros paraphrasis* (Pesaro, 1588), p. 4.

32 On Galileo's time in Padua see A. Favaro, *Galileo Galilei e lo Studio di Padova*, vols. I and II (Padua, 1966); S. Drake, *Galileo at Work. His Scientific Biography* (Chicago, 1978), pp. 18–156.

33 Only G. Lazara has attested to the fact that Zonca was a mathematics teacher; see "Memorie cert". We do not know when or where he taught.

of canonical and civil law at the university and participated along with Galileo and other colleagues in founding the *Accademia dei Recuperati*.[34] By contemporary standards Padua, at the end of the 16th century, was a small city with a population of about 40,000.[35] I find it difficult to imagine that people interested in the same issues, belonging more or less to the same professional and social class, and separated only by a slight difference in age (in 1592 Galileo was 28 and Zonca 24) could not have known about each other. It is not improbable that Vittorio personally knew Galileo, or knew someone from his entourage, or had read one of the versions of his lecture notes on mechanics which, as we know, circulated in numerous copies. The fact that Zonca does not cite Galileo is not surprising. The authority of the pseudo-Aristotelian *Meccaniche* may have seemed to him a more than adequate scientific grounding. And the Paduan architect may not have been up to the task of recognizing the recent Archimedean breakthrough. Moreover, before 1606 Galileo had not published anything and was not yet a recognised authority in the years Zonca was writing *Novo teatro*, before his death in 1602.

While Zonca never cited Galileo, neither did Galileo cite Zonca. This may seem obvious, but it deserves some attention. *Novo teatro* was published in Padua in 1607, five years after the author's death, when Galileo was still teaching in Padua, which he then left for Florence in 1610. It is difficult to imagine that Galileo never saw this work, reprinted in 1621. From time to time the great scientist – who in 1593 had built and patented a "structure" to raise water – took an interest in projects of technicians and inventors in order to urge them to take into account the principles of mechanics when constructing machines, if they did not want "to spend time, effort and money in vain." Certainly he acknowledged the "many advantages and great utility" that could derive "from mechanical instruments in various manual crafts, and one could hope to get other advantages from perfectly intelligent experts of that mechanical science." But he was wary of those who "took to developing new inventions out of a certain natural talent alone, but without recourse to mathematical

34 A. Maggiolo, *I soci dell'Accademia patavina dalla sua fondazione. Accademia patavina di scienze, lettere ed arti, già dei Recovrati* (Padua, 1983), p. 373. Antonio Zonca's affiliation with the Accademia is from 25 November 1599, as is Galileo's. According to A. Favaro, Antonio Zonca was one of the university's most renowned jurists (*Galileo Galilei e lo Studio di Padova*, vol. II, p. 20).

35 In 1558 the chief magistrate Bernardo Zorzi calculated that Padua had a population of over 38,000. Eighteen years later (1576) the deputy chief magistrate Pietro Sanudo stated that it had 36,000 according to "the latest descriptions." See *Relazioni dei Rettori Veneti di Terraferma*, vol. IV; *Podesteria e Capitanato di Padova*, ed. A. Tagliaferri (Milan, 1975), pp. 50 and 67.

principles, which intrinsically demonstrate the nature of the primary and most elementary instruments of which all other machines are composed."[36]

Given this orientation – which was already contained in the *Mecaniche* – there is no doubt that had Galileo read *Novo teatro* with patience and sympathy, in spite of the mediocre and convoluted Italian in which it was written, he would have praised it for its commitment to linking "machine science" to the construction of machines. And he would have done the same for the engineer Buonaiuto Lorini's work on the *Fortificationi* (Venice, 1596) which explicitly used Guildobaldo's theoretical reflections.[37] These are obviously hypothetical and ambiguous considerations. As far as I know, none of Galileo's contemporaries cited *Novo teatro*. Certainly much of the documentation, particularly if handwritten, by now is destroyed, and other material simply lost. After a long and inconclusive search, I can only hope for new, more successful research.

Nevertheless, this hindrance cannot prevent us from detecting a certain affinity or assonance of themes between Galileo and Zonca. Indeed, in a caption in the *Novo teatro*, Zonca touches upon an issue at the heart of Galileo's last work. I refer to *Discorsi e dimostrazioni matematiche intorno a due nuove scienze* (*Discussions and mathematical demonstrations regarding two new sciences*) (1638). At the beginning of this book Galileo set himself a goal that was different but close to Zonca's: to use real machines and the practical experience of artisans to investigate the "reasons for effects that are not only wondrous, but also hidden and almost unthinkable."[38] Galileo's visits to the Arsenal of Venice and his frequent contacts with the *proti* (artisans) there led Galileo to consider them "capable of teaching many things to speculative theorists ... and in particular on matters relating to mechanics; here [in the Arsenal] every

36 "spender vanamente il tempo, le fatiche ed i denari"; "i molti comodi e di grandissima utilità"; "in diverse arti manuali dagli'istrumenti mecanici, ed altri se ne possono alla giornata sperare dai professori perfettamente intelligenti d'essa scienza macchinatrice"; "s'applicano a nuove invenzioni svegliati solamente da certo natural talento, ma privo della regioni mattematiche, le quai intrinsecamente dimostrano la natura dei primi e semplici strumenti dei quali le altre macchine si compongono" (G. Galilei, "A proposito di una macchina per pestare," *Le opere di Galileo Galilei*, vol. VIII [1933], p. 585); translation by the author with the help of Patrick Leech. See also pp. 321, 348. See also in the same volume, "A proposito di una macchina con gravissimo pendolo adattato ad una leva," pp. 571–84. On Galileo's patent see W. Theobald, "Ein Venezianisches Patent Galileo Galileis," *Beiträge zur Geschichte der Technik und Industrie*, vol. 17 (1927), 24–29.

37 B. Lorini, *Delle fortificationi* (Venice, 1596), pp. 171–172, 181.

38 "ragione di effetti non solo maravigliosi, ma reconditi ancora e quasi inopinabili" (G. Galilei, "Discorsi e dimostrazioni matematiche intorno a due nuove scienze," *Le opere di Galileo Galilei*, vol. VIII, p. 49). But it should be noted that the theoretical bases of the two new sciences had been developed during the fruitful years of his teaching in Padua. On the Venice Arsenale see M. Aymard, "L'arsenale e le conoscenze tecnico-marinaresche. Le Arti," *Storia della cultura veneta*, 3/II (1980), 289–315.

kind of instrument and machine is continually put to work by numerous great artisans. Learning from the observations made by their predecessors and by their own continual attempts at understanding, they arrive at highly expert and refined analysis."[39] No doubt belonging to this group of constructors or artisans (*proti*) of "very expert and very refined discourse" was that "good old man" to whom Sagredo – one of the leading figures in the *Discorsi* – attributes the assertion regarding machines that "one should not project from small to big, because many machine inventions work on a small scale, but not on a large one."[40] Based on this formulation Galileo proposed to demonstrate the mathematical reasons whereby "the larger machine, built with the same materials and the same proportions as the smaller one, in all other conditions would correspond with the right symmetry to the smaller one, except for robustness and resistance."[41]

I will not engage with Galileo's profound reflections, developed from the starting point of his analysis of levers to his investigation of the resistance of materials in the specific case of the shaft loaded to the top.[42] Instead I would like to point out that Zonca reached a conclusion similar to that of the "good old man" of the Arsenal. In one of the captions, he notes that when moving from drawing to constructing machines:

> you have to give the right proportion to all the parts, as this profession [architecture] teaches for every machine and construction, so that they will function without fail, because it has been seen that some constructions and machines, when made to operate, did not work. And this was clearly due to not having chosen the right measurements and understanding their proportions, *and this has happened to many people who made many models of machines which worked when they were small but did not succeed when larger, as you often see in constructions where the lever is used*, which is strong enough if it lifts the right proportion of weight but

39 "Largo campo di filosofare a gl'intelletti specolativi ... ed in particolare in quella parte che mecanica si domanda; atteso che quivi ogni sorte di strumento e di machina vien continuamente posta in opera da numero grande d'artefici, tra i quali, e per l'osservazioni fatte da i loro antecessori, e per quelle che di propria avvertenza vanno continuamente per sé stessi facendo, è forza che ve ne siano de i peritissimi e di finissimo discorso" (*Discorsi e dimostrazioni matematiche*, p. 51).

40 "non bisogna argumentare dalle piccole alle grandi, perché molte invenzioni di machine riescono in piccolo, che in grande non poi sussistono" (ibid.).

41 "la machina maggiore, fabbricata dell'istessa materia e con l'istesse proporzioni che la minore, in tutte l'altre condizioni risponderà con giusta simmetria alla minore, fuor che nella rubustezza e resistenza" (ibid.).

42 See Galluzzi, *Momento*, pp. 246–259.

> if it is too weak or if it is made to lift too heavy of a weight, it immediately buckles and breaks.
>
> *Novo teatro*, p. 108[43]

This comment is convoluted and does not state how proportions and measurements should actually be calculated. Rather, it sums up the centuries-long experience widespread among architects and builders of machines, which is also mentioned in Vitruvio.[44] Zonca knew that when moving from small to large dimensions, proportions needed to be redefined according to criteria that could not be purely geometric. The reference to levers could suggest knowledge of Galileo's work. But there is no proof of this because in a conceptually similar context both Lorini and a chapter from the pseudo-Aristotelian *Meccaniche* also refer to levers.[45]

So far I have connected Zonca's mechanical knowledge to treatises on mechanics. This list must also include those authors of books on machines who had already incorporated some paradigms of the principles of mechanics into their works. In addition to Vitruvio, these sources include Lorini – but with some doubt because he is never cited in *Novo teatro* – and Jacques Besson, author of *Theatrum instrumentorum et machinarum* (1569) which Zonca cites and read probably in the Italian translation of 1582.[46] Moving further back in

---

43 "se li devono dare tutte le sue parti proportionate, sì come questa Professione insegna, che si debba fare in ogni Machina, et Edifitio tale, acciò possino riuscire sicuramente, perché si sono veduti alcune volte Edifitij, e Machine, quali messi fuora in opera non <sono> riusciti, e di ciò s'è veduto chiaramente esser stato cagione il non haver ben partito le misure, e conosciuto le loro proportioni, *e questo è avenuto a molti che havendo fatto molti modelli di Machine, picciole sono riuscite, ma grandi non li sono altrimente riuscite, sì come spesso si vede nelli Edifitij dove entra la lieva*, la quale sta forte a quanto peso proportionatamente può sostentare, ma se aviene che sia debole, o che venghi ad esser troppo il soverchio della fatica, subito cede, e si rompe."

44 *De Architectura*, x 16. Vitruvio wrote: "Nonnulla vera sunt quae in exemplaribus videntur verisimilia, cum autem crescere dilabuntur" (but there are some which are promising in sample, but collapse when they begin to increase in scale"). There is no doubt that Zonca had this passage in mind as well as all of ch. 16 of *De Architettura*.

45 See the pseudo-Aristotelian *Meccaniche*, *Quaestio XVI*. In the introduction to *Fortificationi*, Lorini had criticized those "who trust in the ease shown by small models" and do not take into account the "effects of the lever". On this topic see S. Di Pasquale, "L'uso dei modelli nella costruzione della cupola di S. Maria del Fiore," *Atti del Dipartimento di Costruzioni dell'Università di Firenze*, (pre-print), February, 1984. Both Luca Pacioli and Leonardo were among those who considered the risks of constructing based on models.

46 On Besson's mechanics see A.G. Keller, "A Manuscript Version of Jacques Besson's Book of Machines with his Unpublished Principles of Mechanics," *On Pre-modern Technology and Science. Studies in Honor of Lynn White Jr.*, eds. Bert S. Hall and Delmo C. West (Los Angeles, 1976), pp. 75–103. We should also consider that O.V. Biringucci was advised to enrich his translation of *Parafrasi* by Piccolomini with "a collection of all the machines and instruments in use." But he had decided, as he states this in the dedication "To the

time, we encounter the most significant figure: Francesco di Giorgio Martini. The mechanical analysis of the relationship between weight on the circumference of a wheel and weight on the axle of the wheel, which I attributed to Guidobaldo and Galileo, could also have been adopted from the tradition of the *codici martiniani*. The same applies when Zonca explains how that relationship should be "practically" understood. Martini wrote:

> As I said before, if I put one *libra* of weight on the circumference of a wheel, how many *libre* can that shaft lift? Do as follows … let's say that the diameter of the wheel is ten arms, and the diameter of the shaft is one arm … first take half of the shaft that will be half an arm, and that much is the leverage of that shaft. Then take half of the diameter of the wheel that is five arms. Now look at how many times half an arm fits into five arms, which will be ten times, and that will be how much the shaft of that wheel will be able to lift. So you see, for each *libra* of weight on the circumference of the wheel, the shaft will lift ten *libre*.[47]

The analogies seem clear. This confirms Zonca's dependence on Martini, already shown by Ladislao Reti based on a comparison of drawings.[48] But this poses other questions. Where does Martini's mechanical knowledge come from? It seems obvious that he knew the writings of medieval authors on weights. But how did the *de ponderibus* works – all or some of them – get into the hands of the Sienese architect? To these questions there are still no answers. After all, the entire history of the "tradition" of Martini's drawings, preserved in dozens of codices, still has to be put in order, selected and interpreted. This work is a

readers," to treat this material "in a special book where I will put all sorts of machines, old and new, for water, weights, for grinding, and for war; and I will think about Vitruvio's last chapters which are so obscure. In this way study, experience and the experts in this profession will show me something more, and these mechanical principles of Aristotle will take hold and provide the basis for the book on machines".

47 "Mettendo siccom'è detto una libra di peso in su la circunferrenzia della ruota, quante libre in sullo stile levarà? Farai così … poniamo che sia una ruota ch'el diametro suo sia braccia dieci, e 'l diamitro dello stile braccia uno … in prima piglia el mezzo dello stile che sarà mezzo braccio, e tanto è la lieva del detto stile. Dipoi piglia el mezzo del diamitro della rota che viene a essare braccia cinque. Ora guarda un mezzo braccio quante volte entra in braccia cinque che v'entrarà volte dieci, é tanto arà di lieve in su lo stile la detta rota. Siccome vedi, per ogni libra di peso che serà in su la circunferenzia della ruota leverà libre dieci in su lo stile" (F. Di Giorgio Martini, *Trattati di architettura, ingegneria e arte militare*, ed. Corrado Maltese [Milan, 1967], I, pp. 141–142).

48 L. Reti, "Francesco di Giorgio Martini's Treatise on Engineering and its Plagiarists," *Technology and Culture*, IV (1963), 287–298.

necessary preparation for examining the sources on mechanics, both classical and medieval, of Francesco di Giorgio Martini and reconstructing his influence throughout the 16th century.[49]

Various voices can be heard in *Novo teatro*, not all of them clearly identifiable or separable. These voices define the genealogical density of the text, its intertexuality, and by their very ambiguity they provide a composite record of superimpositions that can be interpreted in different ways.

The steps for disassembling machines into their elemental parts, analysed earlier, are interwoven with other types of classifications, which acquire importance in the case of grain mills. In describing them, rather casually, Zonca proposes a brief taxonomic analysis of their "types" (*Novo teatro*, p. 15). The "types" of mill are distinguished first by whether they are set in motion by "animate forces" or "inanimate forces." While mills that have an "animated motor" are driven by "men, or animals of various species," the others, driven by inanimate forces, are moved by wind or water. Water-powered mills are of three types. 1) those called "in some places in Italy ... a Coppello" (with containers) are powered by mountain water collected in containers and "made to descend through canals"; 2) those with "dead water [perpetual motion] and various types of water tanks, which by themselves conduct the water to transmit motion"; and 3) mills powered "by running river water." The latter mills are of two distinct types: those at "ground-level," built "stably" on riverbanks, and those "built over boats," which "are in the middle of rivers and connected with chains to the shore or to a bridge." This basic taxonomy is then enriched with other important specifications. Mills powered by "animated bodies" (men or animals) are divided into three groups according to whether the movement comes from a vertical wheel, a sloping wheel or a wheel "parallel to the horizon" (*Novo teatro*, p. 26). Whereas wheels with containers received water from above, the others received it from below. Table 11.1 illustrates the different "types" of mills that are essentially based on the analysis of motors, or "forces" or "types," according to a method that was still applied at the beginning of the 19th century in famous treatises on mechanics.[50]

49 I have separated the scientific-mechanical tradition from the technological one for ease of explanation, but the two aspects should be analysed together.

50 M. Hachette wrote in the "Préface" to his *Traité élémentaire des machines* (Paris, 1811): "On sait que les seuls moteurs applicable aux machines sont les animaux, l'eau, le vent, les combustibles; la notion des ces moteurs détermine la forme des machines qui en reçoivent directement l'action" ("One knows that the only motors applicable to machines are animals, water, wind, combustibles ; knowledge of these motors determines the form of the machines which receive directly the action").

TABLE 11.1 'Force' or 'form' of mills (grain mills)

"Animate force"		"Inanimate force"				
Human	**Animal**	**Wind**	**Water**			
		(Wind mill)	Mountain water collected in containers (wheels take water from above)	"Dead Water"	"Running Water" (wheels take water from below)	
					Mills on land or immobile	Water mills or mobile

SOURCE: ZONCA, *NOVO TEATRO*, XXII

It would be interesting to reconstruct the historical process for the formation of this taxonomy. Here I limit myself to recalling that for centuries juridical science distinguished between mills on land ("immobile") and water mills ("mobile"). Since the time of Bartolo da Sassferrato, jurists had classified mills as mobile and immobile. This distinction had important consequences on the nature of property and its hereditary transmission.

Giovan Battista Ripa, a jurist from Pavia and contemporary of Zonca, summed up the dominant doctrine as follows. Only "immobile" mills, which as a rule could only be inherited through male lineage, could be enfeoffed. The others, "mobile" mills, which could even be sold informally by guardians, followed the female line.[51] This distinction suggests an interesting intersection between technological and juridical thought, a dialogue between two cultures often considered farther apart than they actually were.[52] It is not improbable that architects and engineers helped to clarify the different technical nature

51 G.B. Ripa, *In primam et secundam infortiati partem commentaria* (Venice, 1575), p. 64. There is a vast literature on this topic. See the bibliographies of J. Heringius, *De molendinis eorunque jure* (Lyon, 1625) (*Quaestiones* V *and* VI), and A. Gobius, *Tractatus de aquis* (Bologna, 1673). Contrary to prevalent belief, Baldo degli Ubaldi argued that all mills could be enfoeffed because "omnes res a quibus fructus percepitur inter immobilia computantur" ("all possessions are counted among the property of those who receive the income"). (F. Corti, *Tractatus feudorum*, [Cologne, 1562], part I, f. 25*v*).

52 Legal and water power interests are interwoven in the work by G.B. Barattieri, *Architettura d'acque* (Piacenza, 1656). Barattieri, "an educated engineer from Lodi," provides a brief

TABLE 11.2 Operation of machines

Moves on its own	On its own does not move (animate motion)			Or has inanimate motion			
	"With reason" (humans)		"Without reason" (animals)	Air		Fire	Water
				"free"	"closed"		
The "little figures … taught by ancient Greek Erone"	Machines for peace: pulleys, levers, wheels, hoists	Machines for war: battering ram protective screens mobile towers catapult slings	Moved by two- and four-wheeled wagons, metal drums, shafts, shields and reels.	Wind mill	a. "Movement spiritali" of Erone that "with the force of air produces different voices and sounds." b. Machines of Agricola for removing bad and noxious air from mines and inserting good air.	A turn-spit that operates by the "movements of smoke"	"Wheels to grind grain to saw wood, to press cloths, to 'pound' pieces to make paper to strike iron"

SOURCE: VITTORIO ZONCA, *NOVO TEATRO*, XXIII

historical sketch of the relationships between water-power and law starting with Bartolo. He believed that in dividing the land after floods "the work of a jurist" as well as that of "a surveyor" were necessary (p. 83). It is well known that for "visits" of waters, a water-power architect was often accompanied by a lawyer.

of mills, and jurists used these classifications to codify the distinctions in the conceptual categories of law.

But Zonca could not be satisfied with a taxonomy that – based on the notion of the (flour) mill – excluded other types of mills: paper mills, fulling mills, pressing mills, spinning mills and so on, Thus a second, more comprehensive classification was developed, based on the notion of "machine." This redefinition of the taxonomic principle tended to work around embarrassing aspects of the Italian language, which did not allow for the formation of words beginning with the term "mill," in order to cover a vast range of productive sectors. To understand the problem it is useful to bear in mind that in German *follo* (fulling mill) is *Walckmühle* (Mühle = mill); *maglio* (trip hammer) is *Hammermühle*; and *cartiera* (paper mill) is *Papiermühle*. Similar examples can be taken from English. In Italian, as in other Romance languages, with its stronger identification of mill with grinding grains, there is less flexibility for diversified semantic combinations.

In 1625 the German jurist Johannes Heringius compiled a taxonomy that defined mills according to: 1. 'type' (wind, hand, water, etc.); 2. 'matter' defined either as the material to be processed (*Öhlmühle* [oil]) or as the instrument used for production (*Stampfmühle* [stamp]).[53] Classifications of this type, which Heringius and subsequent German jurisprudence proposed, were never imitated or taken up by Italian jurists.[54] This significant absence helps us to understand Zonca's second taxonomic operation, from which emerged classifications based on different types of production, and therefore the role of processing machines.

According to this new classification (*Novo teatro*, p. 92) "All machines," whether for utility or for pleasure, were classified according to three fundamental types: 1. those "that move themselves"; 2. those "that do not move themselves"; and 3. those "that have beneath them certain things that give them movement." Proceeding from this preliminary systematization, Zonca constructed a series of sub-classes illustrated in Table 11.2. This table includes among the hydraulic machines, along with "wheels for grinding grain" (grain mills), also fulling mills, paper mills, bellows, saws and "other types" of machines. For organizational reasons, the flour mill is reduced to a place inside a small box.

53 J. Heringius, *De molendinis*. See *Quaestio v.*

54 Francesco Maria Pecchio – who knew and cited Heringius – acknowledged in his treatise *De molendinis* the existence of different types of mills. He wrote: "Plura enim sunt genera moendinorum" ("there are indeed many kinds of mills"). These included "molendinum fullonicum" ("the fulling mill") or "pannificium" ("cloth-making mill"), the mill "sericum et illud in quo pulvis tormentarius construitur" ("the silk mill and the one in which gunpowder is made"). But then he added that of these mills "non erit sermo in praesenti tractatu" ("will not be the topic of the present treatise"). His analysis is in fact limited to flour mills (F. M. Pecchio, *De aqueductu et molendinis*, t. III, lib. IV [Pavia, 1680], pp. 233 ff.).

In Zonca's comments on the drawings, in addition to the two general taxonomies he introduced other partial taxonomies. Thus screws are divided into three types: "screws with just one head (using the vocabulary of a master artisan) are usually used to move very heavy weights. ... Screws with two heads, these are used with arquebuses, so that they can remove the bullets from them. ... Screws with four heads are usually used with printing presses that print letters in books" (*Novo teatro*, p. 4).[55] Zonca actually expresses his intention to write a work on the differences among screws "and how they are made ... since no one else has dealt with this matter even though it is necessary" (*Novo teatro*, p. 66), despite it being mentioned in the works of Besson and Vitruvio.[56] Unfortunately this treatise on screws has not been found, and it may never have been written. This seems to be equally true for his research on "the manufacture of watches," which was supposed to be a part of – if I read correctly – the *Novo teatro* (p. 97). On various types of wheels, Zonca reports what he read in the pseudo-Aristotelian work, differentiating "three types of circular movement around their centers." In the first "the circumferences move around the centers, pulling them along like the movement of wagon wheels"; in the second movement "the same circumferences move around the same center, with the center staying still, like the wheels of pulleys"; in the third "the circumferences move around their centers, equidistant on the floor, where they are placed, as with the wheels for making clay vases" (*Novo teatro*, pp. 97–98).[57]

According to Franz Reuleaux, up until the end of the 17th century authors of books on machines considered "each machine as a whole, and the parts that composed it were made only for that machine. Thus they definitely did not have the idea, or had it only rarely, of differentiating those parts in the machines that we call mechanisms. A mill was a mill, a printing press was a printing press and nothing else. This is why in the old books we find each machine described separately from the others and with an analysis that goes from the first to the last component."[58] According to Reuleaux, only with

55 "Vite a un sol capo (per parlar con vocabolo maestrale) et queste si costumano ne i movimenti de i gravissimi pesi ... Vite a dui capi, et queste si fanno in servigio de gli archibugi, onde si cavano le palle da essi ... Vite a quattro capi, le quali si costumano fare ne i torchi, che stampano le lettere de i libri."

56 Galileo was also interested in the construction of screws. See letters from January 17 and August 23, 1602 in *Le opere di Galileo Galilei,* vol. X (1934), pp. 86 and 90. In Venice in 1615, the *De cochlea libri quattuor* by Guidobaldo was published. On the history of screws see W. Treue, *Kulturgeschichte des Schraube* (Munich, 1955). On screws with four threads, which Zonca had perhaps described first, see M. Audin, "L'imprimerie," *Histoire générale des techniques*, t. II, *Les premiéres étapes du machinisme*, ed. M. Daumas (Paris, 1965), p. 670.

57 A similar description can be found in the pseudo-Aristotelian *Meccaniche. Quaestio VIII*.

58 F. Reuleaux, *Cinématique. Principes fondamentaux d'une théorie génerale des machines*, translated from German by A. Debize (Paris, 1877), pp. 10–1.

Leupold's great multi-volume work which began to appear in 1724 do we see representations of mechanisms separated from the machines. I think I can state that *Novo teatro* already demonstrates a departure from the idea that every machine is a unique composition in its category.[59]

It is difficult for us now to perceive the (relative) novelty of Zonca's thoughts, marginalized since their publication by the great scientific debates of the time and irreparably hidden by the successive cultural stratifications. The link between theory and practice, like that between science and technology, is a theme that no longer surprises us. Zonca affirms this link, which before Francis Bacon was one of the motifs of writers of mechanics, and which he practiced because it was inherent in his professional qualification. As he acted, so would "all those mechanics who understand the theories and principles of the Machines. And where there are difficulties in those [machines] they will know to increase or to diminish power in their operations, and as to their parts, according to where they should be installed, and if there is appropriate need" (*Novo teatro*, pp. 43–44).[60]

But who are these mechanics? Zonca does not answer this question directly. The sparse annotations in *Novo teatro* offer a sketch not unlike those of other writers and architects such as Guidobaldo, Piccolomini, Pigafetta, Barbaro, and Lorini outlined in the second half of the 16th century. The mechanic is not a *uomo 'mechanico'* (mechanical man) nor is he a pure mathematician. In addition to the principles of mechanics, he has to be able to draw and have a certain practical experience: in short, judgment. His professional profile, similar to that of architects and engineers, is not defined by what he can do with his hands, but by the knowledge of mathematical science and design applied to the manual crafts.[61] Only the connection between these different fields of knowledge could enable one to accomplish those "various and secure operations" that are, as clearly expressed in the subtitle [Machines and Buildings], the book's ultimate purpose.

All the considerations expressed so far could provide the outline of the basic structure of the text. In other words, my reflections may clarify the categories

59 Leonardo had already accomplished the same operation, but at a very different level of detail and completeness. See L. Reti, "Technology," under *Leonardo da Vinci, Dictionary of Scientific Biography*, ed. Ch. Coulston Gillespie (New York, 1970–1976).

60 "tutti quei mecanici, i quali intenderanno le teoriche, et le ragioni delle Machine. Et dove in quelle occorreranno difficoltà sapranno nell operationi accrescere, <o> diminuire le forze, et i membri loro, secondo i luoghi ove si collocheranno, et il bisogno opportuno."

61 See P. Rossi, *I filosofi e le macchine (1400–1700)* (Milan, 1962), pp. 11–67. For the history of the word "mechanic" see M.L. Altieri Biagi, "'Vile mecanico'," *Lingua nostra*, XXVI, 1965, dossier 1, 1–12.

the author used to construct his own discourse. However, it would be wrong to reduce the interpretation of the text to these categories, omitting the work's discordances and conflicts. The staging of *Novo teatro* is not abstractly unitary. It is composed of a myriad of intertextual weavings, insertions and tensions. In fact, the text oscillates between two approaches. On the one hand we have the author's citations and drawings copied (or imitated) from other drawings. On the other, the drawings represent things he observed, machines he saw working in actual places, in urban or rural settings sometimes specifically indicated. Close examination reveals that eleven of the drawings were copied from other drawings. Who originally made those drawings is not stated, with one exception: "New invention of mills for grinding, transported onto the battlefield. Invented by Signor Pompeo Targone, engineer of the Most Excellent Signor Ambrosio Spinola, general of the Catholic Majesty in Flanders." This drawing (between pp. 88 and 89) has no glossary; nor does the drawing that immediately precedes it: "Machine that transports soil from one place to another," also attributed to a military engineer.[62] The two machines for "turning spits" refer to a printed book, *Arte di cucinare* (*The Art of Cooking*) by Bartolomeo Scappi, "the secret cook" of Pope Pius V.[63]

We know for certain that the last seven drawings of *Novo teatro* were diligently copied from Francesco di Giorgio Martini's treatises. It is impossible to know which of Martini's codices Vittorio used. I like to think it was the one in the University Library of Padua. Of all Martini's manuscripts that I have consulted, the one in Padua is the only one that contains a rapid sketch of what in *Novo teatro* is called "Mill moved by animal power" (p. XXVI). This drawing does not belong to the Martini tradition and could have been sketched by Zonca himself.[64]

62 We know only of one work by Pompeo Targone, *Les inventions et machines admirables du sieur Pompée Targon intendant des ingenieurs de France Dressés de nouveau contre la ville de la Rochelle* (Paris, 1622).

63 B. Scappi, *Opera* (Venice, 1596). One of the two machines had already been drawn by Leonardo (Edizione Nationale dei Manoscritti e dei Disegni di Leonardo, *Il Codice Atlantico*, diplomatic and critical transcription by A. Marinoni, vols. I–XII [Florence, 1975–1980], f. 21 back, vol. I, p. 58). Table II (p. 13) of "Gates to contain water" (p. 12) which Zonca copied from life (at Dolo or Stra), had also been drawn by Leonardo (*Il Codice Atlantico*, f. 656 r.-a, vol. VIII, pp. 90–1).

64 The attribution to Martini is improbable. The codex (B.U.P., Ms. 764, f. 111*r*) arrived in a mutilated state. It contains numerous drawings, but not the text. The code was purchased in the 19th century from a Venetian antique shop. I am grateful to Alexander Keller and Raffaele Vergani who drew my attention to this manuscript.

In other drawings direct observation is always present, yet this does not exclude the influence of models and literary suggestions. Several times Zonca explicitly indicates where he conducted the observation. Thus when he describes the *vita perpetua* (endless screw) capable of lifting "very heavy weights" – up to 20,000 *libbre* – he states that after being used at "a very large plant in the city of Padua," it was "completely replaced by the use of winch and pulleys that did the same work" (*Novo teatro*, p. 1). The second machine, in which horsepower replaced human energy, is described as "very easy ... and inexpensive," and "more practical" than the *vita perpetua* it replaced (*Novo teatro*, p. 7). On the "sluices to contain the water of some rivers for various needs" (*Novo teatro*, p. 9), Zonca says that they were similar to the locks constructed on the Brenta River and on the "division of the Brenta ... for navigating to Venice" (*Novo teatro*, p. 11); the first lock was near Padua and the other two at Stra and Dolo. The *Carro delle Zaffosina*, the mechanical device at Fusina used to lift boats and transfer them from the Brenta river to the Lagoon, was five miles from Venice (*Novo teatro*, p. 59).[65] At the border of the lagoon of Venice, near Fusina, Zonca saw – as had the German architect Heinrich Schickhardt before him – the "Wheel to raise water" for supplying Venice (*Novo teatro*, p. 62).[66] The two architects drew the essential mechanisms of the structure in so similar a manner that leaves no doubt of its location, which Zonca did not indicate. We already know that the "Machine to full cloth" (p. 43) was located in Padua. The "Mill made with animal motion" ground "wheat in the city of Venice rather conveniently" (p. 26).[67]

---

65 The idea of drawing both the locks on the Brenta and the mechanism at Fusina could have been suggested by Piccolomini's *Parafrasi*, where both constructions are cited and partially analyzed (*Parafrasi di Monsignor Alessandro Piccolomini*, pp. 61 and 65). It was said about the locks at Dolo – according to a malicious rumor reported by Zonca – that it was superfluous for navigating and was there "for nothing else than to make the clearer water go to Venice's lagoon to prevent it from alteration" (*Novo teatro*, p. 11).

66 On the supply of water to Venice, see M. Costantini, *L'acqua di Venezia. L'approvvigionamento idrico della serenissima* (Venice, 1984). Schickhardt's drawing was published by M. Eckoldt, "Der Brenta-Kanal bei Venedig in der deutschen Reise und Fachliteratur des 16–19 Jahrhunderts," *Technik Geschichte*, xxxv, 1968, no. 2, p. 92. Schickhardt had also rapidly drawn the *Carro di Fusina*. On the wheel to "raise the water" of the Brenta see also G. Ceredi, *Tre discorsi sopra il modo d'alzar acque da' luoghi bassi* (Parma, 1567), p. 17.

67 The existence and (relative) frequency of this type of mill in the Po valley, Venice (near the church of Saints Giovanni and Paolo), Turin, and Barcone (Piacenza) is attested to by several 16th century authors including Giuseppe Ceredi (*Tre discorsi*, p. 50). See A. G. Keller's interesting article "The Oblique Treadmill of the Renaissance: Theory and Reality," *Transactions of the International Symposium on Molinology*, 2 (Viborg, 1971), 225–231. According to G.A. Borgnis (*Traité complet de mécanique appliquée aux arts* (Paris, 1818), p. 33) this mill was still common "dans la Romagne et dans plusieurs autres provinces

In the absence of explicit textual indications and other convincing sources, such as Schickhardt's drawing, it is better not to add to this list. Nevertheless we can reasonably affirm that the majority – twenty in all – of the remaining drawings refer to the area around Venice, without excluding the existence of drawings of machines located in other areas. One could conclude that Zonca sketched "his" machines from observation, in the same way that he drew maps. Unlike Francesco di Giorgio Martini, he made no pretence of originality.[68] It is no coincidence that his name never appears in the registers of the Senate of Venice requesting patents and privileges as an inventor of new machines.[69] On the contrary, he frequently drew on acquired knowledge, common practice and the opinions of "masters." Thus the wheels of water-powered mills should have a diameter "of twelve to fourteen feet" according to a "proportion ... [that] is commonly used for everything," and should turn "toward the right, since this is also common practice" (*Novo teatro*, p. 16).[70] The handle of the "Machine for sharpening weapons" had to have "a bend as is the ordinary custom" (p. 40). To determine the number of "fins" ("wings") on water wheels, one should accept the view and the "judgment of the Master" (*Novo teatro*, p. 31).[71] In the description of the *Mangano per dare il lustro* (a pressing machine to full the cloth), he emphasizes the importance of the "role of workers" because that is what "the Masters say" (*Novo teatro*, p. 54). Regarding presses "for making wine," Zonca declares that they could be "seen in many places, because they have been in use for a long time" (*Novo teatro*, p. 48).

These homages to current practice are significant. But it would be wrong to conclude that Zonca limited himself to copying indiscriminately what he saw.

---

d'Italie." This is a curious piece of information and in spite of research conducted in Romagna, I have not been able to verify it. Perhaps the information was imprecise.

68 F. di Giorgio Martini, *Trattati*, pp. 492–493.

69 This assertion is based on the register of all industrial privileges issued by the Senate of Venice from 1570 to 1610. This investigation is part of a broader research project financed by the C.N.R. (National Council of Research). See R. Berveglieri, C. Poni, "Three Centuries of Venetian Patents (1474–1796)," *Acta Historiae Rerum Naturalium necnon Technicarum*, special number 17 (Prague, 1982), 381–391.

70 Zonca, see also pp. 19, 31, 83, and 87. Only in one case – when he describes a wheel with containers for collecting water – does Zonca present (p. 23) wheels with a much bigger diameter: 16–20 feet. On the size of water wheels and for other important aspects of flour mills see L. Makkai, "Productivité et exploitation des sources d'energie (XVIe–XVIIe siécles)," *Produttività e tecnologie nei secoli XII–XVII*, ed. S. Mariotti, Istituto Internazionale di Storia Economica F. Datini di Prato, Atti delle 'Settimane di Studio', vol. 3 (Florence, 1981), pp. 163–181.

71 On the same page he asserts that the "master" would also have to decide on the number of *bolzonelli* (spokes) to insert on the water wheel. Sometimes the "master" is not the artisan who constructs the machine, but the person who runs it (p. 83).

On the contrary, he selected, modified, and improved. Among the "types" of mills he chose as the "best" and the "most used" were those "so necessary for human life" (*Novo teatro*, p. 15). In the description of the "Wheel for hollowing out lead for glass windows" he states that "of the many similar machines I have seen, this is one of the most beautiful and ornate" (*Novo teatro*, p. 80). On the other hand the drawing of the *Carro* near Fusina was instead modified to improve its functioning and "not complicate the right side" (*Novo teatro*, p. 60). The fulling mill in Padua, whose measurements he calculated, was improved by adding a second wheel with containers which would mechanically conduct water to a point at which it would become an essential part of the production process. This functional combination, which often escaped readers' attention, brings to mind many questions. Did he see this? Or is this Zonca's only silent invention? Sometimes the literary source and the observation of reality overlap, with interesting results. Thus Zonca invites the reader to compare the "Wheel to raise water," referring as we know to direct observation, to a similar machine of Vitruvio, whose conception he implicitly disapproved (*Novo teatro*, pp. 62–63). The "Machine to grind powder for cannons" is presented as a variation of a machine published by Giorgio Agricola (*Novo teatro*, p. 86).

This method of selection, of inclusion and exclusion, merits closer attention. It reveals processes of centralization and unification with which a formal grounding of technical knowledge is obtained. This contrasts with the actual pluralities, particularities and discordances of actual techniques. The object or the machine chosen is appropriated and modified in the drawing, invested with specific mechanical theories, taken out of its social background, inscribed into particular taxonomic sequences, and integrated into the structure of the treatise. This is Zonca's "theater", both counterposed to and at the same time tied to the multifarious reality from which it is separated.

In *Novo teatro* the centralizing effort is both constantly disputed and systematically defended. Thus the *"tavola" del torchio per stampare* (the table of the printing press) should be "cast in metal so that it is smoother and the letters printed evenly." It would not be advisable to make it either of wrought iron – "since it would not be possible to flatten it equally with the hammer" – or of stone – because it is – "breakable" – and not even of wood. But whoever would want to make it out of wood would have to use olive wood (p. 65). The pivots of the wheel used "to hollow the lead" must be "made of a single piece together with the wheel, and pounded ... and of good steel." If they were welded to the wheel they would not last long "nor ever compare to those made of one piece"

(*Novo teatro*, p. 80).[72] In the *Soppressa per dar il lustro a le tele* (press to polish canvas) one should not use "iron nails but ... wooden pegs so that when closed the plates are smoother and even" (*Novo teatro*, p. 46). The *Trombe da ruota per cavar acque* (Containers to extract water), round in the drawing, could also be made square "and perhaps will be more secure and more easy to make as I have seen, and they are amazingly successful" (*Novo teatro*, p. 111). And the container with which "to extract water" could have a different form from that in the drawing and made "longer, triangular, or with the rims more curved so as to hold a greater amount of water" (*Novo teatro*, p. 113). In short, along with the repeated emphases on centralizing and uniformity in the discourse, there continually emerges a recognition of the plurality and decentralized nature of technical solutions. It is evident that the forces of technological centralization of *Novo teatro* operate in an environment of factual plurality, with reference to a complex stratification that represents only one aspect. And that is the "best" aspect and its dominant character, Zonca emphasizes, because it ensures "varied and secure operations" within a reality that is multiple.[73]

The turn to pluralism reappears in the technical vocabulary which combines Greek, Latin and vernacular (Italian) terms, and also the jargon and/or dialect of the *maestri*. Thus *ergata*, a scholarly Greek term, is translated into *argana* (hoist or winch) as "the vulgar call it," if it is made up of a circular shaft standing upright. If, however, the circular shaft is parallel "to the ground," some would call it *sucula* (from Vitruvio) but the more modern ones would use "*naspo* [reel], or *molinello* [mill]," or "*cavallette, capre* or *gaverne* [jargon for winches], and in those places where it is necessary to let water drain slowly ... *sborradori*" (*Novo teatro*, p. 10).[74]

These frequent superimpositions make Zonca's style difficult, with the complicated and varied paths in his discourse. In little more than a page – the average length of his descriptions – one sees terms from the principles of

---

72 Even the bend of the "iron handle [crank]" of the "machine to sharpen weapons" had to be "pounded with a hammer and not welded out of two pieces, because there was the risk, while using it, that it would break" (p. 40).

73 I constructed the relationship between the factual plurality of techniques and the centralizing effect of the "theater" by freely using the considerations on the language-dialect relationship developed by M. Bakhtin, *Estetica e romanzo* (Turin, 1979).

74 On the richness of Zonca's lexical material see M.L. Altieri Biagi, *Galileo e la terminologia tecnico-scientifica* (Florence, 1965). More in general on technical terminology see G. Hollister-Short, "The Vocabulary of Technology," *History of Technology*, Second Annual Volume (1977), 125–155, and M.L. Biagi, "La prospettiva storico-linguistica nella ricerca sulla scuola galileiana," *La Scuola galileiana. Prospettive di ricerca*, eds. G. Arrighi, P. Galluzzi, M. Torrini, E. De Angeli and L. Belloni (Florence, 1979), pp. 165–177.

mechanics, from the *maestri* and from the *pratici* (practicians), together with reflections on common usage, on measurements. A whole world, still disorganized, crowds onto these pages with its own demands, to which the author concedes a strong, albeit subordinated yet intriguing, expressive autonomy.

These relationships guarantee, in their extreme dialogical variety, the materiality and individuality (although reformulated and emphasized) of the drawings of structures and machines. These detailed descriptions further enable the viewer to better perceive these machines, as many examples indicate. Water wheels should be made of oak, with the exception of the fins [parts of the water wheel in contact with water] which should be made of fir, a tender and light wood (*Novo teatro*, pp. 20 and 32); millstones should be made of "Istrian stone" (*Novo teatro*, p. 84); for "for the mechanism that turns the *spiedi* (spit), "thin tinplates" from Germany should be used (*Novo teatro*, p. 93);[75] the *vasi* (receptacles) of the machine that grind "the powder for the cannons" should be of "high quality metal so that when you grind it the powder does not catch fire and burn up, as happened sometimes when they were made of other material" (*Novo teatro*, p. 87). In constructing the sluice gates one should be aware "that wood in water never swells in length, but swells in thickness";[76] therefore the single planks and pieces should be assembled "diagonally" so that the effects of humidity and swelling would not impede "the gates from closing" (p. 11).

Less numerous are the calculations of the cost of installing the machines. A "mill moved by animal power" would cost "approximately four hundred *scudi*" (*Novo teatro*, p. 27). A "press to make oil" would cost three hundred ducats, sixty of which "for the work of the *maestri*" (*Novo teatro*, p. 52). The cost of a silk mill with four *varghi* (processing compartments) according to the estimate of "some who have had these machines made" was "one hundred ducats without the wheels, *timpani* (shields) and *rochelli* (bobbins) that are outside the spinning machine" (*Novo teatro*, p. 72). The profitability of machines is analyzed only once. According to the *practici* who had first-hand knowledge, with a "mill moved by animal power" based on an average production of ten bushels of wheat per day, it was possible to earn 15 *lire* plus 30 *libbre* of flour, against a daily cost of one *zecchino*, equal to the cost of maintaining two pair of oxen,

75 More than once Zonca shows admiration or consideration for "German inventions" (pp. 89 and 86). Giuseppe Ceredi also praised German techniques (*Tre discorsi*, pp. 13–4, 32–3, 45).

76 "di buon metallo, accioché pestando la polvere non getti fuoco, et s'abbruggi, come è intervenuto alcuna volta, quando sono stati fatti d'altra materia"; "che 'l legno stando in acqua per l'humidità non cresce mai per la sua longhezza, ma ben si gonfia per la sua grossezza."

the miller's pay and duties (*Novo teatro*, p. 27). For another machine, "*l'argana* for teasling woolen cloth," Zonca clearly points out its economic advantages. By using it, "one man in a short amount of time can work on many lengths of cloth and much better than the Masters were accustomed to do in the past, because after raising their arms to hang up the cloth they had to pull it down to teasle it, all with great exertion and much cost" (*Novo teatro*, p. 97).[77]

Having demonstrated the intertextual complexity of the *Novo teatro*, I should turn to an analytical examination of individual drawings. But that is beyond the scope of this work. Instead I will concentrate on one drawing: the silk mill (*Novo teatro*, pp. 68–75, images p. 68 and 74). This round-shaped machine marks the high point of technology in the Po valley and in Europe between the 14th and 18th centuries, which justifies this choice. It already represents the factory system (especially in the evolved form of the silk mills "alla bolognese").[78] The entire process of production, with the sole exception of doubling, was mechanized. The task of the workers (men and boys) was to feed the machines and tie the threads when they broke. We do not know how or where Zonca managed to observe "his" silk mill, which differed from those "alla bolognese." Nonetheless, the decision to publish the silk mill – new and essentially different from the tradition of the illustrations of Martini or Leonardo – is consistent with the emphatic open-mindedness of the *Novo teatro* to processing machines.

On the external circumference of Zonca's silk mill formed by two *varghi* (processing compartments, one above the other), were 36 *naspi* (reels) (18 per *vargo*) on which 216 threads (6 threads for each reel) were twisted and wound contemporaneously. I note that Zonca did not draw the machine from an external point of observation (whatever that would be). He first separated the *ghirlanda* ("garland," the inner part), that is the mechanism that transmits movement, from the (external) processing machine in which it was contained. In the two drawings he clearly distinguishes both the inner part and the external processing machine from the water wheel (the power source). This significant

77 This machine (gig mill) had been prohibited by law in England in 1552 (P. Mantoux, *La révolution industrielle au XVIII siécle* [Paris, 1959], p. 424). It was only in 1672 that at Schio (Vicenza) the first fabric brusher powered by a water wheel appeared (W. Panciera, "Articolazione della produzione e livelli tecnologici delle manifatture laniere di Schio nella seconda metà del secolo XVIII," *Quaderni Storici*, vol. 20, no. 59 [1985], 403–426). Writing about another machine, the "wheel-powered containers for drawing out water," Zonca asserts that "it will ease workers' efforts by one half" because "a man alone at the wheel will do more than two with a *strambucho*" (*Novo teatro*, p. 111).

78 On silk mills see Poni, *La seta in Italia*, ch. 1. For details on the technological and organizational differences between the different types of silk mills see Poni, "Piccole innovazioni e filatoi a mano: Venezia (1550–1600)," *Studi in memoria di Luigi Dal Pane*, pp. 371–389.

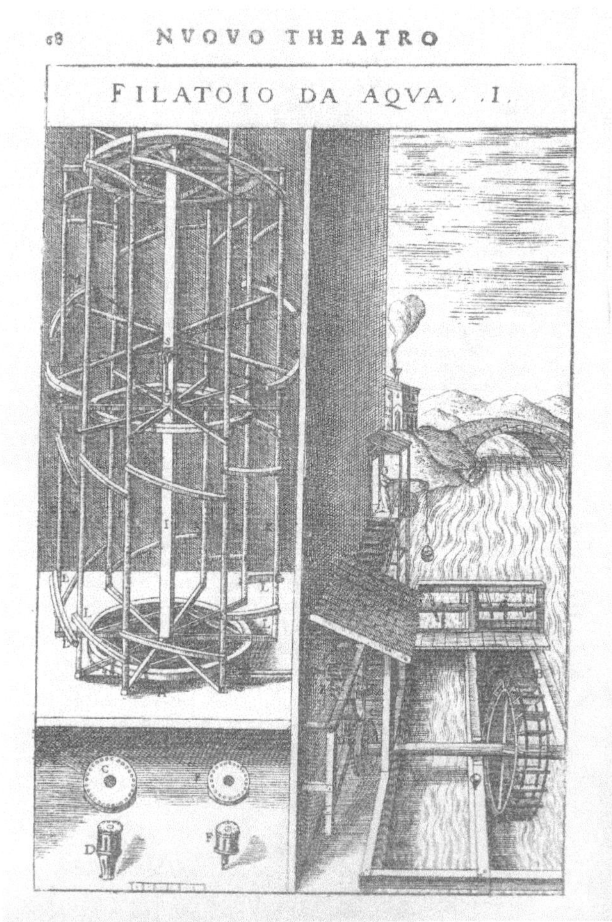

FIGURE 11.4 Water-powered silk mill I
SOURCE: ZONCA, *NOVO TEATRO*, P. 68

analysis occurs only once in *Novo teatro* and only for this machine. This was not by chance. If Zonca had not proceeded in this way, if he had simply presented the machine as it was, the drawing would not have depicted – and one would not be able to read – the individual parts of the various mechanisms. But the moment he carried out his reflection on the separation of the parts of the machine he struck at the heart of its fundamental originality, namely the autonomous functioning of the mechanism that transmits movement and the separation of this mechanism from the hydraulic wheel and the (external) processing machine.

FIGURE 11.5 Water-powered silk mill II
SOURCE: ZONCA, *NOVO TEATRO*, P. 74

Zonca is acutely aware of the importance of the operation carried out that he uses and emphasizes it in the written text. First he analyzes the "*ghirlanda* structure" (the machine that transmits movement), and only after having described it fully does he begin to analyze the "other structure that encircles it, which contain the *varghi* within which the rows of reels and bobbins operate."[79]

79 Before Zonca, only the German architect H. Schickhardt had managed to analyze a silk mill in detail. See his ingenious sketch in Poni, *La seta in Italia*, image 8 (between pp. 296 and 297).

But this high level of awareness has its limits and weaknesses. For example Zonca did not choose the model well (perhaps he could not do otherwise). Already by the 16th century, maybe earlier, the structure of the silk mill in Bologna had attained a particularly high technological level with the introduction of mechanical winders and bobbins to spin quality organzine. These innovations, jealously guarded by the city of Bologna (spies who attempted to divulge the secret were threatened with the death penalty), were brought to Venice only in 1604, when Ottavio Malpigli from Modena asked the doge for the privilege for the silk mill "alla bolognese" (equipped with bobbins and mechanical winding).[80] Due to the opposition of the Venetian spinners who felt threatened by this decidedly labor-saving machine, it took eight months to obtain the patent. It is unlikely that Zonca's drawing – without bobbins and mechanical winding–was taken from Malpigli's licence. A hypothesis of this sort comes up against insurmountable chronological and technical difficulties. By the end of the 16th century numerous Bolognese "machinists", in challenging the prohibition, had introduced the technical know-how of their mill into other areas (such as Modena, Trento and Faenza), so it would not be rash to assert that the flow of information from Bologna had reached Padua, possibly in incomplete form. The fact that in the San Giacomo parish in Padua where Zonca lived there was a spinning mill where the "spinner Vincenzo Bologna" resided hints at a trail worth exploring.[81] Nevertheless I do not believe this should lead us to change the date of 1634 as the beginning of the widespread diffusion of silk mills "alla bolognese" in the Venetian state.[82] In other areas of Italy's Po valley this machine was introduced even later, as in Piedmont, where Giovan Francesco Galleani obtained the patent in 1674.[83] And it was only in 1718, after a period of industrial espionage in Italy (probably in Piedmont), that John Lombe introduced it in England, building a large silk mill in Derby (with mechanical winding and bobbins), described by Paul Mantoux as "une véritable usine, la première qui ait existé en Angleterre" ("a veritable factory, the

80 Archivio di Stato di Venezia, *Senato Terra*, b. 172. Malpigli's request was registered on March 10, 1604. See also Poni, *La seta in Italia*, ch. 6.

81 Vincenzo Bologna is recorded as having baptised his daughter Maria on May 19, 1591, in Padua'sArchivio Vescovile e Biblioteca Capitolare di Padova (hereafter A.V.B.C.P.), *Registri delle parrocchie soppresse, S. Giacomo, Baptizatorum 1564–1596; mortuorum 1578–1596*, reg. 1, unnumbered sheet in the year listed. On July 25, 1596 one "Giuliano da Bologna, spinner" had baptized his daughter Altobella (ibid. in the year listed).

82 Poni, *La seta in Italia*, ch. 6, pp. 266 ff.

83 Poni, see in this volume, ch. 7, pp. 189, 206–7.

first that existed in England").[84] This innovation was so prized that in 1732 the English parliament granted Thomas Lombe – John's heir – the sum of 14,000 pounds sterling as an award for merits acquired and for renouncing the patent. But was such a large sum really justified? And was it really necessary to cross the Channel and the Alps to obtain the know-how of Italian silk mills? Would it not have been sufficient to use Zonca's drawings? Some time ago Sir George Clark, posing these questions, pointed out that a copy of *Novo teatro* has been in the Bodleian Library (Oxford) since 1620 on one of the shelves "accessible to any reader."[85]

To this question, which was never resolved, one must respond "yes": it was necessary to cross the Channel, and for several good reasons. We must remember that John and Thomas Lombe's silk mill, defined in English sources as "alla piemontese" (in the 18th century this name indicated an improved mill compared to the Bolognese model), was more complex and different from Zonca's. In addition to the mechanical winder and reels (as in the mills "alla bolognese") it also contained several small innovations that improved its operation.[86] This simple fact suffices to justify Lombe's espionage travels. To this one can add, paraphrasing *Novo teatro,* that Zonca got rather lost in the "beautiful, marvellous. ... water-powered spinning plant," and its many movements of "wheels, shafts, casters"[87] Certainly the separation between the processing machine and the machine that transmitted movement gave to the drawing a high level of clarity. But despite this choice Zonca did not succeed in analyzing correctly the connections between the two machines at three crucial points, corresponding to three crucial errors.

The first error relates to the *tiranti* (tie-rods) of the *straffinazzi* (modern word, *strofinazzo,* counterweights) that are set in the wrong place. If the *ghirlanda* (inner structure) turns from left to right, they should be placed at the other end

84 P. Mantoux, *La révolution industrielle*, p. 189. See also W.H. Chaloner, *People and Industries*, (London, 1963), pp. 8–20.

85 G. Clark, *Science and Social Welfare in the Age of Newton* (Oxford, 1969), pp. 37–38.

86 The differences between Piedmontese and Bolognese silk mills were first identified by F. Robecchi, "Insediamenti produttivi bresciani nel Settecento. Mulini da seta e preindustrializzazione," *Le alternative del Barocco* (Brescia, 1981), p. 289. The differences are in "small" details.

87 On the disconcerting complexity of silk mills we have the beautiful testimony of Cristobal de Villalon (who visited Bologna around the middle of the 1500s). According to Villalon, Bologna's silk mills were "una gerigonza que yo no la se explicar mas de que es un sutilissimo ingenio" ("'a jargon' that I cannot explain more than that it is a very subtle ingenuity") (*Viaje de Turquia* [Madrid, 1919], p. 102). A few years ago Marcel Bataillon proposed to attribute *Viaje de Turquia* to Andrea Laguna. See J. Lafaye, *L'itinéraire intellectuel de Marcel Bataillon: du sens litteral à la mémoire de Marcel Bataillon* (Paris, 1979), pp. 72 ff.

of the counterweight, and not where they are found.[88] The second error is that the "*cintura di corame* (leather belt), that is placed outside the *fusi de' rochelli* (spindles of the bobbins) to twist the silk," Z, is drawn only as a detail. It never appears, neither in its function as a rotating band, nor in the drawing of the processing machine or the machine that transmits power. Given this absence, it could not be easy to determine where the belt should be placed nor how it would function. The third error is a series of misunderstandings about how the reels functioned. The *ruota dentata* or *stella fissa* (gear wheel or "fixed star") G is not placed where it should be, in the center of the *bolzoniera* (spoked wheel) but on the outside. Even the smaller gear wheel H, to be affixed to the linchpin of the reel, is not where it should be, below and not above the gear wheel G, which moves it. With the help of glossaries and comments that correct some of the errors of the drawing it would have been possible to put the gear wheel G back in the center of the *bolzoniera.* But it is more difficult to determine the correct position of the second gear wheel H, even though Zonca's comment confirms that the drawing of this wheel is "flawed" (although he does not say how). These errors are resolved incorrectly in the overall drawing, where the axles of the reels are fixed directly to the center of the *bolzoniera*, whereas the gear wheels H no longer have any function and are hanging to the left of the reels.[89]

Apart from these errors, which only expert technicians (such as the Bolognese machinists or as John Lombe became) could have corrected, a more general observation of the drawings should be made. From these drawings presented in a natural perspective, it would not have been possible to construct any machine without the contribution of the knowledge and practical experience of the *maestri*, "experts" and "mechanics" to whom the *Novo teatro* was addressed (but who were not necessarily the purchasers of the book).

88 To more easily understand Zonca's mistakes on the spinning mill – too tall in Image I on p. 68 (Image 11.4) and very much out of proportion to the Image II on p. 74 (Image 11.5) – compare it to the image of the silk mill in the *Encyclopédie* (see Image 13.2 p. 357). There are other errors in the drawing in *Novo teatro*. For example, door B of the lock (p. 9) opens in the wrong direction (towards the outside instead of inside). But I believe most of the errors are concentrated in the two figures of the spinning mill.

89 I could not have carried out this detailed analysis without the precious help of a group of technical experts from the Istituto Tecnico Industriale Aldini Valeriani in Bologna, who constructed a large functioning model of a silk mill. Along with these experts I would like to thank Roberto Curti, Director of the Museum "Macchine, Scuola, Industria" in Bologna, who promoted the initiative, and Flavio Crippa, Director of the Museo Civico-Setifico of Abbadia Lariana (Como), who communicated to me penetrating observations of the technical details of silk mills and Zonca's errors.

Regarding the "machine to grind powder" Zonca wrote: "this device is very beautiful, and easy, and so clear, that any mediocre *maestro* would know how to build it" (*Novo teatro*, p. 86). And in another passage, commenting on the "structure to raise and drain out water": "in a single view one cannot show all the effects, nor all the parts of the instrument, but it is enough so the experts can easily understand all the parts and operations" (*Novo teatro*, p. 101).[90] Since all (or nearly all) the drawings depict just one view, we can conclude that only "experts" could have used the drawings of machines to go from observation to execution, with the help of information and instructions in the captions, glossaries, drawings of sub-groups and proportions to scale.

Thus Zonca created a complicated exchange with the masters. On the one hand, as shown in the previous pages, they provided him with information that is woven into *Novo teatro*. On the other hand they received a body of knowledge in return – modified by its impact with theory – which "still" needed their collaboration to be put into practice. This latter qualification functions at the margins of the text like an apparently innocent and obvious referral to the outside. But it is instead full of meaning. It traces the borders of an opaque zone: the masters' ability to construct, that remains beyond the scope of *Novo teatro* and is not revealed. The silence surrounding that jealous know-how that apprentices learned during their long years in the workshops, represents an implicit acknowledgement of the secrets of the trade and the authority of the masters. The procedures of initiation and transmission of the innermost secrets of "worker" knowledge are neither communicated nor altered. Instead they operate within a complex cultural exchange that, precisely because of this absence of communication, creates the network of reciprocal services connecting the author and the masters. This relationship cannot exist where the exchange of knowledge is used to violate and expropriate the "talismanic" knowledge that must only be passed on through codified rites and initiations.

This mode of exchange of knowledge as it appears in *Novo teatro* is in contrast to that found in the great *Encyclopédie*. Denis Diderot would have wanted to divulge "all the professional secrets" of artisans "sans aucune exception" ("without exception"), given his profound desire for knowledge. Instead he had to contend with workers' suspicion of inquiries and "l'absurdité de leurs mensognes" ("the absurdity of their lies").[91] The artisans refused to transform

---

90 "Edificio per alzare, et seccare l'acque"; "in una sol vista non si possono mostrare tutti gli effetti, né meno tutte le parti dell'instrumento, ma basta che da huomini intendenti, saranno facilmente conosciute tutte le sue parti, et operationi."

91 All Diderot's citations are taken from the entry *ENCYCLOPÉDIE* in the *Encyclopédie*, vol. V, pp. 646–647. See ch. 13 in this volume.

themselves into informers and to collaborate with the scientific project of the *Dictionnaire raisonné des Sciences, des Arts et des Métiers*. They remained silent or they mockingly gave wrong information, making fools of the *Encyclopédie* interviewers, drawing their prying eyes and ears into wily traps. After publishing the first four volumes of the *Encyclopédie* (from the letter A to E), Diderot was forced to acknowledge that some entries, such as the article BLANCHISSERIE DE TOILES (fabric bleaching) did not even have "l'ombre du sens commun" ("a shadow of common sense"), whereas other entries, like in the article BRIQUE (brick) were full of "bévues grossiéres" ("gross errors"). This required a change in the form of investigation, redefined in an inquisitorial sense also to circumvent the "bad" memory of the workers and their lack of "bonne foi" ("good faith"). But Diderot asked above all for understanding and sympathy from his hypothetical collaborator for all the errors he fell into and all the disappointments he experienced in his relations with the artisans. He wrote: "It is especially when he will have walked through the workshop for some time, with money in hand, and when they will have made him pay dearly for the most ridiculous falsehoods, that he will learn what type of people the Artists are, especially in Paris, where they look at every man who questions them with some curiosity as an emissary of the tax farmers, or as a worker who wants to open his own shop."[92]

These problems, embedded in the very roots of the *Encyclopédie*, did not exist for the author of *Novo teatro*. In contrast to Diderot and his collaborators, Zonca was not an intellectual "external" to the world of work. He did not have to resort to hired informers, and he did not intend to overstep the critical threshold beyond which began the domain of the masters' rites of initiation and authority. The pages of *Novo teatro* restore to us an image of a technician able to synthesize information and whose professional practice (not of one engaged in a publishing project) put him in direct contact with workers and masters whose professional secrets he respected. Diderot on the other hand, starting with the "matières grèges" ("raw materials"), wanted to investigate systematically not only production costs, construction methods and instruments, but bodily gestures, "manoeuvres" ("movements"), the masters' "tours des mains" ("manual dexterity"), up to the point of detecting in their motions

92 "C'est sur-tout quand il aura parcouru pendant quelque tems les ateliers, l'argent à la main, et qu'on lui aura fait payer bien chèrement les faussetés le plus ridicules, qu'il connoîtra quelle espece de gens ce sont quel les Artistes, sur-tout à Paris, où la crainte des impôts les tient perpétuellement en méfiance, et où ils regardent tout homme qui les interroge avec quelque curiosité comme un émissaire des fermiers généraux, ou comme un ouvrier qui veut ouvrir boutique."

"un movement indifferent d'une precaution essentielle" ("a movement different from an essential precaution"). These observations reveal profound cognitive differences between *Novo teatro* and the *Encyclopédie*, and the existence of areas of study – such as the theoretical foundations of technical knowledge, procedures for their transmission, etc. – which deserve further exploration.[93]

At this point one may ask what the relationship was between *Novo teatro* and the historical epoch in which it was written. Some years ago Friedrich Klemm proposed linking *Novo teatro* to a particular artistic culture, Mannerism, due to the links drawn between fantasy and technique, nature and artifice. This is an interesting insight that Klemm detects in the drawing of the "machine that turns spits with the movement of smoke," where the hand of a classical-style statue holds the spit of a rotisserie while four dolphins form the pedestal.[94]

To me it seems useful to connect *Novo teatro* to the historical epoch Carlo Cipolla defined as "the San Martino summer [Indian summer] of the Italian economy," a period of 'late flowering' that goes from the middle of the 16th century to the first decades of the 17th century.[95] In this light, *Novo teatro* can be seen as emblematic of the productive structure of Italian industry, especially in the Po valley. On the one hand, it underlines the need to improve the level of use of available energy (especially hydraulic), by applying the principles of mechanics to the construction of machines. On the other hand, it shows the industrial potential of processing machines. The hydraulic spinning mill, already a factory system, can be considered the epitome of technological goals achieved at that time.[96] However, it would be wrong to equate the assessment

93 This way of interpreting the role of work in the *Encyclopédie* is extraneous to all Diderot specialists and the Enlightenment culture. These pages had already been written when I read the pre-print of C. Koepp's article "The Alphabetical Order: work in Diderot's *Encyclopédie*" which, with sources similar to my own, arrives at similar conclusions (see *Work in France. Representations, Meaning, Organization and Practice*, ed. S.L. Kaplan and C. Koepp [Ithaca 1985]). See also in this volume ch. 13 on the *Encyclopédie* and the crafts.

94 *Novo teatro*, p. 91. F. Klemm, "Technische Entwürfe in der Epoche des Manierismus besonders in der Zeit zwischen 1560 und 1620," *Zur Kulturgeschichte der Technik* (Munich, 1979), p. 155. One could add that in this same drawing the figure of the "Sprecher" (speaker) appears, who (turning his back to the audience) indicates, with raised arms, the action that takes place in the incision. According to S. Sypher (*Rinascimento, Manierismo, Barocco* [Padua, 1968], pp. 166–167), the "Sprecher," an ambiguous figure hovering between art and life, between depiction and reality, had been introduced by the Mannerist painters. Another "Sprecher" appears in *Novo teatro*, p. 82.

95 *Storia dell'economia italiana*, ed. Carlo Cipolla (Turin, 1959). See the editor's important *Introduzione*, especially pp. 16–18.

96 Other interesting machines are the flour mill (p. 14), in which a single water wheel, thanks to "a steep slope, and an abundance of water" also powers a small mallet and a spring for sharpening blades; the mangle (p. 56) that shows how to reverse the movement of the

of a contemporary historian (Carlo Cipolla) with the awareness that Zonca had of the epoch in which he lived. It would be even more arbitrary to imagine that Zonca had complete knowledge of his epoch. Such knowledge was not an issue for him, and was beyond his scope.. Thus we do not know how detailed his perception of reality was.

We do know that in the 16th century ideas were beginning to circulate in Europe asserting the superiority of modernity over antiquity based on geographical explorations and technical progress.[97] In Italy the most important and best known exponent of this thought was Alessandro Tassoni.[98] Even before him the Oratorian, Tommaso Bozio, learned follower of Filippo Neri, criticized and rejected the doctrine of senescence and the decline of the world (according to R.F. Jones "the direct antithesis of the idea of progress").[99] In two of Bozio's works, published in 1591 and 1595, he asserted the technological and scientific superiority of: 1. the moderns over the ancients; 2. the European peoples over those of Africa and Asia; and 3. the people who remained faithful to the Catholic church over those who became Protestant.[100] This last point had been developed as part of a theological polemic regarding the "signs" of the true church.

In Bozio's work the topic of technological and scientific progress as a sign of superiority takes an unusual turn. When he describes the "machinas et mechanicorum constructionem et usum" ("machines and construction and use of machines") he asserts that contemporaries already prevailed over

---

processing machine without changing the direction of the motor's movement; the mill (p. 21) equipped with a mechanical sifter, of which only the mechanized wheel has been drawn. The mechanical sifter, presented as a German invention, was drawn in full some years later by F. Veranzio (*Machinae novae*, s.n.t. [Venice, 1615–1616], figure 28).

97 See J.A. Maravall, *Antiguos y modernos. La idea de progreso en el desarrollo inicial de una sociedad* (Madrid, 1966), and A.G. Keller, "Mathematical Technologies and the Growth of the Idea of Technical Progress in the Sixteenth Century," *Science, Medicine and Society in the Renaissance*, vol. I (London, 1972), 11–27.

98 A. Tassoni, *Dieci libri di pensieri diversi* (Venice, 1627). See in particular the last chapter "Discorso degli ingegni antichi e moderni."

99 R.F. Jones, *Ancients and Moderns. A Study of the Rise of the Scientific Movement in Seventeenth Century England* (Berkeley, 1965), p. 28; see also the entire second chapter.

100 T. Bozio, *De signis Ecclesiae Dei* (Rome, 1591), I, pp. 237–243; idem., *De novo et antiquo Italiae statu adversus Machiavellum* (Rome, 1595), pp. 346–371. For an analysis of Bozio's arguments see C. Poni, *Economia, Scienza, Tecnologia. La teologia polemica di Tommaso Bozio* (Bologna, 1966). Bozio's theses profoundly influenced George Hakewill, one of the strongest supporters in England of the superiority of moderns over the ancients. On Hakewill see Jones, *Ancients and Moderns*, pp. 29–40; Jones did not reconstruct Hakewill's dependence on *De signis*.

the Greeks and Romans "inter quos principem locum tenet post Tartaleam cadanumque, Guidus Ubaldus e Marchionibus Montis, cujus extant doctissimi mechanicarum libri" ("among whom the first place, after Tartaglia and Cardano, is held by Guidobaldo Del Monte, who wrote very learned books on the mechanical arts"). These names are followed by those of Giorgio Valla and Giuseppe Ceredi for the machines they designed to lift water, and Michelangelo Buonarroti, constructor of an "eccellentissima" machine to lift weights, and Juanelo Turriano, inventor of the planetary clock.[101]

These ideas on the progress of science and technology probably circulated, through diverse paths, in the cultural milieu of Padua. They may have provided Zonca with plenty of stimuli for understanding the importance of the existing industrial structures surrounding him in his city and which he could see every day. It is important to keep in mind that 16th century Padua was a major textile center. In 1554 mayor Marc'Antonio Grimani calculated that Padua's wool merchants invested annually about 50,000 ducats purchasing raw wool and another 50,000 to "process the wool and make fabrics and hats, which … expenses are a benefit for the poor who live off the work of their hands." The processing of wool – spinning, weaving, dyeing, and finishing – provided subsistence to an "infinity of persons. And this 'Arte' also attracts many to live in the city and increases the number of people by the day."[102] Based on a widespread urban-rural putting-out system (and the centralization of finishing operations in numerous plants, including hydraulic-powered ones, such as fullers) Padua's wool industry fed a major export business with the Levant.[103] Thus it was true what Matteo Dandolo said when, presenting a report to the Senate of Venice in 1547 at the end of his term as harbor master in Padua, he declared that the wool industry was, together with the university, "the soul of the city."[104] If we read *Novo teatro* from the perspective of Padua's textile industry, we can better understand Zonca's attention to mangles, fullers, and presses for "polishing," and machines for teaseling cloth.

101 T. Bozio, *De novo et antiquo Italiae*, pp. 360–361. On Turriano's clocks see J.A. Garcia-Diego, *Los relojes y automatas de Juanelo Turriano* (Madrid, 1982).

102 *Relazioni dei rettori Veneti di Terraferma.*, IV, pp. 42–43.

103 Specifically, 1,500 high value cloths with a unit value of 40 ducats and 2,000 lower value cloths with a unit value of 16 ducats were produced annually.

104 Ibid., p. 17. Towards the second half of the 18th century it was estimated that Padua's wool industry employed about 18,000 people; see L. Dal Pane, *Storia del lavoro in Italia dagli inizi del secolo XVIII al 1815* (Milan, 1944), pp. 64–65.

But Padua was not only a wool city. It also produced a moderate amount of raw silk.[105] It was not by chance that Ottavio Malpigli decided to build in Padua (probably after 1604) the first silk mill "alla bolognese" in the Venetian state.[106] In addition to textile machines, other water-powered industrial plants were located within the ancient city walls: machines for grinding powder, at least one power hammer with four wheels with an attached blade-sharpening workshop, and a large number of flour mills.[107] In the waters of the Brenta, one of the waterways that crossed the city, 30 hydraulic mills were crowded together near the Molino Bridge to supply the city with flour.[108] It is not an exaggeration to state that Padua had one of the highest concentrations of urban water wheels in the Po valley.[109] But we cannot verify what this situation meant for Zonca. From the windows of his house he could see the water wheels at the Molino Bridge, and he had to cross this bridge every time he went from his house to the city center, towards the *palazzi* of the rich and powerful, and the markets. Did he ever stop to talk to the millers who lived in his same parish and went to his same church?

On Vittorio's life I was able to find only scarce and fragmentary information. The best documented event is his burial, proven by two independent sources. In the *Libro dei morti* (Book of the Dead) of the Health Office of the Padua municipality, on 15 November 1602 it states: "Vittorio Zunco age 34. He was ill for a long time with 'mal di flusso'. Visited by the most excellent Vigonza, San Giacomo."[110] The second source is the Registry of the Dead of the parish of Giacomo: "Messer Vittorio Zonca, sculptor, about 30 years of age. Lived in the Torrazzo, died in the union of the Holy Church, and was buried at San

---

105 *Relazioni dei rettori Veneti di Terraferma*, IV, p. 43. Padua's rapidly growing silk production had in 1554 reached a value of about 50,000 ducats, equal to the value of raw wool processed in the city.

106 A.S.V., *Savi alla Mercanzia*, New series, *Oro in Foglia – orsogli alla bolognese*, b. 117. The news is contained in a letter from December 1634, in which the *Savi alla Mercanzia* (the Venetian Trade Authorities) presented a proposed law to the Senate to promote the diffusion of silk mills "alla bolognese". For an analysis of the controversy see Poni, *La seta in Italia*, ch. 6, pp. 271–274.

107 *Relazioni dei rettori Veneti di Terraferma*, IV, pp. 64, 69.

108 A. Portenari, *Della felicità di Padova* (Padua, 1623), p. 112.

109 Bologna, with 300 water wheels around the middle of the 16th century, had more than Padua. [See ch. 10 in this volume.]

110 A.S.P., *Archivio Civico Antico, Ufficio di Sanità di Padova, Libro dei Morti* (*1595–1602*), no. 464. "Mal di flusso" could have been dysentery or pulmonary disease. This source as well as the following one (note 102) was known to Beck, *Beiträge zur Geschichte des Maschinenbaues*, p. 293.

Bernardino on 15 November 1602."[111] From these sources we can deduce his date of birth: around 1568.

[...]

His father, Girolamo, probably born in Bergamo, had been granted "cittadino originario" status in 1569 (perhaps a necessary requirement for being admitted to the guild).[112]

[...]

The *Torrazzo* (bell tower) where the Zonca family lived was an old *palazzo* of the 13th century[113] The fact that the Zoncas lived in a noble house with a tower and had the right to be buried at the church of San Bernardino, where at least from 1630 a gravestone appeared which cites the family name, appears as a sign of the upward mobility of a recent immigrant family.[114] The erudite Paduan Cesare Malfatti wrote either at the end of the 16th century or at the beginning of the 17th century): "These (the Zoncas) were special; two of them became Jurists, left artisanship and commerce, lived very civilly" ("civilmente").[115] This latter definition seems borrowed from the legal language of the time and validates an identification of a sort of urban middle class between the nobility and the populace.[116]

---

111 A.V.B.C.P., *Registri delle parrocchie soppresse, S. Giacomo, Baptizatorum 1596–1621; Mortuorum 1597–1620*, reg. 4, unnumbered sheet in the year listed.

112 A.S.P., *Archivio Civico Antico, Prove di Nobiltà*, vol. 105, Index. See in the index the proof of nobility in 1787 of the notary Liberale Zonca who may have belonged to the same family as Vittorio (G. Vedova, *Biografia degli scrittori padovani*, vol. II [Padua, 1836], p. 454).

113 The expression is used on 6 March 1594 by the priest of San Giacomo, on the occasion of Cecilia Marieta Campora's baptism to distinguish Vittorio Zonca's residence (*il Torrazzo*).

114 On the gravestone were the words: "Heredes ex testamento quondam Eccellentissimi Pauli Zonca Juris Utriusque Doctoris Posuerunt. Anno Domini MDCXXX" (The heirs by will of the late most excellent Paolo Zonca, Doctor of both Laws [civil and church law] laid this stone. A.D. 1630). The inscription is reported by G. Lazara, "Memorie certe," and by G.A. Tommasini, *Urbis Patavinae descriptiones sacrae et profanae* (Padua, 1649), p. 143. For more information on the church of San Bernardino see P. Brandolesi, *Nuova descrizione delle pitture, sculture, architetture ... e d'altre cose notabili di Padova,* in B.U.P., ms. 3239, unnumbered sheet. In San Bernardino the wool guild had erected its own chapel (Rizzoli, *L'Università dell'Arte della lana*, pp. 122–126). Unfortunately the church was destroyed in the 19th century. The area of the ancient monastery was at Via Zabarella 54, the current site of the *Intendenza di Finanza* (Inland Revenue Service).

115 C. Malfatti, "Cronichetta overo epitome delle famiglie che hora sono nella città di Padoa" (24 February 1598), in B.C.P., B.P. 15.1239. Before 1550 the name Zonca appears several times in the *Acta graduum* of the University of Padua. But these may refer to another family than Vittorio's. See *Acta graduum academicorum Gymnasii patavini ab annum 1501 ad annum 1550*, ed. Elda Martellozzo Farin (Padua, 1982) (index).

116 On the concept of "living civilly" see G. Trebbi, "La cancelleria veneta nei secoli XVI e XVII," *Annali dell Fondazione Luigi Einaudi*, vol. XIV (Turin, 1980), 72–77, 122–25, passim,

Vittorio also participated in this upward mobility. This is revealed by his request for the title of architect, which he obtained in 1597. Two years later he worked as a *perito straordinario* (expert consultant) on the visit to the Tartaro River. According to G. Lazara, mentioned above, he was Padua's *proto* (chief engineer). These titles, and in particular the latter two, could appear to be interchangeable. But were they? A recent essay by Lionello Puppi acknowledges a certain confluence between the professions of *proto* and *perito*, at least in the 18th century.[117] But the same author shows that for centuries these two roles remained relatively separate. Whereas the office of *pubblico proto* (chief city engineer) required "precise professional training in architecture" (and the duty to supervise the maintenance of public buildings as well as designing and supervising construction sites), a public *perito*'s tasks initially were confined to land surveying. And it was only at the end of the 16th century that the tasks of a *perito* came to include cartographic registration, structural building surveying, and the "evaluation of delicate issues related to water." Thus it seems that the title of architect, which Zonca assumed in 1599, was closer to that of *proto* than *perito*. No record of Vittorio's activity as a sculptor or teacher of mathematics, has been found, nor have his school records. Since at one point he cites Vitruvio in Latin (p. 66) we can assume that he had assimilated the basics of a language that was part of the culture of Padua's "civil" class.

It is my impression that *Novo teatro* had a relatively broad circulation. This is proven by the three editions (1607, 1621, 1656) and the number of exemplars that survived. Who bought it? Did it have a popular circulation? And in which areas? In spite of extensive investigation in European and American libraries I do not feel adequately prepared to answer these questions. On the other hand, it is possible to reconstruct the influence of Zonca's work on the literature of "theaters of machines" in the 17th and 18th centuries. The contours of this influence, particularly on German technical culture, are known.[118] In 1612–1614, more than half of Zonca's drawings (28 out of 42) were incorporated into Heinrich Zeising's *Theatrum machinarum* (divided into seven parts).[119]

and A. Ventura, *Nobilità e popolo nella società veneta del '400 e '500* (Bari, 1964), p. 88–92, 303–37, passim and bibliography.

117 L. Puppi, "Il Collegio dei 'pubblici periti' a Padova dal XVI al XVIII secolo," communication presented at the colloquium *Les villes et la diffusion de l'innovation en Europe occidentale*, Paris 30 Nov.–1 Dec. 1984.

118 Beck, *Beiträge zur Geschichte des Maschinenbaues*, pp. 392–3; the entry "Zeising" in F.M. Feldhaus, *Die Technik der Vorzeit der Geschichtlichen Zeit und der Naturvölker* (Leipzig and Berlin,1914); and Reti, "Francesco di Giorgio Martini's Treatise."

119 H. Zeising reproduced the following drawings from *Novo teatro*: pp. 1, 3, 9, 12, 14, 25, 42, 45, 47, 50, 58, 61, 64, 76, 82, 85, 88^1, 88^2, 91, 94, 96, 100, 103, 105, 107, 110, 112, 114. The seven

The German architect generally copied the machines precisely, with just one exception: that of the fulling mill, in which the second wheel is missing. A curious and perhaps revealing absence, as is the absence of the two drawings of spinning mills.[120] On the other hand these editions were enriched with decorative backdrops, with numerous "indicators" of Nordic style landscapes and architecture. The glossaries and comments were shorter than those of Zonca. The theory of machines, instead of being spread throughout the comments as in *Novo teatro*, was judiciously collected in the first part or first chapter, which obviously served as an introduction. Zeising acknowledged his debts to Tartaglia, Ramelli, Brivius and many others. He never mentions Zonca. Nor does the architect Georg A. Boeckler, author of a book on machines published in 1661, which reproduced just eight of Zonca's drawings, three of which did not appear in Zeising's work,[121] a clear indication that Boeckler had direct knowledge of *Novo teatro*. Through these two authors Zonca's drawings became known to the "mathematician and mechanic" Jacob Leupold, who copied several of them in his *Theatri machinarum*.[122] Leupold – a scrupulous author – often cited his sources. But since he had no direct knowledge of Zonca, he instead cited the intermediaries Zeising and Boeckler. In total, Leupold unknowingly reproduced eight machines from *Novo teatro*. A modest

drawings from p. 100 to p. 114 are taken from Martini. Zeising sometimes made small adjustments. Thus for example the "wheel for raising water" (p. 61) pours water into a wooden container instead of a "*burchiella*" (boat for water provisioning in Venice).

120 The first printed drawing of a silk mill appeared in Germany at the beginning of the 18th century. See the "Italienische Fillatorio" in F.P. Florini, *Oeconomus prudens et legalis oder Allgemeiner Klug und Rechts-Verständiger Hausvater*, VI (Nuremberg, 1705).

121 Boeckler reproduced the fulling drawings from *Novo teatro*: pp. 18, 33, 36 (not copied by Zeising) and pp. 82, 85, 91, 94 and 105. The fulling mill is one of Zonca's machines that Boeckler did not copy. He preferred instead O. De Strada's fulling mill (*Künstliche Abrisz aller Hand-Wasser-Wind-Rosz und Handt Mühlen* [Frankfurt am Main, 1627]), which is smaller and does not have the second wheel (n. 72). This is an interesting choice. Boeckler writes that he could have represented "plures fulloniarum molarum species" (many kinds of fulling mills), but that he decided to leave them out because they were "vulgares et obviae" (common and obvious), and also to save on printing costs (p. 23). To understand Boeckler's choice we can add that De Strada is his main source.

122 On Leupold see K. Mauersberger, "Das Werk Jakob Leupolds (1674–1727)," *Vorfeld der Maschinenwissenschaften*, in *Dresdener Beiträge zur Geschichte der Technikwissenschaften*, fasc. 5, 1982, 84–102, and L. Hiersemann, *Jacob Leupold. Ein Wegbereiter der technischen Bildung in Leipzig* (Leipzig, 1982). These writings were kindly brought to my attention by U. Troitzsch. See also E.S. Ferguson, "Leupold's Theatrum Machinarum. A Need and an Opportunity," *Technology and Culture*, vol. 12 (1971), 61–69.

and culturally not very significant presence in a work whose author already drew and commented on Newcomen's machines.[123]

In contrast, Zonca had no influence on books about machines published in Italy in the 17th century.[124] In only two later manuscripts did I find proof of his influence. The first, in chronological order, is *L'annotomia delle artiglierie* by the Bolognese "bombardier" Giuseppe Antonio Baraldi, compiled before 1704. This voluminous work includes seven drawings from *Novo teatro*.[125] The second manuscript, possibly from the first years of the 19th century, is entitled *Libro di meccanice o sia machine*, by the architect from Cesena, Mauro Guidi, and contains rough sketches of 23 of Zonca's drawings.[126] This is obviously a late compilation, without comments or indications of scale.

I will close this brief list with the name of John Wilkins. In the drawings of his *Mathematicall Magick*, none of the machines of *Novo teatro* are to be found. But he cites Zonca in a long list together with Ramelli, Besson, Vegezio and Lipsio, writing: "I ... willingly acknowledge myself a debtor to them for many things in this following discourse."[127]

---

123 In *Theatrum Machinarum Generale oder Schauplatz des Grundes Mechanischer Wissenschaften* (Leipzig, 1724), Leupold copied Zonca's drawings from pp. 25, 91, 100 and 105; in *Theatrum machinarum hydrotechniacarum. Schauplatz der Wasser-bau-kunst* (Leipzig, 1724), the *Carro di Fusina* is depicted. In *Theatrum Machinarum hydraulicarum oder Schauplatz der Wasser-künste*, t. I–II (Leipzig, 1724–25), drawings from pp. 25, 100, 112, and 114 appear; in *Theatrum Machinarum oder Schauplatz der Heb-Zeuge* (Leipzig, 1725), "*Vite perpetua*" appears. In *Theatrum Machinarum Molarium*, the scale drawing from p. 25 and Pompeo Targone's "*Nova inventione*" are depicted.

124 I am referring essentially to the works of G. Branca, *Le macchine* (Rome, 1626), and F. Veranzio, *Machinae novae*, s.n.t. [Venice 1615–1616]. The latter, born in Sebbenico where he became bishop, was politically active in Hungary. Thus Veranzio was not Italian. His technical work is nevertheless strictly tied to Italian mechanical culture. See. L. Makkai, "De Taccola à Veranzio. L'ingénieur de la Renaissance en Hongrie," *Histoire économique du monde méditerranéen 1460–1650. Mélanges en l'Honneur de Fernand Braudel* (Toulouse, 1973), pp. 337–347.

125 G.A. Baraldi, "L'annotomia delle artiglierie osservate minutamente dall'occhio di Felsina," Biblioteca Universitaria, Bologna, ms. 220. Baraldi copied the drawings from pp. 1, 19, 82, 85, 88[2], 100, 101, 107, and 114.

126 M. Guidi, "Libro di meccanice o sia machine," Biblioteca Comunale, Cesena, ms. Atlante 40. On Guidi, see A. Lenzi and A.M. Matteucci, *Cosimo Morelli e l'architettura delle Legazioni Pontifice* (Imola, 1977), pp. 110, 128–131.

127 J. Wilkins, *Mathematicall Magick or the Wonders that may be performed by Mechanicall Geometry* (London, 1648), p. 7. On J. Wilkins see C. Webster, *The Great Instauration. Science, Medicine and Reform (1626–1660)* (London, 1975), pp. 163–4, 171–172, and passim. Wilkins, one of the Bacon's followers at Oxford, probably read the Bodleian Library's copy of *Novo teatro*. An indirect reference to Zonca may be contained in *Explication des modeles des machines et forces mouvantes que l'on expose à Paris* (Paris, 1683), where on p. 48 a "Moulin ambulant pour suivre une armée" is noted, attributed to M. Tarragon.

This research, done by patiently leafing through some tens of copies of *Novo teatro*, looking for comments and annotations, produced only modest results. It seems that only one machine produced appreciable reactions: the last one which portrays a perpetual motion of Martinian origins, whose dissymmetry Zonca had pointed out. In Florence's Biblioteca Marucelliana there is a copy of the third and last edition of 1656 on which an anonymous hand had written: "The idea is nice. But the effect is awful. One couldn't have done worse. This one hasn't studied the laws of the air. Oh what an ox! Oh what an ass!" And then "It's not worth anything. No, even worse! O what an idiot! It goes against all the nature of hydraulics as we now know it!" A significant and exasperated assessment, probably from the second half of the 17th century. In another copy in the Vatican Library, below the perpetual motion machine, is the laconic annotation: "Laborat in falso principio" ("He labors under a false principle").[128]

In Zonca's "theater," as in the other "theaters" of maps and urban images of the 1500s, the element that justifies the title is the dominant role of drawings.[129] But too often the drawings, which ensured the success of several publishing efforts, were used or rather plundered in banal ways, as stray objects for illustrative and decorative purposes, thus removed from their verbal context. With few exceptions, this is particularly true of Zonca's work. Unscrupulous sellers took the book apart to throw single, detached images onto the antiquarian market. And many of these detached images taken from *Novo teatro* appeared in diverse and rich histories of technology.

In this study, the first one in nearly four centuries since the death of Zonca, I proceeded in the opposite direction. I tried to understand the *Novo teatro* in its multiform stratification, deconstructing the text and reorganizing a complexity that is almost "hidden" in its original form. But beyond the text I also examined the problem of its relationship to what is external, to that multiple reality – industrial and social – that explain the "scenes" even if they do not appear on the "stage." The themes of this study are played out thanks to these inter-weavings, constructed with patience. An attempt, however it may succeed, at reconstructing history. Or a reference point for other reading strategies.

---

128 In yet another copy from the Vatican Library (Cicognara v. 970) the perpetual motion has been replaced by the drawing of a "New way to raise water by itself by one third," Rome 1616, by G. Finugio dedicated to Federico Cesi.

129 See A. Ortelius, *Theatrum Orbis Terrarum* (Antwerp, 1570).

CHAPTER 12

The Craftsman and the Good Engineer: Technical Practice and Theoretical Mechanics in J.T. Desaguliers

Carlo Poni

The relationship between technical practice and theoretical mechanics has, at least since Galileo Galilei, often been seen as a complex and difficult one. The great scientist, who in 1593 constructed and patented a machine for lifting water,[1] often warned technicians and inventors not to ignore the principles of mechanics if they wanted to avoid "to spend time, effort and money in vain" when constructing machines.[2] He saw "the many conveniences and uses" that "mechanical tools" would bring to "many different manual crafts, in addition to the others which may be expected from those practitioners (*professori*) trained in mechanical science." He was mistrustful, though, of those who "took to developing new inventions out of a certain natural talent alone, but without recourse to mathematical principles, which intrinsically demonstrate the nature of the primary and most elementary instruments of which all other machines are composed"[3] He thus attacked, vehemently on occasions, those *professori* who invented and built engines with the aim of increasing their motive power. According to Galileo, no motive power, whether that of a horse, a man or an ox, could be increased by any transmission mechanism. On the other hand, astounding results could be obtained by following the Archimedean principle according to which weights on a lever were in an inverse relation to each other with regard to their distance from the fulcrum. That is, if two weights on scales were balanced, a very small weight would be

1 W. Theobald, "Ein Venezianisches Patent Galileo Galileis," in *Beiträge zur Geschichte der Technik und Industrie*, vol. 17 (1927), 24–29. On the Venetian patents, see R. Berveglieri and C. Poni, "Three Centuries of Venetian Patents (1474–1796)," *Acta Historia Rerum Naturalium necnon Technicarum*, Special Issue 17 (Prague, 1982), pp. 381–393.

2 G. Galilei, "A proposito di una macchina per pestare," *Le opere di Galileo Galilei*, Nuova ristampa dell'Edizione Nazionale, vol. VIII (Firenze, 1933), p. 585; translation by Carlo Poni with the help of Patrick Leech. As far as I know, this essay has never been translated into English. See also p. 290.

3 Ibid.

 | DOI:10.1163/9789004713277_014

sufficient to change the equivalence of the forces, with the result that huge weights could be lifted.[4]

These objections to the use of "a certain natural talent" did not prevent Galileo from drawing on commonly-used machines and the practical experience of artisans in order to investigate the "reasons for effects that are not only wondrous, but also hidden and almost unthinkable."[5] Galileo recommended visits to the Venice Arsenal and constant consultation with its foremen (*proti*) as this would give rise to "a large field to speculative minds for philosophizing, and particularly in that area which is called mechanics, inasmuch as every sort of instrument and machine is continually put in operation there. And among its great number of artisans there must be some who through observations handed down by their predecessors as well as those which they attentively and continually make for themselves, are truly expert and whose reasoning is of the finest." However well-trained and experienced, though, not even these *proti* were able to escape from the "idle notion of the common people" when they hazarded explanations of the resistance of solid bodies to breaking.[6]

Galileo's views on artisans were thus twofold. On the one hand he mistrusted those who embarked upon "new inventions" without "mathematical principles." On the other he praised those who continued in established technical skills while at the same time rejecting the explanations they gave to their operations. His was not, though, merely sterile criticism. Galileo brought new mathematical and scientific requirements into the world of the mechanical arts, but he also introduced technical problems into the academy. A new natural science capable of helping artisans and mechanics in their efforts to invent and innovate was created, though not without considerable controversy and disagreement.

It should be remembered, however, that engineers and architects with a variety of skills and practical knowledge of the principles of mechanics had existed since the fifteenth century. This can be seen, for example, from the extraordinary collection of technical manuscripts produced by the engineers of the Siena school, attributed by nineteenth-century scholars to Francesco di Giorgio Martini. [...] The Martinian tradition was familiar with the principle

4 For these topics, see P. Galluzzi, *Momento, Studi Galileani* (Rome, 1979).

5 G. Galilei, "Discorsi e dimostrazioni matematiche intorno a due nuove scienze," *Le opere di Galileo Galilei,* vol. VIII, p. 49.

6 Ibid., pp. 49–50. For the English translation, see G. Galilei, *Two New Sciences. Including Centers of Gravity and Force of Percussion*, translated, with introduction and notes by Stillman Drake (Madison, 1974), p. 11.

that the weight of a pound, applied to the circumference of a wheel, moved a very much heavier weight placed on its axis, according to the relation between the radius of the wheel and the radius of the axis.[7] This can also be found in the *Novo Teatro di Machine et Edifizii* of the Paduan architect Vittorio Zonca published in 1607. This relatively little-known architect, who was really more of an engineer, dedicated himself to applying the principles of mechanics to the construction of machines in order to help them improve the way they worked. In this way elements of calculus were added to the stock of repeated and accumulated practices. In particular, he suggested a way of to improve a "hydraulic machine for fulling clothes" already in operation in Padua. To make it work "properly" it would be sufficient to double the diameter of the wheel submerged by the exceptional flow of water. If the wheel were made larger in relation to its axis it would acquire greater power but would lose speed. He therefore advised an increase in the numbers of cogged levers on the axis for moving the hammers on the fulling machine so as to allow it to "work quickly and efficiently" again.[8]

These examples serve to focus our attention on the relationship between scientists and technicians or artisans, a subject examined in an excellent article by Rupert Hall ("The Scholar and the Craftsman in the Scientific Revolution").[9] My research, however, has excluded the work of the technicians and artisans who constructed scientific and laboratory instruments used by scientists, an area that has been extensively studied.[10] Instead, I shall concentrate on the

7 F. Di Giorgio Martini, *Trattati di architettura, ingegneria e arte militare*, ed. C. Maltese (Milan, 1967), vol. 1, pp. 141–142. See B. Gille, *Les ingénieurs de la Renaissance* (Paris, 1964) and *Prima di Leonardo. Cultura delle macchine a Siena nel Rinascimento,* ed. P. Galluzzi (Milano, 1991). On the relationship between the Italian technical literature of the fifteenth and sixteenth centuries (on fortification, gunners, hydraulics) and the origin of early modern science see L. Olschki, *Geschichte der Neusprachlicfien Wissenschaftlichen Literatur.* Erster Band (*Die Literatur der Technik und der angewandten Wissenschaften van Mittelalter bis zur Renaissance*) (Heidelberg, 1919); Zweiter Band (*Bildung und Wissenschaft in Zeitalter der Renaissance in ltalien*) (Leipzig, 1922); Dritter Band (*Galilei und seine Zeit*) (Halle, 1927). See also the critical analysis by H. Floris Cohen, "Galileo's ups and downs in the Historiography of the Scientific Revolution," *Italian Scientists in the Low Countries in the XVIIth and XVIIIth centuries*, eds. C.S. Maffioli and L.C. Palm (Amsterdam-Atlanta, 1989), pp. 16–18.

8 For the possible relations between Zonca and Galilei (who never mentions the Paduan architect) see in this volume ch. 11, pp. 285, 288–292, 298 (note 56).

9 R. Hall, "The Scholar and the Craftsman," *Critical Problems in the History of Science*, ed. M. Clagett (Madison, 1962), pp. 3–23.

10 See M. Daumas's excellent *Les instruments scientifiques au XVIIe et XVIIIe siècles* (Paris, 1953). There have been a large number of inventories of instruments and brief biographies of their makers since this study, among them E. Zeiner, *Deutsche und Niederlandische Astrononische Instrumente des 11–18 Jahrhunderts* (Munchen, 1956); E. G. Taylor, *The*

ways scientists contributed to the invention of new machinery, or how they improved the use of old machinery; and what scientists thought of those technicians who were also entrepreneurs and constructors of machinery with concrete industrial applications, such as supplying a city with water, mine drainage, the optimal functioning of existing machinery and others.

This is not a new topic, but one in which much remains to be done. Here I will limit myself to examining the work of an English scientist writing in the period before the onset of the industrial revolution, John Theophilus Desaguliers. Desaguliers was of Huguenot origin, a Protestant minister, a Grand Master (since 1719) and reformer of the Grand Masonic Lodge of London, member of the Royal Society since 1714 and later its secretary, and active popularizer of the *Principia* of Isaac Newton, whose pupil he had been.[11] Strongly philanthropic and convinced, as were all the English Newtonians, that the knowledge he possessed was socially useful, Desaguliers was one of the first, in 1710, to hold courses in experimental physics at Oxford and later, from 1713, in London, to a paying public of widely differing social origins.[12] As Musson and Robinson

---

Mathematical Practitioners of Tudor and Stuart England (Cambridge, 1970); J. Brown, *Mathematical Instrument-Makers in the Grocers' Company 1688–1900* (London, 1979). See also *Storia delle Scienze, Gli strumenti*, ed. G.L.E. Turner, series editor P. Galluzzi (Milan, 1990).

11 According to Margaret C. Jacob (*The Radical Enlightenment. Pantheists, Freemasons and Republicans* [London, 1981], p. 112), "over a fourth of early Masonic membership also belonged to the Royal Society, with Desaguliers as the most active and prominent leader in both camps."

12 On the life of Desaguliers, see *Dictionary of National Biography*, ed. L. Stephen, vol. 16, (London, 1888), pp. 400–401; A. Rupert Hall's entry in the *Dictionary of Scientific Biography*, ed. Ch. Coulston Gillispie, vol. 4 (New York, 1971), pp. 43–46. On his freemason activities, see D. Campbell Lee, *Desaquliers of No. 4 and his services to Freemasonry* (London, 1932); W.R. Hurst, *An Outline of the Career of John Theophile Desaguliers* (London, 1928); Jacob, *The Radical Enlightenment*, pp. 109–141; idem., *The Cultural Meaning of the Scientific Revolution* (New York, 1988), pp. 126–127, 143–44, 155 and passim. With J. Anderson, Desaguliers published *The Constitution of Free Masons, containing the History, Charges, Regulations ... of that most Ancient and Right Worshipful Fraternity* (Dublin, 1730). According to N. Hans, *New Trends in Eighteenth Century Education* (London, 1951), the public attending his lectures included "merchants, craftsmen and clerks." The course fee was three guineas, the first guinea to be paid on enrollment, the other two at the first lecture. See J.T. Desaguliers, *A Course of Mechanical and Experimental Philosophy. Cours de Philosophie mecanique et expérimentale* (London, 1720). On the scientific and organizational activities of the Royal Society, see J. H. Heilbron, *Physics at the Royal Society during Newton's Presidency* (Los Angeles, 1983), pp. 31–33, 91–96 passim. The dates of the nomination of Desaguliers to the Royal Society and to the Grand Lodge of London can be found in J. R. Clarke, "The Royal Society and Early Grand Lodge Freemasonry," *Transactions of Quatuor Coronati Lodge*, vol. 80 (1967), p. 115. Jacob (*The Radical Enlightenment*, p. 125), has pointed out that under the guidance of Desaguliers and Reverend J. Anderson, "masonic lodges became places

have pointed out, he was not a pure theorist without practical engineering experience,[13] but was rather constantly concerned with the need to link theory and practice, teaching and experimentation. After publishing a few short physics manuals for his students,[14] in the 1720s he began writing a major work in two volumes which would include all his experience as teacher and scientist, entitled *A Course of Experimental Philosophy.*

In the "Preface" to the first volume (1734), he declared his own satisfaction at having begun his one hundred and twenty-first course, having been in any way "instrumental to the improvement of others," and having trained at least eight of the eleven or twelve European professors capable of holding courses in experimental physics. He also expressed his pride in the discoveries of his students, from which he himself had learned.

Remarking on the moral character of the scientist, he stressed the disinterested nature of scientific research. The discoveries of students and colleagues, rather than leading to envy as in all other professions, were welcomed as "new acquisitions by all lovers of natural knowledge, the profit being shared in common, while the discoverer has only the honor of the invention."[15]

In order to win over a non-specialist public, Desaguliers decided to write in a somewhat wordy but essentially simple and clear language, not encumbered with too many mathematical formulas (confined for the most part to the notes at the end of each lecture or chapter). The first volume was meant to treat the principles of mechanics, machine friction and Newton's three laws of motion; the second, hydrostatics, pneumatics, hydraulics and optics. It was

---

where gentlemen, whether lowly or titled could receive a minimal instruction in mathematics, listen to lectures on the new science, or make up for what they did not know in science by participating in a movement that claimed to be descended from the earliest practitioner of applied mathematics – the masonic architect."

13 A. Musson and E. Robinson, *Science and Technology in the Industrial Revolution* (Manchester, 1969), pp. 37–40, passim.

14 Besides the manuals and works cited by Musson and Robinson, see also *A System of Experimental Philosophy prov'd by Mechaniks,* ed. P. Dawson (London, 1719). This work was republished the same year with corrections approved by the author under the new title of *Lectures of Experimental Philosophy* (London, 1719). A complete collection of Desaguliers' work should also include the writings published in the *Philosophical Transactions* of the Royal Society.

15 J.T. Desaguliers, *A Course of Experimental Philosophy,* vol. 1 (London, 1734). The quotations are from the *Preface.* Diderot expresses a similar idea in the entry "Arts" of the *Encyclopédie.* One of the eight students capable of holding courses in experimental physics was the Swede, Marten Triewald, who lectured in Edinburgh (1724) and later in Stockholm (1728). See S. Lindquist, *Technology on Trial. The introduction of Steam Power Technology into Sweden (1715–1736)* (Uppsala,1984), pp. 183–214.

in this form that the work was presented to its subscribers for their approval. The first volume came out only after some considerable time, and completion of the second volume was even slower and more laborious. It was finally published in 1744, without the chapter on optics but with an extra one on hydraulic machinery.

Frequently criticized for negligence because of the increasing delays in finishing this second volume, Desaguliers defended himself in the "Preface" from those readers who might have disapproved of the alterations made to the project to which they had subscribed. He claimed that the alterations had been requested by the majority of the subscribers and by friends who, aware that he had dedicated several years to the study and analysis of hydraulic machinery, had persuaded him to carry out a detailed study of a certain number of "engines to make the practice of so useful an Art easy." His main justification for the alterations and substitutions was that only by abandoning the chapter on optics had it been possible to find the space (about a hundred pages and twenty-five illustrations) to show in detail exactly what each machine could do. This know-how would provide the reader with all the necessary arguments for revealing and rejecting the astonishing but dishonest promises of the uneducated and deceitful entrepreneurs ("mechanical undertakers").[16] He continued: "This is a very necessary caution, for there are several persons who have money that are ready to supply boasting engineers with it, in hopes of great return, and especially if the project has the sanction of an Act of the Parliament to support it, and [then] the Bubble becomes compleat and ends in ruin."[17] This unusual self-justification indicated precisely the social uses of

16 Desaguliers, *A Course,* "Preface," vol. 2 (1744), p. vi. In the French edition of the *Course,* "undertaker" is translated as "entrepreneur". This term was probably used for the first time in France by Barthelmy de Laffemas at the beginning of the seventeenth century in the form of "entre-preneurs" (B. de Laffemas, *Lettres et exemples de la feu Reyne mère comme elle faisoit travailler aux manufactures* [Paris, 1602], p. 24). In 1603, the same author used this word in the form "entrepreneur" together with the word "entreprise" (idem., *Le plaisir de la noblesse et autres qui ont des eritages aux champs sur la preuve certain et proffict des étauffes et soyes qui se font à Paris* [Paris, 1603], p. 7). For Laffemas, the "entrepreneur" is one who combines labor and proprietors' resources for productive ends. In England, the term "entrepreneur" widely substituted the word "undertaker" only in the second half of the nineteenth century (J.W. Gough, *The Rise of the Entrepreneur* (London, 1969), pp. 11–17). From this point on, the term "entrepreneur" will be used except when directly quoting Desaguliers.

17 Desaguliers, *A Course,* "Preface," vol. 2, pp. vii-viii. Desaguliers justified the delay by explaining that he had had to resolve the dispute "about the force of bodies in motion," a problem deriving from Galileo, which divided European scientists into two camps. While the Italians, Germans and Dutch held that force was equal to "the product of the mass into the square of the velocity," the French and the English measured force "by the product of

scientific knowledge, in this case in a polemic with entrepreneurs, as well as its economic importance. As regards the chapter on optics, the author advised the public to buy Smith's manual[18] or to read Newton's account in the *Philosophical Transactions.*

It is not clear whether the subscribers, whom Desaguliers freed from their promises to buy the second volume, were entirely satisfied with the alterations made. Nevertheless the work represented the peak of the great professor's experience as scientist and teacher and had enormous success, being translated quickly into several languages.[19] The space given to the analysis of machinery and the beautiful illustration no doubt contributed to its success.

Like Galileo, Desaguliers expressed his contempt for those who build new machinery without any training in theoretical mechanics: "There is a great deal of room for ignorant enterprising people to exceed one another in mechanical defects." The "engine makers" (smiths, carpenters and turners) plagiarized each other just like poets and writers. What was worse, they often misused the ideas they had stolen. Desaguliers backed up this statement by citing the case of an "undertaking plumber" who applied a flywheel (speed regulator) he had seen on another machine to his own machine in order to increase its power. The result was precisely the opposite to what he had imagined. Called in to give an opinion, Desaguliers had the flywheel removed, and the machine, lightened of the extra weight, could be run by an animal motive power 75% less than before.[20]

---

the mass into the simple velocity" (ibid.). On publications by subscription in England, see W. A. Speck, "Politicians, Peers and Publication by Subscription (1700–1750)," *Books and Their Readers in Eighteenth-Century England,* ed. I. Rivers (Leicester, 1982,) pp. 47–68, and in the same volume, G.S. Rousseau, "Science Books and their Readers in the Eighteenth Century," pp. 197–255. The expression "bubble" (fraudulent speculation) almost certainly refers to the South Sea Bubble and the Bubble Act of 1720. In the "Preface" to the second volume of *A Course,* Desaguliers explains that if it had not been for the intervention of a certain peer who happened to be an expert in mechanics, Parliament would have granted a patent to a defective hydraulic machine, with disastrous economic consequences, as "a great many persons were ready to subscribe considerable sums to the project, which money of course would all have been lost, and perhaps some families ruin'd" (ibid.). See also vol. 2, p. 416.

18 The work mentioned is R. Smith, *A Compleat System of Opticks in Four Books, Viz A Popular, a Mathematical, a Mechanical and Philosophical Treatise* (Cambridge, 1738).

19 The second volume was translated into French under the more modern title of *Cours de Physique experimentale,* 2 vols. (Paris, 1751). The same year saw the appearance of the first translations into Dutch (*De naturkunde vit ondervindingen opgemakt,* 3 vols. [Amsterdam, 1751–1756]).

20 Desaguliers, *A Course,* vol. 2, p. 413. The passion of Desaguliers for the use of machines in his experimental lectures can be clearly seen in a letter sent to the President of the

Despite these criticisms, he admitted that there were "projectors" who were responsive to the needs of the "buyers of their engines" and who had such a "strong natural genius for mechaniks that without any previous knowledge of mathematiks and philosophy [they] have performed great works and built [...] rules upon facts and observations." Examples were Hadley and Sorocold, "the only engine makers of any note of the last age in England, who never fail'd of success in their undertakings, because their chief view was that the works might be brought to perform, before they considered what profit they should get by them." Now, however, he continued, there was an overabundance of "engineers [...] and projectors only considering what they shall get by a piece of work or what advantage may be made of a cried up undertaking." He criticized this new generation of entrepreneurs, thirsty for money and lacking professional responsibility, for having also ruined many people by convincing them to invest in costly and unworkable projects.[21]

According to Desaguliers, nearly all plumbers and mill constructors called themselves "engineers" even though the majority of them were incapable of measuring the quantity of water necessary for moving different types of

Royal Society on 29 April 1728 (University Library, Cambridge, Mss. ADD 4007, f. 669). Two historians have taken up the defense of practical engineers from the attacks in *A Course*. According to Lionel Th. C. Rolt (*Great Engineers* [New York, 1963], pp. 26-27), Desaguliers "refused to credit the fact that an ill-educated country blacksmith (Savery) could possibly succeed, where the best scientific brains of the day, including a fellow of the Royal Society, failed." According to H.W. Dickinson (*A Short History of the Steam Engine* [Cambridge, 1939], p. 22), "the doctor (Desaguliers) seems to have been only ready to detract the performances of others than himself, and to attribute bad motions to them" (the practical engineers).

21 Desaguliers, *A Course*, vol. 2, pp. 414–415. Desaguliers' judgments can be contrasted with those of the French mathematician, Ph. De La Hire (*Traité de mécanique* [Paris, 1695], pp. 3–4), more favorable to the artisans. Sorocold and Hadley's London Bridge waterworks had been presented by H. Deighton in an article in the *Philosphical Transactions* (vol. 38), 1731, 5–12. The Reverend Mr. Holland, too "had a very great genius for mechanics, but was no philosopher, so as to be able either to calculate the force of a power or to apply it to the best advantage" (Desaguliers, *A Course*, vol. 2, p. 521). By the eighteenth century, the term "projector" had taken on a negative meaning. Some continued to distinguish "honest projectors" from the others, however. See D. Defoe, *Essays upon Several Projects or Effectual Ways for Advancing the Interest of the Nations* (London, 1702), pp. 31–55. A decisive re-evaluation of "projectors" as innovators was carried out by J. Bentham in his *Defence of Usury* (1787) (in *Economic Writings*, ed. W. Stark, vol. 1 [London, 1952], pp. 167–171, 177). See also E. Pesciarelli, "Da Cantillon a Smith: considerazioni sull'origine della teoria dell'imprenditorialità," *Annali di Storia dell' Impresa*, vol. 2 (1986), 487–507; and ibid., "Smith, Bentham and the Development of Contrasting Ideas on Entrepreneurship," *History of Political Economy*, 21 (3), (1989), 521–536.

hydraulic wheels.[22] They calculated the force of a stream of water by sight and "he that has most practice is likely to succeed." The new machine "undertakers," then, unlike those of the previous generation, were only concerned with profit and gave little attention to the quality of their work. These "men of practice" called themselves "engineers," but they had nothing to do with the true "ingénieurs" who had received "a proper education for the Sciences."[23] To whom sometimes he refers as "good engineers."

The distinction between the French and English terms that Desaguliers makes here derives from his knowledge of and admiration for the French technical and scientific schools such as the *École d'Artillerie,* whose training of military engineers included a solid grounding in theory. He was also careful to keep up with the scientific literature of his country of origin. He was an active translator of French works particularly in the period 1711–1718 and made frequent, though not always explicit, references to the work of the French scientists of the Paris *Académie des Science.*[24] The greater weight given to the word "ingénieurs" can be traced, more particularly, to the title and subject matter of two works which he admired: Belidor's *La science des ingénieurs*

22 B.F. Belidor (*Architecture hydraulique*, vol. 2 [Paris, 1739], p. 379) also distrusted the tinsmiths. "Je dirai seulement que la plomberie, étant une profession qui n'est guère connue que de ceux qui l'exercent, il convient d'éclairer de près les ouvriers qu'on employera, et d'exiger de maîtres une garantie de 4 ou 5 ans, qui justifie la bonté de leur ouvrage" ("I will only say that for plumbing, being a profession that is hardly understood except by those who practice it, one should closely examine the workers that one employs, and demand of the masters a guarantee of 4 to 5 years [of experience] to assure their good work"). According to D.S.L. Cardwell (*Technology, Science and History* [London, 1968], p. 72), Belidor was one of Desaguliers French correspondents.

23 Desaguliers, *A Course*, vol. 2, p. 415. On the history of engineering, see H. Straub, *A History of Civil Engineering* (Cambridge, Mass., 1964); W.H.G. Armytage, *A Social History of Engineering* (Cambridge, Mass., 1962); D.S.L. Cardwell, *The Organisation of Science in England* (London, 1972); *Architekt und Ingenieur. Baumeister in Krieg und Frieden*, Einleitung U. Schutte, Austellung des Herzog August Bibliothek Wolfenbüttle (Braunschweig, 1984); A. Picon, *Architectes et ingénieurs au siècle des Lumières* (Marseille, 1989); A. Buchanan, *The Engineers. A History of the Engineering Profession in Britain 1750–1914* (London, 1989).

24 In 1711 Desaguliers translated J. Ozanan's *Traité de fortification* with an appendix on Vauban's fortification methods. The following year he translated Ozanan's *Méthode générale pour tracer des cadrans sur toute sorte de plans;* in 1713 N. Gauger's *La mécanique au feu;* in 1718 E. Mariotte's *Traité du mouvement des eaux*; and in 1742, J. Vaucanson's *Le mécanisme du fluteur automate.* See also W.H.G. Armytage, *The French Influence on English Education* (London, 1968), pp. 14–17 passim. The first edition of Belidor's *Science des ingénieurs,* which I have not been able to consult, was published in 1729.

dans le conduite de travaux de fortification et d'architecture (Paris, 1739) and the *Ingénieur françois ... avec la méthode de Monsieur de Vauban* (Lyon, 1738).

The severity of Desaguliers'criticisms of the "mechanical undertakers" was a continuation of a tradition which originated in Galileo. It may also have been part, though, of a more direct and bitter dispute between artisans and experimental philosophers. The latter were accused by the "men of practice" of being "men of theory," by which was meant that "many things which are true in the theory do not answer in the practice." Desaguliers rejected this accusation with indignation, though recognizing that it was "as common as it is false."[25] He himself had been involved in a frustrating controversy with a "man of practice." On 9 January 1725, the surveyor John Warner launched a fierce criticism of Desaguliers' project for supplying the city of London with water by diverting the Fraye and Cowley water courses. According to Warner, Dr. Desaguliers had calculated the capacity of the two courses so incorrectly that it suggested that he "had more regard to the currency of his project than to the quantity of the current." While Warner opposed the project on behalf of a Mr. Home, solicitor or owner of grain mills which would be at risk if the plan were carried out, Desaguliers acted on behalf of a society of "gentlemen." In the course of the dispute Warner did not hesitate to use strong language, denouncing "the machinations and evil designs of some projectors who ... have certainly no other view but their own private gain notwithstanding their specious pretenses of benefiting the public."[26] Desaguliers reacted to these violent attacks with detachment and tolerance. In a letter of 12 January 1725, he wrote to a mediator to inform the mill owner that he was prepared to discuss his project with him and that "if I cannot make good all that I have asserted, I have the authority from the Gentlemen principally concerned ... that they will drop their design."[27]

The details of this meeting, which was to have taken place prior to a second meeting with a Parliamentary Commission, have not been traced. We do know that the plan to supply London with water on which Desaguliers had worked went ahead in the end, although it is not certain whether this was in the form which Warner had criticized. It is not improbable that the millers were able to protect their interests. Desaguliers, on the other hand, seems to have lost his house in Channel Row (Westminster) which was demolished in order to

25 Desaguliers, *A Course*, vol. 2, p. 415.

26 British Museum (henceforth B.M.) *Ms. Landsdowne*, DCCCXLI, 51, f.113, John Warner's letter of 9 January 1725. The attacks on the "men of practice" in *A Course* may perhaps be seen as the continuation of this dispute.

27 B.M., ibid., 53, f. 117, Desaguliers' letter to W. Boyer of 12 January 1725.

make room for the new water course. Further research would be necessary to clarify the precise role of Desaguliers in this affair and to gauge the effect it had on him.[28]

After attacking the "man of practice," Desaguliers also criticized, in the spirit of Francis Bacon, those pure mathematicians who had little familiarity with either applied mathematics or with "mechanical performances." It was no surprise that they too were unable to carry out their projects, their designs being too vague. Even if they calculated correctly the intensity of the force to be applied, they left the construction of the machines to simple workmen. These workmen, moreover, had caused the failure of more than one project either because of technical incapacity or through plain dishonesty, in order not to have to admit the success of projects that they themselves had not elaborated.[29]

What sort of qualifications, though, should an entrepreneur or constructor of hydraulic equipment or machinery have, according to Desaguliers? First, the "undertaker" had to have a good knowledge of the professions of the mason, mill constructor, smith and carpenter. He also had to know the resistance and solidity of materials and how to draw a general plan of a whole machine down to the last detail. He had to be able to draw the smallest parts on a larger scale so that it was possible to analyze a project piece by piece *before starting work on it.* The drawings had to be carried out using the same techniques which the French *ingénieurs* used for the construction of fortresses and which the entrepreneurs who constructed the major public works used to elaborate their *devis,* a detailed plan in various scales indicating also estimated costs.[30] Besides this,

28 D. Campbell Lee, *Desaguliers of No. 4,* passim. I am not entirely certain that he lost his house during the course of these works.

29 Desaguliers, *A Course,* vol. 2, pp. 415–416.

30 Ibid.. Desaguliers' comments on the *devis* owed much to Belidor's *La science des ingénieurs,* the sixth and last chapter of which is entitled "La manière de faire des devis." These detailed plans were considered necessary by the provincial intendants in order that they could proceed to tender public works. In *Architecture hydraulique* (vol. 2, p. 249), Belidor too criticized those architects and engineers who provided their workers with "ni devis ni desseins" ("neither estimates nor designs"). Sebastiano Serlio's major work of the sixteenth century had already introduced drawings of houses and buildings which were real, finished projects from which the architect could make a direct estimation of the costs (S. Serlio, *Architecturae Liber Septimus* [Frankfurt, 1575], edition consulted *Il settimo libro,* in *Tutte le opere* [Venice 1584], p. 44). See also A. De Cerceau, *Livre d'Architecture* (Paris, 1559), which contains a list of projects of 50 buildings from the simplest to the most complex (to be found also in Serlio's *Sesto Libro,* left unpublished but of which De Cerceau was aware), containing also a calculation of the *toise* (unit of measurement equal to six feet) for each project. According to De Cerceau, if the *toise* of the building was known, it would be possible to "connaistre la dépense qu'il convient faire" "(to know

the entrepreneur (or good engineer) had to have a grasp of applied mathematics (that is, of theoretical mechanics) sufficient to calculate the effects of the force applied and the losses due to friction. If he oversaw the work properly, that is, if he directed the site personally, the workmen would not be found lacking in either ability, honesty or diligence.[31]

But how could it be possible to combine so many different areas of knowledge and expertise, those more or less of the civil engineer? It was not only a question of overcoming the division between manual and intellectual labor. It was also necessary to change the forms and means of the transmission of knowledge within the artisan crafts. Traditionally, a carpenter learned his trade in the carpenter's workshop, the smith in the forge and so on. The artisans did not only run the workshops, they were also teachers. The workshop was not only a place of production but also a school in which exams were taken after years of apprenticeship. For young trainees, passing this exam by producing a masterpiece marked the end of a phase of their life. Having successfully undergone this rite of passage, they acquired the right to open a workshop, although this was not always possible. Those who opened a workshop became a full master craftsman with the right to take on and train new apprentices and to pass on the skills of the profession.[32]

---

the expense that was suitable to make" ["Preface"]). On Serlio, see M. Carpo, *Metodo e ordini nella teoria architettonica di Sebastiano Serlio,* unpublished Ph.D thesis, European University Institute of Florence (Fiesole, 1990).

31 Desaguliers, *A Course,* vol. 2, pp. 415–416. Desaguliers used his skills as an experimenter also to criticize the erroneous conclusions of other scientists. On 11 December 1739, for example, he invited friends and colleagues to his house in order to show them the errors which Claude Perrault had committed. Perrault claimed to have invented a machine "which will act without friction [...]. This, were it true, would be a great improvement and of vast service in mechanical works [...]. I am sure he is mistaken, and I can both demonstrate mathematically and experimentally by models wherein he is deceived" (B.M., *Ms. Sloane,* 40050, f. 244). Desaguliers discusses this theme also in the *Philosophical Transactions.* "Les machines qui élèvent des fardeaux sans frottement" ("The machines that raise weights without friction") are described by C. Perrault in *Recueil de plusieurs machines de nouvelle invention* (Paris, 1700). For the analysis of friction, see Amontons, "De la resistance causé dans les machines tant par le frottement des parties qui les composent que par la roideur des cordes qu'on y employe et la manière de calculer l'un et l'autre," *Histoire de l'Académie Royale des Sciences avec les Mémoires de mathématique et de physique,* (1669), 3d ed. (Paris, 1732), pp. 206–227 of the *Mémoires.*

32 Y. Deforge, *Le grafisme technique. Son histoire et son enseignement* (Mâcon, 1981). Eugene S. Ferguson, "La fondation des machines modernes: des dessins," *Culture technique,* no. 114 (1985), 183–207. According to Locke, poor children should be sent to learn a trade as early as possible (see *Some Thoughts Concerning Education* [1693], Appendix A, "Working Schools" (Cambridge, 1880), pp. 189–191.

This means of transmission, however, had the defect that it was not capable of teaching the same person the rudiments of three or four different trades. It was usually only in the workshops for the construction of cathedrals, castles and palaces, mills, ships and canals where the conditions for the transmission of a wide range of skills could be found. These, though, were relatively closed worlds, limited by and large to architects, their assistants and most direct helpers. The training of technicians in a variety of fields required the creation of new training institutions capable of transmitting extensive and formal knowledge in specific subjects and disciplines (technical drawing, mathematics, physics, mechanics) along with the experience of the workshop and the laboratory. This need was met in the nineteenth century with the foundation of technical-industrial schools with varying difficulties and specializations. However, the long period of incubation of new methods of transmission of technical knowledge reaches back to the seventeenth century, and the idea of the compilation of a "History of Trades" encyclopedia, of Baconian inspiration. In 1647, Samuel Hartlib suggested to Boyle that he should encourage William Petty to compile a "History of Trades." Petty himself had suggested to Hartlib, in his first printed work, the foundation of a new college where manual crafts could be taught even to the elite, non-artisan classes. Little more than a decade later, as Michael Hunter pointed out, the Royal Society of London, on the prompting of a generous patron, John Cutler, gave Robert Hooke the task of holding a number of lectures at Gresham College in London, on the "history" of technical practices. Hooke, however, was either not able or not willing to take up this proposal, too involved in elaborating the fundamental principles of physics to describe specific practices or else unable to teach "the operative part" of technical practice. There may have been other reasons as well for his refusal. Hooke realized, as is clear from a letter written in 1683 quoted in full and discussed by Hunter, that his course on craft technology had met with disapproval from both artisans and gentlemen, due to jealousy and disdain respectively.[33]

It would not be difficult to provide further examples of a general mistrust between scientists and artisans. Desaguliers himself wanted to have a better understanding of the technical practices of the artisans, although he realized that this was not easy. He wrote: "There is a combination among most workmen to make a mystery of their Arts; and they look [upon] him as a false brother who lets gentlemen into their manner of working and the knowledge of the price of all materials."[34] This same difficulty, the reluctance of the

33 M. Hunter, *Establishing the New Science. The Experience of the Early Royal Society* (Woodbridge, 1989), p. 37, 286–314, passim.

34 Desaguliers, *A Course*, vol. 2, p. 415.

artisans to let their know-how range beyond the confines of their corporations, was encountered also by Denis Diderot when compiling his *Encyclopédie.* In the third volume under the entry ARTS he invited the artisans to take part in the great encyclopedic project of advancing knowledge, to "ne pas faire périr avec eux les découverts qu'ils feront" ("not to let the discoveries they make perish with them") and to subordinate "l'intérêt d'un seul à l'intérêt de tous" ("the interest of one to the interest of all"). In return for this collaboration, the academicians would free them from prejudice, and help them to perfect and render intelligible their arts.[35] A few years later, however, when writing the entry ENCYCLOPÉDIE for the fifth volume, Diderot had to admit that a great many artisans refused to supply information. They remained obstinately silent in the face of the questioning of the encyclopedia investigators or made fun of them by giving false information, telling "les faussetés les plus ridicules" ("the most ridiculous falsehoods"). According to Diderot, some of the entries of the *Encyclopédie* did not even have "l'ombre du sens commun" ("the shadow of common sense") whereas others were full of "bévues grossières" ("gross errors").[36]

---

35 *Encyclopédie*, ARTS, vol. 3. See in this volume, ch. 13 on the writings on different crafts in the *Encyclopédie.*

36 For this conflictual reading of the relations between Diderot and the artisans, see ch. 13 in this volume, and C. Koepp, "The Alphabetical Order. Work in Diderot's *Encyclopédie,*" in *Work in France. Representation, Meaning, Organizations and Practice,* eds. S. L. Kaplan and C. Koepp (Ithaca, 1986), pp. 229–257. According to Diderot, the reticence of the artisans was particularly strong in Paris "où la crainte des impôts les tient perpetuellement en méfiance, et où ils regardent tout homme qui les interroge avec quelque curiosité comme un émissaire des fermiers généraux ou comme un ouvrier qui veut ouvrir boutique" ("where the fear of taxes makes them perpetually suspicious, and they look upon every person who questions them with curiosity as an emissary of the farmers-general or as a worker who wants to open up his own shop"; see the article ENCYCLOPÉDIE in *Encyclopédie*). This explanation is significant but inadequate. Diderot did not realize that his questions violated the corporate practices of the transmission of technical know-how and posed a threat to the still dynamic ancient order of the workshops. However, the lowering of the barriers which protected the artisanal crafts facilitated and accelerated, during the course of the eighteenth century, the gradual spread of technical information to scientific circles. The practical results of this should be judged case by case. Besides A.E. Musson and E. Robinson's *Science and Technology,* see also R. Hahn, *The Anatomy of a Scientific Institution. The Paris Academy of Science (1666–1803)* (Berkeley, 1971); A. Braccesi, "lstanze pratiche e conoscenza formale nello sviluppo della meccanica e della termodinamica," *La Società* (1979), no. 1, 95–105; Ch. Coulston Gillispie, *Science and Polity in France at the End of the Old Regime* (Princeton, 1989); R. Hahn, "Science and the Arts in France: the Limitations of an Encyclopedic Ideology," *Studies in Eighteenth-Century Culture,* vol. X (1981), 77–93; P. Mathias, "Who Unbound Prometheus? Science and Technological Change 1600–1800," *Science and Society 1600–1900,* ed. P. Mathias (Cambridge, 1972), pp. 54–80.

Such resistance, though common, cannot be considered the only response of the artisans to enquiries about working techniques. If they were approached in the right way, artisans could be persuaded to cooperate in unveiling the mysteries of their profession. Not all the entries in the *Encyclopédie* contain "bévues grossières," and this is true also of the *Descriptions des Arts et Métiers* approved by the Paris Académie de Sciences and compiled with the crucial assistance of scientists such as Duhamel de Monceau and J. Lalande. According to Lamoignon de Malesherbes, when members of the *Académie* started to visit the "ateliers pour voir travailler les ouvriers et faire connaître au public leurs procédés" ("the workshops to see workers at work and make their methods of work known to the public") they were astonished to see

> plusieurs de ces artisans quitter le rabot et la lime pour prendre la plume, et composer eux mêmes des traités raisonnés de leur art, qu'on croiroit l'ouvrage de mathematiciens ou de physiciens consommés.[37]

Where have these treatises ended up? Were they perhaps used as sources by Duhamel de Monceau in his description of twenty trades, or by Lalande, who described nine? Here, in fact, we face a question requiring careful and detailed analysis. According to Charles Coulston Gillispie, at least forty of the treatises or pamphlets of the *Descriptions des Arts* were written by amateurs, artisans, manufacturers and so on. The best of these treatises was undoubtedly that on stained glass by Pierre le Vieil, "the last surviving master of a craft fallen into desuetude."[38]

---

37 "several of these artisans leave the plane and the file to take up the pen and themselves compose well thought-out tracts about their art that one believed to be the work of a consummate mathematician or physicist" (G.-C. Lamoignon de Malesherbes, "Mémoire sur la liberté de la presse," in *Mémoires sur la librairie* [Paris, 1809], pp. 269–70). The manuscript on which the publication is based is dated 1788 (Bibliothèque Nationale de Paris, Ms. Fr., Collection Anisson, 22182). Lamoignon de Malesherbes was one of the twelve honorary members of the *Académie des Sciences.* See Gillispie, *Science and Polity in France,* p. 82 passim.

38 On the *Descriptions des Arts et Métiers* see Gillespie, *Science and Polity,* pp. 348–356, passim. The idea of describing the artisan crafts was widespread in eighteenth-century France. Joubert de l'Hiberderie, fabric designer and author of *Le dessinateur pour les fabriques d'étoffes d'or, d' argent et de soie* (Paris, 1765) justified his publication on two grounds. First, it could help the Lyon weavers avoid making the same mistakes as their former masters in Italy, who were forced to work hard "avec une peine infinie et avec peu de succès" ("with a great deal of hard work and little success") when setting up the looms because they had not retained "aucun vestige, aucun écrit qui put leur rappeler comment on montoit un tel métier." ("any vestige, any writing which could help them recall how one could mount such a loom"). De l' Hiberderie continues: "C'est pour cela que j'ai décidé que mon

In the introduction to the first volume of the *Descriptions* edited by J.E. Bertrand, an anonymous author (perhaps Bertrand himself) confidently emphasized the practical utility of the collection. Artisan know-how, translated into a precise, detailed and intelligible language, would be of benefit to those artisans able to read and who wanted to "s'instruire sur leur métiers, abréger ou simplifier leur manoeuvres, en connoître les raisons, apprendre à perfectionner leur ouvrages" ("instruct themselves on their craft, to shorten or simplify the movement of their hands, to understand the reasons, to learn and improve their work"). The *Descriptions* would be even more useful to those *fabricants* (putting-outers) who employed artisans and workers but who were interested little in production techniques as long as the goods they had commissioned could be sold at a profit. The anonymous writer contrasted this by now anachronistic image of the intermediary between production and the market who contributed nothing towards the "perfection de la manufacture, qu'il ne connoît quelque fois que comme marchand et qu'il n'a point étudié comme practicien" ("the perfection of manufacturing, whose only knowledge was that of a merchant and had not at all studied as a practitioner") with the more modern image of the entrepreneur interested "à connoitre les détails du métier" ("to know the details of the craft") and thus able to manage his workers and to improve manufacture. This new figure of the manufacturer would have the task of cutting production times by introducing an efficient division of labor. In his firm,

> l'ouvrage le plus simple passe successivement par une multitude de mains avant que d'être fini. Chaque opération occupe un ouvrier différent qui, en le répétant sans cesse, apprend à le faire avec autant de

ouvrage devint public pour le bien des jeunes artistes et celui des Arts en général, à fin de transmettre à la posterité les différents genres d'étoffes qui se fabriquent à Lyon" ("it is for this reason that I decided that my work should become public for the benefit of young artists and for the Arts in general, in order to transmit to posterity the different kinds of fabrics which are made in Lyon"). The second reason stemmed from the psychological frustration de l'Hiberderie had encountered in his youth as an apprentice designer. His older and more experienced masters, in fact, responded to his eager questioning with a wall of silence, either through ignorance or through not wanting to "m'expliquer par quelle voie" ("explain to me in which way") they had developed their skills. The author added that he had written the book "pour m'instruire moi même, pour faire passer à mes confrères le fruit de mes études et engager par ce moyen quelqu'un d'eux [...] d'en former progressivement un corps d'ouvrage qui puisse être utile aux manufactures et agréable aux amateurs" ("in order to teach myself, to transmit to my fellow workers the fruit of my studies and by this means engage some of them [...] gradually to form a work corps that can be useful to manufacturing and agreeable to non-professionals") (pp. ix- xiii).

> vitesse que d'exactitude. [...] C'est ainsi que l'étude de l'Art, rendue facile par des bonnes descriptions peut éclairer, diriger un fabricant qui, sans ces secours, s'en tiendroit peut-être toujours aux routes battues, quoique inexactes.[39]

The similarities between the proposals of the *Descriptions des Arts et Métiers* and the Smithian model of the division of labor are important signs of more modern thinking.[40]

These examples show that it was not impossible to collect the information necessary to explain the secrets of the Arts and to spread the knowledge of new technologies. Desaguliers, however, partly because of the type of work he was writing, did not attempt to bring to light the more or less secret working practices whose negative consequences he had indicated. He criticized their secrecy but was more interested in describing new technologies. The last chapter of *A Course,* in particular, is mainly devoted to the description of machinery and plants built between 1680 and 1740. This chapter, which takes up around

---

39 "the most simple work passes successively from a multitude of hands before being finished. Each operation occupies a different worker who, on repeating it continuously, learns to do it with as much speed as exactitude. [...] It is in this way that the study of Art, made easy by good descriptions can enlighten, direct a manufacturer who, without these aids, remains perhaps always on beaten paths, even if inexact" ("Introduction" to the *Description des Arts et Métiers,* faites ou approuvées par Messieurs de l'Académie Royale des Sciences de Paris, nouvelle édition, vol. 1, ed. J.E. Bertrand [Neuchatel, 1771]). This edition is different in several places from the original folio *Cahiers.* I have not been able to consult the Moutard edition. The text of the "Introduction" was republished in part in the *Supplement au Mercure* of 23 June 1787. On the complexity of the problem of the transmission of technical know-how, see J. Perrin, "The Inseparability of Technology and Work Organization," *History and Technology* no. 1 (1990), 1–13.

40 Towards the end of the eighteenth century an important avant-garde didactic innovation took over from the *Description des Arts:* the machine display cabinet of the Paris Conservatoire des Arts et Métiers, and with it the idea of transmitting technical know-how through *de visu* observation. This involved practical demonstrations, the forerunners of the subsequent applied science courses. These new means of education, closely linked to the invention and diffusion of the new machinery of the Industrial Revolution, were in turn replaced by more efficient educative processes in the nineteenth century – technical schools fully equipped with workshops for youths who had completed primary school. In certain key sectors such as mechanics and metalworking, the workshop apprentice began to be replaced by the school apprentice, who had been taught theory, technical drawing and had been given some experience of manual work. This process, whose distant roots I have indicated, was not confined to England and France. Research should be widened to the rest of Europe. One of the most important works in this respect is that of J . Leupold (in several volumes) which, at the beginning of the eighteenth century, attempted to combine a scientific approach with a practical ability in machine construction.

a third of the entire volume, draws heavily on such figures as Henry Beighton, inventor of four machines, and Bernard F. Belidor, from whom Desaguliers takes his description of two French hydraulic plants. The latter were Francini's machines, one built in the garden of the Bibliothèque Royale in Paris and the other the huge hydraulic plant at Marly, the most famous and admired of its time. Desaguliers had spent eight days at Marly examining in detail the colossal plant. For all the machines described – mills, fire pumps, pile drivers, cranes, hydraulic plants, Savery's and Newcomen's machines and so on – Desaguliers gave indications as to the place of construction, the name of the constructor and the owner, the way they worked (with the help of drawings) and the mechanical principles on which they were based, together with the relevant mathematical calculations (not always confined to the notes).

Many of these machines received serious criticism while others were recognized as near perfect. Among the latter were the water mill built by Henry Beighton at Ban Pool in Warwickshire and the water wheel ("breast wheel") invented by Henry Baker, "whose skill in mechanics as well as all parts of mathematics and philosophy is well known." Sometimes Desaguliers made brief comparisons of the efficiency of different hydraulic plants. After criticizing the inefficient arrangement of certain parts of thc Marly plant with its 14 wheels, he compares it with the excellent construction of a similar plant on the Thames (London Bridge) by Sorocold which supplied the city with water. The latter lifted almost three times as much water as that of Marly with four wheels. He then notes, quoting Belidor, that the Marly plant cost around 4 million pounds. The same results could have been obtained using just one of Newcomen's steam engines at a cost of 10,000 pounds.[41] Desaguliers concerned himself, then, not only with the technical efficiency of plants but also their cost and profitability.

Of all the machines considered, the one which attracted Desagulier's attention the most was the steam engine, from the first attempts of the Marquis of Worcester to Thomas Savery, Thomas Newcomen, down to the later improvements that he himself had proposed working alongside s'Gravesande. In these pages, Desaguliers reveals himself in several guises: historian, scientist,

41 Desaguliers, *A Course,* vol. 2 pp. 530–531. The Marly machine worked badly because it had been built "by an ordinary man of Liège, who was entirely ignorant in mathematics." As a result, though it had "many excellent contrivances" it was unable to lift "all the water that it shou'd do, because the workman did not know how to calculate, so as to give the power of the river Seine its utmost advantage" (ibid., vol. 1, p. 69). Belidor had already given a sarcastic and critical opinion of the Marly machine, which made "autant de bruit dans le monde" ("so much noise in the world") (*Architecture hydraulique,* vol. 2, pp. 195–203).

entrepreneur and (good) engineer. From 1718 onwards he had constructed seven "fire engines," one built for Peter the Great, another set up in his own back garden in Chanwell Row by Gun Jones.[42]

Desaguliers' work as a scientist, entrepreneur and experimenter may be seen as carrying out a "metaproduction function," that is, the exploration of the production possibilities which can be obtained by developing existing technical and scientific knowledge, and attempts to modify or overcome certain institutional obstacles such as the rules for the transmission of technical know-how.[43] His aim was to prevent "great works or manufactures" being built "in such a manner that the great part of the intensity of the power is uselessly spent [...] as for example when there are unnecessary frictions arising from ill contrivance of the whole engine, or the wrong figure of some of its parts, or the bad performance of the workman, or if men or horses exert but a small part of that strength which they might apply without weariness or inconveniency. Then the skill of a good engineer may be advantageously applied in changing the form or altering the parts and motions of a machine."[44]

Desaguliers' technical and scientific know-how are naturally limited by the period in which he lived: he died some decades before the onset of the Industrial Revolution. This does not mean, however, that he was not acquainted with the factory system already in existence in England at the beginning of the eighteenth century in the form of the great silk mill built by the Lombe

42 Among the machines described, there is no mention of the one for which Desaguliers received a patent on 25 July 1720 together with the "instrument maker" William Vreen and the "copper smith" Daniel Niblet. This was "a new invention for making the steam and vapour of boyling liquor useful for many purposes and particularly for drying malt, hops, starch and other humid substances, and for baking, brewing, distilling" without the risk of fire (B.M., *Ms. Eg. Ch. 7686*). The patent can be found in B. Woodcroft, *Alphabetical Index of Patentees of Inventions,* (London, 1969). Instead he describes a ventilator intended for changing the air in a sickroom or mine which was to be presented fully in the *Philosophical Transactions.* Stephen Switzer's description of steam engine construction is based on the information and technical analysis of Desaguliers and Hauksbee. The particular steam engine Switzer describes (*A General System of Hydrostatics and Hydraulics, Philosophical and Practical* [London, 1729]), was exhibited in Channel Row and was the subject of some of Desaguliers' lectures, given to an audience of potential buyers interested in the "supplying of great quantities of water, draining mines and other uses in which the engine may be of service" (*The Daily Post,* 30 January 1721; quotation from I. Inkster, *Science and Technology in History. An Approach to Industrial Development* [London, 1991], p. 314).

43 I have taken the concept of metaproduction function from V. Ruttan and Y. Hayami, *Agricultural Development* (Baltimore, 1971), pp. 53–54.

44 Desaguliers, *A Course,* vol. 1. p. 69.

brothers and modelled on the Italian silk mills.[45] He described a distinctive characteristic of the new machinery by noting that in order to twist a thread, using the previous technology, the hand of a worker had to turn half a pound (the weight of a spindle) while the same hand was normally capable of lifting a weight of up to 25 pounds. Only a machine could liberate the power of a hand "before misapply'd or not employ'd at all." This had been done "at Derby in a very ingenious manner by the Messieurs Thomas and John Lombe, who have employ'd the force of a water wheel to the working of Italian silk, so as to lose or mispend no part of the power." This was, however, a somewhat biased analysis although original and characteristic of a mind trained in applied mathematics. The advantages of powered machines are underlined because they replace the work of the hand, used at only 2% of its force, as if the task of the hand were simply that of lifting weights. This ignores several issues: the new role of work, now given the task of feeding and controlling the machinery which twisted the silk; the organization of the new system, involving the overseeing of the work of hundreds of workers (men, women and children); and finally the structure and operation of the machinery. Desaguliers dedicates a few lines only to the transmission of movement: "One water-wheel communicates motions to all the rest of the wheels and movements of which any one may be stopp'd separately and independently of the rest." It might be asked why this brief description is not followed by a fuller and more detailed account accompanied by drawings. Desaguliers anticipates this question by explaining that he was prevented from describing this "curious" machine by the prohibition of their owners, who did not want "to have a description of the whole engine or any [of] the movements of it made public."[46]

Desaguliers did not seem to realize that this was in effect a justification of those technical secrets which he had so criticized among the artisans and

45 The history of this machine (in England) can be found in nearly all the manuals of the history of the Industrial Revolution, from Paul Mantoux to Peter Mathias. [For a comprehensive history of this machine and of the silk industry in Italy, see C. Poni, *La seta in Italia. Una grande industria prima della rivoluzione industriale* (Bologna, 2009).]

46 Desaguliers, *A Course*, vol. 1, pp. 69–70. Instead of describing how the mill machines worked, Desaguliers published, and he was the first to do so, the number of cogs (26,586) and movements (97,746). These data were later published in the fourth edition (1742) of Daniel Defoe's *Tour thro' the Whole Island of Great Britain*, being absent in the first edition of the *Tour* (the only one edited by Defoe himself) and only added subsequently by later editors. None of the historians who have quoted these figures from Defoe have recognized the debt to Desaguliers. On the various editions of the *Tour*, see G.M. Barringer, "Defoe's A Tour thro' the Whole Island of Great Britain," *Thoth, Journal of the English Graduate Group*, vol. 9 (1968), 3 ff.

which he saw in other contexts as constituting an obstacle to technical progress. This episode reveals ambiguities and contradictions. Desaguliers demands transparency from the artisans but accepts the opacity of a machine which, for the first time in history, replaced the work of hundreds of silk throwers with its own mechanisms. Two hands are needed to spin or twist (or "throw") silk thread, whereas the machine constructed by John and Thomas Lombe twisted thousands of threads mechanically. Desaguliers makes no justification for this ambiguity in his writings, distancing himself from the obvious desire of the "undertakers" (like the artisans) not to reveal the secrets of their trade.

In or around 1719 Desaguliers, together with a "mechanical workman" who used to assist him in his courses and friends such as the Marquis Lord Tullibardine, Dr. Alexander Stuart and Dr. Pringle, had not hesitated to mix with the crowds at Haymarket in London in order to spy on the feats of strength of a German Samson.[47] Desaguliers wanted to explain the mechanical principles that allowed men of normal physical capacities to lift enormous weights, win contests easily against apparently stronger challengers, and develop strength equal to that of a horse or four men (with the help of the right equipment).[48] The observations on the exploits of the Samson are reported in *A Course* and in the manuscripts of the Royal Society in a style which is close to parody despite the intentions of the author.[49] Desaguliers and his four helpers ("very curious persons") positioned themselves around this Samson in order to observe the posture of his body from different angles. After repeated observations, and having memorized his movements, they attempted to imitate him. In short,

47 Dr. Alexander Stuart was the author of the *Dissertatio medica inauguralis de structura et motu musculari* (Lugduni Batavorum, 1711), an argument which he took up again in the *Three lectures on Muscular Motion read before the Royal Society in the Year 1738 … being a supplement of that Year* (London, 1739). This supplement can be found also in volume 40 of the *Philosophical Transactions.* Dr. Pringle could be the Dr. J. Pringle, author of *A Rational Enquiry into the Nature of the Plague …* (London, 1722). The presence of "Samsons," jugglers and tightrope walkers at the London fairs is well documented by T. Frost, *The old showmen, and the old Londaon fairs* (London, 1874), pp. 19, 52–55, 144–145, 170–171 passim.

48 For the scientific analysis of the operations of animate bodies, Desaguliers relies on G.A. Borelli, *De motu animalium* (Rome, 1680) and Ph. De La Hire, "Examen de la force de l'homme pour mouvoir des fardeaux," *Histoire de l'Académie Royale des Sciences avec les Mémoires de Mathematique et de Physique* (1699), pp. 153–162 of the *Mémoires*. According to Borelli, "Animalium operationes sunt a causis et instrumentis et rationibus mechanicis" ("the workings of animals have mechanical causes, means, and reasons"). Only the use of the principles of mechanics (levers, wedges, screws and so on) could enable us to read the "codex divinus in animalibus conscriptus" ("the divine book written in animals") (ibid., p. 3).

49 Desaguliers, *A Course,* vol. 1, p. 255. See also the whole of Lecture IV.

Desaguliers too exhibited himself as a Samson, although rather than showing himself to the crowds at Haymarket he would do so at the Royal Society or to the audience of his "experimental lectures." His aim was to show how, by moving the body according to the principles of mechanics, it was possible for even a professor to lift the largest of weights and carry out other feats of strength with, of course, the help of the same equipment used by the German Samson (see Figures 12.1 and 12.2).

The followers of the lectures were encouraged to do the same to prove how "any person of ordinary strength ... can easily do all that the German above mentioned used to do." On at least one occasion, the Marquis of Tullibardine successfully challenged the Samson of Haymarket to a trial of strength (and ability). The story concludes with a comment which could be interpreted as a justification of espionage. Desaguliers writes: "I don't hear that any of these Samsons have attempted since to impose upon people in the same manner in or near London." To reveal the secrets of the Samsons who exhibited themselves in public, it was implied, was to disabuse and enlighten the public. In the case of the silk mill constructed at Derby, however, this duty to share technological secrets was subordinated to a private obligation, to the promises Desaguliers made to Thomas Lombe before and during his visit to the factory.

These two cases would seem to suggest that it is social relations and the way in which they are perceived and lived that dictate the conditions that lead to the divulgation and spread of technical processes. This is particularly clear when different groups enter into conflict with each other. An important case described by Desaguliers was that of Richard Newsham,[50] an "engine maker," who was tried at the Court of Westminster on the charge of having repaired badly a hydraulic machine belonging to the Shadwell Company. It was only with great difficulty that the technicians appearing in support of Newsham were able to persuade the lawyers, and that the lawyers in turn were able to convince the court, that Mr. Newsham had worked well applying correctly the scientific knowledge that was available at the time. This case, summarily reported by Desaguliers (but which would repay examination in the court records) points to the crucial importance of civil litigation for the understanding of technical and mechanical processes.

50 Richard Newsham was the inventor of an improved fire-fighting machine (Desaguliers, *A Course*, vol. 2, p. 505).

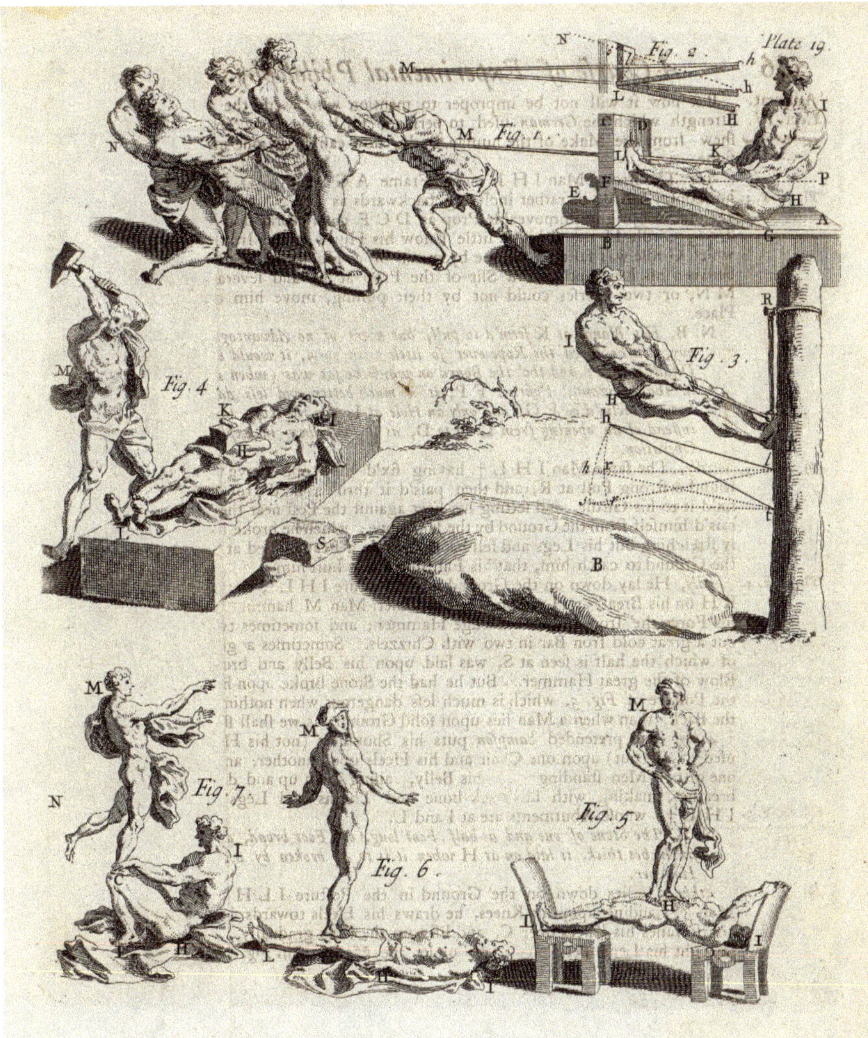

FIGURE 12.1 Postures of the body I (according to the principles of mechanics: lever, wheel, etc.) and apparata to multiply muscular power
SOURCE: DESAGULIERS, *A COURSE IN EXPERIMENTAL PHILOSOPHY*

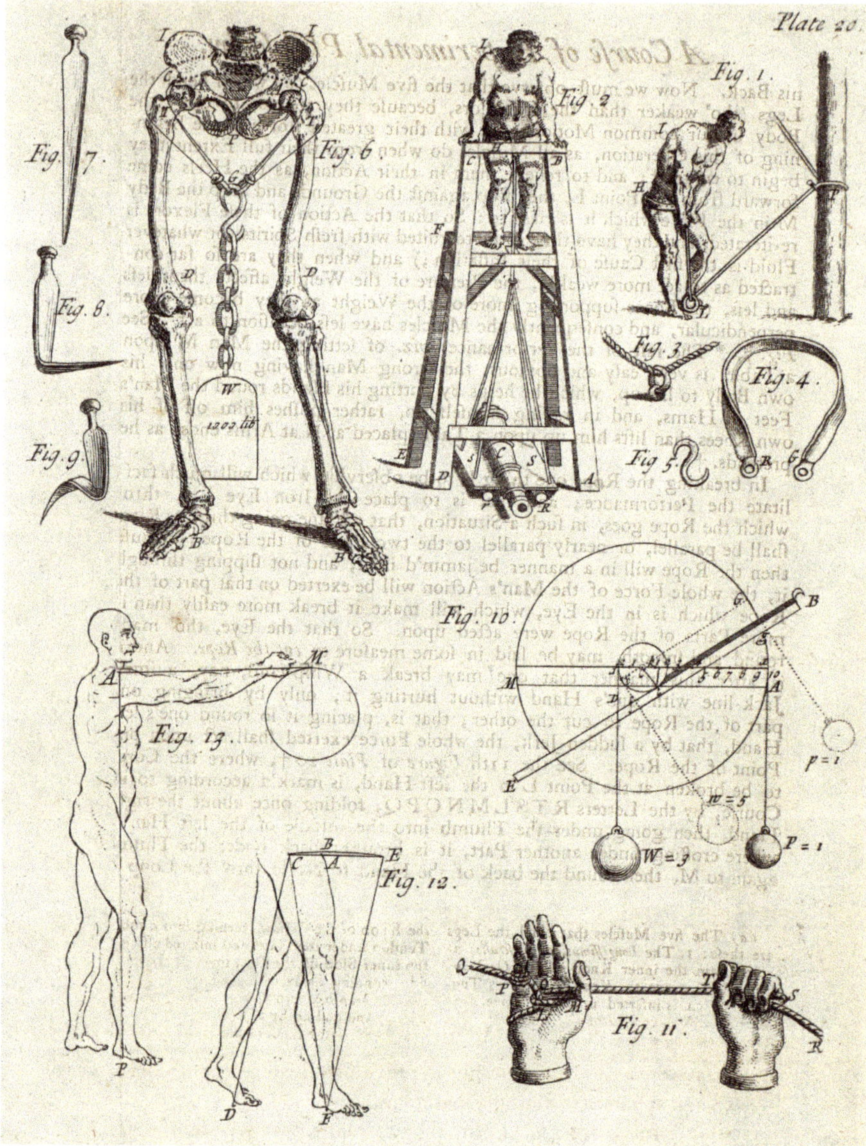

FIGURE 12.2 Postures of the body II (according to the principles of mechanics: lever, wheel, etc.) and apparata to multiply muscular power
SOURCE: DESAGULIERS, *A COURSE IN EXPERIMENTAL PHILOSOPHY*

CHAPTER 13

The Worlds of Work: Formal Knowledge and Practical Abilities in Diderot's *Encyclopédie*

Carlo Poni

In October 1750, Denis Diderot published a *Prospectus,* an eight-page folio booklet, announcing the forthcoming publication of the *Encyclopédie, ou dictionnaire raisonné des sciences, arts et métiers*.[1]

According to the *Prospectus,* the subject matter of the *Encyclopédie* would be divided into three areas: the sciences, the liberal arts and the mechanical arts. Traditionally, these activities had not been given equal treatment. Much had been written on the sciences and on the liberal arts, but almost nothing on the mechanical arts. He continued: "Of those who have written on them, one had insufficient knowledge of what he wanted to write about [...]; another only touched upon the subject, treating it from the point of view of the grammarian or linguist rather than that of the artist; and a third did better, because he was closer to the world of work, but at the same time was so summary in his treatment that the activities of the artists and the descriptions of the machines [...] took up only a very small part of his work."[2]

In order to obtain information on the technical practices of the workshops, Diderot had decided to turn directly "to the most accomplished artisans of Paris and of the kingdom." He wrote: "We have taken the trouble to go into their workshops and ask them questions, write under their dictation, develop their thoughts, find terms appropriate to their arts, copy and improve their drawings, talk to those from whom we had received written accounts and – an almost indispensable precaution – correct by means of a series of long interviews what others had insufficiently, obscurely and sometimes incorrectly

1 D. Diderot, *Prospectus,* in *Oeuvres complètes de Diderot,* J. Assèzat, ed., vol. XLLL (Paris, 1876), pp. 129–145. This work (dated 1750) announced the publication of the first volumes of the *Encyclopédie, ou Dictionnaire raisonné des sciences, des arts, et des métiers, par une société des gens de lettres. Mis en ordre et publié par M. Diderot,* 17 vols. (Paris 1751–1765), and is partially reproduced in the "Discours préliminaire" by d'Alembert published in vol. 1. See in particular pp. XXXIII–XLI and XLIII–XLIV.

2 *Prospectus*, p. 140.

 | DOI:10.1163/9789004713277_015

described."[3] Diderot, in short, was one of the first to use the oral survey both to obtain precise information and to check on the information he received.

It was true that some artisans were literate. But, according to Diderot, "most of those who exercised the mechanical arts have chosen them only through necessity and work out of instinct. Out of a thousand, scarcely a dozen can be found capable of expressing themselves clearly about the objects that they make." He continued: "We have come across artisans who have worked for forty years with almost no knowledge of their machines." He admitted, however, that the artisans worked with highly original instruments and carried out complex operations "very difficult to describe by those who are not artisans," who did not personally operate the machines with their own hands and see an object take shape under their own eyes.[4]

These ideas put forward first in the *Prospectus* were taken up in a more analytical manner in the first volume of the *Encyclopédie* under the entry *ART*. Here Diderot looked into the distinction between the liberal and the mechanical arts. The former were based on intellectual rather than manual activity, "while the mechanical arts were instead the fruit of manual rather than intellectual activity." According to Diderot, "this distinction between the liberal and the mechanical arts, although well founded, has had appalling effects, embittering wellrespected and useful men, reinforcing in us who knows what natural laziness which has inclined us too much [...] towards the belief that a constant and continuous manipulation of material and physical objects [...] is damaging to the human spirit; that to practice and even to study the mechanical arts means lowering oneself to things which demand hard work, base thinking, difficult presentation, and which concern unlimited numbers and dishonorable trade." This prejudice had negative social repercussions. "It fills the city with proud and superfluous thinkers and the country with petty, lazy, indolent and haughty tyrants."[5]

According to Diderot, it was finally time to give due justice to artisans. "The liberal arts," he wrote, "have celebrated themselves too much. Now they should stir themselves to save the mechanical arts from the humiliation to which they have been too long consigned by prejudice. It is the responsibility of the king to protect them and to rescue them from the misery in which they languish. The artisans feel themselves humiliated because they have been held in contempt. [...] Let us teach them to have greater esteem for themselves. This is the only

3 Ibid.

4 Ibid., pp. 140–141.

5 *Encyclopédie*, vol. I, *ART*, p. 714.

way that better work can be obtained from them. Someone should leave the bosom of the academy and descend to the laboratories, collect the works of the Arts and show them to us in a book which encourages artists to read, philosophers to think usefully and the powerful to put to good use their authority and their wealth."[6]

This topic was taken up once more under the entry *MÉTIER* ("Craft"). "This term will be used to indicate any profession that requires the use of hands which is limited to a certain number of mechanical operations aimed at the production of a single object and which the worker repeats without rest. I do not know why a mean idea is associated with this word. It is from the trades that we receive all the necessities of life. Anyone who visits the workshops will immediately see usefulness combined with clear proof of wisdom." He continued: "Antiquity transformed into divine beings those who invented the crafts. The following centuries cast into the dust those who perfected them."[7]

Diderot's intention was to bring together members of different crafts in order to give greater dignity to the weaker ones. This was at the basis of the general project for the mechanical arts. He warned that the history, that is, descriptions of nature without that of the arts would be incomplete.[8] He was aware that it was not possible to improve practice without theory, or indeed to have theory without practice. Each craft had its own distinctive features related to the materials, instruments and body movements that could only be learned through practice. This led Diderot to conclude that only a tradesman with rational capacities could talk with proper knowledge of his trade.

In the meantime, he attempted to define the difference between the geometry (or mechanics) of the artisans and that of the academicians, starting with the observation that the "elements of the geometry of the academicians were the simplest and least complex part of the geometry of the workshop." He continued: "Those who know only pure geometry are usually clumsy, while the artisan who knows only experimental geometry, based on practice, is a very limited worker." But he followed this immediately by saying astutely that the artisan could do without the pure geometry of the academy through his practical intuition of certain fundamental questions such as friction. Diderot ridiculed those who, with no experience, drew up designs of machines on paper which could never work. And he warned, making reference to Galilean physics, that some machines worked when they were small but not when they were large.[9]

---

6 Ibid., p. 717.

7 Ibid., vol. X, *MÉTIER*, p. 463.

8 Ibid., vol. I, *ART*, p. 715.

9 Ibid., p. 716.

lt is worth remarking here that his use of the words "artisan" and "artist" was not accidental. The term "artisan" indicated workers in mechanical arts which require "less intelligence." Thus it was said that a good shoemaker was a good artisan, and that a good watch- or clockmaker was a great artist. More generally, the title of "artist" was given to those who were expert in mechanical arts that were half practical and half speculative.[10]

At this point in his thought Diderot emphasized the deep and widespread ignorance of the technical practices necessary to produce the objects required for everyday life (clothes, beds, shoes, tables, doors, candles). This prompted the idea of sending artists into the workshops to sketch machines and instruments for use in the *Encyclopédie*. "Nothing that could help a clear visual representation has been omitted," be added.

The entry *ART* concluded with a thorough analysis of the superiority of one manufacture over another that could be attributed partly to "the excellence of the materials" ("la bonté des matières") and partly to the speed of the work and the perfection of the finished product. According to Diderot, the latter depended entirely on the number of workers employed. When a large number of people were employed in an industry, each operation was carried out by a different person. "Each worker carries out one, and only one operation throughout his life. And he will do this well and rapidly. Those who worked best will also cost the least. In any case, taste and fashion will always improve when there is a large number of workers, because it is highly likely that there is one among them who is able to reflect, combine and finally find the means to raise himself above his companions." Thus an individual's means of upward social mobility was to be found through innovation, through saving on raw materials, introducing new machinery, or suggesting a "more comfortable way of working" ("une manoeuvre plus commode"). But especially important, according to Diderot, were the advantages of large-scale production. If foreign manufacturers "do not equal our Lyon manufactures this is not because elsewhere they do not know how work was carried out there. Everywhere there are the same looms, the same silks and more or less the same practices. But only in Lyon are there 3,0000 workers in the same place, working in the same industry."[11]

The advantages of the division of labor were emphasized by Alexandre Deleyre who, in his entry *ÉPINGLE* ("Pin"), analyzed the production of pins. The editor (perhaps Diderot), commenting on this entry, praised Deleyre because he managed to raise himself to the highest contemplation of Francis Bacon's

10 Ibid., p. 745. l have not always maintained this distinction.

11 Ibid., p. 717

philosophy, and at the same time lower himself to the most minute details of mechanics. Each pin went through numerous operations which resulted in pins of different qualities and prices depending on their length and width. This work, Deleyre stated, "is all the more difficult because only the habit of the eye or the hand can subject the worker to this rule."[12] The illustrations accompanying the entry *ÉPINGLE* represented the several phases of production. Pinmaking, traditionally very strong in Paris, was dependent on *laiton* (brass wire) imported from Sweden and subsequently refined in the forges and the French *tréfilerie* (workshops producing wire). But since the cost of living had risen in Paris, the production of pins had decreased dramatically and had shifted above all to Laigle and other towns in Normandy where labor was cheaper.[13]

The idea of Diderot and Deleyre on the advantages of the division of labor anticipate the major cultural transformation that culminated in the construction of classical political economy. This analysis of the positive results of the division of labor reappeared in the first chapter of Adam Smith's *The Wealth of Nations* (1776). According to Smith, one worker on his own could with difficulty make one pin a day. But if the manufacture of pins was given to ten men, each worker carrying out at the same time successive operations for each pin, the average production of pins per day per worker would increase to about twelve pounds of pins. Since one pound consisted of more than 400 moderate-sized pins, those workers would have made more than 40,000 pins a day, in other words on average approximately 4,800 pins per day per worker.[14]

The entry *ENCYCLOPÉDIE*, in the fifth volume, introduces a major change of perspective. Diderot admitted, first of all, in response to numerous criticisms, that the entry *ART* contained some analyses and descriptions which could hardly be worse, although he also gave examples of others which could hardly be better.[15]

In a relaxed but self-critical manner, he recognized that in future the informers for the *Encyclopédie,* responsible for the entries relating to artisans – and the instruments and machines for manual work – should be chosen from among experts in scientific disciplines such as mineralogy, chemistry, physics, mechanics and geometry. This ideal interviewer, highly professional and with technical and scientific knowledge, would be able to identify immediately the

---

12 Ibid., vol. V, *ÉPINGLE*, p. 808.

13 Ibid.

14 A. Smith, *The Wealth of Nations*, ed. E. Cannan (London 1961), vol. I, pp. 11–12. See also R. Scazzieri, *A Theory of Production Tasks, Processes and Technical Practices* (Oxford 1993), pp. 38–41.

15 *Encyclopédie*,vol. V, *ENCYCLOPÉDIE*, pp. 646–647.

quality of the raw material used by the artisans, to understand straightaway the reasons behind a host of operations, and to reveal the secrets and the mysteries of the trade. He would not allow himself to be led on by the workers, not fail to notice the skilled hand movements ("les tours des mains"), be able to distinguish without difficulty an unimportant movement from an essential precaution, and make a true calculation of the mechanical forces, tempering the rigor of mathematical hypotheses. Armed with this elaborate knowledge, this ideal interviewer would submit the artisans to questioning on the raw materials used, the prices at which they were bought, and their place of origin. He would, moreover, reveal "the absurdity of their lies."[16]

This was a major accusation, and one directed above all at the artisans and the artists, the same whom Diderot had defended against the arrogance of the liberal arts. In fact despite all the care and attention that had been taken, a number of "gross untruths" (as, for example, in the entry *BRIQUE* ["Brick"]) had slipped into the *Encyclopédie,* while the entry *BLANCHISSERIE DES TOILES* ("Fabric bleaching"), and others went beyond all common sense. The ideal interviewer (Diderot himself or his collaborators) would soon have realized, after spending time in the workshops of the artisans, that he had paid "dearly" ("l'argent à la main") for the most ridiculous falsehoods.[17]

Diderot had seen, then, what sort of people artisans were, particularly in Paris, where fear of taxes kept them in a permanent state of alarm, and where they always took those asking questions to be agents of tax collectors or other craftsmen wanting to open shop. It was better, according to Diderot, to shift the survey from Paris to the provinces, where "you could ask people who were not suspicious. Where money is rarer and time cheaper, it appears to me evident that we can learn with less expense (or we can obtain more reliable information)."[18]

We do not know whether Diderot really put this option into practice. If he did, though, it would have been an error, since Paris and Lyon were the most highly industrialized cities in France. Wrong too was the idea that the artisans took the *Encyclopédie* interviewers to be tax collectors or craftsmen who wanted to open shop, as we will see shortly.

Continuing his exploration of the differences between artisans and scientists, Diderot observed, as an astute sociologist, that the origins and progress of an art were different from the origins and progress of a science. "Scientists

16 Ibid., p. 647.
17 Ibid.
18 Ibid.

converse with each other, write to each other, make their discoveries known, contradict each other and are contradicted. These discussions and papers describe facts and give dates. Artisans, on the other hand, live their lives ignored in obscurity and isolation. All those who work at a craft do so for their own gain. They do almost nothing for their glory. There are inventions that remain buried in the memories of families for centuries, handed down from one generation to another or else degenerate without anyone knowing with any precision who made a certain discovery or when."[19]

Diderot's sincerity and irritation were deep. But he did not realize that artisans were not only shopkeepers who produced for the market. They were also master-artisans who transmitted knowledge of their craft to their apprentices in a training period that lasted from five to seven years. The workshop, in short, was also a school, although of a special type. The transmission of technical practices took place by means of imitation. The apprentices learned their craft miming and copying the movement of the hands, the legs and the bodies of their masters. It was a tacit knowledge, tacitly transmitted, and ended with an examination by members of the guild. The examination was not oral and certainly not written, but practical. The aspiring artisan had to produce a "masterpiece" that varied from one craft to another. For example, those who wanted to become master shoemakers had to make a shoe in a given time under the supervision of the examination commission headed by the Rector of the guild and its older members. Not without reason the artisans feared that opening up other channels of training would diminish their social prestige and reduce available cheap trainee labor.

It is clear that one of Diderot's main objectives was to rationalize the movements of the workers' body with the aim of increasing productivity and the quality of work, and thus also of the product. This became a focus of attention at the beginning of the twentieth century in the work of the American engineer, F.W. Taylor, the inventor of the scientific organization of work. Both Diderot and Taylor came up against the resistance of workers to these processes of rationalization.[20]

It was precisely on this ground, under the entry *CHEF D'OEUVRE* ("Masterpiece"), that the *Encyclopédie* attacked the guilds. It was an insidious attack directly aimed at the figure of the master artisan responsible for transmitting the secrets of the craft, and one which took all value away from the practice. If the journeyman (*ouvrier*) who sought to become a master knew

19 Ibid.

20 F.W Taylor, *The Principles of Scientific Management* (New York, 1911).

his craft well, it was pointless examining him. If he did not have the expertise he should not be turned down or even prevented from opening up shop. This *ouvrier* would soon become known as a bad worker and be forced out of business. Not the guild but competition would expel the incompetent artisans from the market.[21]

The attack on the corporations was more subtly argued, more balanced and richer in the entry *MAÎTRISES* ("Masterships") written by Faiguet de Villeneuve. According to him, masterships had been introduced partly to verify the professional skills of those who engaged in the Arts, but even more to encourage emulation, order and fairness. Unfortunately, over time the *maîtrises* had been transformed into shrewd monopolies, damaging to the national interest. Instead of formulating wise rules for regulating the commerce of a great people, the *maîtrises* had fomented ignorance, bad faith and laziness. According to Faiguet de Villeneuve (quoting Furetière, *Dictionnaire universel* [Paris, 1690]), the corporations were nothing but "cabals, places of drunkenness and monopolies." The richest and the strongest excluded the weakest and gained control of everything. The only remedy was to introduce freedom and competition in all the Arts.

Moreover, the apprenticeship was too long, with damaging side effects on social behavior. It prolonged male celibacy, with negative consequences on population growth. Strong, promising youths were forced to emigrate, a clear and dishonorable loss for the country. Instead, solid advantages should be offered to "conjugal unions," that is, giving *maîtrises* to married workers for free or for low fees, which would include their widows and sons. The licenses to open shops should be taken out of the hands of the guilds and given to a "municipal chamber" made up of five or six aldermen. Faiguet de Villeneuve strongly attacked the rules that prohibited widows from inheriting their husbands' shops unless they married journeymen belonging to the craft to which the dead man belonged.[22]

Was it really necessary to produce a "masterpiece" in order to guarantee perfection in the art? Faiguet de Villeneuve said no. Accuracy and honesty in doing good work were sufficient. Fortunately, these qualities were within reach even of the mediocre. It was not necessary to put on the market only artistic wonders ("les prodiges de l'Art"). Those working for ordinary people could be happy with small earnings. The "good worker [...] the man of taste

---

21 *Encyclopédie*, vol. LLI, *CHEF D'OEUVRE*, p. 273.

22 Ibid.,vol. LX, *MAÎTRISES*, p. 912. See S. Kaplan, *La fin des corporations* (Paris, 2001), pp. 28–29.

and genius would soon be known for his talents and he would employ them for the wealthy [...] and discerning."[23]

Diderot was ready to go to extremes to break through the secretiveness of the artisans, even going so far as to ask the government to authorize the *Encyclopédie* interviewers to enter the workshops "to see the artisans work, to ask them questions and to draw the tools, machines and the workplaces." He continued: "There are circumstances in which the artisans are so impenetrable that the shortest way would be to enter the workshop directly as an apprentice or to put a spy in there. There are few secrets that would not come to light in this way. It is necessary to divulge all these secrets, without exception."[24]

Nevertheless, Diderot recognized that these objectives were not shared by everybody. Some thought the *Encyclopédie* should "only be a vast manuscript safely shut away in the king's library and inaccessible to other eyes. Thus a book of the state and not of the people."[25] It would be a work made inaccessible to the eyes of artisans, for fear that the "knowledge of the nation, its secret transactions, its intentions, its industry, its resources, its mysteries, its enlightenment and its arts would be disseminated outside the kingdom," to the detriment of French superiority over neighboring and rival nations. Diderot rejected this strategy. With fierce sarcasm he denounced those "good citizens" who instead of enlightening foreigners wanted to spread darkness and barbarism among them in order to dominate more easily the rest of the world. These "good citizens" were portrayed as "the most malicious men." It is not easy to forget these pages, some of the most important in the whole of the *Encyclopédie,* and ones which raised France to the role of guide to humanity.[26]

Diderot's ideas on mechanics are part of a scientific tradition that has its roots in the mechanics of Galileo Galilei and later developed by others, including the English scientist J. Th. Desaguliers, a pupil of Newton. Galileo often admonished artisans not to ignore the principles of mechanics when constructing machinery, so as not to lose time, energy and money. He recognized the many advantages and great utility that a number of crafts might obtain from mechanical instruments, and other benefits they might hope for with the help of intelligent *professori* (artisans) of mechanical science. But he distrusted those who "took to developing new inventions out of a certain natural talent alone, but without recourse to mathematical principles, which intrinsically

23 Ibid., esp. p. 913.
24 Ibid., vol. v, *ENCYCLOPÉDIE*, pp. 646–647.
25 Ibid., p. 647.
26 Ibid.

demonstrate the nature of the primary and most elementary instruments of which all other machines are composed." This led Galileo to attack, sometimes with heavy sarcasm, those *professori* who projected and constructed machines with the aim of increasing their motor power. According to Galileo, motor power – of a horse, a man, or an ox – could not be increased by any transmission mechanism. But extraordinary results could be had following the teachings of Archimedes, using the principle that the weights on the lever were each in an inverse relation to the distance from the fulcrum. Thus if two weights on the scales were in equilibrium, only a very small weight would be enough to alter the balance of the forces. This principle could be used to raise extremely heavy weights.

These arguments against the use of "natural talent alone" did not prevent Galileo from using everyday machines and the practical experience of artisans to investigate the "reasons for effects that are not only wondrous, but also hidden and almost unthinkable." A visit to the Arsenal in Venice and the time passed with its "proti" ("artists") were recommended by Galileo as a "a large field to speculative minds for philosophizing, and particularly in that area which is called mechanics." Nevertheless, although they were highly competent and could speak well, even these artisans repeated "idle notion[s] of the common people" when they offered explanations concerning the "resistance of solid bodies." Galileo's position on the artisans, in short, developed in two main directions: reserve towards those who made "new inventions" but who had no "mathematical principles," and praise for those whose work was based on practical experience but who lacked theoretical grounding. These distinctions and criticism introduced new mathematical and scientific requirements into the world of the mechanical arts, at the same time bringing technical problems into the world of academic culture. This gave rise (although with frictions and conflicts) to a new science of nature, capable of helping artists and mechanics in their efforts at innovation.[27]

---

27 For the above see G. Galilei, "A proposito di una macchina per pestare," *Le opere di Galileo Galilei*, vol. VIII [1933], p. 585, translation by Carlo Poni with the help of Patrick Leech; G. Galilei, "Discorsi e dimostrazioni matematiche intorno a due nuove scienze," *Le opere di Galileo Galilei*, vol. VIII [1933], p. 49. English translations in G. Galilei, *Two New Sciences. Including Centers of Gravity and Force of Percussion*, translated, with introduction and notes by Stillman Drake (Madison, 1974), pp. 11–12. See also G. Galilei, *Le meccaniche*, ed. and introd. Romano Gatto (Florence, 2002), pp. 54–77; E. Giusti, "Il ruolo della matematica nella meccanica di G. Galilei," *Galileo Galilei e la cultura veneziana* (Venice, 1995)), and pp. 290, 292, 324 above.

Following the example of Galileo, J. Th. Desaguliers wanted to know better the technical problems of artisans and artists. But he recognized that this objective was not within easy reach. "There is a combination among most workmen to make a mystery of their Arts: and they look upon him as a false brother, who lets gentlemen into their manner of working, and the knowledge of the price of all the materials." Like Galileo, Desaguliers did not hesitate to show his contempt for those who constructed new machines without having received any training in theoretical mechanics. Caftsmen who "plagiarized" from each other also misapplied that borrowed knowledge, with results often the opposite of what was sought. Yet he also tried to discover the technique of a German "Samson" who performed at Haymarket moving huge weights.[28] Desaguliers went with friends to observe closely his movements and the tools he used. They learned and showed how even a person of normal strength could repeat the same feat as "Samson" using the same tools and moving the body according to mechanical principles.[29]

Whether Diderot tried to apply to the movements of the artisans of Paris the observational method that Desaguliers used to analyze the movements of the body of the London Samson is an open question. But such observation in the open air could not be transposed to the confined and badly-lit space of the artisan workshop, where it would not be possible to reconstruct the triangulation of observation that had allowed Desaguliers and his friends to uncover the secrets of the Haymarket Samson.

In the corpus of the *Encyclopédie*, the entry *HORLOGERIE* ("Watchmaking and Clockmaking") occupies a special place in constructing a synthesis of science and technical practice, although starting from the point of view of science. Those who studied to be watchmakers first of all had to become good "geometers, mechanics and physicists" disposed to understanding "the spirit of principles" and with the talent to apply them.[30]

The watchmaker, for example, could not limit himself to reproducing watches and pendulums mechanically, as often had been done, with little

28 J.T. Desaguliers, *A Course of Mechanical and Experimental Philosophy*, vol. 2 (London, 1744), p. 415. The presence of "Samsons," jugglers and tightrope walkers at the London fairs is well documented by T. Frost, *The old showmen and the old London fairs* (London, 1874), pp. 19, 52–55, 144–145, 170–171 passim. [See also ch. 11, esp. pp. 373–374.]

29 For a more extensive account of Desaguliers see ch. 12 in this volume.

30 Unlike all the other arts, the clock- and watchmakers referred to themselves in a particular way. Many clock- and watchmakers appear with their own name, or even as authors of treatises on their trade. It is enough to mention here A. Thiout, P. Alexander, Julien le Roy and Enderlin (*Encyclopédie*, vol. VIII, *HORLOGERIE*, pp. 305 and 309).

understanding of theoretical principles. This was the limit of the *ouvriers*. The man of genius instead had to understand and use the laws of movement, employing the simplest and most efficient means. This was the way to train "artist watchmakers." But first, it was necessary to seek out the individual's natural inclinations, his talents, and then to teach him practical mechanics, in particular regarding friction, the identification of the different properties of metals, the dilating effects of heat and so on.[31]

Once this practical and technical knowledge had been acquired, the watchmaker as a geometer could construct the machine (the watch) according to the laws prescribed by theory. Thus he should be able to calculate the curvature of the escapement, and as a mechanic he should be able to evaluate the forces in play. Theoretical knowledge could only be acquired gradually. In the same way, sophisticated manual techniques were acquired through repeated use. These results could be obtained more rapidly with rules which were made clear.

In practice the watchmakers' guild made a sharp distinction between the *ouvriers* and the artists. The artists, also called "clock engineers," had some knowledge of theoretical mechanics and were also versatile workers who designed the numerous components of the watch and did a variety of tasks. *Ouvriers* produced the different parts of watches which the artists assembled, and only at this point could they correct the errors of the *ouvriers*, constructing, where it was lacking, the mutual compatibility of the parts – "the soul of the machine."[32]

The production of watches was carried out with a different form of manufacturing cooperation compared to that of pinmaking. The latter encouraged a vertical process of work. The same iron thread went through numerous successive phases before reaching its final form. The production of watches, on the other band, brought together different workers with different skills. Some made the pendulums and the wheels, others the escapement and the face, others still the case, the pendulum, the spiral springs. I believe that these specialists did not work together under the same roof in a large manufactory, but instead in their workshops. We must also remember that some of the parts of the watch often came from Geneva or London. The spiral springs, for example, made with high-quality steel, had to be well-tempered "so that they could give back all the charge that they received."[33]

31 Ibid., pp. 306–307.

32 Ibid., pp. 307–308.

33 Ibid., p. 308.

Specialization was the monopoly of men, but only for the mechanical parts. Women made the hands of the watch or clock as well as the watch and clock cases. The polishers and the gilders were also women. The quality of the finished product as a whole was attributed to the high quality of the workers, "who do the same thing throughout their life."[34]

French watch- and clockmaking was divided into three main sectors: (1) the clocks of belltowers, towers and castles; (2) upright clocks; and (3) pocket watches. The making of upright clocks was subdivided into sixteen subsectors, each the responsibility of specialists who were mainly men. The making of pocket watches was subdivided into twenty-one subsectors, each of which was managed by *ouvriers en petit* who specialized in the production of wheels, cogs, escapements, watch faces, hands, cases, chains (often gold or gold-plated). Alongside these specialists were a large number of *ouvriers* (workers) who made only the instruments used by the watch and clockmakers.[35]

Watchmaking was not limited to "machines that measured time"; rather it was considered as part of the science of motion. On the perfection of the art and its practitioners depended instruments for astronomy, navigation, mathematics and machines for physical experiments. Not by chance, the enterprising watchmaker George Graham of London was received into the Royal Society. High quality results, of course, were not within the reach of everyone. This was the field of superior minds, intelligent and dextrous artists captivated by their love of their work and their art, full of self-regard and up-to-date with the latest innovations.

According to the author of the entry on watchmaking, who separated the artist of genius from the "workers and charlatans," it was necessary to entrust

34 Ibid. According to Marx, specialization in work tools is linked to the emergence of "partial" workers. Their coming together to form a trade takes the form of heterogeneous manufacturing (K. Marx, *Capital. A Critique of Political Economy*, vol. 1, ed. Ernest Mandel, trans. Ben Fowkes [London, 1976], Book I, ch. 14, section 3, pp. 461–470, passim). On the history of clockmaking, see, C.M Cipolla, *Clocks and Culture* (1300–1700), (London, 1967); D. Landes, *Revolution in Time. Clocks and the Making of the Modem World* (Cambridge, Mass. 1983). The entry *HORLOGERIE* in the *Encyclopédie*, includes analysis and data not yet used in historical research.

35 Ibid. vol. VIII, p. 307. Antoine Thiout, *Traité de l'horlogerie mécanique et pratique*, vols. 1-2 (Paris, 1741; Julien Le Roy, *Avis contenant les moyen de régler les montres tant simples qu'à répétition* (1741); Le Roy also republished [Henri Sully], *Règles artificielles de temps augmentée de quelques mémoires sur l'horlogerie* (1737).

the management of the guild of watch- and clockmakers to the most intelligent and qualified members, who would select the talented artisans and prevent entry to those "poor workers" who would only set back "the progress of the art which they tend to destroy."[36]

Once again with the aim of deepening the gulf between workers and artists, the writer denounced those who had chosen the art of watchmaking only from a desire to become rich, having neither taste, nor ability, nor talent. A second group attempted, but with little success, to assimilate the principles of the art. Only a small group, composed of intelligent artists with particular abilities, could be considered capable of discovering new principles or developing those already acquired. Singled out for praise were those who dedicated themselves to perfecting the art. This spirit of emulation was not native to France: in large part it was due to the immigration to Paris of English artists such as Sully.[37]

After distinguishing artists from workers, the author of the entry complained of the privileges of the Beaux Arts artists (painters, sculptors, architects) compared to the artist watchmakers. The former received not only encouragement and high earnings but also acquired the reputation and wealth that followed merit, while artist watchmakers lived in obscurity, exposed to the imitations of plagiarists, charlatans and "merchant workers." Despite this, the French watchmaking industry, although never helped by the state, had progressed, surpassing in quality its English counterpart.

This entry closed with a proposal to establish a Society or Academy to promote and bring about innovations, in effect resuscitating the Société des Arts earlier set up under the protection of the comte de Clermont. Clockmaker members were expected to inform their colleagues of the innovations being introduced and to register them in the archives of the society. This practice, pursued by a number of astute clockmakers, would strengthen the position of French clock-making on the intenational market. Nothing carne of the scheme, however, due to irresolvable conflicts among the founders.[38]

In the entry *COMMERCE*, the *Encyclopédie* broached a development of great historical importance. In the words of the author [François Véron de Forbonnais], "the economy of human labor consisted in its substitution by machines and animals." But this substitution could take place only when the expansion of export trade required more workers than those available on the market. Once full employment was achieved, it would be possible to introduce machinery to economize *on* human labor, increasing at the same time

36 *Encyclopédie*, vol. III, *HORLOGERIE*, p. 309.

37 Ibid.

38 Ibid. pp. 309–310.

production for export. Labor-saving devices would thus not affect employment, particularly in areas in which the expert legislator was able to redirect the labor force from one sector to another in response to demand.[39]

The author of the entry *INDUSTRIE*, the chevalier de Jaucourt, directly defended "the utility of the inventions of industry" and rejected the notion that machines would take away from workers their means of subsistence. It was true that the competitive advantage of an innovating country would not last long. Sooner or later, foreigners would obtain technological secrets. But it was better to be a "first comer," anticipating innovation, rather than copy the innovations of others to compete on the market. Innovative countries would be rewarded with sure profits. *Ceteribus paribus*, the nation in which industry was the freest would also be the most innovative.[40]

Also with the aim of increasing export trade, the article "Industry" argued that it was necessary to abolish customs duties at the frontiers and redirect goods to navigable canal networks to reduce transport costs. The author of the entry *COMMERCE* forcefully stated that intelligent peoples either suppressed customs duties or calibrated them to the trends of international markets.

These visions of French achievements in the international market appeared encouraging. Among the obstacles to this goal was the high interest rate in France, at least five percent, in comparison with countries with which France competed, England and Holland, where the rate was around three percent. One result was that investment in France was discouraged, resulting in fewer jobs available and less competition.

In order to encourage agriculture, manufacture and commerce it was necessary to lower the interest rate, kept artificially high because of investments in 50–60,000 unproductive venal offices. The author of this entry INTÉRÊT (ÉCONOMIE POLITIQUE) foresaw the destabilizing effects of such a grave but necessary decision. He advised that this operation be preceded by some positive signal to reinforce credit, such as reducing the *taille* tax (on peasants) and suppressing other taxes onerous on the people and meager as government revenue. In the meantime he advised lowering the interest rate to four percent. According to the author, such a policy would give a new lease of life to

39 Ibid., vol. III, *COMMERCE*, p. 697.

40 Ibid., vol. VIII, *INDUSTRIE*, pp. 694–695. In England, the introduction of machines is discussed favorably by J. Cary, *A discourse concerning the East-India Trade shewing it to be unprofitable to the Kingdom of England, being taken out of an essay on trade* (London, 1696), pp. 99–100 and by H. Martin, *Considerations upon the East India Trade* (London, 1701), pp. 581–590.

agriculture, industry and commerce as well as benefit state finances by reducing the cost for loans.[41]

The entry *MANUFACTURE [RÉUNIE, DISPERSÉE]* ("Manufacture, concentrated, scattered") gave an anonymous contributor the chance to take up again the topic of the division of labor. Investments in medium or large industries, he argued, satisfied different needs, essentially those of employing at the same time a large number of workers distributed in diverse tasks which would decrease the cost of production as well as the time entailed in production. Location of these businesses would depend principally on the local supply of labor, but also on the presence of raw materials, above all iron mines, which attracted capital for the construction of foundries, forges and drawing mills. The same was true for the deposits of clay used in the production of porcelain.

These firms and their products could be worthwhile only on certain conditions: that they not be exposed to the caprices of fashion, should guarantee steady profits, and be linked to efficient transport routes. They also had to be protected by the government, which should reduce duties on raw materials and cost of transport, as well as grant privileges and exemptions. Nevertheless, these privileges and exemptions, useful for encouraging emulation and promoting talents, if applied badly, could disadvantage other professional groups no less useful. In this connection the author, recognizing the need for medium and large industries that Colbert had promoted in the time of Louis XIV, complained that little or nothing had been written on those structures.

This entry also distinguished analytically between "concentrated manufactures" ("manufactures réunie") and "scattered manufactures" ("manufactures dispersées"). "Concentrated manufactures" employed a considerable number of workers under the same roof. The work rhythms were regulated by the ringing of a bell. Workers were subject to rigid discipline under the eye of supervisors who treated them harshly and had an air of superiority. Wage levels were differentiated according to qualifications. In a porcelain manufactory, the furnace tenders received a lower wage than the painters who decorated the plates and tiles. These centralized plants struck the imagination and excited considerable curiosity.

The contributor also noted that these industries were based on large investment in fixed capital for the construction of the buildings. They required heavy expenditure in maintenance, and high salaries for the managers, cashiers, bookkeepers, clerks and supervisors. All this expenditure – including daily wages – had to be paid for by the outgoing goods that were often unable to

41 *Encyclopédie*, vol VIII, *INTÉRÊT*, pp. 826–827.

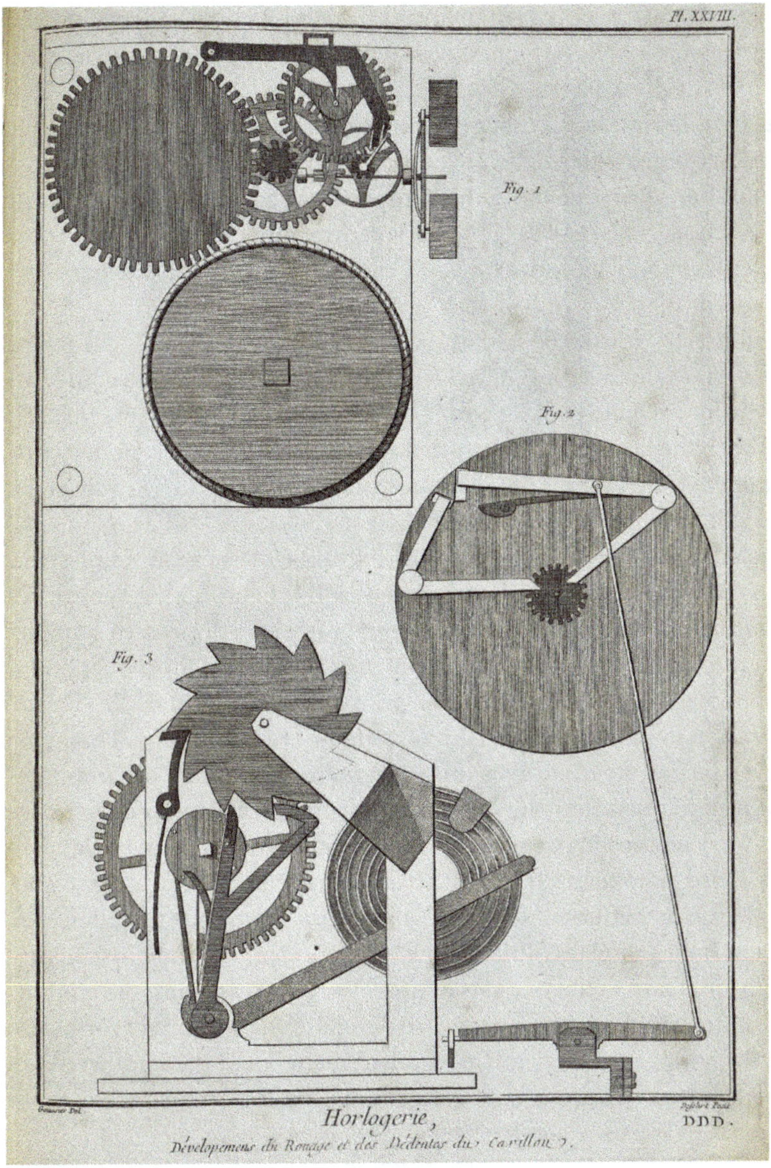

FIGURE 13.1 Clockmaking, the gearwheel and teeth of a tower bell
SOURCE: D.DIDEROT, *ENCYCLOPÉDIE, OU DICTIONNAIRE RAISONNÉ DES SCIENCES, DES ARTS, ET DES MÉTIERS, PAR UNE SOCIÉTÉ DES GENS DE LETTRES. MIS EN ORDRE ET PUBLIÉ PAR M. DIDEROT*, 17 VOLS. (PARIS 1751–1765)

compete with the low prices of small firms. And despite rigid supervision and control, management in large manufactures faced insuperable problems, such as theft of material by workers.

At times of unfavorable fluctuations in trade, manufacturing entrepreneurs were sometimes obliged to sell below cost in order to pay daily wages. A considerable number of first generation entrepreneurs had failed. Those of the second generation, who had bought the failed manufactures cheaply, could sustain themselves only by correcting abuses and managing the business simply and economically.[42]

Small industries "scattered" widely over an area were not subject to the same exorbitant costs that had ruined large manufactures. Anyone could buy raw materials for weaving (wool, cotton, silk) and work on it at home on their own looms with the help of children, other members of the family or dayworkers (*compagnons*). This sector of small producers provided the woven serges, velvets and small woolen and silk cloths.

This type of organization was particularly advantageous in the countryside, where labor could not be usefully employed in the fields all the months of the year. During the winter, in particular, some members of peasant families, rather than not work, found it beneficial to work on looms for production for the market. Since this work was not the principal occupation of the household, the peasant families could be content with low remuneration. This activity could even be perceived as "a rest from the more taxing work of farming."[43]

It might also happen that the labor force of this "scattered" manufacture could, with work on the loom, earn more money than with work on the land. In these cases, these "half-peasants" might abandon agriculture altogether to concentrate full time on better-paid work: manufacture. This advantage, however, would not last long. In the medium to long term, food prices would rise in proportion to the increase in the "industrial" workforce. At this point, the employment pendulum would swing back towards agriculture. In reality, according to this author of *MANUFACTURE*, those who had abandoned the land would in the meantime have lost the desire to cultivate it. This last comment is without doubt the mark of keen sociological insight.

42 Ibid., vol. X, *MANUFACTURE*, pp. 60–61.

43 Ibid., pp. 61–62. These analyses call to mind the theory of rural protoindustry elaborated by F. Mendels and H. Medick. See, F. Mendels, "Protoindustrialization. The First Phase of the Industrialization Process," *Journal of Economic History*, 32 (1972), pp. 241-61; idem., *Industrialization and Population Pressure in Eighteenth-Century Flanders* (New York, 1981); P. Kriedte, H. Medick, J. Schlumbohm, *Industrialization before Industrialization* (Cambridge, 1981).

The writer was nevertheless convinced that things could not go well where cultivation of the land was not the occupation of the greatest number, augmented with some textile work especially in the winter months when the land could not be worked. These mechanisms had given encouragement to small manufactures that could cause large manufactures to fail with a single weapon: low prices. Yet some large manufactures failed for the simple reason that they were large: their size incurred heavy debts and price competition undercut their profit margin.

Nevertheless, the author praised those concentrated manufactures that not only were successful in producing for the market, but which did honor to the nation, "like the delicate cloths of Abbeville" introduced by the Dutch manufacturer Van Robais. In such cases, for the production of high-quality textiles, it could be convenient to build large factories. Since no single individual could obtain the capital required, it was necessary to have recourse to state financing. This type of investment could be justified only if sales could be guaranteed through the production of low-quality and low-priced goods for the internal market and high-quality and high-priced goods for the international market. Despite this intelligent line of argument, the writer also believed that if the capital spent to set up concentrated manufactures had been distributed widely "among the people," the results would have been just as positive.[44] Still, the author contended, for fine cloths such as those of Abbeville, it was useful to establish large manufactures. Here the complexity of diverse organizations of work are alluded to and are linked to diverse organizations of the market.

The entry *SOIE* ("Silk") is one of the longest, about thirty pages, and also one of the most important for its analysis of innovative processes.[45] Some of these innovations, imported from Piedmont, involved the early phases of the industrial processing of silk: from reeling – when cocoons are placed in tanks of boiling water to form the thread and then wound on a reeling machine – to the twisting ("throwing") of these threads in the mechanical silk mills "alla piemontese." According to the author of this entry, French practices of reeling were considerably improved under the influence of the "Manifesto del Consolato di Torino [...] per la filatura delle sete" of 29 May 1720. This treatise

44 On the centralized manufacturing of the Van Robais of Abbeville and Amiens, see G. Martin, *La grande industrie en France sous le règne de Louis XV* (Paris, 1900), pp. 273, 322 passim; P. Deyon, *Amiens capitale provincial* (Paris, 1967), pp. 68, 74, 141, 143, 192. On the Van Robais, see also T.J Schaeper, *The French Council of Commerce 1700–1715. A Study of Mercantilism after Colbert* (Columbus, Ohio, 1983), pp. 170–172.

45 *Encyclopédie*, vol. XV, *SOIE*, pp. 268–306.

proposed reducing the number of threads worked on at the same time from six to two. The attention of the female spinners, concentrated only on two threads, allowed the thickness of the thread to be made uniform, stronger, and finer.

The Piedmontese regulations also decreed that these spinners could not be paid piece rates but should be paid "by the day and with good wages so that they would work with care."[46] These new regulations reduced productivity calculated by pounds but increased productivity in terms of the quality of the products, resulting in a higher price. According to a group of French merchants, the silk spun with the Piedmontese reeling machines at La Sône in Dauphiné by the brothers François and Fleury Jubié sold in 1745 at up to 16 livres a pound compared with the 9–10 livres for silk spun by traditional methods, whose "grossness" and "defects" the merchants denounced.[47]

According to the great technician Jacques Vaucanson, the Piedmontese regulations were "the most beautiful and the most ample." But he also argued that they would be most successful when the processes of reeling and twisting were concentrated under the same roof, enabling entrepreneurs to verify and control the quality – the uniformity and fineness – of the thread that the use of Piedmontese water-powered silk mills promised.[48]

In these silk mills "alla piemontese," which can already be classified as a factory system, the whole productive process of twisting was mechanized. The task of the worker was to feed the machines with raw thread exactly as it was spun, to knot the thread when it broke, and to place the thrown thread into the appropriate baskets. The thread from these baskets was then used for weaving, an operation largely concentrated in Lyon, which from the end of the seventeenth century had begun to dominate the world market for woven silk with

46 See "Il Manifesto del Consolato di Torino […] per la filatura delle sete del 29 maggio 1720" and the second "Manifesto del Consolato di Torino […] dell'8 aprile 1724," both published in F. A. Duboin, *Raccolta per ordine di materie delle leggi […] emanate dai Sovrani della Real Casa di Savoia*, t. XVI, vol. XVIII (Turin, 1849), pp. 163–191. An English travelling merchant wrote from Hamburg in April 1728: "It is impossible that silk can be used in lieu of Piedmontese silk for making alamode, lustring, pardessus […] because there is no silk in the world so apt, so clear, so fine" (Public Record Office, Board of Trade C.O. 388 Correspondence, vol. 27, c. 110).

47 Archives Nationales, Registre du Bureau du Commerce, F 92, cc. 178–180.

48 J. Vaucanson, "Construction d'un nouveau tour à filer la soie des cocons," *Histoire et Mémoires de l'Académie Royale des Sciences* (Paris, 1749), pp. 142–154. 1749 was not the year of publication but the year in which the treatise was presented to the Académie Royale des Sciences. Idem., "Construction de nouveaux moulins à organsiner les soies," *Histoire et Mémoires de l'Académie Royale des Sciences* (Paris, 1757), pp. 161–165. Idem., "Nouvelle construction d'une machine propre à moirer les étoffes de soie," *Histoire et Mémoires de l'Académie Royale des Sciences* (Paris 1767), pp. 5–13.

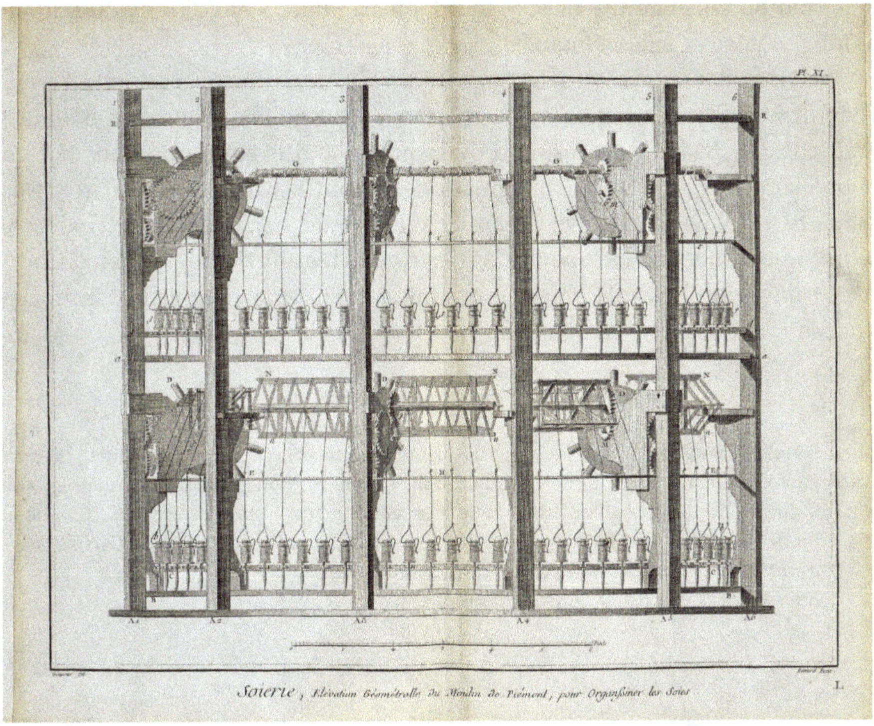

FIGURE 13.2 Silkmaking, geometrical image of the silk mill of Piedmont producing organzine
SOURCE: *ENCYCLOPÉDIE O DICTIONNAIRE RAISONÉE DES SCIENCES, DES ARTS ET DES MÉTIERS*

"les modes de Paris faites à Lyon."[49] It was in Lyon, too, where new types of looms were experimented and diffused, beginning with the loom invented by Jean Baptiste Garon in 1717. According to the *Encyclopédie,* in just a few years no fewer than 10,000 of these looms were sold in Lyon, thanks also to the drop in price from 45 livres to 7 livres and 10 sous. Another innovative loom was the one constructed by Baptiste Falcon, which exploited the ideas of Basil Bouchon and applied to the loom perforated cards capable of memorizing the designs and transmitting the information in order to transfer the designs automatically onto the fabrics.[50] To encourage Falcon, the new regulations for the Lyon silk industry that Vaucanson drafted in 1744 permitted master weavers,

---

49 See chap. 9 in this volume.
50 *Encyclopédie*, vol XV, *SOIE*, pp, 300–301.

who traditionally had the right to four looms, to have an additional fifth loom as long as it was a Falcon loom.[51]

The chevalier de Jaucourt, in the entry *INDUSTRIE*, distanced himself from Diderot when he distinguished "arts" from industry. The arts became identified with the Beaux Arts inspired by exquisite and lively sentiments and an appreciation of genius and imagination. In contrast to the Beaux Arts was industry with its distinctive meaning that would become classic. Industry represented "mechanical operation of nature." This affirmation signaled a profound mutation towards a new economic system drawn explicitly from the English model.[52]

---

51 See A. Doyon, L. Liaigre, *Jacques Vaucanson mécanicien de génie* (Paris, 1966), p. 227. Paulet, a silk merchant, unfairly criticized the low innovation potential of the French silk industry. But he recognized that there were some extraordinary exceptions, "tel que le métier à la Falcon, à la Manger et ceux montés à la Regner". See M. Paulet, *L'Art du fabricant d'étoffe de soie. Seconde partie* (Paris, 1789), p. 867.

52 *Encyclopédie*, vol. VIII, *INDUSTRIE*, pp. 694–695.

PART 4

Methods

CHAPTER 14

The Name and the Game: Unequal Exchange and the Historiographic Marketplace

Carlo Ginzburg and Carlo Poni

Let us begin with a rather trivial observation. During the past half century, there has been a definite imbalance in the historiographic exchange between Italy and France. Italy has received much more than it has given. We shall not linger over the reasons for this. We shall limit ourselves to recalling that even in a case like this, the history of historiography, in the traditional sense of the term, shows its own limitations. Only an analysis hinging on the "social use of historiography" (as Krzysztof Pomian pointed out in a general way some years ago)[1] is adequate to the task of reconstructing the terms of a relationship that goes well beyond the research of individuals and of research and teaching organizations, to involve basic political choices and, ultimately, whole societies very different from one another.

The persistence of this basic imbalance, naturally, does not mean that the relationship between Italian and French historians—or, more specifically, the French historians connected with the *Annales* group—has remained unchanged over these fifty years. It is our conviction that today we are entering into a brand new phase, tied to the emergence, in part still embryonic, of new directions in research. Because these new directions will be our concern here, the discussion will be more prognostic than diagnostic.

We have talked about unequal exchange and the historiographic marketplace. A dependent country, though, does not necessarily mean a poor country, for it is well known that Italy's historiographic dependency goes hand in hand with its extraordinary richness in the very documentary material without which the historian cannot work. (We are thinking here not only of the documents preserved in archives and libraries but also of the countryside, of the shape of the cities, of the people's ways of conducting themselves: all of Italy can be—and has been—seen as one enormous archive.) Years ago, Franco Venturi spoke with bitter irony of Italian libraries and archives as terrain that had been subjected to extensive rather than intensive cultivation.[2] Changing

1 K. Pomian, "L'histoire de la science et l'histoire de l'histoire," *Annales E.S.C.*, vol. 30 (1975), 952.

2 F. Venturi, *Settecento riformatore: Da Muratori a Beccaria* (Turin, 1969), pp. XVII–XVIII.

 | DOI:10.1163/9789004713277_016

the metaphor a little, we could define the Italian archives as precious deposits of primary materials, in large part never mined.

The gap between primary materials such as archival sources and the possibilities for their mining has become particularly apparent during the very period that has witnessed the almost universal triumph of quantitative history. Subjective resistance to that triumph, tied to a cultural tradition still today imbued with idealism, should not be ignored. But limiting ourselves to that resistance alone, as often happens, would be one-sided and, in its own way, idealistic.

Quantitative research on any large scale presupposes considerable financial investment and *équipes* of researchers—in a word, an advanced research organization. A study like the one bravely done by Elio Conti may be considered representative, especially when put next to that by Christiane Klapisch and David Herlihy on the Florentine tax census of 1427.[3] When employed shrewdly, French-American capital and the computer make possible undertakings that would be impossible for a single individual. (What interests us here is the difference in scale between the two kinds of research, rather than a comparative analysis of the results achieved.)

Research into the history of property and population shows that quantitative history is alive and well. Also very much alive is serial history: the quantitative study of an extended period, which has now shifted from the study of prices (the old point of departure) toward changes in production, analyzed through tithes and account books. Without doubt, we owe valuable results to the powerful investigative tools provided by serial history—for example, the discovery of structural change in demographic crises, from the catastrophic mortality crises of the cruel seventeenth century to the less weightily Malthusian crises of "morbidity" of the eighteenth century.

We are not risking too much, however, if we state that the quantitative study of an extended period can also obscure and distort facts. Prices, food, and mortality are matters that take on significance over the short period especially if we want to analyze the way in which political power reacts to economic fluctuations and food crises, such as through price controls, building up of reserves, requisitions, or buying grain on the foreign market. In looking at an extended period of time, as Steven Kaplan pointed out, it is difficult to understand the day-to-day problems of survival. We tend to think in terms of ten-year averages

3 D. Herlihy and C. Klapisch-Zuber, *Les toscans et leurs familles* (Paris, 1978). Now in an abbreviated translation as *Tuscans and Their Families: A Study of the Florentine Catasto of 1427* (New Haven, 1985). Elio Conti completed a study of *L'imposta diretta a Firenze nel Quattrocento (1427–1497)* (Rome, 1984).

and moving averages reported on semi-logarithmic graphs. Lived experience (undoubtedly an ambiguous expression) is largely relegated to the margins. This "long-run approach can generate an abstract, homogenized social history, devoid of flesh and blood and unconvincing despite its scientific cachet."[4]

All the same, we believe that serial quantitative history is by now part of "normal science," in Thomas Kuhn's sense,[5] and that the enormous amount of material preserved in Italian archives must be examined in order to verify the paradigms and rules of the serial approach, in order to articulate, demonstrate, delimit, and manipulate them. (Let us make clear that, in this context, the term *paradigm* has a meaning both weaker and more metaphorical than that given it by Kuhn; historiography remains, despite everything, a pre-paradigmatic discipline.) A part of the scholarly community must dedicate itself either totally or partially to this kind of research.

Other themes and other kinds of research are, however, already coming to the fore. In particular, we see the emergence in several aspects of historical research characterized by analysis, at extremely close range, of circumscribed phenomena—a village community, a group of families, even an individual person. This can be explained for reasons both intrinsic and extrinsic to the discipline. We will begin with the latter, the extra-historiographic reasons.

In recent years, several very different phenomena, such as wars in Southeast Asia and ecological disasters (oil spills), have revived discussion of strategic objectives long discounted and therefore long unanalyzed, whether of socialism or of unlimited technological development. It would not be going too far out on a limb to suggest that the growing fortunes of microhistorical reconstructions are tied to growing doubts about the established procedures of macrohistory. Precisely because we are no longer so sure that the game is worth the candle, we are persuaded to reanalyze the rules of the game. We are tempted to compare the optimism, whether for reform or revolution, of the fifties and sixties with the radical skepticism of the late seventies, a skepticism destined probably to grow more intense in coming years. That microhistorical investigations often take as the object of their analyses the themes of the private, the personal, and the lived experience, the same themes forcefully proposed by the women's movement, is no coincidence, since women constitute, without doubt, the group that has paid the highest price for the development of human history.

4 S. L. Kaplan, *Bread, Politics and Political Economy in the Reign of Louis XV* (The Hague, 1976), pp. xx-xxi.

5 T. Kuhn, *The Structure of Scientific Revolutions*, 2d. ed. (Chicago, 1970).

The increasingly close connection between history and anthropology is both symptom and instrument of this awareness. (In this case, too, we have a relationship of imbalance, in spite of the growing interest in history on the part of such anthropologists as Jack Goody.)[6] Anthropology has offered historians not only a series of themes largely overlooked in the past—from kinship relationships to material culture, from symbolic rituals to magic—but also something of much greater importance: a conceptual frame of reference, whose outlines we are only now beginning to make out. The demise of the ethnocentric illusion (which, paradoxically, coincided with the unification of the global market) has made untenable the idea of a universal history. Only an anthropology saturated with history or, what is the same thing, a historiography saturated with anthropology will be adequate to the task of rethinking the multimillennial endurance of the species *Homo sapiens.*

Thirty years ago, in an article later reprinted as an introduction to the *Anthropologie structurale* collection, Claude Lévi-Strauss wrote that "the famous statement by Marx, "Men make their own history, but they do not know that they are making it," justifies, first, history, and, second, anthropology. At the same, time it shows that the two approaches are inseparable."[7] The desired convergence of history and anthropology still has many obstacles in its path: first among them is the difference between the documentations used by the two disciplines. The complexity of social relationships, reconstructible by the anthropologist through fieldwork, contrasts sharply with the one-sidedness of the archival sources that must serve as field material to the historian. Each of these sources, born of a specific social relationship and, more often than not, sanctioned by an institution, can offer legitimacy for the researcher's specialization. One is a historian of the church or of technology, of business or of industry, of population or of property, of the working class or of the Italian Communist party. The motto for this kind of historiography could be, "Don't let your left hand know what your right hand is doing." This fragmentation reflects the fragmentation of the sources. The church records introduce us to individuals at birth or death, as parents or children; the property registers, to individuals as owners or tenants; the criminal records to individuals as plaintiffs or witnesses in a trial. This way, however, we risk losing the complexity of the relationships that connect any individual to a particular society. This is true even of those sources richer in unpredictable data, such as criminal or inquisitional proceedings, which, particularly the latter, are the closest thing

6 J. Goody, *The Domestication of the Savage Mind* (Cambridge, 1977).

7 C. Levi-Strauss, *Structural Anthropology* (Garden City, N.Y., 1967), p. 24.

we historians have to the modern anthropologist's field study. But if the area of research is sufficiently circumscribed, then the individual documentary series can transcend time and space in a way that permits us to find the same individual or group of individuals in different social contexts. The thread of Ariadne that leads the researcher through the archival labyrinth is the same thread that distinguishes one individual from another in all societies known to us: the name.

The use of names to open up new fields for historical research is not new. Nominative demography (Henry's study of Crulai, for example)[8] has led to a noted shift of perspective in the area of historical demography and to a new object of investigation: the reconstruction of families. But nominative methodology can be carried well beyond the strictly demographic sources. In the church records of rural parishes in sharecropping areas—the district around Bologna comes immediately to mind—next to the names and surnames of the "manager" (*reggitore*, the head of the household) and of the members of his family, there are also the names of the farmhouse and of the cultivated land (Red House, White House, the Palace, etc.). Taking this place-name as a guide, it is not hard to find in the property registers (and thus in another archive) an important piece of information: the size of the farm. Next to the name and to the land dimensions in the register, we find the name of the landowner. From here, from this name, we can go back to the private archive for that property for which, if we are lucky, we can find in the administrative registers the annual farm accounts and, together with the name of the sharecropper and of the land that he farms, also the annual account of crop production, divided according to crop types (grain, hemp, corn, vine, timber) with the halving of the gross product and the account of the farm debt for each landholding and for each tenant-farmer family. In other words, we find a series of facts (usually, but not always, covering a brief period) with which it is possible to reconstruct the interconnections among diverse conjunctures.

The journey of investigation, obviously, can begin at any point in the chain. The best point of departure is probably not the archive of the parish but that of the large property. The latter includes the names of peasants and the names of places that we can seek with greater hope of success in other archival sources, such as parish and property registers, in which, in principle, there should be listed the names of all the families and all the landholdings. Applying an analogous procedure to notarial records, it is possible to reconstruct the

8 L. Henry, *La population de Crulai, paroisse normande, Travaux et documents de l'INED* (Paris, 1958).

matrimonial strategies among families that were allied or related. The course of this research can be carried even further by going to episcopal ecclesiastical archives and there looking for dispensations allowing marriage between blood relatives. Once again, the guiding thread is the name.

As we have already indicated, this game of rebuff and rebound does not necessarily close the door to serial investigation, if it is useful. A series, particularly if it has not been manipulated, is always useful. But the center of gravity for the kind of micro-nominative research proposed here resides elsewhere. The lines that converge upon and diverge from the name, creating a kind of closely woven web, provide for the observer a graphic image of the network of social relationships into which the individual is inserted.

Studies of this kind are also possible in the case of individuals belonging to those social strata characterized by greater geographical mobility. Here, certainly, we must proceed a little more tentatively, entrusting ourselves to the particular case at hand and to good luck. But once again the name serves as a valuable compass. Let us take Costantino Saccardino, a distiller and professional jester, tried for heresy by the Inquisition of Bologna and condemned to death together with three followers in 1622.[9] The trial proceedings, unfortunately lost, created a notable echo: civic chronicles in manuscript as well as printed narratives provide further details of the event and its protagonist. It turns out that Saccardino had lived in Venice and a probe into the archives of the Venetian Inquisition brings to light a group of denunciations with which he was charged. One brief mention shows Saccardino in Florence, serving the Medici in the role of jester, and, in fact, his name can be found among the recipients of payments by the court in the first decade of the seventeenth century. From a bibliographical check one discovers a small treatise on medical arts that he published, concluding with a list of clients cured and healed, similar to other records drawn up by Bolognese notaries that mention these clients by name. This list is confirmed by an examination of the notarial sources preserved at the State Archive of Bologna. One document, however, refers to a corresponding record drawn up some years before by a notary in Ferrara. Bit by bit, a biography, albeit fragmentary, emerges from the network of relationships that circumscribe it.

For all their dissimilarities, the two studies we have outlined have two elements in common: their reference to the lower strata of society and their use, as guiding thread, of the name. Several years ago, describing the state of

9 For a brief look at the research referred to here, see C. Ginzburg and M. Ferrari, "La colombara ha aperto gli occhi," *Quaderni storici*, vol. 13, no. 38 (1978), 631–639. [The Dovecote Has Opened Its Eyes - Eds.]

prosopographical studies, Lawrence Stone distinguished two currents: one, qualitative, concentrated on the study of elites (political, cultural, etc.) and the other, quantitative, aimed at investigating broader social groups.[10] Our present proposal would combine the non-elitist perspective of the second current with the particularized analysis of the first to achieve a prosopography from below (analogous to that proposed by E. P. Thompson), one opening out into a series of case studies but never excluding, as we have said, serial research.

It is obvious that a prosopography from below should take as its objective a series of case studies. An investigation that is both qualitative and exhaustive will be able to examine only entities that are numerically circumscribed—elites, in other words. The problem, then, will be to choose from the mass of available data those cases that are relevant and significant.

Are they significant in the sense of statistical frequency? They will not always be, because there also exists what Edoardo Grendi has called, with an apt oxymoron, the "normal exception."[11] We can assign at least two meanings to this expression. First, it designates documentation that is only apparently exceptional. Stone pointed out the singular fact that the only subordinate groups about whom it is sometimes possible to collect a good deal of information are all "minority groups, which are by definition exceptional since they are in revolt against the *mores* and beliefs of the majority."[12] But an examination of criminal trials before 1800 (before, that is, the figure of the professional criminal had been established in the modern sense of the term) leads the researcher to less pessimistic conclusions. The overwhelming majority of these trials concern very common and often unimportant crimes, such as brawling, petty thievery, and so forth, carried out by absolutely unexceptional individuals. It is no paradox to affirm that in preindustrial societies a certain type of transgression constituted the norm, in fact, even if not in law.

But the "normal exception" can also have another meaning. If the sources are silent about or systematically distort the social reality of the subaltern classes, then a truly exceptional (and thus statistically infrequent) document can be much more revealing than a thousand stereotypical documents. As Kuhn has shown, it is the marginal cases that challenge the old paradigm, and for this very reason they help to forge a new, richer and more nuanced one. They serve in other words as clues or signs of a hidden reality that generally does not emerge from the documentation.

10 L. Stone, "Prosopography," *Daedalus*, vol. 100 (1971), 46–79.

11 E. Grendi, "Microanalisi e storia sociale," *Quaderni storici*, vol. 12, no. 35 (1977), 512.

12 Stone, "Prosopography," p. 59.

Coming from very different backgrounds and working on very different themes, both authors of the present essay have found themselves recognizing the decisive importance of those traces, those clues, those details previously overlooked, which upset and throw into disarray the superficial aspect of the documentation.[13] Beyond this, it is possible to reach a deeper, invisible level, the one comprising the rules of the game, "the history that men do not know they are making." At this point we recognize the echo of lessons, at the same time different and connected, taught us by Marx and Freud.

Microhistorical analysis is therefore Janus-faced. On one side, operating as it does on a reduced scale, it often makes possible a reconstruction of lived reality that is inconceivable in other kinds of historiography. On the other side, it sets out to investigate the invisible structures within which that lived reality takes shape. The implicit model is the relationship between *langue* and *parole* formulated by Saussure. The structures that regulate social relations are, like those of the *langue*, unconscious. Between the form and the substance there is a gap that scholarship aims to fill. (If reality were transparent, and therefore instantly knowable, Marx said, critical analysis would be superfluous.) For this reason we propose to define microhistory, and history in general, as the *study of lived experience* [*scienza del vissuto*], a definition that seeks to comprehend the reasoning of both the supporters and the enemies of the integration of history with the social sciences, and for this, no doubt, it will not be pleasing to either side.

The term *structure* is ambiguous. Although historians have identified it primarily with extended duration, perhaps the moment has come to emphasize instead, within the notion of structure, that characteristic of system that, as Roman Jakobson has shown, includes synchrony as much as diachrony.

In no case can microhistory limit itself to verifying, on its own scale, the macrohistorical (or macroanthropological) rules that have been elaborated elsewhere. One of the first discoveries of the student of microhistory is the rare and sometimes non-existent relevance of the analyses (to begin with the chronological ones) elaborated on the macrohistorical scale. From this the comparison takes its decisive importance. In this connection we can note that comparative history, unpopular in Italy is on the rise in France.

---

13 See Carlo Ginzburg, "Spie. Radici di un paradigma scientifico," *Rivista di storia contemporanea*, vol. 7 (1978), 1–14. The best translated version is "Clues: Roots of an Evidential Paradigm," in *Clues, Myths, and the Historical Method*, trans. John Tedeschi and Anne C. Tedeschi (Baltimore, 1989,) pp. 96–125. See also C. Poni, "Innovazione contadina e controllo padronale," paper presented to the Arbeitsprozesse colloquium, Gottingen, June 22–28, 1978.

The history of Italy is a polycentric history, as demonstrated by, among other things, the series of documents preserved in the archives of the peninsula. It is our belief that today microhistorical investigations constitute the most appropriate way to mine this extraordinary accumulation of primary material, a method more appropriate and more accessible also to craftsmanlike ways of gathering.

In this sense, perhaps, we can be allowed to look forward in the coming years to an exchange between Italian and French historiography that is less unequal than in the past and that will strengthen further the collaboration between the two.

CHAPTER 15

The Silk Mill: A Path of Research

Carlo Poni

Let me reconstruct the path of my research. My work was not constructed on a hypothesis. It was built step by step, one small part after another, with changes sometimes unexpected and fortuitous.

My interest and curiosity about silk mills goes back to the 1960s, when I read for the first time a classic of modern history, the book of Paul Mantoux, *La révolution industrielle au XVIIIème siècle* (1905). In the first chapter of the second part of this book Mantoux writes that in 1717, after a trip to undertake industrial espionage in Italy, a certain John Lombe set up in England, in Derby on the Derwent River, a true factory, the first established in that country.

That building, constructed fifty to seventy years before the beginning of the Industrial Revolution, was 500 feet long, five stories high and had 460 windows. Inside were large cylindrical machines, rotating on vertical axes moved by water wheels which gave the desired twisting to hundreds of silk threads. These threads were gathered together in skeins ready for sale. According to Daniel Defoe, the author of *Robinson Crusoe*, these machines were composed of about 25,000 wheels and 97,000 other components and produced about 73,000 ells of thread every day.[1]

John Lombe and his brother Thomas earned enormous sums in a few years. In 1732 the English Parliament paid to Thomas Lombe, the heir of John, a sum of 14,000 pounds sterling in recognition of their value and in exchange for renouncing their patent of invention.

According to Mantoux this machine – the silk mill, which would introduce the factory system – foreshadowed the Industrial Revolution but did not yet initiate it. Silk thread had a limited market and its impact on the whole economy could not have the same effect as was the case later with cotton. Furthermore this machine did not undergo substantial improvement as occurred with cotton spinning towards the end of the century.

Nevertheless, we can say that the silk mill was the *first model* of the factory system, and models are important. The silk mill was already a form of

1 "Ell. A measure of length, varying in different countries. The English ell = 45 inches", *Oxford English Dictionary*.

 | DOI:10.1163/9789004713277_017

completely mechanized production, leaving to the workers the sole task of introducing the material and knotting the threads when they broke.

The Italian silk mills, like that of John Lombe, employed hundreds of workers, giving rise to new problems, namely the discipline and control of work. These problems either did not exist or had a different character in craft shops. In the latter the "master", working together with the apprentices, instructed and controlled them at the same time. The factory system introduced a completely novel system of work: hundreds of workers were engaged in different tasks, and each part of the work process had to be controlled. A specialized corps of supervisors was needed.

The existence of the silk mill as a model had a certain importance in the industrial history of England. The "water frame" of Arkwright, which mechanized the spinning of cotton and inaugurated the Industrial Revolution, was set in motion with energy provided by water wheels operating in a mill similar to that of Lombe. Since cotton fibers are short, at the moment of twisting the fiber must be kept firm so that it does not break when it is drawn out. Arkwright resolved this technical problem with the use of special rollers. This problem does not exist for silk: the silk worm forms a thread that is naturally long. The silk mill only provides various twistings to the thread to make it more resistant, preparing it for weaving.

These technical comparisons (and differences) do not exhaust all the relations between silk mills and cotton mills. Almost all those who invested capital in cotton mills between 1770 and 1780, and worked as directors, had begun as owners of silk mills, including Arkwright. This experience was fundamental for acquiring the ability to manage large firms with hundreds of workers.

Information on John Lombe comes from the autobiography of the eighteenth-century writer William Hutton, who at the age of seven was sent to work in Lombe's mill. His experience as a spinning worker reveals many particulars about Lombe's trip to Italy for the purpose of industrial espionage, as well as the operation and discipline in the mill in Derby.

When I read this account, at the beginning of the 1970s, I was interested in the history of agriculture and I considered the silk mill as a curiosity that did not relate to my research. Of course, I knew that at the end of the fourteenth century a silk spinning mechanism existed in Italy, in Lucca, but I did not know how it was made; above all it did not enter my mind that the English machine of the eighteenth century could in some manner be linked to that old medieval spinning device. Another obstacle, purely epistemological, was the fact that historians conduct their research in chronologically defined spheres: medieval, modern, contemporary.

To move from the eighteenth to the fourteenth century would have entailed not only a leap in time but also a shift from one corporation of historians to another. For these reasons it was not easy to connect these two items of information. I have to say that others had written on the silk mill, but without knowing the history of Lombe, and therefore without connecting the Italian data with the English (among the few exceptions I may point out the work of Corrado Barbagallo).[2]

Before beginning my research I thought of silk spinning as a Lucchese-Bolognese peculiarity. I did not believe that machines had existed also in other areas, the Veneto or Lombardy. I was so uninformed as to consider it a local characteristic, a species of a great cocoon that contained two cities – Bologna and Lucca – with their techniques. In short, not only did I not see the link between these machines and the Industrial Revolution, I did not even pose the question of the existence of similar machines in other parts of Italy. To tell the truth, I could have had some more precise idea of the technology and functioning of this mill because Vittorio Zonca, author of a *Novo Teatro di machine et edificii* (Padova, 1607), had already made a design of it and explained it. I have to add that only some years later did I succeed in overcoming the enormous difficulty involved in reading this important book. In the seventeenth century Italian technical language was not yet formed and lacked a codified form. A screw was called *verme* or *coclea*; the axle of a wheel was *peritrochio*. To orient myself in the jungle of words I had to ponder over the same problems as those who in that century translated into Latin and Italian the mechanics of Aristotle and Archimedes; I had to go to the origins of the technical-scientific language that was emerging precisely at the beginning of the seventeenth century and to which Galileo Galilei had made a great contribution.

Following the itinerary of a historian of agriculture, I had read towards the end of the 1950s the *Ricordo d'agricoltura* of Camillo Tarello, in which the author pointed out that the Venetian Senate had granted to him a "privilege" (*brevetto*, i.e. patent) for having invented a new method of cultivating the land. It seemed an interesting lead, and I began to do some research on this theme in the State Archives in Venice. In this way, from 1962 I began to collect and classify the agricultural-industrial patents. In the course of this research I found a patent granted in 1604 to the Modenese Ottavio Malpigli to introduce in the Venetian State the silk mill "alla bolognese". This source suggested that the silk mill "alla bolognese" existed already in Modena. So I began to make new connections,

2 Corrado Barbagallo, *Le origini della grande industria contemporanea: 1750–1850* (Florence, 1929–1930).

to place my work within a larger geographical space. The Venetian sources in addition underlined the social consequences of the new technology. The local spinners strongly opposed the introduction of the Bolognese silk mill which, by increasing the productivity of labor, would cause unemployment and poverty. The Venetian Senate resisted this corporative opposition and granted the patent.

Continuing my work and concentrating on the Venetian research, I discovered in the Archives of the Cinque Savi alla Mercanzia (Venetian Board of Trade) an enormous quantity of information. In the Venetian area the silk mill spread with difficulty between 1604 and 1634, but afterwards, with overwhelming force, tens of silk mills sprang up in the countryside of Bergamo and Brescia, and of Bassano and elsewhere in the Veneto region. By now the idea that the silk mill had been a limited monopoly in a few areas definitely faded from my mind. I then discovered that this great technical expansion came about on a wave of increased production of raw silk in the Venetian State, going from 500,000 *libbre* annually in the sixteenth century to 2,500,000 *libbre* in the eighteenth century.

Through these same sources I further discovered that around the year 1720 in the western area of the Po valley, from Turin, another type of silk mill arrived that was called "alla piemontese" or "alla torinese" and which was considered as an improvement on the silk mill "alla bolognese." In 1970 I presented the results of my first studies in the Venetian area at an International Congress of History of Industrialization held in Lyon.

The construction of large silk mills especially in the Venetian and Piedmontese areas, which employed tens or hundreds of workers, required a substantial investment of capital. Did this involve capital of bourgeois origin? An economic historian in the 1960s would have been strongly tempted to respond "yes". But the facts differ. Especially in the Venetian area it was nobles who established these mills. The habit of thought that certain manuals of history instilled about the relation between social class and economic development had to give way to more flexible thinking. For centuries in Lucca, for example, the great merchant-entrepreneurs were nobles.

Continuing to study the Venetian sources I became aware of another interesting fact: there were different types of silk mills, some with water wheels and others without, some with mechanical winding and others without, etc. Silk mills were scattered throughout northern Italy. But many signs indicated an enormous pressure to acquire the Bolognese technology (and in the eighteenth century the Torinese technology). The machines "alla bolognese" were in effect the most sophisticated and the best. But what were the differences among the various types of mills? The sources in Bologna offered no indications; in fact they revealed themselves to be the most uninformed, opaque and least transparent. Bologna for centuries was obsessed with the idea of having to defend the "know-how" of its silk mills from real and imagined industrial spies. Knowledge of this machine was so internalized that even traces of it vanished in the archival documentation of the city. From being the center of the diffusion of the new technology of the silk mill between the sixteenth and seventeenth centuries, Bologna became an empty point of research. My attempts at classification failed one after another. Not one taxonomy that I elaborated held up against the apparent incoherence and dispersion of the sources.

Rather disappointed with this failure, in 1971 I accepted the invitation of Saint Antony's College to spend an academic year in Oxford. There I began to read and study in the Bodleian Library, seeking documentation in the diaries of English visitors to Italy and Europe. I thought that observations by "external eyes" would be able to gather distinctive features of little or scarce significance to "natives". In this way I ended up discovering the travel diary of an anonymous English silk merchant who came to northern and central Italy in 1676. This manuscript can be considered a true and precise survey of the production of thread and the spinning mills made on behalf of a commercial company.

This was in effect a fundamental document because this technical observer, required to inform about the quality of goods, pointed out the best areas of production, describing the characteristics of the various manufacturing processes and the *typology of different silk mills*. And so I found, well-made and ready for use, that classification that so often I had vainly attempted to construct. According to the anonymous English merchant, the three fundamental differences among the silk mills were the absence or presence of water wheels, mechanical winding, and spinning bobbins (*rocchelle*).

Only the machine "exactly alla bolognese," different from the others, was equipped with all three characteristics. This discovery permitted me to classify the silk mills, identifying technological and dimensional differences. The water wheel enlarged the size of production (up to one-hundred workers); mechanical winding concentrated within the firm operations otherwise given to women engaged in cottage industry; and reeling permitted higher quality spinning.

How was the organization of work and the productive process structured? To this question I would respond with sources found in the Academy of Sciences in Turin. The smallest productive unit included eight workers (*incannatori*/winders), four men working at the spinning machine and one at the twisting machine. Therefore the Turin mills, to function, needed at least twenty workers distributed in four principal jobs: winding, spinning, doubling, twisting. If the mill increased in size, the number of workers increased in the same proportion. If the business became very large, supervisors were introduced. For very large mills – I found one in Piacenza in the eighteenth century that employed some hundreds of workers – the direction was separated from the manual productive process and included eight clerical workers, two bookkeepers, one director, vice-director and other personnel. In Gorizia, in another large mill in 1712, I found a sign characteristic of the new mode of production: a set of factory regulations. These rules indicate that one part of the workforce slept in premises within the enclosure of the mill, which was surrounded by a large wall; a bell regulated the time of work, break time and prayer. Since young men and young women worked in the mill, it was forbidden to "speak of love". There were also provisions for penalties for those who did not do good work and also a prison for those who robbed. This business, in other words, had small jurisdictional power: disobedient workers and robbers could be incarcerated for small periods of time.

On the basis of these studies and with the great quantity of information collected I could publish in 1976 a comprehensive article entitled "The origin of the factory system: technology and productive organization in the silk mills of northern Italy 17th-18th centuries".[3] In this article I pointed out that already at the end of the seventeenth century large structures existed, such as the one that Lombe constructed in England; and I could substantiate that the model of the factory system was born at least one-hundred years earlier in Italy. This model was not limited to two or three examples. There were about a hundred large mills, many more medium-sized mills, and a host (perhaps as many as a thousand) of small ones.

Pondering the problem of the relation between the origin of the factory system and the process of industrialization, I avoided the temptation of identifying the existence and diffusion of the factory system in Italy with the Industrial Revolution. The Industrial Revolution cannot be identified with the introduction of this or that machine (the fulling mill, the silk mill or the water frame). In the same article I described the diffusion in Italy during the sixteenth-seventeenth centuries of mechanized spinning as a paradoxical phenomenon, as it was accompanied by a major process of deindustrialization. By the end of the seventeenth century Italian textiles did not succeed in withstanding – or withstood less well on the international market – competition from the great woven silks of Lyon. The large diffusion of silk mills between the seventeenth and eighteenth centuries and especially at the end of the eighteenth century

3 Published in Italian, "All'origine del sistema di fabbrica: tecnologia e organizzazione produttiva dei mulini da seta nell'Italia settentrionale (sec. XVII–XVIII)," *Rivista Storica Italiana*, III, (1976), 447–497. See Poni, *La seta in Italia*, ch. 1.

coincided with the decline of the production of the finished product. From northern Italy large quantities not of finished goods but of spun thread went to the industries in Lyon and in England. In Italy the diffusion of the factory system did not bring together the processes that led to the Industrial Revolution. Absent were those dynamic elements – as Mantoux analyzed – that would be present in England at the end of the eighteenth century.

Finally, after having acquired extensive information about the area of diffusion in Italy of the silk mill, and after having clarified to myself the central importance of the history of this machine, I directed my research back to Bologna, stimulated by the studies that Alberto Guenzi contemporaneously began to carry out on the man-made hydraulic system of the city.[4] After analyzing the Venetian and Piedmontese areas, after studying the large mills of Faenza and Piacenza, I felt ready to address the case of Bologna that I would not have been able to understand had I not completed this long tortuous course of research.

In an article entitled "Expansion and decline of a large industry: silk spinning in Bologna between the 17th and 18th centuries"[5] and published in 1983, I finally wrote about the Bolognese silk mills at the end of the seventeenth century and followed their decline through the eighteenth century.

From this brief reconstruction of the progression of research one can draw some insights on how the "laboratory" of the historian functions. It is not basically very different from that of scientific and technical research. One has to wrestle with one's own ignorance, rapidly cast away hypotheses that do not work, have patience and imagination in combination, be prepared to draw the maximum advantage from fortuitous and casual inferences, and be open to new knowledge that challenges old learning.

4 A. Guenzi, "L'area protoindustriale del Canale di Reno in città nel sec. XVIII," *Problemi d'acque a Bologna in età moderna* (Atti del colloquio, 10–11 ottobre 1981), Istituto per la storia di Bologna (Bologna, 1983), pp. 173–200.

5 Published in Italian, "Espansione e declino di una grande industria: la filature da seta a Bologna fra XVII e XVIII secolo," *Problemi d'acque a Bologna in età moderna,* pp. 211–287. See Poni, *La seta in Italia,* ch. 3.

Postscripts

CHAPTER 16

Remembering Carlo Poni

Carlo Ginzburg

1. I had known Carlo Poni for some time already when, in the mid-1970s, we began to attend the meetings of the editorial board of *Quaderni storici*. I had liked him from the first, and we now became friends, our friendship nurtured by the differences in our backgrounds and our interests.

In 1978, during a meeting of *Quaderni storici* in Rome, Carlo pointed out the possibility of using given names as clues to link different archival collections. I should make clear that this itself is not a memory but an inference from the clear memory I have of walking with Carlo after the meeting—we were in Piazza del Gesù—and saying to him that he should write an essay on the topic. He answered that we should write the essay together. Back in Bologna, when we began to work on the project, Carlo suggested the title: "Il nome e il come." (As we all know, he liked proverbs and folk sayings: "Fossi e cavedagne benedicon le campagne," the title of Carlo Poni's second book, was a proverb roughly translatable as "Ditches and headlands bless the countryside.")[1]

The papers presented at the meeting in Rome were published in the 39th volume of *Quaderni storici*, entitled "Farms and Microhistory," which Carlo edited. In the paper that Carlo presented at the meeting in Rome, I glimpsed a unifying (historiographic, perhaps even theoretical) thread. Shortly thereafter we decided to turn the fruit of our shared labor into a presentation on "*Les Annales* and Italian Historiography" at a conference in Rome in January 1979. This choice shaped our presentation, starting from the subtitle (Carlo's idea, if memory serves me right, like the title): "Unequal Exchange and the Historiographic Market." Not long afterward, our discussions turned a very short paper into a quietly forceful proposal to view in a new light the balance of power between the center (French historiography linked to the *Annales*) and the periphery (Italian historiography in all its variety). In the translations that followed, "Il nome e il come" became, if not a manifesto, then a mini-manifesto of microhistory. The title of the French translation (1981)—"La

1 Carlo Ginzburg and Carlo Poni, "Il nome e il come: scambio ineguale e mercato storiografico," *Quaderni storici*, vol. 14, no. 40 (1979), 181–190 [translated in chapter 14 of this volume]; C. Poni, *Fossi e cavedagne benedicon le campagne* (Bologna, 1982).

 DOI:10.1163/9789004713277_018

micro-histoire"—announced it in no uncertain terms.[2] In German the question mark that followed the noun—"Was ist Mikrogeschichte?" attenuated the form without changing its substance.[3] The translations that followed reproduced the original title more or less literally (though in some cases, given my limited knowledge of certain languages, I am unable to check the literalness of the translation).[4] But in those years "Il nome e il come" was widely read as a concise presentation of the historiographic project known as "microhistory." This point merits further consideration.

2. In our essay we linked "the growing fortunes of microhistorical reconstructions to growing doubts about the established procedures of macrohistory" (namely, socialism or unlimited technological development). "Precisely because we are no longer so sure that the game is worth the candle, we are persuaded to reanalyze the rules of the game."[5] Today, thirty years after the fall of the Berlin Wall, faced with an ever-worsening environmental crisis, I stand by those words. I think Carlo would, too.

Carlo's idea to follow the trail of names as a way of overcoming archival and disciplinary barriers was presented as one possible strategy in "historical research characterized by analysis, at extremely close range, of circumscribed phenomena—a village community, a group of families, even an individual person."[6] A paragraph that Carlo edited took up a theme that he had hinted at in his introduction to the volume of *Quaderni storici* dedicated to "Farms and Microhistory": the reconstruction of families as a way to link data from parish records to data in cadastral registers and notaries' archives.[7] There followed a paragraph in which I mentioned a work in progress on an individual, Costantino Saccardino: a converted Jew, a jester and distiller by profession, condemned to death by the Inquisition in Bologna in 1622.[8] But when I wrote

---

2 "La micro-histoire" *Le débat*, no. 17 (1981), 133–136.

3 "Was ist Mikrogeschichte?" *Geschichtswerkstatt*, no. 6 (1985), 48–52.

4 "Il nome e il come" has been translated into the following languages: French, German, English, Portuguese, Spanish, Korean, Catalan, Chinese, Georgian.

5 See p. 401 above.

6 Ibid.

7 Carlo Poni, "Azienda agraria e microstoria," *Quaderni storici*, vol. 13, no. 39 (1978), 801.

8 For the first formulation of that research, see Carlo Ginzburg and Marco Ferrari, "La colombara ha aperto gli occhi," *Quaderni storici*, vol. 13, no. 38 (1978), 631–639 [see note 14 in chap. 14 in this volume]. The attempt to retrace Saccardino's trial led me in 1979 to write a letter to Pope John Paul II in which, calling myself "a Jew, an atheist, a scholar of history," I asked him to open the Central Archive of the Congregation for the Doctrine of the Faith (formerly known as the Holy Office) to scholars. The trial records were not found, but the letter, as Cardinal Ratzinger (the future Pope Benedict XVI) publicly declared in 1998, contributed to the opening of the Archive.

"even an individual," I also had in mind Menocchio, the Friulian miller at the center of my book *The Cheese and the Worms* (1976).

3. In 1978 the debate on microhistory had just begun. One of the most important contributions to the debate was Edoardo Grendi's essay "Microanalysis and social history" (1977). From that piece, over the course of a lively discussion with Carlo on case studies and their implications, I quoted (here I am obliged to use the first person) a passage that was destined to become famous: "The challenge will therefore be to select, from the mass of available data, relevant, significant cases."

Significant in the sense of statistically frequent? Not always. There are also cases of what Edoardo Grendi called, in a vivid oxymoron, the "normal exception."[9] But let's read on in Grendi's essay. After mentioning "the possibility of characteristic 'revelations' (especially in court papers)" Grendi observes:

> Characteristically the historian works with many indirect witnesses: in this situation the exceptional document can turn out to be exceptionally 'normal,' precisely because it is relevant.[10]

Only now, forty years later, do I realize that Grendi's sentence, which had impressed me deeply, reworked (and partly revised) his critique of *The Cheese and the Worms*. In his introduction to the volume of *Quaderni storici* entitled "Famiglia e comunità" (1976) Grendi had objected that the dichotomy that I posed "between anonymity in the crowd and the exceptional, exemplary individual" was incomplete, and that "resorting to exceptional cases narrows the scope of what the historian can know, because it requires exceptional documentation."[11] In 1978 he acknowledged that exceptional documentation could give the historian access to larger, more "normal" phenomena. So I had argued in my book. I had used certain trials of the Inquisition ("court papers"), presenting them as exceptional documents:

> The paucity of witnesses on the behavior and the attitudes of the lower classes in the past is surely the first—but not the only—obstacle in the

9 See p. 405 above.

10 E. Grendi, "Microanalisi e storia sociale," *Quaderni storici*, vol. 12, no. 35 (1977), 506–520, in particular p. 512.

11 E. Grendi, introduction to "Famiglia e comunità," *Quaderni storici*, vol. 11, no. 33 (1976), 891. For a response to Grendi's observation on the "anonymity of the crowd," I would refer the reader to my critique in the introduction to *The Cheese and the Worms* of François Furet, who also wrote about anonymity.

> way of this kind of research. But there are exceptions to this rule … This exceptional trial [the first of Menocchio's trials] ended with a no less exceptional sentence (accompanied by a lengthy recantation).[12]

I had thus argued that this exceptional documentation (no less than the individual whom it concerned) offered interpretative possibilities with far-reaching implications:

> An almost exclusively oral culture like that of the lower classes of pre-industrial Europe tends to leave no traces, or, at best, leaves deformed traces of itself. Hence the explanatory power of a borderline case like Menocchio's.[13]

A singular case: a miller who had read the *Fioretto della Bibbia* and the *Decameron*, who debated with the inquisitors as an equal on chaos and the creation of the world. But the "barrier that Menocchio unconsciously interposed between himself and the printed page" was informed by "a culture far different from that expressed on the printed page: an oral culture" that was deeply rooted in the European countryside.[14]

In "The Name and the Game" we made the following observations about "the exceptional normal," the striking oxymoron coined by Grendi:

> If the sources are silent about or systematically distort the social reality of the subaltern classes, then a truly exceptional (and thus statistically infrequent) document can be much more revealing than a thousand stereotypical documents. As Kuhn has shown, it is the marginal cases that challenge the old paradigm, and for this very reason they help to forge a new, richer and more nuanced one. They serve in other words as clues or signs of a hidden reality that generally does not emerge from the documentation.[15]

4. "Clues or signs": I was looking back at *The Cheese and the Worms*, which had been published three years earlier, and at the same time I was anticipating

12 Carlo Ginzburg, *Il formaggio e i vermi* [1976], new ed. (Milano, 2019), pp. 13, 113.
13 Ibid., p. 154.
14 Ibid., pp. 42, 138.
15 See p. 405 above.

the essay “Clues: Roots of an Evidential Paradigm,” which was coming out just then.[16] Carlo responded right away to this flight toward generalization:

> Microhistorical analysis is therefore Janus-faced. On one side, operating as it does on a reduced scale, it often makes possible a reconstruction of lived reality that is inconceivable in other kinds of historiography. On the other side, it sets out to investigate the invisible structures within which that lived reality takes shape. The implicit model is the relationship between *langue* and *parole* formulated by Saussure. The structures that regulate social relations are, like those of the *langue*, unconscious. Between the form and the substance there is a gap that scholarship aims to fill. (If reality were transparent, and therefore instantly knowable, Marx said, critical analysis would be superfluous.) For this reason we propose to define microhistory, and history in general, as the *study of lived experience*.[17]

As I reread these words I seem to hear Carlo's voice. I remember that period of collaboration, which never recurred, with great fondness. By following the traces of the given name Carlo had come to formulate a definition of history in general—an unpredictable outcome. But Carlo was, as those who knew him, who read him then and who read him now, nothing if not unpredictable.[18]

16 Carlo Ginzburg, “Spie. Radici di un paradigma indiziario,” in *Crisi della ragione. Nuovi modelli nel rapporto tra sapere e attività umane*, ed. A. Gargani (Torino, 1979), pp. 59–106.

17 See p. 405 above. In his valuable work, *A micro-história italiana. Escalas, indicios e singularitades* (Rio de Janeiro 2006), p. 331, Henrique Espada emphasizes the novelty of the definition of history as "the study of lived reality," tentatively attributing it to me. I am pleased to correct his conjecture, based on my recollections.

18 See A. Torre, “In ricordo di Carlo Poni,” *Quaderni storici*, vol. 53, no. 158 (2018), 317–321.

CHAPTER 17

In Praise of Carlo Poni

Edmund Leites

In a conversation with the former president of a major United States corporation who knew that I was planning to attend a meeting to honor Carlo, he wanted to know about the man and the work I so admired. I thought I would do so by telling him about some of Carlo's essays.

I began with "Peasant Tricks and Landlord Strategies in the Bolognese Countryside." An astounding essay—a rethinking of the place of peasant tricks and deceptions from the end of the 16th century to the 1920s. I first heard it forty years ago, when he delivered it as a talk to the Wednesday Social Science Luncheon of the Institute for Advanced Study, at Princeton, where we were both Fellows. Reading it years later, it remains for me as humane and perceptive as ever.

I have always felt that Carlo's success as an historian of the silk industry has unfortunately led to an insufficient appreciation of his work on the history of the changing agricultural ways of this city's countryside. In my recent rereading of this essay, I asked myself, who else has seen, so clearly, that while many of the demands of the socialists in the difficult twelve-month strike of 1920 outside the walls of Bologna were rooted in the demands of day-laborers, particularly in the world of large-scale rice cultivation, what the socialists called for would also have freed the peasants from the need for theft and tricks. Instead of stealing, hiding produce and so on, to defend themselves from hard times (something the landlord was often advised to accept), they would have had the acknowledged right to minimal subsistence in times of dearth.

Next, in my account of Carlo's work, I turned to "Fashion as Flexible Production: the Strategies of the Lyon Silk Merchants in the Eighteenth Century." It is not unknown now, and was well-known then, that the Lyon silk merchants, from the close of the 17th century, used annual product differentiation to create great difficulties for the merchants of other silk producing cities, including Bologna. What Carlo makes us see is that this use of annual change in product survived as a successful tool of the Lyon silk merchants because of the special and prestigious place in the industry given to the over one hundred designers of silk fabrics. They were often the merchants themselves, or

 | DOI:10.1163/9789004713277_019

the partners of merchants, and they maintained an intimate and continuous relation to France's cultural capital, Paris. No similar relation of cities existed for any other silk producing center. It's a brilliant article.

Finally, I talked about "The Worlds of Work: Formal Knowledge and Practical Abilities in Diderot's *Encyclopédie.*" I see Carlo, in many ways, as the true and admirable heir of Diderot in relation to the worlds of work—and more humane, in his investigations, than Diderot himself. When Diderot wanted to know how artisans actually worked, how they made what they did, he understood that they had a strong interest in keeping their trade secrets secret, unlike scientists, who, in Diderot's words, "converse with one another, write to each other, make their discoveries known, and contradict each other or are contradicted." Yet, as Carlo says, that's not at all fair to the artisan. He observes that for the skilled craftsman, "the transmission of technical practices takes placed by means of imitation. The apprentices learned their craft by miming and copying the movement of the hands, the legs and the bodies of their masters. It was a tacit knowledge, tacitly transmitted, and ended with an examination by members of the guild"—and the creation of a "master-piece." Here is a full-fledged and honest ethic, and is it not how we would do it, if we sought to be as good as Carlo? Would we not begin by imitation, and conclude in the hope that we had made something as good as he has, which would receive the kind of praise we give him today?

I spoke to my friend in this manner, in the hope of communicating the grounds of my admiration of Carlo. And after patiently listening, he replied, "Oh, I see, he describes the way the world really works."

Well, yes.

How do we, or how did Carlo, come to know the way the world really works? In contemporary macro-economics, and in the attempt of a significant group of American economists to apply their notion of economic man to apparently non-economic spheres of life, say, romance, the overwhelmingly dominant premise is that the world actually works the way it *must* work, according to the model of markets that neo-classical theory embraces. The foolishness of the idea that neo-classical economic theory knows how the world must work is all too evident these days. How did Carlo come to avoid looking at the world in this way? How did he come to see it as it really is?

Let me offer to you some of my preliminary, and tentative, answers to these questions.

To say that he wants to know how the world really works is to say, first, that he wants to assemble more than details, wants to create more than an historical record. He has demonstrated, again and again, an interest in providing descriptions which involve a high degree of abstraction. Deception, honesty, standards, trust, measurement, the culture of cities and the culture of industries, secrets, imitation as a way of teaching and learning—all these terms illustrate the level of abstraction Carlo seeks to achieve in his descriptions of the ways men – and women – work and trade. His abstraction, however, is not mathematical. If you will, it is the kind of abstraction Aristotle sought in his reflections on human life, say, in his *Ethics*, or *Politics*, or in his survey of Greek constitutions. Aristotle was a notorious student of documents and data, and a man who longed for the abstraction. So is Carlo.

I note that Carlo's early studies were in philosophy. In his own work as an economic historian, he achieved a level of philosophical intelligence which is rare in the discipline of philosophy itself. It is this level of abstraction which makes Carlo's studies a challenge to the orthodoxy of neoclassical economics. Not because Carlo directly challenges this orthodoxy, but because he offers better descriptions, on the same level of high abstraction as neo-classical economic theory, of how people have worked, made, traded, invented, trusted, deceived, fallen behind or gotten ahead of one another. It would be a great loss if his writings were seen only as an exceptional contribution to the history of Italian agriculture and industry before the era of industrialization. It is such a history, but it is much more. His work is an exemplary description of "the way the world really works."

There is something more to be said about the motive forces in Carlo's work. In a splendidly insightful introduction to Carlo's book, *La seta in Italia*, Carlo Ginzburg writes that we find "un'esperienza di recerca profondamente originale, condotta con un energia e un'intelligenza quali s'incontrano di rado" ("an experience of profoundly original research, conducted with energy and intelligence that is rarely found"). When I read an essay by Carlo, I encounter, first, a complex subject matter, exquisitely illuminated through research that is copious and startlingly inventive. But, second, in reading Carlo, I find an author full of humanity, kindness, and love for the people who populate his world, people who struggle, create, and devise methods for coping with, or changing, sometimes with great cunning, the ways they organize their economic life.

I cannot think of a writer who surpasses Carlo in revealing both a delicate love of technologies and economic arrangements *and* an expansive love of the men and women who create and transform these arrangements. It is this love, I believe, which has enabled Carlo to achieve what so few do: a description of how the world works.

Emerson, somewhere, says that when we read a book, we want to encounter a man thinking, in the movement of his thought. In Carlo's work, we certainly encounter such a man. Yet, beyond what Emerson asks for, we also meet a man loving, sympathetic to the comedies, trials, and cunning ingenuity of our lives; lives lived not only in their unique specificities, but in the larger and common world of changing economies and technologies. I would say that Carlo's singular achievement lies in uniting the life of the scholar and the life of the lover. It is not surprising, therefore, that in reading Carlo we come to love him.

CHAPTER 18

Between Practice and Theory: An Appraisal

Roberto Scazzieri

The scholarly contribution of Carlo Poni, which this volume presents in its thematic breadth and methodological complexity, is a subtle interplay of different points of view called upon when interpreting the world of human practice as it unfolds through production, cultural frameworks, and economic institutions. The worlds of work relate to the worlds of theory through actions in which human capabilities transform material conditions either directly or indirectly by the operation of tools and machines. Capabilities induce material transformations by the interplay of dispositions and reflection, in which bodily affordances interact with tacit knowledge and reasoning along a continuum that connects the visualizations of technical practices of workers, landowners and entrepreneurs with the generalizations and theories of technologists and scientists.

The structure of the volume emphasizes the uniqueness of Carlo Poni's blending of different points of view in his handling of human practice in the production sphere. Part One ('Peasants, Landowners, Agronomists') calls attention to the interplay between the multiple visualizations of production processes by distinct groups of actors, the conflicts inherent in those alternative visualizations, and the strategies adopted by social groups in pursuing their objectives, while acknowledging the coexistence of different and conflicting interests in the same social context. The paper "Peasant Tricks and Landlord Strategies in the Bolognese Countryside" (in this volume, ch. 1), which Poni presented at the Princeton Institute of Advanced Study in 1980 and never published before, examines the complex intermingling of trust and mistrust characterizing the organization of agricultural work in a sharecropping regime. This investigation brings to light what was, in Poni's words, "a dual path between the moral and the deviant, the visible and the invisible, and which not only uncovers the contradictions in the relations of production between landowners and peasants, but also analyzes the contradictions within the very system of productive forces expressed in the daily practice of work and of the control of workers" (p. 11).

The chapters "Between Agriculture and the Manor: Structure, Strategy and Ambiguity in Agostino Gallo's *Dialogues*" (ch. 2) and "Environmental Crisis and the Shifting Practice of Property Rights: the Bolognese Marshlands, 17th to

 | DOI:10.1163/9789004713277_020

19th Centuries" (ch. 3) call attention to alternative visualizations of production arrangements under different social and environmental conditions. Gallo's *Dialogues* emphasize the ambiguity inherent in a landlord's point of view that blends "theory" (in the form of the agronomic reconstruction of agricultural tasks) with the goal of managing agricultural practices according to an effective pursual of economic interests. In contrast to other agronomic expressions of the landlord's point of view, such as those brought to light in the previous chapter, Gallo's argument represents an 'epistemological breakthrough' (p. 36), with its emphasis on avoiding the harsh treatment of sharecroppers while also encouraging the direct involvement of proprietors in modifying the traditional sharecropping system, taking it towards a more "rational" organization of agricultural practices. "Environmental Crisis and the Shifting Practice of Property Rights: the Bolognese Marshlands, 17th to 19th Centuries" (co-authored with Roberto Scazzieri) addresses the shifts in the visualization of production arrangements generated by a crisis in which the transformation of previously fertile agricultural land into marshland made property rights no longer enforceable without contestation. In this case, different social positions generate conflicts beyond the organization of production and the distribution of yield and extend to the identification and enforcement of property rights in a radically modified natural setting. Indeed, the environmental change brought to light the contrast between the private and the collective organization of property, also because the practice of the latter had not entirely disappeared in the marshlands between Bologna and Ferrara due to the limited survival of an alternative mode of ownership.[1]

The concluding chapter in Part One of the volume ("Family and '*Podere*' in Emilia-Romagna: Peasant Sharecroppers," ch. 4) shifts attention to the internal structure of peasant families in the sharecropping context of the Emilia-Romagna region of Italy. Here the different points of view of men and women respectively lead to the coexistence of conflict and compromise within the sharecropping production unit of *podere*. Gender cleavages generate different and sometimes opposing viewpoints that find a contested synthesis in the long-run time horizon associated with the conditions for the intergenerational survival of the household.

Part Two of the volume ("Artisans, Workers, Merchants") turns to the issue of managed contest and conflict in early modern manufacturing production. Here Poni's attention focuses on the coexistence of alternative points of view

---

1 P. Grossi. *An Alternative to Private Property: Collective Property in the Juridical Consciousness of the Nineteenth Century* (Chicago, 1981).

adopted by different actors and social groups because of their distinct positions in the production process. A classic instance of different roles in manufacturing activities is provided by the guild organization of trades. The study of manufacturing organization in early modern Bologna casts light on the network of production in a society characterized by a strongly hierarchical pattern of division of labor. The two chapters "Norms and Disputes: The Shoemakers' Guild in Eighteenth-Century Bologna" (ch. 5) and "Local Market Rules and Practices: Three Guilds in the Same Line of Production in Early Modern Bologna" (ch. 6) consider the interplay and conflicts within and among guilds engaged in different stages in a single line of production. The first addresses the conflicts arising within the domain of activities controlled by a particular city guild (the shoemakers' guild) and identifies "major strains" between urban and rural craftsmen, between shoemakers and cobblers, and between the bottom and top layers of the guild's hierarchy. The second paper switches attention to the connectivity between three guilds (butchers, tanners, and shoemakers) linked together by the trading and processing of skins. Here Poni examines the conflicts arising at the interfaces between the guilds, in which the different role of each guild in the line of production leads to conflicts that may be interpreted in terms of the economic theory of bilateral monopoly. In the example that Poni examines, these conflictual roles were managed in a relational framework governed by political authority and aimed at maintaining the steady flow of materials-in-process from one stage of production to another in spite of market fluctuations. This approach to internal conflicts within the city's production structure reveals a "network of dependence and compensation" based on the awareness of mutual obligation as a necessary condition for social stability.

The other three chapters of Part Two ("'Measure for Measure': From Fine Thread to Rigid Labor Control. Changing Conditions of Work in Silk Factories" (ch. 7),"Technology, Organization of Production, and the Gender Division of Labor" (ch. 8) and "Fashion and Innovation: Strategies of Lyon Silk Merchants in the eighteenth century," ch. 9) examine the interplay between technical change, the internal organization of the productive unit, and the division of labor under conditions of increasing market orientation of production activity. In "Measure for Measure" Poni reconstructs the organizational and technological transformations of the silk industry in seventeenth- and eighteenth-century Italy as the industry moved from piecework to daily wages and started introducing the factory form of production. These changes were "interrelated and connected" (p. 179) but were not a single process. The transition to the factory system only affected the mechanical spinning sector, while the introduction of daily wages initially affected only the reeling stage in connection with a technological innovation that allowed the production of a new type of thread (fine, regular and round), and thus a new range of textiles. This chapter reconstructs the interdependence between technological change and the organization of labor, analyzes the relationship between remuneration of work and workshop arrangements, and brings to light the complex interplay of discipline and workers' resistance that characterized the introduction of a more concentrated organization of production.

The chapter "Technology, Organization of Production, and the Gender Division of Labor" reconstructs the interplay between market impulses and the reorganization of production processes through changes in technology and in the gender division of labor. This paper focuses on the transformation of tasks conducted in the silk production process (spinning and weaving) under conditions of technical change. The introduction of new tasks and the reorganization of existing ones led to changes in the division of labor between sexes and age cohorts, particularly through the upgrading and/or downgrading of certain tasks as well as their assignment to a different gender or age cohort. This highlights a multi-layered relationship between technical transformation, the identification of productive tasks, and the assignment of tasks to capabilities within the productive establishment.

The chapter "Fashion as Flexible Production" examines the prerequisites and consequences of a dynamic market strategy based on the "planned and programmed" transformation of production lines and finished products. Emphasis is on the linkage between the competitive strategy centered on the annual changes of fashion, the development of sophisticated capabilities (those of designers) that were directly instrumental to that strategy, and the introduction of a flexible production machine (the Jacquard loom) at the beginning of the nineteenth century. Unlike the case of Bologna, in which the market strategies of the different stakeholders were embedded within a multi-layered relational structure aimed at social stability, the case of Lyon is an instance of a successful attempt to combine flexible manufacturing with the ability to steer consumer demand by following and also inducing transformation in taste, and ultimately turning uncertainty into a fundamental component of the merchants' competitive strategy.

Part Three ("Engineers and Theorists") introduces abstraction as an essential element of human practice in the material sphere. In this section, we find multiple explorations of the ability to "extract" general principles from manual operations and to turn those principles into instruments for improvement of production. The chapter "The Synergy between Two Innovations: Canals and Silk Mills in Bologna" (ch. 10, co-authored with Alberto Guenzi) considers an issue that is at the origin of the medieval industrial transformation of

Bologna: the local government's decision to construct a canal bringing running water to the heart of the walled city. The subsequent introduction of the silk mill as a technical artifact producing energy without direct human involvement turned the spinning of threads into a mechanized and more productive operation. Here public intervention (the building of a fundamental energy infrastructure) allowed the successful introduction of the technological innovation (the silk mill) that sustained Bologna's manufacturing activities for several centuries.

The chapter "Behind the Scenes: The Staging of a Theater of Machines" (ch. 11) directly addresses the nature of artifacts. Poni considers theatres of machines as mechanical spaces derived from the rational reconstruction of human motions and aimed at enhancing the reach of human activity by introducing "intermediate motions" independent of human intervention. This chapter introduces the issue of machinery as "applied theory" and illustrates the extent to which Renaissance thinkers and engineers considered it possible to conceive of and construct mechanisms capable of harnessing movement into artificial channels and so make more effective the achievement of specific purposes.

The next chapter in this section ("The Craftsman and the Good Engineer: Technical Practice and Theoretical Mechanics in J.T. Desaguliers," ch. 12) considers the intrinsic ambiguity of the relationship between theory and practice when dealing with the organization of production processes. The paper links its argument with Galileo's criticism of the ignorance of "artificers" regarding theoretical mechanics while also calling attention to Galileo's interest in their inherited knowledge and direct experience in using instruments and machines. After discussing Galileo's criticism of "artificers," the paper considers the view of the 18th century English scientist J.T. Desaguliers, who was critical both of "mechanical undertakers" and of pure mathematicians unaware of the specific circumstances making mechanisms work or not work. In Desaguliers's view, the good constructor of machines should combine knowledge of theoretical mechanics with understanding of the solidity and resistance of materials, and with the ability to assess a project before starting to work on it. This would require a deep transformation of the channels for the transmission of knowledge within the productive unit: the education of artisans in the general (theoretical) principles governing the performance of tasks would require a period of general education in technical-industrial schools training young people destined to a variety of trades. However, this approach would entail a different pattern of division of labor, which was incompatible with the closed and secretive apprenticeship system characterizing artisan workshops. This difficulty reflected the interplay between controlling the production process and governing apprenticeship training. In turn, that interplay was at the root of artisans' lack of trust in the external "reconstruction" of their technical practices and became a major obstacle to the discovery of general principles governing production activity.

The last chapter in Part Three ("The Worlds of Work: Formal Knowledge and Practical Abilities in Diderot's *Encyclopédie*") deals with technical practices as processes in which the deliberate arrangement of tasks may coexist with unintentional operations and transformations often concealed to the artisan. The chapter starts with Diderot's observation, in the *Prospectus* announcing the forthcoming publication of the *Encyclopédie*, that scholarship had overlooked technical practices (what Diderot calls "the activities of the artists and the descriptions of the machines" – p. 375) while devoting great attention to the sciences and the liberal arts. Diderot's project was to turn technical practices unaware of themselves into rational arrangements of tasks, so that the inventions of the artisans could become available to the public and be rescued from secrecy and eventual oblivion. However, as Poni points out: "[t]he workshop [...] was also a school, although of a special type. The transmission of technical practices took place by means of imitation. The apprentices learned their craft miming and copying the movement of the hands, the legs, and the bodies of their masters. It was a tacit knowledge, tacitly transmitted, and ended with an examination by members of the guild. The examination was not oral and certainly not written, but practical" (p. 381). In other words, the transmission of tacit knowledge by imitation of body motions allowed artisans to bypass the divide between the formal knowledge of principles governing actions and the unintended consequences of those actions when performed under given material circumstances.

Part IV ("Methods") directly addresses the methodological conceptions and criteria underlying Carlo Poni's contributions to economic and social history. The chapter "The Name and the Game: Unequal Exchange and the Historiographic Marketplace" (co-authored with Carlo Ginzburg) calls attention to the relationship between concealment and disclosure and emphasizes the vital role of exception and surprise in making apparent inner structures that would otherwise go unnoticed. Here we find an explicit consequence of Poni's philosophical anthropology, in which awareness and formal knowledge coexist with a world of practice grounded in lack of awareness and tacit knowledge. In Poni's view, fundamental socioeconomic and cultural structures are seldom apparent, and often exert their influence through indirect routes channeled through practice. The latter may be inconsistent with, or resistant to, attempts to make sense of it in terms of explicit and formal knowledge. A case in point are the manifold instances of conflict that Poni detects behind social practices such as the peasant "tricks" and the artisans' unwillingness to open apprenticeship training to formal education outside the workshop. Alternatively, the haggling and compromises characterizing the relationship between guilds within the same line of production, and the public authorities' interventions to regulate them, may signal the persistence of relational structures aimed at social cohesion as a higher-order objective beyond the need to face market pressures. This paper makes explicit Poni's and Ginzburg's view that the close focus of micro-history allows a reconstruction of human practices and beliefs that would otherwise be impossible. At the same time, that close focus may bring to light 'invisible structures,' which are not immediately apparent and yet may exert a fundamental influence on the unfolding of individual lives and social dynamics.[2]

The last chapter of Part Four ("The Silk Mill: A Path of Research," ch. 15) provides a reflection on the part of the author on his own approach to the investigation of socioeconomic structures and of their transformation over time. A crucial point of this chapter is its emphasis on combinatorial imagination, on the role of serendipity in allowing the researcher to take advantage of change 'interferences,' and on the role of intellectual track changes that make possible the utilization of unexpected evidence and the questioning of established points of view.

Taken in their unity, the essays in this volume outline a research framework of impressive depth and scope. The core of this framework is the reconstruction of multi-layered human practices, the intertwining of awareness and unawareness in the unfolding of actions, and the consequences of this for the dynamics of structures. This attitude to social investigation opens up a variety of research avenues, some of which are pursued in this volume. The same framework is at the root of the three lines of inquiry and institution building that gave a distinctive mark to Carlo Poni's activity in the last decade of his activity at the University of Bologna and at the other centers of academic work with which he was associated at that time (primarily Clare Hall in the University of Cambridge). One of these strands concerns the investigation of *patterns of interdependence* in their relationship with the emergence and

2 C. Ginzburg, "Postscriptum: Ricordando Carlo Poni, a Rereading of 'Il nome e il come'," *Quaderni Storici*, vol. 54, no. 161 (2019) 552–556; see in this volume, ch. 14, p. 406. Idem, "Some queries addressed to myself," *Balzan Papers*, I, (2020 [2012]), 283–291. In the 2019 paper, Ginzburg calls attention to Poni's belief that the deep structures regulating social life are fundamentally concealed from social actors' view and that scholarly investigation should aim at filling the gap between "form" and "substance" (see Ginzburg, "Postscriptum: Ricordando Carlo Poni", p. 555 and "Some queries addressed to myself").

evolution of production and market networks. The analysis of economic networks often considers the existence and evolution of connections in terms of a well-defined set of relationships between actors or processes. Production networks often presuppose a fixed set of identities and connections, without directly considering the complex internal structure of individual and collective actors, in which relational dispositions may be manifold and not always active at the same time. Such an approach, in general, has paid little attention to the changing identities of production units, and to the evolving pattern of their interaction over time. The inherent "redundancy" of any given set of connections may be associated with flexible units and variable connections in a production network.[3] Connections may be intermittent and the "nodes" within any given network may not be fixed at any given time.[4] In general, any given actor (such as a household or a firm) may be associated with a complex bundle of dispositions and capabilities which are not always active at any given time. It follows that connections between actors may be intermittent rather than permanent, and that emergent networks seldom conform to a preconceived pattern of interaction. As a result, the process by which actions are conducted within a given set of connections is not clearly distinguishable from the process by which those connections came into existence. It often happens that the process leading to a certain action cannot be distinguished from the discovery that a certain pattern of connectivity is possible. In many cases, the structure and evolution of production connectivity does not conform to the model of an organizational network: connections may be intermittent, and a given action may often be a novelty, rather than the application of a well-defined decision rule.

3 H. Simon, "Architecture of complexity," *Proceedings of the American Philosophical Society*, vol. 106 (1962), 467–482, and M. Landau, "Redundancy, rationality, and the problem of duplication and overlap," *Public Administration Review*, vol. 4 (1969), 346–358. See also: *Production Networks: Market Rules and Social Norms*, C. Poni and R. Scazzieri, eds. Eleventh International Economic History Congress, Milan, 12–16 September 1994. Session C.11; *Mercato e forze locali: il distretto industriale*, G. Becattini, ed. (Bologna, 1987); G. Lorenzoni, *L'architettura di sviluppo nelle imprese minori* (Bologna, 1990); P. Bianchi, *Produzione e potere di mercato* (Rome, 1991); Bianchi and L.M. Miller, "Innovation and Collective Action: the Dynamics of Change," *Structural Change and Economic Dynamics*, (June, 1996), pp. 193–206; M.H. Lazerson, and G. Lorenzoni, "The Networks that Feed the Industrial District. a Return to the Italian Source," *Industrial and Corporate Change*, (June,1999), pp. 235–66; C. Poni, "Comparing Two Urban Industrial Districts. Bologna and Lyon in the Early Modern Period," in P.L. Porta, R. Scazzieri, and A. Skinner, eds., *Knowledge, Social Institutions and the Division of Labour* (Cheltenham, 2001), pp. 199–227.

4 S. Alliney, "Intermittent causality: on some possible representations of processes of change," University of Bologna, Faculty of Economics (11 December 1996), mimeo.

Since the early 1990s these themes became enmeshed with an interest in the social and political conditions of open-ended connectivity and were the focus of a research seminar on *Foundations of Markets and Social Norms*, which Carlo Poni convened at the University of Bologna in collaboration with Stefano Zamagni and myself and within the framework of the Bologna-Cambridge-Harvard senior seminar network. The seminar explored themes such as the relationship between awareness and unawareness in Spinoza's analysis of human dispositions,[5] the relationship between social norms, markets and productive practices,[6] the implicit morality of the market,[7] the relationship between connectivity and the market order in Friedrich von Hayek,[8] and in Adam Smith,[9] the classical roots of the concept of benevolence,[10] conceptions of civil society in their relationship with the political order,[11] the role of passions, and of their mutual balancing, as the foundation of "civil life."[12]

Interest in the conditions for the emergence and maintenance of networks leads to a consideration of the *dimensions of trust*, which became another characteristic strand of Poni's inquiry into human conduct within social structures. This is because the exploration of connections presupposes a belief structure in which actors may expect the new connections to take place. However, the trust required by connections may vary depending upon the structure of the "possibility space" in which connections may develop. In the case of a

5 H.-J. Wagener, "[De] Cupiditate et Potentia: the Political Economy of Spinoza," *The European Journal of the History of Economic Thought*, (1994), 475–93 (presented at the Bologna-Cambridge-Harvard Senior Seminar Network, Bologna, 21 January 1993).

6 C. Poni, "Markets, social norms, and productive practices in an eighteenth-century industrial district: the case of Lyon," Bologna-Cambridge-Harvard Senior Seminar Network, Bologna, Academy of Sciences, (11 February 1993), mimeo.

7 S. Zamagni, "The Limitations of the Indirect Morality of the Market," Bologna-Cambridge-Harvard Senior Seminar Network, Bologna (3 May 1993), mimeo.

8 J. Birner, "'Put asunder to be join joined again?' Neural Network Theory and Social Science," Bologna-Cambridge-Harvard Senior Seminar Network, Bologna (13 January 1994), mimeo.

9 E. Rothschild, "The Bloody and Invisible Hand," Bologna-Cambridge-Harvard Senior Seminar Network, Bologna (24 February 1994), mimeo.

10 G. Vivenza, "The Classical Roots of the Concept of Benevolence," Bologna-Cambridge-Harvard Senior Seminar Network, Bologna (4 May 1994), mimeo.

11 E. Leites, "Prospects of an American Identity: the Lincoln Conception of Civil Society," Bologna-Cambridge-Harvard Senior Seminar Network, Bologna (19 May 1994), mimeo; N. Matteucci, "Hayek e la società civile" [Hayek and civil society], Bologna-Cambridge-Harvard Senior Seminar Network, Bologna (1 June 1994), mimeo; L. Ornaghi, "The Mirror of Politics: Civil Society and Its Image," Bologna-Cambridge-Harvard Senior Seminar Network, Bologna (20 April 1994), mimeo.

12 M. Torrini, "La *Vita civile* di Paolo Mattia Doria" [The *Vita civile* of Paolo Mattia Doria], Bologna-Cambridge-Harvard Senior Seminar Network, Bologna (25 May 1994), mimeo.

"tight" possibility space, new connections presuppose the belief in deterministic processes, or at least the belief that probability distributions are known to actors. The new connections are those that can be more easily predicted based on existing social knowledge, and they are likely to be "strong" considering that, in general, they would materialize within the existing economic and social networks. In the case of a "loose" possibility space, on the other hand, trust is associated with the expectation that new connections may arise quite independently of existing linkages and networks. Trust in this case does not presuppose a tight belief structure, and new connections may arise even if individuals and groups are unknown to one another before a connection materializes. In fact, the dimensions of trust are manifold, and may involve complex mutual influences between trust and mistrust. The research seminar on *Dimensions of Trust*, which Carlo Poni convened in the mid-1990s at the University of Bologna in collaboration with Stefano Zamagni and myself and within the framework of the Bologna-Cambridge-Harvard senior seminar network, explored manifold features of trust in its relationship with the dynamics of social structures. An important theme discussed at that seminar was the relationship between trust and mistrust, which initially led to the investigation of issues such as simulation and dissimulation, the relationship between oath and contract, trust as the outcome of translation, trust and trustworthiness, and the relationship between trust and political obligation.[13] Subsequently, the seminar moved to the consideration of themes directly related to social structures such as benevolence and trust, mistrust, mistrust between equals and trust between unequals, trust, reciprocity, and civil society, loss of culture and loss of trust, trust and the tolerance of uncertainty, market haggling, trust, and the "equilibrium of lying."[14] The seminar continued into the late 1990s

13 M. Pesce, "Simulation and Dissimulation," Bologna-Cambridge-Harvard Senior Seminar Network, Bologna (20 April 1995), mimeo; P. Prodi, "Oath and Contract," Bologna-Cambridge-Harvard Senior Seminar Network (16 May 1995), mimeo; F. Perlin, "Translation and Trust," Bologna-Cambridge-Harvard Senior Seminar Network, Bologna (25 May 1995), mimeo; J. Brewer, "Trading in Intangibles and the Art Market," Bologna-Cambridge-Harvard Senior Seminar Network (1 June 1995); Ornaghi, "Political Obligation and Trust," Bologna-Cambridge-Harvard Senior Seminar Network (6 June 1995), mimeo.

14 Vivenza, "Benevolence and Trust," Bologna-Cambridge-Harvard Senior Seminar Network, Bologna (27 May 1996), mimeo; Rothschild, "Mistrust," Bologna-Cambridge-Harvard Senior Seminar Network (29 April 1996), mimeo; G. Alberti, "The Structural Conditions of Mistrust," Bologna-Cambridge-Harvard Senior Seminar Network (16 April 1996), mimeo; Zamagni, "Civil Society between Democracy and the Civilizing Process: the Role of Reciprocity," Bologna-Cambridge-Harvard Senior Seminar Network (15 May 1996), mimeo; Leites, "Loss of Culture and Loss of Trust," Bologna-Cambridge-Harvard Senior Seminar Network (23 May 1996), mimeo; G. F. Lanzara, "Trust, Learning, and Institutional

discussing issues ranging from the breakdown of trust, and a translation-based theory of trust, to proximity and tyranny, pure trust and cautious trust, and the relationship between trust and reputation.[15] Subsequently, the seminar turned to themes such as trust, flight and intellectual migration, redistribution and trust, trust and the risk of distance, the limitations of trust and governance in a production network, the relationship between trust and the density of interpersonal connections, and the mutual implication between passions, reasons, and the development of the self.[16] In the early 2000s the seminar developed a focus on the epistemics of social confidence, the relationship between "form" and "substance" in reasoning concerning fairness, and the coexistence of compromise and conflict (peace and war) under conditions of fuzzy borders and divided sovereignty.[17]

Gradually, an important focus of the *Dimensions of Trust* seminar had become the study of *social structures at the interface between lack of awareness*

Dynamics," Bologna-Cambridge-Harvard Senior Seminar Network (3 June 1996), mimeo; N. De Marchi, "Dealing Credibly in 17th Century Netherlandish Art Markets," Bologna-Cambridge-Harvard Senior Seminar Network (17 June 1996), mimeo.

15 P. Seabright, "Organized Crime and the Breakdown of Trust in the Former Soviet Union," Bologna-Cambridge-Harvard Senior Seminar Network (14 April 1997), mimeo; Perlin, "A Theory of Trust: Speech, Translation and Civil Representation," Bologna-Cambridge-Harvard Senior Seminar Network (21 April 1997), mimeo; Alliney, "Proximity and Tyranny: Institutional Trust and Repression," Bologna-Cambridge-Harvard Senior Seminar Network (5 May 1997), mimeo; P. L. Sacco, "Pure Trust versus Cautious Trust in Risky Environments," Bologna-Cambridge-Harvard Senior Seminar Network (20 May 1997), mimeo; C. Muldrew, "The Currency of Credit and Personality: Belief, Trust and the Economics of Reputation in Early Modern English Society," Bologna-Cambridge-Harvard Senior Seminar Network (10 June 1997), mimeo.

16 H. Hagemann, "Trust and Flight: German Intellectual Emigration after 1933," Bologna-Cambridge-Harvard Senior Seminar Network (2 March 1998); A. Petroni, "Redistribution and Trust," Bologna-Cambridge-Harvard Senior Seminar Network (18 May 1998), mimeo; Muldrew, "Trust and the Risk of Distance: the Problem of Mercantile and Trade Credit in the Early Modern Period," Bologna-Cambridge-Harvard Senior Seminar Network (1 June 1998), mimeo; Lazerson, "The Limitations of Trust. Why Firms Need Controlling Companies," Bologna-Cambridge-Harvard Senior Seminar Network (22 June 1998), mimeo; L. Bruni, and R. Sugden, "Moral Canals: Hume, Smith, and Genovesi," Bologna-Cambridge-Harvard Senior Seminar Network (11 January 1999), mimeo; Muldrew, "From 'light cloak' to the 'iron cage'. The Development of Self-control and Savings in 17th and 18th Century England," Bologna-Cambridge-Harvard Senior Seminar Network (5 June 2000), mimeo.

17 Alliney, "'You're thinking like me, then I trust you.' Reflections on the Epistemics of Social Confidence," Bologna-Cambridge-Harvard Senior Seminar Network (19 June 2000), mimeo; G. Levi, "An Economics of Fairness," Bologna-Cambridge-Harvard Senior Seminar Network (12 June 2000), mimeo; R. Ellenblum, "Medieval Borders, Crusader States, and Trust," Bologna-Cambridge-Harvard Senior Seminar Network (21 May 2001), mimeo.

and reflexivity. This had been a central theme of Carlo Poni's research since his interest in the relationship between hidden conflicts concealed in material culture and their representation at the level of formal knowledge (see above). Now the consideration of that relationship became increasingly associated with an interest in the conditions leading to the opening (or closing off) of social interdependencies. This exploration took advantage of Poni's long-standing interest in the links between human skills, body practices and theoretical understanding (reflexivity). In a presentation at the history of science seminar at Bologna, Poni had related the reconstruction of technical practices to Paolo Mattia Doria's distinction between actions based on thinking and actions based on dispositions independent of reflexivity.[18] The subsequent exploration of this theme in the late 1990s and early 2000s involved close interaction with the Bologna mathematician Stefano Alliney, the economic and social historian Frank Perlin (at that time a frequent visitor to Bologna University), and myself. Alliney contributed to our exchanges with his interpretation of the topological theory of proximity spaces, which involves overcoming the Euclidean conception of distance.[19] In Alliney's interpretation, proximity spaces suggest a theory of society based on the possibility of multiple linkages, plasticity of focusing, and tacit dispositions. In this perspective, the capability of identifying stylized facts by means of pre-analytical schemes is a necessary condition for developing the "induction of a topology."[20] Frank Perlin was at a relatively early stage of his life-long research trajectory on "difference as virtue"[21] and called our attention to the role of translation as the constitutive condition of social connectivity.[22] In Perlin's

18 Poni, "Macisti e schermidori. Scrivere e descrivere le pratiche tecniche" ["Strong Men and Fencers: Writing and Describing the Technical Practices"], Bologna, History of Science Seminar (22 March 1994), mimeo; see P.M. Doria, *Discorsi critici filosofici* (Venezia, 1724). Doria draws attention to fencing as an example of the relationship between habit and effective action: '[a]ll habits, which depend on the body, would be poorly executed by us if the mind wants to reflect at the same time as the habits are working. If a fencer wants to reflect on the laws by which he must strike a blow at the same time as he strikes it, the motion will stop in him of those animal spirits, which [are] necessary to execute the action with speed, and he would no longer be able to strike the blow' (Doria, 1724, p. 67).

19 Alliney, "Per una interpretazione della topologia della prossimità" [For an interpretation of the topology of proximity], University of Bologna, Faculty of Economics (June 1996), mimeo.

20 Idem, "You're thinking like me" (19 June 2000).

21 Perlin, "Difference as Virtue. Representation, Translation and the Idea of the Social Contract'," contribution to the workshop *Structural Change, Civil Society and Sustainability*, Enschede, Universiteit Twente (4–5 October 1996).

22 Idem, *City Intelligible. A Philosophical and Historical Anthropology of Global Commoditization before Industrialization* (Leiden, 2020).

view, the consideration of translation devices is of crucial importance due to the need of "redefining, the very conception of the significance, function, status, and thus nature and origins, of 'frontiers' of all kinds, and of the forms of communication traversing them."[23] As for myself, I was developing an interest in the varieties of modes of reasoning within the social space, which I found closely related to a multidimensional approach to distance and to the vital role of translation as interpretive device.[24] Carlo's contribution provided a fundamental connecting frame for those intersecting lines of exploration, both with his uniquely detailed knowledge of the relationship between technical practices, trading arrangements, and social structures, and with his deep interest in the conceptualizations developed within anthropology, philosophy and economic and social theory. In this way, our interactions came to build on the economic theory of production, structural interdependencies, and modes of exchange,[25] the theory of framing and institution building,[26] the analysis of analogical reasoning under fundamental uncertainty,[27] and the cultural study

---

23 Ibid., p. 102; idem, *'The Invisible City': Monetary, Administrative and Popular Infrastructures in Asia and Europe, 1500–1900* (Aldershot, 1993); idem, *Unbroken Landscape. Commodity, Category, Sign and Identity: Their Production as Myth and Knowledge from 1500* (Aldershot, 1994).

24 R. Rossini Favretti, G. Sandri, and R. Scazzieri, "Translating Languages: an Introductory Essay," in *Incommensurability and Translation. Kuhnian Perspectives on Scientific Communication and Theory Change*, eds. R. Rossini Favretti, G. Sandri and R. Scazzieri (Cheltenham, 1999), pp. 1–29; Scazzieri, "Economic Beliefs, Economic Theory and Rational Reconstruction," ibid., pp. 289–306; idem, "Patterns of Rationality and the Varieties of Inference," *Journal of Economic Methodology* (2001), 105–110; idem, "Analogy, Causal Patterns and Economic Choice," *Stochastic Causality*, eds. M.C. Galavotti, P. Suppes and D. Constantini (Stanford, 2001), pp. 123–139.

25 J. Hicks, *A Theory of Economic History* (Oxford, 1969); A. Quadrio Curzio, *Rendita e distribuzione in un modello economico plurisettoriale* (Milan, 1967); idem, Quadrio Curzio, "Technological Scarcity: an Essay on Production and Structural Change," in M. Baranzini and R. Scazzieri, eds., *Foundations of Economics. Structures of Inquiry and Economic Theory* (Oxford and New York, 1986), pp. 311–38; L.L. Pasinetti, *Lectures on the Theory of Production* (London, 1977); idem, *Structural Change and Economic Growth. A Theoretical Essay on the Dynamics of the Wealth of Nations* (Cambridge, 1981); Scazzieri, *A Theory of Production. Tasks, Processes, and Technical Practice* (Oxford, 1993); D.C. North, *Institutions, Institutional Change and Economic Performance* (Cambridge, 1990); idem, *Understanding the Process of Economic Change* (Princeton, 2005).

26 M. Aoki, *Toward a Comparative Institutional Analysis* (Cambridge, 2001).

27 J.M. Keynes, *A Treatise on Probability* (London, 1921); G.L.S. Shackle, *Imagination and the Nature of Choice* (Edinburgh, 1979); P. Suppes, "Freedom and Uncertainty" in H.G. Natke, and Y. Ben-Haim, eds., *Uncertainty: Models and Measures, Mathematical Research* (Berlin, 1997), pp. 69–83.

of dialogues and interfaces in a multidimensional social sphere.[28] On a personal note, those years of intense and forward-looking explorations were a fundamental building block of lines of inquiry that I subsequently pursued along a variety of directions, often in collaboration with senior and younger colleagues.[29] Most recently, the relationship between human dispositions, the plurality of actors' points of view, and social interdependencies has provided the focus of investigations into the political economy of structural transformation and the constitution of political economy, suggesting a direct link to the multiperspective approach to social practices and structures of which the essays in *The Worlds of Work* provide an outstanding example.[30]

28 M. Bakhtin, *The Dialogical Imagination: Four Essays*, M. Holquist, ed., C. Emerson and M. Holquist, transl. (Austin, 1981); J. Goody, *Capitalism and Modernity: the Great Debate* (Cambridge, 2004).

29 M.C. Galavotti, R. Scazzieri, and P. Suppes, eds., *Reasoning, Rationality and Probability* (Stanford, 2008); Scazzieri, A.K. Sen, and Zamagni, eds. *Markets, Money, and Capital: Hicksian Economics for the Twenty-first Century* (Cambridge, 2008); Scazzieri and R. Simili, *The Migration of Ideas* (History of Science Publications, 2008); S. Marzetti Dall'Aste Brandolini and Scazzieri, eds., *Fundamental Uncertainty: Rationality and Plausible Reasoning* (Houndmills, 2011); A. Pabst and Scazzieri, *The Constitution of Political Economy* (Cambridge, 2023); Baranzini, C. Rotondi, and Scazzieri, eds., *Resources, Production and Structural Dynamics* (Cambridge, 2015); I. Cardinale, I., D. Coffman, and Scazzieri, eds., *The Political Economy of the Eurozone* (Cambridge, 2017).

30 Cardinale, "Beyond Constraining and Enabling: Toward New Microfoundations for Institutional Theory". *Academy of Management Review*, 43, 1 (2018), 132–155; Cardinale and Scazzieri, "Sul ritorno dell'economia politica," *Rendiconti, Istituto Lombardo Accademia di Scienze e Lettere, Classe di Lettere e Scienze Morali e Storiche*, 150, (2016), 69–91; Cardinale and Scazzieri, 'Explaining Structural Change: Actions and Transformations'. *Structural Change and Economic Dynamics*, (2018) https://doi.org/10.1016/j.strueco.2018.12.002; Cardinale and Scazzieri, eds., *The Palgrave Handbook of Political Economy* (London, 2018); Baranzini, "Socio-economic Structures and Long-term Dynamics," *Rendiconti della Classe di Scienze Morali, Storiche e Filologiche*, Atti della Accademia Nazionale dei Lincei, serie IX-vol. XXXI (2021), 245–255; Bianchi and S. Labory, "L'economia politica dell'industria," *Rendiconti della Classe di Scienze Morali, Storiche e Filologiche*, Atti della Accademia Nazionale dei Lincei, serie IX-vol. XXXI (2021), 211–224; Cardinale, "'Structural Political Economy: Particular Interests, Systemic Interests, and the Structure of Division of Labour," *Rendiconti della Classe di Scienze Morali, Storiche e Filologiche*, Atti della Accademia Nazionale dei Lincei, serie IX-vol. XXXI (2021), 257–274; Cardinale, and J. Runde, "From Dishwashing to Dishwasher Cooking: on Social Positioning and How Users Are Drawn Towards Alternative Uses of Existing Technology," *Cambridge Journal of Economics*, 45(4), (2021), 613–630; L. Costabile, "La teoria politica della divisione del lavoro," *Rendiconti della Classe di Scienze Morali, Storiche e Filologiche*, Atti della Accademia Nazionale dei Lincei, serie IX-vol. XXXI, (2021), 225–229; A. Pabst, "The 'Body Politic' and Political Economy," *Rendiconti della Classe di Scienze Morali, Storiche e Filologiche*, Atti della Accademia Nazionale dei Lincei, serie IX-vol. XXXI (2021), 231–238; M. Pianta, (2020) "La *Political Economy* su scala mondiale," *Rendiconti della Classe di Scienze Morali, Storiche*

In the 1990s and early 2000s, the close intertwining between practice and theory as intellectual objects characterizing Carlo Poni's contribution to scholarship combined with institutional involvement both at the level of local material culture and at the level of academic life in its interdisciplinary and international dimensions. Both aspects of Poni's lifework are central to the reconstruction of his scholarly contribution. In the former, Poni played a leading role in the establishment of the Museum of Peasant Civilization (*Museo della civilta' contadina*) and of the Museum of Industrial Heritage (*Museo del patrimonio industriale*) in Bologna. In the latter, Poni's active involvement was central to the launching in 1993 of the collaboration through visiting fellowships between Clare Hall, Cambridge, and the University of Bologna (the *Bologna-Clare Hall Fellowship Scheme*), which is still providing a much-valued avenue of intellectual exchange. His contribution was also central to the establishment of the *Institute of Advanced Study* at the University of Bologna, the first such institution in Italy, which started operating in 2000–2001 and to whose early activity Carlo devoted years of constant attention and advice in his capacity as one of the founding Institute's Resident Fellows.

In recognition of Carlo Poni's contribution to scholarship, in 2005 the Accademia Nazionale dei Lincei awarded him the "Antonio Feltrinelli Prize for Social, Demographic and Economic History."

---

e Filologiche, Atti della Accademia Nazionale dei Lincei, serie IX-vol. XXXI, (2020), 239–244; Scazzieri, 'Ripensare l'economia politica: strutture analitiche e contesti', *Rendiconti della Classe di Scienze Morali, Storiche e Filologiche*, Atti della Accademia Nazionale dei Lincei, serie IX-vol. XXXI, (2021), 175–210; Scazzieri and Quadrio Curzio, "Sulla complessità teorica e storica dell'economia politica," *Memorie*, Atti della Accademia Nazionale dei Lincei, serie IX-vol. XLV-fascicolo 1, (2022), 13–37; Pabst and Scazzieri, *The Constitution of Political Economy. Polity, Society and the Commonweal,* (Cambridge, 2023). Cardinale and Scazzieri, "Architectures of Production and Industrial Dynamics: A Task-Function Theory of Structural Change", *L'industria. Rivista di economia e politica industriale, nuova serie,* vol. xliv, 4 (2023), 559–582.

Index, *Worlds of Work*

Agriculture, Agronomy, Landowners, Peasants, Sharecroppers, Sharecropping
  Agriculture--Sharecroppers, Sharecropping 12–19
  Farming and household
    Patriarchal family structure
      Community of goods among brothers, obstacle to accumulating wealth and becoming freeholders 95
      Death and succession 94–100
      Different family units 72
      Female and child labor 88–89
      Inchiesta Agraria (1881) 71, 83–84, 94, 97, 101, 102, 104
      Marriage, dowries, inheritance 72, 97–100
      Reggitore, father, authority over work and family 71–74, 84
      Reggitrice, wife, authority over women and domestic matters; widow loses status 71–73, 84
      Sons, different work roles 72, 74, 92, 103
      Trebb, winter evening gatherings of peasants in cowsheds 93–94
      Weakening of patriarchal family structure 101–102
  Sharecropping, an agrarian system
    Italy, predominant in Po region 14th-16th centuries until 20th century 73–74, 76–77, 81–83, 91–92
    Landowners—urban nobles, non-nobles, church institutions 73–74, 77
      Annual contract for farmland (*podere*), controlled peasants' work 12–14, 89, 104–105
      Received half annual production; payments in money, in kind, free services 13
    Peasants 73–74, 77, 79–82
      Annual contract, renewal or eviction 13, 19, 92–93, 105
      Deceits, tricks, thievery 14–19
      Farm (*podere*)--small, scattered, subsistence economy 12–14
      Non-farm work prohibited 89
      Provided labor, work instruments, half the seed and half to all the oxen 12
      Received half annual production 13
      Relations withs landowners 14–15, 23, 32–33, 35, 45, 48, 53
      Rent in cash, debt payments; additional payments (*patti*)--payments in kind, free services 13
      Views on peasants--Church, theater 19–21
    Sharecropping transformed, 19th century 21–25
      New agricultural cultivation landowners introduced 22–23, 104
      Reforms in sharecropping proposed
    Sharecropping ended, late 19th century-20th century 102–106
      Decline in sharecropping, increase in wage-earning farm workers 102
      Industrialization, new work opportunities 106
      Opposition of peasants, influence of socialist movement 23–24
      Sharecropping contracts eliminated, outlawed (1964) 100
Agronomists, Agronomy
  Gallo, Agostino
    Cloth store owner; petty nobleman; gentleman farmer 28–30
    Dieci Giornate della vera agricoltura e piaceri della villa,1564 (*Ten Days of Real Agriculture and the Pleasures of the Manor*) 26

Agronomists, Agronomy (*cont.*)
Addressed to noble and urban owners of large country properties 30, 32–44, 46–47, 50–52, 54
"Capitalistic" farming 34–39
Increase profitability, investment 36
"Modern" agricultural practices to best cultivate fields 35–36, 40–45
Multiple crop rotations foretell the agricultural revolution 39–43
Peasants paid in money 31–32, 34
Replace sharecropping with personal management (*boaria*) 34
Dual image of peasants 31–32, 35–36
Manorial life and pleasures 50–52
Norms for good landowners, more just treatment of peasants 30–35, 47
Italy, Po Valley (late 16th century-first-half 17th century)
Agronomy of landed proprietor against agricultural practices of peasants 11–12
Tanara,Vicenzo, *L'economia del cittadino in villa* (*The Economy of the City-Dweller in the Countryside*), 1644 11–12
Landlord control over peasants 16–17
Paternalistic concern for peasants 19–20
Peasant agriculture—cunning, laziness 14, 16–18, 24
"True" agriculture, hard-working, Roman model 12
Scientific agronomy and capitalistic agriculture, late 18th century 21–22
New agronomy, Society of Agriculture; new agriculture, 19th century 22
Berti Pichat, Carlo, Bolognese agronomist (mid-19th century) 79, 81, 84
Re, Filippo, *Elementi di agricoltura* (*Elements of Agriculture*, 1815) 21–22
Artisans, Crafts, Corporations/Guilds
Bologna, 17th–18th centuries
Guild system
Bilateral institutional monopoly 155, 158, 174, 428
Guild rules and market forces 164–166
Reciprocal obligations 146
Conflicts within guilds; Rights of guilds underlay disputes
Entry, fee payment, membership 155
Guild members and guild council 115–116, 129–138
Masters' authority over journeymen and apprentices 138
Oligarchical structure 115, 168
Strategies of attack and defense 116
Work disputes between guilds
Cobblers, limited to repair used shoes 125–126
Inequality--rich and powerful tanners, poor tanners 165–168, 170–171, 174
Master shoemakers and cobblers 125–129
Master shoemakers, exclusive right to make and sell new shoes 125
Making and use of leathers, butchers, shoemakers, tanners 143, 146–149, 151–154, 156–163
Rights of guilds underlay disputes 164
Shoemakers' guild, composition 114–115
Tanners, rich and powerful craft 150
Urban shoemakers against rural shoemakers 116–122, 124–125

Culture, meanings and relations
High culture 24, 113
Legal culture--lawyers and artisans
Lawyers engaged in disputes; artisans adopted legal language 119–120, 139–142, 151–152
Popular culture, artisans, peasants 24–25
Interaction with dominant classes 24
Work culture 5, 36, 113–114, 116, 141–142, 181, 209–210, 363, 380–381, 386

Desaguliers, John Theophilus, scientist, entrepreneur, experimenter
- *A Course of Experimental Philosophy*, 2 volumes (1734) 355
  - Construction of machines must be based on scientific principles, knowledge of mechanical operations and theoretical mechanics 361–362
  - Criticism of artisans who kept secret knowledge of their craft 363
  - New training institutions must include workshop practices and scientific knowledge 363
- *Descriptions des Arts et Métiers*, Paris, *Académie des Sciences* 365
  - Artisans described different trades; knowledge used to improve production and division of labor 366–367
- Lombe's silk mill factory 369–371
- Machines and plants built 1680–1740 367–368
  - Interest in hydraulic machines and especially steam engines 368–369
- "Metaproduction function" 369
  - Use of existing technical and scientific knowledge to explore production possibilities 369
- Popularizer of Newton's *Principia*; taught experimental physics 354
- Samson at Haymarket London (how the human body can move according to mechanical principles) 371–372
- Technical practice and theoretical mechanics--antecedents: Giorgio Martini, Galileo, Zonca 352–353

Diderot, Denis
- *Encyclopédie ou dictionnaire raisonné des sciences, arts et métiers*
- *Prospectus*, purpose of the *Encyclopédie* (1750) 375–376
  - Make known to the public information on mechanical arts, machines and work practices 375–378
- Diderot, on artists/artisans 376–378
- Artisans transmit knowledge only to train apprentices in their workshops 381
- Fear public knowledge of their work practices 386
- Knowledge of mechanical work must be known to the public 379–380, 383
- Scientists spread knowledge and ideas; artisans embrace secrecies 380–381

Encyclopédie, articles
- *Art*, Diderot 376–377, 378
  - Distinction between liberal arts and mechanical arts 376
  - Favored large-scale production and division of labor 378
- *Chef d'oeuvre* ("Masterpiece") 381–383
  - Attacked system of guilds and master artisans 381
  - Competition, not masterpiece, will eliminate bad workers 386–387
- *Commerce*, François Véron de Forbonnais (machine production to economize on human labor) 388–389
- *Encyclopédie* (critical of artisans' untruths due to fear of tax collectors and competing artisans) 379–381
- *Épingle* ("Pin") Alexandre Deleyre (advantages of division of labor) 378–379
- *Horlogerie* (Watchmaking and Clockmaking); Scientific knowledge and specialized workers ("artists") with technical practice necessary 385–388
- *Industrie* Chevalier de Jaucourt (Abolish customs duties; Defended machine production and freedom for industry to advance innovation) 389
  - Distinguished "arts" (Beaux Arts) from industry ("mechanical operation of nature") 396

Encyclopédie, articles (*cont.*)
Intérêt [*Economie Politique*] ("Interest [Political Economy]"; Lower interest rate to advance agriculture, industry and commerce) 389–390
Maîtrises (Masterships) Faiguet de Villeneuve Critical of apprenticeship requirements; freedom and competition to combat monopolies by masters 382–383
Manufacture [*Réunie, Dispersée*] ("Manufacture, concentrated, scattered"; large industries in factories with division of labor and control of workers; small industries in countryside [protoindustry]) 390–393
Métier (Craft; work requiring the use of hands in mechanical operations) 377
Soie ("Silk"), Lyon example 393–396. *See* Silk, Silk Manufacturing, Lyon, France
Environmental Crisis and Property Rights, Bolognese Marshlands
Appropriation 60–61
Closed mode 60
Instability 61–62
Open mode 60
Commons (common-access resources)
Decomposition 62
Environmental crisis and property rights 55–69
Liquid commons (in Bolognese countryside) 55–69
Marshlands, modes of appropriation 55–69
Marsigli's *De Agri Bononiensis Palustris Historia* 62
Open wetlands, and modes of appropriation 55
Taxonomy 56–57, 63
Transformation of property rights 56–57
Property rights 55–69
Centers of gravitation of entitlements 59
Common property 55
Declarative speech acts 65
Delimitation 60–61
Delineation 60–62
Disappearance 59
Economic theory 57
Enforcement 56–63
Environmental constraints 56
Exploratory and aggressive enforcement 62
Nesting structure 66–67
Open-access resources 55
Relational arrangements 66
Seasonal 63
Social conflict 62–63
Wetlands economy
Modes of appropriation 63

Fashion (*See* Silk, Silk Manufacturing, Lyon, France)

Gender division of labor (*See* Silk, Silk Manufacturing)
Guilds, city government, papal authority
Guild autonomy decreased 115, 125
Guilds subject to authority of Papal Legate and municipal government
Pricing disputes 147–155, 157, 160, 166, 170–171
Principles of moral economy 174
Legate and municipal authority in disputes 116, 121–125
City authorities supported urban shoemakers to defend urban industry 129
City failed to reform guilds 135
Legate gained power over Senate and shoemakers' guild 121–125
Legate supported country towns to make quality shoes 122–125
(*See also* Artisans, Crafts, Corporations/Guilds)

Historians, Historiography, and Theorists
Bakhtin, Mikhail, parody and plurivocality 25, 142n, 332n, 439n
Bergeron, Louis, late forms of proto-industry 234–235

Braudel, Fernand, traditional clothing, fashion 241
Conti, Elio, Klapisch, Christiane and Herlihy, David, Florentine taxation 400
Goody, Jack, interest in history among anthropologists 402
Grendi, Edoardo, "Microanalysis and social history", "normal exception" 405
Hall, Rupert, "The Scholar and the Craftsman in the Scientific Revolution" 355
Henry, Louis, nominative demography 403
Hjelmslev, Louis, metonymies (paradigmatic relations) 16
Jakobson, Roman, structure as synchrony-diachrony 406
Kuhn, Thomas, "normal science", paradigms and marginal cases 401, 405
Lévi-Strauss, Claude, convergence of history and anthropology 402
Mantoux, Paul, the Industrial Revolution in the eighteenth century 1–9
Marx, Karl, reality not transparent 406, 414, 420
Mauss, Marcel "reciprocal obligations" 144
Mendels, Franklin, protoindustry 235
Polanyi, Karl, "market embedded in society" 144, "great transformation" 244
Pomian, Krzysztof, the "social use of historiography" 399
Saussure, Ferdinand de, relationship between *langue* and *parole* 16, 406, 414, 420
Simmel, Georg, fashion 241
Stone, Lawrence, prosopographical studies—elites, broader social groups 405
Taylor, F.W., early 20th century, scientific organization of work 381

Industrial Revolution 22, 24, 238, 303, 354–355, 366–370, 408–410, 413–414

Lombe, John and Thomas, first mechanized silk mill in England, 1717 296, 337–338, 369–371, 408–410, 413
Lyon (*See* Silk, Silk manufacturing)

Microhistory/Macrohistory 399–407
- History and anthropology
  - Themes from anthropology now in history 402
    - Kinship, material culture, symbolic rituals 402
- Microhistorical investigation
  - "Hidden reality" revealed through marginal cases 405
  - Lived experience (*scienza del vissuto*) 406
    - Reveals invisible structures of lived experiences 406
  - Nominative methodology/micronominative 403–404
    - Name as guiding thread, personal, family, place 403–404
    - Reconstruction of personal and social relationships 404
  - Prosopographical studies 405
    - Elites, broader social groups 405
    - Serial history 400–401

Poni, Carlo
- From historian of agriculture to historian of silk
  - Learning about silk mills, England and Italy 408–410
  - Research in State Archives in Venice 410–411
  - Silk mills' classification 412
    - Mills "alla bolognese" (Technological transformation—water-powered mechanization) 411–412, 414
    - Mills "alla piemontese" (work organization, large factories) 411–413
    - Origin of factory system 413
  - Silk mills spread in northern Italy, 16th-18th centuries 413
  - Silk mills not an Industrial Revolution; but foreshadowed the Industrial Revolution 413–414

Silk, Silk Manufacturing: Italy
Bologna
Handwork—traditional silk making, females worked at home, raised silkworms, reeled thread 214
Machine production—silk mill "alla bolognese". *See* image 212
mechanized twisting (1341) 215 and winding, mid-15th century 217
mills with larger work force increased production 216
silk mills with "no human labor" (1481) 289–290
Network system—silk in international trade, organzine and voile 297
Secrecy of silk mill technology
Bologna manufacturers and city government opposed silk manufacturing in the countryside 219
Revealing the technology a crime punished by death 296
Urban industrial concentration, late 17th century 295–298
significant population engaged in the silk industry 297, 299
vertical integration of spinning and winding, greater output, improved quality 296
Water power and machine production
canals and underground conduits for industry unique to Bologna 292–295
city with most water wheels, greatest number and size of industrial factories (late 17th century) 292, 295
oldest water-powered silk mills (late 14th century) 296
silk mills 90% of water-powered factories 295
Decline of Italian silk industry 302–303, 413–414
Expansion and competition, northern Italy
Lombardy 230–232
Late 17th century-18th century, Bergamo 203; Como, Lecco 229–230
19th century, Lombard countryside main producer of silk in Italy 229
Provinces of Bergamo, Como, Milan—2/3 of Italy's production capacity 229
Province of Como: Como, Varese, Lecco, most productive manufacturing region 229
Province of Lecco—increased mechanization, lighter mechanicaltwisting frames eased work for women 232;
Greatest silk producer in Italy 230–232
Modena (1501), Trento (1538), Faenza (1559–1561) 215
Piedmont: Turin (1664), Racconigi 223
Innovations in spinning "alla piemontese" 1667
Governing authorities encouraged advanced technology; fines and warnings against opponents 203–204, 225
Improved quality of thread 203–204. *See* image, 395
Pay changed from piece work to daily wage 204
Piedmontese technology introduced in Bologna, (1750), a large mill, finer thread 191
New technology and daily wage introduced in France 204–205
Vaucanson promoted Piemontese technology 205, 224, 394
Verticalization of production—spinning and twisting in same mill; improved quality, greater worker control 205, 220
increase in size and number of mills, surpassed Bologneseproduction and technology 224
Venice (1604), Venetian state (1634) 220, 337, 345, 411
Mills spread in countryside, late 17th century 220

Gender division of labor
Bologna, northern Italy
Hand work at home—women raised silkworms, did reeling 214–220
Mechanical winding displaced female hand winding at home 296
Men and boys in mills 233
Boys did mechanical winding 218
Men did twisting and skilled weaving 218
Women paid less than men 216
Women's work at home continued
"Doubling" thread, weaving voile; increase of women weavers 215–218
Florence: women worked at twisting machines 229
Lombardy, mid-19th century
Bergamo
17th-18th centuries, prohibited female mechanized winding to protect home winders 225
Increase of women in factory work. "doubling" and reeling 226–227. *See* image, 213
Como, Lecco—Men cultivated the land, women did mechanical winding in factories 233, girl factory workers lived in silk mill dormitories 234
Lecco—Women and girls, half the twisters in mills; home winding ended 231–232
Married men, did agricultural work or better-paid work, some in silk mills 234
Married women mainly did agricultural work, some returned to factory work 234
Women ended factory work, age 20–23 233
Women paid less than men and boys 216, 225, 231–232
Piedmont
Racconigi—men, women, children employed; women earned less than boys 223–225
Veneto: Vicenza—girls and boys did mechanical winding 221, 225
Silk, Silk Manufacturing: Lyon, France
Fashion not luxury 239
Fashion as rapid change, distinct from luxury 239–242
ideas of Fernand Braudel, Georg Simmel 241
Societies with social mobility, influence of custom and religion replaced by wealth 242
Innovative silk production—annual change of fashion, late 17th century 239, 243
Advanced planning in design and color of flowered silk fabrics
Customer preferences for silk fabric, patterned silk and fashionable clothes in silk 282
Jacques Savary, *Le parfait négociant* (1675), noted annual change of fashion 280
Lyon and Paris--Artistic and commercial dominance
Lyon fashions sold as "modes de Paris faites à Lyon" ("fashions of Paris made in Lyon") 272
Role of designers unique in Europe 272–277
Long years of study of design; annual trips to Paris to visit art collections; immersion in Paris culture
Artistic and practical knowledge of needs and expectations of silk market; collaboration with weavers; discussions with merchants, buyers 257–261, 263–264, 275
Maximum publicity to promote new annual designs—dolls (*poupées*), fashion journals, pre-production samples 264
Lyon's business strategy
Barriers to entry 238, 244, 257
Centralized decision-making 242
Dialogue between producers, designers, elites on tastes of consumers 243

Silk, Silk Manufacturing: Lyon, France (*cont.*)
 Dominate the international market 243–244
 Entrepreneurial strategies 238
 Flexible production 238–239, 277
 Market segmentation 238, 271
 Monopolistic competition 238–239, 244
 Product quality and differentiation 238–239, 243–244, 247, 263, 265, 271, 275–279
 Transactions costs 158, 238
 Lyon's silk industry, merchants and workers
 Grande Fabrique, Community of Merchants and Master Workers in Silk 251–252, 256–257, 262, 274, 282
 Maîtres, small independent weavers (*Petite Fabrique*) 251–253
 Maîtres gardes, heads of the Community 251–254, 270
 Maîtres ouvriers, majority of weavers, independent piece-rate workers, received designs and raw materials from *fabricants* 250–253
 Marchands fabricants, rich entrepreneurs engaged in putting-out system 250–253
 Merchants and weavers, conflicting economic interests 251–254
 Disputed claims of responsibility for success of Lyonnais patterned silk
 Fabricants gained greater importance
 Ouvriers' work and professional mobility obstructed 250
 Technological innovations and inventions
 Delasalle, Philippe (1770), use of perforated cards to change the design without resetting the loom 276–277
 Falcon, Baptiste (11720's), use of perforated cards on the loom to transfer designs onto the material 276, 395–396
 Jacquard, Joseph-Marie, invented Jacquard loom (1801), use of punch cards to transfer designs to the cloth 276–277, 285

Vaucanson, Jacques de, invented automatic loom 205, 276, 395–396

Wages
 Piece work 179–185, 192, 207
 Regole, Farra 208, 210, 223
 Wages and piece work 204–205
 Wages for daily work replaced piece work 179–180, 204–205, 209, 398, 436
 Improved work outcome; increased control of labor; greater value produced 203–205
 Spread of daily wages to France 205
 Women paid less than men. *See* Gender Division of Labor
Waste (*Cascami*)
 Waste in the silk industry, spinners versus merchants 193–200, 204–205, 208
 Catholic moral theology, "just wage", "moral economy of work" 199–200
 Regole of Farra denied right to waste 208; Senate decree on waste 199–200
 Waste increased when wages fell 200; daily wages reduced waste 204–205
 Waste worked by peasants 237
 Worker control 180–181, 296
 Architecture of factories: walls, dormitories, horizontal structure 208–209, 221–222
 Masters controlled apprentices and journeymen 138, workers use of waste 196
 Regulations of work time, discipline of behavior, punishment 208, 220, 222–223
 Vertical integration, large factories, control of workers' accuracy 206–209

Zonca, Vittorio
 Architect-engineer of machines 304–305, 347

Aim: improve construction of machines to improve their functioning 312–314
Taught mechanics, University of Padua, (1592–1602), contemporary with Galileo 316–320
Influences in Padua
Major textile center (wool) with water-powered industrial plants 344–345
Rich reflections on mechanics 314–316
Mechanical thought before Zonca 305, 311, 314–316
Mathematics applied to mechanical thought 312, 315–316, 319–321
Novo teatro di machine et edificii (*New Theater of Machines and Buildings*) [Padua, 1607] 304
Drawings
Drawings suggested improvements in machine operations 330–333
Elements that transmit motion 322–324
Machines and maps with scale 306–307
Silk mill drawings (Depiction of separate parts of the machine facilitated understanding of its functioning) 334–339
"Six classes" (*ragioni*), basic parts in all types of machines 311
Grain mills, classification by force of movement 322
Qualifications to be a "mechanic" 327
Principles of mechanics applied to production techniques to improve efficiency of machines 313
Tacit acknowledgement of trade secrets of masters and apprentices 340–342
Novo Teatro in contemporary culture
Mannerism 342
Carlo Cipolla, "late flowering" of Italian industry 342
Superiority of modernity over antiquity—science, technology, geographic explorations 343–344
"Theaters of machines", 17th–18th centuries
Influence on German technical culture 347–349
Zonca family, social ascension 345–347
Uncle of Zonca and Galileo among founders of *Accademia dei Recuperati* 317

Index, *Postscripts*

Ginzburg, Carlo
joint project on microhistory 417–418
(*See also* Microhistory above)
"normal exception" (Grendi, Edoardo) 419–420
research strategy—follow names in historical research 418
reconstruct lived reality, connections to larger social structures 421

Leites, Edmund
copious research with illuminating understanding of complex subjects 424
historical descriptions with a high degree of abstraction 423
"how the world really works" 423
men and women at work described with a high degree of non-mathematical abstraction 424
insight on lives and work of peasants 422
senstive understanding of work practices of artisans and their secrecies 423
writings reveal "a delicate love of technologies and economic arrangements *and* an expansive love of the men and women who create and transform these arrangements" 424

Scazzieri, Roberto
Analogical reasoning, 438
and uncertainty 438
and social dialogues 439
Artifacts 430
and rational reconstruction of human motions, 430
and Galileo's criticism of "artificers" 430
and Desaguliers' criticism of artificers and pure mathematicians 430
as "applied theory" 430
Bologna-Cambridge-Harvard Senior Seminar Network 434
Clare Hall, University of Cambridge 432, 440
Dispositions, and reflection 426, 433, 434, 437, 439
Environmental crisis 55–70, 418, 426–427
Formal knowledge 431, 437
and informal knowledge 431, 437
Informal knowledge 431, 437
and disclosure of hidden social structures 432
and formal knowledge 431, 437
and surprise 431
and tacit knowledge 431, 437
Interdependence
and market networks 433
and intermittent connections 433
and open-endedness of connectivity 433–434, 437
Manufacturing production 427–431
and infrastructure (Bologna canals) 429–430
and guild organization 427–428, 429
and social conflict 428
and social stability through compensation 428
Peasant households 427
and intergenerational survival strategies 427
and gender cleavages 427
Practice, in its relationship to theory 430–431
Property rights 427
Reasoning, in its relationship to practice 430–431
Serendipity, and combinatorial imagination 432
as heuristic device 432
Social conflict, and production organization 434
Social structures
disclosure of 431
and intermittent connectivity 433
and theory of proximity spaces 437
their relationship to awareness and reflexivity 43

Surprise and disclosure of hidden social structures 43

Tacit knowledge 426, 432
 and disclosure of hidden social structures 431
Technical change
 and flexible production 429
 and gender division of labor 427, 429
 and infrastructure development 429–430
 and the internal organization of the production unit 428–429
 and market orientation 429
 and partial transition to the factory system 428–429
 and social conflict 429
 and the work process 429
Technical practice and the deliberate arrangement of tasks 431
 and unintentional operations 431
Theory, its relationship to practice 430–431
 and extraction of general principles from manual operations 429–431
 (*See also* Practice, in its relationship to theory)
Trust
 and forms of production organization 434, 436
 and mistrust 426, 435–436
 and translation 435–438

Viewpoints
 and environmental crisis 427
 and interpretation of human practice 430–431
 and social conflict 426–429

www.ingramcontent.com/pod-product-compliance
Lightning Source LLC
LaVergne TN
LVHW022042061125
825117LV00004B/74